Teaching Team Sports

A Coeducational Approach

Joan A. Philipp, PhD
Youngstown State University
Jerry D. Wilkerson, PhD
Texas Woman's University

Human Kinetics Books
Champaign, Illinois

Library of Congress Cataloging-in-Publication Data

Philipp, Joan A., 1930-
Teaching team sports : a coeducational approach / by Joan A.
Philipp, Jerry D. Wilkerson.
p. cm.
Bibliography: p.
ISBN 0-87322-259-8
1. Physical education and training--Study and teaching
(Secondary)--United States. 2. Coeducation--United States.
I. Wilkerson, Jerry Diana, 1944- . II. Title. III. Title: Team
sports : a coeducational approach.
GV365.P48 1990
796'.071'273--dc20 89-7533
CIP

ISBN: 0-87322-259-8

Developmental Editor: June I. Decker, PhD
Copyeditor: Bruce Owens
Assistant Editors: Timothy Ryan and Valerie Hall
Proofreaders: Greg Teague and Linda Siegel
Production Director: Ernie Noa
Typesetter: Angela Snyder
Text Design: Keith Blomberg
Text Layout: Tara Welsch and Jayne Clampitt
Cover Design: Jack Davis
Illustrations: Era Hartford and Elizabeth Schwarz
Printer: Versa Press

Printed in the United States of America

10 9 8 7 6 5 4 3 2 1

Human Kinetics Books
A Division of Human Kinetics Publishers, Inc.
Box 5076, Champaign, IL 61825-5076
1-800-747-4HKP

Contents

Preface

We wrote this book to help physical education teachers prepare units of instruction for team sports for middle and high school students. This book presents comprehensive instructional material suitable for teaching each of the sports from beginning through advanced levels. Included are offensive and defensive strategies that may be used for class play and interscholastic competition. Some of the team sports are especially appropriate for coeducational classes. Teaching activities that are new to students, such as field hockey and speedball, enables everyone to start at the same skill level. This enhances coeducational classes. The introductory chapter provides general suggestions for implementing team sports in coeducational classes or teams. To meet the needs of specific groups, teachers can select appropriate goals and objectives from those listed. Ideas in each chapter will also help the teacher provide the best learning opportunity for all students in the coeducational setting. These suggestions relate to class organization, skill practice, and game play.

Students in methods classes or those entering their first teaching experiences will find this book especially useful when organizing course material, planning teaching sequences, and learning to analyze sports skills. The teaching progressions suggest logical plans for the presentation of skills. The sections on practice drills offer a selection of patterns for practicing the skills. Classes that need a lot of practice may use most of the drills, whereas those that progress more rapidly would use only those appropriate for their instructional needs.

This first section of the book includes a chapter on principles and observation of movement to help teachers and coaches recognize movement variations more skillfully. This will assist them in observing ineffective movement patterns and making positive corrective suggestions.

Fundamental movements are grouped and analyzed to demonstrate the relationships among various skills. Those who understand the similarities and differences among skills can plan learning experiences that take advantage of the transfer effects of some skills while avoiding or moderating the interference effects of other skills. The fundamental movement chapter serves as a reference for the descriptions of specific skills included in the sports chapters. It can also help the beginning teacher, recreation leader, or performer understand the fundamental skill elements combined in specific team-sport skills.

The technique descriptions for each sport offer a concise analysis of the motor skills involved in that sport. A comprehensive knowledge of biomechanics is not necessary to interpret these analyses, although an understanding of fundamental movement patterns would be helpful.

Instructional suggestions to address common skill problems follow the analysis of the skills. These suggestions will help the instructor evaluate the skill patterns and suggest ways that students may improve. They are not all-inclusive but rather represent the more common types of movement difficulties within that specific skill.

Some of the basic rules of the sport are included in each sport chapter. Because rule changes occur frequently in some sports, the reader who is interested in the details of the rules is referrred to the national organization of the specific sport, the National Federation of State High School Associations, or the American Alliance for Health, Physical Education, Recreation and Dance. These last two organizations publish rules for many team sports. The rules of speedball have changed little since its origin, although modifications are made to fit different playing or teaching situations. The rules of flag and touch football also vary throughout the country. The inconsistencies in these two sports reflect the lack of interscholastic competition in them.

Acknowledgments

The authors wish to express appreciation to the following individuals: Margaret H. Meyer and Marguerite M. Schwarz for their inspiration and permission to use material and the format from their book *Team Sports for Girls and Women*; Carol Pope for typing and editing; Elizabeth Schwarz for art work; Era Harford for the graphics; Nan Reeveley for typing; Gordon Longmuir for suggestions and ideas for the soccer chapter; Wilma Thompson for support and encouragement; and the students at Texas Woman's University who served as subjects and photographers. We also wish to thank the reviewers for their thorough and helpful analyses. Without the assistance of all these individuals, this manuscript might never have been completed.

Part I

Concepts and Methods

Chapter 1
Introduction to Teaching Team Sports

Team sports should be an important component of the coeducational physical education program because of the unique contributions such activities can make to personal development and the integration of the individual into the cooperative experiences necessary in a democratic society. The value of team sports for boys has long been put forth as a means of helping youngsters develop the interpersonal skills needed for success in a competitive and corporate world. More girls are now entering the career-oriented world, and they should be taught the same social interaction skills that boys have been expected to learn.

Team sports help young people of both sexes to (a) develop leadership and followership skills, (b) become an integral part of a team, (c) learn to work together to achieve a desired outcome, (d) recognize the goals of the group and place these goals ahead of personal glory, (e) develop a spirit of competition and a willingness to strive for a goal, (f) accept a challenge, (g) develop a feeling of belonging to a group, and (h) understand loyalty. Team sports can also improve *cardiorespiratory efficiency* and *neuromuscular* control. Additionally, the successful development of basic motor abilities such as *flexibility*, *agility*, *balance*, *strength*, and *coordination* generally enhance a person's self-concept and feelings of worth.

Team Sports in the Curriculum

Analysis of the characteristics of children informs us that the upper elementary and early secondary school levels are excellent periods to emphasize team-sport activities. Students in their 11th and 12th years are strongly interested in group work, cooperative effort, and peer approval. Team sports provide a natural outlet for this interest. The middle school student has the capacity to refine motor skills and learn strategy and team play (Williams, 1983). Therefore, an emphasis on team activities for Grades 5 through 8 is recommended by physical education curriculum theorists (Annarino, Cowell, & Hazelton, 1986; Melograno, 1979; Nixon & Jewett, 1964; Willgoose, 1984). Team sports would still constitute a significant part of the program in Grades 9 and 10, especially in schools having large classes. These activities would also be included to a lesser degree in Grades 11 and 12, where advanced skills and strategies could be taught.

In a daily program of physical education, a variety of team sports can be taught effectively. However, the program that is conducted only 2 or 3 days each week must be more selective and perhaps would cover only two or three team sports per year with some repetition from one year to the next and with one or two new activities being added as some are phased out. A typical middle school and secondary school curriculum might include the team sports illustrated in Figure 1.1. If some of the team sports were not available for scheduling, others would be substituted. Other units such as rhythmics, aquatics, self-testing activities (conditioning, gymnastics, etc.), and individual sports would round out the program.

Teaching Progressions

Team sports should be developed progressively. The gross motor skills (e.g., passing, catching, dribbling, and striking) should be taught to elementary school children. The more refined movements (e.g., performing the jump shot, heading, flicking, and spiking) should be taught to upper middle school or high school students. Team play and strategy would also be developed in the secondary schools. A comprehensive physical education curriculum plan would have children beginning to explore fundamental movement patterns in the early grades (kindergarten through second). Students would then

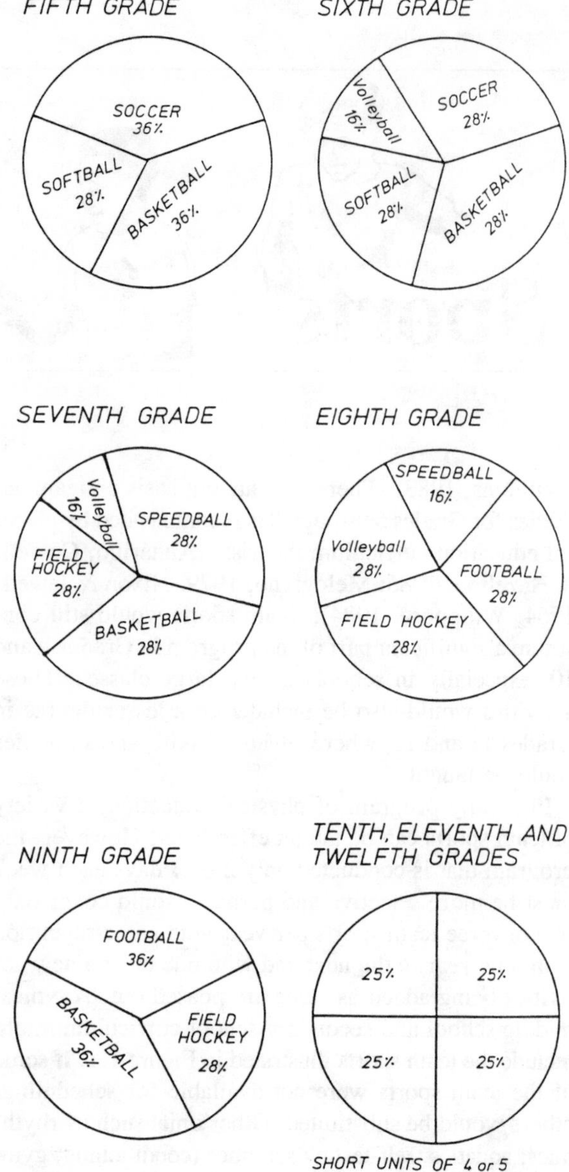

Figure 1.1. Team-sport time allocations for Grades 5 through 12

move into those fundamental skills needed for sports activities in Grades 3 through 6 before team sports are introduced in Grades 5 through 8 and refined in Grades 9 through 12.

Middle school youngsters would usually start with the sport-specific beginning skills. Intermediate skills would be introduced to those who had previous experiences in that sport, whether they be seventh and eighth graders or high school students. Advanced skills should be reserved for those with 2 or 3 years of prior experience or for players on interscholastic teams.

Coeducational Considerations

Most elementary school programs involve coeducational classes. If this coeducational situation is carried on into the middle school or junior high setting, there are fewer problems than if boys are separated from girls for part of the time and then reintegrated. The students who are accustomed to being in classes together can be encouraged to develop cooperative, helping attitudes toward one another rather than competitiveness. Team sports can act as a medium to develop an individual's empathy toward others and to teach young people tolerance and acceptance of individual differences.

The primary problems that occur in coeducational classes at the secondary school level result from our culture, which encourages (almost mandates) boys to practice and participate in team sports outside of school but discourages (or restricts) girls from participating in them. Therefore, many boys develop a higher skill level than do most girls and are not challenged by coeducational competition. If our school programs moved away from the traditional "big three" of basketball, football, and softball to emphasize different team sports, girls would not be at such a disadvantage from the start. Field hockey, soccer, and speedball are appropriate for this purpose.

Accommodating Varying Skill Levels

Classes can also be organized in a manner to enhance learning for the skilled and the unskilled. When players must go one-on-one with an opponent, pair them so they are of comparable ability, just as a basketball team does when competing with another team. Students can be paired in different ways for different activities according to individual traits or abilities. Examples of this pairing are matching for speed in soccer, for height in basketball, and for hitting ability in softball. More suggestions for equalizing game play will be found in each sport-specific chapter. When a player does not directly oppose another, as in volleyball or softball, try to equalize the teams by distributing some skilled and unskilled players on each team.

The use of stations when organizing a group can also allow for a variety of skill levels. In this technique, separate activities are planned for different areas of the gymnasium. One pattern has students move from one station to another, practicing the skills assigned to each respective station. Another pattern makes use of four to eight stations in progressive skill levels. All students start at Station 1, where a simple skill is executed. Those who perform that skill successfully move on to Station 2, which demands executing a more difficult skill. Progression to additional stations involves increasingly difficult skills. Students who cannot perform the skill at a station must stay there and practice it. Criteria for mastery or moving on to the next station should be specified (e.g., making three out of five lay-up shots for basketball). The last station should be of sufficient difficulty to challenge the highly skilled. After all students have mastered a skill, that station should be eliminated and new ones added to introduce more difficult skills.

Sometimes special rules may need to be established to assure equality of play. It is much better to have students internalize cooperative, nurturing behavior than to establish rules that require it, but sometimes this is necessary for a short period of time. An example of this type of rule is requiring that at least one girl hit the volleyball before it is sent over the net. Another example is requiring a novice to handle the ball before a shot at the goal is taken in basketball. These are artificially imposed situations that do little to improve the skills of these players and that interfere with the flow of play of skilled players. They should be avoided whenever possible.

Another solution to the problem of the skilled versus the unskilled is to group the students according to skill levels based on skill tests or performance observations. This allows the students to compete with others of comparable skill. The poorly skilled will not be overwhelmed or ignored by those of greater ability. The highly skilled will not be bored but will be challenged to strive to improve their skills. Organizing classes in this manner requires more work and planning by the teacher but results in an improved learning experience for the students.

Separate tournaments based on skill levels may be established within the class. This would be especially useful in large schools where two or more classes are scheduled during the same period. Regrouping the students homogeneously by skill level (not by gender) allows one teacher to work with the more highly skilled and to present advanced material to challenge the learner. During the same time, the other group or class learns basic skills and knowledges while having the opportunity to cooperate and compete within the scope of their capabilities. Educators must take care that this procedure does not result in de facto segregation.

A variation used successfully by some physical educators requires cooperative effort within a team to bring all players to a desired skill level before game play is permitted. Squads or teams comprised of players of varied skill levels are established near the beginning of a sport unit. Criteria for skill performance are set, and all members of a team (or a certain percentage such as 75% or 90%) must achieve these minimum skills before a team may begin game play. This usually results in the skilled players helping the less skilled so that all can progress to game playing.

Conscientious teachers of team sports must assess the achievements of the students in each class and strive to provide a learning experience suitable to their needs. The curriculum should develop progressively from basic sport skills to advanced skills that require teamwork and strategy. Teaching basic skills and then throwing out the basketball or assigning sides and then throwing out the ball and bat are not enough. Physical education teachers must teach, and they must do it competently, just as coaches must coach competently. As students move from grade to grade, they should be presented with more difficult skills, complex strategies, and knowledges. They should be expected to develop more mature behavior patterns and to accept more responsibility for both their own advancement and that of their classmates. When physical education programs are worthwhile and effective, young people will learn to incorporate physical activities into their lifestyles and enhance the quality of their lives.

Evaluation in Coeducational Classes

Throughout the elementary grades and into middle school, both boys and girls can be evaluated using the same measures. However, some adjustment or careful selection of tests used to measure skill achievement at the high school level may be needed. Although the emphasis in physical education would be on motor development and fitness, evaluation should encompass all three domains of learning: motor, cognitive, and affective.

Motor skills can be evaluated by the use of (a) skills tests (standardized or teacher devised), (b) incident charts, (c) successful task completion (e.g., making two out of five shots in basketball), (d) the standing or rank achieved in competition with classmates, (e) personal improvement, or (f) observations made by the teacher. The first five of these suggestions for evaluation are objective measures, whereas the last item is subjective. Because subjective measures are affected by observer bias, it is difficult to justify using this measure exclusively when determining grades.

Cognitive learning can be evaluated through written examinations, verbal quizzes, and observation of compliance with the rules and use of strategy in game play. Tests should be given after a unit of instruction has been completed or just before tournament play begins to determine whether students know the rules, techniques, and necessary strategies for successful team play.

Care must be taken when selecting skills tests for use at the high school level to avoid tests that are affected by strength, weight, or height. Human growth studies reveal significant differences between most males and females in their middle to late teens. Males are usually taller, heavier, and stronger than females; and therefore would have a distinct advantage over the female classmates in tests such as a distance throw or the volleyball spike. Tests evaluating accuracy (free throw shooting) or control (dribbling a ball) provide more equitable measures of achievement for all students.

Students who are accustomed to expect physical education to be an enjoyable learning experience will be more attentive and willing to develop new skills and knowledges. Evaluating the achievements of youngsters is not only a means of assessing progress but also a motivating device.

Terminology

Cardiorespiratory efficiency—Interaction of the circulatory system (the heart) and the respiratory system (the lungs)

Closed skill—A skill that is always performed the same way regardless of its use in a game or contest (e.g., bowling, free throw shooting)

Flexibility—A measure of the range of motion possible in a specific joint

Movement efficiency—Proper execution of a skill with minimum effort through conformity to good body mechanics

Neuromuscular—Involving the interaction of the nervous and the muscular systems

Skill—A purposeful combination of movements to accomplish a specific objective or goal

Strength—The ability to overcome a resistance (force or load) once

References

Annarino, A., Cowell, C., & Hazelton, H. (1986). *Curriculum theory and design in physical education* (2nd ed.). Prospect Heights, IL: Waveland Press.

Melograno, V. (1979). *Designing curriculum and learning: A physical coeducation approach.* Dubuque, IA: Kendall/Hunt.

Nixon, J., & Jewett, A. (1964). *Physical education curriculum.* New York: Ronald Press.

Willgoose, C. (1984). *The curriculum in physical education* (4th ed.). Englewood Cliffs, NJ: Prentice-Hall.

Williams, H., (1983). *Perceptual and motor development.* Englewood Cliffs, NJ: Prentice-Hall.

Selected Readings

Dougherty, N., & Bonanno, D. (1979). *Contemporary approaches to the teaching of physical education.* Minneapolis: Burgess.

Jewett, A., & Bain, L. (1985). *The curriculum process in physical education.* Dubuque, IA: Wm. C. Brown.

Rink, J.E. (1985). *Teaching physical education for learning.* St. Louis: Times Mirror/Mosby.

Seidentop, D., Mand, C., & Taggart, A. (1986). *Physical education: Teaching and curriculum strategies for grades 5-12.* Palo Alto, CA: Mayfield.

Chapter 2
Principles of Movement and Observation

Practitioners in physical education and sport are confronted with leadership and teaching responsibilities in an immense variety of physical activities. It is essential that the practitioner have a strong theoretical base of knowledge about physical and sport activities. Beyond acquiring knowledge, the practitioner must apply that knowledge to a variety of physical skills in educational, clinical, and recreational settings. Foundational knowledge about how people move is essential to everyone who works with physical skills or human movement. Authors such as Cooper, Adrian, and Glassow (1982), Wickstrom (1983), and Broer & Zernicke (1979) suggest that the study of human movement begin with an attempt to identify basic movement patterns. Fundamental movement patterns are the language of movement. A thorough knowledge of those patterns facilitates a better understanding of the more complex sport-specific skills performed in team sports. It is the purpose of this chapter to discuss and define the terminology of movement, define the structure and complexity of sport skills, discuss the general mechanical principles that apply to movement, and suggest an observational plan for analyzing sport skills.

Fundamental Terms

A prerequisite to the discussion of fundamental movement patterns and sport-specific skills is a brief description of the terminology related to the structure of human movement. Terminology may vary depending on the author or the source; the following terminology will be used in this text.

Basic Movement

A *basic movement* is defined as any simple change in position of the anatomical segments of the body. Daniels (1984) defines a basic movement as one that cannot be broken down into a smaller or simpler form without changing the action. Examples of basic movements are *flexion* and *extension* of the arm around the shoulder, flexion and extension of the forearm around the elbow, *lateral flexion* of the trunk or head, *inward or outward rotation* at the shoulder or hip, transfer of weight, and maintaining a specific *static position*. These basic movements and others can be found in the fundamental patterns.

Fundamental Movement Pattern

A *fundamental movement pattern* is a series of basic movements combined in a temporal and spatial sequence that accomplishes a general purpose. The fundamental pattern is a general pattern of movements utilized in the fundamental skill. Fundamental patterns have very generalized purposes, such as locomotion of the body, control of the body, or manipulation of an object or the body.

Fundamental Skill

The adaptation of a fundamental movement pattern for the purpose of accomplishing a more specific objective is defined as a *fundamental skill*. These common motor activities are the foundation of more advanced and highly specific sport skills. For example, the fundamental skills of throwing, striking, pushing, carrying, and holding share the common general purpose of manipulation of an object and therefore are members of the family of manipulative fundamental movement patterns. Uniqueness exists within each fundamental skill grouping, defined by *range of motion*, plane of motion, and different environmental constraints. Additional examples of fundamental skills are running, jumping, stopping, starting, pivoting, catching, trapping, and landing.

Sport-Specific Skill

A *sport-specific skill* is a highly defined fundamental skill or a combination of several fundamental skills with a very specific purpose. Further defining distinctions of a sport-specific skill are (a) the constraint of spatial dimension or playing area, (b) the constraint of playing time, (c) the uniqueness of sport equipment and its limitations, (d) the constraint of the playing rules, and (e) the range of motion and speed of movements used in the skill. These constraints on the skill prescribe the unique movement to be applied in solving the specific sport-environmental problem for the performer.

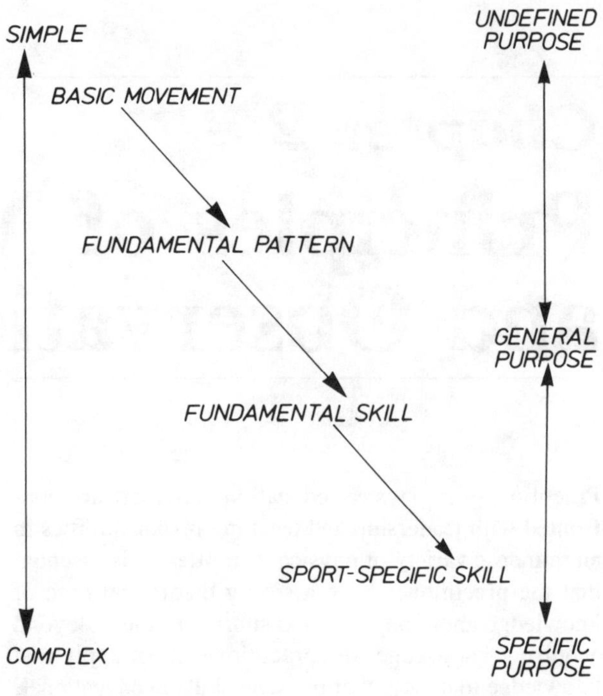

Figure 2.1. Skill structure

Skill Structure

Sport skills are built from sound performance ability of the fundamental skills. This idea is based on the principle of development, which states that development proceeds from simple to complex, from homogeneous to heterogeneous, or from general to specific. The primary hierarchical form of movement skill is illustrated in Figure 2.1.

The illustration of each of these terms is consistent with the definitions defined previously as well as with the theory of general-to-specific development. Each level of movement depends on the successful attainment of the movements above it.

Several characteristics of movements or skills differentiate the degree of simplicity or complexity in the specific movement skill (Figure 2.2). The more complex a movement is, the more control is required for its execution. *Control* is defined here as the ability to restrict the speed, range of motion, and precise timing of the individual component parts of the movement. Degrees of freedom in movement refers to the number of *body segments* utilized in a movement. The more complex the skill is, the more degrees of freedom that will be utilized in the movement. The more simplistic the skill is, the fewer degrees of freedom that will be required in the skill execution.

In addition to these qualities of motion, the number of component parts of a skill helps define simplicity versus complexity. The more component parts or fundamental skills that are incorporated into a sport-specific skill, the more complex and difficult the movement task will be. The levels of complexity of several basketball skills are illustrated in Figure 2.3. The addition of component parts in a skill requires the application of addi-

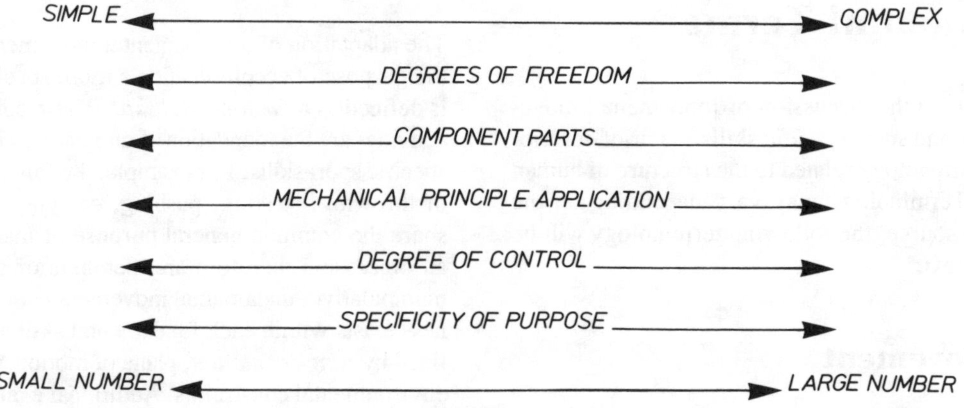

Figure 2.2. Complexity versus simplicity in sport-specific skills

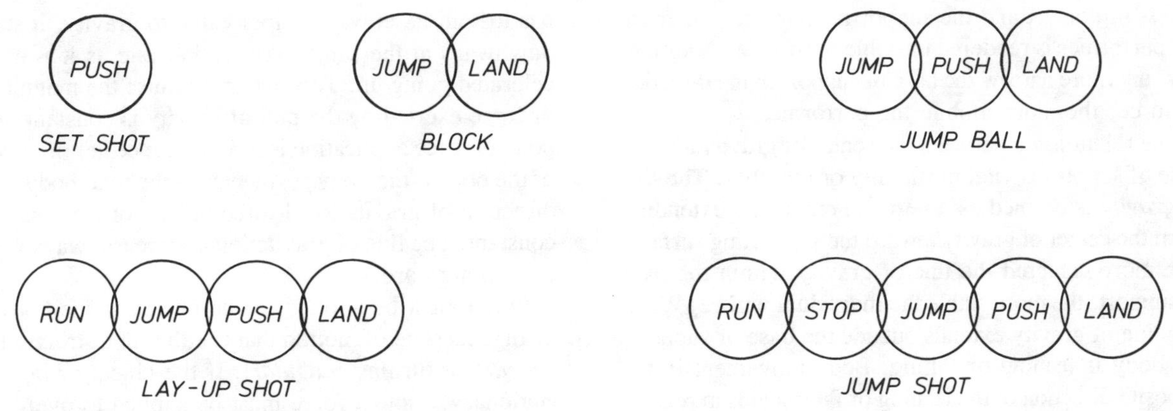

Figure 2.3. Examples of sequentially combined fundamental skills to create sport-specific skills

tional mechanical principles and further defines the complexity of the skill. Sport skills are usually more complex as the purpose of the skill becomes highly specific.

Some qualities of movement are sought at any level of movement-skill complexity. The qualities of efficiency of motion and coordination are essential at each level of movement. The exceptional performer masters each level with economy of motion and displays refined coordination. The attainment of these qualities at each developmental level enhances one's ability to achieve and master the next level with the same preciseness. These qualities are highly related and generally are attained simultaneously. Kelso (1982) defined *coordination* as the function of constraints of all free variables of a movement into a purposeful action. *Movement efficiency* is the proper execution of a skill with a minimum amount of effort through conformity to good body mechanics. This requires the proper application of the mechanical concepts of movements, which is discussed next.

Mechanical Principles

The laws of mechanics must be applied to movement so that one can move effectively and accomplish the specific goal of the skill. The general understanding of mechanical principles is important in recognizing their diverse applications to a variety of team-sport skills. The mechanical concepts pertaining to movement are grouped into theme topics for clarity and for purposes of discussion.

Center of Gravity and Balance

The earth exerts a pulling force on all bodies and objects on its surface. This pull of *gravity* exerts a vertical downward force on all body parts or segments. The *center of gravity* of the total body is that point inside or outside the body or object where all things are equally balanced or where gravitational pull is concentrated, a point around which the body or object could be balanced. The center of gravity is dynamic or movable in that any movement of the body parts away from the center, or *midline*, of the body causes the center of gravity to shift in the direction of movement proportional to the distance and the amount of mass (weight) displaced. External weight, such as a sport implement, adds to the total body weight and affects the location of the center of gravity, displacing it in the direction of the added weight. The body's balance remains more stable when an object is carried or held close to the body's center of gravity.

The control of the center of gravity provides the performer with *stability*, or balance, while stationary or moving. Stability is maintained when opposing forces acting on the body are equal. The manipulation of the center of gravity provides the performer with a means to cause movement, or *mobility*. For example, the larger the *base of support*, the more stable the body will be. The reverse of this would be decreasing the size of the base of support for the purpose of making the body unstable for the initiation of motion. Stability and mobility are inversely related. The principles of stability or balance can be reversed in their applications to affect motion or cause mobility.

The base of support is any body part or object in contact with the supporting surface and the adjacent area between the points of contact. The larger this base of support is, the more stable the body will be. There must be considerable friction between the points of contact and the supporting surface for a widening of the base to be effective. If the base of support is extended in the direction of force application or force absorption, more stability will be achieved. The reverse of these principles renders the performer mobile. The smaller the base of support and the less the amount of friction between the points of contact and the supporting surface, the more the performer is rendered unstable or mobile. Additionally, the more narrow the base of support in the direction of force, the more mobile the performer.

The relationship between the center of gravity and the base of support is vital to stability or mobility. The *line of gravity* is defined as a perpendicular line extending from the center of gravity toward the supporting surface. The more centered the line of gravity within the base of support, the more stable the individual will be. When this line of gravity extends outside the base of support, the body is leaning or falling. Body movement in the opposite direction of the leaning or falling aids in regaining balance or stability. In some activities, such as walking and running, the center of gravity is continuously shifting, and balance is regained by establishing a new base of support under that shifting base of support.

There are other situations in sports in which balance is affected by the type of movement the individual performs. Balance is precarious when moving in a *rotary* manner. Focusing on stationary objects aids in maintaining dynamic balance during these situations.

Force

Force is defined as a push or pull exerted on a body or an object. Force applications are essential in order to create movement. Any change in the state of motion or nonmotion is the result of the application of force. Forces are classified as either internal or external. An *internal force* is created by the contraction of muscles, causing body segments to move, slow down, or stop moving. An external force is a push or pull that originates outside the body and is exerted on the body or an object. External forces may come from another performer, gravity, the wind, a supporting surface, or other environmental sources.

Four characteristics of force help to describe the specific application of force: (a) the magnitude of force, which describes the amount, or quality, of force being applied; (b) the direction of force application, defined as the direction of force application on the body or object; (c) the point of force application, which defines the location on the object or body where the force application occurs; and (d) the *line of force*, which is a line extending from the point of force application indefinitely in the direction of force application. The line of force helps interpret the result that occurs due to force application.

The force of gravity limits performance as it pulls the body or object downward toward the center of the earth. Force must be applied to change the *velocity* of the body or an object. Gravity decelerates an object or the body on its upward flight in airborne situations. Once an object has lost all its upward velocity due to gravity, it starts downward at the same acceleration rate as it was decelerated going up. This occurs because the magnitude of force exerted by the pull of gravity is constant. The point of force application is through the center of gravity of the object, the body segments, or the total body. The direction of gravitational force or line of force is also constant. The line of gravitational force is always vertically downward.

Force must be applied for an object or the body to change its state of motion that is either in a straight line (*linear*) or turning (*angular*). If the object or body is stationary, enough force must be applied to overcome the mass or weight (*inertia*) of the object or body to make it move. If the object or body is fixed at one end (e.g., the foot planted in a pivot step), enough force must be applied to overcome the object's or body's reluctance to rotate (*moment of inertia*). If the object or body is moving, force must be applied to increase or decrease the linear or angular velocity, causing the object or body to speed up or slow down, respectively.

Increasing the distance over which the force is applied increases the amount of force that is generated. This additional force increases or decreases the rate of velocity for the purpose of either acceleration or deceleration. The greater the range of motion over which the force is imparted, the greater the distance will be in which to generate force. This increase results in the additional force that affects the motion of the object or body. Additionally, a greater number of body parts (levers) simultaneously or sequentially used provides an extended amount of time available for building or depleting force. Time to build force is especially important when creating force to move stationary objects or bodies.

When the body or an object is acted on by a force, the resulting acceleration and change of speed is proportional to the mass. The more mass (weight) an object or the body has, the more force that is necessary to change its present movement behavior. It takes more force to move or stop a heavy object or body than a light object or body. Once the movement is started, it takes less force to maintain the speed than to change that speed. The final direction of a moving object or body is the resultant of the magnitude and direction of all forces that have been applied to that object or body.

When several forces are applied sequentially, each succeeding force is applied at a point when the preceding one has made its greatest contribution. This concept is visible when observing individual body parts or segments in their movement behaviors. When several body segments are used in a movement skill in succession, each contributes to the motion by accelerating until a peak accelerate is achieved, which is generally a half to a third of its range of motion. Another body segment will begin its contribution at this point. Segments continue this pattern until all segments involved have made their contributions.

Force should be applied as directly as possible to an object or the body through its center of gravity in the intended direction of movement. This assures the intended direction, economy of effort, and minimum rotation (unless that is the purpose of the skill). When an object is lifted or pushed, the amount of force necessary to move that object increases as the distance of the object from the body's center of gravity increases. This concept is especially important when moving heavy and bulky objects.

Force dissipation in such fundamental skills as landing, catching, and trapping is achieved by application of force in the opposite direction of movement for the purpose of overcoming its *momentum*. When absorbing force, one should receive the force through gradual reduction so that the shock is dissipated over as long a distance and time as possible. The shock of an object or body can be diminished by absorbing it either over a greater distance, over a greater area, over a greater period of time, or with any combination thereof. When a greater distance is needed to absorb force, a longer period of time is also usually necessary. Absorption of force over a greater area is generally accomplished by the use of such sports equipment as softball gloves, knee pads, and shin guards.

Newton's Laws of Motion

Sir Isaac Newton formulated three basic laws of motion that apply to all objects or bodies under the influence of gravitational pull. All sport movements are influenced by these laws or principles of motion and are therefore important in understanding human movement.

Newton's first law states than an object or the body continues its present state of rest or motion unless acted on by a force. A force must be exerted on an object or the body to change its motion, direction, or speed. This resistance to change is *inertia*, and it varies proportionally with the mass (weight) of the object or body. This law also applies to body segments, objects, or the total body in rotational types of motion.

A force is necessary to change the present state of motion or velocity of an object or the body either positively or negatively. Acceleration is the change of speed or velocity of an object or the body. This increase in velocity is referred to as *positive acceleration*; the decrease or slowing down is *negative acceleration*, or *deceleration*. The amount of speeding up or slowing down is directly proportional to the amount of force applied. To increase the rate of speeding up or slowing down, one must apply increasing amounts of force. The amount of mass of the object or body influences how much force must be applied to accelerate positively or negatively. A large mass requires more force application than does a smaller mass for the same rate of acceleration. Therefore, Newton's second law states that the acceleration of a mass is directly proportional to the force applied and is inversely proportional to the mass.

Newton's third law states that for every action there is an equal and opposite reaction. Actions and reactions are forces. Therefore, for every force exerted by the body, there is an equal and opposite force exerted on the body. The human body is put into motion or motion is diminished due to this law. An example of the application of this principle is the pushing against the earth that occurs in jumping. The more downward vertical force applied to the earth, the more upward vertical force reaction occurs. Therefore, a performer's pushing downward and backward creates an upward and forward reaction. This principle also applies to rotary, or angular, motions. The more force applied, the more angular force reaction occurs. In addition, the farther away from the axis of rotation the force is applied, the more angular reaction occurs in the body or object.

Levers

A *lever* is a simple machine utilized externally and internally by the body in human movements. The purpose of a lever is to gain some mechanical advantage. A lever has a rigid bar, fulcrum, point of force application, central point of resistance, force arm, and resistance arm. The rigid bar can be the bones of the body when the lever is internal or an implement when the lever is external. The joints of the body are the fulcrum in the internal lever and the point around which rotation occurs in the external lever. The point of force application is the attachment of the muscle by the tendon to the bone in the internal lever and the point of force application by the body or object in the external lever. The resistance point is the central point of balance of the weight of the body segment in the internal lever or the center of all body parts and objects being supported by the body part in the external level. The resistance arm is the distance between the fulcrum and the resistance. The force arm is the distance between the fulcrum and the point of application of force. There are three types of levers based on the location of these component parts (Figure 2.4).

A requirement of the first-class lever is that the fulcrum be positioned between the resistance and the point of force application. The closeness of the fulcrum to either the point of force application or the center of resistance dictates the mechanical advantage the lever has.

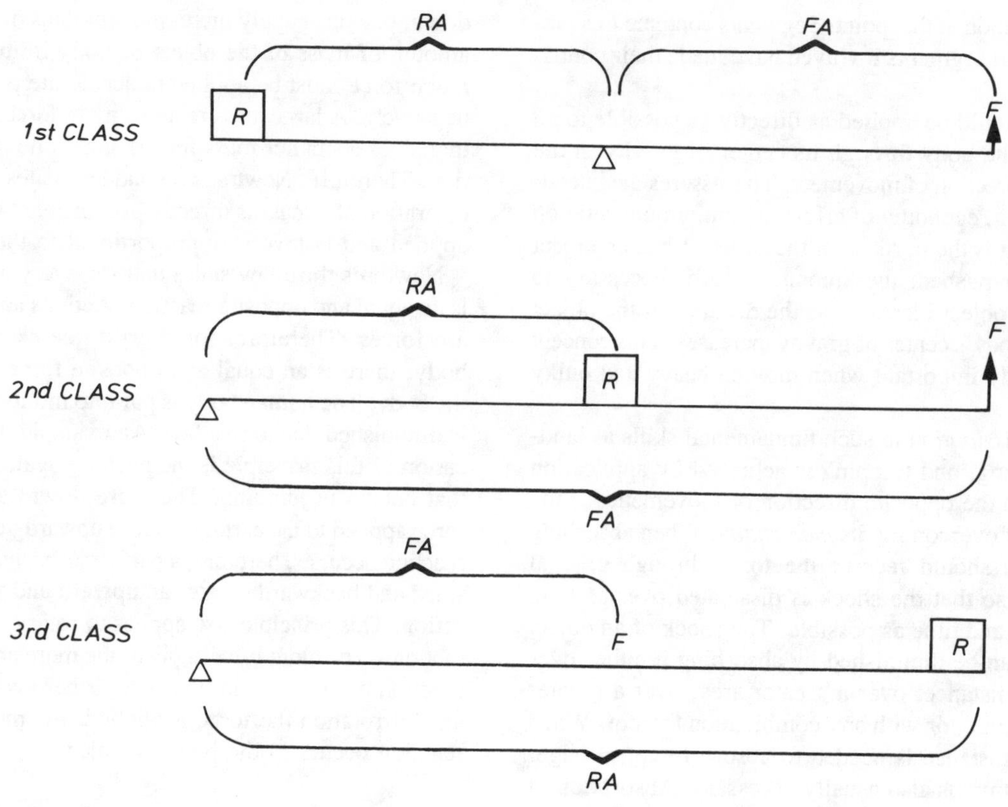

Figure 2.4. Lever classifications: R = resistance, F = force, Δ = fulcrum, FA = force arm, RA = resistance arm

When the fulcrum is closest to the resistance, the mechanical advantage becomes the ability to overcome a large resistance with a small amount of force. When the fulcrum is closest to the point of force application, the mechanical advantage becomes the ability to produce speed of motion, although large amounts of force must be applied. When the resistance multiplied by the resistance arm ($R \times RA$) is equal to the force multiplied by the force arm ($F \times FA$), then balance is the advantage. Movement occurs when levers are unbalanced. Motion described as angular occurs when the internal levers of the human body are unbalanced.

A requirement of the second-class lever is that the resistance be positioned between the fulcrum and the point of force application. In this lever, the force arm is always larger than the resistance arm. The mechanical advantage in this lever is the ability to overcome a large resistance with a small amount of force.

A requirement of the third-class lever is that the point of force application always be positioned between the fulcrum and the resistance. In this lever, the resistance arm is always larger than the force arm. The mechanical advantage in this lever is the production of speed in movement, but it demands large amounts of force. Most internal levers in the human body are third-class levers.

The human body is a system of levers functioning together to accomplish any given task. For example, when kicking a ball the leg consists of three levers working in combination with one another to produce the fast-moving distal extremity (foot) that will contact the ball. The thigh, lower leg, and foot are separate levers functioning in this system. These anatomical levers function sequentially to produce the whipping action of the leg to impart the largest amount of force to the ball. The upper-body anatomical levers function the same way in throwing types of movements.

Integration of Linear and Angular Components

When a lever is rotating around the fulcrum with a constant angular speed, the linear speed of any point on the lever is proportional to the distance from that point to the fulcrum. The linear motion at the distal end of a lever is larger than the linear motion at the fulcrum, or point of rotation. The linear motion at the distal end of the lever can be increased if the length of the lever is increased. When the force applied to the lever is uniform and the lever is decreased in length, the angular speed will increase. Therefore, a performer can change the distribution of mass about an axis of rotation by shortening the lever length (by pulling body parts toward the center of the body) and thus proportionally increase the angular velocity.

Most human movements are a combination of several angular movements that result in a linear motion. The integration of linear and angular motion occurs often to optimize performance. Angular motions of the legs create a linear total body motion of the human body in running. A shortening of the arm lever in throwing occurs to increase the angular speed with which the arm is moved forward toward the point of contact or release. A lengthening of the arm lever (extension of the elbow and flexion of the wrist) occurs just prior to contact or release to create the largest amount of linear speed to be transferred to the ball or object.

Momentum

The momentum of the body or an object is the product of its mass (weight) and velocity (speed). The momentum expresses the amount of motion a body or object possesses. The momentum of a body or object can be changed by increasing or decreasing the mass or velocity. In most movement skills the mass is redistributed or the velocity is changed to alter the momentum of the body or object. The momentum possessed by a lever (body limb or implement) can be transferred to an external object or the body. The momentum of the arm is transferred to the ball in throwing. Momentum is also transferred from the leg to the ball in kicking. The momentum of an implement such as a bat can be transferred to the ball in softball batting. The momentum of several body parts can be transferred to the total body, causing the body to become airborne, as seen in jumping. When the transfer of momentum is for the purpose of making the body airborne, the transfer of momentum must occur at the instant of takeoff for maximum transfer of momentum.

Follow-Through

Follow-through in any movement skill is the phase of motion following the *force-production phase* of the motion. Follow-through is a continuation of the motion that prevents a decrease in velocity of body parts during the force-production phase, helps prevent injury, and places the body in position for the next sport skill. The follow-through motion permits maximum speed to be generated during the action phase of the skill by decelerating the body parts after the action phase is completed. Follow-through also prevents injuries caused by the abrupt stopping of body parts or the total body. Generally, follow-through helps to position the player for the next skill sequence to be performed.

Projectiles

There are many different *projectiles* in team-sport activities. Projection of the body as well as of objects such as a softball, soccer ball, football, field hockey ball, basketball, and volleyball occur in team-sport activities. The force to project the body or an object must be greater than the inertia of the projectile and any external forces restraining the body or object. The larger the velocity of the object just prior to release or contact, the greater the resultant velocity on the object. The general purposes of projection are projectile speed, distance, and/or accuracy. The direction of an object is determined by the point of force application on the body or object. Force application on the body or an object (except through the center of gravity of that body or object) will cause it to rotate. The farther from and less perpendicular to the center of gravity the point of force application occurs, the more rotation is imparted on the object.

An object moving in a circular path will begin to move in a straight line from the point of contact or release. The path of an object when projected is determined by the amount of velocity and the angle at contact or release. The greater the air resistance, the more the path of the body or object will depart from the original path. The lighter the weight and the larger the surface area of the projectile, the greater the air resistance on that object will be and the more the path of the object will be altered.

If the purpose of the projection is speed rather than distance, the angle of projection should be as close to the horizontal as possible while still achieving the desired distance. If the purpose of projection is distance, the optimal angle of projection is 45°. This angle may be altered due to additional outside forces. If the purpose of projection is vertical lift, the optimal angle approaches 90°.

Spin and Angle of Rebound

When the body or an object approaches a surface that has a greater resistance than its own, it will rebound off that surface. The normal angle of rebound will be at the same angle from which it approaches the surface but in the opposite direction (rebound) (Figure 2.5). The normal angle of rebound can be altered due to *spin*, defined as a rotating of an object while airborne, and/or the elasticity of the object and the resisting surface. The angle of approach will play a role in determining the location and amount of depression of the body or object.

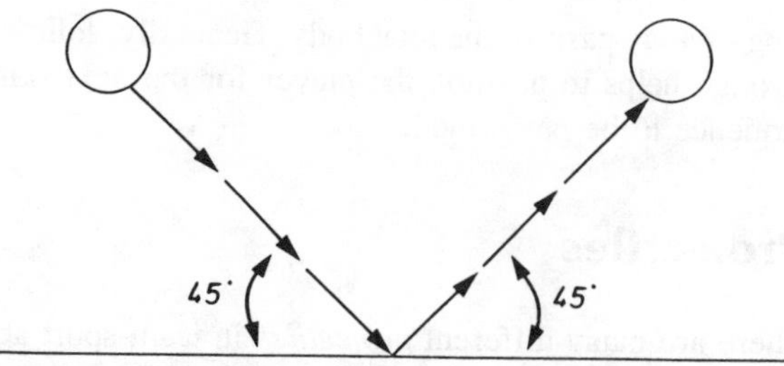

Figure 2.5. Normal angle of rebound

The more depression, the more the object will react to that depression. The smaller the angle of approach to the surface, the greater the depression of that surface and the greater the rebound will be. For practical purposes, the angle of rebound is approximately equal to the angle of approach when spin is not a major influence.

When an object is in flight with no spin, the object will move or curve in the direction of the most powerful outside force (e.g., gravity or wind). To project an object without spin is very difficult. Air resistance against the surface of the object will cause some spin even when trying to project the object without spin. Any object will tend to spin toward the side of least pressure. The spin on an object will cause a change in the *frictional forces* between the object and the resisting surface when rebounding. This change in frictional force changes the angle of rebound. Any object spinning in one direction will curve and rebound in the direction of the spin. An object with *top spin* will have an increase in forward friction. This is caused by the object rotating toward, and therefore spending more time in contact with the resisting surface. This will cause a decreased or lower, angle of rebound (Figure 2.6). The object with *backspin*

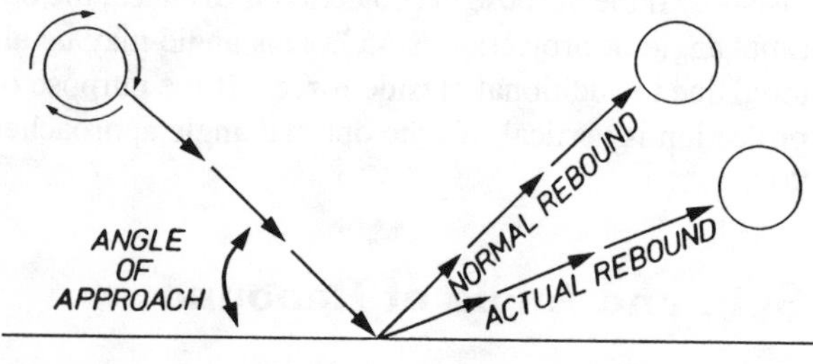

Figure 2.6. Lower angle of rebound

will have an increase in backward friction. This is caused by the object rotating against, and therefore spending less time in contact with, the resisting surface. This will cause an increased, or higher, angle of rebound (Figure 2.7).

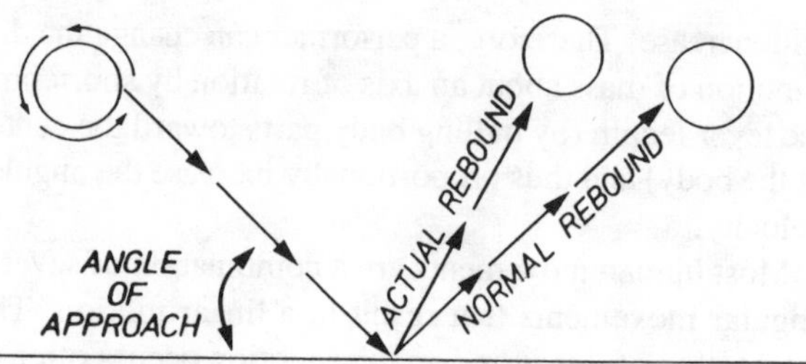

Figure 2.7. Higher angle of rebound

Observation and Analysis of Skills

The observation and analysis of movement skills are an everyday professional responsibility of the practitioner. The learned skill of observation occurs on a daily basis for most professionals. Correct and accurate observation must be learned through structured experiences. The analysis and assessment of skills are also professional responsibilities in two types of situations. First, the analysis of motor skills is preliminary to teaching motor skills. A skill must be thoroughly understood before the practitioner can structure appropriate activities for the learning environment. Second, an analysis can also be utilized to assess an individual's performance level. The assessment can be performed to detect correct and incorrect performance elements that can be be employed in the instruction of that individual to improve performance. Analysis and assessment are also utilized to evaluate and grade individual students.

One approach to the observation and analysis of motor skills involves the two general procedures of preplanning and observation. Preplanning involves gathering information pertaining to the sport-specific skill for the purpose of building a skill framework or structure that permits the practitioner the opportunity to understand the skill thoroughly and to form an objective set of performance expectations. This procedure is utilized in preparation for teaching or observing. The observational procedure is performed on the basis of structured preplanning. The practitioner can then observe and assess with more objectivity.

Preplanning

Preplanning involves several procedural steps in the gathering of information. The steps are executed in the following order:

1. Identify the skill to be analyzed.

2. Determine the general purpose of the skill.
3. Reconstruct the skill with the sequencing of the fundamental movement patterns utilized in the skill.
4. Determine the special circumstances in which the skill is performed and may affect the skill execution.
5. Determine the specific performance goal.
6. Design the skill model relative to performance expectations.
7. Construct observational questions based on the designed skill model.

The first step is to identify the sport-specific skill to be taught or observed. Once the skill is identified, the general purpose of the skill needs to be clarified. General purposes could be locomotion, body control, or object manipulation. The purpose of locomotion would be to transpose or move the body from one location to another by means of walking, running, or jumping. The purpose of body control would be to maintain balance/stability or agility while stopping, starting, or changing direction. The purpose of object manipulation would be to control objects through carrying, pushing, throwing, striking, or receiving-of-force movements. Object manipulation for receiving of force can also include the receiving of force of the total body in landing.

The next procedural step is to break down the specific skill into fundamental movement components. The reconstruction of the skill with fundamental movements facilitates a better general and mechanical understanding of the skill. When this procedure is followed for a variety of sport-specific skills, the practitioner begins to recognize the similarities and dissimilarities between and among skills from the same general fundamental movement pattern. A model of skills that progresses from simple to complex begins to emerge and permits understanding of the skill objectively without preconceived ideas prejudicing the practitioner. The practitioner should list the component skills in the order of execution. A more thorough understanding of the skill can be accomplished by answering the following questions:

1. Which fundamental movements or skills are utilized as the preparatory motion, force production, and follow-through of the total skill?
2. How much does each fundamental component contribute to the total skill?
3. What are the sequences of joint action in each component from the beginning until the end of the total skill?
4. How are smooth transitions made between the fundamental components?
5. What range of motion should be expected in each moving region of the body?

The next procedural step in preplanning involves identifying special circumstances in which the skill is performed. These can be grouped into the categories of performer-imposed characteristics and environmental-imposed circumstances.

Age and ability level are special circumstances imposed by the performer. Performance expectations should be altered to match the individual performer's characteristics. Expectations based on the optimal performances of top athletes can be detrimental to other age groups such as the young and the very old as well as the less mature. Performer characteristics should be taken into consideration when planning the learning environment or observing and evaluating the performer.

The environment surrounding the execution of the skill imposes limitations, including the playing environment and the connective skills executed before and after the skill. The playing environment limits performance of a skill by the rules of the game, the dimensions of the playing area, and the sport equipment utilized in the skill performance. These limitations need to be taken into consideration when formulating the skill expectations. Changes in technique execution may occur due to pre- and postskill execution and should also be taken into consideration when formulating the skill expectations.

The next procedural step of preplanning is to determine the specific performance goal of the skill. These goals are measures of successful performance and are more unique and specific to the activity and performing circumstances. The performance goal could be as specific as scoring points by putting the basketball through the goal or as general as gaining some advantage in the activity. Other examples of performance goals are accuracy and placement of an object, velocity of an object, vertical or horizontal movement of an object or a body, change in direction, quickness in a short time period, velocity at takeoff or over an extended period of time, the connecting of two skills, and maintaining balance. The performance goal assists in defining the specifics of skill execution.

The next procedure in preplanning is to design a skill model with performance expectations when all elements and circumstances surrounding the execution of that skill are taken into consideration. This provides the practitioner with an objective understanding of the skill and a set of reasonable expectations for the performer(s). The final step in the procedure of preplanning is to construct a list of observational questions based on skill technique, physiological prerequisites, skill perception, and performer motivational level. Specifics on each of these levels of observation follow.

Observational Procedures

Several visual observation plans are available in the physical education literature (Brown, 1984; Daniels, 1984; Hay & Reid, 1982; Hoffman, 1984). The visual observation plan presented here is illustrated in Figure 2.8 in a flow-chart format similar to Hoffman's (1984). The initial observation is for making an evaluation of the total skill and determining the success or failure of the specific goal of the skill. The observer should ask whether the goal was achieved. If the goal was achieved and the performance optimal, then move on to the next

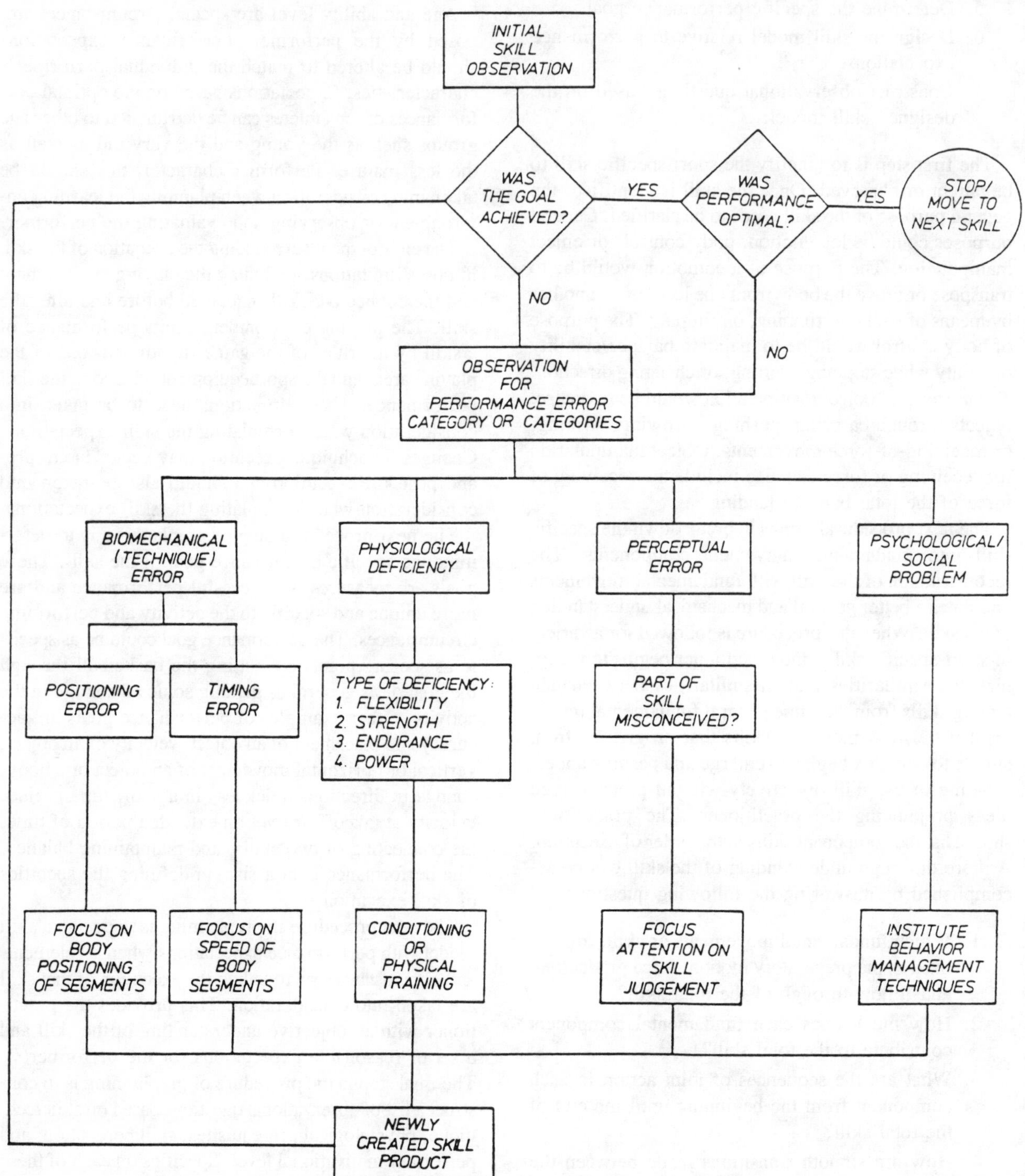

Figure 2.8. Observational flow chart

skill or performer. If the goal was not achieved or the performance not optimal, then another observation is necessary to determine the type of performance error.

Certain factors will enhance the observer's ability to see and evaluate a skill. The first point is that the observer must view the skill performance several times to make accurate judgments about the performance. The second consideration is where to position yourself for the best possible view of the performer. The position should be one that permits a view of the total movement and gives ample environmental view to link the skill with the surroundings and the specific purpose of the skill. A position without distracting objects or other performers is helpful in concentrating on the observation task. During observation, it is best to pick out objects, such as walls, that give you vertical and horizontal reference points from which to make associations of the skill relative to the space in which it is performed. Several angles of observations might be necessary to evaluate the performance fully. Once positions for observation are decided on, the observer should mentally review the performance expectations set during preplanning before beginning the observation.

The observer should concentrate on the separate components of the skill in the order of occurrence. This involves first evaluating the *preparation phase* and then proceeding to the force-production phase and finally the follow-through phase of the motion. The observation of each component of the skill should progress from the slowest-moving parts (*proximal*) to the fastest-moving part (*distal*). The observer should try to determine the source of the performance error. The errors in performance are generally under one of four categories: (a) biomechanical, or technique; (b) physiological; (c) perceptual; or (d) psychological/social. It is possible for performance difficulties to be from two or more of these categories when skill execution is performed badly.

Biomechanical Errors

Biomechanical, or technique, errors are categorized as either body-positioning or timing errors. Body-positioning errors involve the observation of the prevailing body positions during the preparation, force-production, and follow-through phases. The observer should pay special attention to the sequence of joint action and the range of motion in each of the joints. Additionally, any extemporaneous or unnecessary motion can detract from or limit the performance. Observers need to be aware of two types of extemporaneous motion: (a) those motions that limit or detract from the execution of the skill, and (b) those that merely define style in the skill (they do not interfere with achieving the goal).

Observers should also pay special attention to such things as the use of opposition; head motion, which generally leads the movement; and hip motion, which generally indicates the total body center-of-gravity movement. Special attention to the direction of moving body parts and to the direction of force application in a skill will help the observer determine whether proper force production is occurring in the skill. The observer should define the force-production requirements of the skill as this helps define the sequential body-segment pattern in the skill. For example, some skills require an all-out maximum production of force (ballistic) such as jumping, blocking, and throwing. Other skills require accuracy, which requires controlling the range of motion, which in turn decreases the force production with special emphasis on the timing of the skill. A need for both force production and accuracy (kicking) requires a compromise or a balancing of these components. The observer should be aware of the compromise between and among elements to help accomplish the specific goal of the skill.

The observer should attend to the stability or mobility of the performer. Assessment of the stability needs of the performer will dictate the movements. Observation of the center of gravity relative to the base of support will indicate the level of stability or balance. *Weight transfer* is an indication of stability or mobility changes. All body positioning that is incorrect should be referenced with the mechanical principles being violated. Emphasis on the incorrect body positioning to the performer should be reinforced with the mechanical principle application, thus providing the practitioner with reasons for movement change. Performers soon learn to apply the mechanical principles to other movement problems. Body-positioning errors can be corrected by emphasizing the body-segment corrections needed and providing mechanical explanations and practice situations.

Timing errors center around the speeds of individual body segments and of the total body. Quickness or slowness of body segments should be observed. The observer should also pay special attention to any pauses or slowing of body segments during continuous motion. If pauses occur, the movement will appear jerky or arhythmical. The more force production needed in a skill, the faster the action of body segments will be. Motion should be slowest in the proximal body parts (center) and fastest in the distal body parts (extremities). Additionally, speed of motion should progress from slow to fast in most skill movements.

The proper timing of body segments relative to one another is essential in many sport skills. Blocking actions of the body are created in some skills to provide a strong or stable base on which other body parts can pull. *Blocking* is defined as stopping the movement of one body segment or segments prior to the conclusion of the skill. In throwing types of motion, the hips move in a *counterclockwise* direction (for a right-handed thrower) and stop once facing the direction of the throw. The blocking of the hips in this movement provides a strong base on which the throwing arm can complete the throwing motion. In kicking, the thigh slows considerably when perpendicular to the ball, providing a strong base on which the lower leg and foot swing through to make contact with the ball.

In some sport-skill movements it is essential for some body segments to lag behind others in the movement. In throwing, the hand and lower arm stay behind the upper arm and shoulder. Opening at the elbow (extension) and wrist (flexion) carries the ball into position for release with the greatest speed. In kicking, the lower leg and the foot stay behind the hip and thigh. The opening at the knee and ankle moves the leg toward the ball for the contact.

Agility movements require rapid change in the speed and timing of body segments. Failure of agility movements generally result from inaccurate decisions as to when to speed up or slow down in movement sequences. Quickness is essential in agility movements, which indicate rapid timing or speed changes. All timing errors are also related to mechanical principles that can explain the reasons for timing changes. Mechanical principles should be used to explain timing errors to the performer and followed with opportunities for practice.

Physiological Errors

Physiological errors are caused by performer deficiencies. A performer may have difficulty in movements due to a lack of flexibility (range of motion in specific joints), strength, endurance, or power. When such physiological deficiencies exist, correction involves physical training programs that focus specifically on that deficiency. Performance can be enhanced by improving the physiological prerequisites to the specific sport skill.

Perceptual Errors

Perceptual errors can be a misinterpretation of the skill execution or a judgment error. Performers may not recognize the components needed to perform a skill, and these must be brought to their attention. For example, the beginning softball pitcher who has difficulty throwing the ball horizontally without an arc will often try to throw a curve ball, not realizing that the ball will not curve unless thrown fast enough to cause a lot of air friction. Some basketball players attempting the jump shot mistakenly do a one-hand push shot. They have failed to perceive the hesitation between the jump and the shot that makes the shot so difficult to block. The practitioner must be able to provide the critical feedback necessary to supplement the performer's naive skill perceptions.

Psychological Errors

Psychological or social problems in performance arise due to motivational or attitudinal problems. When these types of problems exist, behavior management is the best procedure. Some behavioral problems such as showing off can be handled easily by the instructor or leader by consulting with the performer or by withholding the attention the performer seeks. When the problem is one of self-confidence, performers must be encouraged to develop more positive attitudes toward themselves and their chances of success. Ziegler (1987) has studied this area and offers suggestions for the practitioner.

Once the performance errors are detected and analyzed, the practitioner must incorporate some instructional procedures for correcting the errors. Once a new skill product is produced, the procedure starts over again. The newly created skill is observed again for goal accomplishment. If the skill is optimal, then the observer proceeds to a new skill or performer. If the skill is still not optimal, then the observational evaluation begins again.

Terminology

Acceleration (positive acceleration)—An increasing rate of change of velocity (speeding up)

Acute angle—A small or the smallest possible angle between two lines of interest

Agility—The ability to change movement direction very quickly

Angular motion—Movement of an object or body in a turning motion around an axis

Backspin—Movement of the top of a spinning object toward the back of the object or the point of projection

Base of support—Any body part or object in contact with the supporting surface and the adjacent area between the points of contact

Basic movement—Any simple change in position of the anatomical segments of the body

Blocking—Stopping the movement in one body segment or a group of segments prior to the conclusion of a skill

Center of gravity—The point inside or outside a body or object where all things are equally balanced or where gravitational pull is concentrated

Clockwise—Rotational motion in the normal movement direction of the hands of a clock

Control—The ability to restrict speed, range of motion, and precise timing of components of a movement

Coordination—The function of constraints of all free variables of a movement into a purposeful action (Kelso, 1982)

Counterclockwise—Rotational motion opposite the normal movement direction of the hands of a clock

Deceleration (negative acceleration)—Changing the rate of velocity or speed in a negative direction (slowing down)

External force—A force applied outside the performer from another performer, gravity, wind, the supporting surface, or another environmental source

Follow-through—The continuation of a motion after force has been applied, an object has been released, or impact has occurred

Force—A push or pull exerted on a body or object

Force absorption—The action(s) used to dissipate the force of an object or a body; the deceleration to zero velocity of an object or a body

Force production phase—The time within a skill when the actions produce force that is directed to the accomplishment of the specific goal

Frictional force—Adhesiveness between two surfaces

Fundamental movement pattern—A series of basic movements combined in a time and spatial sequence that accomplishes a general purpose

Fundamental skill—A fundamental movement pattern designed to accomplish specific objective

Gravity—A vertical downward force on all objects and bodies

Impact—Contact between two objects, an object and a body part, or a body and its supporting surface

Inertia—The reluctance of an object or body to do anything other than what it is presently doing; the amount of inertia is generally the mass (weight) of the object or body

Internal force—Force generated by contracting muscle from within the body

Lever—A simple machine comprised of a rigid bar, a fulcrum, a point of force application, a central point of resistance, a force arm, and a resistance arm that creates a mechanical advantage

Linear movement—Movement of an object or body in a straight line

Line of force—The direction in which force is applied to propel or stop an object

Line of gravity—An imaginary line that extends from the body's center of gravity downward toward the supporting surface

Mobility—The ability to create a state of motion

Moment of inertia—The amount of force needed to overcome an object's or body's present state of angular motion

Momentum—The product of the mass (weight) and velocity (speed) or an object or a body, expressing the amount of motion the object or body possesses

Preparation phase—The time within a skill that positions the body and each of the individual segments in an appropriate position to initiate force; precedes the force production phase

Projectile—Any object or body that becomes airborne

Range of motion—The total angular movement in degrees of a specific joint in a particular motion

Rotary movement—A turning motion around an axis, which can be either stationary or moving

Sidespin—Lateral rotation of an object to the right or left

Spin—The rotation of an object

Sport-specific skill—A highly defined fundamental skill or a combination of several fundamental skills with a very specific purpose (usually related to one sport)

Stability—An equilibrium of opposing forces acting on a body

Topspin—Movement of the top of a spinning object toward the front of the object or away from the point of projection

Transfer of weight—A shifting of weight that changes the line of gravity relative to the base of support

Velocity—The rate at which an object or body moves through space relative to time (speed)

References

Broer, M., & Zernicke, R. (1979). *Efficiency of human movement* (4th ed.). Philadelphia: W.B. Saunders.

Brown, E. (1984). Kinesiological analysis of motor skills via visual evaluation techniques. *Proceedings of the Second National Symposium on Teaching Kinesiology and Biomechanics in Sports*, **2**, 95-96.

Cooper, J., Adrian, M., & Glassow, R. (1982). *Kinesiology* (5th ed.). St. Louis: C.V. Mosby.

Daniels, D. (1984). Basic movements and modeling: An approach to teaching skill analysis in the undegraduate biomechanics course. *Proceedings of the Second National Symposium on Teaching Kinesiology and Biomechanics in Sports*, **2**, 243-246.

Hay, J., & Reid, J. (1982). *The anatomical and mechanical bases of human motion*. Englewood Cliffs, NJ: Prentice-Hall.

Hoffman, S. (1984). The contributions of biomechanics to clinical competence: A view from the gymnasium. *Proceedings of the Second National Symposium on Teaching Kinesiology and Biomechanics in Sports*, **2**, 67-70.

Kelso, J. (1982). Concepts and issues in human behavior: Coming to grips with jargon. *Human motor behavior: An introduction*, 21-58.

Wickstrom, R. (1983). *Fundamental motor patterns* (3rd ed.). Philadelphia: Lea & Febiger.

Ziegler, S. (1987). Negative thought stopping: A key to performance enhancement. *Journal of Physical Education, Recreation, and Dance*, **58**(4), 66-69.

Selected Readings

Groves, R., & Camaione, K. (1975). *Concepts in kinesiology*. Philadelphia: W.B. Saunders.

Kreighbaum, E., & Barthels, K. (1985). *Biomechanics: A qualitative approach for studying human movement* (2nd ed.). Minneapolis: Burgess.

Phillips, S., & Clark, J. (1984). An integrative approach to teaching kinesiology: A lifespan approach. *Proceedings of the Second National Symposium on Teaching Kinesiology and Biomechanics in Sports*, **2**, 19-23.

Piscopo, J., & Baley, J. (1981). *Kinesiology: The science of movement*. New York: Wiley.

Stoner, L. (1984). Is the performer skilled or unskilled? *Proceedings of the Second National Symposium on Teaching Kinesiology and Biomechanics in Sports*, **2**, 233-234.

Chapter 3
Fundamental Movements

Fundamental movement skills are the building blocks on which sport skills are constructed. The understanding of fundamental skills enhances an individual's ability to interpret, observe, and evaluate more advanced and highly specific motor activities such as those utilized in team sports. The purpose of this chapter is to introduce the fundamental skill techniques, discuss mechanical principles that are essential to skill success, explain the purposes and variations of each skill, and present possible key questions to be used for evaluation when the skill is performed as a more advanced team-sport skill. All instructions are presented for the right-handed performer and should be reversed for the left-handed performer.

Locomotion

Locomotion is defined as the displacing, or moving, of the body from one location to another. These types of movement patterns are the most fundamental physical movements in most team sports. The most basic means of locomotion is walking. The specific fundamental skills of locomotion discussed are walking, running, and jumping.

Walking

Wickstrom (1983) describes walking as the most natural form of upright locomotion. The skill of walking is considered to be a cycling motion with progressive, alternate leg action. A full cycle of walking consists of a support phase and a swing phase for each leg. Cycling movements consist of both sides of the body performing the same movement but in opposition to each other. The action of opposition as well as the alternating action of the arms and legs provide for dynamic balance in this skill. The distinguishing features of walking that separate it from other forms of locomotion are the momentary double support in which both feet are in contact with the supporting surface in addition to the continuous contact of one of the feet with the supporting surface.

Technique Description

The technique of walking is described relative to one leg during 1 full cycle. The leg experiences two phases in the walking skill. The first phase is the support phase, in which the foot is in contact with the supporting surface. The support phase begins when the foot strikes the supporting surface and is called *heel-strike*. Immediately following heel-strike, the hip extends while the knee and ankle flex slightly in order for the body to move directly over the total foot. At this point the knee and ankle reverse direction of motion by extending and pushing against the support surface to propel the body forward and upward. It is during this time that momentary double support occurs. The pelvis shifts laterally toward the support foot and tilts downward on the opposite side. Extension of the hip, knee, and ankle continue until the body moves so far forward that the foot breaks contact with the supporting surface. As the foot leaves the supporting surface, the swing phase of the leg begins. The swing phase consists of a slight backward swinging followed by a full forward swinging of the leg to prepare for the next heel-strike. Knee *flexion* occurs during the swing phase in order for the foot to clear the supporting surface; then the knee swings forward and extends in preparation for heel-strike, and the motion begins its cycle again. During the total cycle, each arm is synchronized with the opposite leg.

Mechanical Principles

The following are mechanical principles that apply to the fundamental skill of walking. Unique applications of the following principles are necessary for specific team-sport skills.

Application of Force. When a body is acted on by a force, the resulting acceleration (change of speed) is proportional to the body's mass. The final direction of a body is the resultant of the magnitude and direction of all forces. These forces are necessary to overcome the inertia of the body and initiate motion. It takes less force to maintain a given speed than to accelerate or decelerate the walking motion.

Action/reaction. For every action or force there is an equal and opposite reaction or force. When the walker pushes backward and downward, the reaction is a forward and upward motion. The most efficient walker has a minimum upward motion and a maximum forward motion.

Equilibrium in Motion. Balance is regained by establishing a new base of support under a shifting center of gravity. Walking is a continuous shifting forward of the center of gravity in a falling motion. Balance is regained by establishing a new base of support. Balance is also enhanced by the alternate and opposite movements of the legs and arms.

Purposes and Variations of Walking

The purpose of walking is to displace one's body from one position to another at a moderate or slow speed. The walking skill is utilized in most team-sport activities. Any step movements, such as the crossover steps in volleyball, sidestepping in goalkeeping, and lunge-type movements in all sport activities, are variations and applications of the walking skill. Walking is employed frequently as a means of connecting two or more sport skills in the game or competitive setting.

Key Analysis Questions

The following are questions for the observation and analysis of the general skill of walking. Specific questions for unique applications of walking are based on the specific goal of the skill as utilized within the specific team sport.

1. Does the body center trace a flat curve when observed in the walking skill?
2. Does the trunk remain upright with only small amounts of flexion and extension?
3. Does the head bob up and down unnecessarily?
4. Does the performer have the appropriate range of motion of the limbs during the movement?
5. Does the performer strike the surface with the heel and then roll over the entire foot?
6. Does the performer toe in or toe out during the walking movement?
7. Do the performer's arms move in opposition to the legs?
8. Do the arms have a rhythmic pendulum-type swinging action?
9. Does the movement flow continuously, or are there momentary pauses in the movement?

Running

Running is another cyclical movement with the arms and legs performing repeated actions and moving in synchronous opposition. Running is a variation in the fundamental patterns of both walking and jumping. The run is performed with exaggerated walking movements but at a much faster pace. Slocum and James (1968) defined running as a series of smoothly coordinated jumps executed from one foot to the other foot. That which distinguishes the run from the walk is the period of time in which the body becomes airborne. Further, that which distinguishes the run from the jump is the continuous motion of the run as opposed to the regaining of balance after landing in the jump.

Technique Description

The run is a cycling movement skill in which the arms swing through an arc and in opposition to the movement of the legs. The trunk appears totally upright during level running, but there is a very slight forward lean throughout the skill. The run consists of support and nonsupport phases. The support phase begins with a striking of one of the feet with the supporting surface. The support leg begins flexion at the hip, knee, and ankle in order to help the total body rotate over the support foot. Once the body is in position over the support foot, extension at the hip, knee, and ankle help to propel the body forward and upward into nonsupport, or the flight phase. The recovery (opposite) leg is swinging forward and extending at the knee in preparation for the next support phase. During knee extension of the recovery leg, the support leg experiences flexion at the knee with backward movement or *hyperextension* at the hip until it breaks contact with the supporting surface. This breaking with the supporting surface begins the nonsupport phase, where the body becomes airborne. The knee continues to flex as the heel approaches the buttocks.

Mechanical Principles

The following are mechanical principles that apply to the fundamental skill of running. Unique applications of the following principles are necessary for specific team-sport skills.

Application of Force. Force must be applied to change the body's state of motion. The runner pushes downward and backward with the support foot, creating an upward and forward reaction. The line of force is from the center of gravity through the foot. This line in relationship to the supporting surface creates the angle of takeoff in this leaping motion. The resultant acceleration of the run is proportional to the magnitude of force applied and is inversely related to the mass (weight) of the runner. The more horizontal or forward the resultant is and the less vertical or upward the resultant, the more efficient will be the runner.

Angular and Linear Integration. A performer can change the distribution of mass (moment of inertia) about an axis of rotation and proportionally change the angular velocity. The runner flexes the knee to shorten the radius of the lever and therefore increase the angular velocity. This action rotates the legs quicker and increases the stepping frequency. This integration of the angular motion increases the overall linear velocity of the total body.

Momentum. The human body is frequently put into motion by transferring momentum from a part of the body to the total body mass. When the body becomes airborne, the transfer of momentum must occur at the instant of takeoff. The more time that the body is airborne in relationship to the time spent in support, the faster the run will be.

Equilibrium in motion. Alternate and opposite motions of the arms and legs promote equilibrium during the movement. The base of support is always changing with a rapidly moving center of gravity. This motion gives the needed factor of mobility, which is opposite in execution to stability.

Purposes and Variations of Running

The purpose of running is to displace the body from one position to another at a moderate to fast speed. The primary purpose of running in team sports is locomotion from one part of the playing area to another. Most team sports require a sprint or a fast run between locations on the playing area in order to be positioned properly for the next offensive or defensive strategy. A specific utilization of the fundamental pattern of running in team sports is baserunning in softball.

The fundamental skill of running varies with the speed of the run. The smallest possible amount of time in nonsupport produces a version of running referred to as *jogging*. As the speed of the run increases, various aspects of the technique change in proportion to the increase of speed. Those aspects that increase with proportional increases of speed are range of motion in the arc of the swinging arms, stride length, and flexion of the knee during recovery. Less upward and downward motion of the total body also accompanies faster speeds. The heel of the recovery leg comes closer to the buttocks as the speed of the run increases. Characteristics of the slower pace are a shorter stride, more bouncing motion, less range of motion in the arm swings, and less knee flexion.

Key Analysis Questions

The following are questions for the observation and analysis of the general skill of running. Specific questions for unique applications of running are based on the specific goal of the skill as utilized within the specific team sport.

1. Does the runner's body appear to glide across the surface with minimal upward and downward motion?
2. Does the runner's flexion at the hip, knee, and ankle vary appropriately with the intended speed of the run?
3. Does the runner fully extend the support leg at takeoff?
4. Does the runner's foot land directly under the body?
5. Does the trunk lean slightly forward in level-surface running?
6. Does the trunk lean vary appropriately with uphill and downhill running?
7. Do the runner's arms swing slightly toward the midline of the body with bent elbows and in opposition with the legs?
8. Does the runner eliminate any exaggerated rotary or twisting actions around the trunk and hips?

Jumping

Jumping is a fundamental skill that is used in a variety of recreational and team sport activities. This locomotor skill involves projecting the body into the air. The laws that govern any projectile apply to the jump due to the airborne state of the body. Purposes of jumping vary tremendously, but all jumps include a takeoff, flight, and a landing phase. Most jumping skills designate a controlled reestablishing of contact with the supporting surface.

Technique Description

The jump begins with flexion at the hips, knees, and ankles during the preparatory crouch. During the preparatory phase, the arms move down and backward in preparation for the forward swinging motion. The thrust that projects the total body in the air is generated by a forceful extension at the hips, knees, and ankles. During this forceful extension, the arms swing forward and upward in the direction of the jump. The body is extended at takeoff and at the initial touchdown on landing.

Mechanical Principles

The following are mechanical principles that apply in general to the jumping fundamental pattern of movement. Unique applications of the following principles are necessary for specific team-sport skills.

Application of Force. The final direction of a moving body is a resultant of the magnitude and direction of all forces that have been applied to the body. The force should be applied directly through the center of gravity and at the appropriate angle for accomplishing the specific purpose of the skill. The resultant force applied affects the acceleration of the center of gravity, which is in proportion to the mass of the body.

Sequential/simultaneous Force Application. A greater number of body parts (levers) used increases the amount of available time to build force. The greater the range of motion of these levers over which the force is imparted, the greater the motion of the body. Sequential applications of force by levers act as the means to apply thrust to the body and cause it to be airborne. The more explosion and force needed for the jump, the more simultaneous is the application of force from the lower extremities (levers) during extension.

Momentum. The heavier the body is, the more force will be necessary to overcome its inertia. The lower extremities transfer their momentum to the total body to make it become airborne. The transfer occurs at the instant of takeoff. Once the body is airborne, gravity limits its flight by pulling it back to the surface. This accentuates the need for a large acceleration at the time of takeoff. Transfer of momentum by the arms to the total body also occurs.

Balance/equilibrium. The base of support must be stable in order to have a firm base on which to apply force. Positioning of the arms during the preparation provides balance so that force production can be effective.

Purposes and Variations of Jumping

The purpose of jumping in general is to displace the total body center of gravity a specified amount in the desired direction. Specific purposes of the jump might be to achieve vertical height or horizontal distance. It is important for the performer to control the magnitude of force production and the angle of projection to achieve the specialized purpose of the jump.

The jump can be executed from one or both feet, and landing can be on one or both feet. Specific variations of the jump include the hop, the leap, and the hurdle. When the performer takes off on one foot and lands on the same foot, the variation is a hop. When the takeoff is from one foot and the landing occurs on the opposite foot, it is a leap or hurdle. The jump can also be performed by taking off from one or both feet and landing on both feet simultaneously.

Key Analysis Questions

The following are questions for the observation and analysis of the general skill of jumping. Specific questions for unique applications of jumping are based on the specific goal of the skill as utilized within the specific team sport.

1. Does the performer utilize an appropriate stance from which to apply force?
2. Does the performer take a preparatory crouch position of sufficient depth?
3. Does the performer utilize the appropriate amount of trunk flexion that corresponds to the directional purpose of the jump?
4. Does the performer synchronize the arms with the legs appropriately?
5. Does the performer take off from both feet simultaneously when appropriate?
6. Does the performer extend fully at takeoff?
7. Does the angle of takeoff correspond with the purpose of the jump?
8. Does the performer maintain control in the air and on landing?

Body Control Movements

Body control movement patterns are best characterized as efforts or movements to maintain balance, to maintain control or stability while in motion, and to redirect motion of the total body. The general categories of body control movements are balance and agility types of fundamental movement skills.

Balance Movements

Balance is basic to all sport movements. Sport movement activities require varying amounts of stability or instability. Principles pertaining to stability can be reversed in their interpretations for the principles that provide instability or mobility.

There are two distinct classifications of balance skills: static and dynamic. These types have been defined and described by Espenschade and Eckert (1967): "The maintenance of a particular body position with minimum of sway is referred to as static balance while dynamic balance is considered to be the maintenance of posture during the performance of motor skill which tends to disturb the body's orientation" (p. 163).

Balance is affected by both mechanical and neuromuscular factors. Mechanical factors of levers, forces, motion, and center of gravity affect a performer's balancing ability. Awareness of balance means a physical understanding and awareness of the center of gravity in relationship to the base of support. Balance is affected by the mass of the object, the dimensions of the base of support, the location of the center of gravity, and the location of the line of gravity relative to the base of support.

Balance is a precarious physical ability that is controlled by neuromuscular factors such as the stretch reflex, the proprioceptors, the reticular formation of nerve cells, and the kinesthetic sense supplied through the vestibular apparatus of the ears and eyes. Kinesthetic sense is the mechanism by which the performer has a sense of body position in the environment. Balancing ability can be improved through physical activity.

Technique Description

The technique of balance involves the performer's ability to adjust the center of gravity relative to the base of support regardless of being stationary or in the act of moving. A performer can enhance balance by enlarging the base of support, lowering the center of gravity, maintaining the center of gravity over the base of support, and maintaining the line of gravity within the base of support. The more centered the line of gravity is within the base of support, the more stable the body. Other movements enhance balance but are applicable to specific types of sport movements. Reversal of the principles of balance will render the performer instable or mobile.

Equal and opposing forces on the body produce stability or balance. Opposing forces are constantly at work on the body, and when these opposing forces are equal, equilibrium (or balance) is achieved. Instability or mobility is achieved when the opposing forces are not equal. When the performer experiences undesirable instability such as falling or leaning, balance can be restored by movement of body segments in the opposite direction of falling or leaning.

Mechanical Principles

The following are mechanical principles that apply in general to balance-type movements. Unique applications of the following principles are necessary for specific team-sport skills.

Base of Support. The larger the base of support in the direction of movement, the more stability available for the performer. Friction between the base and the supporting surface is necessary for stability. Balance can be regained by establishing a new base when the original base is lost. The nearer the center of the base is to the line of gravity, the more stable the body will be.

Opposition of Motion. Any movement away from the midline of the body disrupts the equilibrium or balance. This can sometimes create a situation of excessive leaning or falling. Balance can be restored by moving body parts in the opposite direction or by establishing a new base of support under the shifting center of gravity.

Application of Force. When opposing forces acting on the body are equal, stability is maintained. When opposing forces acting on the body are unequal, motion is created.

Purposes and Variations of Balance Movements

The purpose of balance is to maintain a state of equilibrium when the body is either stationary or in the state of motion. Static and dynamic balance are two distinct variations of balance.

The three- and four-point stances in football activities are examples of static balance in team sports. Static balance is essential to the goalkeeper's stance in soccer or field hockey and also to the guarding stance in basketball. Dynamic balance is essential to successful performance in most team sports.

Key Analysis Question

The following are questions for the observation and analysis of the general movement category of balance movements. Specific questions for unique application of balance are based on the specific goal of the skill as utilized within the specific team sport.

Static Balance

1. Does the performer use an appropriate stance width?
2. Does the performer stagger the stride or base of support in line with the oncoming force or the application of force?
3. Does the performer maintain the center of gravity centered over the base of support?
4. Does the performer maintain the line of gravity within the base of support?

Dynamic Balance

1. Does the performer maintain symmetry of the body and limbs while in motion?
2. Does the performer maintain control of the body while moving?
3. Does the performer utilize the balance principles for stability?

Agility Movements

The precise application of timing, balance, and muscular control supplies the performer with the attributes for successful execution of agility movements. Agility is the fundamental pattern of altering the direction or the state of motion of the human body. These types of movements are essential to team-sport activities. Agility movements provide the strategies for movement redirection and are a means for connecting movement skills. These movements provide performers with the ability to position themselves strategically in the activity or game.

Technique Description

Agility movements that alter the state of motion of the human body are initiated with either short or long strides. The short stride is utilized to accelerate the body quickly. This involves shifting the center of gravity forward and outside of the base of support. The performer pushes vigorously against the supporting surface in a downward and rearward direction. The reverse of this is the act of decelerating the body quickly, which is referred to as *stopping*. This is accomplished by reaching out with one foot or increasing the *stride length*. Forward motion is resisted by planting the forward foot and permitting some slight flexion of the knee to absorb the forward momentum. The friction between the foot and the supporting surface acts as a force in opposition to the forward force.

The pivot and the *dodge* are created by turning or pushing off a planted foot without coming to a stop. These movements are initiated by direct downward force to the supporting surface with the planted foot, which becomes the axis of rotation. The hip, knee, and ankle may have to flex somewhat to absorb any excessive forward force. When the non-weight-bearing foot is lifted from the surface, all momentum is transferred to the planted foot. Any directional change can now occur with a swinging action of the free leg. The performer can shift the movement around the foot or in a diagonal direction. It is because of such movements that body direction can be altered.

Mechanical Principles

The following mechanical principles are used for starting, pivoting, and dodging. Principles for stopping motions are the reverse of these as well as those stated for balance.

Base of Support. The smaller that the base of support is and the more shift of movement that occurs away from the midline of the body, the more mobility of the body there will be. The farther the center of gravity is from the center of the base of support, the more mobile the performer will be. A shift of the center of gravity outside the base of support creates a falling or leaning position, which promotes motion.

Application of Force. The body moves when the forces acting on the body are unequal. Movement in the opposite direction of intended motion provides an equal and opposite reaction that creates unequal forces acting on the body. Small amounts of friction between the feet and the supporting surface also act as a means of rendering the body mobile.

Purposes and Variations of Agility Movements

The purpose of agility movements is to alter the rate or direction of the acceleration of the human body. These movements are utilized for (a) directional change, (b) connecting skills, (c) quick positioning, and (d) deceiving the opponent. The variations center around the quality of the movement or the change in direction in the movement. Changing the quality of the movement involves changing from a state of movement to one of no movement (stopping) or from a state of no movement to one of movement (starting). Another variation is changing the direction of movement. This variation requires the movement to be an axial rotation around a point such as the foot. Directional change around one foot is called *pivoting*. Dodging is redirection of movement with quick directional steps that are created by shifts of the center of gravity within the base. The base is a planted foot that acts as an axis point from which the motion is initiated.

Key Analysis Questions

The following are questions for the observation and analysis of general agility movements. Specific questions for unique applications of agility are based on the goal of the skill as it is utilized within the specific team sport.

1. Does the performer appropriately manipulate the center of gravity over the base of support?

2. Does the performer utilize the appropriate forward stepping in stopping and starting?
3. Does the performer utilize the proper trunk lean in stopping and starting?
4. Does the performer rise from the starting position smoothly or abruptly?
5. Does the performer utilize hip, knee, and ankle flexion to decelerate the body in stopping?
6. Does the performer sufficiently plant the foot in all agility skills?
7. Does the performer utilize most of the forward momentum in redirecting the line of motion in pivoting and dodging?
8. Does the performer demonstrate body control in the agility movement?

Manipulative Patterns

Objects or bodies lend themselves to various types of manipulation. Success in most sport activities depends on the efficient and effective manipulation of objects or bodies. *Manipulative* fundamental patterns are performed for the purpose of controlling or giving impetus to an object or a body with the body, body parts, or implements. All the basic manipulative patterns are grouped into four categories: carrying and holding, pushing, throwing and striking, and receiving force.

Carrying and Holding

The fundamental patterns of carrying and holding involve maintaining continuous contact with an object or implement while manipulating it and the body. These patterns generally involve grasping and securing an object or implement while moving.

Technique Description

This technique encompasses grasping and securing an implement or object. The object or implement is secured by reaching and grasping with body parts. The object or implement is held against the body for the most stability. Varying degrees of object or implement stability are achieved by the amount of body surface area or parts securing the object or implement. When mobility of the object or implement is needed, reversing these motions is necessary. Mobility requires the movement of the implement or object away from the body.

Mechanical Principles

The following are mechanical principles that apply in general to carrying and holding fundamental movements. Unique applications of the following principles are necessary for specific team-sport skills.

Object Stability. Stability of an object is maintained if the object is secured close to the body's center of gravity. External weight added to the body becomes part of the total weight and affects the location of the center of gravity, displacing it in the direction of the added weight. If the object is close to the center of gravity, then it remains fairly consistent with its normal position. This object positioning facilitates the ease of performing other movement patterns.

Application of Force. The heavier the object is and the faster it is moving, the more force is necessary to overcome its inertia. The amount of force increases as the distance between the object and the body's center of gravity increases.

Stability/Mobility. A performer needs to increase the base of support and to position that base in the direction of force application when stability is desired. Mobility can be initiated by reversing these principles and promoted by narrowing the base and shifting the line of gravity outside the base of support.

Purposes and Variations of Carrying and Holding

The purposes of carrying and holding are the (a) securing of an object or implement, (b) controlling an object or implement while manipulating it, and (c) manipulating an object or implement efficiently while performing other movement patterns such as running. The most important purpose is object or implement control.

Grasping involves securing an object between body parts. Carrying and holding vary according to the body parts used in controlling the object or implement. Stability and mobility of an object or implement exist on a continuum. Stability is obtained by using the largest number of body parts possible to secure the object or implement. Examples of this concept are rebounding in basketball when surrounded by the other team and maintaining control of the football in the same type of situation. When mobility of an object or implement is needed, the object is grasped with a small number of body parts and a small body surface area. An example of this concept is grasping a softball with the thumb and fingers.

When both security and the ability to move the object or implement quickly are needed, a secure grasp is maintained in such a manner that a smaller grasp can be achieved quickly. An example of this is carrying a field hockey stick. The performer secures the stick at the handle with one hand and cradles the shaft with the other hand. Mobility of the stick is achieved by dropping the cradling hand or sliding it up to the hand on the handle.

Key Analysis Questions

The following are questions for the observation and analysis of the general carrying and holding fundamental patterns. Specific questions for unique applications of carrying and holding are based on the specific goal of the skill as utilized within the specific team sport.

1. Does the performer utilize the appropriate amount of body parts in securing the object or implement?
2. Does the performer keep the object or implement close to the body for stability or away from the body for mobility as required by the situation?
3. Does the performer hold or carry the object or implement in such a way that restricts other movement patterns?
4. Does the performer maintain balance or use the object or implement in appropriate ways to help maintain balance throughout the total movement being executed?

Pushing

The fundamental pattern of pushing involves the manipulation of an object by movement directed away from the body. Pushing involves the continuous contact with an object while manipulating it away from the body. The action involves extension against the object in a straight line.

Technique Description

The technique of pushing starts with flexion of the upper extremities in preparation for the force-production phase of the movement. Force production is accomplished by extension against an object. The amount of force production is proportional to the speed of the upper extremities during the extension. Follow-through of the upper extremities in the line of motion is necessary for maximum application of force. This continuous motion permits the performer to apply the largest force (acceleration of segments) at the moment of object release. Continuous motions after the release (follow-through) permit gradual deceleration of the upper extremities.

Mechanical Principles

The following are mechanical principles that apply in general to the pushing fundamental pattern of movement. Unique applications of the following principles are necessary for specific team-sport skills. All concepts covered on projectiles and their spin and angle of rebound apply to the pushing pattern (see p. 13).

Application of Force. The final magnitude and direction of the resultant force applied to an object is the summation of all forces and directions of forces applied. The greater the range of motion over which the force is imparted, the greater the motion will be of the object. The more flexion occurring during the preparatory phase, the more distance for extension is possible in the push. The force should be applied through the center of gravity of the object in the intended direction. The heavier the object, the more force needed to overcome its inertia and set it into motion.

Sequential/Simultaneous Force Application. Several forces are applied by the body segments of the upper extremities during the pushing pattern. The forces are generally sequential with each individual body segment making a contribution. The more force needed for the push, the more simultaneous and the faster the segments must act to produce force.

Balance in Motion. Stability is necessary in the pushing pattern for applying force substantially. Size, positioning, and direction of the base of support are important for establishing a firm base from which the performer can push.

Momentum. Momentum can be transferred from a moving lever to an external object. The more force production required, the more levers (body segments or total body) are needed to contribute to the transfer of momentum to the object.

Follow-Through. The follow-through in pushing permits the performer to apply maximum force without decelerating at the instant of release.

Purposes and Variations of Pushing

The purpose of pushing is to give impetus to an object, resulting in movement or projection of that object. The specific purpose of projection varies with the goal of the specific sport skill. The movement goals for the object might be (a) vertical height, (b) horizontal distance, (c) precision or accuracy, (d) speed of object movement, or (e) combinations of these goals.

Variations of the pushing pattern in team sports are numerous. The pattern varies depending on the body parts utilized in pushing. Most pushing patterns occur with the upper extremities. Utilization of other body parts in these patterns is common in soccer, where the knee and shoulder are used for pushing.

The use of the upper extremities in pushing vary regarding the use of one or two arms in the execution.

One-handed pushes are common in basketball. Examples of a one-handed push include the dribble, the bounce pass, the shoulder pass, and the set shot. Two-handed pushes are less common in basketball but more so in field hockey. Examples of two-handed push skills in field hockey include the dribble and the push pass.

Key Analysis Questions

The following are questions for the observation and analysis of the general skill of pushing. Specific questions for unique applications of pushing are based on the specific goal of the skill as utilized within the specific team sport.

1. Does the performer flex the extremities or other body parts sufficiently for proper range of motion for the force-production phase of extension?
2. Does the performer use the appropriate stance?
3. Does the performer utilize the transfer of body weight with the appropriate timing when large force production is necessary?

Throwing and Striking

Throwing and striking are grouped together as one general movement classification because of the large number of commonalities shared between the two, from similar spatial patterns to shared purposes and types of variations.

Throwing and striking are acts of propelling an object by means of bodily movement. Both movement patterns involve the accumulation of increasing velocities of successive or simultaneous body segments that terminate at the distal end of the body or implement.

Most forms of throwing and striking involve the utilization of the upper extremities to propel an object. Unique striking patterns such as kicking, blocking, and butting, which employ body parts other than the upper extremities, are discussed separately.

Pattern Classification

There are different classifications of throwing and striking movement patterns based on the movement of the arm relative to the body. This classification is basically a spatial configuration that enhances the understanding of the movement pattern and the application of mechanical principles.

The throwing and striking skills in which the rotating arm moves around the shoulder primarily above the horizontal are classified as an overarm throw or strike. These same types of motion, but below the horizontal, are classified as an underarm throw or strike. When the arm rotates about the shoulder and moves in the general area directly horizontal to the body, these skills are considered to be members of the family of sidearm throws and strikes.

Purposes of Throwing and Striking

Commonality in purpose is also shared by the throwing and striking movement patterns. The general purpose of throwing and striking is to project an object through space. The specialized or specific goal might be (a) maximum horizontal distance, (b) maximum vertical height, (c) precision of projection or accuracy, (d) maximum object speed, or (e) any combination of these goals.

The specific goal of a sport skill affects the degree of application or importance of any specific mechanical principle to the movement. The goal is also affected by the uniqueness of the movement and differentiates that movement from other skills in the same general movement classification.

Mechanical Principles

The patterns of throwing and striking utilize the same mechanical principles of motion. The degree of application of these mechanical principles differentiates the specific throwing and striking skills from each other. The following principles apply to all throwing and striking skills as do all principles of projectiles, spin, and angle of rebound covered previously (see p. 13).

Application of Force. A greater number of body parts and/or implements (levers) that are sequentially used increases the amount of available time to build force. In addition, the greater the range of motion and speed of these levers, the greater the force that is available for transfer to the object. The resultant force is directly proportional to the size and the number of forces applied.

Force Direction. Force application to an object needs to be applied directly through the object's center of gravity in the intended direction. The amount of force needed for a specific object depends on the mass (weight) of that object.

Linear and Angular Integration. The linear and angular components of the upper extremities must be utilized in order to actualize the best performance possible. Linear and angular velocity are inverse when utilizing a lever (arm or implement). The shorter the lever is, the more angular motion there will be. The longer the lever is, the more linear speed there will be at the distal end of the lever. In some forms of throwing and striking, the lever length is decreased in order to increase the angular (turning) speed around the shoulder. Just prior to *release* or contact, the lever is opened (lengthened) for increasing the linear speed of its distal end. This increases the amount of momentum available for possible transfer to the object. Some throwing and striking skills use other body parts (hips or pelvis) to add force without shortening the lever.

Momentum. The momentum accumulated by the upper extremities is transferred to the object. In striking, the momentum of the object or implement before impact is equal to the momentum after impact. The performer tries to transfer most of the momentum to the object and a minimum amount to the implement. This is the law of conservation of momentum.

Follow-Through. A follow-through motion in both throwing and striking ensures that the center of the arc of motion occurs at the moment of release or contact. This permits the performer to produce the maximum force and speed for transferring to the object. Follow-through also helps prevent injury by providing the movement time to dissipate the force generated for release or contact.

Stability/Mobility. Varying degrees of both stability and mobility are essential in throwing activities. All principles of instability or mobility are utilized for creating or starting the movement and creating force, but stability is required just prior to release or contact as it provides the performer with a firm base on which the whipping or slingshot type of final motion can occur for transferring the maximum velocity to the object.

Stability is mandatory, and all principles of stability apply for most of the striking movements. Without a firm base, the force production would be minimized.

Overarm

The overarm throwing and striking pattern involves a complex integration of movements by individual body segments. The distinguishing feature of this throwing and striking classification is the complete rotation of the upper arm. The arm moves above the horizontal in a lateral and backward motion during the preparation. Forward and medial motion occurs during the force-production or the action phase. Pelvic and spinal rotation also assist in the force production.

Technique Description. The stance or base of support varies relative to the throwing or striking skill being executed. Body weight is rocked or shifted backward on one or both feet during the preparation. The hips, spine, and shoulders rotate clockwise or backward as the throwing or striking arm is retracted to the maximum backswing position. The force-production phase begins with a forward body-weight shift. The typical overarm throw with one arm begins with the pelvic rotation in a counterclockwise direction accompanied by forward and medial upper-arm movement. Immediately following this motion, the trunk moves counterclockwise, which facilitates the forward motion of the throwing arm and positions the upper arm for the rapid extension of the elbow just prior to release. This sequential motion creates a whipping action, which permits maximum force production to be transferred to the object.

The pattern of movement in the two-handed throw is different than that of the one-handed overarm throw. Both arms retract over the head to the maximum backswing position. Forward motion of the arms continues with extension at the elbows until release. Body-weight shift contributes significantly to the force production in this type of overarm throw.

In both types of throwing or striking patterns, the arm(s) continue forward and downward with medial motion occurring after release or contact until the momentum of the arm(s) is dissipated. Follow-through in both patterns is essential to accuracy and maximum force production of projection.

Variations of Overarm Throwing and Striking. There are many variations of the overarm throwing and striking pattern. One of the differentiations in the overarm pattern is whether the object is being struck or released. In addition, further differentiation is made relative to the utilization of one or two hands in the pattern.

The most typical throwing pattern is the overarm one-handed throw such as that utilized in softball and football. The basketball overarm pass is another variation of the overarm throw. Overarm throws with two hands include the basketball and the speedball two-handed overhead pass, the soccer throw-in, and the soccer goalkeeper's throw.

Many striking skills in volleyball utilize the overarm pattern. These are all striking skills due to the rules prohibiting the throwing of the ball. One-handed striking skills in volleyball include all variations of the overarm serve, the spike, and the attack hit, or smash. Two-handed striking skills in volleyball include the overhead pass (front set) and the back set.

Key Analysis Questions. The following are questions for the observation and analysis of the general skill of overarm throwing and striking. Specific questions for unique applications of the skill of overarm throwing or striking are based on the specific goal of the skill as utilized within the specific team sport.

1. Does the performer utilize a stepping action when appropriate? Is the stepping leg opposite the throwing or striking arm?
2. Does the performer use an appropriate range of motion in the trunk and hips that could restrict the range of motion in the arm?
3. Does the performer utilize a full range of motion in the shoulder and not shorten the backswing?

4. Does the performer adequately flex at the elbow and wrist with outward rotation at the shoulder during the preparatory action?
5. Does the performer use a whipping action of the arm or implement with the more distal body segments or implement lagging behind the adjacent proximal body segments?
6. Does the performer fully extend at release or contact?
7. Does the performer release or contact the object when it is tangent or at the appropriate angle to the target? Was the release or contact early or late?

Underarm

The distinguishing feature of the underarm movement pattern is the movement of the arm below the horizontal during the force-production phase of the motion. The underarm throw and strike can vary in complexity depending on the number of rotating body segments integrated into the movement. The primary rotation occurs around the shoulder, but additional rotations at the forearm, hand, and pelvis can increase the application of force. The pelvic rotation is generally facilitated by a transfer or shift of the body weight. Additional force production can be generated by increasing either the range of motion or the velocity of the body segments.

Technique Description. The underarm throwing and striking movement patterns begin with a shift of weight rearward and a clockwise rotation of the pelvis. The preparatory motion of the arm generally involves extension of the elbow with motion occurring primarily around the shoulder. The vertical height of the backswing can vary from waist height to a full circling motion by the arm. Force-producing action is initiated with rotation of the pelvis forward or counterclockwise with the weight of the body transferred toward the point of release or contact. The arm moves rapidly down and forward until release or contact occurs. The number of body segments employed in the motion affects the force-production capabilities. The release or contact is usually parallel with the line of the trunk or slightly beyond that line. The forward motion of the arm after the release or contact is continued until the momentum of the arm is dissipated.

Variations of Underarm Throwing and Striking. Categorization of specific underarm throwing and striking skills is also typified by the use of one or two arms in the execution of the skill. The typical underarm throwing pattern is the softball pitch. Additional variations of the one-arm throw are the basketball underhand pass and the basketball hook pass. The two-handed underarm throws are seen primarily in football and include such skills as the lateral pitchout, the centering snap, and the handoff.

In the striking pattern, the variations also extend from skills employing one or two hands. The typical one-handed striking skill is the underarm volleyball serve. Two-handed striking movements may be observed in the field hockey skills of dribbling and driving as well as in the volleyball skills of bumping, passing, and digging.

Key Analysis Questions. The following are questions for the observation and analysis of the general skill of underarm throwing and striking. Specific questions for unique applications of the skill of underam throwing and striking are based on the specific goal of the skill as utilized within the specific team sport.

1. Does the performer demonstrate a stepping forward action when appropriate for the skill?
2. Does the performer have an appropriate step length when the step is utilized? Is the stepping leg opposite the throwing or striking arm?
3. Does the performer shift body weight rearward onto the back foot during the preparatory action and forward onto the front foot during the force-production action?
4. Does the performer use an adequate amount of pelvic rotation for the specific sport skill?
5. Does the performer demonstrate an appropriate range of motion or vertical lift on the backswing?
6. Does the performer restrict the movement in any of the joints?
7. Does the performer adopt an appropriate range of motion and speed of motion of the upper extremity?
8. Does the performer fully extend the arm(s) at release or contact?
9. Does the performer release or contact the object when it is tangent to the target? Is the release or contact early or late?

Sidearm

The sidearm pattern is utilized in a large number of throwing and striking sport skills. The distinguishing feature of the sidearm pattern is the limitation of rotational action occurring at the shoulder joint. This constraint facilitates controlling the arm in a horizontal position relative to the body. The arm is also held fairly stable throughout the motion. The primary force production results from pelvic rotation, which turns the trunk, arm, and/or implement toward the direction of projection of the object to be struck or released.

Technique Description. The sidearm throwing and striking pattern begins with a backward shift of weight and a clockwise rotation of the hips and trunk. The force-production phase of motion is produced primarily by forward and counterclockwise rotation of the hips and trunk. This motion carries the shoulder, arms, and/or implement counterclockwise in the direction of the object to be struck or released. During this rotation, the body weight is shifted forward. The hips or pelvis lead the turning action before other body parts start to rotate. There is a slight lagging behind of the upper arm, forearm, hand, and implement. The hips or pelvis stop rotation first and create a blocking situation or a firm base on which the arm can rotate until release or contact. This type of action is referred to as *blocking*. Rotation of the arm continues after release or contact until the momentum of the arm is dissipated.

Variations of Sidearm Throwing and Striking. The sidearm throwing and striking patterns have many variations. Sidearm throws are generally utilized in sports that also use the overarm throw. The most common sidearm one-handed throws are seen in softball and football. The goalkeeper in soccer also uses the sidearm throw extensively. One-handed striking is used in the volleyball sidearm serve, and the two-handed strike is used in softball batting.

Key Analysis Questions. The following are questions for the observation and analysis of the general skill of sidearm throwing and striking. Specific questions for unique applications of the skill of sidearm throwing and striking are based on the specific goal of the skill as utilized within the specific team-sport skill.

1. Does the performer demonstrate an appropriate length of stride (size of base of support) for the movement skill?
2. Does the performer appropriately shift the body weight forward for the release or contact?
3. Does the performer rotate the pelvis rapidly toward the object?
4. Does the performer utilize a blocking action at the hips in order to create a firm base against which the whipping arm or implement can pull?
5. Does the performer rotate the arm or implement rapidly toward the release or contact?
6. Does the performer rotate the arm or implement through the appropriate range of motion?
7. Does the performer restrict the motion in any of the joints?
8. Does the performer utilize an appropriate speed of motion in order to meet the purpose of the skill?
9. Does the performer have the arm fully extended at the time of release or contact?
10. Does the performer release or contact when the object is tangent to the target? Is the release or contact early or late?

Specialized Forms of Striking

Striking can be performed with all body parts; which are used would be dictated by the type of sport activity being performed. Most striking skills are performed through the use of the arms or the implement. Other types of striking that are specialized are blocking, butting, and kicking, and these use either the lower extremities or the total body. These specialized forms of striking are discussed separately because of their uniqueness.

Blocking and Butting

The fundamental patterns of blocking and butting are defined as patterns that stop or give impetus to another body or object. These movement patterns are further differentiated from other patterns because the total body is used to stop or give impetus to an object or the body.

Technique Description. The technique of blocking or butting begins with flexion of the hips, knees, and ankles. The arms vary in preparatory motion depending on the specific sport skill being performed. Body parts flex for the preparation of force-producing extension movements. The body moves into total extension, which resembles an uncoiling of the body toward the object or body. Continuation of the motion in the line of extension is maintained until the total momentum is dissipated.

Mechanical Principles. The following are mechanical principles that apply in general to the skills of blocking and butting. Unique applications of the following principles are necessary for specific team-sport skills.

1. Balance/equilibrium. Balance is important in these fundamental movement patterns for the purpose of establishing a firm base on which to apply or receive force. The larger the base is in the direction of force application or absorption, the more stable it is and the more force absorption and application capabilities that are possible for the performer.
2. Application of force. The final direction and magnitude of force on an object or the body is determined by all forces applied, and the resulting acceleration or change of velocity and is proportional to the mass. If the body or object is to be moved the largest possible distance, then the force should be applied as directly as possible through the center of gravity of the object or body. If rotation of the object or body is desirable, then force should be applied as far away from the axis of rotation as possible. Other means of inducing rotation are transferring momentum from a part of the body to the total body as well as stopping or checking the linear velocity at an extremity.

3. Linear and angular integration. The greater the number of body parts (levers) sequentially used over the largest possible range of motion, the greater the application of force on the object or body. Linear velocity is increased by extending the distance over which force is imparted or by lengthening the lever or lever system.
4. Momentum. Momentum is transferred to an object or the body by moving levers. In blocking and butting, the transfer of momentum is the most effective when it occurs at the point of maximum velocity.

Purposes and Variations of Blocking and Butting. The general purpose of blocking is to stop an object or the body. The specific purpose of butting is to give impetus to an object.

The variations of these patterns are defined merely as to which pattern is being utilized. The blocking pattern is used extensively in football activities, such as in shoulder blocks and two- or three-point-stance blocks. An example of butting is heading or head volleys in soccer.

Key Analysis Questions. The following are questions for the observation and analysis of the general skills of blocking and butting. Specific questions for unique applications of the skills of blocking and butting are based on the specific goal of the skill as utilized within the specific team-sport skill.

1. Does the performer adopt an appropriate amount of body flexion for the needed force production?
2. Does the performer extend body parts at the appropriate time and with enough speed?
3. Does the performer apply force throughout the movement in the line of extension?
4. Does the performer achieve the specific goal of the sport skill?

Kicking

Kicking is a unique form of striking in which the lower limbs are used to impart force to an object. The movement skills used in kicking vary by amount of force imparted to a ball that is stationary or moving. In another variation of kicking, the goal is to give impetus to a ball that is dropped from a height. The movement pattern of kicking is essential to success in team sports such as soccer, speedball, and football.

Technique Description. The preparatory action begins with a step forward with that foot opposite the kicking foot. The foot is placed slightly to the rear and lateral to the object to be struck or to the area rear and lateral to where the object would drop if airborne. This stepping action facilitates the rotation of the pelvis clockwise (for a right-footed kicker), which opens the hip area for a powerful rotational motion toward the object. During the step and pelvic rotation, *hyperextension* at the hip and flexion of the knee of the kicking leg are positioned appropriately for the force production. The height of this backswing is dependent on the amount of force production needed to execute the skill.

The force-production phase begins with a downward and forward swing of the leg accompanied by a counterclockwise rotation of the pelvis toward the object. The leg demonstrates a whipping action characterized by sequential utilization of the body segments of the leg. The first movement is flexion of the hip until the thigh comes forward and is approximately perpendicular to the ground. The thigh then stops rotation at the hip, creating a firm base against which the lower leg can pull when opening or extending. This is the blocking action of the thigh. Extension at the knee then opens the leg as it swings toward the object until contact is made. The leg follows through the arc of motion until the momentum of the leg is dissipated.

Mechanical Principles. The following are mechanical principles that apply in general to the kicking fundamental pattern of movement. Unique applications of the following principles are necessary for specific team-sport skills.

1. Balance/equilibrium. The final step or width of stance just prior to the kicking action is increased in the direction of the force application. There must be considerable friction between the front foot and the surface to provide a firm base from which to swing the kicking leg. The stepping action provides balance and lowers the center of gravity toward the base for additional stability. This stability is especially needed during the rapid swinging action of the kicking leg. Utilization of opposition keeps the body or pelvic region open to permit a large range of motion and does not restrict the action of the kicking leg.
2. Linear and angular integration. Linear and angular motions are integrated for effective performance in kicking in much the same way as they are utilized in throwing. Decreasing the lever (leg) length increases the angular speed of cocking the leg and the forward swinging action of the same leg. The potential linear velocity of the end of the lever (foot) is increased by lengthening or uncocking the lever just prior to ball contact.
3. Leverage. The greater the number of body parts (levers) sequentially utilized through their largest possible ranges of motion, the better are the possibilities for greater motion of the object or body. The greater the motion of the leg, the more potential there is for acceleration. The more

acceleration of the mass of the leg, the more force produced. The levers sequentially apply force to create the largest possible force on the ball. This is the sequential timing of the uncocking action of the leg.

4. Momentum. The linear force of the distal end (foot) of the lever (leg) is transferred to the object. This force should be applied as directly as possible through the center of gravity of the object in the intended direction.

Purposes and Variations Of Kicking. The purposes of kicking are identical to those of all throwing and striking skills (see p. 29). The specific goal of kicking is (a) maximum horizontal distance, (b) maximum vertical height, (c) precision in ball placement or accuracy, (d) maximum ball speed, or (e) any combination of these purposes.

The variations of kicking are differentiated by the amount of force production necessary for success. Less forceful kicks, such as the soccer dribble, are centered around accuracy. Those skills that requires moderate force and accuracy are soccer and speedball passes. The skills that require some accuracy but tremendous amounts of force are placekicks and punts in soccer and football.

Key Analysis Questions. The following are questions for the observation and analysis of the general skill of kicking. Specific questions for unique applications of the skill of kicking are based on the specific goal of the skill as utilized within the specific team sport.

1. Does the performer have an appropriate final approach step length?
2. Does the performer place the support foot slightly behind and lateral to the area of ball drop or the actual ball?
3. Does the performer utilize the arms in opposition with the legs for balance?
4. Does the performer open the body sufficiently for the appropriate range of motion?
5. Does the performer execute the appropriate amount of backswing for the force production necessary in the skill?
6. Does the performer utilize the blocking principle and whipping action of the leg adequately?
7. Does the performer contact the ball in the proper area of the ball for the appropriate angle of trajectory?
8. Does the performer utilize follow-through for dissipation of force?
9. Does the performer follow through toward the midline of the body?

Receiving Force

The action of receiving force involves the deceleration (slowing down) or stopping of either the body or an object in flight or motion. The general purposes of receiving force are dissipation of the force and control of the airborne or moving object or body. Receiving-force fundamental movement patterns are catching, trapping, and landing.

Mechanical Principles for Receiving Force

The mechanical principles for catching, trapping, and landing are very similar, so the mechanical concepts are presented together for all receiving-force types of movement patterns.

Application of Force. A force must be applied in the opposite direction of flight of an object or the body to decrease the velocity or decelerate it. This force should be applied to an object or the body as directly as possible through its center of gravity.

Force Application

The shock of catching or landing is diminished by absorbing it over a greater distance, a greater area, a greater period of time, or any combination thereof. When an object or the body is acted on by a force, the resulting deceleration and change of speed is proportional to the mass of the object or body. The heavier the object or body and the faster it is moving, the more force necessary to overcome its inertia and decelerate the movement.

Balance/Equilibrium. During the act of catching or landing, balance is essential for maintaining control for the subsequent movement. The width of the base of support must be sufficient for force absorption and in line with the path of the object or body.

Catching

The fundamental skill of catching is defined as the controlling of the kinetic energy of an object through the effective positioning of the hands and body parts. *Retraction* and grasping are utilized for stopping and controlling the object. Using body parts such as the foot, thigh, chest, and lower leg to control the object are examples of *trapping*, a variation of catching used mainly in soccer and speedball.

Technique Description. The technique of catching or trapping begins with positioning the hands or body parts in an effective position for receiving the object. This positioning generally involves moving the receiving body parts toward the object. The feet are positioned in a stride position toward the moving object for stability. Retraction and grasping are utilized for effective reduction of the shock of impact and dissipation of the kinetic energy of the object. Control of the object is achieved through force absorption, which is increased by extending the distance over which the force is absorbed. This increase is accomplished by retracting or flexing the extended body parts or retracting the total body by taking steps backward. Enlarging the area over which the force is received gives the performer another means of increasing control. Equipment such as the softball glove and football pads are employed for this purpose.

Purposes and Variations of Catching. The purpose of catching or trapping is to control the movement of an object in motion or flight. This manipulation of the object is achieved through the controlling of the force of the object. Reasons for controlling the object are varied, but generally they are for stopping or redirecting the object.

Variations of catching and trapping are best defined relative to use of the hands or other body parts for controlling the object. Catching in softball is a common example of this pattern in team sport activities and is accomplished through the aid of a glove for the purpose of enlarging the area over which force is received. Devices such as gloves are used when the momentum of the object is greater than an individual can absorb without protection. Catching a football with the hands does not require the use of a glove because there is less object momentum and a softer surface to be contacted.

Trapping is accomplished with the hands or other body parts. Typical types of trapping include the use of body parts such as the chest, thigh, lower leg, or knee in soccer. A variation of trapping with the hands is the trapping of grounders in softball.

Key Analysis Questions. The following are questions for the observation and analysis of the general skill of catching. Specific questions for unique applications of the skill are based on the specific goal of the skill as utilized within the specific team-sport skill.

1. Does the performer position the body in line with the direction of the object path?
2. Does the performer utilize an appropriate stride width?
3. Does the performer extend the hands or body parts toward the object?
4. Does the performer position the receiving body parts in a proper extended position to receive the object?
5. Does the performer move through an appropriate distance and at an appropriate speed to dissipate the force of the object?
6. Does the performer gain control over the object?

Landing

Landing is a specialized form of receiving force. The performer must control the body through dissipation of force, which is created by the body weight (mass) descending from a height. The acceleration of the body toward the supporting surface is proportional to the height from which the body is descending. Body control and balance are achieved through gradual deceleration of the body during and immediately following impact.

Technique Description. The performer prepares for impact by extending the legs or reaching for the supporting surface. The legs are at an angle to the surface. The angle of the legs to the surface is dependent on the amount of vertical and horizontal momentum the body possesses. The angle is close to 90° if the largest amount of momentum is vertical. The angle decreases as the horizontal component of momentum increases. This means that the performer extends the legs forward for the landing. The more horizontal momentum that is present, the more distance is necessary to dissipate this horizontal momentum by the performer. A more vertical position also maximizes the vertical distance in which the performer can dissipate the vertical downward momentum. Once impact has occurred, the body continues on the line of motion, yet with deceleration. Deceleration is created by resisting but permitting slow flexion at the hips, knees, and ankles. The arms reach forward to help maintain balance on landing.

Purposes and Variations of Landing. The primary purpose of landing is to dissipate the momentum of the body falling downward toward the surface. Variations of the landing are based on the ratio of vertical to horizontal momentum the performer has at the moment of impact. Landing from a vertical height, such as from a tip-in or a jump ball in basketball, is slightly different than landing with both vertical and horizontal momentum, such as that in a long-jump type of activity.

Key Analysis Questions. The following are questions for the observation and analysis of the general skill of landing. Specific questions for unique applications of the skill are based on the specific goal of the skill as utilized within the specific team-sport skill.

1. Does the performer extend the legs toward the landing?
2. Does the performer flex at the hip appropriately for the type of landing being experienced?

3. Does the performer flex against the impact of landing?
4. Does the performer reach forward with the arms for maintaining balance on landing?
5. Does the performer maintain balance and stability throughout the landing?
6. Does the performer recover quickly from the landing and appear to be in position for the next movement skill?

Terminology

Abduction—Movement away from the midline of the body through the frontal plane

Acute angle—A small, or the smallest possible, angle between two lines of interest

Adduction—Movement toward the midline of the body (generally the return of an abducted limb to the anatomical position)

Balance—The maintenance of equilibrium while one is stationary or moving

Ball trajectory—The flight path assumed by an airborne ball

Body segment—Any individual body part that is separated from other body parts by a joint, or articulation (e.g., hand, forearm, upper arm, trunk, thigh, shank, foot, head)

Cycling motion—Repetition of action on alternating sides of the body

Depression—Pressing (the shoulder girdle) downward

Distal—Farthest from the center or midline of the body

Dodge—A sharp, angular move to change direction to avoid an opponent

Elevation—Lifting (the shoulder girdle) upward

Eversion—Outward movement of the sole of the foot

Extension—Any movement resulting in an increase of a joint angle (opening or straightening)

Feint (fake)—A short preliminary move with the ball, head, arms, or foot used in an attempt to confuse and misdirect an opponent

Flexion—Any movement resulting in a decrease of a joint angle (closing or bending)

Forward stride—A step in a forward direction

Hyperextension—An extension motion greater than 180° or the anatomical position for a joint

Inversion—Inward (medial) movement of the sole of the foot

Inward (medial) rotation—Movement of a limb or body part inward around the long axis

Lateral—To the outside or away from the midline of the body

Lateral flexion—Sideways movement of the head or trunk

Lateral (outward) rotation—Movement of a limb or body part outward around the long axis

Locomotion—Displacing or moving the body from one location to another

Manipulative skill—A skill performed to control and/or give impetus to a body or object

Medial—To the inside or toward the midline of the body

Medial rotation—Movement of a limb or body part inward around the long axis. Same as inward rotation

Midline—An imaginary line that separates the body into equal right and left halves

Open hips—Position of the hips which permits the most rotation in the force production phase of a skill

Outward (lateral) rotation—Movement of a limb or body part outward around the long axis. Same as lateral rotation

Place kick—A kick of a stationary ball from the ground

Planted foot—The foot positioned for full contact with the supporting surface

Pronation—Turning (the palm of the hand) inward and downward; opposite of supination

Proximal—Closest to the center or midline of the body

Release—When a ball leaves the hand(s)

Retraction—The act of withdrawing an object, implement, or body part (generally for the purpose of force absorption or dissipation)

Static position—A position in which an object or body segments remain motionless

Stride length—The horizontal distance traveled in one full step on each side of the body

Supination—Turning (the palm of the hand) upward and outward; opposite of pronation

References

Espenschade, A.S., & Eckert, H.M. (1967). *Motor development*. Columbus, OH: Charles E. Merrill.

Slocum, D., & James, S. (1968). Biomechanics of running. *The Journal of the American Medical Association*, **205**, 97-104.

Wickstrom, R. (1983). *Fundamental motor patterns* (3rd ed.). Philadelphia: Lea & Febiger.

Suggested Readings

Broer, M., & Zernicke, R. (1979). *Efficiency of human movement* (4th ed.). Philadelphia: W.B. Saunders.

Cooper, J., Adrian, M., & Glassow, R. (1982). *Kinesiology* (5th ed.). St. Louis: C.V. Mosby.

Groves, R., & Camaione, D.N. (1975). *Concepts in kinesiology*. Philadelphia: W.B. Saunders.

Hay, J., & Reid, J. (1982). *The anatomical and mechanical bases of human motion*. Englewood Cliffs: Prentice-Hall.

Kreighbaum, E., & Barthels, K. (1985). *Biomechanics: A qualitative approach for studying human movement* (2nd ed.). Minneapolis: Burgess.

Kruger, H., & Kruger, J. (1982). *Movement education in physical education: A guide to teaching and planning* (2nd ed.). Dubuque, IA: Wm. C. Brown.

Luttgens, K., & Wells, K. (1982). *Kinesiology: Scientific basis of human motion* (7th ed.). Philadelphia: W.B. Saunders.

Noble, L., & Eck, J. (1984). Piagetian learning paradigm for teaching mechanical concepts. *Proceedings of the Second National Symposium on Teaching Kinesiology and Biomechanics in Sports*, **2**, 35-42.

Stoner, L. (1984). Is the performer skilled or unskilled? *Proceedings of the Second National Symposium on Teaching Kinesiology and Biomechanics in Sports*, **2**, 233-234.

Chapter 4
Planning Practice and Drills

We all tend to enjoy doing those activities that we do reasonably well. Those movement skills that are incorporated into a person's lifestyle that contribute to personal well-being and health usually are the ones that have provided successful experiences in the past. Physical education classes must seek to provide satisfying movement experiences for young people so that involvement in physical activity will become an integral part of their everyday lives. As Bain (1980) proposed, we must attempt to make movement so significant that it becomes an essential phase of living, such as eating, resting, or personal hygiene. The approach to teaching movement skills must be interesting and challenging and must provide a measure of success to the learner, without which the learner will soon lose motivation and become disinterested. The teacher must provide encouragement and should plan simple practice *drills* that allow small successes at first, followed by more complex activities that challenge the learners and encourage them to further achievements. Once they have mastered the basic skills, they can move into game situations with a better opportunity for success, which may promote a lifetime involvement.

Drill Selection

Drills and practice patterns should progress from those that work on one or two skills, to those that require several skills, and finally to those that simulate the game situation. If the actual game requires the participant to use open skills (those that vary from situation to situation, such as a player dribbling a ball in a game), then the practice drills should culminate in an activity that is similar to the game.

Skills that are learned in closely controlled settings often disintegrate when the performer is placed in a less controlled game situation. The practice of *closed skills* (those performed the same way each time without interference by others or the environment, such as a volleyball serve) would not need to be practiced under such variable conditions. However, the teacher should be aware of the boredom involved with doing the same thing repeatedly and may wish to change practice patterns to remotivate the learner. The effective teacher or coach plans skills practice in such a way that students feel they have achieved some success, have understood how the skills fit into the game, and are eager to move ahead.

The most effective way to learn a motor skill is to practice it physically. Teachers should keep this in mind and move students into practice situations as quickly as possible. Explanation, demonstration, or presentation of the problem should not consume half the class time. Get the students moving! If you have sufficient equipment and space, let each person have a ball to practice individual skills. The more practice trials each person gets, the sooner the skill will be mastered. Pair the students to work on passing- or catching-type skills and use small groups whenever possible to learn teamwork strategies before going into the game situation. Always plan to maximize each student's practice time as much as possible.

Students who have mastered the beginning skills should not be required to go through the simple skill drills again each time the sport is taught. Plan more advanced practices for the more advanced students. The same drills done repetitively year after year do not contribute to the motivational level of the learner or to the development of skills. As drill patterns are learned, renewed motivation can be created by introducing competition in the form of relays or adding a scoring procedure to the activity.

Whenever there are enough balls for half the group and space to spread the class out, students should be paired for ball-handling practice. This permits more practice for each person than would occur in small-group work (five to eight per group). Many discipline problems can be avoided by reducing waiting time and keeping students actively involved in the skill practice. The paired-practice formation should be arranged so that all balls are moving back and forth in the same direction to minimize the danger of students being hit in the back or side by errant balls. Spacing of participants depends on their skill levels; that is, poorly skilled must be placed farther apart for safety.

Basic Drill Patterns

The usual teaching situation requires that students share equipment and work in limited space. In these cases, squad or group drills provide suitable means for practice. Some of the common patterns of simple drills are illustrated and discussed here. These drills can be adapted to allow practice of many skills in different sports. They can be used by beginners to learn new skills or by advanced players to warm up before a game or strenuous practice. These drills can be converted into contests by adding restraining or target lines and specifying the number of trials, counting the number of successful repetitions within a certain time period, or determining which group completes a circuit first. Drills specific to each sport and skill are included in each sport-specific chapter. The diagrams throughout this book will use the legends in Figure 4.1.

Single Column or Relay

Players stand behind one another facing in the same direction (Figure 4.2). Beginning with Player X1, each player takes a turn and goes to the end of the *column*. The distance to the turning line depends on the activity to be practiced.

Column With Leader

The leader is positioned at a designated distance from the squad. The leader faces the squad and gives each player a turn at the pass or throw. Players may return to the end of the column (Figure 4.3), follow the pass to a position behind the leader, or replace the leader (Figure 4.4).

Single Line

Players stand side by side (Figure 4.5). The object is started with Player X1 and is passed from player to player. The drill may finish when the object reaches Player X5 or when it has been returned again to Player X1.

Leader and Class

The class stands in a single line or a semicircle, and the leader stands in front of and facing the class (Figure 4.6). The leader continues as leader until each player has had a turn; then the leader may be changed.

X	=	A position of a player.
X (open line on left)	=	A player facing ———→ (direction of open line).
X (open line on right)	=	A player facing ←———.
———→	=	Path of ball.
— — →	=	Path of a moving player.
······>	=	Path of a ball carrier.
MWWWWM	=	Dribbled ball.
ᗰ	=	Pivot by a player.
X or D	=	Defensive player.
X or O	=	Offensive player or opposite team player.
———→|	=	Block or obstacle which stops the ball or player.
~~→	=	Path of punted or kicked ball.

Figure 4.1. Legends

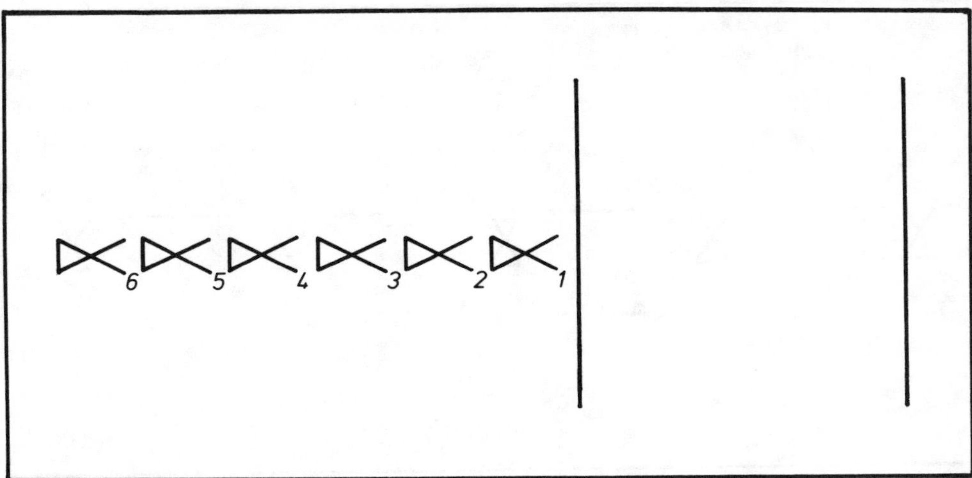

Figure 4.2. Single column or relay

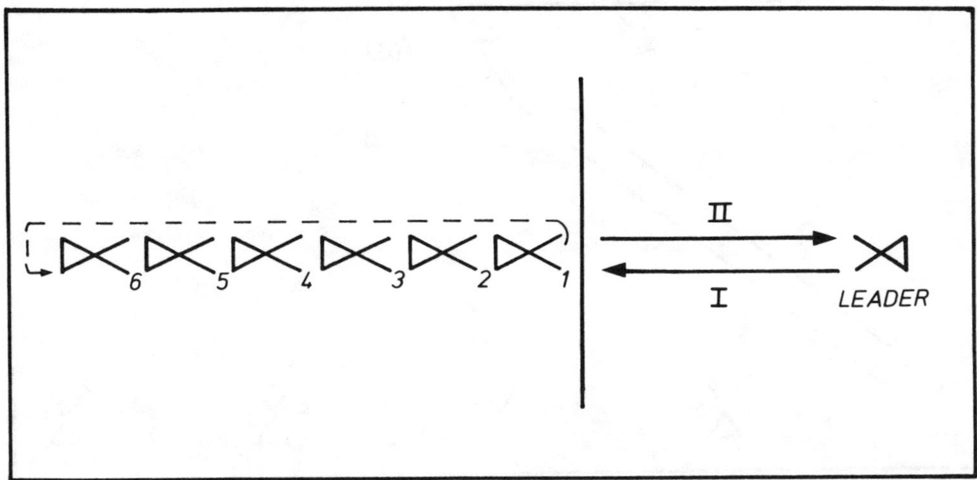

Figure 4.3. Column with stationary leader

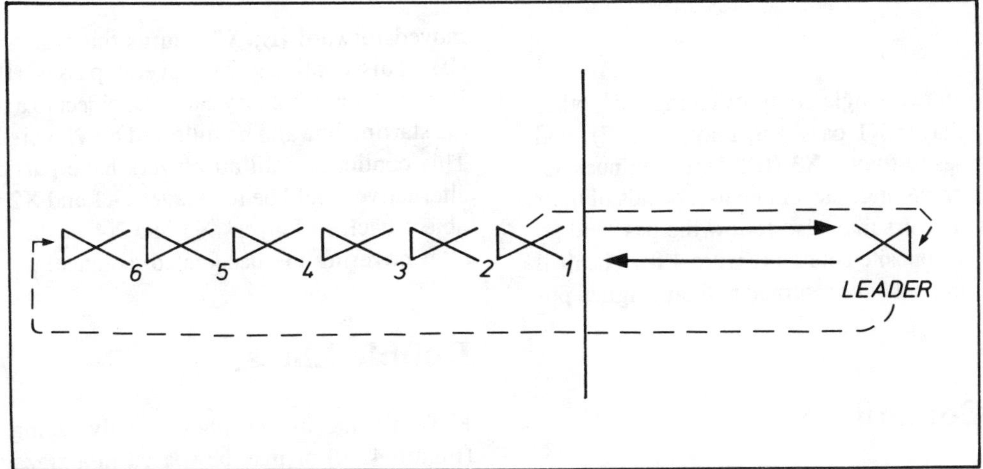

Figure 4.4. Column with changing leader

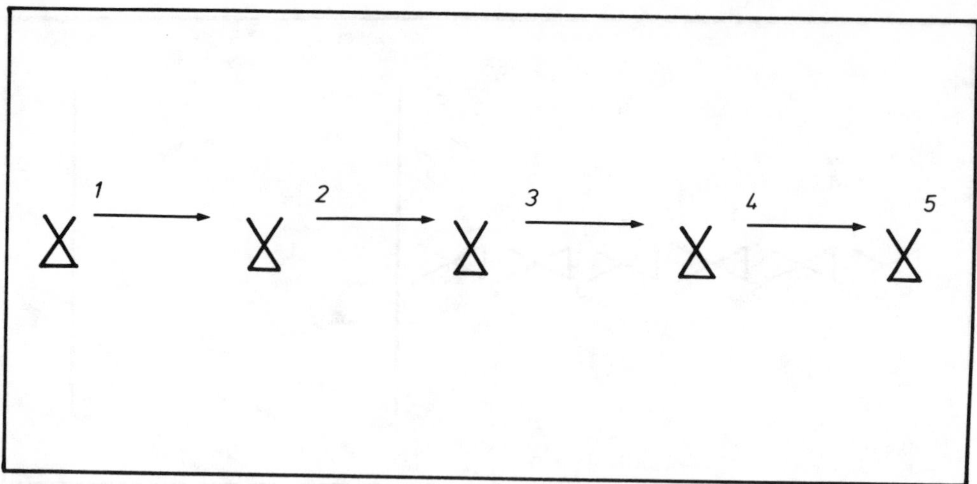

Figure 4.5. Single line

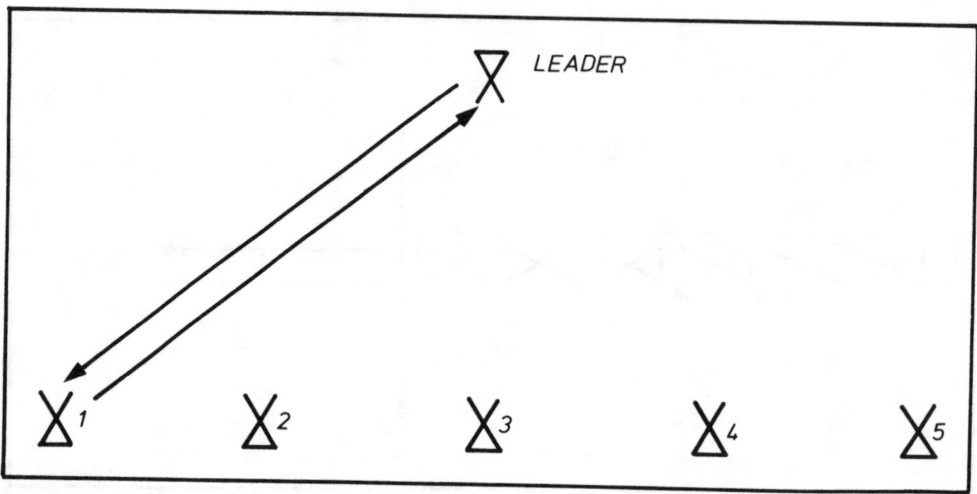

Figure 4.6. Leader and class

Shuttle

Individuals form two single columns facing each other (Figure 4.7). Player X1 passes to Player X2 (I), and Player X2 passes to Player X3 (II). This continues sequentially. After passing, players go to the ends of their own columns. Players may also follow the pass and go to the end of the opposite column (Figure 4.8). The drill may continue until all have returned to their original positions.

Double Column

Players stand in double columns (Figure 4.9). Player X1 passes diagonally forward to Player X2 who has moved forward (I); X2 returns the pass to Player X1 (II). This continues for several passes (III and IV). Players X1 and X2 may carry the object to a line opposite the starting line and be followed by Players X3 and X4. This continues until all players have participated. An alternative would be for Players X1 and X2 to carry the object back to Players X3 and X4 at the starting line after covering the designated distance.

Double Lines

Players stand in two lines directly facing each other (Figure 4.10) or may be spaced in a zigzag formation (Figure 4.11). The object is started with Player X1, who passes to Player X2. Player X2 passes to Player X3. This

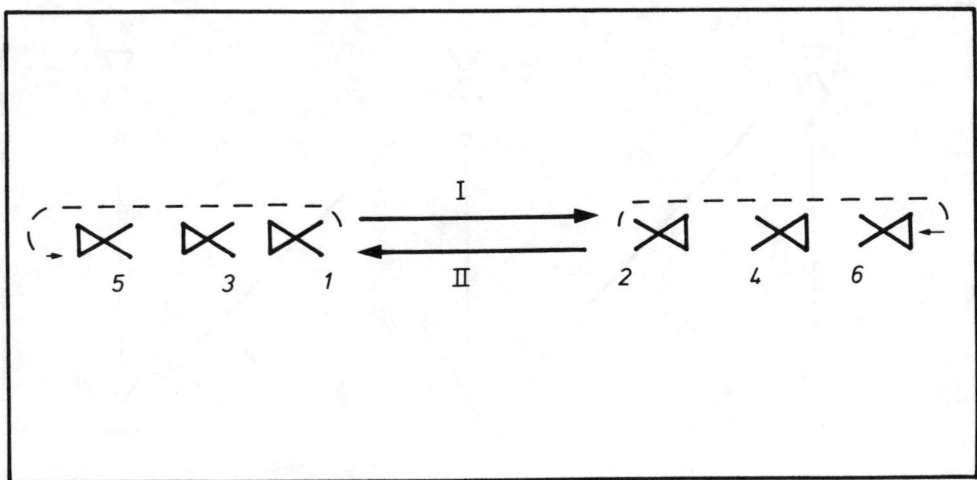

Figure 4.7. Shuttle

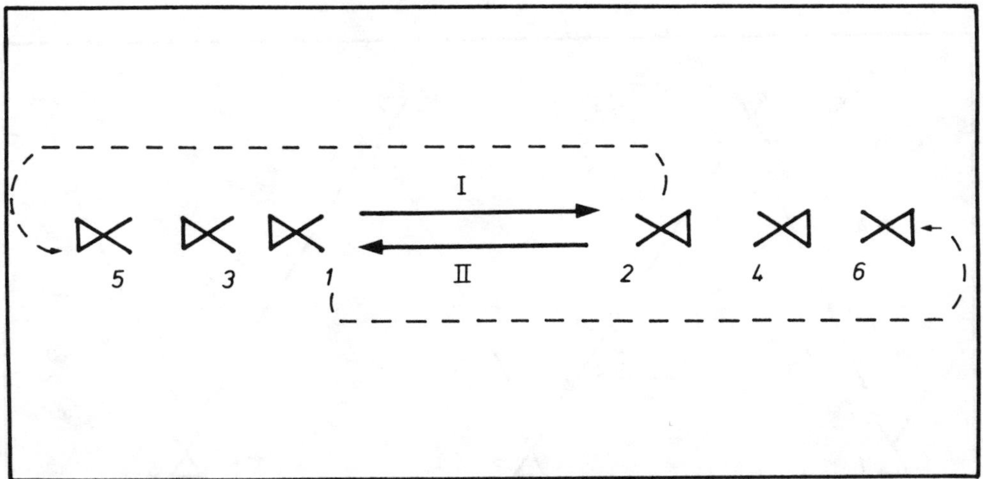

Figure 4.8. Shuttle with column exchange

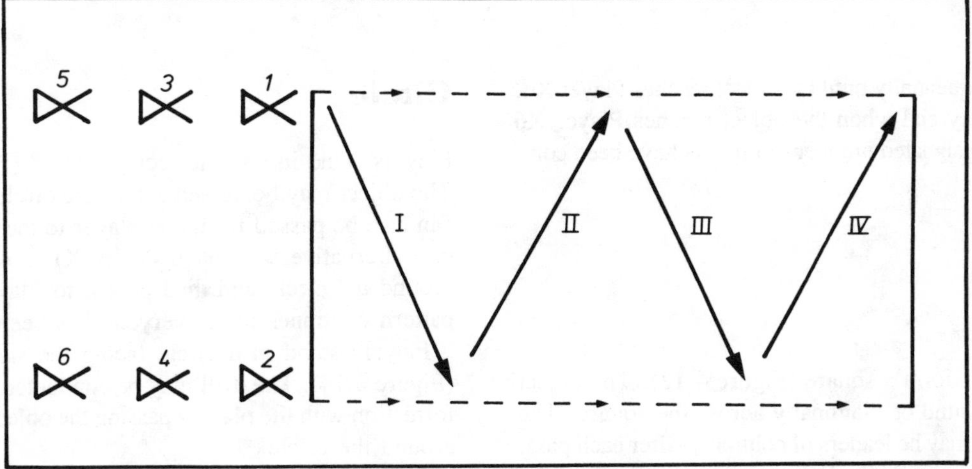

Figure 4.9. Double column

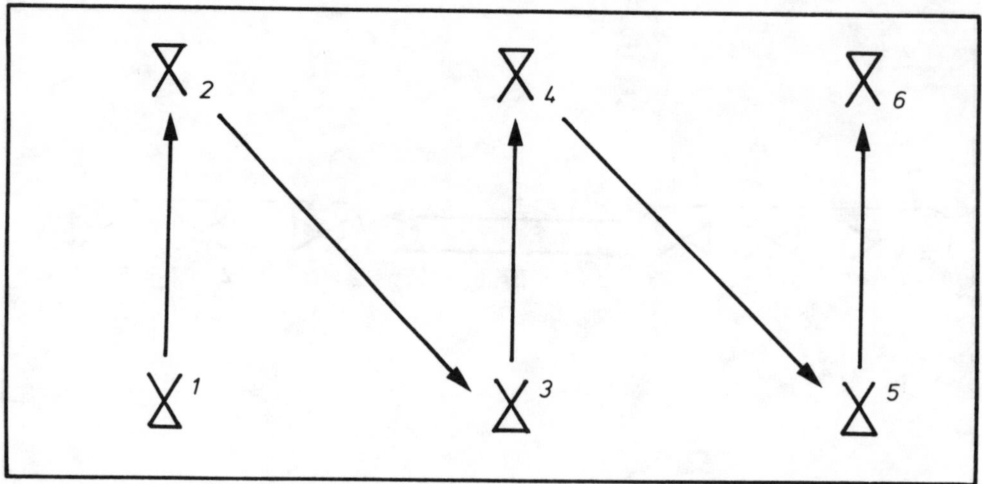

Figure 4.10. Double lines

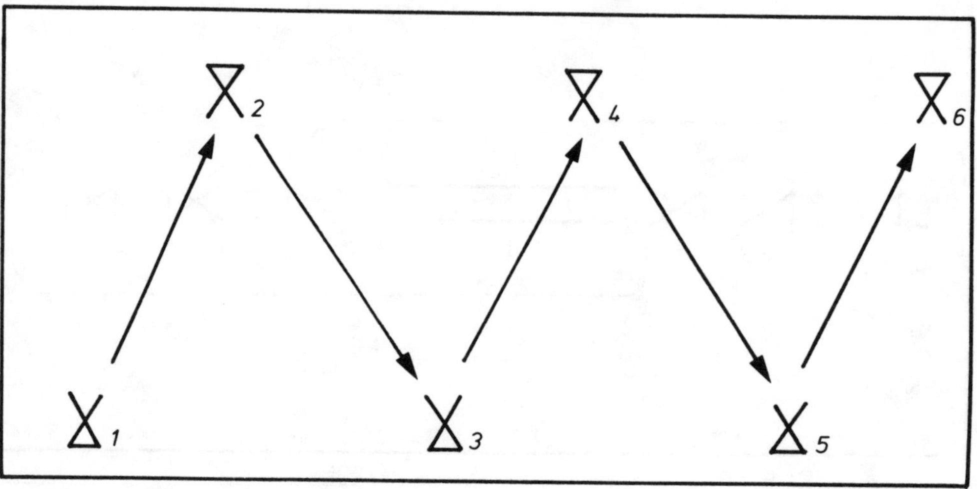

Figure 4.11. Double lines (staggered)

continues sequentially until the object reaches Player X6. The drill may end when the object reaches Player X6 or when a designated number of circuits have been completed.

Square

Four players form a square (Figure 4.12). The object is passed around or diagonally across the square. The four players may be leaders of columns. After each pass, the passer goes to the end of the same column, and the next person becomes the new passer.

Circle

Players stand in a circle facing inward (Figure 4.13). The object may be passed across the circle. The object can also be passed from one player to the next. A second alternative is to have Player X1 move the object around the circle and then pass it to Player X2. This pattern continues until everyone has been the passer.

Players stand in a circle facing the same direction (Figure 4.14). The drill may be conducted as a moving formation with the players passing the object as they run around the circle.

A third formation may be used from the circle by placing a leader in the center (Figure 4.15). The object is

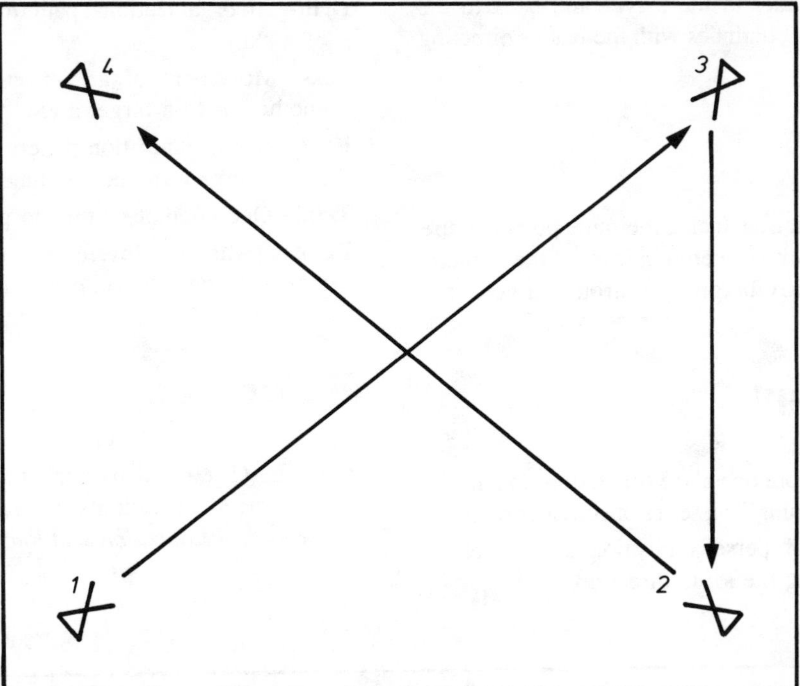

Figure 4.12. Square

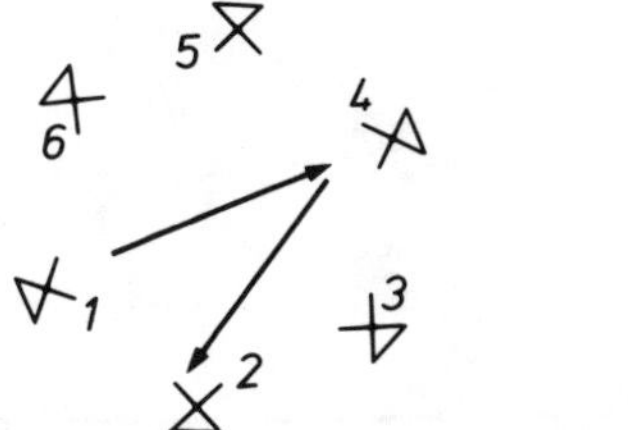

Figure 4.13. Circle formations (facing inward)

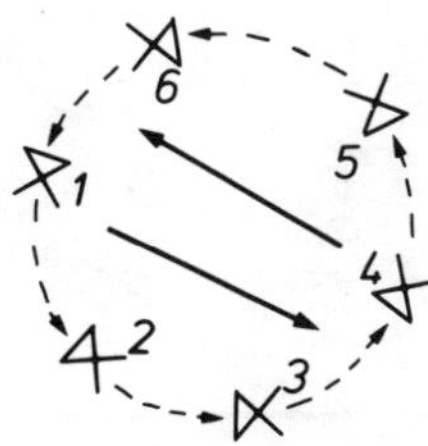

Figure 4.14. Circle formations (facing counterclockwise)

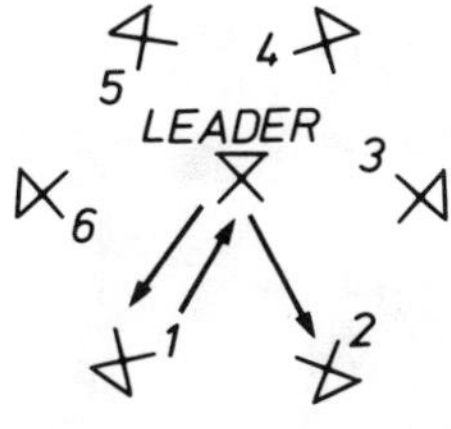

Figure 4.15. Circle formations (leader in center)

passed from the leader to the player and back to the leader. This pattern continues with the leader directing the passes.

Semicircle

Players form a semicircle facing the same point (Figure 4.16). A leader may be centered in front of the semicircle, or the squad may be grouped around a goal.

Terminology

Circuit—Moving from one place (or station) to another (as in "circuit training"); a series of activities or tasks

Column—A line of persons positioned one behind another, all facing the same direction

Drill—An organizational pattern that facilitates practice of a skill

Pass—Movement of an object from one person to another or to a target area

Relay—An organization pattern in which members of a team take turns performing a skill

Trial—One attempt or turn to perform a skill

Zig-zag pattern—Movement in alternating directions to the right and left while moving forward

Reference

Bain, L. (1980). Socializing into role of participant: Physical education's ultimate goal? *Journal of Physical Education and Recreation*, **51**(7), 48-50.

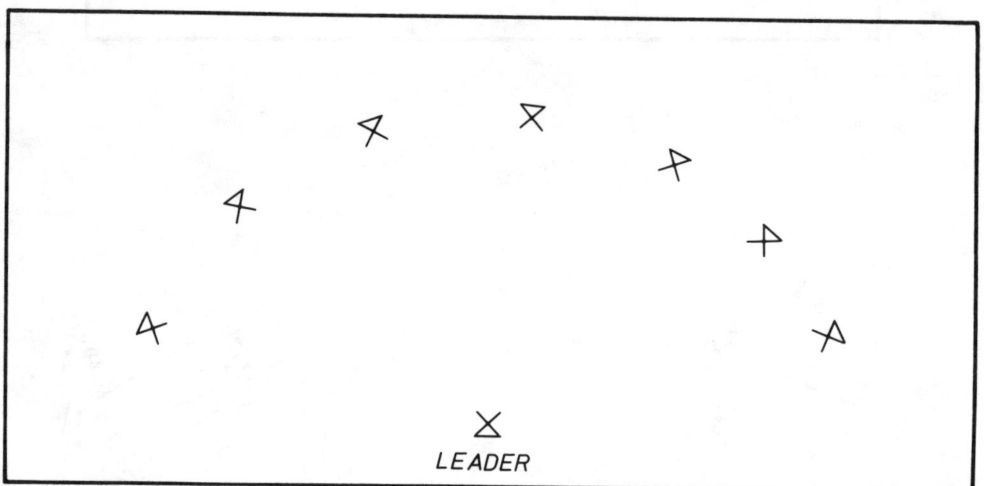

Figure 4.16. Semicircle

Part II

Team Sports

Chapter 5
Basketball

Basketball was devised in 1891 by Dr. James A. Naismith, physical education director at the YMCA College in Springfield, Massachusetts, as an outgrowth of a project to create an interesting game to encourage young men to participate in indoor exercise and recreation programs during the winter. The first games were played with a soccer-type ball (some say football) using peach baskets as goals. There was no limit to the number of players on a team in these early games. This was soon changed, however, and within a few years the five-player game was accepted for men.

Naismith proposed 13 rules for basketball. The game and these rules were first publicized in 1892 in a YMCA magazine that circulated throughout the country. The game quickly caught on and spread to other YMCAs, playgrounds, and schools. The first intercollegiate game was held in 1896 (Yale vs. Connecticut Wesleyan).

In 1892, Senda Berenson of Smith College, recognizing the merits of basketball, modified the rules and introduced the game to Smith's women students. Under the leadership of Berenson, a group of women educators revised some of the original rules and published the *Basketball Guide*, the first such rule book for women, in 1901.

These early rules required six players per team rather than five and restricted players' movements to only one division of the court. The court was divided into three parts until 1938, when it was changed to a two-part division. Players assigned to one division could not move into any other division. In 1962, the roving player was added. This allowed two players to play on both the front- and the backcourt so a team could develop a four-player offense and defense. Finally, in 1971 the rules were revised to reduce the number of players to five and to eliminate most of the differences between women's and men's rules. However, some areas of the country still play the six-player divided-court game.

Men's intercollegiate rules were established to govern college play in 1904. Other groups, such as the YMCA and the Amateur Athletics Association, had their own variations. These groups standardized most of the rules for men in 1915, although some minor variations continued to be allowed. With the exception of the 3-point play, the major rules for men have not changed much in recent years, although small revisions are made annually by national rules committees for high school and college play.

Rules for high school basketball are published annually by the National Federation of State High School Associations. Rules for college men and women are published annually by the National Collegiate Athletic Association.

Purposes and Values

Basketball requires the development of cardiorespiratory endurance and the fundamental motor skills of balance, agility, and general forms of locomotion such as jumping and running. Arm and shoulder strength in addition to eye-hand coordination are enhanced by the throwing and basket-shooting activities. Leg strength is developed through running as well as jumping. The use of peripheral vision when dribbling or seeking pass outlets is essential and should be encouraged.

Conditioning for this sport should begin before the actual games are played. If players have been involved in other vigorous activities such as soccer, speedball, or conditioning exercises, they will be able to participate more fully at the start of the unit. Otherwise, cardiovascular developmental activities should precede game situations.

Preliminary activities taught to children in elementary school enhance later motor development in basketball skills. Elementary school children should work on dodging, jumping, and the basic ball-handling skills of throwing, catching, and dribbling. As they gain control and strength, goal shooting should be added.

Middle school students should work on perfecting basic skills and learning simple offensive and defensive strategies such as effective 1-on-1 guarding techniques and *outlet pass* patterns. Game play is essential to this age group, although lengthy endurance activities should not be permitted in the regular class setting. The opportunity and time for proper conditioning is not available in the average physical education or recreation situation.

Students involved in interscholastic athletics or outside league play may have the time and facilities for the long-term conditioning program necessary for advanced play.

The Game

Basketball is played by two teams attempting to score points by throwing the ball through the hoop at one end of the court while trying to prevent the opponents from scoring points in a similar manner at the other end of the court. Each team is comprised of five players who must pass, hand, or dribble the ball to advance it toward their *own goal* (basket) which is being defended by the opponents. The opponents attempt to intercept the ball and move it toward the opposite end to score in their goal.

Each goal made from the playing court counts 2 points. Goals made by free throws awarded when the opponents foul count 1 point. The team scoring the most points in the allotted time wins. Some rules for advanced players allow 3 points to be scored by long shots made by players who shoot from at least 19 ft 9 in. away from the basket rim.

High school games and those for younger players are usually played in quarters. College and adult games consist of two 20-min halves. If the score is tied at the end of the regulation playing time, one or more overtime periods are played.

Violations are offenses that result in loss of possession of the ball (commonly called *turnovers*). Examples include (a) taking steps while holding the ball; (b) dribbling the ball, catching it, and dribbling again; (c) causing the ball to go out of bounds; (d) stepping on or over a boundary line while holding the ball; and (e) holding the ball too long under certain circumstances. When a player commits a violation, the opponents throw the ball in from out of bounds at a point near where the violation occurred.

Fouls are more serious offenses such as personal contact with the opponent (*pushing*, *blocking*, and *holding*), or *unsporting behavior* such as delaying the game, having too many players on the court, or using abusive language. Fouls are usually penalized by awarding the opposite team *free throws*. Generally, each team is allowed a specific number of fouls before the free throw penalty is put into effect. Individual players are allowed five (six in some cases) fouls, after which they are ejected from the game.

Playing Area

The regulation basketball court is divided by a center line (Figure 5.1). At each end is a designated lane area

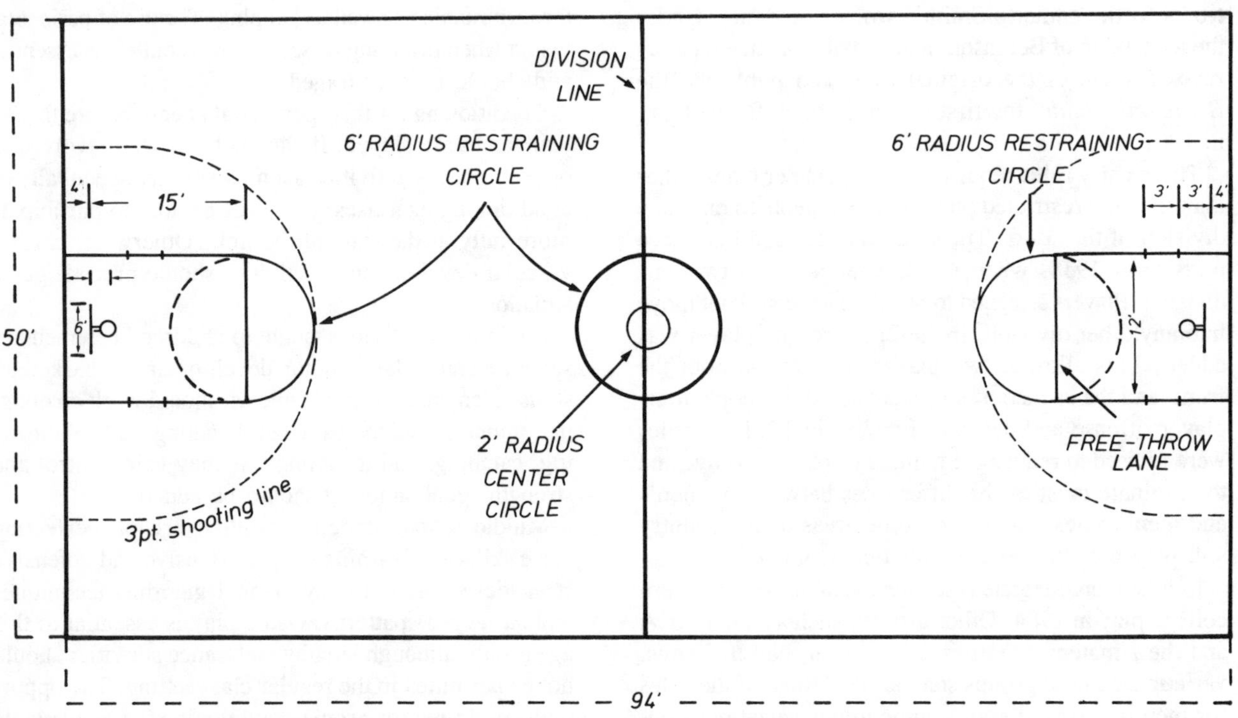

Figure 5.1. Basketball court

marked on the floor under the basket. This area is 12 by 19 ft, and it delineates the *free throw lane*. Circles with a 6-ft radius are marked in the center and at each *free throw line*.

The basketball court should be 94 ft by 50 ft, although this can be modified to fit the area available. Even if the court must be shortened to fit the space, try to retain as much width as possible. Reducing the width by more than 10 ft interferes with the development of advanced strategy and should not be done when working with advanced skills. For elementary school students, a smaller space is quite suitable. Courts should have at least 6 ft of out-of-bounds space around them, especially at the end lines under each basket. If this space is unavailable at the end lines, heavy padding should cover the wall to a height of 8 ft.

Equipment

The following is a description of the equipment necessary for basketball. Standards for equipment and recommendations on equipment use are also included.

Backboards and Baskets

The backboards may be rectangular or fan shaped and are generally made of plastic or glass, although wood is still used in some cases. One is attached at the center of each end of the court so that the lower edge of the board is 9 ft above the court and 4 ft inbounds from each end line. The basket is attached to the backboard at a height of 10 ft above the court surface and 6 in. from the backboard. The inside of the basket ring is 18 in. Nylon or cotton mesh nets should be suspended from rims to slow the ball down as it passes through the basket. Wire mesh is sometimes used for outdoor play areas, but these may be somewhat hazardous for older or taller players who may catch fingers in the wires. Basket rims should be orange in color.

Basketballs

Basketball covers may be made of rubber, leather, or synthetic material. For official tournament play, leather balls are usually mandated. For class play and skill learning, rubber or synthetic balls are appropriate. These balls are usually less expensive than leather balls and therefore more of them may be purchased for less money. One ball for every two players is desirable to maximize participation and learning, but one for every five or six players is manageable.

Official balls come in two sizes. Those for boys and men should weigh between 20 and 22 oz and have a circumference between 29-1/2 and 30-1/4 in. Those for girls and women should have a circumference between 28-1/2 and 29 in. Children with small hands will be able to handle the smaller balls more easily; therefore, they are recommended for use in elementary schools, middle schools, and perhaps even in high schools. The smaller ball is mandated in varsity play for girls and women in some leagues. For general secondary school use, there should be some balls of each size so players can choose the one they find more comfortable to handle.

Pinnies

Pinnies or vests provide appropriate means of distinguishing one team from another during game play and should be available as supplementary equipment. They can be purchased from sporting goods stores or homemade from cotton fabric. Stitching or painting large numbers on the pinnies makes them more versatile but is not essential.

Suggestions for Coeducational Play

One of the best ways to overcome the difference in skill levels among students in classes is to limit competition and encourage cooperation. Students can learn to help one another improve if the teacher or coach organizes the group in an appropriate manner. For example, a station arrangement can be used for practice where a small group of students (squad) is assigned to work at each station. These stations might consist of set-shot shooting at one basket, lay-up shooting at another basket, target passing using two different types of passes at the third and the fourth stations, dribbling around obstacles at a fifth station, and a shuttle dribble at a sixth station. The class is then divided into six squads, one at each station. Minimum performance criteria are set for each station. As each person achieves that performance level, he or she must then help the others in the squad achieve the same level. All members of a squad continue to practice at one station until all (or perhaps 75%) can do the skill, after which they move on to another skill. The minimum performance expected must be adjusted to suit the class. Seventh graders might be expected to make one out of four short set shots, whereas tenth graders should be able to make at least three out of five shots.

When some players in the class are considerably more highly skilled than others, two levels of performance criteria (Level I and Level II) may be needed. The highly skilled must perform the Level II criteria, and those assigned to the Level I group will have less rigorous tasks. The Level II players might have to make five out of five short set shots, whereas the Level I performers must make only three out of five. The Level II performers may have to perform the obstacle dribble in 10 seconds, whereas the Level I players have 20 seconds. These are only examples of how the levels may differ. Teachers will have to experiment to determine valid criteria.

One way to set up the criteria is to select one skilled and one intermediate performer and have them do the skills involved. Use their scores as guides to determine the skill level to be achieved for each group. It would be best to set the expected scores a little below those achieved by the test performers. For example, if the skilled dribbler (Level II) did the shuttle dribble in 10 seconds and the less skilled (Level I) did it in 20 seconds, a fair minimum score for Level II might be 15 seconds and for Level I, 25 seconds. Using somewhat more lenient scores than those achieved by the experimental performers allows more performers to achieve success. If the instructor finds that the minimum performance levels are achieved too easily or are too difficult, they can be readily adjusted before the next lesson.

Another way to utilize the station technique of organizing is to set up several stations of increasing difficulty for each skill. Minimum performance objectives are established for each station. Performers start at the least difficult one and move on to the next only after having reached the specified objectives. In order to avoid all students starting at one place and then standing around to wait for a turn, assign small groups to start at different skills. There might be three levels of difficulty for passing: (a) chest pass at a 3-ft-square target from 15 ft; (b) bounce pass at a 2-ft-square target from 15 ft; and (c) overhead pass at a 2-ft-square target from 20 ft. The criterion level could be four out of five passes. Those assigned to passing would start at Station 1 and proceed to Station 2 and then to Station 3. Another group would be assigned to start at Station 1 of several dribbling stations while others could be at shooting stations.

This style of class organization expects that students can monitor their own performance and practice what they need. When students are not mature or self-disciplined enough to do this, it is less effective. Teachers may be able to make use of squad leaders or student assistants to supervise each station. The student leader could be given a list of the persons in the class and then observe the players at a station and check when the performer reached the minimum criteria at that station. This arrangement would enable the teacher to circulate throughout the gymnasium, critique various students' performances, and encourage on-task behavior.

Some variations of the regulation basketball game provide for more equitable competition between boys and girls. One of the best of these is sometimes called *zone basketball*. In this game the court is divided into 9 (or 12 in large classes) equal areas with shoe polish, tape, or water-color paint. One player from each team is assigned to each zone, and all must stay in their own zones. This allows players within a zone to be matched according to height and skill. This game also encourages passing and reduces the problems of a few players dominating play. Because some players are in zones far from the basket at which their team is shooting, they never get a chance to try for a basket. Therefore, a rotation system should be used so that all players get an opportunity to play in zones near the shooting end and in zones near the defending end of the court. Rotating after 5 to 7 min of play accomplishes this in the usual 40-min activity period.

There is a line-type variation of basketball similar to line soccer that can be used to cope with skill differences in coeducational play. In this variation, the class is divided into two or four boys' teams and the same number of girls' teams. An equal number of boys' and girls' teams is assigned to one of two major class divisions: A or B. Two girls' teams (or two boys' teams) from opposite divisions are assigned to the basketball court to play a game while the remaining players line up along both sidelines out of bounds.

The sideline players should alternate the A and B players. The players on the court may dribble, pass to each other, or pass to the sideline players as they move the ball into shooting position. The sideline players may only receive and pass the ball, and may not dribble, shoot, or travel with the ball. After the first two teams have played for a short while, they move to the sidelines, and two teams of the opposite gender go onto the court. This continues until all teams have had a chance to play on the court.

Mixing boys and girls together on each team usually provides the best opportunity for girls to improve their skills unless the boys are permitted to dominate play and never pass to the girls. Equating teams by distributing players by skill and height establishes teams of comparable playing ability. This assignment of players may be necessary to equalize play rather than allowing students to choose their own teams. If the boys refuse to pass the ball to the girls, it may be necessary to institute a rule that states the girls must handle the ball before a basket is attempted. However, this is an artificial technique and should be eliminated as soon as possible.

The *1-on-1 defense* is a better system to use than the *zone defense* when teams have a diversity of skill levels. The functioning of these systems is discussed later in this chapter. The 1-on-1 system allows an individual to be assigned to guard an opponent of comparable ability. The zone system may result in a short, unskilled player having to defend against a tall, skilled opponent, which is undesirable.

Teaching Progressions

Skills in this chapter are grouped according to fundamental movement relationships to one another and commonality of purpose for ease of understanding and analyzing. This does not imply that the skills should be presented to students in that order.

The following outline presents recommended progressions for teaching basketball skills. Strategies should be introduced into practice and team play as the need arises and as skills develop. When working with novices, only those skills listed for beginners should be taught. The intermediate players would review the beginning skills and move on to the next level. Advanced players quickly review the beginning and the intermediate skills, but most of the instructional time should be spent on the advanced skills and strategies. These progressions may need to be varied to accommodate individual groups or classes (see chapter 1 for ideas for organizing classes with students of different skill levels).

Progression for Beginning Players

I. Passing and catching
   - A. Chest
   - B. Two-handed overhead
   - C. One-arm push (shoulder)
   - D. Bounce

II. Dribbling using each hand

III. Pivoting

IV. Shooting
   - A. Set (short-to-intermediate distance)
     1. Two-handed (weaker players)
     2. One-handed (stronger players)
   - B. Lay-up
   - C. Shooting games

V. Rebounding

VI. Jump Balls

VII. Guarding: 1-on-1

VIII. Game play
   - A. Lead-up games
     1. 3-on-3
     2. Half-court games
   - B. Full-court game

Additional Skills for Intermediate Players

I. Passing and catching
   - A. Baseball (overarm)
   - B. One-arm underarm

II. Dribbling
   - A. Shifting from one hand to the other
   - B. Protecting the ball

III. Feinting

IV. Shooting
   - A. Longer set
   - B. Moving

V. Begin game play

VI. Rebounding (blocking out)

VII. Guarding: Zone defense

VIII. Tournament play

Additional Skills for Advanced Players *

I. Passing and catching
   A. Hook
   B. Long fast-break passes

II. Shooting
   A. Jump
   B. Hook

III. Guarding (more zone defenses)

*It is recommended that game or modified game play become part of each day's lesson after 2 or 3 days of review and new material being presented.

Techniques and Practice

Passing and Catching

Passing and catching should be taught together. The various types of passes should be introduced separately and practiced one at a time for beginners. In a review of passing and catching with older, more experienced players, two to four different passes can be presented in rapid sequence and followed by drills organized for the practice of all passes simultaneously.

Passing

The act of *passing* is a purposeful projection of the ball between teammates to transfer possession of the ball. Different types of passes are used for varying distances between teammates and varying game circumstances. Good passing requires accuracy, proper timing, appropriate speed, deception, and choice of a suitable pass. The passing skill is essential to the well-played game.

Chest Pass. This is the most basic pass used in basketball (Figure 5.2). The chest pass is for short, unobstructed distances (10 to 20 ft) between teammates. This pass is a pushing fundamental skill (Figure 5.2).

The stance is approximately shoulder width with one foot slightly forward. Both hands hold the ball at about abdominal level or in the vicinity of the chest. The fingers are positioned on the sides of the ball and are spread, the thumbs are pointing inward or behind the ball, and the elbows are flexed and close to the body.

The force production phase begins with a step forward on the front foot or with a forward shift of body weight. The use of the forward step is optional. The arms are lifted upward while simultaneously extending at the elbows and pushing the ball away from the body at about chest level. The wrist and fingers perform a snapping action to add velocity to the ball. The snapping is a rapid *pronation* (palms turned outward) at the wrist with finger

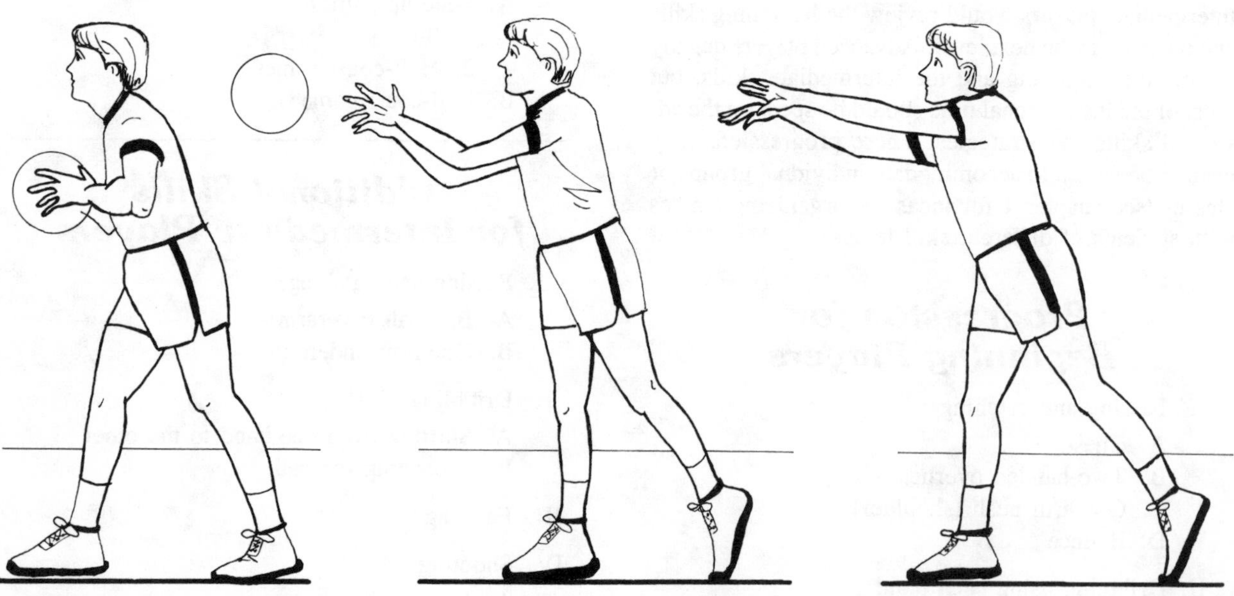

Figure 5.2. Chest pass

extension. The ball flight is direct and fast, and the target is just below the chin of the receiver.

The follow-through consists of a continued forward motion of the arms toward the intended direction of ball flight. At the conclusion of the follow-through, the palms of the hand should be facing outward and the thumbs facing down.

Bounce Pass. This is a pass in which the ball is pushed to the floor before reaching the receiver. It is utilized when an opponent is obstructing the passer or the intended receiver and is especially appropriate when the guarding opponent has the arms up. The bounce pass can be executed with one or both hands and is considered a pushing fundamental skill.

The two-handed bounce pass is almost identical to the chest pass, but the starting position is lower in the chest pass. The direction of the arm extension and follow-through is toward the intended area of ball strike on the floor, or approximately three quarters of the distance between the passer and the receiver or at least closer to the receiver than to the passer.

The one-handed bounce pass is held with both hands to position the ball to the side. The pushing hand is held behind the ball while the other hand is under and slightly to the front of the ball. The nonpushing hand comes off the ball as the pushing arm and hand begin extension. All other aspects of the one-handed bounce pass are identical to the two-handed bounce pass.

Two-Handed Overhead Pass. The two-handed overhead pass is utilized for passing over an opponent's head. This pass is a two-handed overarm-throwing fundamental skill.

The ball is held overhead with both hands. The fingers and thumbs are spread behind and to the sides of the ball. The arms are held extended or slightly flexed directly overhead or slightly in front of the head. The stance can be either parallel or in a shoulder-width stride with one foot ahead of the other.

The preparation for the pass begins with a retraction of the arms to slightly behind the head with the elbows slightly flexed. This motion is created by hyperflexion at the shoulders and flexion at the elbows.

The force-production phase is initiated by either a forward shift of body weight or a forward step. At this same time, a forward extension at the shoulders moves the arms toward the release point. The arms are also extended at the elbows. Just prior to release, a vigorous snapping of the wrist (*abduction*/radial deviation) occurs.

The follow-through is executed primarily at the wrist in its already established motion. Some follow-through of the shoulders forward (extension) might occur, but too much could cause the player to foul a nearby defender.

Shoulder or One-Arm Push Pass. The shoulder push pass is executed from in front of the shoulders with a pushing action. This pass is performed in the same way as the one-handed bounce pass with the exception of ball-flight direction and ball positioning just prior to the pushing action.

The ball is held with both hands. The pushing hand is positioned behind the ball and the other hand on the front of or under the ball. The ball is brought to above and slightly in front of the shoulder of the pushing arm. Force production can begin like other passes with a forward body-weight shift or forward-stepping action. The arm extends and directs the ball away from the body and in the direction of the intended receiver.

Baseball or Overarm Pass. This type of pass is used for long passes downcourt. The baseball pass resembles the motions executed in an overarm throw. This pass is an overarm throwing fundamental skill.

The stance is a forward stride. The throwing arm retracts behind the head with a rearward shift of body weight and opening (clockwise rotation) of the hips (right-handed throw). The shoulder horizontally abducts, and the elbow flexes. The throwing hand holds the ball underneath. The nonthrowing arm is held in front of the body. This positioning is identical to that of overarm throwing with the exception that the forearm is not laid back as far.

Force production is begun with the counterclockwise rotation of the hips and a forward weight shift or forward stepping. The rotating hips bring the trunk around toward the ball release. The upper arm rotates forward from the shoulder. Soon after this, the elbow begins extension. Just prior to release, the wrist extends. The point of release should be out to the side of the body and tangent to the target. The angle of trajectory is commensurate with the distance the ball is being thrown.

The follow-through is a continuation of the arm moving in the intended direction of ball flight. The wrist rotates medially, or toward the midline of the body, (pronation) with the fingers pointing toward the direction of ball flight.

One-Handed Underarm Pass. The one-handed underarm pass is also referred to as a shovel pass. It should be used for short to medium distances (5 to 25 ft). Long underarm passing is especially dangerous due to the many opportunities for interception. This pass should be used when a player is caught in a low body position and must transfer possession of the ball immediately. This pass is an underarm throwing fundamental skill.

The most accommodating stance for this pass is a forward stride with the forward foot being opposite the side of the throwing action. This permits the hips to be open (rotated *clockwise* for a right-handed thrower) for the fullest range of motion possible in rotating toward the ball release. The ball is generally held in both hands for stability until the force-production phase of the throw begins. The preparation phase begins by positioning the ball to the preferred throwing side of the body. The body weight is shifted rearward onto the back foot.

The force-production phase of the throw starts with a forward shifting of the body weight, counterclockwise rotation at the hips, and dropping the nonthrowing hand from the ball. The initiation of the forward swinging motion of the arm occurs first at the shoulder. Some elbow extension can occur if the elbow was flexed during preparation. However most of the forward swinging action of the arm occurs due to flexion at the shoulder. The ball is released at the center of the arc created by the swinging arm. The center of the arc should be tangent to the desired target (waist of receiver).

The follow-through is a continuation of the already established swinging action of the arm. The body weight should be on the forward foot.

Hook Pass. The *hook pass* involves a certain amount of risk. Extending the ball to the side with one hand places the ball in a convenient position for an interception (Figure 5.3), so the hook pass is not used frequently but only in special situations. There are two situations in which the hook pass is especially effective. The first is when the defender is guarding especially close without other opponents nearby. The second is when *rebounding* the ball. When a player is airborne in a rebounding situation, the hook pass helps avoid bringing the ball down into a crowd of opponents.

The ball is held in the throwing hand out to the side between waist and shoulder height. The ball can be held against the forearm by flexing at the wrist. The fingers are spread and underneath the ball.

Force production begins either with a swinging action of the shoulder when airborne or with a forward step on the opposite side of the throwing arm when passing with the foot in contact with the floor. The ball is elevated by an upward swinging action of the arm at the shoulder (abduction). The elbow is held in an extended position. The free arm is extended to the side when feasible for balance.

The ball is released overhead and parallel with the floor. The throwing hand moves under the ball to impart force and backspin on the ball by snapping (flexing) the hand at the wrist. Backspin provides for the most control of the ball. The follow-through continues in the already established line of action.

Common Movement Problems and Suggestions. The following are common difficulties encountered in passing. Additionally, suggestions are included for instruction.

The objective of passing is to deliver the ball to the receiver without communicating the pass type or the in-

Figure 5.3. Hook pass

tended receiver to the opponent. A crisp (fast) pass is necessary to accomplish this. The following are suggestions for increasing the speed (velocity) of passing.

- The forward stepping action that is deliberate (fast body-weight shift forward) creates a faster pass. When a one-handed pass is used, the player should step forward on the foot opposite the throwing arm.
- An increased speed of knee extension, shoulder rotation, and prescribed elbow and wrist action will increase the velocity of the passed ball.
- If speed of passing is the main objective, then shorter passes are advisable.
- Ball control is frequently lost due to imparting too much spin on a thrown ball. If any spin is to be imparted on the ball, it should be backspin. Too much spin of any type makes catching difficult.
- Beginners should focus on two-handed and short-distance passes for accuracy and speed of delivery. One-handed and longer passes are more suitable when ball control has been established in the other passes.
- Players should have many experiences passing the ball various speeds. If the receiver cannot catch the ball due to the positioning of the ball or the speed of delivery, then the pass is unsuccessful. Individual practice can be accomplished by passing against a wall.

Common movement problems are found in the chest pass and the bounce passes. The following are common difficulties to consider.

- One reason for not applying sufficient force (speed) on the ball is not keeping the elbows close or into the sides of the body. Indirect force application occurs with the elbows out. The elbows close to the body permit most of the force application to be directly behind the ball for the pushing motion.
- Incorrect *ball trajectory* is generally caused by improper hand placement on the ball and incorrect follow-through direction. Emphasis should be placed on keeping the thumbs behind the ball. In addition, only the fingers (not the palms) should be in contact with the ball. Follow-through should always be in the direction of ball trajectory and the target.
- In the bounce pass, the ball should rebound about waist high for the receiver. The ball will rebound at approximately the same angle as it was projected to the floor. Players need experience with passes of varying distances to acquire the proper judgment in a variety of passing situations within game play.

Common movements are found among the two-handed overhead pass, the shoulder push pass, and the baseball pass. The following are common movement problems and suggestions for these passes.

- The forward step is especially helpful in these passes for increasing the application of force (speed) to the ball. Emphasize the step until the player has sufficient strength to perform with or without the step.
- Proper positioning of the elbow relative to the ball is important in the execution of these passes. The elbow stays in front of the ball until after release for the two-handed overhead and the baseball passes. The elbow should be positioned behind the ball in the one-handed shoulder and the chest passes.

Common movements are found in the underarm skills of the one-handed underarm and hook passes. The following are common problems and suggestions for these passes.

- In the underarm pass, accuracy can be enhanced by flexing the forward knee slightly just prior to release. This flattens the throwing arc made by the hand and increases the time available to make an accurate release.
- Both passes have more accuracy when the fingers are straight (extended) and pointing in the direction of ball flight at release.
- A late release will cause the ball to be projected downward in the hook pass and vertically upward in a one-handed underarm pass. The reverse occurs when the release is early.

Catching

Catching is the act of receiving or gaining possession of a thrown ball. The primary result of an inaccurate catch is fumbling the ball and possible loss of possession. Catching is a receiving-force fundamental skill.

The catching technique begins by positioning the body in a stance that can dissipate the largest amount of ball force. The stance is a shoulder-width forward stride in the direction of ball flight.

Preparation for catching is achieved by shifting the body weight forward and reaching toward the ball. The arms should be relaxed with the fingers pointing upward for receiving at waist height or above or pointing down for receiving below the waist. The thumbs are together and behind the ball when receiving a ball at waist height or above. The little fingers are together behind the ball when receiving below waist height.

Dissipation of force or stopping the ball flight for controlled possession begins with flexion of the elbows and shoulders. This is done slowly while resisting the ball flight and shifting the body weight rearward. This motion is referred to as "giving" with the ball. The ball is brought to the stomach (center of gravity of the body) for the greatest control and protection. The body weight may be shifted rearward onto the back foot or a step backward may be taken to provide more dissipation of ball force.

Common Movement Problems and Suggestions. The following are common movement difficulties encountered when instructing players on the catching technique. Additionally, suggestions are given for instruction.

- When the player fails to catch the ball, it is possible that the receiver did not focus on the ball during the entire flight. Emphasize continuous visual focus on the ball.
- A stance that permits a large base of support in the direction of ball flight provides more distance over which the performer can move in the direction of ball flight without losing balance. This also provides a longer time period to dissipate the force of the ball.
- Players should be instructed to pull the ball toward the center of the body for the most ball control and protection.
- A common problem is to have the ball rebound off the fingers. This can be caused by moving toward the ball when contact occurs or by holding the fingers extended stiffly at the moment of impact. The reach for the ball should occur before contact. The arms should be moving in the same direction as the ball on contact until the catch is completed. Another possible cause of the ball rebounding off the fingers is pointing the fingers toward the back of the ball. This is generally caused by holding the hands too close.

Passing and Catching Practice Drills

The following are practice drills for passing and catching. Various passing skills can be practiced with each of the drills unless a specific drill is indicated.

Paired Stationary. The following are paired stationary practice drills for passing and catching. Paired drills maximize individual practice time.

1.0. To increase each student's time on-task and assure maximum opportunity to handle a ball, students can be paired for practice. Any large ball might be used if there are insufficient basketballs. Soccer balls, volleyballs, and playground balls work quite well. With younger children or novices the lighter-weight balls allow them to practice the skills longer without fatigue or fear of hurting the hands when catching.

With mixed-skill groups, a skilled player could be paired with an unskilled player and encouraged to help that player improve. Challenge may be added to the passing by having each pair count the number of successful passes made and comparing these numbers with other pairs in the class. The more skilled player must then throw the ball "sympathetically" so that the less skilled partner can catch it. Emphasize that a good passer must throw passes that can be caught.

1.1. Very large classes might be divided into groups of three or four. Two players are then spaced apart in the gym as for paired practice, and the other one or two persons are positioned behind the passers. One player passes to a partner and then steps behind the waiting player, who steps up to receive the pass back to that side of the gym. Passes continue back and forth, alternating receiver and passer each time. This requires players to stay involved in the activity rather than standing around waiting for a turn.

Group Stationary. Paired practice situations would be ideal here, but most classes do not have the luxury of sufficient equipment and space. The drills suggested require one ball for every group of five or more players. Obviously, the smaller the group size, the more individual practice available. These drills can be used to practice all types of passes.

1.0. Circle Formation (Figure 4.13). Pass the ball back and forth across the circle. Start with the circle about 10 ft in diameter for beginners and widen it as skill increases. Specification of the type of pass makes the drill highly structured. Varying the type of pass permits more realistic game-type practice. Competition may be added to improve motivation as skill improves. This could be done by having each group count the number of successful passes completed within a specific short period of time or by having each group count the number of successive passes completed. In the latter case, counting must start over if the ball is dropped. The use of the elimination pattern, in which the group that drops the ball must stop and sit down, is not recommended because those who need the most practice get the least.

2.0. Circle Formation (Figure 4.13). The ball is passed around the outside of the circle. Players must make a large circle so they are at least 8 ft from the adjacent players. The use of the pivot could be introduced with this drill. The addition of a second ball on the opposite side of the circle would increase the amount of practice for each player.

3.0. Circle Formation with Leader in Center (Figure 4.15). One player stands in the center of the circle and passes to each person around the outside. After 1 round (or more if desired) the leader goes to the outside, and another takes the role of leader in the center. Practice continues until each person has had a turn as leader or until the instructor discontinues the drill.

4.0. Double-Line Formation (Figure 4.10). Pass the ball back and forth down the line. At the end of the formation, the ball can be reversed in direction back to the start. For motivation, pass down and back as quickly as possible. The winner is the first team to complete the drill without dropping the ball or the squad having completed the highest number of passes in a specified time period.

5.0. Leader and Class Formation (Figure 4.6). If the skill level is varied within the class, those of higher skill may be selected to be the leader facing the line. Otherwise, each person in the group takes a turn as leader and passes the ball to each person consecutively from one end of the line to the other.

Passing While Moving. As skill levels improve, more emphasis should be placed on passing while moving without illegal traveling.

1.0. Circle Formation (Figure 4.13). Pass the ball back and forth across the circle while all are running or slide stepping clockwise; reverse direction to counterclockwise. Emphasize passing ahead of the receiver.

2.0. Shuttle Formation (Figure 4.8). A player from Column 1 passes to the first person in Column 2 and runs to the end of the opposite column. The first person in Column 2 passes to the second person in Column 1 and runs to end of that column. This continues until all players have a turn. This drill is more effective when there are only three or four persons in each column and the practice becomes a continuous run. The players should be instructed to run past each other on one side only to avoid collisions (e.g., right shoulders).

Variation: Passers go to the end of their own line rather than to the end of the opposite line.

3.0. Double Columns Facing Same Direction (Figure 4.9). The columns are positioned at one end or side of the court about 8 to 10 ft apart. The first person in each line starts running toward the other end of the court, passing a ball back and forth as they run. When working with novices it is sometimes better to have the two passers face each other and do slide steps down the floor. After reaching the far end of the court, players may return around the outside of the court to the end of their line or may form new columns at the opposite end and return after all have done the drill once. If the balls must be returned to be used by another pair, they should be rolled along the sidelines and not allowed to interfere with other groups performing the drill.

4.0. Three Columns Facing Same Direction (Figure 5.4). This is also called the *weave*. Players X1, X2, and X3 all start running down court. Player X2 passes the ball to Player X3 (who has moved ahead) and then runs behind Player X3. Player X3 passes to Player X1 and runs behind Player X1. Player X1 passes to Player X2, who has now moved around Player X3's court position and continued downcourt. Player X1 then runs behind Player X2. This pattern continues the length of the playing area. Remind players to pass ahead of the receiver so they will not have to stop and to always run around and behind the player to whom they passed the ball.

Hook Passing. The hook pass usually follows a pivot or a rebound. Special drills to practice this unique skill follow.

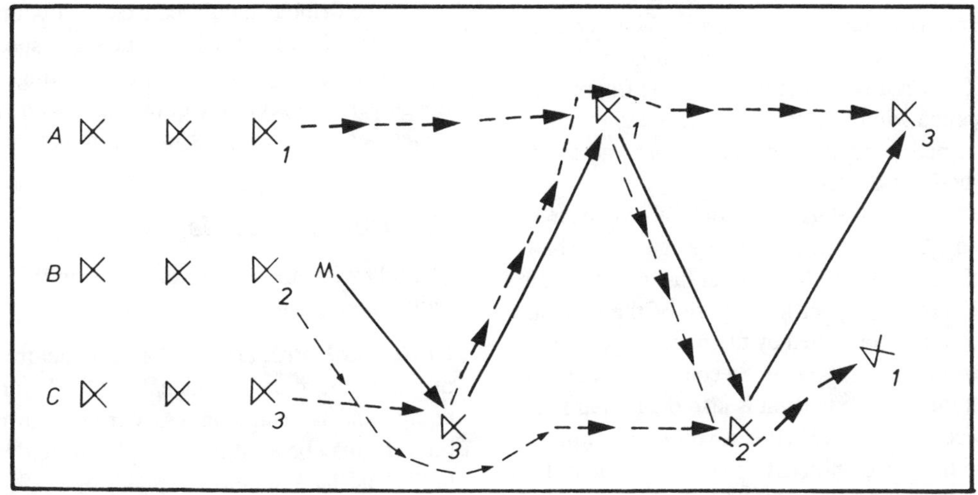

Figure 5.4. Weave drill

1.0. Circle Formation (Figure 4.14). All players are facing counterclockwise. Players are 6 to 8 ft apart. The player with the ball turns to face the center of the circle and hook passes to the player to the left, who catches the ball and turns to hook pass to the next player. This continues until all players have completed a hook pass. A left-handed player turns to face the outside of the circle before passing. If players have learned to pivot, this skill should be used here.

2.0. Double-Column Formation. This is the same as in Drill 3.0 (passing while moving). The players in the right column use the hook pass if right-handed. Left-handed players use the hook pass when in the left column.

Dribbling

The *dribble* is a means of advancing the ball by a series of bounces. The skill is effective when the player is unguarded or is unable to pass the ball. Dribbling is used to advance the ball downcourt, set up plays, or maneuver away from an opponent. The dribble is performed either standing in one place (stationary) or moving (running or walking). The skill involves a pushing action of the ball toward the floor. As the ball rebounds from the floor, the player recovers (receives) the ball with one hand and immediately initiates another push. This sequence of actions is generally done repeatedly.

The stance for the stationary dribble is a forward-stride position. For a low dribble, the knees are moderately flexed, which keeps the center of gravity low for more stability. The knees are only slightly flexed for a higher dribble. The body position requires a constant shifting of the center of gravity over the base of support in a forward direction when the dribble is combined with locomotor movements such as running and walking.

The preparatory motion for the pushing action begins with placement of the fingers and thumb near the top of the ball. The wrist is hyperextended. The fingers and thumb are spread without the palm of the hand touching the ball. The ball is positioned in the front and to the side of the body at contact.

The force production starts with forceful extension of the arm at the elbow, wrist, and fingers against the ball. The ball is directed toward the floor at the desired angle for accomplishing the specific purpose of the dribble. The ball direction is controlled by the fingers and thumb.

The follow-through of the arm is a continued extension toward the floor. This extension is also the preparatory action for receiving the ball after it rebounds from the floor. On contact the dribbler reverses the action of the arm in the direction of ball flight. The elbow flexes, and the force of the ball helps to hyperextend the wrist. This places the arm and hand in the preparatory position to push the ball back to the floor. This cycle permits the dribbler to repeat the skill in a continuous fashion.

Common Movement Problems and Suggestions

The following are common movement problems encountered during the instructional process. Suggestions are presented here also to enhance the learning environment.

- The dribbler can dribble the ball high or low. The lower dribble is easier to control and is used to protect the ball when closely guarded. The higher dribble is used whenever there is not a defender attempting to gain possession of the ball and when the dribbler is moving rapidly downcourt. The higher the dribble, the less knee flexion and the more force production that is necessary. Force production is increased by increasing both the range and the speed of motion in the pushing action.
- Lack of ball control can be caused by several factors. If the player allows the palm to strike the ball (slapping), ball control is lost. Another important factor in ball control is the use of the hand on the ball. All fingers and the thumb must be in contact with the ball and extend against the ball for control. If the ball is pushed too far in front of the body, ball control is lost.
- Sudden changes in speed or direction in the dribble require changing the dribble force production and follow-through. The faster the dribble is executed, the more the ball is pushed in front of the body. The slower the dribble, the more vertical the push will be. When directional change is indicated, the follow-through must change. Directional change occurs by extending the arm at the elbow in the new direction. The faster the locomotor skill while dribbling, the more forward must be the angle of ball trajectory to the floor.
- The dribble should be executed without focusing on the ball. Players should practice with special emphasis on focusing straight ahead while dribbling. This permits the player to observe the other players and avoid an opponent or initiate a pass to a teammate.

Practice and Drills

The following are practice drills for dribbling. Both individual and group drills are presented.

Individual Practice. An unstructured formation provides the most practice for all players if enough equipment is available. Any rather large ball that bounces may be used (such as playground balls, volleyballs, and basketballs).

1.0. Every player has a ball of some sort to dribble around the floor. Emphasize control of the ball with one hand and avoidance of all other participants. Encourage players to use the nonpreferred hand as soon as they become comfortable with the preferred hand. Discourage the use of a two-handed bounce, which is illegal in basketball. As skill levels improve, players should advance from a walking dribble to running while dribbling. Have players practice changing hands during dribbling by bouncing the ball back and forth in front of the body from hand to hand and practice dribbling the ball around the body while standing still.

1.1. A motivational variation can be added by restricting the entire class to a half or two-thirds of the space available to begin dribbling. When a player loses control, the player must retrieve the ball and go to the other end to continue practicing. The last person (or the last few persons) to retain control wins. The practice of eliminating those who lose control by making them sit along the sidelines is poor teaching and should be avoided. Have players practice with the nonpreferred hand also.

1.2. More experienced players can be encouraged to keep the head up and use the body to protect the ball by using this unstructured formation with everyone having a ball. Dribblers try to protect their own ball while trying to reach out with their free hand to tap balls away from all others. If there are insufficient balls for all to participate at once, have a half or a third of the group go first and the others practice later. Several winners could be designated from each group. These players could compete with one another after all groups have had a turn.

1.3. Another variation to encourage general awareness while dribbling is for the instructor or leader to hold up fingers designating numbers 1 through 5. The dribblers must duplicate the number of fingers shown with the free hand and watch for changes by the leader.

2.0. Individual practice can also include dribbling while changing body levels (such as sitting, kneeling, lying down) and dribbling behind the back or between the legs. These latter skills should be practiced only after the elementary skills are mastered.

Group Drills. The following are group drills for dribbling. Ball control with awareness of others simultaneously should be emphasized.

1.0. Column Formation (Figure 4.2). The first person dribbles to a designated line, turns, and dribbles back, handing (or passing) the ball to the next player and going to the end of the column. Variations include the following:

1.1. Dribble down with one hand and dribble back with the other.

1.2. Add a 360° pivot at a certain spot and continue dribbling.

1.3. Add obstacles such as cones or chairs to increase difficulty. Start with two obstacles per column and increase to three or four.

1.4. Place human obstacles (other players) in front of columns. Dribblers must go around the human obstacles and should switch dribbling hands to keep the body between the ball and the obstacle. As skills improve, allow the human obstacle to try to steal the ball or cause a loss of control. A simple restriction at the start of this would be to require the human obstacles to keep both feet stationary, then later allow movement of one foot to increase reach. Remember to rotate the players acting as obstacles into the column so they may practice dribbling. Cones may be used until the human obstacles become involved in the drill by trying to steal the ball.

1.5. All these drills can be made into competitive relays when the skill level warrants working on speed as well as control. With relays, be sure to designate an end line far enough from the wall to allow players to avoid colliding with it.

2.0. Double-Line Formation (Figure 4.11). Lines should be at least 12 ft apart. A player at the end of Line 1 dribbles across and hands the ball off to the person in opposite line, who then dribbles back to the next person in Line 1. Each person takes the place of the person to whom the ball was passed. This pattern continues to the other end of the line and back.

Dribbling Drills With Other Skills. The following are dribbling drills combined with other skills. Practicing other skills simultaneously with the dribble best simulates actual game situations.

1.10. Column Formation (Figure 4.2). The first player dribbles out to a specified distance (about 12 to 15 ft), stops, turns, and passes the ball to the next person in line, who repeats the pattern. A new line may be created where the first player stopped, or that player may return to the end of the original column. Use of a specific pass may be required.

2.0. Double-Column Formation Facing Same Direction (Figure 4.9). Columns of individuals are 8 to 10 ft apart. The first person in Column 1 starts dribbling downcourt. The first person in Column 2 keeps pace. After a short dribble, the ball is passed to the Column 2 person, who dribbles and passes back. This continues to the other end of the court. A shot at the basket may be added to this drill.

3.0. Double-Column Formation Facing Same Direction (Figure 4.9). Columns of individuals are positioned close together. The first person in Column 1 begins to dribble toward the other end of the court. The first person in Column 2 tries to get ahead of the dribbler and deflect or steal the ball. This drill should be practiced after instruction in guarding has been given. Variation: Columns of individuals begin near center court. The guard tries to take the ball away from the dribbler or force the dribbler to the sideline without illegal body contact. After shooting has been introduced, the dribbler may attempt a shot.

Fundamental Movements

Success in basketball is more accessible to those who are agile. Players must be able to change directions or speeds rapidly. These fundamental techniques are centered around the ability to start and stop quickly, run fast for short distances, and change directions quickly by pivoting. The ability to move quickly enhances the player's ability to fake, feint, or dodge the opponent.

The primary consideration in the execution of these skills is body control and footwork. Both qualities are centered around the manipulation of the body's center of gravity over the base of support (stance). When a player wishes to move, an unstable position is created by moving or by changing direction (running, starting, pivoting, and dodging). When a player wants stability, a stable body position is created by maintaining the center of gravity over the base of support (offensive stance and stopping). Sometimes it is desirable to maintain stability but to suggest motion (i.e., fake and feint).

Locomotor Movements

The locomotor movements employed in basketball are walking and running. Walking types of movement are generally used in traveling short distances combined with dribbling.

Quickness in moving from one court location to another is more essential than is speed. The run used in basketball must be controlled so that the player can make quick stops or changes in direction. Full speed in the run is seldom achieved or desirable. The ability to accelerate quickly at any point in the game is the most important aspect of running. Acceleration is achieved by taking a substantial first step with the center of gravity low. Subsequent steps are shorter and quicker. Generally, the trunk is inclined forward from the hips when accelerating, thus limiting the size of forward stride in the run. However, if the player runs to maximum acceleration, the body is primarily vertical from this point on.

When running in a curved path, such as in a *cut*, the runner should accelerate on the curved portion of the run. The center of gravity of the body should be leaning to the inside of the curve. This will facilitate a more rhythmical and faster cut.

Specific technique description and analysis questions of walking and running can be found in chapter 3, as can more detailed discussion of variations and mechanical principles.

Body Control Movements

Good balance is basic in basketball. Controlling the human body is interpreted as maintaining or disrupting the state of body balance. Balance while moving or stationary on the court can enhance or facilitate individual skills.

When a player deliberately creates an unstable body position, motion is created. These types of movements employed in basketball are starting, pivoting, and dodging. There are many situations in which basketball players fight to maintain stability. The stability movement types in basketball are the stance, stopping, and the fake or feint.

Offensive Stance. The body position for the offensive stance is performed in one of two ways, depending on the specific game situation. The most frequent stance is a stride position with one foot slightly forward. The stance is shoulder width or slightly wider. The most important aspect of the stance width is that it be comfortable. The weight is equally distributed over both feet. The center of gravity of the body is low to allow quick changes in the state of motion. The knees and hips are slightly flexed to lower the center of gravity. The arms are held close to the body while the ball is held in both hands. The elbows are flexed with the forearms parallel to the floor. The thumbs are on top of the ball with the fingers spread on each side of the ball. The ball is protected by being kept close to the body. This stance is very versatile, as it allows the player to pass, shoot, or dribble.

The second type of offensive stance is the erect stance. The stance and foot position are identical to the standard stance except for the positioning of the upper body. All body parts are extended with the ball held overhead. The ball is held with the fingers spread on the side of the ball and thumbs pointing rearward. This stance would be used by a tall player when opposing a shorter one or when preparing for an overhead pass.

Stopping and Starting. The art of stopping and starting quickly is a part of the general category of agility movements. Starting involves disrupting the state of equilibrium. A common way to initiate a start is to lean, thus shifting the center of gravity outside the base of support (stance). This places the player in an off-balance body position that is recovered by a step or by establishing a new base of support under a shifting center of gravity.

The stopping action involves the reestablishment of equilibrium from a state of motion. This is directly opposite to starting. There are two primary ways of stopping in basketball. The first is a stride stop. The player shifts the center of gravity or the body weight rearward. To accomplish this, the player takes a long forward stride while leaning backward slightly. This provides a larger distance over which to rock forward while braking, or dissipating the force of the forward movement. The forward foot becomes the plant foot. The braking of the force is accomplished by flexing at the knees, lowering the center of gravity. The second foot comes forward in front of the first foot to plant and create a forward-stride position. Balance is reestablished easier in this stop because the direction of the stride is in the same direction as the action for braking the forward momentum. This is the most common type of stop used.

The second stop is a jump stop (or parallel stop). This stop involves jumping to both feet in a parallel stance. The player takes a last running step into the air with the other foot coming forward to join the first foot. Both feet then come down and plant simultaneously. The key to this stop is a rearward body-weight shift with a reaching-forward action of the legs. The feet must plant ahead of the body so the player can dissipate the forward momentum and stop. Once the feet are planted, a slowing down of the forward body movement is accomplished by flexing at the hips, knees, and ankles. This lowers the center of gravity, initiating the state of equilibrium. This stop is versatile because either foot can be the *pivot foot*.

A stop can occur with or without the ball. However, movements after the stop are illegal when the player has possession of the ball, in which case the first support foot becomes the plant foot or the only foot on which the player can pivot.

Pivoting. The *pivot* skill generally occurs after a stride or jump stop. The pivot, or stationary, foot should be as stable as possible. This implies the slight flexion of the leg on that side to lower the center of gravity. The second step is a swinging action of the opposite foot from the pivot foot in the intended direction. This foot is free to move in any direction around the pivot foot. The swinging foot should be kept low to the floor. Pivoting can be done with or without the ball. If the player has the ball, the elbows should be away from the body to protect the ball.

The different types of pivots are referred to by the direction in which the player pivots. There is a front pivot; a reverse, or rear, pivot; and a sideward, or sideline, pivot.

Faking/Feinting. The *fake* or *feint* is a movement that does not disrupt the equilibrium to the point of losing the stance (balance). A fake can be a movement of the eyes, arms, shoulders, or any combination of these. The movement should be sharp or definite so the movements convince the opponent that the player is going to move in that direction. The fake is performed with or without the ball.

The fake is initiated by a shift of body weight or by a step that is very deliberate and in the direction that the opponent thinks the total body movement will go. At the same time, the player must maintain stability to move in the opposite direction. This stability is maintained by flexing the knees and lowering the center of gravity closer to the base of support (stance). The ability to move rapidly in the opposite direction is due to an action and a reaction. A shift of weight of the foot that is opposite the desired direction permits the player to push against the floor for an equal and opposite reaction that is in the direction the player intends to move. The fake step must be moderate in length. If the fake step or weight shift is too long or far away, the player will have to spend too much time coming back and changing directions. If the fake step is too short, it may not be convincing to the opponent. Different types of fakes are used depending on the game circumstance in which they are performed as well as the body parts used in the fake.

Common Movement Problems and Suggestions. The following are common movement problems that occur when controlling the body. Suggestions for consideration in the instructional process are also presented.

Loss of stability of the basketball player generally results in a violation, a foul, or poor ball handling. Emphasis on the rules of stability should help in these situations. The following are body movements that enhance stability.

- Lower the center of gravity toward the base of support (stance).
- Maintain the line of gravity within the boundaries of the base of support. This is the same as keeping the center of gravity over the base of support.
- Increase the size of the base of support but maintain friction between the feet and the floor.
- Positioning of the base of support in the same direction of any oncoming force will permit the player more time and distance over which to dissipate force. This allows for a large range of motion of the total body over the base of support before the line of gravity moves outside the boundaries of the base of support and renders the player instable.

Basketball players must initiate movements quickly. Slowed movements ''telegraph'' the players' intentions.

Apply the stability principles in reverse to facilitate quick movements. The following are body-positioning suggestions that enhance motion.

- Raise the center of gravity away from the base of support.
- Shift the line of gravity outside the boundaries of the base of support. This is generally accomplished by a body-weight shift.
- Decrease the size of the base of support. Small movements can cause a shift of the line of gravity outside the base of support to create motion.
- Use a base of support that is perpendicular to the desired direction of motion. Again, less body-weight shift is necessary to initiate motion.

Pivoting Practice Drills. The pivot may be practiced in large groups with players scattered out facing the instructor. The instructor could give directions such as "Pivot on the right foot half way around" (180° turn) and then observe and correct the learners while they practice. Change the directions frequently so that the players become comfortable when pivoting on either foot. Give each player a ball (or use imaginary balls) and add a fake (feint) to the practice. Many of the group drills include the pivot with other skills.

Drills for Pivoting and Passing. The following drills are for pivoting and passing. Emphasize the pivot aspects of the drill so that players learn to control the body without committing a traveling foul. Some teachers prefer to have students practice dribbling and stopping before adding the pivots to the movement.

1.0. Column Formation (Figure 4.2). The first person dribbles a ball to a specific area 12 to 15 ft downcourt, stops, pivots, and passes the ball to the next person in line.

2.0. Column Formation (Figure 4.2). The player dribbles toward the opposite end of the court. Each time the instructor blows a whistle, the dribbler must stop the forward momentum, pivot 360° and continue downcourt without stopping the dribble. Variation: Use one blast of the whistle to signal a 180° pivot and two blasts to signal a 360° pivot.

3.0. Circle Formation (Figure 4.14). Players should be 8 to 10 ft apart. The ball is passed around the circle. The player receiving the ball must pivot and pass to the person directly behind.

4.0. Column Formation (Figure 4.2). Space the players 10 to 15 ft apart. Proceed as in Drill 3.0, where the first person has the ball, pivots, and passes to the next person, who then pivots and passes. This progresses until each individual has completed the process. The ball is passed back down the column after reaching the end.

Shooting

The ultimate objective of basketball is to score goals; therefore, practicing shooting is important. Usually, players are very interested in this activity, so motivation is not a problem. Several theories regarding the point of aim when shooting are common. For short shots and lay-ups, the ball is usually banked off the backboard (*bank shot*) and allowed to rebound into the basket. For long shots and those taken parallel to the backboard, the shooter should concentrate on the rim of the basket. Some coaches prefer their players look at the far rim of the basket; others prefer to have shooters look at the near rim and drop the ball over it. Players should determine for themselves which is more effective. When working with beginners, the instructor may prefer to specify focusing on the near (or the far) rim to encourage consistency.

The basic physical law of rebounding must be considered when using the backboard. This law states that the angle of incidence approximately equals the angle of deflection, or, in other words, that the ball will rebound off a solid surface at approximately the same angle as it came into the surface. Players should be taught this. If the ball is thrown against the backboard at a 45° angle, it will rebound approximately 45° in the opposite direction (Figure 5.5). If it is thrown at about a 30° angle, it will rebound approximately at a 30° angle (Figure 5.6). Spin on the ball and ball elasticity will also have some effect on the rebound angle. Therefore, the ball must be aimed at the backboard slightly to the right of the basket for a shot from the right front and slightly to the left for a shot from the left front. The greater the angle from the center of the backboard, the farther to that side the ball should hit the backboard.

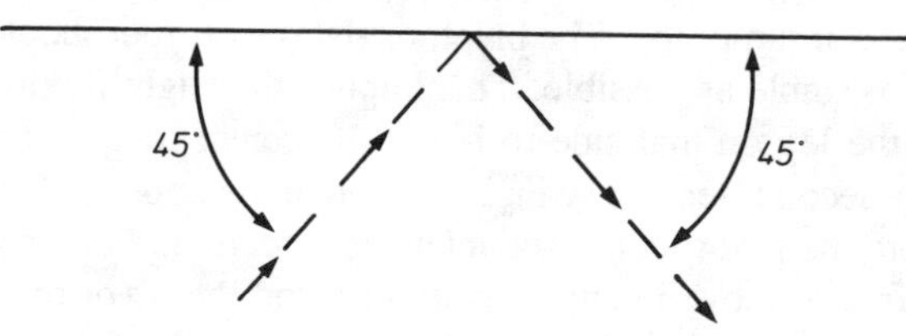

Figure 5.5. Rebound angle: 45°

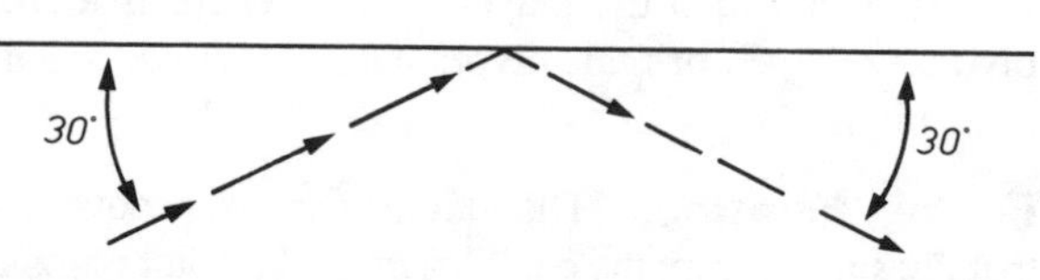

Figure 5.6. Rebound angle: 30°

The arc of the ball is also an important factor. The ball should be arched high into the air so that it comes down toward the basket. This improves the chances of making the basket. Even if the shot is slightly off center, it could rebound into the air and fall into the basket due to backspin on the ball. A shot with a flat trajectory must be perfect to score a goal. If it is slightly low, it will hit the front rim; if it is slightly high, it will rebound hard off the back rim and be difficult to recover.

Young players who have trouble throwing the basketball high enough to reach the basket or players who try to extend their range must learn to use the whole body to maximize the transfer of momentum to the ball. The ankles, knees, and hips should be flexed and rapidly extended, and the body should be thrust upward as the arm or arms extend with the shot. The wrist must be flicked (flexed) and the fingers directed toward the basket. In general, the more body parts involved in the movement, the more force will be achieved.

Shooters must learn to concentrate on the basket and avoid being distracted by noise or nearby movements. The player in a game rarely has plenty of time to prepare for the shot. Initial practice for novices should be done in controlled situations without stress, but the introduction of realistic variables like guards, other players, noise, and pressure should be introduced soon, or the shooters will be unable to perform in game situations. Basketball requires a number of open skills, and the practice situations should simulate game conditions as much as possible.

Skilled players use differential relaxation, which is the ability to relax those muscles not needed for the movement. This conserves energy and allows players to move effectively for longer periods of time without fatigue. Intermediate players should be encouraged to use relaxation techniques whenever possible during play.

Set Shot

Set shots are taken from a stationary position on the court. This shot can be executed with one or two hands. The one-handed set shot is generally preferred and the most common of the set shots. The two-handed set shot is uncommon in basketball today except for the young beginner.

Two-Handed Set Shot. The two-handed set shot is used for shooting long distances or by those who do not have enough physical strength to get the ball to the basket. This shot is a two-handed pushing fundamental movement skill.

The stance for the two-handed set shot is shoulder width and can be either parallel or a forward stride. If additional force is needed to project the ball to the basket, the forward stride provides the best opportunity for generating force in the desired ball direction. The ball is held with one hand on each side with fingers spread and thumbs on the back. The ball is held between waist and chest levels as in the chest shot.

The preparatory movement consists of a slight vertical drop of the ball while in the hands with flexion of the hips, knees, and ankles occurring at the same time. The amount of ball drop and flexion in the lower body depends on the player's distance from the basket or the amount of physical strength of the player. The more distance and lack of strength, the more flexion that will be needed in the preparation. The flexed position provides the player with a larger range of motion for extension, thus helping build momentum that can be transferred to the ball.

The force production phase begins with flexion of the upper body and extension of the body toward the target (basket). Extension occurs at the ankles, knees, and hips of the lower body; flexion of the upper body occurs at the shoulders accompanying extension at the elbows. The ball moves over the head and slightly in front of the body. The hands pronate (turn palms down) at the wrist.

The follow-through is a continuation of the extension, or pushing, of the arms in the intended direction of ball flight. The extension of the lower body at the hips, knees, and ankles may create a lifting of the body off the floor during the follow-through. Release should occur prior to any lift of the body off the floor. If release occurs after the body is airborne, the momentum built from lower-body extension is lost.

One-Handed Set Shot. The one-handed set shot is taken from short to medium distances (5 to 15 ft) from the basket (Figure 5.7). It is usually used for free throws as well as stationary court shots. The one-handed set shot is the most frequent set shot used by physically mature individuals. This shot is a one-handed pushing fundamental movement skill.

The stance for this shot is a forward stride of approximate shoulder width. Some individuals must use a parallel stance, but this is not suggested for beginning and intermediate players. The ball is held in both hands with fingers spread and thumbs to the back. The elbows are held close to the body. This is the same initial positioning as described in the two-handed set shot.

The preparatory motion begins by dropping the ball vertically while turning the hands so the shooting hand is behind the ball and the balancing, or nonshooting hand is in front of the ball. The shooting hand will form a V shape between the fingers and the thumb. The hand position is not centered behind the ball but is shifted slightly to the same side as the shooting hand. In other words, the right-handed shooter will have the right hand on the back of the ball but slightly off center to the right. At this time, the knees flex in preparation for extension.

Force production begins with extension of the lower body and flexion of the upper body. The legs extend at

Figure 5.7. One-handed set shot

the ankles, knees, and hips while the arms flex at the shoulders. The ball moves upward in front of the head during this arm action. The nonshooting hand remains on the ball. Once the ball is positioned, the shooting arm extends at the elbow to push the ball upward off the supporting nonshooting hand. The wrist has a snapping action of flexion and pronation to add momentum to the ball. The fingers are the last to leave the ball before release and help to "steer" the ball.

The follow-through is a continuation of this upper-body movement with a forward body-weight shift onto the front foot. The follow-through motion should be primarily vertical. Any forward horizontal motion may cause the shooter to move into the defender and foul or to step over the restraining foul line in foul shooting.

Practice Drills. The following are practice drills for set shooting. Stationary set shots should be practiced before others are attempted.

Individual or paired practice should be encouraged whenever it is possible to have a ball for every one or two players. Again, the use of volleyballs, soccer balls, or playground balls is appropriate for beginners working on accuracy, but students should not be required to use lightweight balls all the time. A station-teaching arrangement of target practice at walls and basket-shooting practice at the baskets will enable more students to be active at once. Basketballs could be used for shooting, whereas other kinds of balls could be used for accuracy passing at targets on the wall about basket height. Players should work at one station for 5 to 7 min, then rotate to another station to practice another shooting skill or other skill variations.

1.0. Column Formation on Angle to Basket (Figure 5.8). Players are positioned close to basket at about a 45° angle from the end line. The first person in line shoots at the backboard to rebound the ball into the

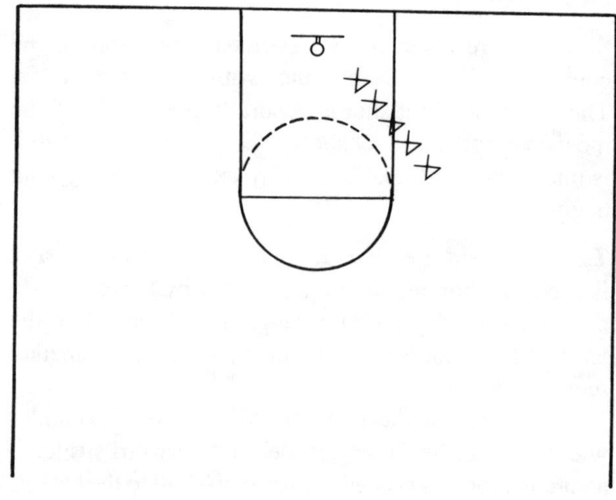

Figure 5.8. Stationary shooting drill

basket. Shooters retrieve their own balls, give them to the next person in line, and go to the end of the line.

Variations include the following:

1.1. A second column of shooters may be positioned similarly at an angle to the left of the basket (Figure 5.9). While the person from one line shoots the ball, the leader of the other line retrieves the rebound. Players could return to their own line or go to the end of the opposite line.

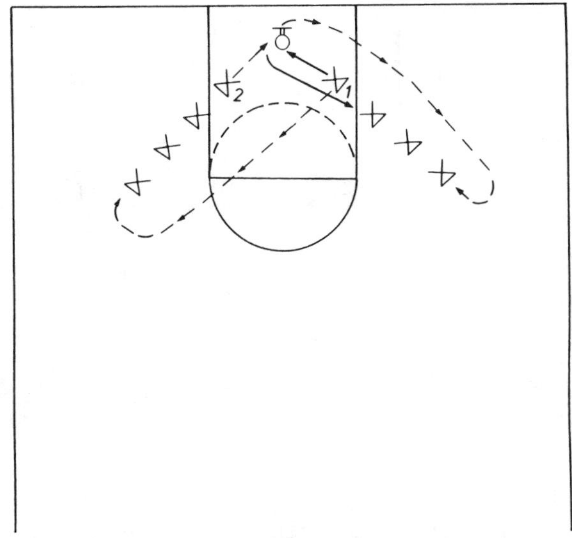

Figure 5.9. Stationary shooting drill with rebounding column

1.2. Each shooter gets three or four turns before giving the ball to the next person.

1.3. For cooperation, encourage players to help one another. See which group can have each individual make a basket first.

1.4. Add scoring and have groups see which team can get the highest score in a given period of time. Be sure they continue to rotate so that each player has the same number of chances to shoot.

1.5. As individuals improve their skills, move lines farther from the basket.

2.0. Column Formation (Figure 4.2). The group is lined up parallel to the end line with the first person standing on the free throw lane line near the basket. The shot is taken without using the backboard. Aim directly at the far rim of the basket. All the variations under Drill 1.0 for the stationary set shot could be added.

3.0. Semicircle Formation in Front of Basket (Figure 4.16). Each player has a ball (or several per group) and practices shooting from individual positions on the floor. Players retrieve their own balls or those closest to them and continue to shoot. Periodically, the players rotate to new positions. The semicircle should be about 4 to 6 ft from the basket for beginners and young children. As individual or group skills and strength improve, move the semicircle farther from the basket.

4.0. Column Formation (4.2). This game is called *Twenty-One*. It is more appropriate for intermediate to advanced players and might be played before class or practice. Because Twenty-One involves a lot of waiting time, it is not a good activity for a large class. Each player in turn gets two shots at the basket; one long and one short. Long shots are usually taken beyond the free throw line or at a comparable distance at an angle to the basket. The successful long shot counts 2 points; the short shot counts 1 point. The object is to score as many points as possible. Competition could be organized among teams or individuals. Variation: Players get two shots each turn, but each person may choose whether to take two long, two short, or one of each. Scoring remains the same with 2 points for a long shot and 1 point for a short shot. The competition could be terminated after each individual in a group completes a set number of attempts or after a specified time period.

5.0. Follow the Leader, or "Horse." This is for more advanced players and involves a lot of waiting time. Thus, it is not suitable for large classes but is fun practice for smaller groups. A chosen leader takes a shot from anywhere on the floor. Each person in the group must shoot from the same spot on the floor. The leader then selects another spot and play proceeds. Players who fail to make a goal from the specified spot receive a letter of the word *Horse* (e.g., the first miss merits an *H*, the second miss *O*, etc.). Players who have completed the word (five misses) are eliminated from the game. Variations include the following:

5.1. If time is limited, the word *Pig* (or any other short word) is used.

5.2. Players may continue in the game until they have six misses rather than five.

5.3. Players who have been eliminated go to another area of the court and continue to practice shooting.

6.0. Designated Spots. Five to eight places on the floor are numbered with tape or water-color paint. Each player must shoot from each spot in sequence until a basket is made. This can be a team-oriented drill, or it can be for individual achievement and practice. Players may take one turn at a time using one ball per group or may use several balls with continuous shooting. The first person to score successfully at each of the numbered points wins the game.

7.0. Free Throw Drills. One player with a ball stands at the free throw line while others in the squad line up on the lane lines. The shooter takes 5 to 10 free throw shots while the others practice rebounding techniques. After the designated number of shots are taken, players rotate, and a new shooter goes to the free throw line.

8.0. Free Throw Shooting Contest. Each player takes 10 to 25 free throws. The player scoring the most free throws wins. While one shoots, other players line up at the lane lines and practice rebounding the balls. Rotate throwers every three to five shots to avoid boredom among the waiting players.

Lay-Up Shot

The *lay-up* refers to a shot taken close to the basket when preceded by a run or a dribble. This is a complex combination of skills, but players experience success with it early due to the better percentages of putting the ball through the basket from close range. The different types of lay-ups are based primarily on the conditions of play. An unguarded lay-up is the easiest, whereas the driving lay-up is more difficult. The latter occurs when the offensive player dribbles rapidly through several players in the attempt to reach the basket and shoot the ball. The technique in any lay-up shot is similar; only the circumstances surrounding the execution are different.

The lay-up consists of a running approach to the basket, a conversion of the forward momentum by a stop, a vertical jump, an underarm throwing or reaching, and a landing combination of fundamental movement skills (Figure 5.10). The technique descriptions and analysis questions for running, jumping, and landing can be found in chapter 3.

The ball is either dribbled or caught at or near the end of the running approach. The ball is secured in both hands close to the body at about waist height just prior to the last step (hurdle) before the jump to shoot. The hurdle step is a long step that places the center of gravity behind the front foot (plant). This places the player in the proper position to transfer most of the horizontal, or forward, momentum in the vertical direction for the jump. The foot opposite the plant foot becomes the driving force in lifting the body vertically for the jump. This leg swings forward and up while the arms bring the ball upward in front of the body by flexion at the shoulders. The ball is protected by keeping it close to the body for as long as possible. The arms continue upward until approximately head height, when the nonshooting hand has the option to move away from the ball. The shooting hand continues to reach upward toward the basket with the ball. The ball is pushed by a flip of the wrist (flexion) or is simply placed by the hand on the backboard just over the outside of the basket rim. The arm is fully extended at release, which occurs close to the vertical peak of the jump.

Figure 5.10. Lay-up

The ball is generally rebounded off the backboard in the lay-up shot. The lay-up should rarely be missed due to the short distance from the basket. Backspin from the wrist flexion enhances the possibilities of the ball rebounding off the backboard into the basket. The rebound from backspin off the backboard's vertical surface pulls the ball downward into the basket. Inexperienced and short players must usually keep the shooting hand behind the ball and push it up to the basket. Tall and experienced players should keep the shooting hand under the ball and lay it up against the backboard.

Lay-Up Shot Drills. The following are drills for practicing the lay-up shot. Players may need to start close to the basket at first and approach with moderate speed. As skill improves, move the players farther from the basket and emphasize approaching with a fast dribble.

1.0. Column Formation (Figure 5.8). Individuals in the column line up at a 45° angle to the right side of the basket. The first person in the column should be 15 to 20 ft from the basket. Each individual dribbles toward the basket and lays the ball up against the backboard, retrieves the ball, and passes to the next person in line, who repeats the pattern. The shooter returns to the end of the column. After several trials from the right side, the column is moved to the left side and then to the center. Note that when moving straight down the center, a rim shot rather than a backboard shot is usually preferred. More advanced players should shoot the left-side lay-up with the left hand and the right-side lay-up with right hand.

2.0. Double-Column Formation (Figure 5.9). One column of individuals is positioned on an angle to the right and another to the left. The first person in one column dribbles and shoots a lay-up; the first person in the other column retrieves the ball and passes it back to the shooters' column. Each goes to the end of the opposite line. Switch the ball periodically so that the retrieving lines become the shooting lines and vice versa. More lay-up practice drills are found under general drills presented later in this chapter.

If players are having difficulties mastering the lay-up sequence of movements, the instructor may wish to teach the skill using the progressive-part approach. Have the student stand at an angle to the basket (to the right for right-handed players and to the left for left-handed players) near the basket as if for a beginning set shot and push the ball against the backboard. Then move back two steps and step forward on the left foot (right-hander), raise the right knee, jump, and shoot. After this is achieved, move back two more steps, take one bounce, jump, and shoot. It is now possible to use the complete running approach with dribbling. Players should achieve reasonable success at each part of the progression before adding another movement.

Hook Shot

This shot is taken at close distances from the basket (within 15 ft). The hook shot is generally executed to avoid a defender guarding closely. The shooter takes one step away from or to the side of the defender and takes the shot. The shooter can take a stationary or a jump hook shot. The arm shooting the ball swings to the side and up (abduction at the shoulder). The arm continues the swing until the release overhead. The technique is identical to the hook pass with the exception of the point of ball release. The hook shot is released earlier than the pass in order to have a higher arc to the basket. For more technique specifics, refer to the technique description of the hook pass (p. 56).

Hook Shot Drills. The hook shot may be practiced using some of the other shooting drills. The following are a few specific drills for the hook shot.

1.0. Double-Column Formation. Players are arranged as in Figure 5.9. Move the columns of players away from the basket near the free throw lane lines. The leader of one column takes two steps toward the basket, turns to face the other column, and receives a pass from that leader. The player then pivots and shoots a hook shot. Both go to the basket for the rebound and return the ball to the next person in the passing column. Have the passing column become the shooting column and vice versa after several turns for each player. Variation: A dribble or one bounce may be added prior to the shot, although many coaches prefer to omit the bounce because inexperienced players tend to use it too often, thereby signaling their moves to the defense.

2.0. The formation described later in this chapter in Figure 5.15 may be used to practice the hook shot. The player from Column 3 may be given the option of a hook shot instead of passing off.

Jump Shot

This is the most frequent shot used by experienced players. This assumes that the players have sufficient strength to project the ball to the basket from a jumping position with a one-handed push. This type of shot is not an appropriate skill for the younger, less physically mature individual.

The jump shot is a stop, jump, and push combination of fundamental movements. The concluding movement of the jump shot is a landing or a receiving of force. The shot is initiated after a momentary stop or redirection of movement. The player either steps to the jumping position on both feet or leaps to this position from a run. Regardless, the player is positioned in a forward-stride or parallel stance with both feet on the floor. The player flexes at the hips, knees, and ankles in preparation for the jump. The ball is held in both hands and close to the body.

The force-production phase of the jump begins with a forceful simultaneous extension of the ankles, knees, and hips. The arms move upward during the jump while maintaining ball possession. The arms position the ball overhead with shoulders flexed, elbows flexed, and wrist hyperextended. As the arms move overhead, the hands are rotated. The shooting hand is positioned behind the ball, and the nonshooting hand is positioned on the front of the ball. The elbow of the shooting arm should stay under the ball. The ball is generally released just after or prior to the peak of the vertical jump. The ball is pushed toward the target by extension at the shoulder and elbow with flexion at the wrist. The shooting technique is identical to the one-handed set shot from this point until the ball is released. Refer to the discussion of the one-handed set shot for specifics related to the technique.

The landing should be a reaching for the floor with the legs and a gradual dissipation of the force through flexion of the lower extremities. For more detailed information on landings, see chapter 3.

Common Movement Problems and Suggestions

The following are common movement problems in shooting. Instructional suggestions are also presented.

- Inaccuracy is the most noticeable problem in shooting. The following are areas of consideration when inaccurate shooting occurs:

a. Shooters should have good control of the ball before the initiation of any shot.
b. Shooters should have a specific target on which they always focus. The shooter needs to concentrate on that target during the act of shooting.
c. The higher the arc in the ball flight, the better opportunity there will be for it to go into the basket. The higher the point of release off the floor, the less arc that is needed in the shot.
d. Use of the backboard increases the possibilities of putting the ball through the basket.
e. Backspin on the ball increases the possibilities of putting the ball in the basket off the backboard.
f. Lack of arm and wrist strength can create a situation where the ball never reaches the basket. The player can be taught to compensate by using more body parts in the movement or to move closer to the basket.

- The nonshooting hand is essential to maintaining control of the ball during shooting.

- Preparatory movements that keep the ball close to the center of the body protect the ball from the defender. This translates into the player using elbow flexion and having a firm grip on the ball.

- The primary focus of body movements during shooting are shoulder *medial* (inward) *rotation* and flexion, elbow extension, forearm pronation, and wrist flexion.

- As distance from the basket increases, the shot requires a larger range of motion of body segments and a higher angle of release.

Moving Shot Drills

Moving drills should be presented after the set-shot practice and after some skill has been achieved. The one-handed set shots may be converted to moving shots easily by moving the shooters farther from the basket and adding a dribble prior to the shot. At the end of the dribble, the ball is raised above the shoulder with the nonshooting hand under the ball and the shooting hand behind the ball. The eyes are focused on the rim of the basket or the backboard, and the shot is taken immediately without pause or hesitation. More momentum can be generated for transfer to the ball than with the stationary set shot by utilizing the momentum of the moving body.

Beginners tend to dribble too far and then find themselves under the basket. To avoid this, the instructor may wish to specify the number of steps to be used with the dribble and to designate a starting position that will require them to end in a reasonable position to shoot.

Care must be taken to avoid *charging*, or running into an opposing guard, when using the moving shot in a game. Beginning with the first practice, players should be encouraged to convert much of the forward momentum to vertical motion to prevent personal contact and to make it more difficult to block the shot.

1.0. Double Formation (see Figure 5.9). Individuals in the column line up 30 ft from, and at a 45° angle to, each side of the basket. The leader of each column has a ball. One leader dribbles to a point about 8 to 10 ft from the basket and shoots a one-handed push shot without stopping to get set. This same player recovers the rebound as the leader of the other column dribbles forward to take a shot. The shooter returns the ball to the opposite column and goes to the end of that line. Play continues with shooters from each column alternating shots. As players become more skilled, the shooting spot may be moved farther from the basket.

2.0. Double-Column Formation. This drill is identical to Drill 1.0, except that a cone or other type of obstacle is placed at the floor position for shooting so that players must stop forward momentum and shoot over the top of an obstruction. When working with advanced players, the jump shot could be used in this drill.

Variation: Add a human obstacle. A stationary guard assumes the position of the obstacle and tries to steal the ball or block the shot.

There are many other types and variations of shooting drills. Additional practice drills for moving shots will be found later in this chapter in the section on general practice drills.

Jumping Skills

The primary purpose of jumping in basketball is vertical lift of the total body to direct, retrieve, or shoot the basketball. Jumping movements for the purpose of shooting are generally preceded by movements such as the run or the dribble. Specific jumps for the purpose of retrieving or directing the ball are primarily performed from a stationary standing position. Vertical lift for reach above the opponent is important when retrieving or directing the ball. The jumping skills in basketball for retrieving and directing the ball are the *jump ball* and the *rebound.*

Generalizations of Jumping

The jump used from a stationary standing position and those used in jump balls and rebounding have the same general movement characteristics and mechanics. The simultaneous application of segmental forces is identical, but correct jumping in these skills within the game situation is primarily dependent on timing. The proper timing of the jumping skill is the most important aspect of the jump.

The jumping stance is a forward-stride position from narrow to shoulder width. If the stance is too wide, force production for the jump will be partially depleted. Both feet should be in full contact with the floor for balance and force-production purposes.

The preparation for the jump begins with the withdrawal of the arms to below the shoulders. Varying positions below the shoulders are possible. This position is dependent on the circumstances of the jump. The lower extremities flex at the hips with the trunk forward. Additionally, the knees and ankles also flex in preparation for the jump.

Jump-Ball Technique

The jump-ball technique combines jumping with a pushing (tapping) fundamental skill. The specific stance for this technique is the standard stationary jumping stance but with possible deviations depending on individual style and comfort. The preparation and force-production phases are the same as those discussed previously in the section on jumping technique.

The most important aspect of this type of jumping is timing. The proper timing should position the player at the apex of the jump when tapping or directing the ball. Generally, the jumping action begins immediately after the ball leaves the hand of the official.

The preferred arm and hand are positioned to the inside of the jumping circle. The tapping hand should stretch and reach upward to its maximum. Dropping the opposite arm down facilitates a higher reach with the tapping hand.

Rebounding Technique

Rebounding consists of jumping combined with reaching and catching to secure the ball after a missed shot. The most important factors are the timing of the jump and the position of the rebounder. A shorter person who gets in good position and who times a jump correctly may be able to outrebound a taller jumper. Offensive rebounding is retrieving your own or your teammate's ball; defensive rebounding recovers the ball after the opponents miss a shot.

Defensive rebounding is easier because the defender usually is in a better position when the shot is taken. The defender should always try to stay between the opponent and the goal. When the shot is taken, the *guard* should pivot to face the basket and try to keep the opposing player from getting close to it. Guards should keep the elbows and legs wide so that the opponents cannot move around them. If the opponent is taller than the defender, the opponent must be kept farther away from the goal than must an opponent who is the same height or shorter.

The eyes should be focused on the basket and the path of the ball monitored closely as it gets there. A ball that hits the front rim will usually rebound well over the head. One that hits the far rim may bounce more than once and fall near the basket area. One that hits the backboard and misses the rim is most likely to fall quickly toward the floor and will rebound at the opposite angle. A flat shot is likely to bounce away from the basket area. Successful players practice watching all types of shots to learn to estimate the probable paths and move into position quickly.

The jump should be timed so that the ball can be caught as high as possible. Reaching up with one hand to pull the ball down toward the other hand is most effective if the player can control the ball with one hand; otherwise both arms must be extended and the reach will be shorter. As the ball is caught, it should be brought toward the waist with the elbows projected out from the sides, the hips flexed, and the shoulders hunched over to protect the ball from the opponents. The offensive rebounder should immediately attempt to shoot again. Even if unsuccessful, the shooter may draw a foul.

The defensive rebounder must try to get the ball away from the basket. The first move might be to pivot away from the basket and the opponent and then either dribble toward the sideline or look for an outlet pass to a teammate near the sideline. The team that wishes to develop a fast break should practice a quick outlet pass and avoid a lot of dribbling. Drills to practice the fast break are presented later in this chapter.

Tall players can afford to be farther away from the basket than can short players. They will also be able to reach over the heads of opponents but must avoid pushing them from behind or allowing the arms to be drawn down over the shoulders of the person in front. In this situation, they must practice lifting the ball back above the head as they catch it as they would push the ball back up to the basket if on offense.

Common Movement Problems and Suggestions

The following are common movement difficulties encountered during the instructional process. Additional instructional suggestions are presented.

The amount of flexion of the lower extremities in preparation for the jump varies depending on the movement preceding the jump. This can change the timing of the jump. The following are principles to consider when instructing in the jumping situation.

- Less lower-extremity flexion is necessary in a jump that is preceded by a run or a hop. In this situation, too much flexion detracts from the vertical lift of the jump by dissipating the forward momentum of the run or the hop rather than transferring it vertically.
- Stationary jumps requires more lower-extremity flexion for generating force. The more time that is taken to build force and vertical distance to push against the floor, the more force production that is possible. The lower extremities should not flex beyond the sitting position (thighs parallel to the floor) due to the added effort of pushing against the floor to elevate the body into the jump.
- The quicker the extension during the force-production phase of the jump, the higher the possibilities for vertical lift. This demonstrates the power of the jumper. When the player flexes the lower extremities of the body too much in preparation, the amount of effort required for a quick extension is increased.
- Jumping should be mainly upward with as little forward motion as possible. This is accomplished by directing one's force application primarily downward for an equal and opposite reaction upward. The angle of takeoff for the jump can be too far forward when the body is not fully extended upright at the moment of takeoff.
- Arms should always be utilized in the jump regardless of the position or the type of jump. The arms facilitate the transfer of momentum from body parts to the total body at the moment of takeoff.
- The eyes should always be focused on the ball. The jump is always begun before the ball reaches its peak or immediately following the rebound of the ball.
- Landing stance from the jump should be shoulder width with weight equally distributed over both feet to be able to respond to the next movement demand.

Rebounding Drills

The following are drills for rebounding. Backboards or walls may be used for rebounding surfaces.

1.0. The class is divided into groups of three players, all of comparable height. Player X1 with a ball stands about 10 ft from a wall. Players X2 and X3 stand side by side about 6 or 8 ft from the wall (Figure 5.11). The player with the ball throws it high against the wall so that it rebounds back (an underhanded throw is best). The other two players try to catch the rebound. They must remain stationary until the ball leaves the thrower's hand, after which they may move to obtain the best position. Rotate throwers so that all have a chance to practice rebounding. If appropriate wall space is unavailable, the backboards may be used. Two groups can function at an individual basket by positioning themselves to either side of the basket. Intermediate players may use the backboard and the basket for this practice, but usually there are too few baskets at which all can practice.

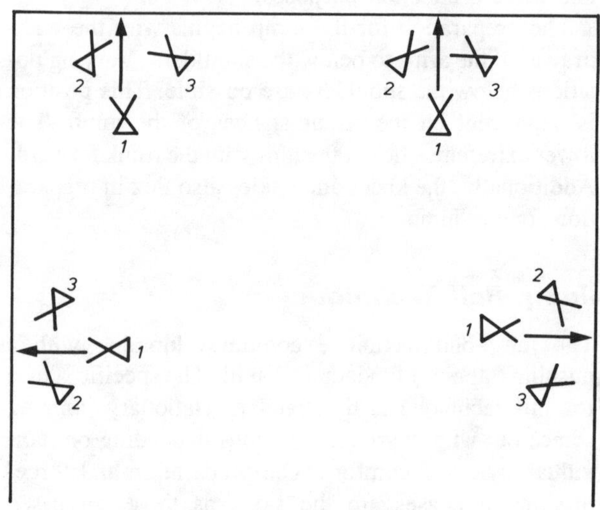

Figure 5.11. Rebounding drill

2.0. Double-Column Formation (Figure 4.9). To accommodate more players, Drill 1.0 can be adjusted by having Players X1, X2, and X3 head the columns. After the first person in each column gets a turn to practice rebounding or throw the ball, that person goes to the end of another column (i.e., Player X1 goes to the column of Player X2, Player X2 goes to the column of Player X3, and Player X3 goes to the column of Player X4).

3.0. Partners. One player (the defender) stands between the basket and the other player, who has the ball. The player with the ball shoots and tries to maneuver around the defender to secure the rebound. This is similar to 1-on-1 play without allowing a dribble. Players switch positions periodically, or the one who gains the rebound becomes the shooter. Variations include the following:

3.1. Allow the defender to try to block the shot.

3.2. For intermediate to advanced players, add a dribble and play the 1-on-1 game. This can be found in the section on guarding.

4.0. Double-Column Formation (Figure 4.9). Individuals in one column line up along each of the free throw lane lines at the basket. A player at the free throw line shoots at the basket, attempting to bounce the ball off the rim. The first person in each column moves to get in front of the other (*blocking out* the opponent) and secure the rebound. The ball is returned to the shooter, and the rebounders go to the end of the opposite column. The next person in each column becomes the next rebounder. The shooter may be a designated player or the last person in one column. Variation: The shooter shoots from an angle to the side of the basket rather than directly in front.

Guarding

The primary purpose of defensive *guarding* is to restrict the opponent from scoring. The use of concentration, correct focusing during the game situation, and quick reactions are essential to being a good defensive player. The defensive stance and footwork continuously change relative to the immediate game action or the defensive plan of the team. The general rule to emphasize in guarding is to maintain proper guarding position between the opponent with the ball and the basket.

Stance Techniques

The defensive stance must be both stable for the purposes of avoiding deception by the opponent and mobile for purposes of quickly moving with the opponent. Thus, stance adjustments relative to the guarding circumstances are needed. Generally, a compromise between mobility and stability is maintained in the guarding stance.

The most common foot positions are the parallel and the stride stances. The parallel stance is slightly wider than shoulder width with the feet parallel and facing forward. This stance enhances quick lateral types of movements. The stride stance is also slightly wider than shoulder width, but one foot is forward. This stance enhances diagonal movements of the guard. A variation of the stride is to turn the rear foot sideward. This permits quick forward and backward movements but poor lateral movements and stability. Regardless of the stance, the knees are flexed to lower the center of gravity for more stability. The player appears to be sitting (Figure 5.12). When stability is needed, the stance is wide with knees flexed to simulate the sitting position. This lowers the center of gravity. In addition, the line of gravity is centered over the base of support. The player must shift the line of gravity outside the base of support to become mobile. With a centered line of gravity, equal amounts of movement can make the player mobile in any direction. When mobility is necessary, the knees are not flexed as much as they are when stability is needed. This trunk position is necessary for quick movements and for following the action of opponents.

Figure 5.12. Guarding positions

The arms are held out from the body. One arm is high and forward toward the opponent and the other low and out to the side. The arm extended up and forward should be on the shooting side of the opponent. Any defensive player should be able to move the arms through an entire range of motion without disrupting stability.

Moving With an Opponent

Once an opponent is moving, the defensive guard must maintain a position between the opponent and the basket. The defensive player must initiate motion quickly to avoid being deceived by the offensive player. This involves moving while maintaining a low center of gravity and making quick movements for directional changes.

The primary motions utilized in following the opponent are sliding steps. The player moves the foot in the intended direction laterally. The other foot closes the gap by sliding in the same direction. The stance position is maintained slightly wider than shoulder width. This involves body-weight shifting. The first slide is accomplished by placing the body weight on the nonsliding foot while the sliding foot moves laterally and close to the floor. Body weight is shifted onto the sliding foot once it becomes positioned and planted. This permits freedom for the other foot to slide toward the planted foot but does not close the stance beyond shoulder width. This is continued repetitively as long as the opponent is moving in the same direction.

When the offensive player moves forward or backward, the defensive player can use stepping actions in either direction to follow the opponent. Generally, steps are not large, as this might place the guard in a too-stable position for moving quickly for a directional change.

Common Movement Problems and Suggestions

The following are general problems encountered by the defensive guard. Additional suggestions for improving guarding techniques are presented.

- The defensive guard should be moving continuously. Players should practice moving in the guarding position in all directions.
- Guards should focus on the body center (waist level) of the opponent. Limb movements are generally not a true indication of the movement to be pursued by the opponent. True movement will involve a definite change in the position of the opponent's center of gravity.
- Arm movements do not detract from stability when the center of gravity is close to the base of support (knees flexed).
- Guarding too close permits the defensive guard to be easily deceived. Generally, a distance of 3 ft is appropriate between the guard and an opponent. Closer guarding is used to force an error by the opponent. This can place the guard in a position that does not permit a quick reaction or recovery to an opponent's quick movement.
- Quick, jerky movements of the guard are an indication of the guard's inability to anticipate the true movement of the offensive player. The guard should relax and move in the direction of the opponent's movement by focusing on the waist level of the opponent. The guard should never move before the opponent does.

Guarding Drills

The following are drills for guarding. One-on-one practice with one shooter and one guard is always more effective if there is plenty of space and equipment.

1.0. Circle Formation (Figure 4.15). "Keep-Away" Game. One person is in the center of a small circle of five or six players. The person in the center tries to intercept passes between players in the circle. When the person in the center gains possession, that person is replaced by the one who last threw the ball. To prevent having one person in the center too long, it may be necessary to put a time limit on center play (e.g., 2 min or 10 passes).

2.0. Team Keep-Away. Divide the class into groups of four or five players (more if necessary). Assign every two groups a limiting space such as half of a court. One group passes the ball around while the other group tries to intercept. Encourage each player to pair up with and guard one opponent. The group that loses the ball becomes the guards, and the other group passes the ball. For advanced players, this can develop into the half-court game. Use pinnies to distinguish between teams.

3.0. Double-Column Formation (Figure 4.8). The individuals in columns are lined up close together near the center of the court. The leader of one column starts to dribble toward a basket. The leader of the other column tries to get in front of and stay between that player and the basket or to force the dribbler to the sidelines and out of shooting range. After reaching the end line or the sideline, players return their balls to the next players in line and go to the end of the opposite column.

4.0. Pass and Guard (Figure 5.13). Arrange four columns of three to five players each. As Player X1 passes the ball to Player X2, Players X3 and X4 run out from their places to guard Players X1 and X2, respectively. Players X1 and X2 try to score while Players X3 and X4 try to intercept or get the rebound. Players rotate to the ends of different columns (e.g., Player X1 moves

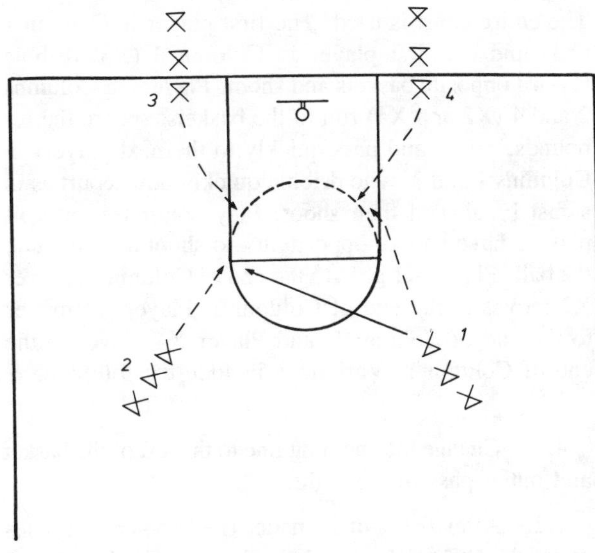

Figure 5.13. Pass and guard drill

to the column of Player X2, Player X2 moves to the column of Player X3, continuing sequentially until all players have rotated).

General Practice Drills

These drills are for group practice of several skills at once. They can be used for class practice after the skills have been taught or for team practice.

1.0. Dribble, Shoot, Rebound, Pass, and Run. Individuals are in two columns at each end of the court near the center line (Figure 5.14). Lead Players X1 and X3 dribble toward the basket, shoot a lay-up, circle behind the backboard, and go to end of the next-numbered column. The first players in Columns 2 and 4 run to the baskets, get the rebounds, pass to the shooting column, and go to the end of the next-numbered column (i.e., Player X1 goes to Column 2, Player X2 goes to Column 3, Player X3 goes to Column 4, and Player X4 goes to Column 1). Players must know the column numbers and go to each column in numerical order so they will all rebound and shoot at each end. This is a good conditioning drill for groups under 25 in number as well as good skill practice. Emphasize keeping on the move. Variation: Instead of lay-ups, players may pause near free throw lines and practice moving shots or jump shots.

2.0. Pass, Cut, Pivot, Shoot, and Rebound. One column of individuals lines up on either side of the court (Figure 5.15). A third column of players lines up under the basket and out of bounds, facing the center of the court. Player X3 moves out to the free throw line, Player X1 passes the ball to Player X3, and Players X2 and X1 cross toward opposite sides of the free throw lane. Player X3 has an option to hand off or pass to either Player X1 or Player X2 or to pivot and shoot. All three players go for the rebound. Player X1 goes to the end of Column 2, Player X2 goes to the end of Column 3, and Player X3 goes to the end of Column 1. The ball is returned to Column 1 or 2.

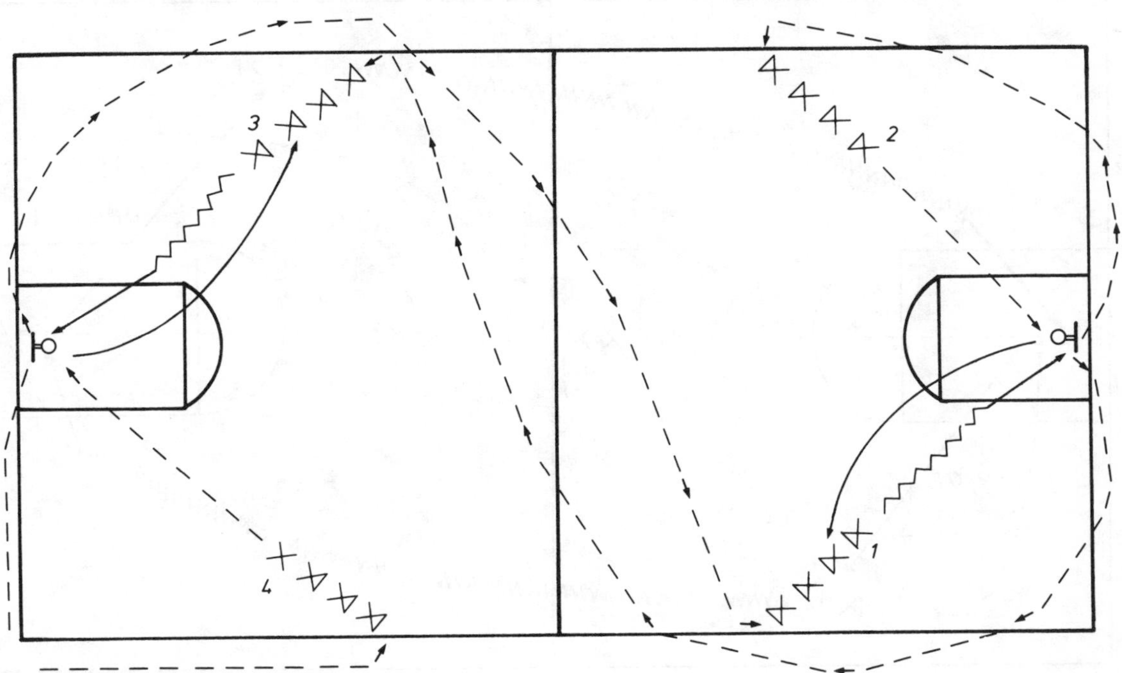

Figure 5.14. Dribble, shoot, rebound, pass, and run drill

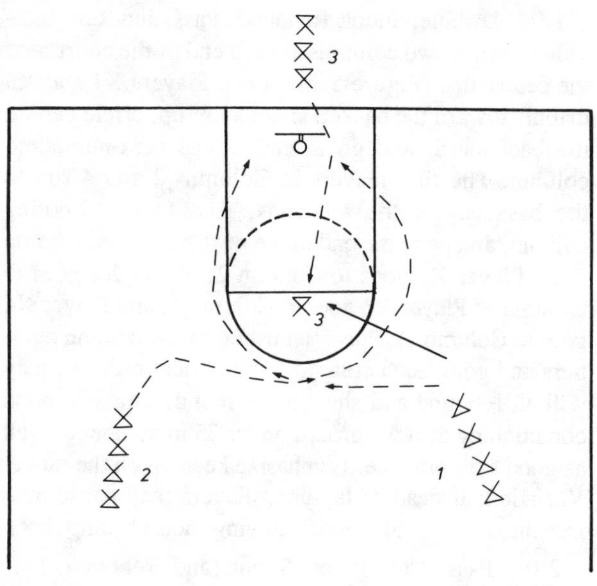

Figure 5.15. Pass, cut, pivot, shoot, and rebound drill

3.0. Dribble, Guard, Shoot, and Rebound. The starting formation is shown in Figure 5.15. Players X1 and X2 dribble and pass while moving toward the basket. Player X3 tries to guard the player with the ball and to intercept or prevent a shot. This is called a 2-on-1 situation.

4.0. Dribble, Shoot, Rebound, Outlet Pass to Fast Break. Squads are arranged in columns (Figure 5.16). The entire court is used. The first player in Column 1 (X1) and the first player in Column 3 (X3) dribble toward opposite baskets and shoot. Players in Columns 2 and 4 (X2 and X4) run to the baskets, secure the rebounds, pivot, and pass quickly to the next players in Columns 1 and 3, who dribble quickly downcourt as in a fast break and then shoot. Play continues until all players have had an opportunity to shoot and rebound the ball. Player X1 goes to the end of Column 2, Player X2 moves to the end of Column 3, Player X3 moves to the end of Column 4, and Player X4 moves to the end of Column 1. Variations include the following:

4.1. Change the shooting line to the left of the basket and outlet pass to the right.

4.2. After the shot is made, the shooter continues under the basket, then curls back even with free throw line. That player receives the outlet pass from the rebounder at Position *OP* and then passes to the leader of the column near the sideline. Young players may need to use this variation rather than try a long pass to the center sideline.

4.3. Columns 2 and 4 become the shooting columns, and Columns 1 and 3 become the rebound columns. Players X2 and X4 dribble and shoot. Players X1 and X3 get the rebounds and pass out to the players in the opposite side columns, who pass back to the players in Columns 2 and 4.

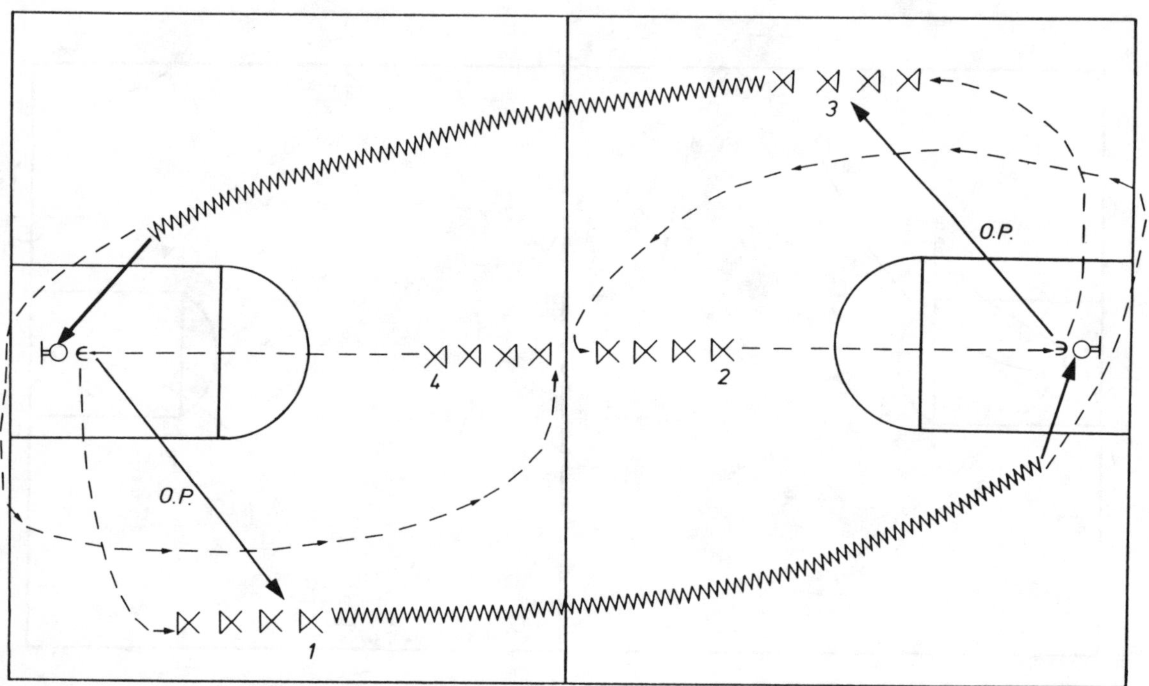

Figure 5.16. Dribble, shoot, rebound, and outlet pass drill (OP = outlet pass)

Offense

Offense begins with simple individual maneuvers designed to get away from the opponent. Players must learn to start in one direction and quickly stop and change directions to elude their guards and be free to receive a pass or shoot. Beginners tend to make small sliding moves, which allow the guards to stay close and defend easily. They must be encouraged to start quickly, get behind the guards, and run several yards before reversing directions. Players should learn to pass and catch on the run. Stationary player are too easy to guard.

Cutting

The *cut* is a rapid move toward the basket. It can be executed by a dribbler who manages to evade the guard and get between the guard and the basket. This is usually done by feinting with the ball, arms, and head in one direction. When the guard moves in that direction, the dribbler may then quickly reverse or pivot to go another way.

The cut can also be done by a player without a ball who seeks to get free to receive a pass. The front, or inside, cut is made by running between the defensive player and the passer (Figure 5.17). Player O1 moves quickly around in front of Defender D1 and tries to get in position to have a direct line to the basket. Player O2 pivots and passes to Player O1 as the guard is cleared. The cutter should fake a move to the other side of the defender before cutting inside. Player O2 may have to pivot to clear Defender D2.

The *back cut*, or *reverse cut*, is done by starting a move inside, then quickly changing directions to go outside or behind the guard (Figure 5.18). Timing is very important. The cutter must be sure that the passer has control of the ball before cutting. The passer must throw the ball ahead of the cutter as soon as the defender is cleared.

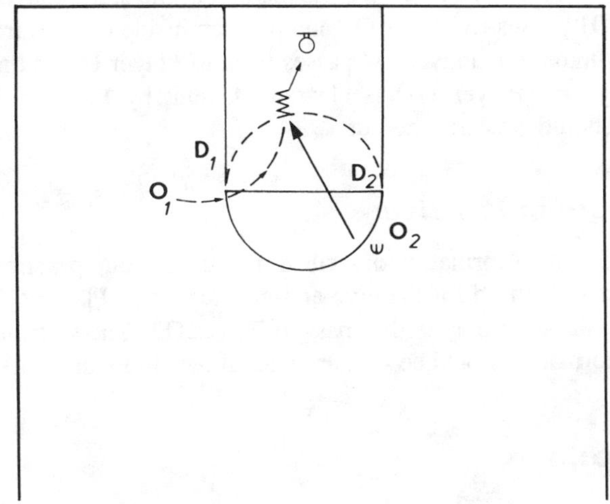

Figure 5.17. Front cut drill

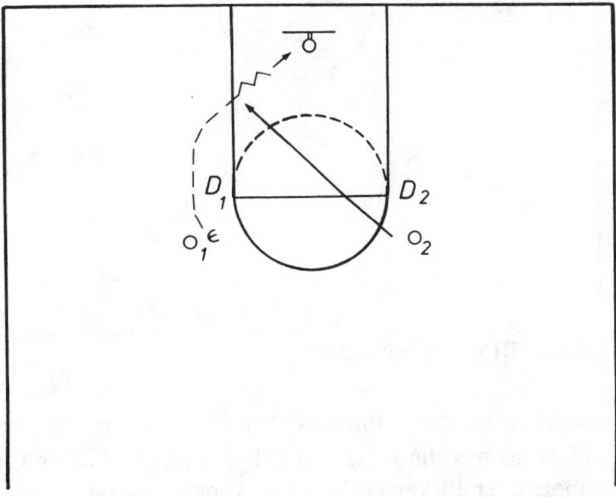

Figure 5.18. Back cut drill

Group Practice

Assign four groups of four to six player at each basket area. Two groups will be lined up behind Players O1 and O2 (Figure 5.17). The other two columns, led by Players D1 and D2, will be along the end line, one at each side of the basket. The first players in Columns D1 and D2 step out onto the court to act as defenders while Players O1 and O2 practice the cut and pass. After a shot at the basket or an interception, the offensive players go to the end of the defender's columns and the defenders to the end of the offensive columns. Then the next person in each group performs the drill. Players should rotate so each has a turn at each position. After practice from the designated side, players in the right column may become cutters and players in the left column passers.

Screening

A *screen* is a legal maneuver to protect your teammate so that a defender cannot get close to stop a dribble or to block a shot. It is especially effective against a 1-on-1 defense.

The *inside screen* requires the screening player to move between the teammate and that teammate's guard (Figure 5.19). There must be no contact between the screener and the defender, so this cannot be done if the

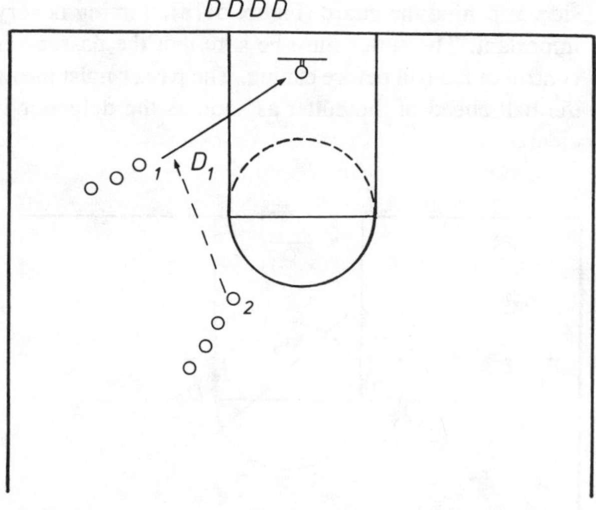

Figure 5.19. Inside screen

guard is too close. Player O2 moves between Players O1 (who has the ball) and D1 and stops. Player O1 shoots over Player O2's head. Another variation is to have Player O2 dribble between Players O1 and D1, then pass or hand the ball to Player O1, who shoots. The screener should face the basket and be ready to go for the rebound.

The *outside screen* has the offensive player move into position behind the teammate's guard (Figure 5.20). Room must be allowed for the guard to turn around. The teammate then moves quickly around the guard, who is screened out and unable to follow the offensive player. If Player O1 has the ball, that player would dribble around Player D1; if not, Player O1 would be free to receive a pass from Player O2 or another teammate.

The *lateral screen* is similar to the outside screen except that it is set to the side of the guard to prevent the player from following the forward, who cuts closely around the screener. Once the screener has established a position beside the guard, the screener must be careful not to move into the path of a guard who tries to go around the screen.

A *moving screen* is legal as long as the screener does not push the defender out of the way or charge. These are usually accomplished by two teammates moving in opposite directions past each other so closely that the defenders are brushed off, leaving one offensive player free to receive a pass or shoot.

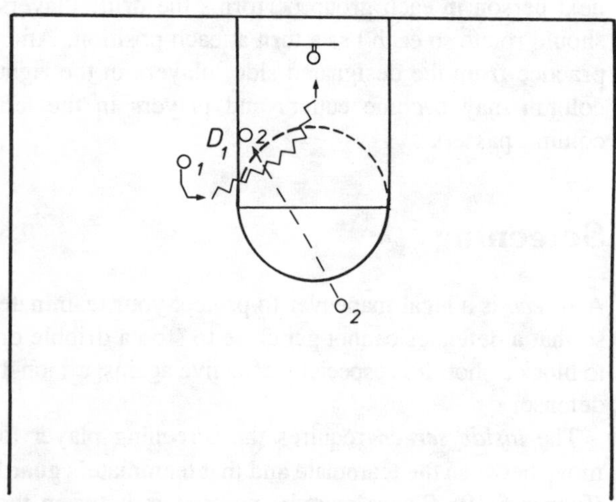

Figure 5.20. Outside screen

Group Practice

Three groups are arranged in columns as in Figure 5.15 with Players O1 and O2 as leaders of two offensive columns and a group of defenders near the end line. As Player O2 receives the ball to start the practice, Player D1 moves into defensive position. Player O2 dribbles between Players O1 and D1 and hands off to Player O1, who shoots over Player O2's head. As an alternative, Player O2 dribbles behind Player O1 and shoots over Player O1's head. Players rotate to another column after completing a turn (i.e., Player O1 moves to the column of Player O2, Player O2 moves to the column of Player D1, and Player D1 moves to the column of Player O1). Variations include the following:

1.1. Set screens and shoot from the other side of the basket.
1.2. Use the same formation for practicing outside and lateral screens.

Give-and-Go

The *give-and-go* is a variation of the cut (Figure 5.17). In this case, Player O1 has the ball at the start. Player O1 passes to Player O2 and does an inside cut toward the basket. Player O2 passes back to Player O1 as the guard (Player D1) is cleared. A feint by Player O1 should precede the cut.

Group Practice

The drill formation described in cutting group practice may be used for the give-and-go except that Player O1 will begin play with a pass to Player O2. The starting formation would be similar to that shown in Figure 5.13.

Pick

The *pick* is a version of a lateral screen. A teammate of the ball handler moves into position to the side and slightly behind the ball handler's guard and assumes a stationary position with a wide stance (Figure 5.20). The ball handler cuts closely around the teammate and dribbles to the basket. The guard is picked off, and the forward gets a clear shot. If the guard tries to push through the blocking offensive player, a foul will occur.

Pick-and-Roll

Alert defenders who are caught in a pick situation will switch to a different player to guard (Figure 5.21). When this occurs, the player who set the pick (screen) should pivot (roll) away from the guard, Player D1, toward the basket and receive a pass from the dribbler. This move is called a *pick-and-roll*. Player O1 has the ball. First, player O2 moves to the side of Player O1's guard (Player D1), and sets a screen (a). Player O2's guard follows (b). Player O1 dribbles around Player O2, picking off the guard, Player D1 (c). Player D2 sees the pick occur and switches to guard Player O1 (d), leaving Player D1 to guard Player O2. Player O2 pivots quickly around Player D1 and cuts toward the basket, receiving a pass from Player O1 (e).

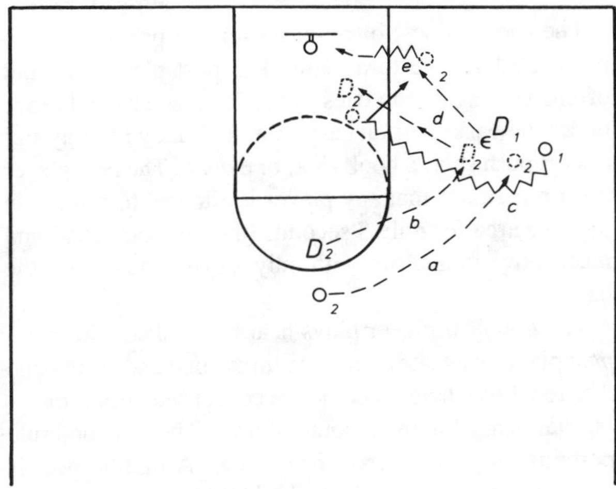

Figure 5.21. Pick-and-roll

The pick or screen may be used anywhere on the court to free a dribbler from the guard. Its use is not limited to the basket area. Players setting the pick may not shift position to obstruct the guards further after their teammates begin the cut.

Weave

The *weave offense* (or figure 8) may be done by three or four players while the other one or two move in and out of the *post* position in the lane or play the corners. The weave is a series of moving screens that attempts to cause confusion among the guards, especially against a 1-on-1 defense (Figure 5.22). The three-player weave begins with Player O1 dribbling toward the side or corner (a). Player O2 moves toward Player O1, passes Player O1 on the side away from the basket, and receives a pass or handoff (b). Player O2 may then use Player O1 as a screen and cut toward the basket or dribble toward the opposite corner of the court. As Player O2 starts to dribble, Player O3 moves past on the side away from the basket, receives the ball (c), and cuts or dribbles in the opposite direction. Player O1 has now circled around and returns to run past Player O3, using that player as a screen and receiving the ball. Whenever any offensive player gets a clear path to the basket, that player should dribble in and shoot.

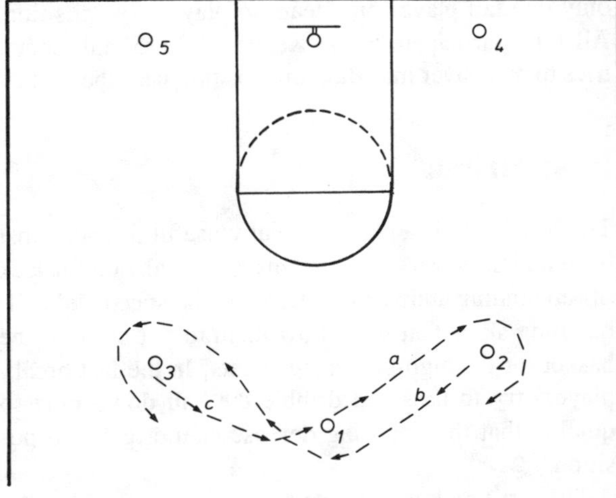

Figure 5.22. Weave pattern

Several key points are important to a successful weave:

- The weaving players must keep moving.
- The player without the ball must run behind and outside the dribbler.
- The handoffs or passes must be made on the outside or away from the guards.
- After receiving a handoff, that player should try to cut around the teammate and toward the basket. If this is not possible, the weave is continued.
- A player who does not receive the ball should continue to run toward the opposite corner of the court, then loop around and come back.
- Weavers must also be alert for an opening to pass to a teammate playing a post position.

- Players need not hand off every time two people run past each other. This is only done in the proper situation because the defense may get careless and leave the dribbler alone, expecting the player to pass.
- An attempt should be made to draw the defense from the center of the court (near the free throw lane) so a cut may be made there.

Practice on the weave may begin early in the program with the passing practice drill shown in Figure 5.4. This will lead into the weave practice drill as described here. Beginners tend to be pushed farther from the basket by the guards when trying the weave. They must be encouraged to cut toward the basket with each handoff. It is best to begin practicing this skill without any guards in place. After the players have mastered the concept of using a teammate as a screen and cutting in behind, add a guard for each of the weaving players.

The four-person weave is appropriate when there is only one tall player on a team to play a post position. All four participate in the weave while the tall center tries to maneuver into shooting position near the basket.

Fast Break

The *fast break* is a play especially useful to teams that have no tall players. Such teams must make up for lack of rebounding ability by developing the speed and ball-handling skills that will allow them to get close to the basket for the high-percentage shots. In the fast break, players try to pass and dribble the ball downcourt so quickly that the opposing defense cannot get into position.

The fast break may be started by a player taking the ball out of bounds after a goal is made, but it usually starts with a defensive interception or a defensive rebound. A *point guard* (the player responsible for the center area near the free throw circle), a *wing*, or another designated defensive player is assigned to start downcourt toward the opposite basket as soon as a teammate secures the ball. The player with the ball immediately passes to the breaking player, who tries to beat the opposing players down the floor. It is better to have two or three players breaking if possible, one in the center and one on each side, as they can then pass back and forth or drive to the basket. When more than one player is involved in the fast break, they must learn to stay away from one another. If they are close together, one defensive player can guard them all, and the break is ineffective.

Group Practice

The following are offensive group-practice drills. Emphasize teamwork during drills.

1.0. Drill 4.0 and its variations in the section on general practice drills are good drills to use here (Figure 5.16).

2.0. Three-Column Formation (Figure 5.23). Player X1 dribbles toward the basket. Players X2 and X3 run somewhat parallel to Player X1 until they near the free throw line, when they curve in toward the basket. Player X1 passes to either Player X2 or Player X3, who shoots. All rebound and continue shooting until a goal is made. Player X1 goes to the end of Column 2, Player X2 goes to the end of Column 3, and Player X3 goes to the end of Column 1. The ball is returned to Column 1. Three more columns could be near the center of the court moving in the opposite direction. This drill moves faster if three or four balls are used at each end. Variations include the following:

2.1. Two columns could be used to practice the two-player fast break.

2.2. Add columns of guards parallel to each of Columns 1, 2, and 3. The guards start down the floor at the same time as the offensive players. They try to catch up and intercept or block the shot.

2.3. Have one or two guards come from under the basket and simulate the 3-on-1 or 3-on-2 situations. This drill would be for intermediate or advanced players.

The use of a post or pivot player can provide an important advantage to a team. The post player is a tall offensive player who tries to evade the guard and move under the basket for an easy shot. This may be a lay-up, a short push shot, a hook shot, or a *dunk*. The post player must remember that any player is allowed to remain in the lane area for only 3 seconds (the *3-second rule*) and must move in and out with only a brief pause near the basket.

The *low-post* player plays near the basket. The *high-post* player stays near the free throw line and, if outside the free throw lane, need not be concerned with remaining stationary for any amount of time. The 3-second rule pertains only to the free throw lane. A middle post is sometimes used between the high- and the low-post positions.

Some teams use both a high post and a low post. Usually, players alternate moving from one side of the basket to the other trying to get free to receive a pass and shoot or to set a screen for a teammate who is cutting toward the basket.

Offense Against a Zone

Many of the maneuvers used against the 1-on-1 defense can be used against the zone defense if players are quick enough or if variations are added. For example, when screening is done, the defense usually switches so the

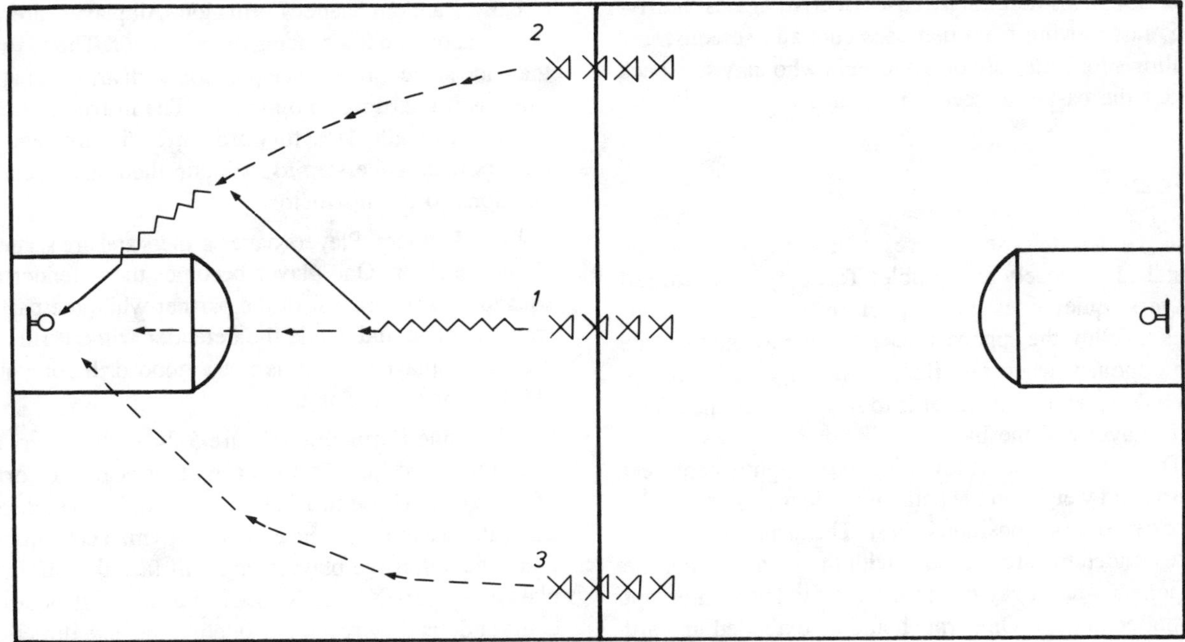

Figure 5.23. Fast break drill

pick-and-roll is more effective. A second cut by another player may be added to complicate the defense's situation.

The more effective offensive moves against a zone defense consist of overloading a zone; using fast, accurate passes; and concentrating on the areas left weak by the zone pattern. Successful long shots are also devastating to a zone defense, but a team cannot always count on accurate long shots.

An *overloaded zone* is one in which two or three offensive players are concentrated in one area in an effort to confuse the defenders so that they do not know who to guard. This should allow one of the offensive players to get free to shoot or to dribble in toward the basket.

In a zone defense, defenders move as the ball moves from side to side. Quick, accurate passes made by the offensive players will cause much movement by the defense. Passing from one side of the floor to the other may tire them or result in an opening in zone coverage.

As an offensive player moves from one zone to another, a different defender becomes the guard. The lines where responsibility shifts (sometimes called *seams*) are often vague. Attackers should play the seam areas as much as possible. Sometimes defenders do not pick up an offensive player soon enough in the zone change, and an opening to the basket can be found.

The offensive team must also analyze the type of zone in use. Each one has certain weaknesses that must be exploited. The best way to beat a zone defense is to fast break down the floor before the defense gets into its zone formation.

Defense

There are two main types of defensive play in basketball: (a) player-to-player, or 1-on-1; and (b) zone. In the former, each defender is paired with an offensive player and is responsible for guarding that person anywhere on the court while trying to prevent that player from getting the ball and scoring. In zone defense, each player is responsible for a specific area of the floor and must guard any opponent who enters that area.

The 1-on-1 system of defense is easier to learn and to use without much team practice. It is frequently used in class play where teammates change often. Each defender is responsible for a specific person and does not have to worry about others. If the teams are relatively equal, opponents can be paired comparably. Play at *midcourt* and in the *backcourt* can be closer, and pass interference is often more effective. Players must be in good physical condition because there is more chasing than in the zone defenses. This defense is effective against outside shooters and is more adaptable than some zone defenses.

Zone defenses base their plans on protecting the shooting areas of the court. The assumption is that players are not a threat until they get within shooting range. As soon as the offensive players go on defense, they run quickly to their own areas of the court and take up their defensive positions without regard for the offense that is moving the ball downcourt. Defenders will guard any opponent who enters their zones as if in a 1-on-1 situation. This defense is most effective against a driving, fast-moving team that uses cuts and screens, and it allows for better use of tall players who may stay back under the basket to secure rebounds.

1-on-1

The 1-on-1 defense requires that the opponents be matched as closely as possible. Tall players guard tall players; quick ones guard quick ones. Each defender tries to follow the opponent when on defense but to evade the opponent when on offense. An important concept for a defender to remember is to stay between the offensive player and the basket.

The stance should be low with knees slightly bent, feet apart, and weight on the balls of the feet (Figure 5.12). A forward-stride position is best. The arms should both be extended toward the sides with the palms facing the opponent when away from the basket to try to intercept or deflect a pass. One arm should be extended upward to block a shot and the other to the side when guarding within shooting range. The arm extended to the side should be the one on the side you think the defender may move or pass (e.g., if near the end line, the arm on the inbounds side). When guarding a player with the ball, the eyes should be focused on the center of the waist of the opponent. Feints (fakes) are usually done with the feet, arms, head, and upper body, but if the waist moves, the player is committed to that direction.

Defensive players should always face their opponents. They should guard loosely (3 to 4 ft away) when the opponent does not have the ball or is far from the basket area. The guard should move in close when the opponent has the ball and is within shooting range or after the opponent has just executed a dribble. If the guard stands too close to an offensive player who is allowed a dribble, it is easier for the forward to cut around the guard and *drive* to the basket.

A sliding step, or shuffle, should be used when guarding closely. The defender must avoid crossing one foot over the other because this limits the ability to move in either direction. While one foot is crossing over, the forward may move toward that side, and the guard, being off balance, will be unable to react in time to stay between the forward and the basket. Even when a player is moving backward and forward, the slide step should be used unless a full-speed run is necessary. When a player moves to the right, the right foot should be back slightly; when a player moves to the left, the left foot should be back slightly.

Practice Drills

The following are practice drills for defensive play. Individual, partner and group drills are presented.

1.0. Random Scatter Formation. All players are well spaced about the floor facing the instructor. They assume the wide stance, bent-knee position with arms out at the sides as if guarding an opponent. The instructor points and moves right, left, forward, or backward, and the players must slide step to maintain their same relative positions to the instructor.

2.0. Partners. Players have partners and are scattered about the floor. One player becomes the defender and tries to stay within 3 ft of the partner while the partner tries to dodge and evade the defender without running into other players. This is not a good drill for young children or large classes.

3.0. Line Formation (Figure 5.24). All players are lined up in two lines facing each other near one corner of the court. Those in Line 1 are the offensive players and will face the opposite end of the gym. Those in Line 2 are the defensive players and will face the offensive players. Players X1 and X2 start sliding on a slant downcourt and, as they reach the sideline, change directions and move in a slant the other way. They continue moving on a slant back and forth until reaching the other end of the court. They return around the outside of the court and go to the end of the other line. As soon as the first pair has moved halfway across the court, the next pair may start so that action is continuous. A cone or a chair at the sidelines may be used to mark the direction change. Remind defenders that the right foot should be back when moving on a slant to the right and the left foot back when moving on a slant back to the left. Variations include the following:

3.1. As players improve their sliding steps, have the offensive player run rather than slide and change directions unexpectedly.

3.2. The offensive players dribble balls while they advance.

4.0. Other guarding drills are described in the drill sections on general practice, dribbling, and offensive practice.

Individual Strategies

Key points to emphasize to the defensive player using the 1-on-1 defense are listed. Many of these also apply to the zone defenders when they are guarding in their own zones.

- Stay between your forward and the basket you are defending.
- Keep a low stance and be ready to move in any direction.
- Keep the arms extended. If you cannot block, you may at least distract.
- Slide step; do not cross one foot over the other.

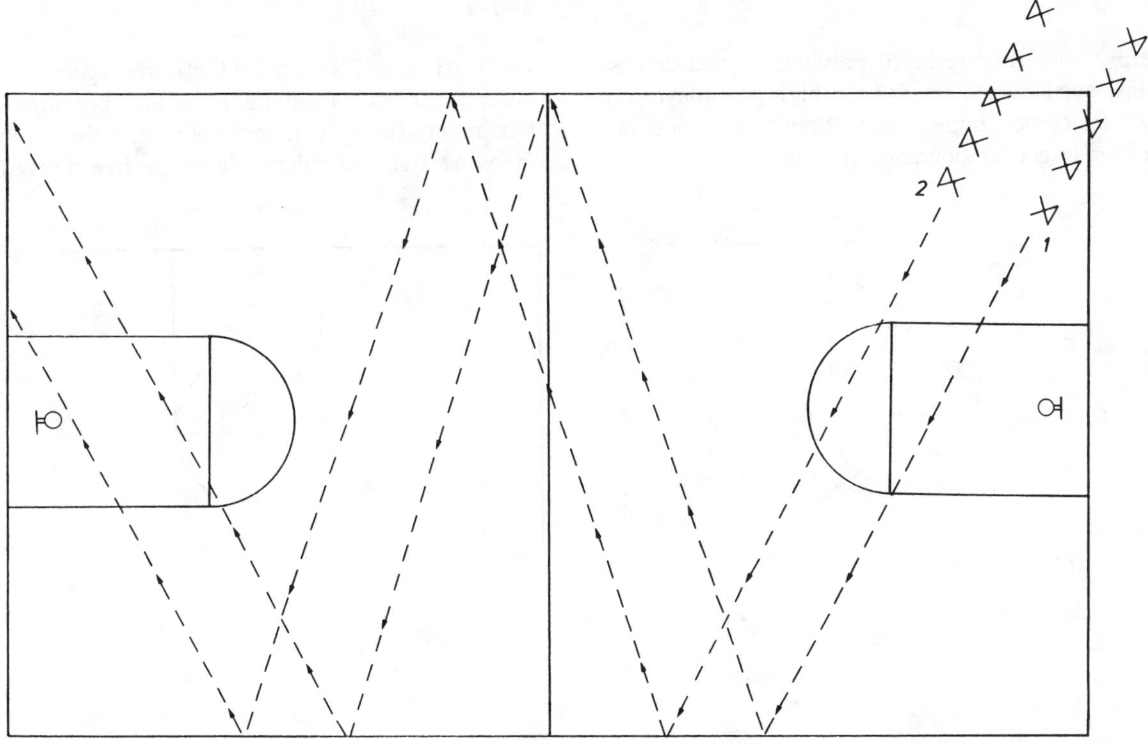

Figure 5.24. Guarding drill

• Be alert to picks and screens. Make plans to switch assignments with another defender if screened out of the play. Verbal cues like "Switch" or "Yours" can be used.

• Focus the eyes on the center of the body of the opponent, but try to use the peripheral vision to monitor other players and the ball.

• Do not play too close to an opponent with the ball unless that player is about to shoot or has completed a dribble.

• Be ready at all times to change from defense to offense.

• Try to secure the inside position at the basket when rebounding.

Zone Defenses

There are several types of zone defenses and variations of each of them. Zone defenses are usually classified by the number of players in each line of defense from the center of the court to the end line under the basket being defended.

The type of zone defense to be used depends on the skills of the defenders and the strategies used by the opponents. A few strengths and weaknesses of each are discussed here.

2-3

The 2-3 zone (Figure 5.25) allows the defenders to have at least two rebounders under the basket at all times. It protects the baseline and the corners and makes low-post play difficult. It may leave the center of the lane open for short shots near the free throw line or double cuts (one cutter following another).

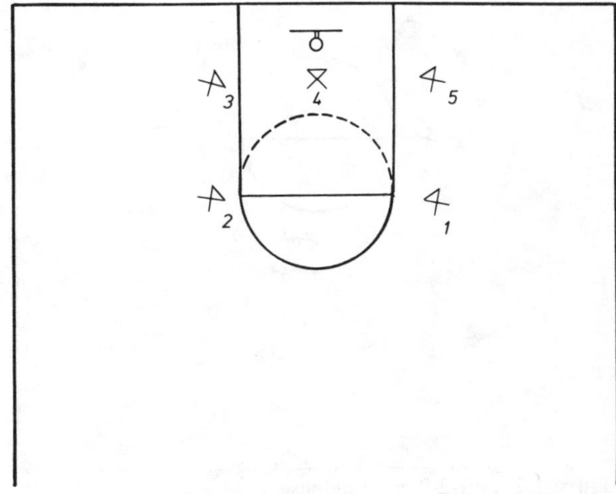

Figure 5.25. 2-3 zone defense

3-2

The 3-2 zone (Figure 5.26) provides a good defense against outside shooters and the high-post player but leaves the corners unprotected. Often there is only one defender in good rebounding position.

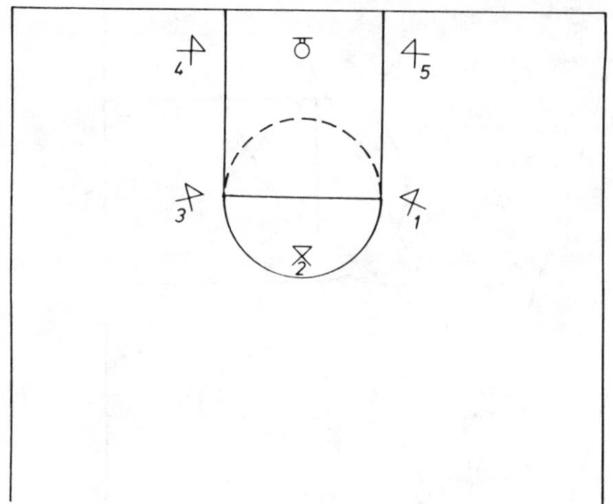

Figure 5.26. 3-2 zone defense

1-2-2

The 1-2-2 zone (Figure 5.27) gives more defensive help under the basket and at the sides but requires one person to guard the entire center area near the free throw circle. A team that has one very quick, competent guard may find this defense effective.

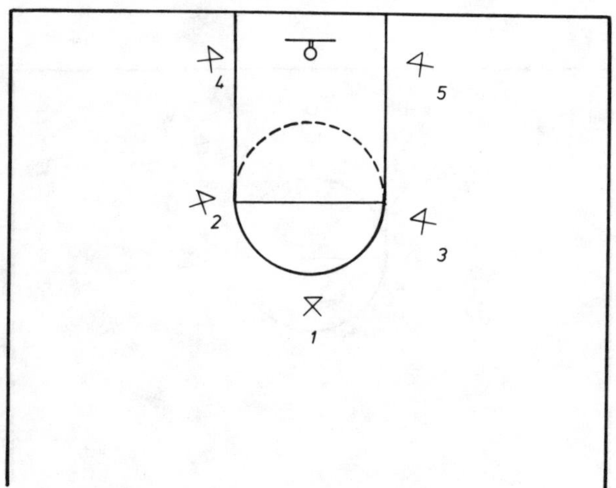

Figure 5.27. 1-2-2 zone defense

1-3-1

The 1-3-1 zone (Figure 5.28) is effective against a strong post player and a cutting team and provides some rebounding strength. It does not protect the corners or the wing areas on either side of the free throw line.

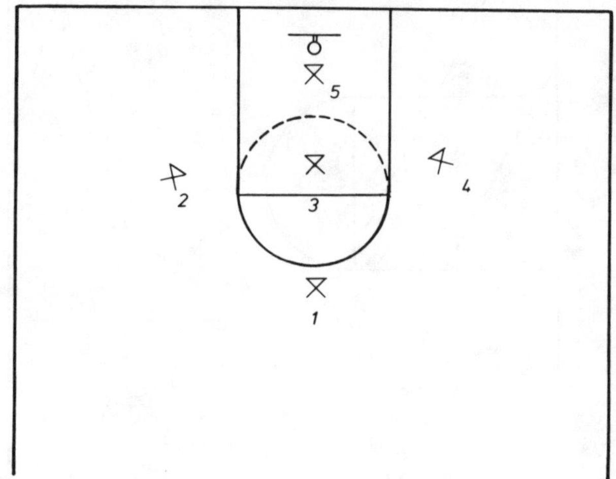

Figure 5.28. 1-3-1 zone defense

2-1-2

The 2-1-2 zone (Figure 5.29) is the most common and allows good coverage of the high- or the low-post player and prevents cutting down the lane. There are usually at least two and often three defenders available to rebound. There is a weakness near the free throw line and along the baseline in some overload situations.

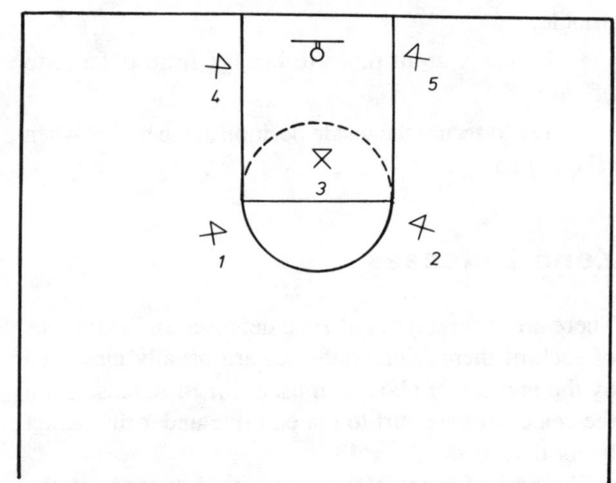

Figure 5.29. 2-1-2 zone defense

2-2-1

The 2-2-1 zone (Figure 5.30) is advantageous to a team that has one tall (and perhaps slow) player and four shorter, fast ones. The one tall player stays under the basket to collect all rebounds while the other four chase or cover outside play. The main problems with this defense are that only one person is in good position to rebound and the corners and baseline are not well protected.

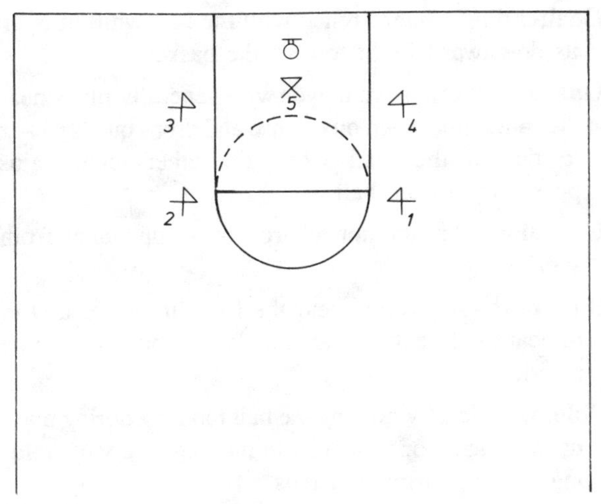

Figure 5.30. 2-2-1 zone defense

Practice Patterns

To practice the zone defenses, defenders are placed on the court in the positions of the selected zone. Three offensive players then move about the court, passing a ball around while the defenders shift to guard the player with the ball. Slow moves and passes will allow the defense time to adjust and the instructor or coach an opportunity to instruct. After the defenders show that they understand what is expected of them, the offensive players move and pass more quickly. One and then two additional offensive players are added to achieve the 5-on-5 situation of the game.

Team Strategies

Important concepts and strategies of zone defense include the following:

- As soon as the other team gains possession of the ball, go directly to your assigned zone as quickly as possible. Turn so that your back is to the basket being defended.
- Within the defenders' own zone area, the skills of guarding covered in the section on individual defense are used.
- The use of a zone defense allows the defenders to conserve energy.
- Position the taller and better rebounders in zones near the basket.
- Practice with your teammates so that all can work together well.
- Try to be aware of everyone in your zone.
- If your zone is overloaded, guard the player nearest the basket or the one most likely to score.
- If another zone is overloaded and no one is in yours, try to assist without deserting your own zone entirely. Be ready to switch back quickly.
- Generally, fewer fouls are committed in the zone defense.

Terminology

Abduction—Movement away from the midline of the body

Assist—A pass to a player who is in position to shoot a basket

Bank shot—A shot at the basket that rebounds off the backboard

Backcourt—The half of the court that is farthest from the basket at which a player is shooting; the half of the court that is being defended

Back cut—Moving quickly (cutting) behind the opponent in an attempt to evade that guard (may be preceded by a fake to the inside)

Ball trajectory—The flight path assumed by an airborne ball

Baseline—The end lines of the court under each basket

Blocked shot—Deflecting or stopping a shot just after it leaves the hand of the shooter or during its upward trajectory

Blocking—Moving into the path of a dribbling player, thus causing body contact (a foul)

Blocking out—Positioning the body near the basket and in front of the opponent to prevent that player from getting a rebound (also called *boxing out*)

Catching—The act of receiving or gaining possession of a thrown ball

Center—A player who generally plays within a few feet of the basket on both offense and defense; usually the tallest player on the team (post or pivot player)

Charging—An offensive player with the ball moving into a stationary player or a player who has an established position (a foul)

Clockwise—Rotational movement in the direction of the hands of a clock

Cut—To move quickly along a new path (usually toward the basket); to elude an opponent; a form of dodging

Double dribble—Dribbling once, stopping, then dribbling again (illegal)

Double post—An offensive pattern using two post players

Double team—Two teammates guarding one opponent

Dribble—A legal means of moving with the ball by using a continuous series of bounces using one hand or the other but never both at once

Drive—An assertive move toward the basket by a person who controls the ball; a rapid, strong dribble toward the goal

Dunk—To push the ball downward through the basket (requires a leap high enough to enable the shooter to reach above the rim)

Faking—Attempting to draw the opponent off balance or out of position by making short, abrupt movements of the arms, ball, head, or one foot; trying to mislead an opponent about where you will move (feinting)

Fast break—A team strategy or play pattern characterized by players changing quickly from defensive to offensive roles and rushing rapidly toward the goal area they are attacking

Feinting—See Faking

Field goal—Any goal scored from the court (other than a free throw) during regular play

5-on-5—Five players opposing five others in a basketball game; often used as a half-court game

Forward—A player who generally plays near the end line to the side of the basket; may also play under the basket

Foul—A serious offense against the rules or illegal contact with an opponent (e.g., using abusive language, pushing); often penalized by awarding a free throw to the offender's opponent

Foul line—See Free throw line

Free throw—An unguarded shot at the basket taken from the free throw line

Free throw lane—The area under the basket delineated by the end line, the free throw line, and two parallel lines connecting the ends of the free throw line with the end line

Free throw line—A line parallel to the end line and 19 feet from it in front of the basket; the line denoting where free throws occur

Frontcourt—The half of the court nearer to the basket at which a team is shooting

Full-court press—A defensive team strategy characterized by having all defenders closely guard their opponents as soon as the opponents gain possession of the ball; defenders closely guarding their opponents over the entire court

Give-and-go—An offensive strategy characterized by a player passing the ball and immediately running toward the basket in an attempt to evade the guard and get free to receive the ball back

Goaltending—Interference with the ball while it is on its downward flight toward the basket

Guard—An offensive player who generally plays near the center line when on offense and drops quickly back to defend the goal when the other team gains possession of the ball

Guarding—An attempt to prevent an opponent from scoring

High post—A position near the free throw line and in or near the free throw lane; a player who plays in this position

Holding—Illegally holding the ball too long during play; preventing an opponent from moving freely by holding with the arms or hands

Hook pass/shot—A pass or shot that is thrown over the head from the side of the player. As the shot is completed, the throwing arm forms a hook pattern overhead

Inside screen—A play in which one player moves in front of a teammate and keeps opponents away while a teammate shoots

Jump ball—A method of putting the ball into play by tossing it into the air between two opponents who must try to gain control of the ball by tapping it to a teammate

Jump shot—A shot taken while the player is jumping in the air (usually a one-handed push shot)

Lane—The area under each basket bounded by the free throw line, the end line, and two (usually) parallel lines connecting those lines (formerly called the *key*)

Lateral screen—A move by an offensive player to assume a stationary position to the inside of the ball-handler's guard so that the ball handler can dribble around the teammate who blocks out the guard

Lay-up—A shot taken from very near the basket following a dribble and a leap toward the basket

Low post—A position close to the basket and in or near the lane (usually played by the tallest player on a team)

Midcourt—The center area of the court

Moving screen—A teammate who moves between the ball carrier and opponents along the same path to protect the moving ball handler

1-on-1—A guarding pattern that assigns each defender a specific opponent (also called player-to-player)

Opponents' goal—The goal a team is defending

Outlet pass—An offensive pass that goes from under the basket toward the sidelines to get the ball away from a crowded, dangerous situation and to initiate movement toward the other basket

Outside screen—Movement by a dribbler to place a teammate between the ball and the basket and to use that teammate to keep opponents away while a shot is taken

Overloaded zone—Two or more members of the offensive team collecting within one of the defender's zone areas

Own goal—The goal toward which a team is shooting

Palming—Placing the palm of the hand under or behind the ball while dribbling and carrying the ball briefly in one hand (illegal)

Passing—Purposeful projection of the ball between teammates

Pick—Dribbling around a teammate so closely that the guard is unable to follow without fouling

Pick-and-roll—An offensive play used when guards avoid a pick by switching to guard a different opponent and the offensive player who blocked out the guard pivots and moves toward the basket (see Roll; Switch)

Pivot—A circular movement around one foot to change directions

Pivot foot—The foot that stays in contact with the floor during the pivot

Point guard—The offensive player who generally plays closest to the center line when on offense; often the team signal caller or director who starts plays

Post—An offensive player who plays near the basket in and around the lane area. Teammates try to pass the ball to this player, who then takes a close shot or passes back out to an unguarded player; the position played by the center or pivot player

Press—To guard closely

Pronation—Turning of the palms of the hand inward and downward

Rebounding—Catching the ball after it hits the backboard or rim but has not entered the basket

Reverse cut—Same as Back cut

Rim shot—A shot that hits the rim of the basket; a shot that just brushes the rim on its way through the basket; using the rim as a target when shooting

Roll—A play, usually used with a pick, in which an offensive player pivots around a guard and runs toward the basket (see Pick-and-roll)

Screen—Interposing a teammate between the ball and an opponent to protect the ball or take a shot

Shot—A legal attempt to throw the ball through the basket

Switch—In the 1-on-1 system of defense, two or more guards changing opponents

Technical foul—A foul against the rules of the game that does not involve personal contact with another player (e.g., having too many players on the court)

3-on-1—One defensive player having to defend against three attacking offensive players

3-on-2—Two defensive players opposing three offensive attackers

3-Second rule—A rule that limits the amount of time that an offensive player may stay in the lane area to 3 seconds (players who move out of the lane may then return for up to 3 more seconds)

Tip-in—A tap or push that returns a rebounding ball toward the basket, usually done at the height of a jump while in the air

Travel—To run illegally with the ball or to move the feet while holding the ball

Turnover—Executing a poor pass or making an error that allows the opponents to gain possession of the ball

Unsporting behavior—Conduct that is unfair, rude, or unseemly or that detracts from the progress of the game

Violations—Minor offenses against the rules that are penalized by giving a throw-in to the opposite team (e.g., traveling, allowing the ball to go out of bounds)

Weave offense—An offensive pattern involving three or more players characterized by a weaving action by the players

Wing—A player who plays near the corner of the court (also called a *forward*)

Zone defense—A defensive system characterized by dividing the court area to be defended into specific section (zones) and assigning one defender to guard whichever opponent enters the area

Selected Readings

Armbruster, D., Musker, F., & Mood, D. (1979). *Sports and recreational activities for men and women*. St. Louis: C.V. Mosby.

Auerback, A. (1975). *Basketball for the players, the fans and the coach*. New York: Simon & Schuster.

Barnes, M. (1972). *Women's basketball*. Boston: Allyn & Bacon.
Casady, D. (1974). *Sports activities for men*. New York: Macmillan
Coleman, B. (1975). *Basketball: Techniques, teaching and training*. New York: A.S. Barnes.
Cooper, J., & Siedentop, D. (1975). *The theory and science of basketball*. Philadelphia: Lea & Febiger.
Ebert, F., & Cheatum, B. (1972). *Basketball: Five player*. Philadelphia: W.B. Saunders.
Mushier, C. (1983). *Team sports for girls and women* (2nd ed.). Princeton, NJ: Princeton Book.
National Association of Girls and Women in Sport (1985). *Basketball guide*. Reston, VA: American Alliance for Health, Physical Education, Recreation and Dance.
Tarkanian, J., & Warren, W. (1983). *Winning basketball drills and fundamentals*. Boston: Allyn & Bacon.

Basketball Skills Errors and Corrections

PASSING (GENERAL)

Error	*Causes*	*Corrections*
Inaccurate		
Ball goes too far left or right of target	• Improper hand placement	• Adjust hand and arm positions behind the ball so that force can be applied in line with the intended line of flight.
	• Incorrect point of release	• Release sooner or hold the ball longer; visualize the planned path of the ball and where the ball should leave the hand(s) to reach the target in as direct a line as possible.
	• Inadequate follow-through	• Reach toward the target with arms; extend the hands and fingers toward the target.
Weak		
Ball falls short of target	• Gripping the ball in the palms of the hands	• Hold the ball in the pads of the ends of the fingers.
	• Inadequate force production behind the ball	• Speed up the extension during the force-production or the action phase of the pass; transfer the body weight forward and/or utilize a forward stepping action (step into it); involve more body parts in the action (hands, arms, trunk, legs).

CHEST PASS

Error	*Causes*	*Corrections*
Inaccurate		
Ball goes to left or right of target	• Thumbs not positioned behind the ball	• Thumbs should point toward each other behind the ball; keep elbows close to the sides.

Error	*Causes*	*Corrections*
Inaccurate		
Ball goes to left or right of target	• Thrown with inadequate amount of backspin	• Push with the thumbs, which should be below the ball's center of gravity.
	• Inadequate follow-through parallel to the floor	• Extend fingers and arms straight toward the target.
Weak		
Ball falls short of target	• Starting with the ball away from the body	• Move ball in close to the body before projecting the ball toward the target.
	• Elbows held away from the body and *not* behind the ball	• Keep the elbows close to the body and the hands behind the ball in the direction of the intended ball flight; if the elbows point out to the sides, the hands will be too far to the sides of the ball, and force will be lost.
	• Knees *not* flexed (bent) during the motion	• Bend the knees and step forward with the throw.
	• Lack of forearm pronation (palms pointing outward)	• Push the ball toward the target by extending the fingers and thumbs forcefully; rotate the hands so their backs are toward each other after release.

BOUNCE PASS

Error	*Causes*	*Corrections*
Inaccurate		
Ball bounces too high or too low	• Starting with the ball too high	• Hold the ball at about chest height.
	• Using an inappropriate spin on the ball	• Keep hand(s) directly behind the ball to avoid spin; topspin will cause the ball to bounce lower than usual, and backspin will cause the ball to bounce higher and to slow down after it hits the floor.
	• Follow-through *not* directed downward in the direction of intended ball bounce	• Reach toward the spot where the ball is to hit the floor, not toward the receiver.
	• Poor placement of the bounce on the floor	• Bounce the ball 4 to 8 ft in front of the receiver for short-to-moderate-distance passes (approximately two-thirds of the distance between thrower and receiver).
Weak		
Ball falls short of target	• Elbows *not* close to the body	• Keep the elbows close to the body.
	• Knees *not* flexed (bent) during the motion	• Bend the knees and step toward the target.

(Cont.)

UNDERHAND PASS

Error	*Causes*	*Corrections*
Inaccurate		
Ball goes too high or to side of target	• Failure to hold the ball with both hands until just prior to release	• Keep the hand that is not imparting force to the throw in contact with the ball to help control it until just before the release; keep the nonthrowing hand on top of the ball.
	• Failure to elongate the arc of the underhand swing	• Flex (bend) the knee of the forward leg as the weight is transferred to it and the throwing arm swings forward.
	• Releasing the ball too late	• Release the ball below waist level (unless a high arc is desired).
Weak		
Ball falls short of target	• Failure to use the opposite leg forward from the throwing arm	• Step forward on the foot opposite the throwing arm.
	• Failure to flex the wrist and extend the fingers	• Point the fingers of the throwing hand toward the target on releasing the ball.

HOOK PASS/SHOT

Error	*Causes*	*Corrections*
Inaccurate		
Ball goes to right or left of target	• Imparting too much spin to the ball	• Use less flexion of the wrist.
	• Failure to look at the target	• Turn the head to the side to look at the target.
	• Failure to bring the arm directly up beside the head	• Straighten the arm as the ball is lifted to shoulder level; as the ball is released, the upper arm is close to the head.
Ball has insufficient loft	• Flexing (bending) the elbow during the over-the-head sweep, causing a flat trajectory or downward path	• Keep the arm straight throughout the shot (the wrist flexion directs the ball).
Weak		
Ball falls short of target	• Failure to extend (straighten) at the knees and rotate the shoulder slightly	• Straighten the legs as the arm extends upward; rotate (turn) the shoulder of the shooting arm inward.
	• Failure to use the entire arm	• Keep the arm straight; balance the ball in the fingers and flex the wrist strongly at release.
	• Failure to get the ball to the basket	• Move more rapidly upward at the shoulder; use this pass only if the distance to the target is less than 10 ft (shorter for novice or young players).

ONE-HANDED SHOULDER (BASEBALL) PASS

Error	*Causes*	*Corrections*
Inaccurate		
Ball falls from hand or is misdirected	• Failure to use the free hand to steady the ball until it starts forward	• Keep nonshooting hand under the ball longer.
	• Hand *not* behind ball	• Place the fingers and the thumb of the shooting hand in line with the directional path to the target.
Weak		
Ball falls short of target	• Throwing-arm elbow *not* behind the ball	• Keep the elbow raised at about shoulder level and behind the body.
	• Ball held in palm of hand	• Keep the ball resting on the fingers only.
	• Using only the arm for force production	• Rotate the hips clockwise during preparation and forcefully rotate counterclockwise for force production. Extend at the ankles, knees, and hips as the pass is made.

TWO-HANDED OVERHEAD PASS

Error	*Causes*	*Corrections*
Inaccurate		
Ball falls short of target	• Hands; including the thumbs, on the sides of the ball	• Move the hands more directly behind the ball so that the thumbs and index fingers can apply force in the desired direction.
	• Ball in line with the elbows throughout	• Lead with the upper arms so that the elbows precede the ball. Final action is a whipping extension of the forearms.
	• Failure to utilize the trunk in a forward whipping action	• Flex the trunk forward to add force. This action should precede the whipping action of the arms.
	• Failure to utilize a forward step with a forward weight transfer	• Step forward toward the target with the throw.

CATCHING

Error	*Causes*	*Corrections*
Lack of control		
Ball does not contact hands	• Failure to focus on the ball during the entire flight	• Concentrate on watching the ball until it touches the hands

(Cont.)

CATCHING (Continued)

Error	*Causes*	*Corrections*
Lack of control		
Ball does not contact	• Inadequate base of support	• Stand with the feet apart in a forward-stride position in the direction of ball flight.
	• Failure to reach toward the ball	• Extend the arms toward the ball with the elbows slightly bent.
Contacts hand but ball is not held	• Catching with a hand on either side of the ball instead of behind the ball	• Hold the palms of both hands toward the ball with the fingers apart but relaxed.
	• Failure to pull the ball toward the center of the body (giving with the ball)	• Flex (bend) the arms as the ball contacts the hands and draw the ball toward the body.
	• Failure to squeeze the ball slightly after gaining a grip	• Close the fingers firmly around the ball.
Ball rebounds off the hands	• Movement toward the ball when contact occurs	• Wait with arms extended until the ball comes to you; do not grab at it.
	• Pointing the fingers toward the back of the ball or making contact with the palms of the hands instead of the pads of the fingers and thumbs.	• Hold the palms of the hands facing the ball; relax the cupped fingers and let ball come into contact with them.
	• Improper hand position for a high ball	• Point the fingers upward with the palms facing the ball and thumbs together.
	• Improper hand position for a low ball	• Point the fingers downward with the palms facing the ball and the little fingers together.
	• Failure to flex the arms, or give, with the ball	• Reach out to make contact; draw the ball toward the body.

DRIBBLE

Error	*Causes*	*Corrections*
Lack of ball control		
	• Slapping the ball or using the palm of the hand	• Cup the hands and contact the ball with the pads of the fingers and thumb.
	• Improper use of the fingers and thumb on the ball	• Spread the fingers and thumb apart.
	• Failure to keep the dribble close to the body	• Bounce the ball about 12 to 18 in. in front and slightly to the dribbling-hand side of the body. This varies with the speed of forward movement of the dribbler.
	• Dribbling too close to the feet	• Bounce the ball to the side of the feet on the dribbling-hand side (see previous correction).

Error	***Causes***	***Corrections***
Lack of ball control		
	• Using the upper arm excessively	• Stabilize the upper arm; restrict motion to the forearm at the elbow and the hand at the wrist.
	• *Not* utilizing the fingers and wrist as the primary means of of control	• Emphasize wrist action with the fingers spread out on the ball.
	• *Not* looking ahead	• Keep the head up; glance down at the ball occasionally.
	• Inappropriate rhythm	• Practice meeting the rising ball with the hand, letting it lift the hand and then pressing it back down.
Poor body control		
Dribbler off balance or unable to move effectively	• Forcing one step for each dribble	• Vary the steps taken between bounces; vary the speed of the walk and run while dribbling.
	• Failure to keep the weight forward	• Flex (bend) the knees and lean the body slightly forward.
	• Failure to use the free hand for balance and ball protection	• Keep the free arm bent and slightly out to the side.
Poor body position		
Ball stolen by opponent	• Failure to keep the head up and maintain focus on the action of the other players	• Try to use the peripheral vision to see what is occurring around you.
	• Inability to dribble with both hands	• Practice with each hand.
Stiff or tense position	• Inability to change speeds and directions while dribbling	• Spread fingers out on ball, absorb force as ball comes up, and direct it downward with a push; select a spot on the floor and practice pushing the ball toward that spot.
Too high		
	• Failure to flex (bend) the knees slightly	• Maintain the body in a slightly crouched position to facilitate rapid movement.
	• Too much force	• Push the ball; absorb the upward momentum by bending the wrist back as the ball comes up to the hand.
Too low		
	• Crouching too low	• Straighten the legs until the knees are slightly bent and the trunk is almost erect.
	• Too little force production on the ball	• Push the ball downward using the hand and forearm.

(Cont.)

JUMPING

Error	Causes	Corrections
Inadequate height		
Failure to secure rebounds or high throws	• Either not enough or too much preparatory flexion in the lower body	• Flex more at the knees, ankles, and hips *or* flex less if crouch is too deep. Preparatory position should *not* go beyond the normal sitting position for a stationary jump and less if the jump is preceded by a run.
	• Failure to extend the lower body rapidly	• Press hard against the floor and extend the body quickly.
	• Inappropriate utilization of the arms	• Start with the arms down and swing them vigorously upward.
	• Failure to project the total body upward in a jump preceded by a run	• Plant one or both feet ahead of the body's center of gravity when moving, lean backward slightly, and bend the knees to convert forward momentum to upward movement.
	• Inappropriate timing	• Jump so that the ball can be contacted at the highest point possible; practice as much as possible in varying rebounding situations.
Hard landings		
	• Inadequate base-of-support width	• Land on both feet with feet apart.
	• Weight *not* equally distributed over both feet	• Get both feet under the body's center as it descends.
	• Inadequate force absorption due to a failure to control speed reduction downward	• Extend legs and feet toward the floor while in the air; absorb impact by flexing slowly at the ankles, knees, and hips.

SHOOTING (GENERAL)

Error	Causes	Corrections
Inaccurate		
Ball goes too far to right or left	• Lack of control or balance before shooting	• Be sure the body is balanced before attempting a shot; widen the stance.
	• Inadequate or lack of focus and concentration on the specific target	• Look at a specific spot on the backboard or rim while shooting
Ball falls short of target	• Insufficient arm and wrist strength to project the ball	• Strengthen the arms and shoulders through exercising; move shooters closer to the basket; bend at the ankles, knees, and hips and use the entire body to project the ball.
	• Inappropriate range of motion in the arm	• Draw the ball close to the body before starting the shot; increase the backswing (preparatory movements).

Error	Causes	Corrections
Inaccurate		
Ball goes too far to right or left	• Insufficient arc on the ball	• Aim higher; push the ball up, not out.
	• Failure to utilize the backboard	• Aim for the backboard when shooting from an angle to the side of the basket; when the ball hits the backboard, it is slowed down and more apt to drop into the basket.
Ball spins	• Inappropriate use of spin	• Keep the fingers behind the ball and avoid having the hand slide off the side of the ball.
Lack of control		
	• Failure to use the nonshooting hand to steady and guide the ball prior to release	• Keep both hands on the ball as long as possible, at least until the one-handed shot is under way. Hold the ball with the fingers and the thumb, *not* against palm.

TWO-HANDED SET SHOT

Error	Causes	Corrections
Inaccurate		
Ball goes too far to left or right	• Failure to push evenly with both hands	• Hold the ball in front of the body with both hands behind the ball; push with both hands.
Ball goes too low	• Starting the release too early when the ball is too low	• Push the ball upward rather than out; keep the ball in the fingers and do not let it rest against the palm.
Weak		
Ball falls short of target	• Failure to use sequential extension (straightening) of the knees and elbows	• Crouch slightly and straighten the legs, hips, and arms sequentially.

ONE-HANDED SET (PUSH) SHOT

Error	Causes	Corrections
Inaccurate		
Ball goes too far to left or right	• Thumb and index finger do *not* form a V on the ball	• Move the shooting hand behind the ball until the V is properly positioned.
	• Index finger *not* in line with forearm and elbow	• Line up the index finger behind the ball.
	• Upper arm *not* parallel to the floor	• Keep the elbow up and out in front of the body; the forearm folds down on top of the upper arm.

(Cont.)

ONE-HANDED SET (PUSH) SHOT (Continued)

Error	*Causes*	*Corrections*
Inaccurate		
Ball goes too far to left or right	• Failure to use nonshooting hand properly	• Place the nonshooting hand slightly to the side and under the ball until the shot begins.
	• Head *not* held steady during the shot	• Focus the eyes on the basket and hold the head still.
Weak		
Ball falls short	• Incorrect foot forward	• Place the foot on the same side as the shooting hand in a forward position.
	• Failure to hold the ball at least as high as the shoulder before beginning the push	• Move the ball to a position just above the shoulder; move the upper arm parallel to the ground under the ball.

LAY-UP SHOT

Error	*Causes*	*Corrections*
Inaccurate		
Shooter in wrong position relative to basket	• Poor angle of approach	• Approach basket from a 45° angle whenever possible.
	• Excessive forward motion and too little upward motion	• Shorten the takeoff step; plant takeoff foot in front of the body to help convert the forward momentum to upward momentum; lift the knee on the shooting side vigorously.
	• Jumping off the wrong foot	• The takeoff foot should be the one opposite the shooting hand to improve balance and maximize reach.
Shooter in correct position but ball not directed toward appropriate target	• Hitting too low or too much in the center of the board	• Focus on a spot on the backboard about a foot above and a few inches to the near side of the basket.
	• Using two hands to lay the ball against the backboard	• Spread the fingers around the ball and control it with one hand.
	• Releasing the ball too soon	• Reach up as far as possible while keeping contact with the ball.
	• Putting excessive spin on the ball	• Place the hand directly behind (or under) the ball; do not allow the hand to slide around to the side of the ball.
	• Removing the nonshooting hand too soon	• Keep the nonshooting hand on the ball to help control it until the ball is raised above the head.

Error	Causes	Corrections
Lack of control		
Ball thrown wildly	• Ball hitting the backboard too hard	• Do not push the ball against backboard if momentum is great; place hand under the ball and "lay" it up.
Ball falls from shooting hand	• Holding the ball too loosely on takeoff	• Keep both hands on the ball until ball is lifted above the head; spread the fingers under or behind the ball and push it.

JUMP SHOT

Error	Causes	Corrections
Inaccurate		
Ball falls short of target	• Improper elbow positioning	• Lift the elbow to about shoulder level as the shot begins; keep the elbow in front of the shoulder and in line with the intended ball path.
	• *Not* utilizing backspin on the ball	• Flex the wrist strongly and let the ball roll off the fingertips.
	• Failure to use pronation (turning palm outward) on the follow-through	• Push the ball strongly with the thumb and index finger; turn the hand so the palm is turned slightly outward after the ball leaves the fingers.
	• Failure to support the ball with the nonshooting hand	• Keep the nonshooting hand under and slightly to the side of the ball until the shot is under way.
	• Forcing the shot when being guarded too closely	• Wait to get balanced before initiating the shot; do not rush the shot.
Ball fails to hit target	• Failure to take the nonshooting hand from the ball prior to releasing the shot	• Drop the nonshooting hand from the ball as the shooting arm is extending toward the target.
	• Failure to hit target area (See also "Faulty foot position")	• Focus on the target; arch the ball; extend the arm and fingers directly toward the target.
Shot blocked	• *Not* releasing the ball just prior to or at the apex of the jump	• Hold the ball longer; wait until after the jump is begun to extend the arm with the shot.
Lack of body control		
	• Faulty foot position	• Point both feet toward the target; place the feet slightly apart with the foot on the side of the shooting arm forward.
	• Excessive trunk rotation	• Draw the shoulder of the shooting arm back slightly prior to the shot but allow no major rotation (twist) of the body.

(Cont.)

HOOK SHOT

(See Hook Pass)

GUARDING

Error	*Causes*	*Corrections*
Losing the opponent		
Poor stance	• Improper stance	• Keep the body upright with the knees slightly bent and the feet at least shoulder-width apart.
	• Failure to keep the head up and watch the opponent	• Keep the head up and watch the opponent's waist; the offensive player may fake with the head, arms, feet, or ball.
	• Failure to use the appropriate arm position	• Extend both arms out from the body; when guarding a player near the basket, keep one arm up to prevent a shot; otherwise, extend both arms out to the sides.
Dribbler gets around the defender	• Inappropriate judgments as to the distance to maintain from the opponent	• Maintain a usual distance of 2 to 3 ft when guarding an opponent; move closer only when the opponent is preparing to shoot or has completed a dribble.
Lack of body control		
	• Crossing the feet	• Use small shuffling or sliding steps.
	• Inability to make quick body movements	• Bend knees slightly and keep weight equally distributed over both feet; take small steps.

Chapter 6
Field Hockey

There is evidence of games similar to hockey being played in ancient times by many nations. The Greeks left pictures in friezes of players who appear to be playing hockey. Many centuries later, the French were playing a similar game called *hoquet*. The games of *hurley* (Ireland), *shinty* (Scotland), *bandy* (Wales), and *hackie* (London) were all field games that resembled modern field hockey.

Until the latter part of the 19th century, field hockey was played only by men. Although India and Pakistan dominated international play for many years, interest in the game has spread throughout Europe, Australia, and New Zealand. Men's field hockey has never developed into a popular sport in the United States.

English women began to have organized hockey teams at Oxford and Cambridge Universities in 1885. In 1895, the All England Women's Hockey Association was founded. This group has been a leader in the promotion of women's hockey throughout the world.

American women's field hockey recognized Constance M.K. Applebee of the British College of Physical Education as giving the primary impetus to the sport in the United States. She demonstrated the game at the Harvard summer school in 1901 and subsequently was invited to teach it to students at several eastern women's colleges, where it was accepted with enthusiasm. Shortly thereafter, hockey clubs for adult women were organized in the Philadelphia area. The sport soon spread throughout the East and the Midwest and later to the West.

The United States Field Hockey Association was formed in 1922 and the International Federation of Women's Hockey Associations in 1927. Since then, periodic international tournaments have been held, with the United States participating. Men's field hockey has been an Olympic sport since 1908, and women's field hockey became an Olympic sport in 1980. Currently, many hockey clubs provide nonschool competition throughout the United States. Most of these clubs are primarily for women competitors.

Field hockey has been an important part of women's intercollegiate sports programs in some areas (especially the East) since the 1960s. The Association of Intercollegiate Athletics for Women organized the first regional and national championships in 1975. These continue under the auspices of the National Collegiate Athletic Association (NCAA). Interscholastic and high school intramural field hockey flourish in some areas of the country.

Success in field hockey requires mastery of skills that are dissimilar to those of other major team sports. This makes it a particularly good coeducational activity because all players begin at the same skill level. Boys do not have the advantage of practicing the stickhandling skills outside of school as they often do with skills for more common sports like softball, football, and basketball.

Purposes and Values

Field hockey is a sport that requires teamwork and a variety of skills. It is a good sport to introduce in seventh or eighth grade and to continue through the curriculum for 3 or 4 years. The skills cannot usually be mastered in one season, so field hockey can remain a challenging activity for some time.

The field formations and general strategies are similar to those used in soccer. Therefore, it is recommended that soccer be introduced first so that players will be familiar with the basic format and will be able to concentrate more on the specific skills needed to move the ball downfield and score goals.

Field hockey is an excellent activity to improve cardiovascular fitness. The actual play periods should be short at the start of the unit unless players are already in good condition. An exercise or fitness unit (or soccer) would be a suitable lead-in activity to prepare players for this sport.

In addition to gross locomotor skills, field hockey promotes the development of (a) fine motor skills such as striking and manipulating an object (the stick and ball), (b) agility, (c) body control, (d) eye-hand coordination, and (e) upper-body strength.

The player who develops finesse and good stickwork can outplay the person who has only strength and power. This makes field hockey an excellent coeducational sport. Further, boys are not usually exposed to the skills outside of school and have not had a head start on mastering the basics. Boys in high school usually are stronger and may run faster than girls of the same age, but agile girls can be competitive in field hockey.

The Game

Field hockey is a game comprised of two teams of 11 players each. A team attempts to score *goals* at the end of the field that the opponents protect while preventing goals at the opposite end that they protect. The team that legally hits the ball into the opponents' *goal cage* more often wins the game. One point is scored for each goal whether scored during regular play or on a *penalty shot*. Official games are generally played in two 35-min halves, although for younger or novice players the time may be shortened. There is no provision for time-outs during play except in the case of injuries. Games that end in ties are not extended into overtime play except certain tournament situations.

At the start of each game, all players must be on their own halves of the playing field. The ball is played by hitting it with the flat side of the field hockey stick. A player must not advance the ball with the feet, the hands, or any part of the body; otherwise, an *advancing* foul is committed. Goalkeepers, however, may kick the ball or allow it to deflect off the body. Players may dribble the ball with their sticks or pass the ball in an effort to get inside the *striking*, or *shooting circle* (a semicircular area in front of the goal). Once inside the circle, players may shoot for a goal using any legal stroke. It should be noted that NCAA rules allow goals to be made from anywhere on the field. Teams are divided into offensive players *(forwards)*, defensive players *(backs)*, *goalkeepers*, and those who back up the offensive players and also help on defense *(links*, *halfbacks*, or as in soccer, *midfielders*).

Playing Area

The playing area is a marked grass or artificial turf field 100 by 60 yd (Figure 6.1). The striking circles delineate the area from which goals may be scored. Goal cages 4 yd long, 7 ft high, and 3 to 4 ft deep are centered at each end of the field. Nets should be attached to the cages to catch the balls that enter. It is feasible for teaching purposes to construct a 2-in. wooden or a 3-in. pipe

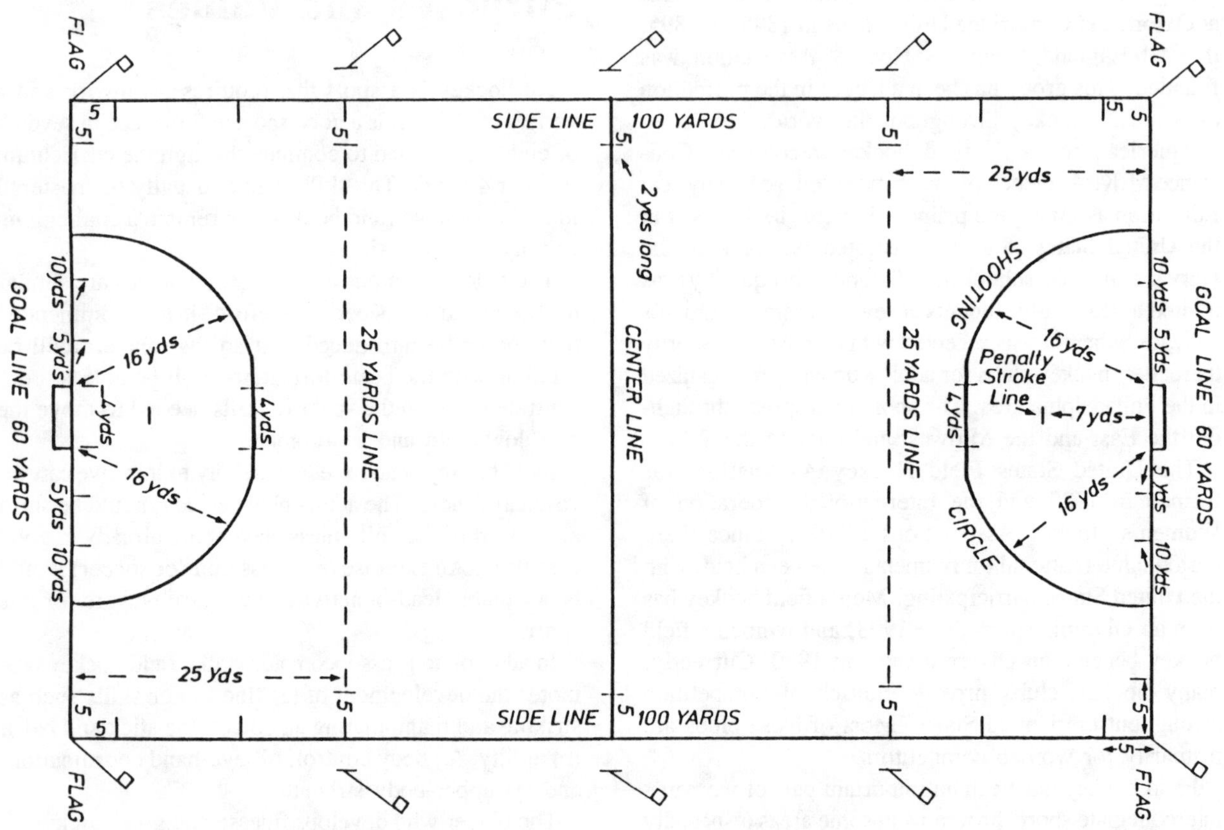

Figure 6.1. Field hockey field with markings

frame to use as goals. For goals made of pipes, slightly larger pipes may be embedded in the ground and the goal frames inserted into these sleeves during the hockey season and removed later. The sleeves should be sunk below the ground surface and capped when not in use to preserve them for future use and to avoid creating a safety hazard if the area will be used for other purposes.

Equipment

The following is a description of the equipment necessary for field hockey. Standards for the equipment and recommendations on equipment use are also included.

Sticks

Field hockey sticks are made with one side of the *blade* flat (*stick face*) and the other side rounded. All sticks are flat on the left side and rounded on the right. They are made of wood but may have plastic inserts as long as these fit into the wood. The minimum weight of the stick is 12 oz. The maximum weight for women is 23 oz and for men 28 oz. No part of the stick may be larger than 2 in. in diameter. Sticks vary in length from about 32 to 40 in. The length of the stick depends on the height of the player; the stick should come about to the hips of the user. Sticks may be cut down for small children to use. There must be no splinters or sharp corners on the stick. Rubber or terry-cloth handle covers are desirable. There should be enough sticks so that each person has an appropriately sized stick to use in class.

Balls

Balls are between 5-1/2 and 5-3/4 oz and are covered with white leather or plastic. The circumference is between 8-13/16 and 9-1/4 in. The Chingford plastic ball is recommended because it is accepted for tournament play and is more durable and less expensive than leather. For class use, it is desirable to have one ball for every two persons, but one ball for every five or six persons is adequate. Hockey balls are generally white, although red or orange ones are appropriate for play on snow-covered fields or to distinguish one team's equipment from another's.

Footgear

Because field hockey is played in all kinds of weather, it is advisable to wear special field hockey shoes. These are made of canvas or leather uppers with rubber-cleated soles. Turf shoes are permitted in some areas. Metal cleats or those used in football shoes should not be permitted. *Shin guards* are available to use in field hockey and soccer and are highly recommended for beginners and young players, as they help prevent painful shin bumps. They are generally made of fabric and have bamboo or firm plastic inserts that strap around the lower leg and protect it against impact with the ball or the stick. Molded plastic forms that fit against the shin inside knee socks also provide good protection.

Goalkeeper's Equipment

Goalkeepers should wear gloves, *goalie pads* (padding that covers the front of the legs), and special shoes. Shoe pads may be worn over regular field hockey shoes if necessary. This is not as satisfactory as having the special shoes, but, for class use, having interchangeable pads is more practical. Masks similar to those used in ice hockey or softball may be worn, especially if the players tend to shoot high shots at the goal. Chest protectors similar to those used in softball may also be worn if desired.

Pinnies

Pinnies or vests are useful for game play to distinguish one team from the other. They may also be used to distinguish forwards from backs when teaching strategy and field coverage.

—— Suggestions for Coeducational Play ——

Distributing players of varying skills levels on each team makes competition more equitable when the time comes for game play. As with other team sports, forming teams early can encourage players to help one another learn as strengthening all teammates will benefit the team.

Minimum criteria for performing basic skills and requiring that all team members achieve the minimum performance level can be established before the team is permitted to move into intermediate skills or game play. Minimum criteria might include (a) passing a ball successfully to a target or a person four out of five times, (b) fielding a passed or driven ball three out of five times without fouling, (c) dribbling a ball around a zigzag or figure 8 course within a prescribed time (the time would depend on the course chosen), and (d) performing a successful straight tackle or *left lunge tackle* three out of five times without hitting or pushing the opponent. The distances, speed of the ball, or time involved will vary with the skill levels of most of the participants. Seventh graders just starting field hockey might have to pass the ball to a target 15 ft away, whereas tenth graders might shoot at a moving target 20 to 25 ft away. The intermediate groups could be given more challenging performance minimums, such as scooping the ball at a target, performing successful dodges, and using a more difficult tackle.

The 5-3-2-1 defensive pattern discussed later in this chapter is recommended for use when teams have equal numbers of skilled and less skilled players. This system calls for five forwards and five backs (three halfbacks and two *fullbacks*) and a goalkeeper. The five backs of one team *mark*, or guard, the five forwards of the other team. The defensive players can evaluate the skills of the opposing forwards and determine who will be responsible for which player. Thus, the more skilled forwards can be covered by the more competent backs. This would function like the 1-on-1 defense in basketball.

Often in coeducational play, care must be taken to provide opportunities for all to participate. One suggestion for accomplishing this is to rotate positions frequently so that the more aggressive do not dominate play. Move the center players to the wing positions or the forwards to the defensive positions and vice versa. It might be necessary to have the girls on a team take all the forward positions for a short period and the boys the back positions. After 5 or 10 min the boys become the forwards and the girls the backs. The opposing team may have girls as backs against a team's girl forwards and boys as forwards against the opposing boy backs. The goalkeeper should also be changed frequently in class play. Too often the goalkeeper position is taken by a youngster who wants to do nothing or by two students who want to stand and talk. It is an important position and should be covered by an attentive, active player. Alternating a male and a female as the goalkeeper may enhance play.

Dividing the field into four or five equal and parallel sections with lines running from end to end is another way to spread out play. Students are assigned to an area and may not leave it. They may move from one end of the field to the other as in regular play, but not laterally out of their assigned segments of the field. This forces ball passing and makes each defender responsible for one specific person (to *cover* the one in his or her area). If the main problem is that the attackers crowd around the ball and chase it all over the field, the forwards may be the only ones assigned to designated areas. The defenders can then use the 1-on-1 type of defense as described later in this chapter.

There are a few rules that may be used to implement coeducational play. These are not recommended unless other means are ineffective for equalizing play opportunities.

- At least one member of each gender must play he ball before a shot on goal may be made.
- Girls must take all *free hits*, *push-ins*, and *corner hits*.
- Girls must field (be the ones who receive) all free hits, push-ins, and corner hits.
- Boys may not drive the ball if they are significantly larger or stronger than the females and are unable or unwilling to exhibit self-control.
- A player who commits a *dangerous hit* into an opponent is penalized by being put out of the game; perhaps by using a penalty box similar to that used in ice hockey. For example, you could impose a 2-min suspension for the first foul, a 5-min suspension for the second foul; and permanent ejection if a third *dangerous hit* or unsafe use of the stick occurs. The team of a suspended player must play with 10 (or 1 less) players. If 2 are suspended, the team must continue with 2 less players. Substitutes for suspended players are not allowed, although they are allowed for ejected players.

Teaching Progressions

Skills in this chapter are grouped according to their fundamental movement relationships to one another and to commonality of purpose for ease of understanding and analyzing. This does not imply that the skills should be presented to players in that order.

Many of the field skills are difficult to master because they are unique and are rarely learned in casual sports play outside of school. Therefore, practice of the beginning skills may have to continue for a longer period of time. Intermediate players may need to continue to practice some basic skills, and even more advanced players should work to refine these skills.

Progressions for Beginning Players

I. Holding the stick

II. Dribbling
   A. Push
   B. Tap

III. Passing
   A. Push
   B. Drive
   C. Scoop (may be held until the intermediate level)

IV. Fielding

V. Tackling
   A. Straight
   B. Left lunge

VI. Goalkeeping
   A. Stance
   B. Fielding
   C. Kick

VII. Bully

VIII. Game play

Additional Skills for Intermediate Players

I. Scoop pass

II. Circular tackle

III. Plays for special situations

Additional Skills of Advanced Players

I. Flick pass

II. Jab tackle

III. Advanced strategies and field-coverage variations

Techniques and Practice

Carrying the Stick

Players must cover large distances on the field hockey playing area. Therefore, running continuously is essential to maintain play. Players must manipulate their implements (sticks) as they run. It is important to carry the stick in such a way that it does not interfere with running yet is usable at any moment.

The left hand is at the top of the stick handle with the right hand 2 in. below the left. The arms are fairly extended and the left arm is slightly diagonal across the body. The stick is carried with the head of the club down and the face of the club forward. This helps the player use the stick quickly.

Common Movement Problems and Suggestions

The following are common movement problems experienced when carrying the field hockey stick. Instructional suggestions are also included.

- Novice players tend to let the stick restrict the movement of the run. The natural rhythm of running must be adhered to. The stick becomes a part of the body and therefore must swing freely while running. Carrying the stick during preliminary running warm-ups is beneficial.
- Some players may appear awkward when making the transition from carrying the stick to lowering and positioning it for striking. Instructors should incorporate practice of striking the ball while on the run.
- The *stick head* should not be held high in the air because this delays movement to the ball and can be hazardous to other players and may result in a *high sticking* penalty

Dribbling

The *dribble* is one of the key skills in field hockey. Its effective use allows a player to control the ball while moving toward the goal or around opponents. Beginners will need to slide the right hand down the stick shaft to improve control. As skill improves and wrists become stronger, dribblers should be encouraged to hold the hands closer to the top of the stick. This allows a more erect posture (the head is held up) as well as a better view of teammates and opponents.

The push type of dribble is used on smooth surfaces such as gymnasium floors and artificial turf. The ball is pushed along by the stick and kept very close to the front right of the dribbler's right foot.

The tap dribble is used on uneven surfaces, such as most hockey fields, and consists of a series of short taps given to hit the ball 1 or 2 ft in front of the dribbler. It is important to keep the ball ahead and to the right of the feet to avoid overrunning or stepping on it. When the dribbler runs fast, the ball is tapped farther in front. This is called a *loose dribble*. It may also be used when there are no opponents near the dribbler.

The stick is held in front and on the striking side of the body (Figure 6.2). The top of the stick is inclined forward with the blade facing forward. The stick is held with the left hand at the top of the handle and with the right hand at the appropriate distance below the top hand. As mentioned previously, the position of the right hand is dependent on the strength and ability level of the player. The strong, experienced player has the hands 1 to 2 in. apart; the weaker, inexperienced player positions them farther apart. The left wrist is very flexed and leads the action. The palm of the right hand faces the direction of the dribble.

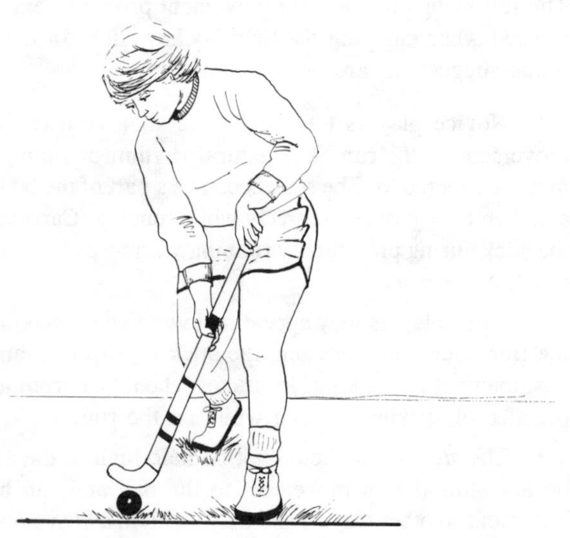

Figure 6.2. Dribbling position with stick

The left elbow is held away from the body and is in front of the action. The trunk is inclined forward or slightly flexed at the hip. The ball is carried (pushed or tapped) directly in front of the right foot.

A series of taps (strikes) or pushes impart force to the ball. The right hand moves forward (elbow extension) as the left hand moves rearward (wrist flexion). The stick acts as a lever with two points of force application. The ball should be struck directly through its center of gravity in the intended direction. The follow-through is a short continuation of the arm motion.

Common Movement Problems and Suggestions

The following are common movement problems in the dribble. Instructional suggestions are also presented.

- The most common problem is the lack of ball control. Generally, players do not keep the ball close and directly in front of the striking side. This can be caused by improper force application to the ball. Practice in a variety of situations that simulate game-pressure situations would be helpful.
- Control of the ball is also possible through the proper execution of wrist flexion in the movement. Players feel awkward with this movement at first but should be encouraged to continue practicing the appropriate technique.
- Players often lose awareness of opponents, teammates, or the ball due to a failure to look up occasionally while dribbling. Emphasize looking up occasionally for the other players.

Practice Drills

The following are practice drills for dribbling. Individual and group drills are presented.

Individual Drills. Individual practice is most efficient if an unlimited amount of equipment and space is available. The following are individual practice drills.

1.0. Each player practices dribbling back and forth between sidelines or around the perimeter of the field. Begin with a walking pace, increase to a slow jog, and work up to a run if possible. Emphasize control rather than speed with beginners.

2.0. A follow-the-leader type game may be played with all dribblers in line behind the instructor or a selected player. The latter is best because the instructor can then observe and critique.

Players can be encourage to practice this skill on their own before class or during recreation time. Obstacles can be added to the dribbling path to increase difficulty.

Group Drills. The following are group drills for dribbling and should be used when equipment or space is limited.

1.0. Shuttle formation (Figure 4.8). Columns of individuals are placed about 30 ft apart. The leader of Column 1 dribbles slowly to Column 2 and leaves the ball for that leader before going to the end of that column. The leader of Column 2 dribbles back and gives the ball to the second person in Column 1 before going to end of Column 1. This continues sequentially until all players have participated. As skill improves, this can be used as a relay.

2.0. Single-Column Formation (Figure 4.2). Columns of individuals are lined up at one end of the gymnasium or at the sidelines of the field. The first person in each line dribbles to a specified line or marker (such as a cone), stops, dribbles back, gives the ball to the next person, and goes to the end of the line. The second person then repeats the drill. When using this drill in a gymnasium, encourage control by prohibiting players from bouncing the ball off the wall. Specify that the players must stop and reverse the dribble before the ball touches the wall. Do not allow the ball to be fielded with the rounded side of the stick. This is illegal. The following variations may be used and can be used as a relay after a moderate level of skill is mastered.

2.1. Place a cone, chair, or player at the turning point and have the players dribble around the object before returning to the start.

2.2. Add three or four more obstacles. Cones, chairs, Indian clubs, or other players may be used. Players must dribble in and out past the obstacles, around the last one, and back to start. Begin by having the players circle the last obstacle in a counterclockwise pattern. For example, if there is an even number of obstacles, pass the first one on the left, the second on the right, and continue in this alternate manner. If an uneven number, pass the first one on the right, the second on the left, and continue in this manner. The counterclockwise turn is easier than a clockwise one.

2.3. Using the obstacle dribble, have players circle the last obstacle in a clockwise pattern. This will be more difficult and require faster footwork.

3.0. Single-Column Formation (Figure 4.2). Several columns of individuals are lined up at one side of the field or one end of a gymnasium. Lines are drawn or marked with cones about 20, 30, and 40 ft from the starting line. These may be marked outdoors by using ropes or cones or by adjusting to the 10-yd markers on a football field. The first player in each column dribbles to the first line, legally stops the ball, dribbles back to the start, reverses and dribbles to the second line and back, etc. That player then goes to the end of the column, and the next player repeats the drill. Two lines instead of three may be designated. This gives the dribbler practice in control, stopping the ball legally, and changing direction. This drill may be used as a relay for intermediate players.

4.0. Single-Column Formation (Figure 4.2). The leader of each column dribbles slowly down the field and back, using one of the zigzag patterns shown in Figure 6.3. The ball is given to the next player, and the dribbler goes to the end of the column. In Pattern A, the ball is dribbled in a zigzag path back and forth. In Pattern B, the ball is dribbled straight ahead and then pushed or pulled directly to the side as if to avoid an opponent. In Pattern C, the dribble is done straight ahead and is interspersed with a series of harder taps or pushes all to one side. Pattern C can be angled either to the right or to the left. Patterns B and C require very agile use of the stick because only the flat surface of the stick is used in hitting the ball.

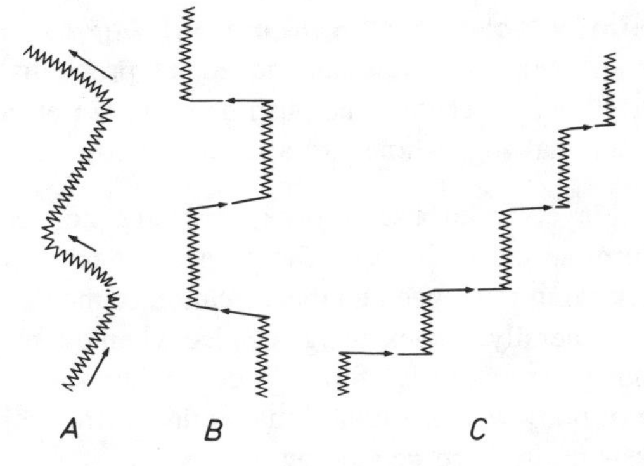

Figure 6.3. Dribbling patterns for practice

In all the drills described, players can share sticks if there are not enough for everyone. As a player goes to the end of a line, that player gives the stick to the next player who needs one. This is far from ideal, however, because it does not permit players to select appropriately sized sticks. Other dribbling practice drills are presented later in this chapter.

Passing and Fielding

Passing involves the transferring of the ball between players. The pass promotes movement of the ball toward the goal. This is done more efficiently by the pass than by the dribble. The pass is a faster means to move the ball and speeds up play. Fielding is the receiving or controlling of the ball once it has been passed to the player. Fielding involves the receiving of force (from the ball) in order to control the ball prior to executing the next movement.

Push

The *push* is a quick and accurate movement that is used for passing and shooting and for expediting a play quickly.

The stick is held with the left hand on top of the stick. The right hand is 3 to 4 in. below the other hand. The top of the stick is inclined forward in the direction of the pass or shot and the blade is in contact with the ball. The forward foot is the foot on the striking side. The trunk is flexed or inclined slightly forward. The back of the left hand and the palm of the right hand face the direction of the hit.

The stick is placed on the ground behind the ball. There is no backswing. Force is applied to the ball by pulling back with the left hand (wrist flexion) and pushing forward with the right hand (elbow extension). The player steps into the push to add to the force application. The stick follows through in the intended ball direction.

Common Movement Problems and Suggestions. The following are common movement problems associated with executing the push pass or shot at goal. Instructional suggestions are also presented.

- Players who use a backswing are no longer performing the push pass. The purpose of not having a backswing is to speed up the execution of the pass or shot. Generally, a backswing is added when the player cannot generate enough force. The stepping action and shift of body weight forward makes up for the lack of backswing in force generation.

- Common execution errors occur in the arm action of the push. The wrist action of the left hand is important in the force production. The wrist action should be a rapid flexion or snapping. The farther apart the hands on the stick, the more mechanical advantage is achieved in the lever (stick).

- Players sometimes position themselves to the ball in a way that makes the movement awkward. When a player pushes to the right, the ball should be outside the right foot, and the toes pointed straight ahead; the body then twists (turns) to the right. When a player executes a backward push, the ball should be behind the right foot, and the toes pointed straight ahead; the body then twists (turns) to the right.

Drive

The *drive* is effective for passing or shooting situations in which a long, hard hit is necessary. It is effective as a pass from the *wing* or the back. The drive is used to clear the ball away from the goal, as a corner hit, or as a free hit. This type of long, hard hit is very effective for shooting.

The player assumes a side-straddle stance with the ball approximately 8 in. in front of the body and nearer to the left foot than to the right foot (Figure 6.4). The stick is held in front of the body at right angles to the ground with the blade surface facing toward the left foot. The left hand is at the top of the handle and the right hand directly below it. The trunk is inclined slightly forward with the shoulders and toes pointing forward.

The stick is drawn backward in line with the intended path of the drive by flexion of the left wrist and hyperextension (bending backward) of the right wrist. The right elbow is flexed and held out from the body to keep the stick from rising dangerously high in the air.

The force-production phase is initiated from a quick backswing by a forward swinging of the stick. This movement is accompanied by a forward stepping action,

Figure 6.4. Right drive

which also causes a forward shift of the body weight. The ball is contacted through the center and behind the ball. The stick is at a right angle to the ground and the arms fully extended at the moment of impact. The wrists snap at ball impact. The snap is created by left-wrist hyperextension and right-wrist flexion simultaneously. The arms and stick follow through by continuing the swing in the intended ball direction.

Common Movement Problems and Suggestions. The following are common movement problems encountered during the drive. Instruction suggestions are also included.

- The most common problem is insufficient force application on the ball. The drive is a power stroke and requires a large magnitude of force application. A weak drive is generally caused by not positioning the hands close together at the top of the stick for the longest lever possible, not swinging through a large range of motion as fast as possible, or not stepping forward into the stroke.
- Striking the ball incorrectly or missing it totally is generally due do not keeping the eyes focused on the ball. Emphasize concentration and continued focus on the ball.
- Keeping the shoulder square and toes forward can prevent the player from creating an *obstruction foul*.

Scoop

The *scoop* is effective as a short pass or a close shot at goal. It is used to dodge over an opponent's stick or to move the ball over rough terrain on the field. The scoop generally follows the dribbling movement.

The player assumes a forward-stride stance with the right foot forward (Figure 6.5). The body weight is forward over the right foot. The ball is positioned about 2 ft in front of and slightly to the right of the right foot. The stick is held in front of the body at an *acute angle* to the ground. The blade of the stick is facing upward in this position. The left hand is at the top of the handle with the right hand slightly farther than midway down the handle. The trunk is extensively flexed or inclined forward.

The *toe* of the stick is placed under the ball. The player performs an upward and forward motion on the ball. The upward motion is created by a downward motion of the left hand and an upward pulling by the right hand. The forward motion is created by extension of the right elbow in a forward direction. The follow-through is a quick continuation of the motion already established by the upper body.

Common Movement Problems and Suggestions. The following are common movement problems associated with the execution of the scoop. Instructional suggestions are also included.

- Failure to lift the ball can be caused by improper placement of the stick blade under the ball or ineffective upward lifting action by the arms and hands.
- Beginners tend to lay the blade of the stick too flat on the scoop with the result that the ball rolls back over the stick.
- Emphasize to players that the scoop is a slow stroke that is low and easily anticipated due to the body positioning. Players should not use the scoop excessively.

Figure 6.5. Scoop

• The follow-through is low. A high follow-through can raise the ball too much. The low scoop is not as easy to intercept as is the high scoop.

• The scoop should first be learned with a stationary ball before using a moving ball.

Flick

The *flick* develops very naturally from the push pass but is considered an advanced skill due to the timing and wrist action required. The flick imparts spin on the ball that aids the player in deceiving the opponent. The flick is used for both passing and shooting.

The flick is executed identically to the push with the exception of the wrist action placed on the ball at contact. The right wrist rotates (pronates), which causes the stick-blade surface to turn over the ball and impart spin. This must be done very rapidly to impart sufficient spin. The blade of the stick turns from right to left over the ball. This causes the blade of the stick to be facing the ground at the conclusion of the stroke. The stick follows through in the intended ball direction.

Common Movement Problems and Suggestions. The following are common movement problems encountered during the flick. Instructional suggestions are also presented.

• The most common movement problem is the lack of wrist rotation at contact. When this occurs, the stroke looks identical to the push stroke, and the ball has no spin.

• When no spin is imparted to the ball but the wrist rotation occurs, the rotation must have occurred during the follow-through and not when the blade was in contact with the ball. Emphasize an earlier wrist rotation.

• A weak stroke will result if the ball is not contacted with the proper part of the stick. Be sure that the toe end of the stick is used.

• Inadequate force application to the ball may also be caused by a failure of weight transfer forward. This is important to force application because there is no backswing.

Fielding

The purpose of *fielding* is to stop a moving ball and then gain control of it. Fielding is imperative to successful team play. Failure to execute good fielding technique generally translates into losing possession of the ball. Every player on the team must be able to field the ball effectively.

A forward-stride stance with either foot forward is assumed. The left hand is at the top of the handle of the stick. The right hand is 6 to 8 in. below the left hand. The body weight is forward on the front foot. The trunk is slightly inclined forward, and the total body is in direct line with the approaching ball.

The stick is at a forward angle with the handle close to the body and the toe of the stick extended forward. The blade surface is facing the approaching ball. The player is reaching toward the ball when contact is made. The stick is retracted once the contact occurs. This is the force dissipation sometimes referred to as giving with the ball. There is no follow-through in this motion.

Common Movement Problems and Suggestions. The following are common problems encountered when executing fielding. Instructional suggestions are also presented.

• A missed ball is often the result of the player failing to watch the ball until it strikes the stick. Emphasize continued focus on the ball.

• When the ball rebounds off the stick, the player has not sufficiently retracted the stick to dissipate the force of the ball. Beginners should start with less forceful ball receiving until the skill is learned. Harder-driven balls can be received after learning the skill technique.

Practice Drills

Passing and fielding should be practiced together so that proper techniques can be used for both. Players should never be permitted to use their hands or feet to stop balls. This would allow them to develop poor skill patterns. The instructor or coach should also try to set a good example by using the hockey stick to pass and field the ball.

Goal shooting consists of passes or drives directed at the goal and can also be practice as specialized passing drills or in the combination drills described later.

Partner Drills. Paired practice is ideal for practicing passing and fielding. However, this requires a ball for every two players as well as sticks for all and a large space to provide safe distances between pairs.

1.0. Partners start 10 to 15 ft apart and push pass (or scoop) back and forth, fielding the ball with the flat side of the stick. As skills improve, players move farther apart to about 25 ft.

2.0. Partners can practice *triangular passes* by running side by side down the field dribbling and passing back and forth. They could use the triangular passing patterns and drills described for soccer in chapter 8.

Group Drills. These drills are suitable for practicing the short passes (push, scoop, and flick) and the drive as well as fielding. To practice the drive, the distance between players should be increased. The flick is considered an advanced skill that requires strong wrists and arms. The flick is not recommended for presentation or practice for the beginner. The push pass and fielding should be practiced first and the scoop added later when fielding a lofted ball is less hazardous.

1.0. Double-Line Formation (Figure 4.10). Lines are about 15 ft apart facing each other. Players pass back and forth down the lines while fielding the ball with sticks before each pass.

2.0 Circle Formation (Figure 4.13). Players pass back and forth across the circle.

3.0. Double-Column Formation (Figure 4.9). Columns of individuals are parallel about 12 ft apart and facing in opposite directions with right shoulders toward each other. Players from Column 1 do right push passes (or scoops) to players in Column 2, who return the ball with right push passes. Variation: Players face the opposite direction (left shoulder toward each other) and practice left passes.

4.0. Shuttle Formation (Figure 4.8). The player dribbles part of the way toward the other column and passes the ball to the next dribbler (see Group Drill 1.0, p. 104).

5.0. Double-Column Formation (Figure 4.9). Pairs of individuals in columns are lined up side by side about 12 ft apart at the center line of the hockey field, all facing the goal line. One individual in each pair of columns has a ball. The leaders of each pair of columns advance toward the goal line, dribbling and passing a ball back and forth. A shot at goal is taken when they get close to it. Individuals in one pair of columns could be placed in the center of the field and another pair halfway between the center and each sideline. Thus there would be six columns, and three pairs of players could start at the same time. Players who have completed a turn should return to their lines around the outside of the field to avoid interfering with the next group of players. The second group could begin as soon as the first three pairs have reached the 25-yd line. The balls will need to be returned quickly to the waiting players if there are only a few balls in use.

6.0. Passing-Shooting Drill. Three columns are positioned near a goal (Figure 6.6). The leader of Column 1 passes the ball to the leader of Column 2 (Pass a) who runs in, fields the ball, and shoots at the goal (Pass b). The leader of Column 3 fields the shot at goal and passes the ball back to Column 1 (Pass c). Each player goes to the end of the higher-numbered column (Player 3 goes to Column 1). If players are reasonably controlled, a second group of three columns may be established at the other side of the same shooting circle.

Dribbling, Passing, Fielding, and Shooting Drills. The following are dribbling, passing, fielding, and shooting drills. Combining skills helps create practice situations that simulate a game.

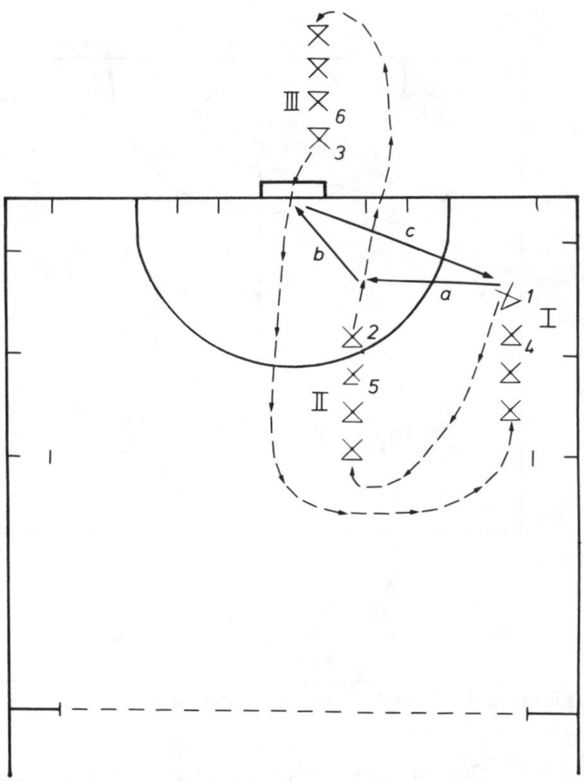

Figure 6.6. Passing and shooting drill

1.0. Column Formation. Individuals in three columns line up about 15 ft apart parallel to each other near the center line of the field (Figure 6.7). Each person in Column 1 has a ball. The first person in each line begins to move downfield, staying even with the others. Player X1 dribbles a short distance, then passes on a diagonal ahead of Player X2, who fields the ball, dribbles, and then passes to Player X3. Player X3 dribbles a short distance and passes on a diagonal back to Player X2, who repeats this procedure and passes to Player X1. This pattern continues until progressing to the opposite end of the field. Be sure the passes are slanted ahead of the runners so they will not have to stop or retreat. The second group may start downfield when the first group reaches the 25-yd line. As the players near the goal line, the one with the ball shoots for goal. Players return around the outside of the field to a different line (e.g., left to center, center to right, right to left). Variations include the following:

1.1. The same drill can be used to practice the dribble and drive by moving the columns farther apart (30 to 40 ft). Be sure that players change columns to practice both right and left drives.

1.2. Add two more columns so that the advancing line will consist of five players as in the traditional forward offensive formation.

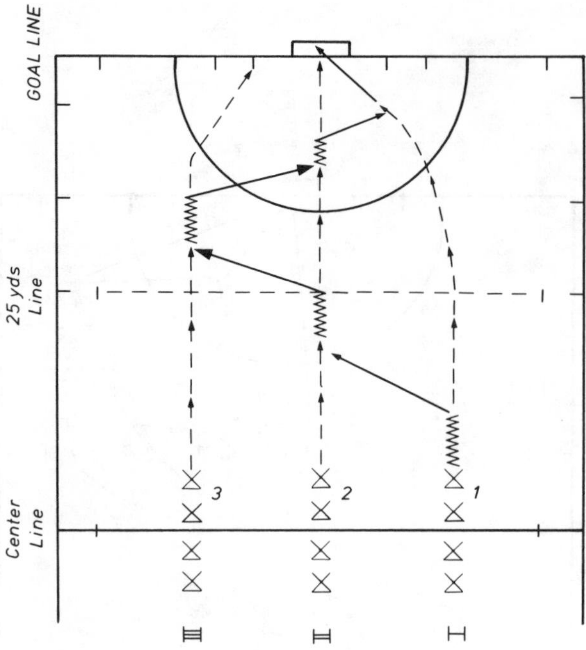

Figure 6.7. Dribble, pass, and shoot drill

1.3. Start at one end of the field and have attack lines move the entire length of the field. Each group starts as the previous line reaches the closer 25-yd line. Players should stay at the opposite end of the field and re-form the columns there. After everyone has completed the drill, repeat the same pattern back to the starting position.

2.0. Circle Formation (Figure 4.14). Six to eight players 6 to 8 ft apart are set up in a large circle with one ball for each circle. All players begin to run slowly in a counterclockwise pattern. The player with the ball dribbles a few feet and passes the ball to another person across the circle. Practice passing ahead of the intended receivers so they will not have to break stride or stop. The player receiving the ball dribbles one or two taps and passes to another in the circle. Variations include the following:

2.1. Call out the name of the intended receiver and practice getting the ball to that person.

2.2. Reverse the pattern to a clockwise run. This is more difficult because it requires a pass to the right and fielding a ball that is coming from the back right.

2.3. Enlarge the circle until players must use a medium or a long drive to pass the ball.

Tackling

Tackling in field hockey does not involve body contact in any way. Rather, it is a means of taking the ball from an opponent who is dribbling. Tackles are usually classified by the approach position. In all tackles, the tackler tries to block or hit the ball when it is not near the dribbler's stick. The more loose the dribble, the easier it is to tackle. The tackler generally tries to take the ball from the opponent and then gain control of the ball or hit it to a teammate.

Straight

The straight tackle is used when the dribbler is coming toward the tackler. The tackler approaches the dribbler and tries to interrupt the dribble or intercept a pass.

The stance is a forward-stride position with the body weight shifted forward toward the front foot. The stick is held perpendicular to the ground. The left hand is at the top of the handle and the right hand 3 to 4 in. below the left hand. The trunk is slightly inclined forward. The tackler is positioned slightly to the right and faces the opponent.

The stick is placed in front of the ball in order to block it. The player pushes into the ball rather than tapping or hitting it. The tackler tries to time the push to intercept the ball after it has left the dribbler's stick. Once the opponent has passed beyond the ball, the tackler proceeds downfield with the ball.

Common Movement Problems and Suggestions

The following are common movement problems when executing the straight tackle. Instructional suggestions are also presented.

- One common problem is when the tackler does not wait for the ball to come off the opponent's stick. Emphasize proper timing and maintaining focus on the ball.
- Beginners tend neither to stay to the right of the dribbler nor to block the ball aggressively. The player must firmly transfer the body weight into the block to block the ball firmly. A firm stance with the body weight forward will help the tackler maintain stick position.
- Players tend to want to hit the ball rather than block or stop it. Emphasize that the block gives more ball control than does a hit.
- The tackler should learn to make the tackle unexpectedly. The tackle should be taught through a progression that enhances the learning of the proper technique. The player should progress from a tackle on a slow dribble to a faster dribble and finally to a dribbler attempting to avoid the tackle.

Practice Drills. Paired practice is an efficient means of learning this skill when there is a lot of equipment.

One player dribbles toward a partner, who approaches and tries to tackle the ball and dribble it in the opposite direction. When one player passes the other, play is stopped; players turn to face each other, then repeat the drill. Each player should have a chance to dribble and tackle. The following are group practice drills.

1.0. Shuttle Formation (Figure 4.8). Columns of individuals are about 30 ft apart. The leader of one column dribbles slowly and loosely toward the leader of the other column, who approaches, performs the straight tackle to draw the ball to the left, and dribbles to the opposite line. The next player then dribbles out to be tackled. Players go to the end of the opposite column. The dribblers should be cooperative at first and allow the tackler to be successful. Variations include the following:

1.1. The dribbler uses a closer dribble but does not otherwise try to dodge the tackle.

1.2. The dribbler tries to avoid the tackle by changing speed or using a pull to the side (dodge).

1.3. Dodging practice may be added here (see the section on dodging).

2.0. Four-Column Shuttle Formation. Players are set up in four columns (Figure 6.8). Columns 1 and 2 are dribblers, and Columns 3 and 4 are tacklers. Players X1 and X2 advance toward Players X3 and X4, dribbling and passing back and forth. Players X3 and X4 approach and try to tackle or intercept a pass. Play stops when the ball passes behind either pair of players. The ball is returned to the next dribblers, and competitors go to the ends of opposite lines.

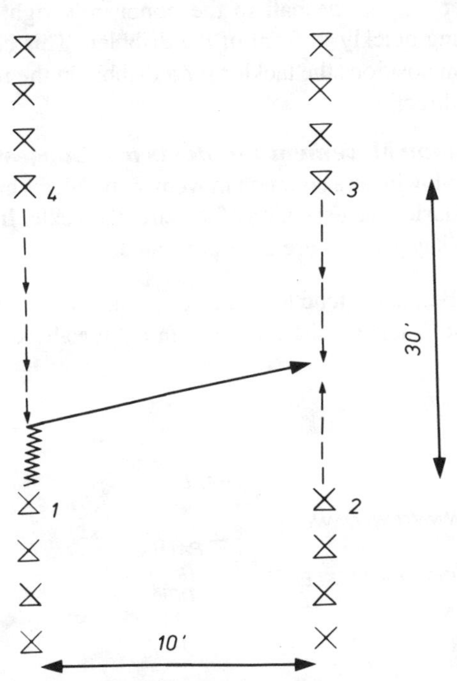

Figure 6.8. Straight tackle drill

3.0. Set up three columns of players as shown in Figure 6.7. Place three more columns of individuals opposite the first three near the goal line. These players will be tacklers. As the dribblers start downfield, the tacklers approach them and try to get the ball. Each tackler is responsible for the opposite dribbler.

Left Lunge

The *left lunge* tackle is used when the dribbler has passed the defensive player. The tackler is running in the same direction and is on the right, or *stick side*, of the dribbler. The lunge is done to the left to interrupt the dribble and cause the ball to be stopped or hit behind both runners.

The stick is carried parallel with the ground with the left hand at the top of the handle and the right hand slightly below the left. The tackler is positioned to the opponent's right.

The stick is extended to the ground and in front of the opponent's ball. The head of the stick travels in a diagonal toward the ground. This is accomplished by an extension of the right elbow. The left hand maintains a firm grip on the handle and helps guide the stick. A lunging step on the left foot occurs during the extension of the stick toward the ball. The ball is blocked by the face of the stick. The follow-through consists of a step on the right so that the tackler can reverse directions.

Less experienced players should be encouraged to keep both hands on the stick to ensure more control. More experienced players who can control the stick with one hand may remove the right hand after the lunge starts and gain more reach by extending the left arm fully.

Common Movement Problems and Suggestions. The following are common movement problems in executing the left lunge tackle. Instructional suggestions are also presented.

- Players tend not to lunge sufficiently and therefore do not place the stick ahead of the ball. Tacklers should practice lunging deep or reaching out to position the stick ahead of the ball.
- Beginners tend to raise the stick too high. Players should keep the stick low and fully extend at the elbow when reaching. This will enhance the possibilities for successful tackling.
- When tackling from behind, players should be careful not to trip their opponents. The overall timing of the skill is very important. The stick should contact the ball when the ball has moved forward off the opponent's stick.
- All players must master the left lunge tackle. It is frequently used by all players. A learning progression with and without the ball as well as slow to fast dribbling should be utilized.

Practice Drills. A mass practice is appropriate for introducing this skill. Players with sticks are dispersed on the field at least 6 ft away from one another. Each player selects a spot on the grass (or places a ball) about 4 ft ahead and 4 to 5 ft to the left of the left foot. The player takes one stride forward on the left foot, swings the stick across in front of the body, and lunges to place the face (flat side) of the stick in front of the selected spot as if blocking a ball. The tackle should be made at a full reach, after which the tackler reverses direction and practices dribbling the ball (imaginary or real) back the other way.

Working in pairs provides the maximum practice in a given period of time. One player dribbles, then the partner approaches from behind on the stick side and performs the left lunge. If successful, the tackler quickly turns around and dribbles back in the opposite direction. The partner then becomes the tackler and tries to regain possession of the ball with another tackle. The following group practice drills can be used to practice the left lunge when equipment or space is limited.

1.0. Double-Column Formation (Figure 4.9). Players in columns are lined up about 6 ft apart. The leader of the left column starts dribbling straight ahead. The first person in the right column runs parallel to the dribbler, executes the left lunge tackle, and returns the ball to the next dribbler. Players go to the end of the opposite column. Dribblers should cooperate and dribble loosely the first few times through the drill. As skill and timing improve, the dribbler should keep the ball closer to the stick and try to retain control. Variation: If the tackler is successful, the former dribbler immediately turns and tackles back. Designate a line about 30 ft from the starting line. The dribbler tries to get the ball over the established finish line; the tackler tries to get the ball back to the starting line. When either occurs, the trial ends, and the ball is given to the next dribbler. Be sure that two players do not monopolize play too long tackling and retackling. After 1 or 2 minutes, give the ball to the next two players in line.

2.0. Two Parallel Columns Facing Opposite Directions. The ball is placed ahead and to the left of the leader of Column 1 (Figure 6.9). Player X1 steps forward, does a left lunge to hit the ball behind, then turns around and dribbles the ball between the two columns. The heavy line indicates the path of the stick as the tackle is executed. Player X1 dribbles past Player X2, who tackles with a left lunge, reverses, and dribbles back between the two columns. Player X3 then tackles Player X2. This pattern continues until all players have participated. Players go to the ends of their own columns after completing a turn.

Circular

The circular tackle is used when attempting to take the ball from the dribbler who is on the right of the tackler and traveling in the same direction. It is an obstruction foul to interfere with the dribbler by reaching across in front and slowing or interrupting that player's running stride. Therefore, the tackler must get a step or two in front of the dribbler and make a circular turn (U-turn), trying to collect the ball as the turn is made, and then dribble it around the dribbler. The ball should remain between the two opponents. If the tackler pulls the ball inward and protects it with a shoulder, it is an obstruction foul, and the other team will be given possession of the ball.

The tackler is ahead of the opponent and to the left. The tackler can also execute this tackle by moving toward the opponent from the left and at a diagonal. The stick is positioned in the hands the same way it is in the dribble or push.

The stick is turned so its face is facing the ball. The tackler pushes the ball to the opponent's right while crossing quickly in front of the dribbler. This circular motion positions the tackler for a dribble in the reverse field direction.

Common Movement Problems and Suggestions. The following are common movement problems encountered during the execution of the circular tackle. Instructional suggestions are also presented.

- Beginners tend to make body contact with the opponent. Tacklers should circle fairly far ahead of the

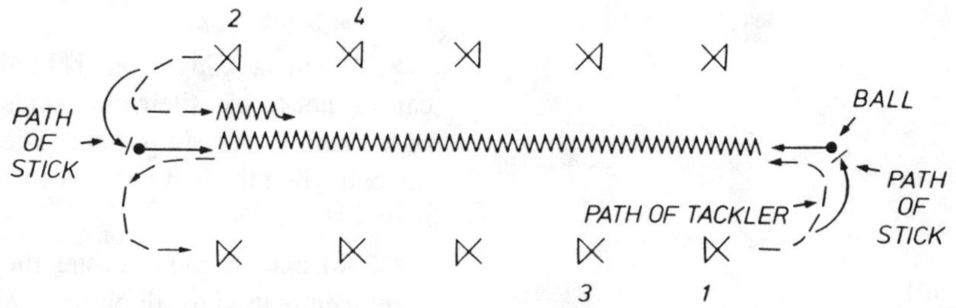

Figure 6.9. Left lunge tackle drill (thin line indicates path of stick for tackle)

dribbler. The beginner can progressively learn how to approach the dribbler closer after the timing of the skill is mastered.

- The face of the club should be facing the direction of the ball tap before turning the body for the tackle. Failure to do this can cause a tap of the ball in the wrong direction.
- The beginner may not make contact with the ball when it is well off the opponent's stick. Emphasis should be placed on meeting the ball beyond the reach of the opponent's stick.

Practice Drills. As with the left lunge tackle, mass practice with or without a ball is a suitable way to start. Paired practice is an excellent way to maximize participation.

1.0. Players spread out on the field at least 6 ft apart with sticks in hand (or faking without sticks). A ball (or imaginary one) is placed ahead and about 4 ft to the right of the right foot. Players move quickly in a circular pattern, turning to the right and keeping the ball between themselves and an imaginary dribbler.

2.0. Paired practice using the drill described in Figure 6.10 is also effective. Player X2 stands with the ball ahead and to the right. Player X1 performs a circular

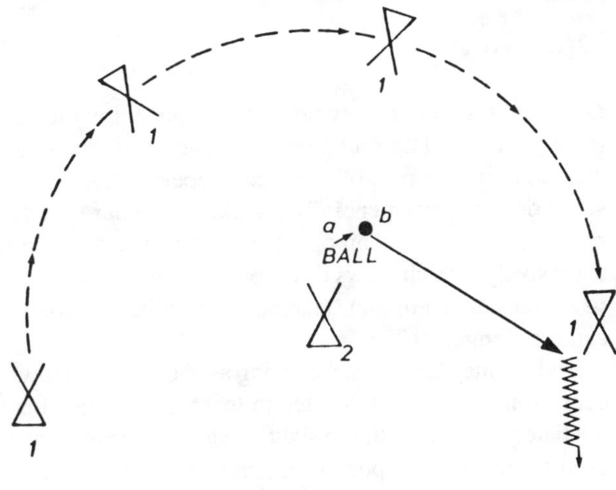

Figure 6.10. Circular tackle drill

tackle around Player X2, who should be stationary for the first few attempts by Player X1 to perform the tackle. The ball may be hit at Point a or Point b, depending on the ball's distance from Player X2's stick. Later, Player X2 dribbles slowly and loosely. Finally, Player X2 dribbles more rapidly. Partners reverse roles so that each has a chance to practice the tackle.

Group practice drills are described as follows. These are used following the individual practice if equipment is limited.

1.0. Double-Column Formation. Players in columns are placed 15 ft apart (Figure 6.11). The sideline and the *alley* line could be used if marked on the field. Player X2 (leader of the right column) passes the ball on an angle ahead of Player X1 (Pass a). Player X1 runs forward, fields the ball by turning the stick so the flat side faces right (b), circles around the ball, dribbles it back (c), and passes to Player X4 (Pass d). Player X4 passes to Player X3, and so on. Players go to the end of the opposite column.

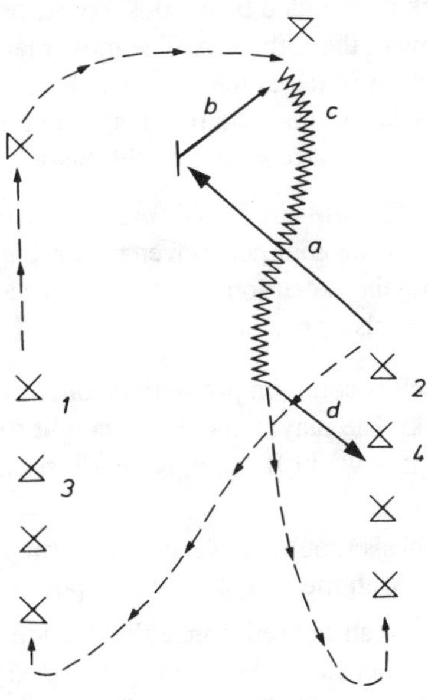

Figure 6.11. Circular tackle pattern

2.0. Double-Column Formation (Figure 6.11). Players X1 and X2 are leaders of columns of four to six persons. Player X1 performs the circular tackle around Player X2 as in Figure 6.10 and returns the ball to the second person in Player X2's column. Players go to the end of the opposite column. Keep the ball stationary on the first trial, but quickly progress to a slow dribble. The players in X2's column should dribble rapidly only after a moderate level of skill is developed. Variation: The players in X1's column may be started 4 to 6 ft ahead of the players in X2's column to give them a chance to make the turn more easily and to discourage shoulder obstruction.

Jab

The *jab* tackle (also known as *job)* is used to interfere with an opponent's control of the ball. It is not a tackle that usually results in control of the ball by the tackler and therefore should be used only when no other options are available to spoil an opponent's progress or shot on goal. It consists of a short poke or a series of pokes at the ball in an effort to interrupt a dribble or pass. It can be done with either hand, but using the left hand allows quicker recovery to a good stickhandling position. Care must be taken to avoid tripping or obstructing an opponent when using the jab.

The jab is executed when the player is parallel with or facing the opponent. The stick is started in the carrying position. The left hand is at the top of the stick throughout the stroke. The left elbow is fully extended and the wrist firm. The body weight is forward over the front foot. The trunk is slightly inclined (flexed) forward.

The stick is extended by a quick extension of the arm at the elbow of the right arm. The movement is a series of jabs with the stick at the ball. The hitting surface of the stick is facing up. The ball may be contacted with the face or the bottom edge of the blade.

Common Movement Problems and Suggestions. The following are common movement problems encountered during the execution of the jab. Instructional suggestions are also presented.

- The most common problem is touching the opponent's stick. The player should be taught to aim at the ball when it is well off the opponent's stick and avoid the stick.
- Emphasis should be placed on a firm grip and extended arm with the face of the club pointing upward.
- The jab can be used from either the left or the right side of the opponent. If the skill is performed to the tackler's left, there is little danger of obstruction. If the skill is performed to the right, there is great danger of obstruction. This is a weak stroke and should be used only in emergencies.
- Emphasize avoidance of the opponent's feet. Tripping or interrupting the opponent's stride is illegal.

Practice Drills. Individuals can practice this skill alone by holding the stick extended at arm's length and nudging a ball along the ground with the bottom of the curved part of the blade. A ball can also be placed on the ground while the player runs past it trying to poke it to the side in passing. This should be practiced from both sides and with each hand.

The following are group practice drills that might be used to practice the jab. Remember to emphasize safe stickhandling.

1.0. Double-Column Formation (Figure 4.9). Individuals in columns are placed about 6 ft apart. The leader of the left column dribbles slowly downfield. The leader of the right column runs alongside and tries to left jab at the ball so the dribbler loses control. Be sure to avoid tripping or obstructing the dribbler. Players return to the end of their opponents' line. After several trials for each person, change the dribbling line to the right column, where the tacklers would be on the left of the dribbler using a right jab. The tacklers must get ahead of the dribbler to avoid illegal interference.

Variation: A finish line 30 to 40 ft away could be designated, and this drill could be used for competition. The dribbler who reaches the finish line gets a point; the tackler who successfully jabs and recovers the ball gets a point. Players could return to the ends of their own columns, and, after performing the drill several times, scores for each team (column) could be compared. Then the dribblers and tacklers switch places. Alternatively, players could change columns after every turn. Team scores could be based on points earned as a dribbler and a tackler.

2.0. Triple-Column Formation (Figure 4.9). Add a third column of individuals beside the other two described. Columns should be about 6 ft apart and all leaders facing the same direction. The leaders of the two outside columns dribble and pass back and forth downfield. The leader of the middle column tries to make them lose control by jabbing at the dribbled ball with the right or the left jab. Players return to the ends of the next columns so that each has a turn at dribbling and jabbing.

Variation: The tackler may also try to intercept the ball as it is passed from player to player.

Dodging

Dodging is a means of avoiding the opponent while retaining the ball. Beginning players should learn the simpler dodges as a part of their skill repertoire. In most situations, players generally should be encouraged to pass the ball to avoid an opponent rather than to dodge excessively, which slows down play. However, players who break ahead of their teammates must be able to execute a dodge.

Dodges may be taught following all the tackles. However, some instructors prefer to teach the dodges immediately following the straight tackle because most are used to evade an opponent in front of the dribbler. A suggested sequence is the dribble, the straight tackle, the stickside dodge, and the nonstickside dodge. This progression presents the offensive move (dribble), the defensive move (tackle), and then the offensive countermove (dodge).

Stickside

The *stickside* dodge, which is done by a quick pull of the ball to the left, is the easiest to perform but also the easiest to stop. The player turns the face of the stick to the left by rotating the wrist. The ball is then pulled left by dragging the ball. The player proceeds with a dribble downfield or passes to a teammate. This must be done very quickly when the opponent is fairly close. An early dodge gives the opponent time to adjust to a new position.

Nonstickside

The *nonstickside* dodge, in which the ball is hit past the opponent on the nonstickside while the dribbler passes on the stick side, is somewhat more difficult both to do and to stop. The player taps the ball to the right and passes right shoulders with the opponent. The dribbler then runs to the ball to recover it and continues dribbling downfield or passes to a teammate. This also needs to be executed quickly and when the opponent is fairly close.

Scoop

The *scoop* dodge, where the ball is lifted over the opponent's stick, is an intermediate skill. The player uses the techniques described in the section on the scoop pass to raise the ball over the opponent's stick.

Reverse Stick

The *reverse stick* tap to the right followed by a pass to the right of the opponent is more difficult and may be left to advanced players. In this dodge, the stick is reversed by rotating the wrist so that the face of the stick is facing the right. The ball is tapped to the right just as the opponent is directly in front of the dodger, who then moves right around the opponent's stick side to recover the ball. The dodger then continues the dribble or passes to a teammate downfield.

In a dodge, the ball should be hit lightly so that it can be easily and quickly recovered. A hard hit on a dodge will send the ball beyond recovery distance and very likely to the opposing backs. The dodge should be started just before the opponent tackles. The direction of the dodge must be disguised. Excessive dodging emphasizes individual rather than team play.

Practice Drills

The following are practice drills for the various dodges. Individual, partner, and group drills are presented.

Individual and Partner Drills. All the dodges can be practiced alone or in pairs. The following are individual and partner drills for dodging.

1.0. When practicing alone, the dribbler should select a spot to dodge around. This could be intersecting lines on the field, a clump of grass, or a cone.

2.0. The use of a human obstacle (partner) is more satisfactory because it provides a realistic situation. The tackler might maintain a stationary position at first to allow the dodger to get the feel of the action. Then the tackler could move only the stick while keeping the feet still. Finally, the tackler could try to get the ball from the dribbler/dodger actively. Students could work all over the field, although it would be safer to have them all moving back and forth the same way. For example, if all were moving east and west, they would be less apt to collide with others than if some were moving at right angles, or north and south.

Group Drills. The following are group-practice drills for dodging. If tacklers were added, most of the dribbling drills could also be adapted for dodging practice.

1.0. Shuttle Formation (Figure 4.8). See Drill 1.0 for straight-tackle group practice, which can be used to practice dodging. As the tackler approaches the dribbler, the dribbler dodges and continues on. The tackler should approach slowly at first and let the dodger achieve a measure of success. The tackler should be less cooperative later and seriously try to get the ball. This formation may be used to practice all the dodges. The stickside and the nonstickside dodges are recommended for beginners. The scoop may be added for intermediate players, and the reverse-stick dodge should be reserved for those even more highly skilled.

2.0. Straight Tackle (Figure 6.8). Dodging can be added to this drill. Players X3 and X4 approach Players X1 and X2, who may either pass the ball or dodge the opponents. It may be necessary to move Columns 1 and 2 farther from Columns 3 and 4.

Goalkeeping

Goalkeepers in field hockey have special privileges not allowed other players. They may *block the ball* with any part of their bodies (including the hands) and kick the ball away. After a goalkeeper stops a shot on goal, the ball may be hit or kicked to the sidelines, a teammate, or an open space. The ball should never be passed in front of one's own goal area. Goalkeepers retain their special privileges only within the shooting circle and therefore should not move outside that area.

The goalkeeper should wear special equipment. Goalie pads to cover the legs and *kickers* (pads with straps) to cover the shoes are absolutely essential. Special goalkeeper shoes may be worn instead of kickers. Older players whose drives are harder and whose goal shots may be lifted should wear face masks and gloves. Some goalkeepers prefer to wear a glove only on the left hand to protect it when fielding the ball. Goalie gloves may be regular sized leather gloves or gloves with special padding to protect the hand. The goalie may not use oversized gloves to extend or widen the hand but may wear specially designed goalkeeper's gloves.

Goalkeepers must learn to play the angles of the goal. They must know when to rush an attacker and when to wait for teammates to tackle. An analysis of the angles of play is presented in the soccer goalkeeping section in chapter 8 (see also Figures 8.11, 8.12, and 8.13).

General Body Positioning

The goalkeeper should stand about 4 ft in front of the cage and slightly to the left of center. This allows for greater stick reach to the right. The stick should be carried in any position below the shoulder. When on defense, goalkeepers should hold their sticks in the right hand and use the left hand to field lofted shots. Many goalkeepers prefer to carry their sticks about halfway down the handle. The knees should be slightly flexed to add stability. The stance is a side-stride position with the feet slightly closer together than shoulder width. The trunk is slightly inclined forward.

Fielding

The goalkeeper typically fields the ball with the stick, the hands, or the front of the lower legs or pads. The most effective fielding technique is the front of the lower legs due to the larger surface area. The hand is used to field lofted balls. Using the stick to field the ball is the most risky means of blocking or stopping the ball. Fielding by means of the stick was covered previously under passing and therefore is not discussed here. Lower-leg and hand fielding follow.

The ball is stopped on the front of the lower legs or pads by bringing the knees and feet together in front of the ball. The knees are slightly flexed with the trunk slightly inclined (flexed) forward. The goalkeeper meets the ball in this position and allows the ball to rebound off the pads. The knee flexion causes the ball to drop to the ground in front of the goalkeeper, who then kicks it clear.

When fielding with the hand, the goalkeeper reaches to meet the oncoming ball with the free hand. Once the ball makes contact with the hand, the hand immediately retracts to dissipate the force of the ball. The goalkeeper then allows the ball to drop to the ground. It is not legal to throw the ball.

Common Movement Problems and Suggestions. The following are common movement problems experienced when performing either lower-legs fielding or hand fielding. Instructional suggestions are also presented.

- Failure to bring the knees and feet together in the front of the lower legs can create a situation in which the ball can slip through the feet and enter the goal cage.
- If the goalkeeper does not retract the hand when fielding with the hand, an injury to the hand can occur. Emphasize that the hand must retract immediately on ball contact.
- Emphasize knee flexion and giving with the impact. This allows the goalkeeper to keep the ball close enough to kick or to sweep aside with the stick.

Kicking

There are several ways for the goalkeeper to *clear* the ball. Generally, the goalkeeper clears the ball with a drive or a kick. The technique, common movement problems, and instructional suggestions for the drive can be found in the section on the drive pass. The kicking method of clearing the ball follows.

The goalkeeper flexes at the hips, causing a forward body lean into the ball after stopping the ball with the front of the legs or the pads. This shifts the body weight forward. The body weight is further shifted onto the nonkicking foot. The kicking foot takes a short, quick backswing. The backswing is accomplished by flexing the knee.

The force production of the kick is created by extending at the knee. The leg swings through the ball. The ball is contacted with the side of the big toe in a clearing kick. The follow-through is short and close to the ground. The goalkeeper should learn to kick with either foot.

The goalkeeper may also use the stick to sweep the ball to the side away from the goal. The stick is held in the right hand and is swept along the ground to push the ball away. This stroke is more natural if the goalkeeper is near the left side of the goal. When the ball is near the right side of the goal, the sweep must be made to the right, not in front of the goal.

Common Movement Problems and Suggestions. The following are common movement problems encountered by the goalkeeper executing a kick to clear the ball. Instructional suggestions are also presented.

- Beginning goalkeepers tend to kick the ball straight ahead, thus positioning the ball for another attempt at goal. Emphasize clearing the ball out to the sides.
- A common problem is lofting the ball, caused by using a high follow-through with the kicking foot. The foot should swing low to the ground, and the body weight should be transferred to the kicking foot immediately after the kick occurs.
- Goalkeepers should be instructed to clear the ball as quickly as possible.

Practice Drills

See the section on soccer goalkeeping practice drills in chapter 8. Goalkeepers should always wear the necessary protective equipment.

1.0. Double-Column Formation (Figure 6.12). Four pairs of cones, chairs, or other goalpost markers are placed 12 to 15 ft out of bounds along the sidelines of the field. Each pair of markers should simulate a goal (12 ft apart). There should be about 20 yd between sets of goals. Two columns of players are lined up opposite each goal and about 20 yd from the sideline. A goalkeeper takes a position a few feet in front of each goal. Players X1 and X2 dribble and pass back and forth until reaching the sideline, where they attempt a shot on goal. The leaders of each of the other pairs of columns do the same, shooting at the goal opposite them. Players may not dribble all the way to the goal. The shots must be taken from the sideline to allow the goalkeeper a chance to field the ball.

Attackers retrieve the ball and return it to the next pair of players in the columns. They then return around the outside of the drill area and go to the ends of the opposite columns.

General Practice Drills

1.0. 3-on-3 (Figure 6.7). Add three more columns of players at the goal line opposite Columns 1, 2, and 3 in Figure 6.7. As Players X1, X2, and X3 dribble and pass toward the goal, the first person in each of Columns 4, 5, and 6 moves out to take a defensive position for a tackle or to intercept and return the ball to the center line (or the 25-yd line). After the ball crosses the goal line or the center line, the players go to the ends of the opposite lines, and six more players begin the drill (three attackers and three defenders).

2.0. 5-on-5 (Figure 8.17). As five attackers dribble and pass downfield, five defensive players start from the other end. Each defender is responsible for the opposite attacker. The defender must tackle that player when the player has the ball and try to intercept passes directed toward that player. The *attack line* tries to score; the defense line tries to get the ball past the center line. For large groups, the attackers may start at the center line. Another group may also start at midfield and move toward the other goal. This allows for 20 players to participate at once (10 on each half of the field). Goalkeepers may be added later.

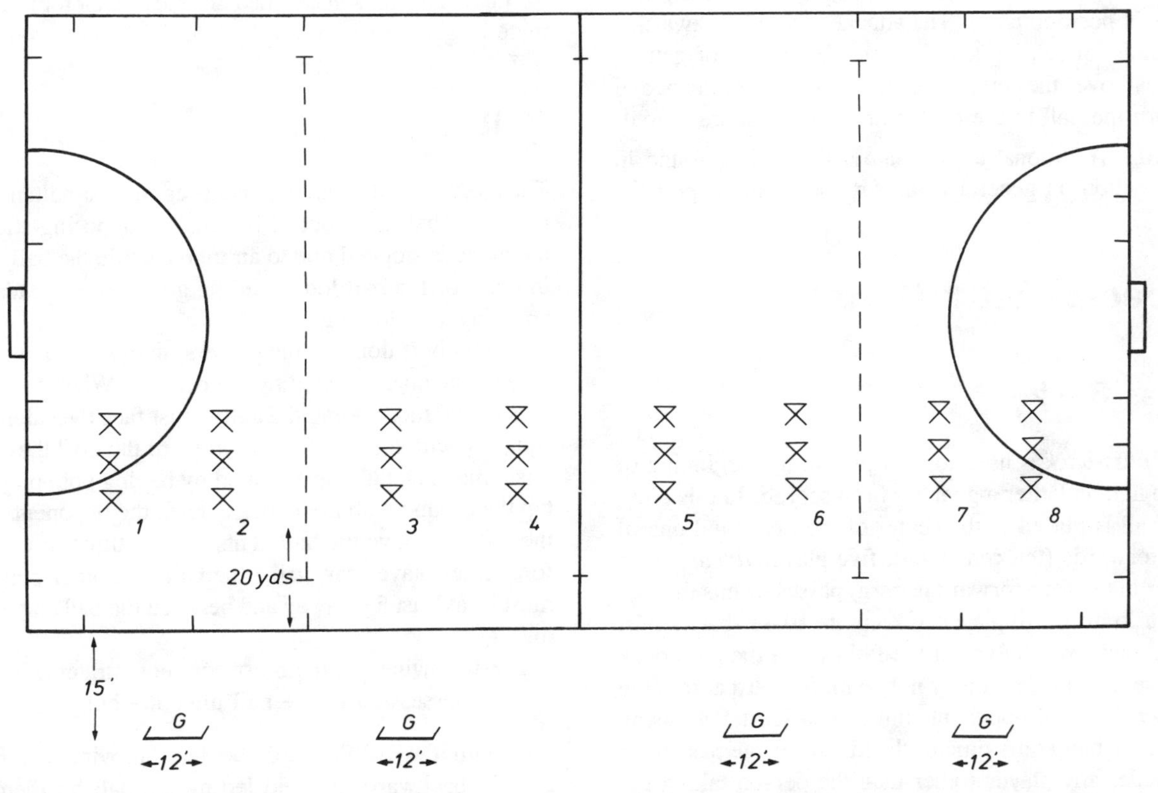

Figure 6.12. Goalkeeper drill

3.0. Five-Player Attack. This can also be used as a four-player attack for teams playing the 4-2-3-1 offensive system (see Drill 2.0). Each player in the right-wing column has a ball. The first player in the wing column dribbles toward the goal line staying near the sideline. The other leaders move parallel with the dribbler in their own areas of the field. When the wing gets about 10 yd from the goal line, the wing sends a long drive across the goal area parallel to the end line. The other players try to field the ball and send it between the goalposts. Players return around the outside of the field to different columns. After several turns, move the balls to the left side of the field and have the left *wings* dribble toward the goal line. The dribblers will have more difficulty centering the ball, but the other offensive players will find it easier to stop the ball and shoot. Groups may be set up on each half of the field working in opposite directions. Variations include the following:

3.1. Use a four-player attack line (only four columns).

3.2. Add defensive players as in Drill 2.0.

3.3. Have the wing and the nearby *inner* pass back and forth downfield before the centering shot is made. This also allows practice of the triangular pass pattern.

3.4. A goalkeeper may be added to defend the goal.

3.5. For team practice, have the forwards compete against the defense using a traditional 5-on-5 or four forwards plus two links against a full defense (see the section on position play). The attackers could be awarded 3 points for scoring and the defense 1 point for getting the ball over the center line. It is easier to intercept and return the ball to the center line than to score a goal.

4.0. Additional appropriate drills will be found in the section on general drills for soccer in chapter 8.

Special Situations

Pass-Back

The *pass-back* is used to start play at the beginning of each half and after a goal has been scored. In this play, the ball is placed in the center of the field, and one of the forwards (the center in a five-player *lineup* or an inner in the four-forward pattern) passes or hits the ball to a teammate. All players (except the passer-back) must be in their own halves of the field when the pass-back is taken, and the ball may not be hit forward across the center line. All opponents must be at least 5 yd away from the ball at the time of the hit. After the pass-back is made, any player (other than the person taking the pass-back) may hit the ball and move about anywhere on the field.

The team taking the pass-back at the beginning of the game is selected by chance. The opposite team is awarded a pass-back at the start of the second half. After a goal is scored, the team not scoring a point restarts play with a pass-back.

The most effective way to utilize the pass-back is with short, fast passes to an inner or the center halfback (or link). Some pass-back play patterns follow.

- Pass back to the right inner, who has moved near the ball 2 or 3 yd from the center line. The right inner passes immediately either to the left inner or back to the center forward, both of whom have started downfield.
- Pass back to the right inner, who passes the ball on a slant toward the opponents' 25-yd line, where the right wing fields the ball.
- Pass back to the left inner, who passes the ball back to either the *center forward* or the right inner or passes to the left wing. The pass-back to the left inner is easier for the defenders to intercept because their sticks are in a better position (flat side toward ball).
- Pass back to center halfback or link. This allows all forwards to move quickly downfield and maneuver to get free to receive a pass. If opponents are marking (guarding) closely, this play is often effective because there is confusion about who should tackle the halfback (or link). That person can then dribble or wait for a teammate to get open.

Bully

The *bully* is used when opponents commit simultaneous fouls, the ball goes out of bounds off opposing sticks, the game is stopped due to an injury while the ball was in play, or the ball lodges in the goalkeeper's pads or any player's clothing.

The bully is done by the players involved in the misplay or the ones selected by the official. When the bully is taken, those doing the bully must face the sidelines squarely with the left shoulder toward the goal they are attacking. The bully is executed by having both players tap the ground with their sticks. Then the opponents tap their sticks above the ball. This is done three times before either player can strike the ball. All other players must be at least 5 yd away and between the ball and their own goal line.

The following are the most common strategies used to gain possession of the ball after the bully.

- Pull the ball toward the feet, moving the feet quickly backward to avoid letting the ball hit them.

• Reverse the stick and pass the ball back to a halfback or link.

• Pull the ball slightly toward the feet and pass ahead and to the left. When using this play, do not allow the shoulders to turn and obstruct the opponent.

• Lift the stick after the third hit and allow the opponent to hit the ball to your halfback. This is effective only if the opponent consistently tries to hit the ball ahead at the end of the bully.

• Vary the rhythm. Start the bully slowly and move very quickly to hit the ball after the third tap of the sticks.

• Place the stick firmly behind the ball after the third tap and trap the ball between the sticks. Then, with a flick or a scoop, lift the ball over the opponent's stick.

• Reverse the stick, give the ball a light tap 2 or 3 ft to the right, then make a quick pass to the right inner. This is for advanced players only.

Sidelines Out of Bounds

When the ball goes out of bounds over the sidelines, play is restarted at that spot by a *push-in* or a *hit-in* by an opponent of the team that touched the ball last. The pass should be taken quickly to prevent the defensive team from getting into position. The ball must not be hit into the air intentionally.

The side halfback or a side back should take the hit. This allows the forwards to move downfield and get into position to receive the pass. All other players from both teams must be at least 5 yd away. The wings might take the pass in when the ball goes out near the opponent's goal line. The links or halfbacks would then move up to assist in the offensive play. The following are several possible ideas for restarting play from the sideline boundary.

1.0. The nearer inner moves to the 5-yd line directly opposite the player taking the hit-in. The wing on that side of the field moves well ahead of the ball. The hitter then has two options: (a) a short pass to the inner or (b) a long pass to the wing (Figure 6.13).

2.0. If play is at midfield or in the opponents' half, the center halfback (link) might come toward the sideline behind the inner, receive the hit-in, and pass the ball downfield to the left inner or wing. This would be especially effective if the defense crowded near the sideline play or marked the offensive forwards closely.

3.0. The same play described in 2.0 could be done with a back if the sideline play were to be taken near the player's own goal line. However, defenders should never execute a long pass across the front of their own goal.

4.0. See Figure 6.14. Near the opponent's goal line, a wing should take the pass-in and utilize the side halfback (a) or the nearer inner (c) as receivers. The center forward (or center halfback) might also cut over to provide another option (b). The forwards should wait until the hitter is ready to hit and then cut into an open space to receive the ball.

Defensive players should mark closely the offensive wing, link, and inner on the side of the field near the play. The defenders should move quickly into position between their own goal and the offensive players because

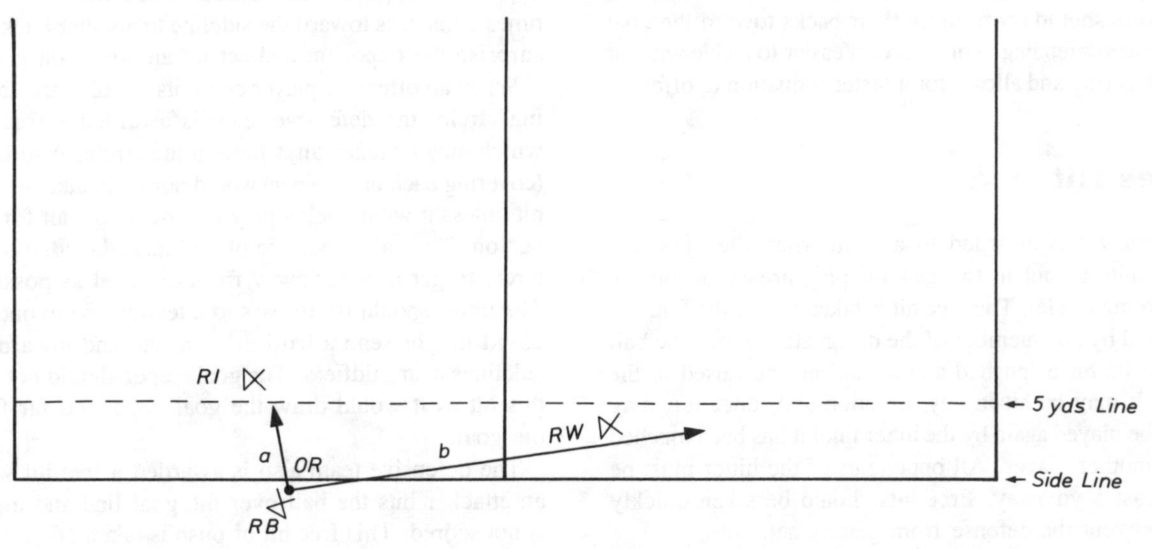

Figure 6.13. Sideline play (RB = right back, RI = right inner, RW = right wing)

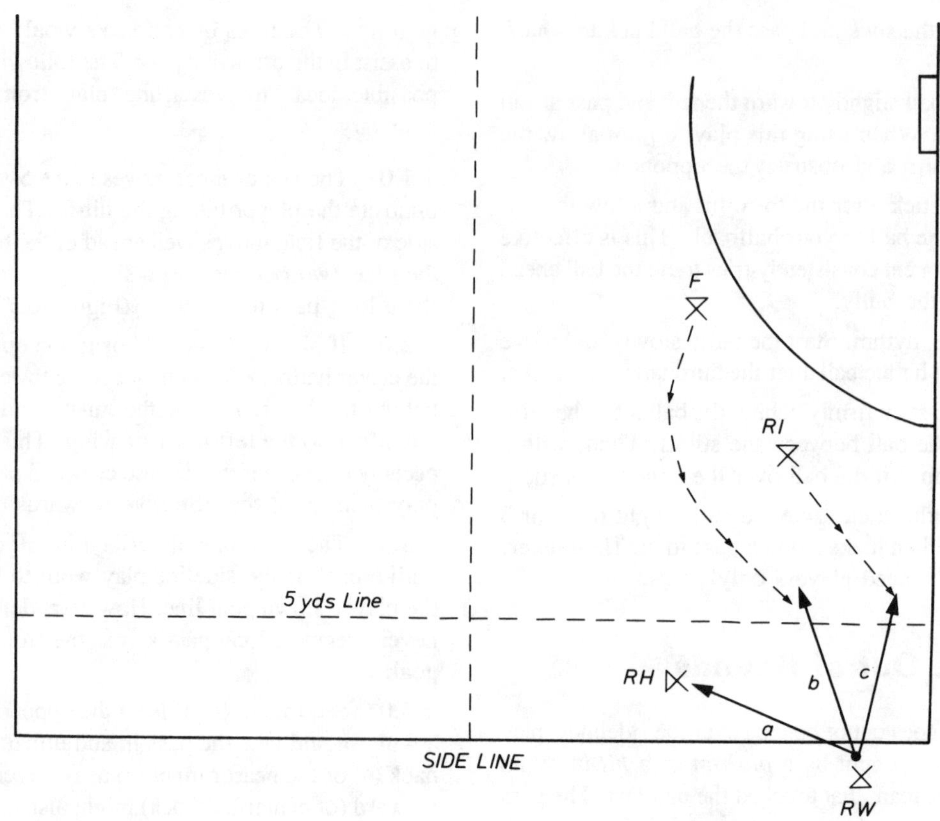

Figure 6.14. Sideline play near opponent's goal line

the offense will try to catch them off guard. Defenders in the center of the field should move toward the sideline play and cover the spaces between their teammates to prevent long passes by the offense. A defensive back should move to a position near the alley line in any offensive player moves along the 5-yd line downfield from the push-in or hit-in. Whenever possible, defensive players should try to place their backs toward the goal they are defending. This makes it easier to tackle without obstructing and allows for a faster transition to offense.

Free Hit

A *free hit* is awarded to a team when the opponent commits a foul in the general play area (outside the shooting circle). The free hit is taken where the foul occurred by any member of the designated team. The ball must be hit or pushed and should not be raised in the air. It may be hit in any direction and, once hit, may not be played again by the hitter until it has been touched by another player. All opponents of the hitter must be at least 5 yd away. Free hits should be taken quickly to prevent the defense from getting set.

Backs usually take the free hits. This allows the forwards to run downfield to receive the pass. The hitter should look ahead to locate teammates, then hit the ball to a space ahead of the receiver. Receivers should never stand and wait for the ball but should move toward it or on an intersecting path. Backs should vary the pattern of the hit. They should not always send the ball toward the left side of the field just because a left drive is easier to perform. Right drives should also be mastered. Sometimes a flat pass toward the sideline to another back will surprise the opponent and set up an attack on goal.

When an offensive player commits a foul in the shooting circle, the defensive team is awarded a free hit, which may be taken anywhere in the circle. A fullback (covering back or *sweeper*) would normally take this free hit unless it would delay play too much to wait for that person. The ball should be placed near the edge of the circle to get it as far away from the goal as possible. The hitter should try to pass to a teammate beyond the 25-yd line or send a hard drive ahead and toward the sidelines near midfield. The goalkeeper should not take this hit as it would draw the goalkeeper too far from the goal.

The defensive team also is awarded a free hit when an attacker hits the ball over the goal line and a goal is not scored. This free hit or push is taken 16 yd from the goal line opposite the spot where the ball crossed the goal line. The offensive strategy used would be the same as that described for the free hit on the edge of the circle.

The defensive team should try to get quickly into position between the goal they are defending and the attackers. Speed is essential because the attackers will try to catch them off guard before they can recover from being on the attack. Halfbacks or links must be especially quick to switch from offense to defense. Defenders near the free hit should mark their opponents as in a 1-on-1 situation. Those away from the ball should watch for open spaces where the attackers may try to cut to receive passes.

Corner Hit

This hit, also called a *long corner*, is taken by the attacking team when a defender unintentionally hits the ball over his/her own goal line and a goal is not scored. The attacking player (usually a wing) places the ball within 5 yd of the nearer corner of the field and hits or pushes it into play. The hitter may not touch the ball again until another player has touched it. All other players must be at least 5 yd away when the hit is taken.

The corner hitter has some choices in placement of the hit (Figure 6.14). The wing may hit the ball to the back (a) or to another forward (b). The plays diagrammed in Figure 6.14 might also be used with the hit coming from the goal line rather than the sideline.

1.0. The ball may be driven across the goalmouth so that a teammate inside the shooting circle can deflect it into the goal.

2.0. A pass to the nearer inner may be made (Pass a in Figure 6.15).

3.0. The link or side halfback may approach for a pass (Pass b in Figure 6.15).

Defensive players should stand with their backs toward their own goal, and each should mark their opposing players carefully. They should position themselves between their opponents and the goal line, a little closer to the ball than to the opponent (Figures 6.15 and 6.16).

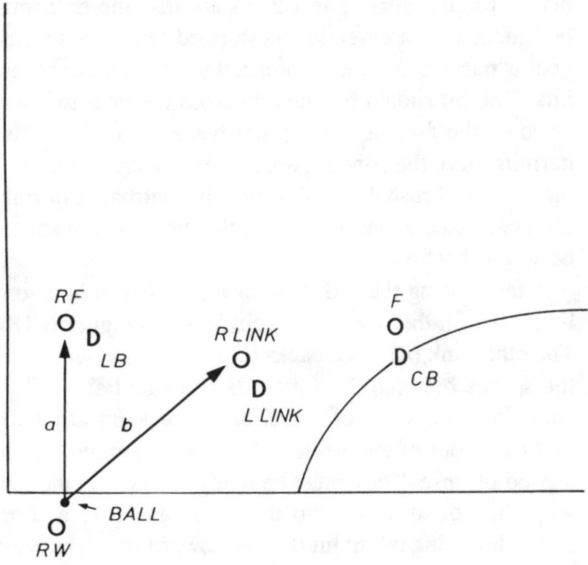

Figure 6.15. Defensive positions for right-corner hit

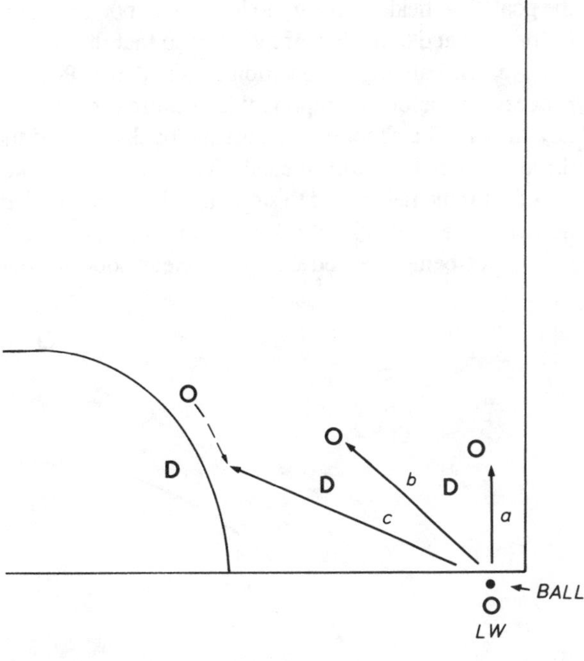

Figure 6.16. Defensive positions for left-corner hit

Penalty Corner

A *penalty corner* is awarded when the defensive team commits a foul within its own shooting circle or intentionally sends the ball over the end line (not between the goalposts). When this occurs, the ball is placed on the goal line 10 yd from the goalpost and an offensive player pushes or hits the ball into play. The attackers may place the ball on either side of the goal. No player other than the hitter may be within 5 yd of the ball. All offensive players must be on the field and outside of the circle. No more than five of the defenders may stand out of bounds behind the goal line. The rest of the defensive team must be beyond the center line when the hit is taken.

A wing usually takes the penalty corner, and the other forwards move toward the ball and spread themselves out just outside the circle. The hitter sends the ball to a teammate, who stops the ball just inside the circle and drives for the goal. The rules state that the ball must be touched by a defender or stopped before a shot on goal is permitted. This is intended to prevent dangerous hits. The hit should be angled across the goal to a forward on the far side if the hitter has a hard drive. This permits more than one forward to have a chance to field the ball as all rush the goal. Offensive halfbacks or links are positioned about 5 yd from the circle in the spaces between the forwards (Figure 6.17).

A team using the link system may wish to have one link (LL) on the edge of the circle also (Figure 6.18). The other link (RL) and backs (CB and LB) would cover the spaces between the forwards and stand about 5 yd back from the edge of the circle to pick up any balls that came out of the circle. The links are important to a good offense. They must be ready to back up the forward line or to move into the circle and take a shot.

The left wing might hit the ball toward the right wing so that all attackers have a chance to try for the ball. Another play pattern is to have one attacker (such as the right inner) field the hit while an adjacent teammate to the left (the left link) steps up and drives the ball toward the goal. The fielder must try to let the ball bounce slightly forward and to the left of the stick so that the shooter receives the ball in good position for the drive. Practice is necessary before attempting this because timing is the key factor. The shooter can start the backswing of the drive as the fielder stops the ball. This allows a quicker shot than if the fielder had to stop the ball and then drive. Sometimes a halfback or link who moves into the circle and is not being marked can get a clear shot at goal.

Defensive players should sprint quickly out to mark the opponents as soon as the ball is hit. The sweeper (D_s) or covering back should move to a backup position as the other backs (and links) move to mark their individual opponents. However, players must always avoid obscuring the goalkeeper's view of the ball. The sweeper may stay near the goal and back up the goalkeeper.

Penalty Stroke

A *penalty stroke* is taken by the attackers when the defense intentionally fouls inside its own circle or a foul prevents a probable goal. The ball is placed 7 yd in front of the goal, and any offensive player shoots with a scoop, a push, or a flick stroke. The shooter may contact the ball only once and may not dribble nor follow up the shot to get a rebound.

The goalkeeper is the only player who may defend against the penalty stroke. The goalkeeper must stand on the goal line and not move either foot until the ball is played, after which the goalkeeper may protect the goal in any legal manner. All other players from both teams must stay beyond the 25-yd line until the play is completed.

A goal is scored if the ball passes into the goal or if the goalkeeper fouls to prevent a goal. Play is restarted with a defense hit taken 16 yd in front of the goal if the ball stops within the circle, is caught or successfully blocked by the goalkeeper, or is passed out of the circle.

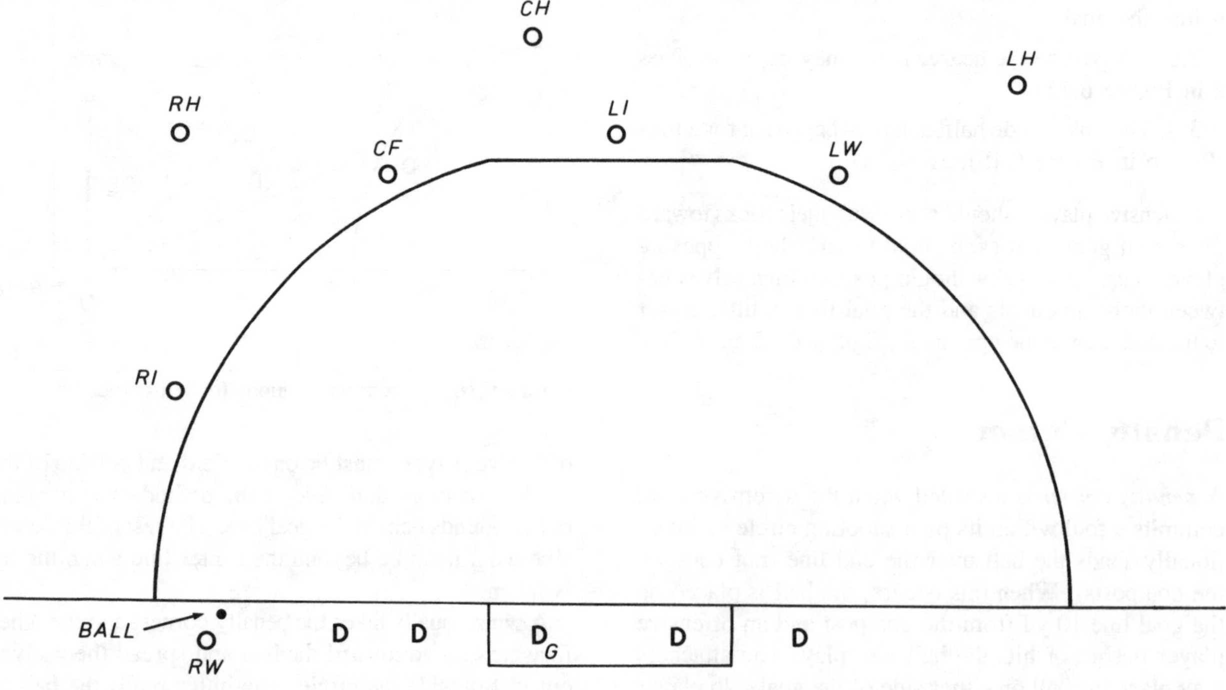

Figure 6.17. Lineup for penalty corner hit by right wing in traditional 5-3-2-G formation

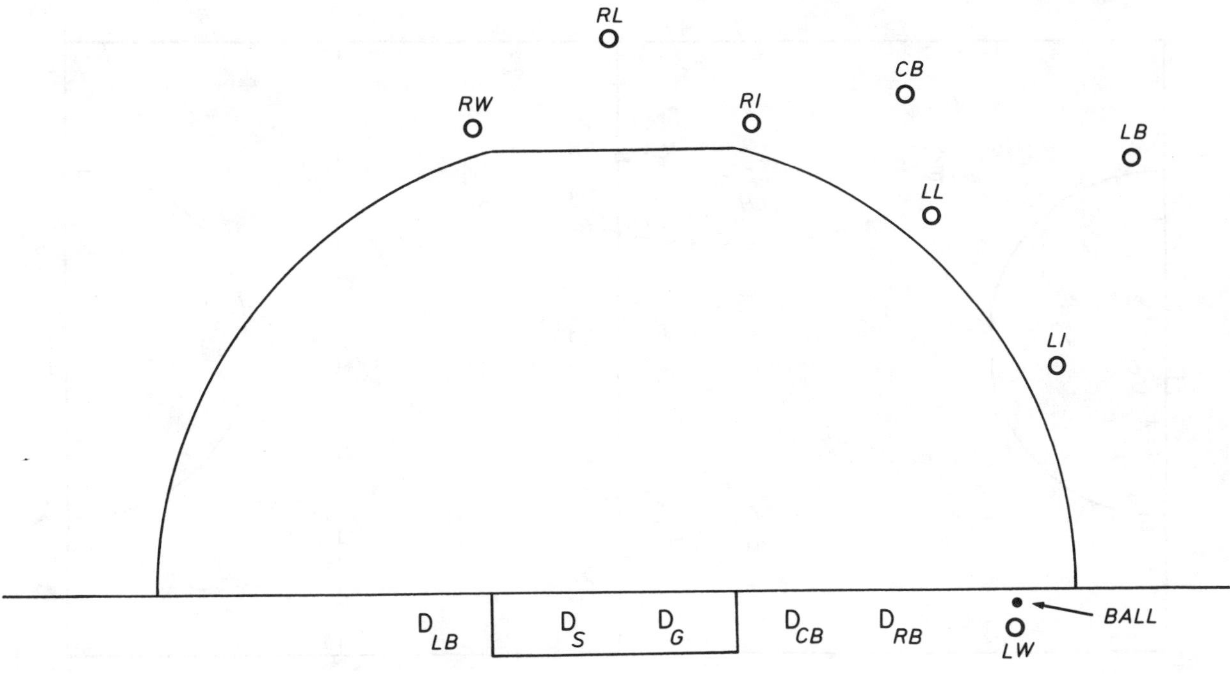

Figure 6.18. Lineup for penalty corner hit by right wing in 4-2-3-1-G formation

The player taking the penalty shot should have strong push or flick stroke. A lofted shot is desirable because the upper corners of the goal are difficult to defend. The best placement is the upper-right corner of the goal (upper left as the shooter views it). The defender carries the stick in the right hand; if the stick is lifted dangerously, it is a foul, and a goal will be awarded. Another good target is the lower-left corner (lower right for shooters). The goalkeeper must move the body to the side and move the stick to the opposite side of the body while avoiding an illegal stick stop.

The goalkeeper should stand on the line slightly crouched with the body weight on the balls of both feet to be able to move in any direction. The stick should be held low with the right hand several inches down the handle. The left hand should be held up about waist or shoulder level to stop high shots. As soon as the ball is touched, the goalkeeper should move in front of the goal line and into the path of the ball, concentrating on blocking the ball. There is no need to kick the ball to clear it from the area.

Position Play

The traditional lineup for field hockey is like that of soccer: the *pyramid lineup*, or the 5-3-2-G pattern (Figure 6.19). More modern play has introduced some variations.

The traditional lineup is recommended for beginners in the class setting. It does not require as much teamwork or player interaction as do some of the other patterns of play. Each of the defensive players is responsible for one of the opposing forwards and can mark that person in a 1-on-1 situation. The dotted lines indicate the forward each defensive player guards. In this lineup, the halfbacks play behind and back up the forward line and, when on defense, guard the opposing wings and center forward. Thus, they play both defense and offense and are often the key to a successful attack by feeding the ball to the forwards.

The fullbacks are mainly defensive players and rarely go much beyond their own half of the field (except if they are unusually fast). When the team is on the attack, one fullback follows the play well downfield to receive any long defensive passes and to send the ball back to the attackers. The other fullback covers or plays back near the 25-yd line or the edge of the circle to defend against any opposing forward who may get a fast break downfield. If one fullback is faster than the other, the faster fullback should be the one to roam to the center line while the other plays the covering position. If they have equal skills, the up, or downfield, player should be the one on whose side the ball is (i.e., if the right wing has the ball, the right fullback moves downfield, and the left fullback covers and vice versa).

The 4-2-3-1-G system (Figure 6.20) is frequently used in competitive play today. It provides for stronger defense and midfield play while depending on four forwards (left wing, left inner, right inner, and right wing) to be the aggressive attackers. It is similar to the bolt system in soccer, which depends more on covering spaces than on marking individual players. It also

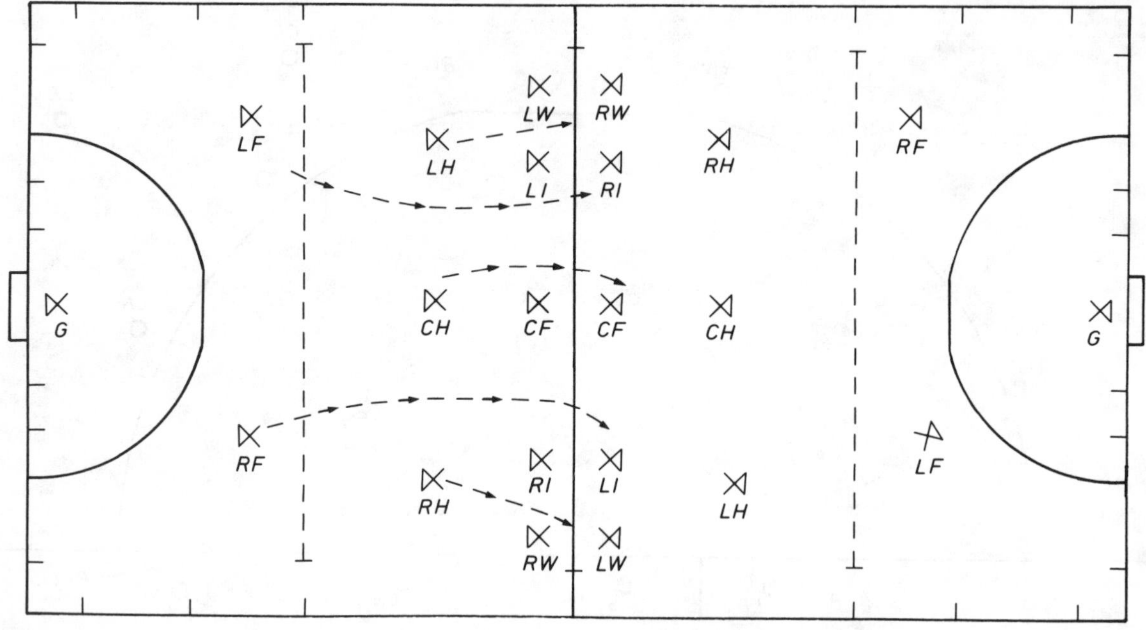

Figure 6.19. Traditional, or 5-3-2-G, lineup (LW = left wing, LI = left inner, CF = center forward, RI = right inner, RW = right wing, LH = left halfback, CH = center halfback, RH = right halfback, LF = left fullback, RF = right fullback, G = goalkeeper)

demands more teamwork and is most effective when players practice working together.

The forwards are the primary offensive players, but the links also contribute significantly to the attack by backing up the forwards and also moving downfield with the forward line. The links must also be ready to assist with the defense. As they follow the forwards, they are the first to get to balls that are passed up by a forward or deflected by tacklers.

The backs (left, center, and right) move downfield behind the attackers and are ready to field all balls that are sent their way by the defense. They are spread out across the field to forestall any breakaways or long passes to opposing wings. They support and feed the attackers in the midfield area but do not usually press the attack. They must be ready to revert to defense and retreat to their own goal area, where they may mark an opponent closely.

The sweeper, like the bolt in soccer, plays the entire field behind the 25-yd line. This person picks up any forward who gets past the backs or any ball that approaches the circle. The sweeper must be ready to move to either side of the field and must try to delay the attackers until other defenders can get back to help the defense. This position is similar to that of the covering fullback in the 5-3-2-G formation.

The 3-3-3-1-G lineup strengthens the play in the center of the field even more (Figure 6.21). The links may move on the attack with the forwards, thereby enhancing the attack. This pattern of play requires links who are fast and have good endurance. It is a better pattern of play for experienced players who practice together than for use in classes or recreational play.

Offense

General Team Strategies

- Move into offensive positions quickly whenever a teammate secures the ball.
- Use triangular passes whenever possible. It is faster to pass and run ahead than to dribble the ball.
- Halfbacks and links should back up the forwards and feed the ball ahead to them.
- Forwards generally do not go back into the halfbacks' areas. They only interfere, and then the backs have no one to pass to when they get the ball.
- Forwards should not go into the shooting circle that their team defends.
- Take all free hits, sideline plays, and corners as

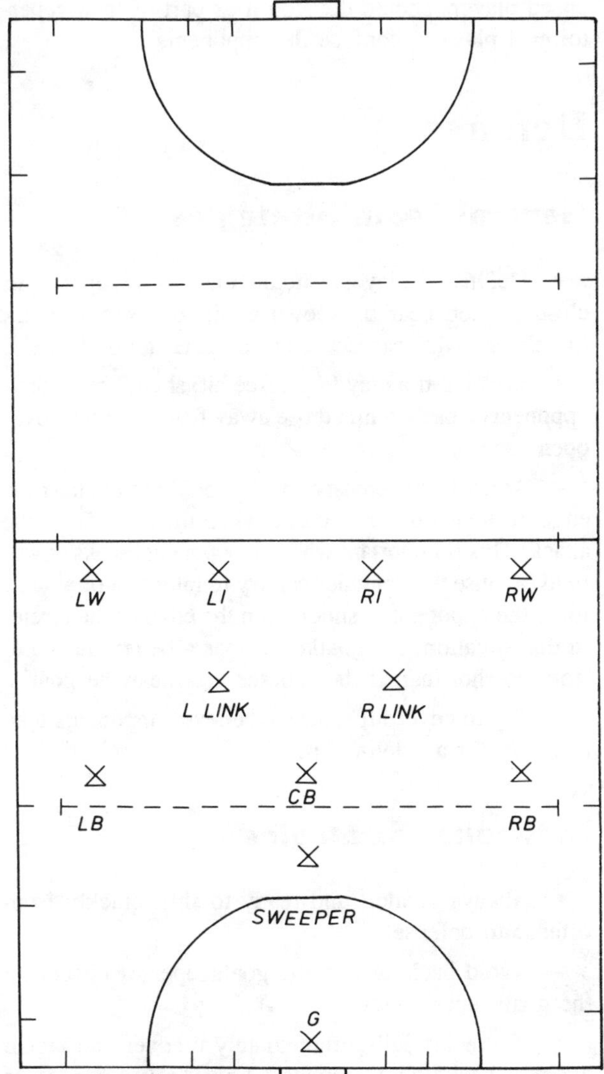

Figure 6.20. 4-2-3-1-G lineup

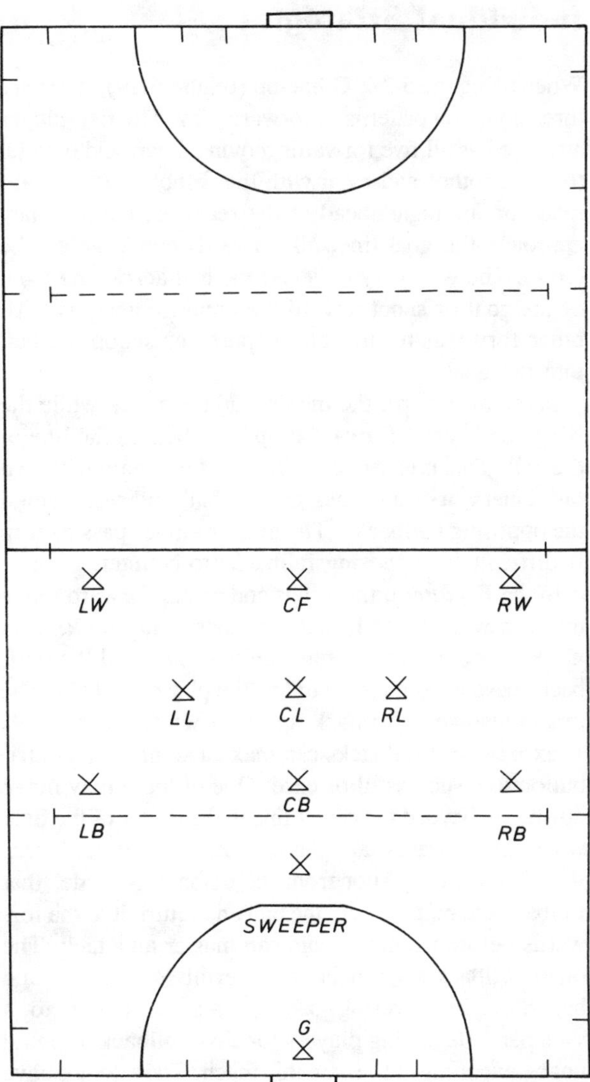

Figure 6.21. 3-3-3-1-G lineup

quickly as possible. The defense may not have time to get set.

- Stay away from a teammate who has the ball. Try to draw the other defenders away from the ball or get free to receive a pass.

- Whenever there is a shot at goal, forwards rush toward the goal with sticks held low in case there is a rebound from a defender. More goals are scored from rebounds than from initial shots.

- The ball should be passed or dribbled near the sidelines when near the goal being defended or between the 25-yd lines. The ball should be played toward the center of the field when approaching the opponent's goal. Attackers must shoot or touch the ball while inside the shooting circle; otherwise, the goal will not count (except in NCAA rules).

- A forward who is successfully tackled should immediately tackle back (i.e., tackle the tackler). This forces the tackler to pass quickly and perhaps inaccurately or to lose the ball.

- When one forward has the ball, all teammates should advance downfield even with and parallel to that player.

- Passes should be angled to a space well ahead of the running receiver so there is no need to slow down or retrace steps.

Individual Strategies

When using the 5-3-2-G line-up (Figure 6.19), there are three common patterns of forward play. The five-player advance has all five forwards moving downfield parallel to one another and even with the dribbler. Passes are made on an angle ahead of the receiver, and, as they approach the goal line, all forwards converge on the circle. The wings try to center the ball across the front of the goal or shoot toward the opposite goalpost. All other forwards try to deflect, push, or scoop the ball into the goal.

In the *M pattern*, the inners lead the attack while the wings and center forward drop back behind the line of the ball. This is especially effective for a team with two fast inners or if an inner got the ball and was behind the opposing halfbacks. The inner-to-inner pass pattern is difficult for opposing fullbacks to counter.

In the *W pattern*, the wings and center forward move up even with the ball, and the inners hang back. This works well when the wings are very fast and the halfbacks have good range to follow the play downfield. The inners also serve to back up the other forwards.

Experienced fullbacks can make a significant contribution to a successful offense. One of them may move downfield beyond the center line in the center of the field when the forwards take the ball near the circle. Then, if a long clearing shot from the defense is made, that fullback attempts to field the ball and return it to the forwards before the other team can muster an attack. The other fullback stays back near her/his *own circle* and becomes the covering back. (This is similar to a sweeper.) Beginning players (or slow fullbacks) should not be encouraged to roam this much. They do not have the skills or the knowledge to know when or how to recover in case of a fast break by opponents.

The 4-2-3-1-G system (see Figure 6.20) and the 3-3-3-1-G system (Figure 6.21) demand that forwards roam farther to the side and be constantly moving. The links and backs (as with the midfielders in soccer) must play both offense and defense and move up- and downfield quickly to attack with the forwards or speed back to defend their own goal. This provide a six-player defense but a weaker forward attack. The play is similar to that described for soccer in chapter 8.

Forwards may confuse the opponents occasionally by *interchanging*, or changing places with another forward. For example, an attacking inner may dribble the ball toward the goal line near the edge of the circle of the field while the wing on that side cuts behind and toward the goalpost. If the backs follow the inner toward the corner, the inner passes to the wing, who takes a shot on goal. Beginners should not try this type of maneuver until they have mastered basic position play. Experienced players should develop it as part of their repertoire of plays to confuse the opponents.

Defense

General Team Strategies

- Defensive players should mark their opponents closely when near their own goal; they should mark loosely or cover spaces when near the center of the field.
- Backs near a play (e.g., free hit) should mark their opponents closely while those away from the play cover open spaces.
- At least one defensive back should remain near the edge of the team's own circle when the team is on the attack. This is important when an opponent breaks downfield because the defender can try to intercept or at least force the opponent to shoot from the edge of the circle. In this situation, the goalkeeper has a better chance to stop the shot than if the shooter gets near the goal.
- Try to cover all spaces whenever opponents take a free hit or a sideline hit.

Individual Strategies

- Always be alert and ready to shift quickly from offense to defense.
- Avoid backing into the goalkeeper or obscuring the goalkeeper's view.
- If a tackle fails, immediately recover and tackle again or back up a teammate who has taken over your job.
- Pass on an angle toward the sidelines near your own goal.
- Never pass across the front of your own goal.
- Try to position yourself so your back is toward your own goal and you are between your opponent and the goal.
- Be persistent and never give up even if passed by your opponent.
- Talk to your teammates so they know what you are planning to do and where you are without turning away from watching the play.

Terminology

Acute angle—A small, or the smallest possible, angle between two lines of interest

Advancing—Stopping or moving the ball into a favorable position with the legs, hand, or body (a foul)

Alley—The area along each sideline within 5 yd of the sideline

Attack line—The row of players attempting to score a goal; the forward line

Backs—Defensive players who generally stay in the half of the field near the goal they defend

Blade—The curved end of the stick used for hitting the ball

Block the ball—To stop the ball with the stick; for goalkeepers only, to stop the ball with the hand, legs, or body

Bully—A means of restarting play after a double foul (or similar situation) in which two opposing players strike the ground and each other's stick alternately three times over the ball and then try to gain possession of the ball

Center forward—The attack player who generally plays about halfway between the sidelines

Clear—To send the ball away from the goal area or to an open space outside the scoring area

Corner hit—A free hit taken near the corner of the field by an offensive player when a defender unintentionally sends the ball over the end line not between the goalposts (also called a *long corner*)

Cover—To protect an area; to back up a teammate who is attempting to intercept or tackle an opponent

Dangerous hit—Lofting a hard-hit ball into another player; driving the ball directly into the legs of a nearby player (a foul)

Dribble—Advancing the ball downfield with a series of controlled taps or pushes with the stick

Drive—A ball hit hard in an attempt to pass or to shoot at the goal

Fielding—The movements performed to stop a moving ball to gain control of the ball

Flick—A pass (usually lofted) that is characterized by the lack of a backswing and a firm twisting of the stick

Forward—An offensive player (attacker) whose primary responsibility is to score goals; a player who leads the attack

Free hit—An unguarded hit awarded to the opponent on the spot where a player fouls (except in the shooting circle)

Fullback—A defensive player who generally plays between the center line and the goal being defended

Goals—Points scored by hitting the ball into the opponent's goal cage in a legal manner (score = 1 point); the framework and netting that define the scoring target (goal cage)

Goal cage—The area described by two posts and a crossbar that define the scoring area; the goal framework and the wire or net attached to the back (out of bounds) of it

Goal line—The end line of the field

Goalie pads—Heavy padded leg guards worn by the goalkeeper; may include padding to cover the shoes (these are sometimes called *kickers*)

Goalkeeper—The one player on a team designated to protect the goal who has special privileges while in the goal area; (e.g., fielding the ball with the legs, body, or hand; also called *goalie*)

Halfback—A midfield player who backs up the forwards on offense and assists the other backs on defense

High sticking—Raising the stick high in the air in a dangerous manner while hitting the ball

Hit-in—See Push-in

Inner (Inside)—The forwards who play between the center of the field and the wings or between the center forward and the wings

Interchanging—Switching positions with a teammate

Jab—A tackle performed by a series of short jabs with the toe or bottom of the stick (same as a *job tackle*)

Kickers—Padding to cover the shoes or the goalkeeper's special shoes to protect the feet

Left lunge—A tackle performed by sweeping the stick to the left while lunging out

Lineup—The pattern or arrangement of players on a team at the start of the game

Link—A player who backs up the forwards or assists with the attack and who also helps defend the goal; a connector between the defense and the offense

Long corner—See Corner hit

Loose dribble—A style of dribble in which the ball is allowed to move well away from the feet

M pattern—An offensive pattern characterized by having the inners lead the attack while the center forward and wings move downfield somewhat behind them; a defensive pattern characterized by having the side halfbacks (or links) play close to the forward line while the fullbacks and center half play back closer to the goal they defend

Mark—To guard an opponent

Midfielders—Players who back up the forwards and assist the backs on defense; links between the forwards and the backs

Nonstickside—Referring to the left side of the player

Obstruction foul—Illegally protecting the ball by imposing the body between the ball and an approaching opponent; pulling the ball around the body or between the feet to prevent an opponent from reaching it

Outside wings—The forwards who play close to each sideline

Pass-back— pass backward from the center of the field to a teammate who is behind the center line; the pass used to start each half and to begin play after each goal

Penalty corner—A free hit taken on the end line 10 yd from a goalpost by an offensive player when a defender fouls in the striking circle (also called a *short corner*)

Penalty shot—A shot at the goal awarded to an offensive player when defenders commit designated fouls in the striking circle

Push-in—Push passing the ball into play from the sidelines after the ball has gone out of bounds at the sidelines

Push—A pass or shot performed by placing the stick against or near the ball and pushing it

Pyramid lineup—An organizational pattern of play characterized by five forwards, three halfbacks, two fullbacks, and a goalkeeper lined up in a pyramid formation from the center line to the goal

Reverse stick—Turning the stick over and moving it to the left or in front of the body with the toe down; to stop or hit a ball that is toward the left of the player

Scoop—A pass that is characterized by a lifting action with the blade of the stick, and that is lofted but not hit hard

Shin guards—Protective gear that fits around the lower legs to prevent injury to the shins

Shooting circle—See Striking circle

Short corner—See Penalty corner

Stick—The object used to control and propel the field hockey ball

Stick face—The flat surface of the curved end of the stick; the striking surface of the blade

Stick head—The curved end of the stick used for hitting the ball

Stick side—The right side of the player

Striking circle—The semicircular area in front of each goal inside which (under most rules) a ball must be touched by an attacker before a goal may be scored

Sweeper—A midfield player who ranges from side to side on the field and tries to intercept all long passes by the opponents; a defensive player who plays near the edge of the striking circle and tackles any opponent who approaches

Toe—The tip of the curved end of the stick

Triangular passes—A series of passes made back and forth by two teammates as they run parallel with each other downfield (two passes from two sides of the triangle, and the running player forms the third side)

W pattern—An offensive pattern characterized by having the center and wings lead the attack while the inners move downfield behind them

Wings—The forwards or attack players who generally play near the sidelines

Selected Readings

Ambruster, D., Musker, F., & Mood, D. (1979). *Sports and recreational activities for men and women* (7th ed.). St. Louis: C.V. Mosby.

Barnes, M. (1969). *Field hockey: The coach and player*. Boston: Allyn & Bacon.

Lees, J. (1942). *Field hockey for girls*. New York: A.S. Barnes.

Mushier, C. (1983). *Team sports for girls and women* (2nd ed.). Princeton, NJ: Princeton Book.

National Association of Girls and Women in Sport. (1986). *Field hockey guide*. Reston, VA: American Alliance for Health, Physical Education, Recreation and Dance.

Field Hockey Skills Errors and Corrections

CARRYING THE STICK

Error	*Causes*	*Corrections*
Restriction of locomotion		
Slow or jerky movements	• Stiff body position while running	• Hold the stick away from the body so it will not interfere with the stride; swing arms freely.
	• Failure to make a smooth transition from carry to hit or tackle	• Keep stick in front of the body so it does *not* interfere with the legs; lean forward from the hips.
	• Failure to use a relaxed grip	• Grasp the stick firmly but not too tightly; bend the elbows.
Slow transition to dribble or pass position		
Ball missed	• Carrying the stick improperly	• Carry the stick so that the blade is slightly above knee level; extend the stick slightly forward and down when ready for action; keep the stick free of the feet; keep the left hand in the dribble position or the pass position at all times so that the stick can be quickly lowered to the ground with the face in correct position.
	• Failure to keep the blade of the stick close to the ground when tackling or receiving the ball or when in the shooting circle	• Extend the stick low to the ground; lean forward; keep the flat side of the stick toward the ball; tighten the grip on the stick; keep both hands on the stick.

DRIBBLE

Error	*Causes*	*Corrections*
Lack of ball control		
Ball missed	• Failure to keep the stick almost perpendicular to the ground	• Press the left hand forward so that it leads the stick; hold the stick with both hands.
	• Failure to keep the stick close to the ground	• Bend forward; keep the blade end close to the ground.

(Cont.)

DRIBBLE (Continued)

Error	*Causes*	*Corrections*
Lack of ball control		
Ball missed	• Failure to hit the ball (overrunning it)	• Focus on the ball closely; bend the head slightly downward but look up frequently; slide the right hand lower on the stick.
	• Failure to use proper wrist action	• Push or tap the ball by using small flexing movements of the wrists.
	• Allowing the ball to get too far to the left	• Press forward with the left hand; be sure the left hand grips the stick correctly; hold the stick so that the flat part faces forward; avoid swinging the stick across in front of the body.
	• Allowing the ball to get too far to the right	• Use the right hand more to push the ball; keep the flat part of the stick facing forward; do *not* allow the left wrist to bend backward.
Ball lost to tackler	• Failure to keep the ball close	• Use proper wrist action (use small flexing movements); keep the ball within 2 or 3 ft of the legs; push or tap the ball; avoid using a backswing; do *not* swing the stick.
	• Improper body position	• Lean forward and bend over slightly; keep the left elbow out in front and the right elbow away from the side; keep the head slightly down.
Loss of spatial awareness		
	• Failure to know field position and location of others	• Avoid holding the head too low; glance up occasionally to survey opponents and field position.

PUSH PASS

Error	*Causes*	*Corrections*
Weak		
Ball fails to reach target	• Failure to utilize weight shift to generate force	• Step forward and shift the weight forward and in line with the pass.
	• Ineffective use of leverage	• Keep the hands apart on the stick handle; push with the right hand and pull with the left hand.
	• Failure to use wrist action	• Rapidly flex the right wrist in a snapping action.
Too hard		
	• Use of too much backswing	• Start the pass by placing the stick behind the ball and close to it; eliminate the backswing.

Error	*Causes*	*Corrections*
Misdirection		
Ball goes to right or left of target	• Improper body position in relation to the ball	• Position the ball at least a foot in front of the leading leg; lean well forward. When pushing to the right, position the ball outside of the right foot; when pushing forward or to the left, position the ball in front of the body.
	• Poor follow-through	• Extend the right arm and the stick toward the target.

DRIVE

Error	*Causes*	*Corrections*
Weak		
Ball fails to reach target	• Inadequate range of motion	• Position the hands close together at top of the stick; rotate the trunk slightly clockwise; swing the stick backward until it is parallel with the ground; keep the right elbow away from the body; swing the stick forward forcefully through the ball.
	• Failure to shift the body weight forward	• Step toward the target with the left foot; shift the body weight forward to add momentum.
	• Improper contact with the ball	• Strike the ball with the center of the blade near the beginning of the curved part.
	• Failure to utilize total body momentum	• Run toward the ball or push the ball a few yards in front (when possible) and run up to it while executing the backswing.
Inaccurate		
Ball fails to go toward target	• Failure to be stable during the swing	• Keep the head over the ball when hitting; shorten or elongate the last step to bring the head over the ball.
Ball hit too hard	• Inappropriate amount of force	• Use the full backswing for hard drives; reduce the backswing for drives to a nearby player.
Poor aim	• Failure to pass ahead of a moving receiver	• Angle the pass well ahead of the running receiver; avoid making the receiver stop or change directions.
Incorrect strike or miss		
	• Failure to maintain focus on the ball	• Watch the ball until contact is made; do *not* look up to find a target after the swing begins.

(Cont.)

DRIVE (Continued)

Error	*Causes*	*Corrections*
Incorrect strike or miss		
	• Topping the ball	• Bend the knees as the last step is taken; keep the head down; swing the stick forward, not up.
Obstruction foul		
	• Interference with an opponent approaching the ball	• Square the shoulders toward the target; keep the toes pointing toward the target.

SCOOP

Error	*Causes*	*Corrections*
Inadequate lift		
Ball does *not* go into the air	• Poor leverage	• Slide the right hand down the stick; lift up with the right hand (flex the wrist) and push downward with the left hand near the top of the stick handle.
	• Improper contact point on the ball	• Place the stick behind and *under* the ball.
	• Failure to use a lifting action	• Lift upward with the right hand.
Ball rolls over the stick		
	• Stick held too flat	• Hold the blade of the stick at about a 30° angle with the ground (back of stick to ground).
	• Too much forward push	• Lift with the forward push; avoid moving the stick to a horizontal position while in contact with the ball.
Too much lift or force		
	• Executing the movement too quickly	• Maintain a slow speed, especially until skilled.
	• Raising the stick too high	• Keep the stick low on the stroke and follow through.
	• Improper body position	• Lean forward and keep the body weight low over the forward foot; avoid standing erect.

FLICK

Error	*Causes*	*Corrections*
No spin on the ball		
Ball lofted too high	• Failure to rotate wrist	• Flex the right wrist and rotate the hand from a palm-up to a palm-down position.
	• Poor timing of the wrist rotation	• Rotate the wrist at the start of and throughout the shot; place the end of the blade against the ball; avoid using a backswing (this causes a hitting action rather than a flick).
	• Failure to stay low to the ground	• Emphasize a low follow-through; keep the stick low for the entire range of motion.
Weak or inadequate force		
Ball goes only a few feet	• Inadequate use of body momentum	• Place the right foot well ahead of the left; transfer the body weight forcefully forward as the stroke begins; keep the knees and hips bent.
	• Improper contact point on the ball	• Place the end (tip) of the flat side of the blade against the ball.
	• Failure to rotate wrist	• Flex the right wrist and rotate the hand from a palm-up to a palm-down position.

FIELDING

Error	*Causes*	*Corrections*
Ball missed		
	• Failure to hold the stick close to the ground	• Bend forward and hold the curved end of the stick about an inch above the ground; keep the flat part of the blade facing the ball.
	• Failure to focus on the ball	• Watch the ball closely; do *not* look up until after the ball contacts the stick.
Ball rebounds too far or in wrong direction		
	• Poor stick control	• Slide the right hand several inches below the left hand on the stick handle; keep the right palm facing forward toward the approaching ball.
	• Poor stick position	• Hold the stick perpendicular to the ground and just above it; press the left hand forward to maintain this vertical position.

(Cont.)

FIELDING (Continued)

Error	*Causes*	*Corrections*
Ball rebounds too far or in wrong direction	• Failure to absorb the force of the moving ball	• Hold the stick well in front of the body with the arms slightly bent; pull the stick toward the body as the ball strikes it.
	• Failure to adjust the angle of the face of the blade	• Hold the stick so that the face of the blade is perpendicular to the path of the ball; when fielding hard-hit balls, press the left hand slightly forward ahead of the blade so that the stick angles downward and backward toward the feet.
	• Improper body position	• Use a forward-stride position with the leading foot in the direction of the ball; help absorb the force of the ball by shifting the weight to the back foot.
	• Unstable base of support	• Flex the knees and widen the stance; keep the weight on the balls of the feet for quick foot adjustment.

STRAIGHT TACKLE

Error	*Causes*	*Corrections*
Lack of ball control		
Ball missed	• Improper grip on stick	• Keep the hands apart with the right hand 4 to 8 in. below the left.
	• Stick held too close to the body	• Hold the stick well in front of the body.
	• Stick held too high	• Keep the stick very close to or touching the ground throughout the tackle.
	• Face of stick laid back	• Press the left hand forward to keep the stick perpendicular to the ground.
Ball *not* controlled	• Failure to control the ball before hitting it.	• Block or stop the ball before attempting to hit or dribble it.
Poor timing		
Tackle missed	• Failure to wait until the ball is away from the opponent's stick	• Watch the length of the opponent's dribble and adjust the approach so that the ball can be attacked when it is not near the dribbler's stick.
Foul made	• Improper body position	• Stay to the dribbler's right; block the ball with a quick reach and transfer of the body weight to the forward foot; stay low and widen the base of support.

Error	*Causes*	*Corrections*
Inappropriate strategies		
Poor balance	• Failure to approach slowly with good body control	• Move slowly toward the dribbler, keeping the body weight low and on the balls of the feet; use small steps and be prepared to change directions quickly; keep the stick close to the ground and well out in front; avoid lunging at the ball.
Slow movements	• Failure to make quick movements at the time of the tackle	• Reach quickly toward the ball; avoid "telegraphing" the move.
Losing the ball	• Striking at the ball	• Block or control the ball before attempting to hit it.

LEFT LUNGE

Error	*Causes*	*Corrections*
Lack of ball control		
Tackle missed	• Failure to lunge sufficiently	• Extend the left arm fully and swing the stick to the left; push the stick out and away from the body with the right hand; release the right hand from the stick as the stick crosses the midline of the body.
	• Poor stick placement	• Aim ahead of the ball to block or stop it.
	• Failure to keep the stick low	• Sweep the stick around just above or along the ground; reach downward and keep the body low by bending at the knees and hips.
	• Failure to intercept the ball	• Wait until the ball is at least 2 or 3 ft in front of the dribbler whenever possible; avoid trying to hit the ball when it is near the dribbler's stick
Interfering with the opponent (a foul)		
	• Lunging too soon	• Wait until you are beside the dribbler before executing the lunge.
	• Uncontrolled swing of the stick	• Keep the stick low to avoid tripping the dribbler; extend the left arm fully and grasp the stick firmly; keep the right hand on the stick (hands together) if the left hand alone is too weak to control the stick.
	• Interrupting the stride of the opponent	• Run beside, not behind, the dribbler; watch for direction changes that might cause you to bump the dribbler.

(Cont.)

CIRCULAR TACKLE

Error	Causes	Corrections
Lack of ball control		
Tackle missed	• Failure to position the face of the stick correctly	• Turn the face of the stick toward the direction the ball should go; tap the ball in that direction.
	• Poor timing	• Contact the ball when it is away from the opponent's stick.
Interference with the opponent		
	• Circling too close to the opponent	• Achieve a position at least one stride ahead of the dribbler before starting to move in front.
	• Improper body position	• Turn toward the dribbler and lead with the left shoulder in making the circle.
	• Failure to push the ball away	• Push the ball to the right; never pull the ball toward you.

JAB

Error	Causes	Corrections
Lack of ball contact		
Tackle missed	• Failure to maintain the proper grip	• Grasp the stick firmly with one hand; extend the arm fully; lay the stick back so the face is up.
	• Failure to jab at the ball	• Push the bottom of the stick at the ball; avoid using a backswing.
	• Poor timing	• Make contact with the ball when it is away from the dribbler's stick; avoid contacting the opponent's stick.
Interference with the opponent		
	• Contacting the opponent's feet (tripping) or stick	• Extend the arm fully and reach to contact the ball when it is out in front of the opponent; use a series of pushes (jabs); avoid holding the stick stationary in the dribbler's path.
	• Pushing the opponent	• Run parallel with the opponent; watch for direction changes that might cause you to collide with the dribbler; when executing a right jab, stay slightly ahead of this opponent and avoid positioning the shoulder in front of the dribbler.

GOALKEEPING (GENERAL)

Error	*Causes*	*Corrections*
Inability to intercept the ball		
Ball missed	• Improper initial position	• Stand several feet in front of the goal, not on the goal line; increase stability by crouching slightly (flex knees) and maintaining the weight equally over both feet.
	• Failure to watch the ball	• Keep track of the ball at all times; pay close attention to the play whenever the ball moves closer than the center line.
	• Improper body position	• Crouch slightly; keep the weight equally over the balls of both feet; hold the free hand about chest high with the palm out; hold the stick in the right hand below waist level and angled toward the ground; keep the knees together.
Body not in line with ball	• Failure to move into the path of the ball	• Focus on the angle of the approaching ball and move toward that side of the goal; move toward the ball to reduce the potential angles for shooting.
	• Poor locomotor pattern	• Move laterally with small shuffling steps, keeping the knees as close together as possible; move forward or backward with short steps; always face the ball; never cross one foot in front of the other while moving into position.
Lack of general awareness		
	• Failure to attend to the play	• Stay on the alert whenever the ball is nearer than the center line; crouch and prepare for quick movements as the ball nears the striking circle.
	• Failure to know where other players are	• Look to see where all opponents are while the ball is still about 25 yd away; as the ball approaches, use the peripheral vision to note nearby players other than the ball handler; keep teammates away from the path between the ball and the goal; know where teammates are (develop some play patterns whenever possible).

(Cont.)

GOALKEEPING AND CLEARING

Error	*Causes*	*Corrections*
Lack of ball control with the legs		
Ball missed	• Failure to stop the ball	• Keep the knees and feet together in front of the body; line up the pads directly in the path of the shot.
Ball rebounds too far	• Failure to control the ball	• When the ball is low, flex the knees to direct the ball to the ground in front of the feet; when the ball is above the knees, give with the ball to absorb force and keep the rebound close to the feet.
Lack of control with the hand, stick or body		
	• Ball rebounding too far forward	• Retract the hand, stick, or body as the ball contacts it; give with the ball; slant the palm, stick, or body part downward to direct the rebound in front of the feet.
Inadequate clearing of ball		
	• Failure to direct the clear appropriately	• Aim to empty spaces toward the nearer sideline; use a low follow-through; control the ball before attempting a kick; kick quickly and firmly.
	• Lofting the kick	• Step forward on the kicking foot immediately after kicking the ball; keep the body weight forward; do not raise the leg or lean backward; sweep the foot through the ball.

Chapter 7
Flag/Touch Football

Touch football grew out of interest in the exciting game of American football developed in the late 19th century. Tackle football required too much equipment and was too hazardous for the average recreational player, so modifications were made so that this game could be played by everyone.

Several variations of touch football require little equipment other than the ball. These include *two-hand touch*, which requires the tackler to touch the ballcarrier with both hands; *one-hand touch*, which requires the tackler to touch the ballcarrier with only one hand; and another variation, *one hand below the waist*, which requires the tackler to touch the ballcarrier below the waist with one hand. These are the football games most commonly played on playgrounds, in intramural leagues, and in community recreation leagues. None permits tackling that knocks down the opponent, and most rules permit only limited blocking or none at all.

The introduction of flag football was an innovation that helped remove much uncertainty and arguments from touch football. When an opponent was able to snatch the *flag* from the belt of a ballcarrier, it was clearly a successful tackle or touch, and the skill and agility needed to protect or grab a flag made the sport more interesting. Flag football has resulted in a game that is more suitable for coeducational play, and it has more standardized rules throughout the country. Flags are attached with either a snap or a Velcro fastening to a belt worn by each player.

Purposes and Values

Football is a very popular fall sport throughout the United States. It has the potential to be an excellent coeducational activity if started in middle school or at the beginning of junior high. Boys usually have the opportunity to develop the throwing, catching, and kicking skills needed for this sport at an early age. Girls rarely have the same opportunity. Therefore, by the early teens, many boys have become rather skilled, whereas girls of comparable age are at the beginning level. If girls are taught the skills in elementary or middle school, they will be able to participate more successfully in competitive football situations in high school.

Football is a spectator sport unsurpassed in the number of people it attracts. It has become a part of our culture in the United States. All young people should have an opportunity to learn about the game and, at least, to become informed observers.

However, football is much more valuable for the individual who plays the game than for the one who merely watches others play. Touch and flag football have become lifetime sports for some people. This involves mostly men, although a few leagues around the country are composed of women or coeducational teams. Football skills contribute to the development of eye-foot coordination, running speed, and strength. Good body control is necessary for successful players, and agility can be improved through practicing the dodging techniques. Conditioning for football can provide a good cardiovascular workout, but the activity itself usually demands only short, vigorous bursts of activity.

The Game

Touch football is a variation of regular (tackle) football modified to make it safer to play without protective equipment. The objective is to carry or pass the ball into the opponents' *end zone* for a *touchdown* while preventing the opponents from taking the ball into the end zone your team defends. The rules vary greatly, and no common set of rules is used throughout the United States. The ball may be advanced by running or passing. The ballcarrier is stopped by being touched by an opponent while carrying the ball. The team scoring the most points within the playing time wins. Ties are not usually played off, although local tournament rules may specify an extension of time, or the winner may be decided by comparing the number of first downs made by each team. This latter plan requires extensive record keeping.

In flag football, the tackle consists of pulling the Velcro- or snap-attached flag from the belt of the ballcarrier. This use of belts and flags provides a more certain way of determining that a tackle has occurred and reduces arguments among young players. It is also safer because there is no reason to hit or push with the hands.

Touchdowns count 6 points and are made by passing or carrying the ball over the *goal line*. A *safety* counts 2 points and is made by tagging a ballcarrier behind the player's own goal line. A *field goal*, if allowed, counts 3 points. A *conversion*, or *point after touchdown* counts 1 point as in regular football. A 2-point conversion may be allowed after a touchdown if the ball is carried or passed into the end zone instead of being kicked after a touchdown. However, most touch or flag football rules make no provisions for field goals and points after touchdowns because many playing areas do not have *goal posts*.

A shoulder *block* is usually allowed, but players may not use their hands and may not leave their feet to block. Ballcarriers may not use their hands to fend off opponents. Some rules do not allow body contact of any sort between opponents to avoid roughness. These rules allow a *screen*, which is set up when players stand or run beside or ahead of a ballcarrier to prevent the opponents from tagging, but neither the blocker (screener) nor the tackler may push the opponent.

Play is started with a *kickoff* (a *punt* or *placekick*) by one team. This kick is usually taken from the 20-yd line or the quarter-yard line. The team receiving the ball becomes the offensive team, and the kicking team goes on defense. After each goal, play is restarted with a kickoff by the team that scored. All players are eligible to receive passes or to run with the ball.

Rule variations that allow the offensive team to retain possession of the ball include (a) gaining 10 yd in 4 *downs*, (b) reaching the second yard marker in 4 downs if the field is marked in 5-yd increments, and (c) reaching the next-closest line if the field is marked in quarters (i.e., 20- or 25-yd lines and a center line). When fields are unmarked or officials are not available, a rule can be used that requires a team to score in 4 downs; otherwise, the ball goes to the opposite team. A team may choose to punt the ball when it does not believe it can make a first down, but it must announce the play in advance. The defensive players may not rush the kicker in an attempt to block, and the offensive players may not cross the *scrimmage line* until the ball has been kicked. Fumbled balls are immediately dead. Possession is retained by the team that fumbled.

Playing time can consist of two 20-min halves, four 10-min quarters, or whatever variations fit the time allotted. Usually 7 to 9 players constitute a team, but for class play as many as 11 or 12 per team are suitable. Free substitution is allowed whenever the ball is not in play.

Playing Area

A flat, grassy area is necessary for touch or flag football. The minimum size is 40 by 80 yd with at least 10 yd around the perimeter. The game can be played on a blacktopped (asphalt) area, but many abrasions and other injuries could occur. A regulation football field is ideal. The field should be marked with 10-yd stripes from end to end, although 20- or 25-yd marks are sufficient (Figure 7.1).

Equipment

The following is a description of the equipment necessary for flag or touch football. Standards for equipment and recommendations on equipment use are also included.

Balls

Regulation leather-covered footballs are suggested for game play in high schools and adult groups. However, these tend to absorb moisture and become hard and slippery if used in wet weather. Rubber or synthetic coverings are more suitable for all-weather play or play on hard surfaces. Beginners and younger children will find the junior-size football more comfortable to use. For instructional purposes and class play, lightweight plastic foam or rubber-covered junior-size balls are highly recommended. However, the use of the 6- to 8-in.-long replicas of a football is not appropriate because they do not require the mastery of kicking and passing skills.

Flags

Sets of belts with short flags attached by snap or Velcro fastenings are available from several sporting goods companies. These can also be made of cloth or flexible plastic strips with Velcro sewed on to the belt and to the end of each strip. A belt with two flags attached (one at each side) is worn by each player, because all are eligible to run with the ball or catch passes.

Pinnies

Pinnies or vests may be needed for touch football but not for flag football. The flags could be of contrasting colors to distinguish one team from the other.

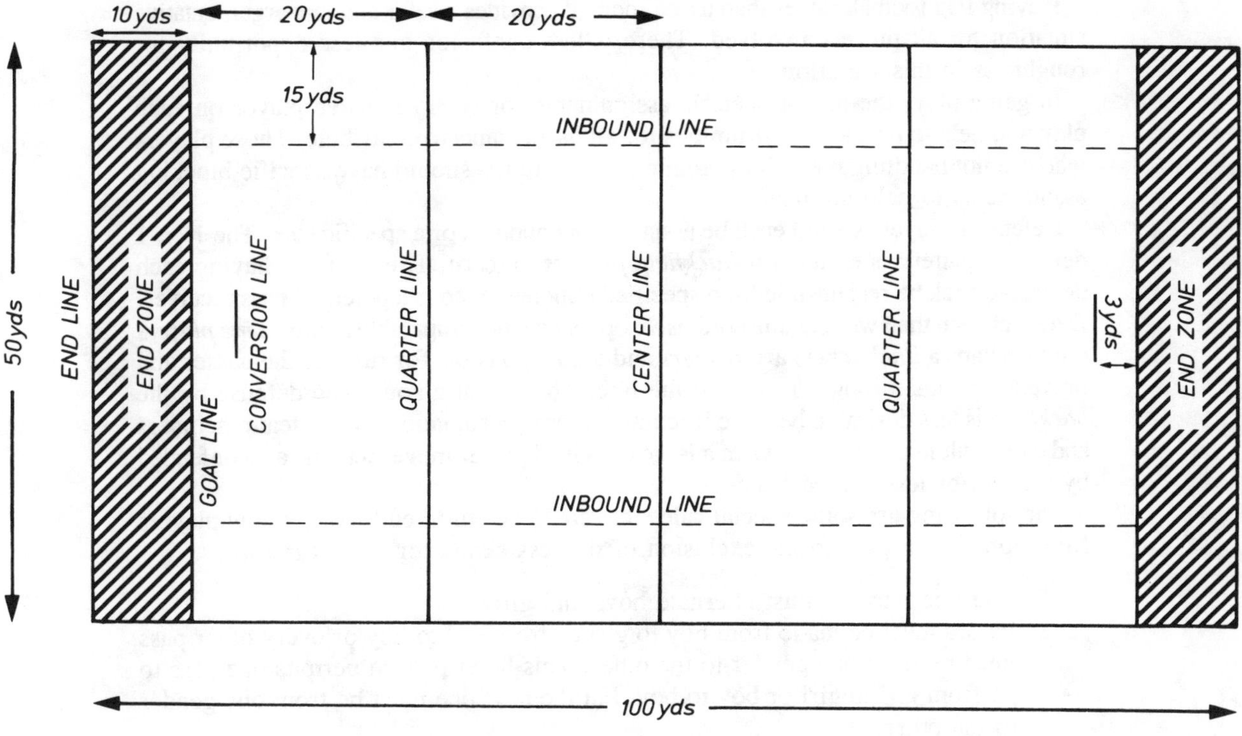

Figure 7.1. Flag or touch football field

Suggestions for Coeducational Play

When the skill levels of some players are significantly higher than those of others, players of comparable ability should compete directly against one another. This can be arranged by balancing teams so that each one has an equal number of skilled and unskilled players. Then players of similar ability would oppose one another in blocking, pass reception (or interception), and other skills of the game.

Players could be divided into homogeneous subgroups according to skill levels when groups are large enough. This could be done readily in large schools where more than one class meets during each period. Simple tests such as a passing test for distance, a pass-catching test, and a blocking-effort evaluation, could be used to determine the groups to which students are assigned. Those of higher skill could be assigned to teams in one division of play (or league), whereas the less skilled players could make up the teams of a second division. Teams would play only those within their own division. A culminating game between winners of each division might be challenging if the skill levels are not too different.

Players could be assigned to teams at the beginning of the unit, and the team players can be made responsible for the achievements of all members of the team. This encourages the more knowledgeable and skillful players to help the others improve. During practice periods, teammates should be encouraged to help one another become contributing members of the team. For example, in leader-class passing drills, the leader could be a more skilled player who would make sure that passes were on target and catchable. Conversely, the weaker players could be the leaders in group drills where the leader gets more opportunity to handle the ball.

Playing flag football rather than touch football provides a safer and less argumentative situation for all players involved. There is less confusion and less opportunity for roughness in this variation.

In game play, the use of specific assignments for each offensive player on each play will help to provide opportunities for all participants to contribute. Those players who are not handling the ball or running pass patterns should have specific blocking assignments to help the team.

Defensive players should each be assigned an opponent or a specific task. The 1-on-1 defensive pattern is easiest for *backfield players* to learn. This requires having each defensive back be responsible for a specified opponent who is a potential pass receiver. Defenders can then work against offensive opponents of comparable ability. *Line players* (and perhaps a *linebacker*) are *rushers* and are responsible for rushing the passer and preventing runs through or around the line. The use of a zone-type defense by the *backfield* is less desirable because it requires more coordination among team members and can result in a mismatch when a large or skilled player moves into the area defended by a small or less skilled back.

The following are some special rules that could be enforced to keep a few players from dominating play to the exclusion of the less skilled or less aggressive.

1. The line players must alternate boys and girls.
2. Passes must be made from boy to girl or from girl to boy or every other pass must be from one gender to the other. This latter pattern permits one pass to go from girl to girl or boy to boy, but the next one must be from one gender to the other.
3. The same type of rule described in Rule 2 can be made for runs by backfield players.

Teaching Progressions

The football skills described are all basic, and most students should be able to achieve adequate levels of mastery. The more advanced students should concentrate on developing more team-play patterns and strategies.

I. Passing and catching
   A. Forward
   B. Lateral
   C. Center

II. Handoffs

III. Ball carrying

IV. Blocking
   A. Screen
   B. Shoulder block (if desired)

V. Kicking

VI. Tagging or grabbing the flag

VII. Game play

Techniques and Practice

Passing

Passing and catching skills should be taught at the same time, as the two skills depend on each other in game play. Emphasis should be placed on learning to throw the football so that it spirals along the longitudinal axis (from tip to tip), thereby sailing farther and being easier to catch. The airborne ball, whether passed or kicked, that rotates end over end encounters more resistance from the air and is much more difficult to catch.

Forward

Any ball that is thrown ahead of the passer or toward the attacking goal is a *forward pass*. The forward pass is an effective means of advancing the ball downfield. Any player on a team is eligible to receive a pass. The passer (usually the *quarterback*) must pass before crossing the line of scrimmage, which is where the ball was placed at the start of the play.

The passer takes the ball in both hands. The throwing hand grips the ball in the middle of the ball with the fingers crossing the laces laterally and the thumb under the ball. The nonthrowing hand acts as a support and a guide until the actual throwing movement occurs. The two hands carry the ball vertically. The trunk and hips rotate clockwise (back/open) to prepare for a right-hand throw. The hands separate, and the nonthrowing arm moves forward for balance and the throwing arm rearward. The ball is moved behind the ear with the elbow flexed (Figure 7.2).

The force-production phrase begins with a forward step on the nonthrowing leg. The trunk and hips rotate forward (counterclockwise). This action also turns the shoulders toward the target and starts the forward shift of body weight. Once the trunk, hips, and shoulders are facing the target, the arm starts its whipping action toward the point of release. The elbow extends rapidly, and the wrist flexes rapidly (snaps) just prior to release. At the time of release, the hand is tangent to the target. The hand comes under the ball to impart lateral spin (spiral) on the ball. The follow-through is a continuation of the arm movement toward the target.

Common Movement Problems and Suggestions. The following are movement problems encountered when performing the forward pass. Instructional suggestions are also presented.

- The throw can lack speed if an improper weight shift or stepping action occurs. Instructors should emphasize the body weight over the back foot (throwing side) at the beginning of the throw. The weight of the body is shifted forward toward the stepping foot (nonthrowing side). The step should be about shoulder width but in a forward stride.
- A firm grip on the ball is essential for distance and imparting spin.
- If the thrower does not have an appropriate backswing, the forward throwing motion will be limited.
- Awkward throws or throws that are ineffective may be caused by the thrower's inability to utilize the whipping action in the throw. Special attention should be given to the sequential ordering of the body in the force-production phase. The hips, trunk, shoulders, upper arm, forearm, and hand move in this order toward the point of release.
- Accuracy in throwing is dependent on the timing of the release. Early releases will cause the ball to have a high trajectory; late releases will result in a low trajectory.

Figure 7.2. Forward pass

Lateral Underhand

The *lateral pass* is made to the side of or behind the passer. The ball may not be thrown so that it goes closer to the goal the team is attacking than the thrower is when making the throw. If this happens, it is considered a forward pass. Only one forward pass is permitted on each play, but a team may pass the ball laterally more than once during a play. The lateral pass is usually done with an underhand motion with one or both hands, although any throw is legal.

When performing the two-handed lateral underhand pass, both hands grasp the ball toward the tip away from the receiver. The arms are retracted down and back toward the body. The thrower steps toward the receiver when initiating the toss. The ball is lightly tossed by extending the arms at the shoulders and elbows toward the receiver. The target is about waist height of the receiver. The follow-through is a continuation of the arms moving toward the receiver.

The one-handed technique begins with the dominant hand grasping the ball. The football is held with the palm of the throwing hand under the ball with the fingers and thumb spread. A simple underhand toss is made and the hand rotates in a counterclockwise manner for a right-handed thrower. This imparts spin on the ball, providing more speed and accuracy, and resulting in a catch that is easier to make.

Common Movement Problems and Suggestions. The following are movement problems of the one- and the two-handed lateral underhand passes. Instructional suggestions are also included.

- A common difficulty is tossing the ball with too much force or without lateral spin. This causes difficulty for the receiver when trying to catch and control the ball.
- Failure to toss the ball with sufficient force is generally caused by not fully extending the arms at release or by restricting the range of movement due to improper body positioning.
- Accuracy can be improved by emphasizing a step toward the receiver with a forward body-weight transfer. A good follow-through also enhances the possibilities for increased accuracy.

Centering/Center Snap

To begin a play other than when a kickoff is taken, a line player must *center*, or *snap*, the ball to a backfield player, who is usually the quarterback. *Centering* involves passing the ball from the ground between the legs to the receiver. It should reach the receiver somewhere between the knees and the chest for ease of handling. More advanced players may wish to try the handoff type of centering used in the tackle football *T formation*. The receiver assumes a position immediately behind the center and takes the ball directly from the hands of the center. The receiver must then move quickly away from the line of scrimmage to execute the play. This is not generally preferred for players of the flag and touch games. Some rules do not even permit this handoff type of play.

The player takes a side-straddle stance with the feet wider than shoulder width. The weight of the body is equally distributed between both feet. The hips and head are held high. Both hands are on the ball as it rests on the ground directly in front of the feet. The dominant hand is positioned toward the front of the ball, and the nondominant hand is centered on the ball with the fingers crossing the laces.

The toss or pass-off begins with flexion at the shoulders when tossing or handing the ball rearward through the legs. If the ball is tossed, the ball is thrown at waist height of the receiver with some spiral spin and not too forcefully. If the ball is handed, it is handed to the quarterback with the laces up and the ends of the ball parallel with the ground.

Common Movement Problems and Suggestions. The following are common movement problems of centering. Instructional suggestions are also presented.

- Problems can be created by an unbalanced stance. If the weight is unequally distributed over both feet, the total movement may appear awkward or uncoordinated.
- If the arms are not swung freely, the timing for the receiver is impaired. Emphasize a smooth swinging of the arms so that the receiver can anticipate the catch.
- The most common difficulty is to throw or hand off the ball with too much force. A hard pass or handoff is very difficult for the receiver to control. Emphasize softness and accuracy in the toss of the center snap.

Handoff

The *handoff* is used as a secure way of giving the ball to another player using the underhand movement. It prevents an *interception* and reduces the chance of a fumble or an inaccurate pass.

The ball is held close to the body with both hands. The foot closest to the direction of the handoff steps forward. The ball is extended to the receiver at waist level. The ball is held until the receiver takes the ball from the hands.

In the handoff, the ball is placed into the midsection area of the receiver, who has one arm horizontal to the ground and underneath the ball and the other arm horizontal and above where the ball will go. As the ball is received, the upper arm clamps down on it, and both hands clasp the ball. Some coaches believe that the arm that is toward the passer should be above the ball and the other arm below it; others think that the elbow of the top arm might interfere with the handoff in this position, so they prefer that the arm that is toward the passer be below the ball.

Common Movement Problems and Suggestions. The following are movement problems encountered when performing a handoff. Instructional suggestions are also included.

- The most common problem of the handoff is faulty timing. The player handing off and the receiver should be synchronized. Practice of the skill without the pressure of a game should help this problem.
- Failure to place the ball in the stomach of the receiver generally results in a fumble.
- The passer must hold the ball firmly until the receiver takes it from the grasp to help prevent fumbles.
- The receiver should accept and cradle the ball with both arms and hands. Trying to grasp the ball with only the hands often results in fumbles.

Receiving

Receiving the ball is a receiving-of-force or catching fundamental movement skill. A player can receive the ball as either a thrown pass or a handoff. The handoff is generally received in the midsection of the body, but the thrown pass can be received above the waist, below the waist, or above the shoulders.

When receiving a handoff from the quarterback or deep back, extend the arms forward toward the player handing off with one arm positioned above the other. If the ballcarrier is approaching the receiver from the receiver's right, the left arm should be under the ball and the right arm held above to clamp down on the ball. As the right arm clamps down on the ball, the left arm flexes (bends) underneath the ball as it is cradled into the stomach. The arms reverse positions when the handoff comes from the receiver's left. As the ball comes to the midsection, pull the ball into the body. If the ball has a lot of force, retract, or give, with the body. The ball should be surrounded with as much body-surface area as possible. The player leans slightly forward to protect the ball further. In other words, the player smothers the ball.

The receiving of a pass is the same for all passes except the positioning of the hands. Players should position themselves in front of the ball. To receive the ball, the player should extend the arms out toward the approaching ball. The palms of the hands are facing the approaching ball with the thumbs toward each other when the ball is above the waist. The fingers are pointing down and the palms facing the approaching ball with the little fingers together when the pass is below the waist. The same hand position is used for the over-the-shoulder catch, but the fingers are directed upward.

In all situations, the receiver dissipates the force of the ball by bringing the ball toward the center of the body. The ball is then positioned in a carrying position as the player continues to run downfield.

Common Movement Problems and Suggestions

The following are common movement problems in receiving a pass or a handoff. Instructional suggestions are also presented.

- Balance and control of the body at all times is essential. Ball control is very difficult if the body is unbalanced.
- Players should maintain focus on the ball at all times. Failure to do so generally results in missing the ball.
- Balls are knocked out of the receiver's hands if the player does not have a firm grip on the ball. Emphasize a firm grip by emphasizing the application of pressure on opposite sides of the ball with the hands.
- Failure to control the ball before resuming a full running stride can cause the receiver to fumble or drop the ball.
- Failure to pull the ball into the center of the body can result in the ball bouncing off the hands.
- Instructors should teach players who cannot reach a pass or handoff directed to them to position their bodies so that any nearby opponents cannot intercept or receive the ball.

Passing and Receiving Drills

Forward Pass Drills

The following are forward pass drills. Both partner and group drills are presented.

Partner Drills. Paired practice for passing and catching provides the most efficient use of time if there is sufficient equipment and space, and when the players are self-directed. The following are partner drills.

1.0. Each pair of players has a football as they practice throwing back and forth. All throws should be going in the same direction (e.g., north and south) to reduce the hazard of balls flying wildly around and hitting other players. Players start about 15 ft apart. After every 5 to 10 throws, players should move two more steps apart until they are about 45 ft apart. Older and more experienced players may be able to increase the distance.

2.0. After this stationary practice, players should practice throwing to a moving receiver. The receiver points in the direction of the intended run. The passer should throw well ahead of the receiver to make the receiver run fast and yet still be able to reach the ball before it bounces. The receiver then becomes the passer and throws the ball back. Some of the following group practice drills are also appropriate for paired practice when there is sufficient space.

Group Drills. The following are group drills for passing and receiving. The distance between the passer and receiver can increase as skills increase.

1.0. Circle Formation (Figure 4.13). Circles are 15 to 20 ft in diameter. Players pass the ball back and forth across the circle. The circles can be made larger if skill warrants it.

2.0. Double Lines (Figure 4.10). Individuals in lines are 15 to 20 ft apart. The ball is passed sequentially back and forth from one end to the other. As skill improves, move the lines farther apart. Variation: Both Drills 1.0 and 2.0 can be used as competitive drills. The players count the number of successful passes in a specified period of time or count the number of successive passes made without error.

3.0. Two Columns at Right Angles (Figure 7.3). The first player in Column 1 passes ahead of the runner (a), who catches the ball and returns it to the next person in Column 1 (b). Players go to the end of the opposite column after completing a turn. Variation: Move Column 2 to the left side and practice catching a ball coming from the right.

4.0. Double-Column Formation (Figure 7.4). The leader of Column 2 runs straight ahead. When the runner gets about 15 ft from the start, the leader of Column 1 passes the football in front of the runner (a), trying to pass the ball so that the receiver can catch it without slowing down. The receiver returns the ball to the next person in Column 1 (b), and each person goes to the end of the opposite column. Variation: Switch passing and throwing lines so that players practice catching over both the left and the right shoulders.

5.0. Double-Column Formation About 5 ft Apart (Figure 7.5). The leader of Column 2 runs straight ahead about 15 ft, then cuts sharply to the left. The passer in Column 1 throws ahead of the receiver (a) and goes to the end of Column 2. The receiver returns the ball to Column 1 (b) and goes to the end of Column 1. With intermediate and advanced players, increase the distance of the pass. Variations include the following:

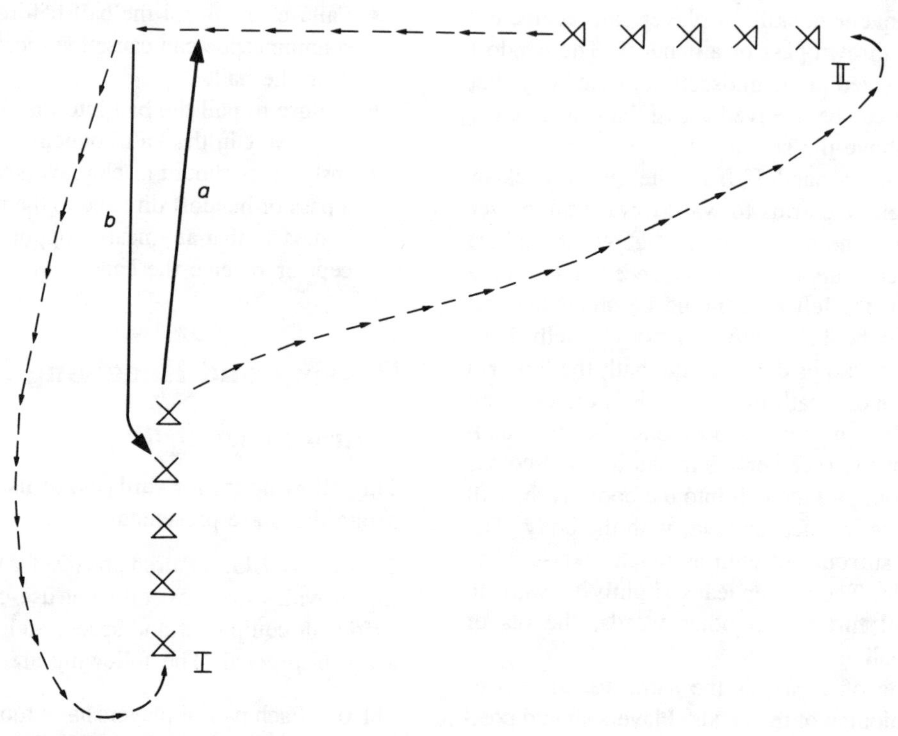

Figure 7.3. Pass to moving receiver

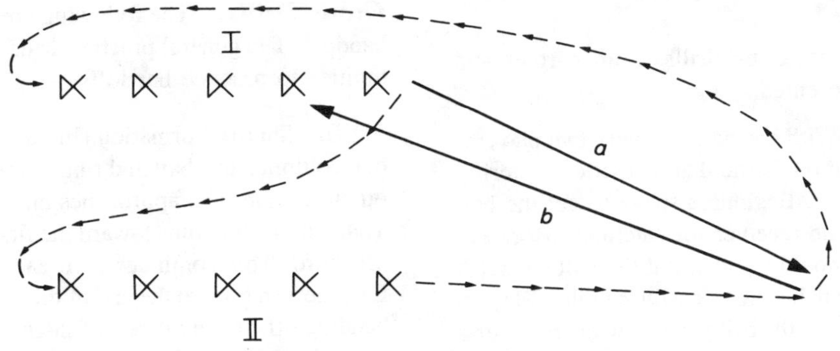

Figure 7.4. Pass to receiver moving away from passer

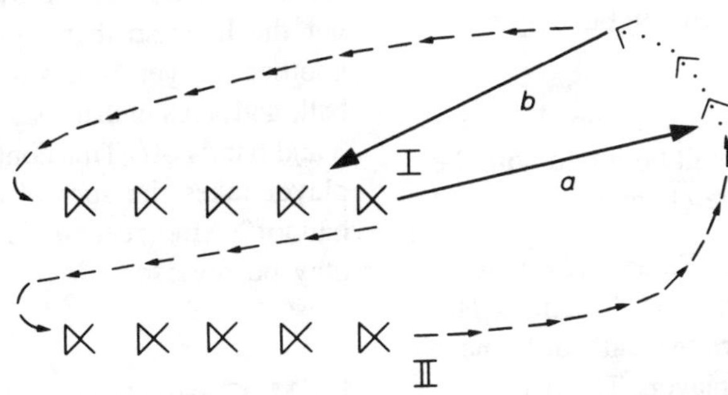

Figure 7.5. Pass to receiver cutting left

5.1. The receiver cuts to the right instead of the left.

5.2. Players in Column 1 become the receivers and players in Column 2 the passers. The receiver runs straight ahead before cutting to the right in front of the passer.

5.3. Use the same formation as in the previous drill, but the receiver cuts to the left away from the passer's column.

Lateral Underhand Pass Drills

The following are drills for the lateral underhand pass. Both partner and group drills are presented.

Partner Drills. If there is sufficient equipment to allot one ball to every two players, partner drills provide the maximum practice opportunities. The following are partner drills.

1.0. Divide the players in partners and place them side by side. Practice lateraling the ball back and forth. Practice throwing to both the right and the left.

2.0. Perform the skill while running side by side or with the receiver slightly behind the thrower. This is a more realistic situation than lateraling while standing still.

Group Drills. The following are group drills for the lateral underhand pass. Lateral passes are not forceful passes and should not be used for long distances.

1.0. Double-Line Formation with Players Staggered (Figure 4.11). Players lateral the ball back and forth and up and down between the lines. Start with lines about 10 ft apart and move back to about 15 ft. Longer laterals are not recommended because of the risk of interception.

2.0. Double-Column Formation (Figure 4.9). Columns of individuals are lined up about 10 ft apart. The leaders of each column begin running downfield, passing the ball back and forth with lateral passes. The passer should move slightly ahead of the receiver before making the pass. After running 40 to 50 yd (about half the length of the field), players should stop and return around the outside of the drill area to the end of the opposite column. Try to have at least three balls per group. Then each pair may start when the pair ahead gets halfway to the stopping line. The players returning to the ends of the columns must pass the ball to the next ones who need them as soon as possible. Additional drills, which include lateral pass practice, will be found with the general practice drills later in this chapter.

Centering Drills

The following are centering drills. Both partner and group drills are presented.

Partner Drills. With one ball for every two players, players scatter about on the field and practice centering the ball to each other. Beginners strive to get the ball a short distance to the receiver for catching. More experienced players should try to spiral the ball so that it goes farther and can be more easily caught. Players should also try to throw the ball just below the receiver's waist. Advanced players may practice centering the ball slightly to one side or the other so that the receiver can stand to the side in the backfield. Remember that players on the offensive team must not be in motion when the ball is snapped (an *illegal motion* penalty) but may move as soon as the ball is released.

Group Drills. The following are group drills for centering. Other centering drills will be found with the general practice drills later in the chapter.

1.0. Single-Column Formation (Figure 4.2). Players are about 8 ft apart and all facing one direction. The first person in the column centers the ball to the next person, who centers to the next player. The drill continues in this manner. Players turn around to face the opposite direction and center the ball back down the column. Increase the distance between players as skill improves. Variation: Competition between columns can be added as motivation. The first column to center the ball all the way down the column and back without error wins.

2.0. Leader-Class Formation (Figure 4.6). The leader is about 10 ft from the class with the back to the class. The leader centers the ball to the person at the end of the line who catches it and passes it back. The leader then centers to the next person. This continues on down the line. The leader then goes to the end of the line and another leader steps out in front of the group and repeats the pattern. Everyone takes a turn at being the leader. Variation: Add competition by seeing which group can complete the *circuit* first or by comparing how many successful centering passes can be made in a given time.

Handoff Drills

The following are handoff drills. Both partner and group drills are presented.

Partner Drills. In pairs, players practice moving toward each other and handing off the ball. Practice handing off and receiving from both the right and the left.

Group Drills. The following are group drills for the handoff. The general practice drills also provide opportunities to practice handoffs.

1.0. Shuttle Formation (Figure 4.8). The leader of one column has a ball and runs toward the leader of the other column who approaches and receives a handoff. That person then runs toward the first column and hands off there. This continues until each player has a turn. Each person goes to the end of the opposite column after handing off. In the interest of safety, players should pass right shoulders at first. Later, change the drill so that players pass left shoulders. This changes the arm positions of the receivers.

2.0. Double-Line Formation (See Figure 7.6). Stagger the lines so that a player is not directly opposite another. Player 1 runs toward Player 2, hands off the ball, and stays in that spot. Player 2 moves toward Player 3 and hands off. This continues on down the line. Each player takes the spot of the person who received the handoff. After reaching the end of the lines, the pattern may be reversed.

Ball Carrying

A team must score points in order to win. Scoring occurs when a team can advance the ball beyond the goal line. One method of advancing the ball is to carry the ball while running. Successful ball carrying is imperative to the successful execution of plays.

The ball should be carried against the body. Additionally, it should be held with one end tucked between the body and the upper arm in combination with the inside of the elbow. The opposite end of the football is held in the palm of the hand with the fingers spread over the end. The runner should carry the ball on the side away from the tacklers (i.e., on the left side if the tackler is approaching from the ballcarrier's right). When a player is surrounded by the opponents, the second hand should be placed on the ball for further protection. Both techniques help to prevent fumbles, although in most touch and flag rules fumbles are ruled dead balls and are returned to the team that fumbled. This eliminates the safety hazard of a pileup as players strive to fall on a fumbled ball.

Common Movement Problems and Suggestions

The following are common movement problems of ball carrying. Instructional suggestions are also presented.

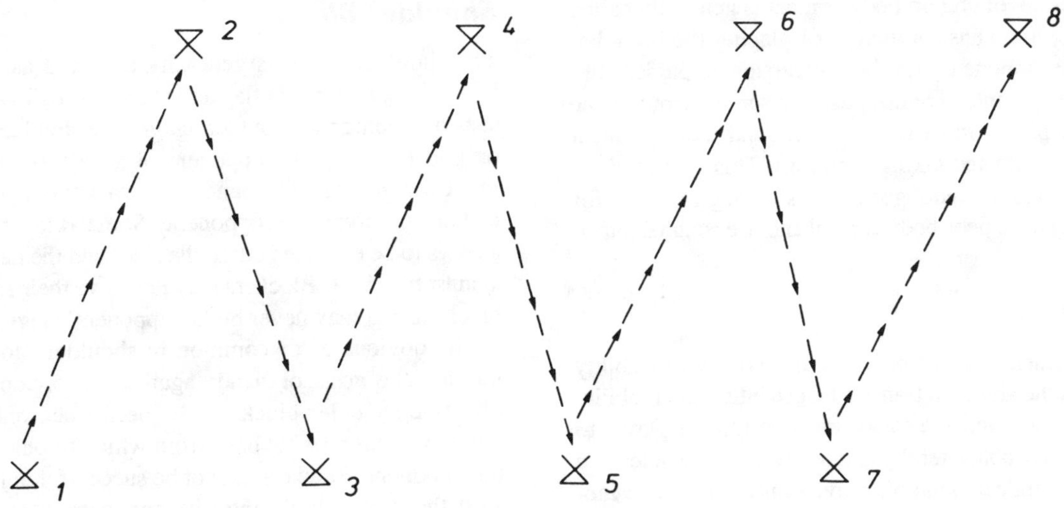

Figure 7.6. Zigzag handoff drill

- Failure to protect the ball can lead to fumbles. Emphasize a firm grip on the ball by applying pressure on the ball against the body.
- Additional protection of the ball by using both hands can help. Proper placement of the hands on the ball is important to cover the largest ball-surface area possible.
- Ballcarriers should be ready to pivot in any direction when approached by the opponent. In addition, failure to transfer the ball from one side of the body to the other can cause difficulties.

Practice Drills

The drills described in the section on tackling can be used for ball-carrying practice. Be sure that players do not attempt to fend off the tackler with one arm extended. This type of movement is illegal. Drills 1.0 and 2.0 can be used for practicing the handoff and for ball carrying.

1.0. Shuttle Formation (Figure 7.7). The columns of players should be 15 yd apart. The leader of Column 1 (Player X1) moves slowly toward the other line carrying a ball. Player X2 moves forward, receives a handoff about 5 yd from Column 2 (a), carries for 5 yd, and hands off to Player X3, who has moved out from Column 1 (b). Players go to the end of the opposite column. This procedure continues until all players have had an opportunity to participate.

2.0. The zigzag drill shown in Figure 7.6 can be used to practice ball carrying as well as the handoff. Emphasize carrying the ball in both hands.

Blocking

The *block* is an offensive skill because it is used by a player on the attacking team to protect a teammate. Some rules do not permit body contact at all while blocking.

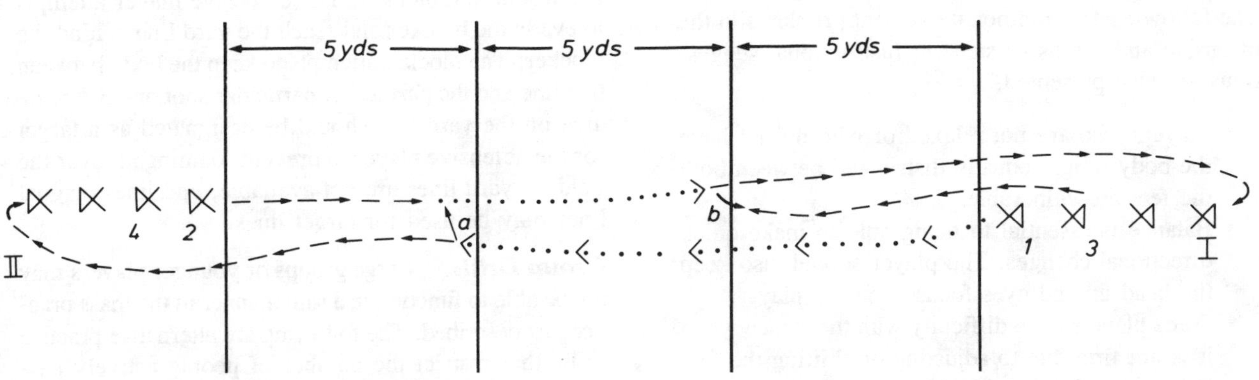

Figure 7.7. Ball-carrying and handoff drill

The block involving no body contact is generally called *screening* and consists merely of placing the body between the opponent and the ballcarrier or passer. Because the opponent cannot push the screener out of the way, the player must try to get around that opponent by quick action and faking (feinting). This type of block is appropriate for younger players or beginners or for those who have poor body control and use rough contact.

Stance

The fundamental stance provides the player with stability as well as the ability to transfer that stability into mobility quickly. The offensive stance must permit the player to move quickly both laterally and backward. The defensive stance is identical to the offensive stance with the exception of a more forward shift of the line of gravity over the balls of the feet. The defensive player must be able to initiate forward motion very quickly.

The feet are in a side-straddle position. The offensive lineperson should have a stance of about shoulder width with the feet flat on the ground. The offensive ends and backs have a stance less than shoulder width and the weight equally distributed between the feet and forward on the balls of the feet. The offensive center has a stance wider than shoulder width and the weight equally distributed between the feet. The defensive lineperson has a stance about shoulder width and the weight equally distributed between both feet and forward on the balls of the feet. The defensive backs have a stance slightly less than shoulder width and the weight equally distributed between both feet. Generally, all players have the knees slightly flexed to add to stability. The arms are hung down from the body by the offensive ends, defensive linepersons, and defensive backs. The center has both hands on the ball. As centers advance in skill, they may use only one hand on the ball; the other hand rests on the adjacent thigh. Offensive backs have the arms across the thighs with the palms of the hands forward.

Common Movement Problems and Suggestions. The following are common movement problems in the offensive and defensive stances. Instructional suggestions are also presented.

- Players who are not relaxed or who do not have the body weight equally distributed between both the feet are vulnerable.
- Balance is essential to being able to make quick directional changes. The player should also keep the head up and eyes focused on the play.
- Some players have difficulty with the stance when it is not firm due to adjusting or shifting the feet before the play is initiated.

Shoulder Block

The shoulder block is generally accepted as the only body block allowed in flag and touch football. This consists of placing the shoulder against the shoulder, chest, or midsection of the opponent in an effort to stop or move that person. The hands and arms may not be used to hold or divert the opponent. Some rules allow the elbows to be extended out to the sides and the hands held against the chest. Blockers may not leave their feet when blocking and may never hit the opponent's legs or back.

The obvious error common in shoulder blocking is moving the arms or hands against the opponent. An effective shoulder block can be performed only when the player has a stable base from which to push against the opponent. Blockers cannot be successful unless they shift the body weight into the opponent.

Practice Drills

The following are blocking drills. Both partner and group drills are presented. Partner drills should be used whenever possible to enable all players to practice simultaneously and to reduce the off-task time.

Partner Drills. Because no equipment is needed to practice blocking, players can be paired. Each person should be paired with another of similar weight and height. Partners stand about 3 ft apart and on a signal take a step or two toward each other and attempt to push the other backward 3 or 4 ft using the shoulder block. If the field is marked with 5-yd lines, one partner could start on each of two adjacent lines, move to make contact between the two lines, and strive to push the partner back over the starting line. Close supervision of school-aged students may be necessary to avoid excessive roughness. Do not let players charge into each other.

Similar pairings and starting points can be used to practice screening (noncontact block) and dodging the screen. One of each pair is designated as the offensive blocker and the other as the defensive player trying to get around the blocker. The defensive player attempts to evade the blocker and reach the yard line behind the blocker. The blocker attempts to keep the body between that line and the partner. A particular spot or a 3-ft wide area on the yard line should be designated as a target for the defensive player to prevent roaming all over the field. If yard lines are not available, end lines or goal lines may be used for target lines.

Group Drills. Large groups or younger players may not be able to function in a safe manner in the mass practice just described. The following are alternative practice drills that restrict the number of people actively participating at one time and thus enable closer supervision.

1.0. Column Formation (Figure 4.2). Divide the class into five columns lined up parallel to one another 6 to 8 ft apart. The leader of each group takes three or four steps forward, turns, and faces the next person in the column. The leader becomes a defensive line player who attempts to reach the third person in the column (the offensive back). The second person in the column is the offensive blocker, who seeks to prevent the defensive player from reaching the third person. After the defensive player has touched the third person in the column or after 30 s have passed, play stops. The defensive line player goes to the end of the column. The offensive blocker becomes the defensive line player, and the next person in the column becomes the new offensive blocker. This continues until all players have had a turn or until the instructor or coach stops play. Note that the defensive line player is attacking or trying to reach the opposing back. The offensive blocker is protecting or defending against the opposing player. Variation: This same drill can be used for screening practice without contact.

2.0. Shuttle Formation (Figure 4.7). Columns of players are lined up 8 ft apart facing each other. The first person in each column moves forward and tries to force the opponent back to that person's starting place using only the shoulder block. Play stops when one person is forced back to the starting line or after 30 s have passed. Contenders go to the ends of their own columns, and the next two players move out to block. Players should walk or move slowly toward each other to prevent hard hits and possible injuries.

Kicking

The two types of kicks used in football are the punt and the placekick. Some rules allow only the punt to be used in flag and touch football. Everyone should learn to kick the ball, although in a competitive situation the best kickers would generally be the ones to perform.

Placekick

The *placekick* is used for the kickoff at the beginning of each half, after goals are scored, for the points after touchdowns, and for field goal attempts. The ball is placed on a kicking tee or held vertically against the ground by a *ball holder* while the kicker steps up and kicks the ball. Players holding the ball for a placekicker should hold one end of the football with only one or two fingers while the other end of the ball rests against the ground. The ball should slant slightly back toward the kicker to improve the loft of the kick. The ball should be held with the left hand for a right-footed kicker and with the right hand for a left-footed kicker so that the rest of the holder's body can lean out of the kicker's way.

Some flag and touch football rules do not permit placekicking. If there are no goalposts on the field, field goals and points after touchdowns are eliminated. Some believe that the injury potential for players who attempt to block placekicks warrants eliminating this strategy from the game. The game does not lose its value or effectiveness if this phase is prohibited. The punt can easily be used for the kickoff, although placekicks usually go farther.

In the placekick, the ball is positioned on a tee or held between one end and the ground by a teammate. The kicker takes several running steps to approach the ball. The nonkicking foot is planted to the side and slightly behind the ball. The kicking leg hyperextends (bends backward) at the hip and flexes at the knee. This cocks the leg rearward in preparation for the force-production phase.

Force production begins with a rapid flexion of the hip. The flexion slows when the thigh is perpendicular to the ground. At this time, the knee whips, or extends rapidly, toward the ball. The foot meets the ball when the leg is fully extended. The ball is contacted with the instep or top of the foot. The follow-through is a continuation of the kicking leg motion in the direction of the kick. The kick should have as much horizontal distance and height as possible because the ball is dead when it hits the ground. Additional information on kicking can be found in chapter 3.

Punt

The *punt* consists of dropping the ball and kicking it before it hits the ground. It is used to move the ball downfield when a team is unable to make the first down needed to retain possession. Whenever a team punts the ball, possession changes hands; the receiving team goes on offense, and the kicking team becomes defenders. The punt may also be used as a kickoff at the start of each half and after a touchdown.

Once the ball is in the possession of the kicker, the ball is held out in front of the body with the laces up (Figure 7.8). The hands are on opposite sides of the ball. With the ball pointing down, the kicker takes a step forward on the nonkicking leg. At the same time, the hip is hyperextended (bent backward) and the knee flexed as in the place kick. The force-production phase begins with flexion at the hip and extension at the knee. At the same time, the ball is dropped. The instep of the foot makes contact with the ball just before the ball reaches the ground. The follow-through is a continuation of the

Figure 7.8. Punt

forward and upward swinging motion of the leg. The follow-through might be so powerful that it lifts the body off the ground. Additional information on kicking can be found in chapter 3.

Common Movement Problems and Suggestions

The following are common problems in kicking. Instructional suggestions are also included.

- The most common difficulty in kicking is the achievement of proper timing. The objective is for the foot to make contact with the ball when at its highest velocity, which is when the leg is fully extended. In addition, the impact should occur when the ball is positioned properly for the desired angle of trajectory. These two events must occur simultaneously in a properly timed kick.
- Players must concentrate and focus completely on the ball throughout the skill. Failure to do so can mean incorrect foot contact with the ball or no contact at all.
- The whipping action of the lower leg is essential to a forceful kick. Force production will be weak if the whipping action is weak.
- When the wind is in the face of the kicker, instruct the kicker to angle the ball trajectory lower than usual. When the wind is at the back of the kicker, the trajectory should be higher than usual.

Kicking Practice Drills

The following are both punting and placekicking drills. Each type of kicking drill is presented separately, although most can be used to practice either kick.

Placekicking Drills. Placekicks are apt to be erratic when beginners try them at first. Therefore, the use of a few balls and more structured group drills is recommended.

1.0. The drills described for punts (see the next section) can also be used for placekick practice. The next player in the column or line steps up to hold the ball for the kicker.

2.0. Two-Line Formation (Figure 7.9). Individuals in Line 1 are lined up at the 10-yd line in front of the goalposts. Individuals in Line 2 are about 15 yd behind the goalposts. A ball holder is designated for each line. This should be an experienced player, if possible. Player X1 attempts to placekick the ball between the goalposts. Players in Line 2 retrieve the ball, give it to their holder, and in turn kick it back. All players (except the holders) receive the kicks, give the balls to their holders, and take turns placekicking for field goals. A second group may be set up at the other end of the field or at other goalposts.

Punting Drills. Beginners are usually erratic at first when punting or placekicking, so they should be far apart for practice. If the space is limited, group practice drills are recommended, as these require the use of only a few footballs at one time and reduce the incidence of injuries.

1.0. Shuttle Formation (Figure 4.7). Columns of individuals are lined up about 20 yd apart. The goal line and the quarter-yard line of a field may be used. The leader of one column punts the ball toward the other column. The leader of the second column catches or retrieves the ball and punts it back. Players go to the end of their own column after completing a turn. When there are several pairs of columns, each pair should be at least 30 ft from the adjacent ones.

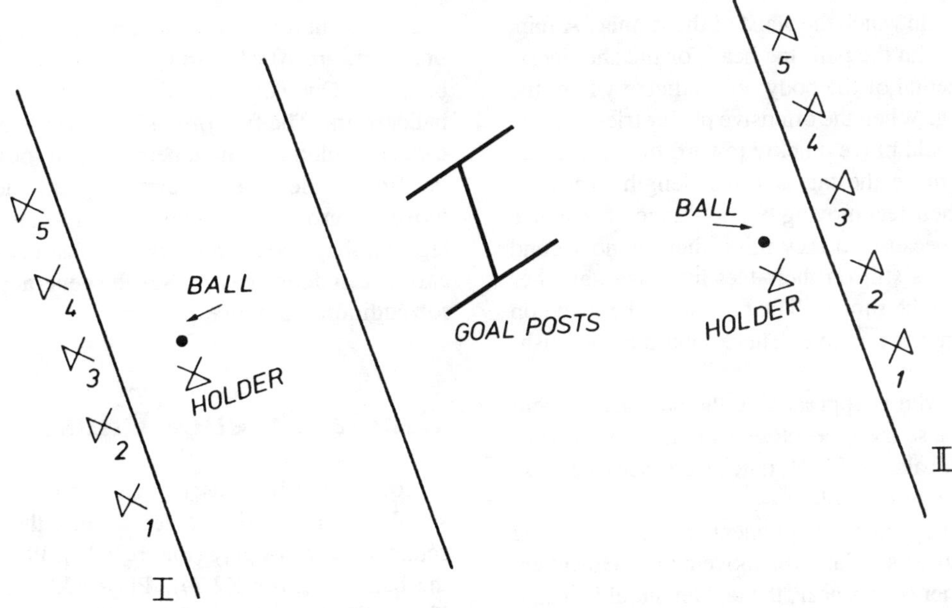

Figure 7.9. Placekick drill

2.0. One-Column, One-Line Formation (Figure 7.10). The first person in Column 1 punts the ball toward Line 2 (a). The player in the line who catches the ball runs toward the column and passes it to the next person in Column 1 (b). The ball may be caught on the fly or after bouncing. The kicker goes to the end of the receiving line, and the punt catcher goes to the end of the kicking column. Be sure that all players in Line 2 get a chance to catch the ball and go to the kicking column.

Tagging or Grabbing the Flag

General Description

Tagging the opponent in touch football requires good body control. If the ballcarrier is approaching, the tackler should be in a slightly crouched ready position with the weight evenly distributed on the balls of the feet in order to be able to move in any direction. The arms should be flexed and out to the sides (abducted) as in the basketball guarding position. As the ballcarrier approaches,

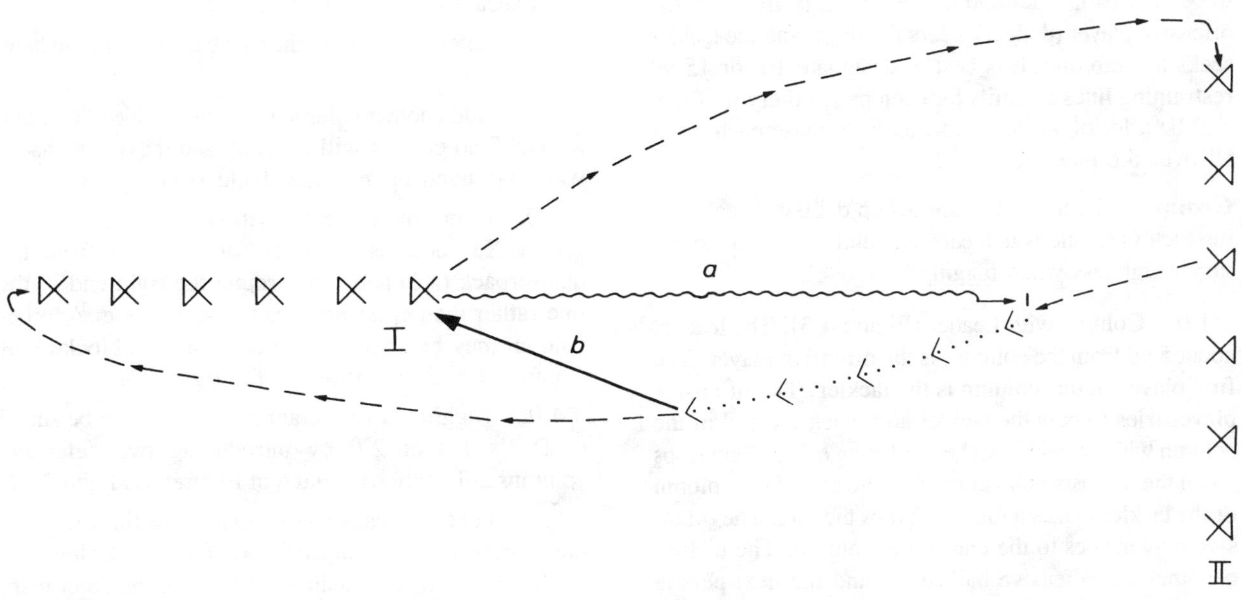

Figure 7.10. Punt drill

the tackler should watch the waist of the runner. A feint may be made with the ball, the head, or the shoulders, but the midsection of the body will indicate where the runner is going. When the offensive player tries to pass, the tackler should move quickly toward the player and reach out to make the tag at arms' length. Tacklers should keep their feet moving but not lunge off balance at the runner because, if they miss, there is no second chance. Tacklers still on their feet may have another chance to catch the runner. The tag should be made on the body whenever possible. There should be no push, just a touch.

The tackler who is approaching the ballcarrier from behind should also try to get close enough to touch without lunging off balance. Short, quick steps help the tackler maintain body control.

Grabbing a flag from the opponent (sometimes called *flagging*) requires similar skill movements. However, as the ballcarrier comes near, the tackler should change the visual focus from the torso to the flag and concentrate on grasping it with one hand.

Tackling Practice Drills

The following are tackling practice drills. Both partner and group drills are presented.

Partner. Paired practice allows efficient use of time when there is enough equipment (flags and belts). The amount of equipment is irrelevant in touch football.

1.0. Partners face each other, and one tries to dodge past the other to reach a designated line or goal area. After a few trials without the ball, the dodger could carry a ball. Change places so that each player has a chance to be both ballcarrier and tackler. If flags are used, the offensive player (dodger) wears the flags, and the tackler seeks to grab one. It is best to designate 10- or 15-yd restraining lines as limits for each pair; otherwise there will be a lot of wasted effort as they chase each other all over the play area.

Group. The following are group drills for tackling. Instructors should watch carefully and prevent unnecessary roughness when tagging.

1.0. Column with Leader (Figure 4.3). The leader, about 5 yd from the column, is the offensive player. The first player in this column is the tackler. The offensive player tries to pass the tackler and reach the end of the column without being touched or losing a flag. Play stops when the offensive player reaches the end of the column or the tackler makes a touch or grabs the flag. The offensive player goes to the end of the column. The tackler becomes the offensive ballcarrier and the next person in line the tackler. The offensive player may carry a ball to practice that skill.

2.0. Shuttle Formation (Figure 4.7). The columns of players are 10 yd apart (yard marks on the field might be used). One column is the tacklers and the other the ballcarriers. The first offensive player tries to reach the tacklers' column without being tagged (or losing a flag); the first tackler tries to prevent this. Tacklers should move toward the opposite column to attempt an early tag, but they should not rush too fast because the ballcarrier can dodge easily. See the general practice drills for additional practice patterns.

General Practice Drills

1.0. Centering, passing, catching, and ball carrying should be practiced together because they make up essential patterns of play (Figure 7.11). Player X1 centers the ball to Player X2 (a). Player X2 passes to either Player X3 (b) or Player X4 (c). Players X2 and X4 start at the line of scrimmage, move when the ball is centered, and run pass patterns downfield. After catching a forward pass, Players X3 and X4 run a few more yards carrying the ball. Each player goes to the end of the next-numbered column (4 goes to 1). The center may remain for several plays and then be replaced.

2.0. Three-Column Formation (Figure 7.12). Player X1 centers the ball to Player X2 (a), who hands off to Player X3 (b), who has cut behind Player X2. Player X3 continues carrying the ball on a run to the left. Player X4 moves downfield to screen or block for Player X3. Players move to the end of the next-numbered column (4 goes to 1). Variations include the following:

2.1. Move Player X3 to the other side of Player X2 and execute a run to the right.

2.2. Lateral the ball to the side back rather than hand off.

2.3. Add another column to the other side of Column 2. Backfield players will cross behind the quarterback, who may hand off to either ballcarrier.

3.0. Using the same formation as in Figure 7.12, Player X3 receives a lateral (or *pitchout*) from the quarterback (X2) and runs around the right end of the line rather than crossing over to the left side. Another column may be added to the right side as blockers or Column 4 may be moved to the right side.

4.0. Tagging or flag-grabbing practice can be added to Drills 1.0 or 2.0 by introducing two defensive columns at Locations 5 and 6 of Figures 7.11 and 7.12.

5.0. Punt and Pass Game. One team lines up near the quarter-yard line on each end of a field. Using only a pass or a punt, each team tries to force the other team back into its own end zone. The ball must be passed or punted from the spot where it is caught or recovered.

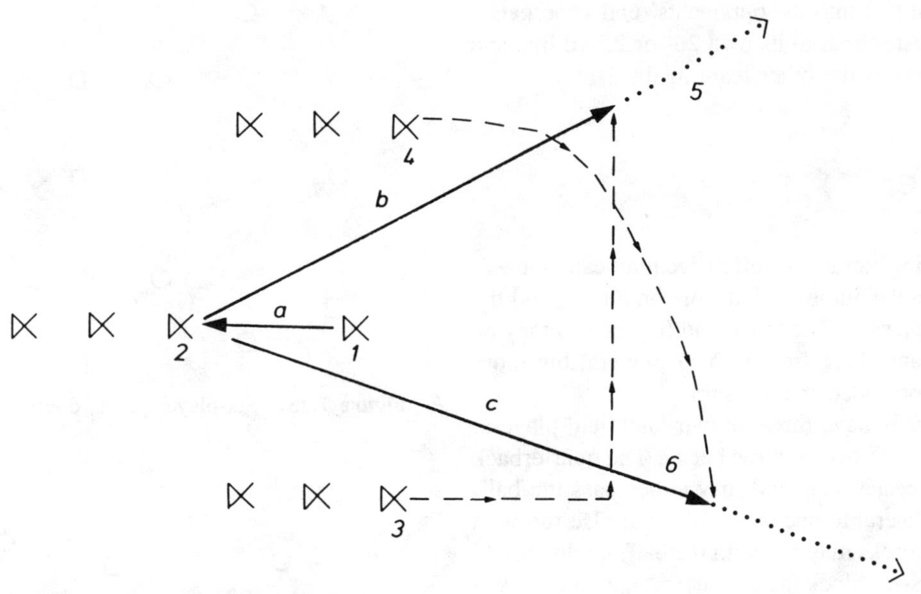

Figure 7.11. Center, pass, catch, and carry drill

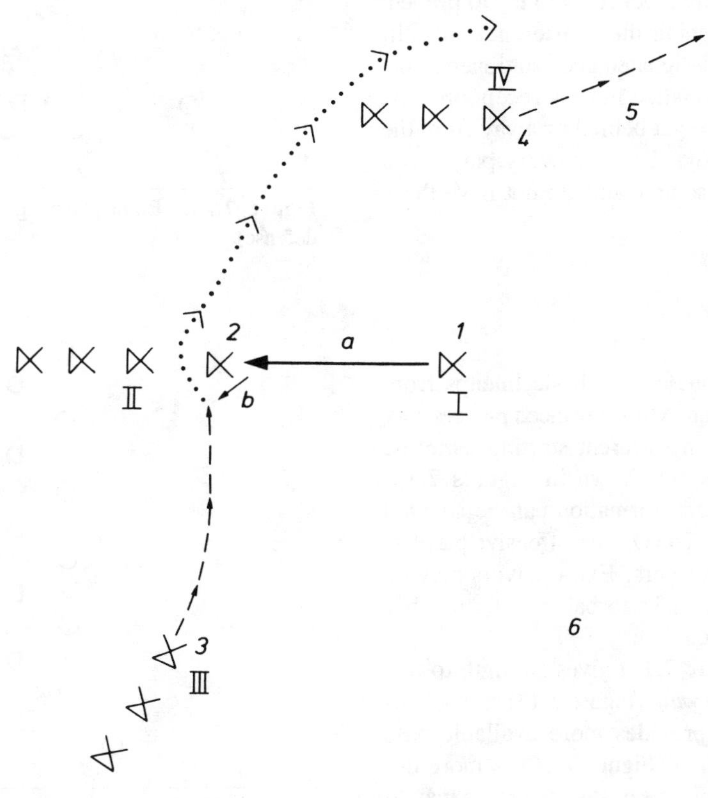

Figure 7.12. Center, hand off, run, block, and screen drill

Two or three steps may be taken when passing or punting, but otherwise players may not move with the ball. Play starts with Team 1 punting the ball from its own 20- or 25-yd line. Team 2 tries to catch or stop the ball as close to the kickoff point as possible, and then kicks or passes the ball back to Team 1. The team that succeeds in getting the ball into the opponents' end zone gets a point and must retreat to its own 20- or 25-yd line and kick off (punt) to the other team again.

Offense

Several starting patterns of offensive play can be used, depending on the number of players on a team and the skills of the players. The touch and flag games may be played with anywhere from 6 to 11 players, but more players can be added if necessary.

Teams usually have three or four backfield players: a quarterback and two or three backs. The quarterback receives the center snap and may either pass the ball, hand off, or lateral to one of the backs or else run with the ball. The backs may run with the ball, go downfield to receive passes, block the opponents, and even throw passes.

The other players, consisting of a center, *tackles*, *guards*, and *ends*, begin each play at the line of scrimmage. These are primarily blockers who try to prevent the opponents from reaching the quarterback or ball-carriers. There may be designated ends stationed at the ends of the line who specialize in pass reception. The end's main job is to try to get behind or away from the defenders to receive a pass. Because every player is a potential pass receiver, some teams do not have these pass-receiver specialists.

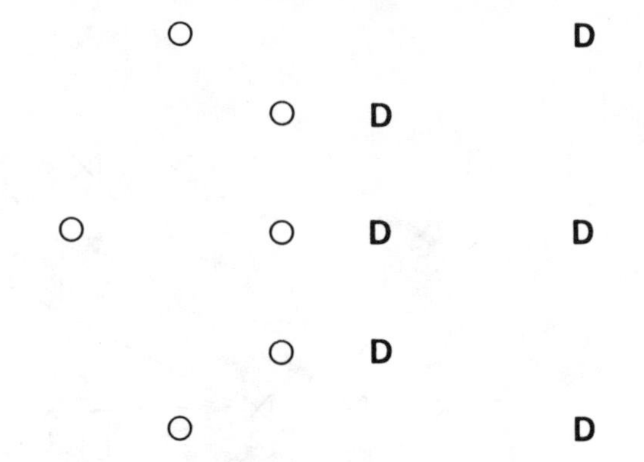

Figure 7.13. Six-player game, double wing (3-3 defense)

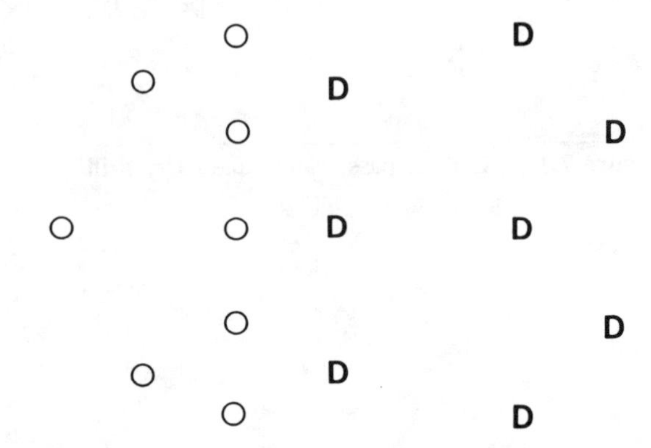

Figure 7.14. Eight-player game, punt formation (3-3-2 defense)

Play Patterns

Teams should develop one or two basic lineups from which various plays are run. More advanced players may wish to have three or four different starting patterns. Typical starting patterns are shown in Figures 7.13, 7.14, 7.15, and 7.16. Each formation can be adapted to any number of players. The O's are offensive players; the D's show defensive players. Extra players may be added as line players or backs to balance the number of players on each team.

The *single wing* (Figure 7.15) gives strength to one side for a run. The *double wing* (Figure 7.13) strengthens each side for runs and provides more available pass receivers. The T-formation (Figure 7.16) is more deceiving because several plays can start the same way to confuse the opponents. The punt formation (Figure 7.14) provides more protection for the quarterback, who may be waiting for a receiver to get downfield.

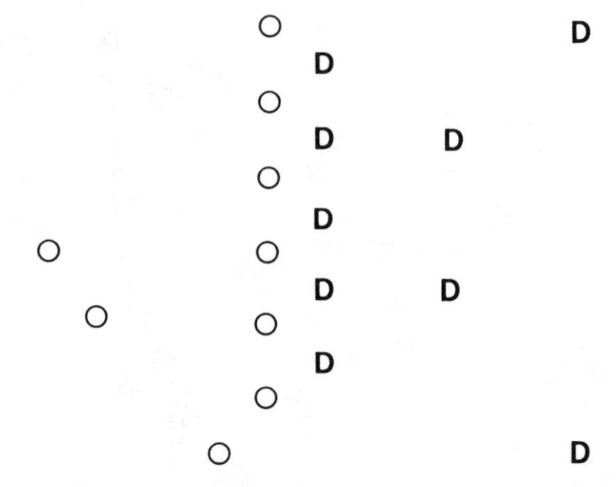

Figure 7.15. Nine-player game, single wing (5-2-2 defense)

A team should have several offensive pass patterns (Figure 7.17). These are paths run by the receivers as they try to evade the defenders. The cuts may be made just beyond the line of scrimmage for short passes or farther downfield for long passes. Passers should try to pass ahead of the receivers so they will not have to slow down or stop. When receivers are having trouble evading the defense, the curl-type pass may be necessary. In this

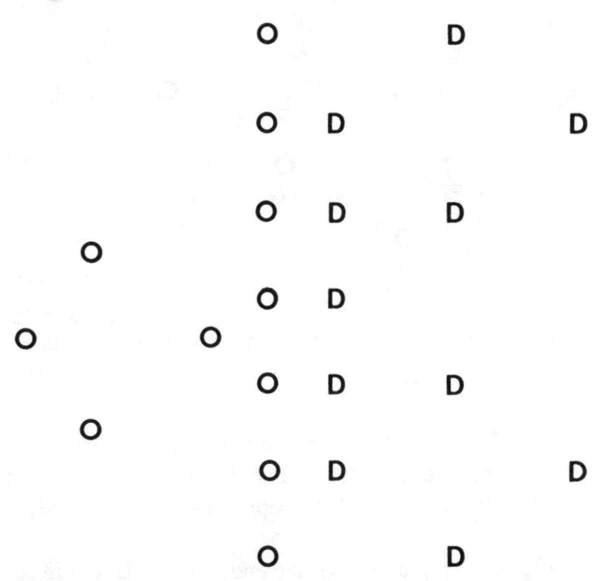

Figure 7.16. Eleven-player game, T formation (5-4-2 defense)

pattern, the receiver circles around and runs back toward the line of scrimmage. The receiver should not run back very far, or very little ground will be gained.

Different players, usually backs and ends, may run these patterns or others. The main advantage of having receivers run set patterns known to the offensive team is that the passer knows where the receiver will be and can throw the ball to intersect the receiver's path. If the passer has to wait to see where the receiver is, the defenders also have time to get to the receiver.

Teams should also have several running plays. In the end *sweep* (Figure 7.18), the line players get outside of the defensive line and block them toward the center while a back carries the ball around the outside of the line. One of the backs may lead the way and block opposing backs to clear the way for the ballcarrier.

Other running plays call for the ballcarrier to run between the opposing line players. The offensive line must block some defenders one way and others the other way (Figure 7.19). Note that the offensive left end blocks the opponent to the outside while the tackle blocks the

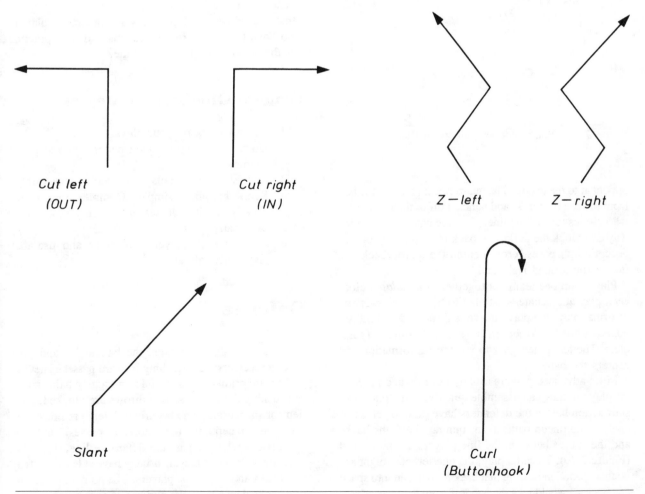

Figure 7.17. Pass-play patterns

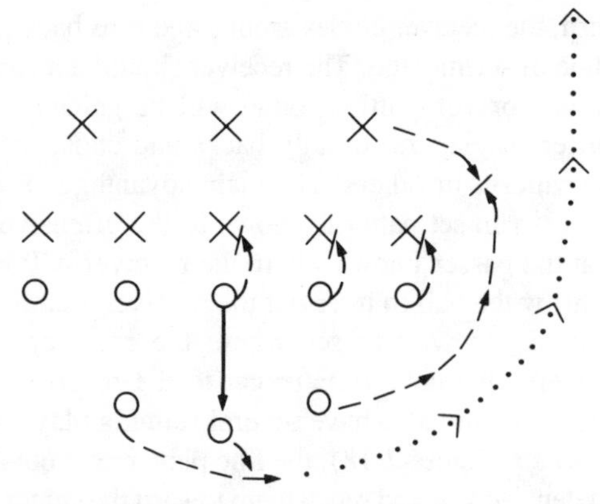

Figure 7.18. Sweep around right end

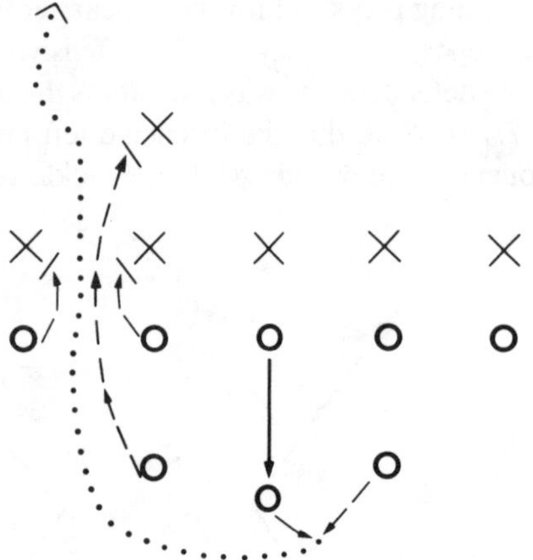

Figure 7.19. Run to left between end and tackle

opponent to the inside. The quarterback receives the ball from the center, turns, and hands it off to the right back, who circles toward the line. The free back may lead the way and block the defensive back from the play or, for deception purposes, cross behind the quarterback and fake a run around right end.

Players on one team get together in a *huddle* before each play and decide what play to try. For classes and informal play, the play pattern is discussed and individuals assigned to do certain things (block, run for a pass, etc.). The team then goes to its starting formation and centers the ball.

More advanced players usually develop and practice set plays so they can assemble quickly, call a play, and start action before the defenders have time to get set or analyze the lineup pattern. In running plays, the backs and the spaces between the line players are numbered (Figure 7.20). To call a play, the quarterback might announce "35," indicating that back #3 will run into space #5. Back #3 would take the handoff from the quarterback

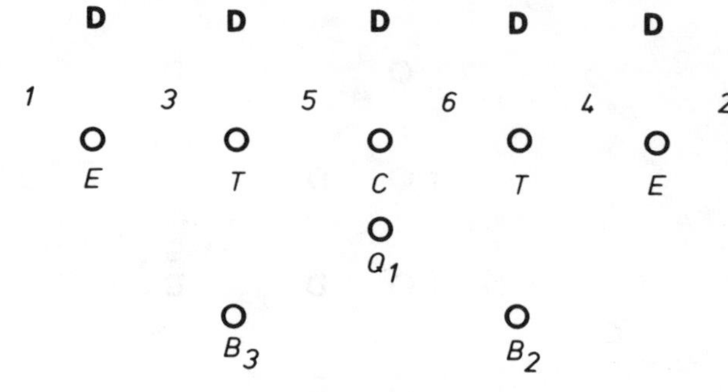

Figure 7.20. Back and space numbers for signal calling

and run between the center and the left tackle (space #5). The center would know to block the opponent to the right and the tackle to block the opponent to the outside or the left.

The passing players and the ends should have different numbers so that these plays could also be called quickly. Memorization of set plays is not necessary for beginners and only complicates the game. Intermediate players may be ready to handle one simple numbering system.

There are many types of numbering systems used. Most should be developed only for advanced players who have time to learn the systems and who practice together over long periods of time.

General Offensive Strategies

1. Learn to mix up your plays.
2. Do not follow a predictable pattern of passing and running.
3. Keep some special plays in reserve to use rarely.
4. Keep the plays simple. Complex maneuvers usually result in losses or broken plays.
5. Be creative.
6. Analyze each player's strengths and use that player accordingly.

Defense

Defense consists of stopping the ballcarrier and preventing receivers from catching forward passes. The line players are primarily responsible for tagging ballcarriers and rushing the passer so that throws are blocked, hurried, or inaccurate. The backfield defenders must prevent pass receptions (or intercept passes) and tag ballcarriers who get past the defensive line.

Teams with 6 to 8 players usually have at least 3 defensive backs and 3 to 5 line players. The number of defensive backs depends on the number of pass receivers the offensive team uses. If the offense uses only the ends and 1 back, or 2 backs and an end, 3 defenders are sufficient. Teams with 9 to 11 players usually need 4 or 5 backs and 5 to 7 line players. Suggestions for defensive lineups are show in Figures 7.13, 7.14, 7.15, and 7.16. These are only suggestions, and lineups should be determined by the skills of the defensive players.

Defensive Patterns

Defensive backfield play may be organized in a 1-on-1 pattern in which each back guards one particular defender (as in 1-on-1 basketball defense) or in a zone defense, in which players are responsible for the opponents who enter their sections of the backfield.

Figure 7.13 shows the 3-3 defense using a 1-on-1 type of defense. Each of the side backs is responsible for the receiver, who starts on the same side of the field. The center back backs up the line play and covers any line player who goes out for a pass.

Figures 7.15 and 7.16 are two examples of zone defensive patterns with five line players, two (or four) linebackers, and two backs. The linebackers tag any ballcarriers who break through the line and defend against short passes just over the line of scrimmage. The backs cover receivers for longer passes on their own sides of the field.

The defensive pattern in Figure 7.14 (3-3-2) can function as 1-on-1 or as a zone. The linebackers guard the ends and the center back if they moved downfield as receivers. The backs guard the two opposing side backs. In a zone, the linebackers defend against the short passes and the backs against long passes.

General Defensive Strategies

1. Line players should persist in trying to reach the ballcarrier. Do not stop with the first block.
2. Linebackers must be alert for short passes or runs.
3. The fastest defensive backs should defend against long pass plays.
4. Defensive backs should stay between the goal they are defending and the opposing players. Never let a receiver get behind you (i.e., between you and the goal).
5. Keep the body under control. Do not lunge extensively or so much that the line of gravity moves out of the base of support, except as a last resort. If you stay on your feet, you may be able to recover and catch a ballcarrier. If you fall, you will never catch the runner.
6. Watch the torso or waist of the offensive player to avoid being faked out of position.

Terminology

Backfield—The area behind the line players; the area where backfield players stand at the start of a play

Backfield players—Halfbacks, fullbacks and quarterbacks; those players who generally start a play from a backfield position; players other than line players

Ball holder—The player who holds the football vertical to the ground for a teammate to placekick

Block—Interspersing one's body between the opponent and the ball or ballcarrier; (may involve body contact as in a shoulder block or it may not as specified by different rules)

Center—To put the ball in play at the start of a down; the person who centers the ball; the offensive line player in the center of the line

Centering—Passing the ball between the legs from the line of scrimmage to a backfield player; used to restart play after the previous play is completed (same as Center Snap)

Center snap—Same as Centering

Circuit—Moving from one place (station) to another as in circuit training; a series of activities or tasks

Conversion—The point-after-touchdown opportunity in tackle football occasionally used in touch and flag football; a placekick attempted from near the goal line to score 1 point after a touchdown has been made

Double wing—An offensive lineup characterized by having an equal number of backfield players and line players on each side of the quarterback (or center)

Down—One complete play or attempt to gain ground; the time from centering the ball until play stops and the ball is dead

Ends—The line players who stand on the ends of the line closest to the sidelines when a play begins; pass receivers

End zone—The area beyond the goal line at each end of the field

Field goal—A placekicked ball that passes between or above the upright posts and above the cross-bar of the goalposts (counts 3 points)

Flagging—Grabbing the flag of the ballcarrier (comparable to tagging in touch football)

Flag—A small strip of fabric worn by flag football players that is attached to a belt by Velcro or snaps

Forward pass—A throw that moves the ball toward the opponents' goal

Goal lines—The lines at each end of the field that a team must cross to score a touchdown

Goalposts—The framework outlining the target area for scoring field goals on points after touchdowns; two vertical posts connected by one horizontal crossbar positioned behind the goal line in the end zone of the field

Guards—The line players who stand on both sides of the center

Handoff—A pass that is not airborne but is handed directly to the receiver

Hike—A term frequently used by the quarterback to indicate that the ball should be snapped and the play started

Huddle—A team conference to determine what offensive pattern or strategy to use on the next play (down)

Illegal motion—Movement toward the line of scrimmage by an offensive player before the ball is centered

Interception—Interfering with or catching a pass intended for an opponent

Kickoff—The kick used to start each half of the game or to start play after points have been scored (the team scoring points must kick to the other team)

Lateral pass—A pass thrown to the side of or behind the thrower

Linebacker—A defensive player who backs up the defensive line

Line players—Players who line up at the line of scrimmage at the start of each play; the center, guards, tackles, and ends in most formations

Offside—An illegal position in which a player is on the opponent's side of the scrimmage line at the start of a play

Pitchout—A lateral pass to a player who is several yards to the side of the passer

Placekick—A ball that is kicked off a tee or from a stationary position where it is being held by another player

Point after touchdown—In some rules, 1 point scored by kicking the ball over the goalpost crossbar and between the goalpost uprights from a spot 3 yd from the center of the goal line

Punt—A ball kicked in the air after having been dropped from the kicker's hands

Quarterback—The player who generally decides what play to use and who usually receives the center snap (the play caller)

Rusher—A defensive player who attempts to run into the opposing backfield and tag the ballcarrier; generally, a line player who rushes into the opposing backfield

Safety—A score counting 2 points made by tagging a ballcarrier behind the goal line the ballcarrier is defending

Screen—A moving block; a block set up by more than one player

Scrimmage line—An imaginary line across the width of the field that marks where a play must start; where the ball was when the previous play ended

Single wing—An offensive lineup characterized by having most of the backfield players and certain line players all on one side of the center

Snapped ball—A ball that has been centered

Sweep—A play in which several offensive players run around one end of the scrimmage line and try to "sweep" the opponents away from the ballcarrier who follows them

Tackle—One of two line players who stands to the outside of each guard in a line of five players or more; stopping ballcarriers by forcing them off their feet (illegal in touch and flag football)

Tagging—Legally touching the ballcarrier to stop play (comparable to the tackle in tackle football)

T formation—An offensive lineup characterized by having the backfield players form a T pattern (usually one in the middle and one on each side) at the start of a play

Touchdown—A score counting 6 points made by carrying the ball over the goal line or throwing the ball to a teammate in the end zone

Selected Readings

Casady, D. (1974). *Sports activities for men*. New York: Macmillan.

Division for Girls' and Women's Sports. (1970). *Soccer, speedball, flag football guide*. Washington, DC: American Alliance for Health, Physical Education, Recreation and Dance.

Little, M., Dowell, L., & Jeter, J. (1977). *Recreational football: Flag and touch for class and intramurals*. Minneapolis: Burgess.

Mood, D., Musker, F., & Armbruster, D. (1983). *Sports and recreational activities for men and women* (8th ed.). St. Louis: C.V. Mosby.

Seaton, D., Clayton, I., Leibee, H., & Messersmith, L. (1974). *Physical education handbook*. Englewood Cliffs, NJ: Prentice-Hall.

Flag and Touch Football Skills Errors and Corrections

FORWARD PASS

Error	*Causes*	*Corrections*
Weak		
Ball fails to reach the target	• Failure to utilize the stepping action and/or forward weight shift	• Step toward the target on the foot opposite the throwing arm.
	• Failure to use enough backswing	• Rotate the trunk so that the shoulder of the throwing arm moves well back on the preparatory phase of the movement; use the force of the trunk rotation and arm-and-shoulder extension to throw.
	• Failure to maintain a firm grip on the ball (see also next cause)	• Spread the fingers along the strings of the football to improve gripping ability with the thumb on the other side of the ball; hold the ball nearer to the tip if necessary to get a good grip.
Poor timing	• Failure to utilize the whipping action of the throwing arm	• Let the elbow lead the arm in a strong forward movement so that the hand holding the ball can be whipped through to the release; use a succession of actions by the trunk, upper arm, forearm, and wrist.
Inaccurate		
Ball goes to left or right of target	• Failure to keep the arm above shoulder level with the elbow up	• Elevate the elbow of the throwing arm to just above shoulder level.
	• Failure to initiate a spiral spin on the ball with the correct hand positioning on the ball and follow-through of the hand	• Flex the wrist on release so that the ball rolls off the fingertips and spirals toward the target; let the little-finger side of the hand lead the motion toward the target.
	• Failure to time the release properly when the ball is tangent to the desired angle of release	• Release the ball at head level or above with the line from tip to tip on the ball pointed directly to the target (or arched upward for a long pass).

(Cont.)

LATERAL UNDERHAND PASS

Error	*Causes*	*Corrections*
Inaccurate		
Ball misdirected	• Failure to utilize a forward stepping action toward the receiver.	• Step toward the receiver on the foot opposite the throwing arm.
Ball wobbles or wavers in the air	• Failure to initiate a lateral spin on the ball by rotating the hand over the ball	• Start with the ball resting on the palm of the hand with fingers spread; rotate the hand to the outside of the ball as it is released; hand is palm down after release with thumb facing the left if right-handed.
Inappropriate force		
Ball thrown too hard	• Too much force on the ball, resulting in poor control for the	• Execute sympathetic passes; throw softly if receiver is close.
Ball thrown too softly	• Failure to apply sufficient force	• Extend the throwing arm toward the receiver; emphasize stepping toward the receiver; increase the backswing of the arm and wrist action.

CENTERING

Error	*Causes*	*Corrections*
Inaccurate		
Ball misses target	• Failure to focus on the target and keep the head down	• Look at the receiver; bend over farther and look between the legs.
	• Failure to hold the ball with the fingers and thumbs spread apart	• Spread both hands around the ball as far as possible; hold one hand on each side.
	• Failure to create a spiral spin on the ball	• Rotate the fingers of one hand over the ball; remove the other hand from the ball as you throw.
Ball thrown too softly	• Failure to swing the arms freely	• Swing both hands between the legs so that the fingers point toward the receiver.
Ball thrown too hard	• Application of too much force	• Look at the receiver before bending over and determine how far the throw must go; practice centering the ball various distances.
Loss of body control		
Ball thrown erratically	• Failure to distribute the weight equally over both feet for a stable base of support	• Bend knees and keep the weight on both feet; do *not* lean on the ball.

HANDOFF

Error	*Causes*	*Corrections*
Loss of ball control		
	• Faulty timing	• Watch the receiver carefully and extend the ball as the person gets 3 or 4 ft away (if running); stand to the side of the receiver to avoid a collision.
	• Failure to place the ball into the receiver	• Push the ball against the stomach or the inside of the bent arm of the receiver; keep it low, near waist level, *not* at shoulder level.
	Failure to hold the ball firmly until the receiver takes the ball	• Maintain hold of the ball until the receiver takes it from your grasp.

RECEIVING

Error	*Causes*	*Corrections*
Loss of body control		
Receiver not in position to catch ball	• Failure to maintain a balanced body position	• Run with short steps when nearing the ball or changing patterns; be ready to jump if necessary; avoid crossing one foot over the other.
	• Turning to watch the passer too soon	• When running a pass pattern, complete most of the pattern before looking back at the passer; do *not* turn and look back over the shoulder while running.
Loss of ball control		
Ball missed	• Failure to maintain concentration on the ball	• Watch the ball as it approaches until it it contacts your hands; try to ignore distractions.
	• Failure to maintain a firm grip on the ball	• Grasp the ball with both hands.
	• Improper position of the hands	• When catching the ball above the waist, point the fingers up and the thumbs toward each other; when catching a ball below the waist, point the fingers downward with the little fingers overlapping.
Ball dropped after contact made	• Failure to protect the ball	• Pull the ball into the center of the body; cradle it and protect it with the arms; tuck one end against the body near the armpit.
	• Failure to control the ball before beginning to run	• Be sure to have a firm grasp on the ball before turning or running; tuck the ball close to the body.

(Cont.)

BALL CARRYING

Error	Causes	Corrections
Loss of ball control		
Ball dropped	• Failure to protect the ball with the body and/or body parts	• Hold the ball between one arm and the body with one end tucked near the bent elbow and the hand on that side over the other end of the ball; place the free hand around and over the ball.
	• Failure to utilize both hands and/or improper placement of the hands on the ball	• Always try to hold the ball with both hands; spread the fingers and thumb around the ball.
Ball pulled away by opponent	• Failure to transfer the ball from one side of the body to the other when directional and/or opponent changes are made.	• When an opponent approaches from the left, carry the ball on the right side of the body and vice versa.

BLOCKING (GENERAL)

Error	Causes	Corrections
Unbalanced		
Blocker pushed away by opponent	• Failure to distribute the body weight over the base of support	• Bend the knees to lower the center of gravity; keep the weight on both feet.
	• Failure to maintain a stable stance	• Keep the body weight low; widen the base of support (wide stance); lean toward the opponent just before contact and avoid shifting the feet.
Blocker eluded by opponent	• Failure to keep head up and eyes focused on the play	• Focus on the waist of the opponent to avoid being pulled out of position by a fake.

SHOULDER BLOCK

Error	Causes	Corrections
Ineffective		
Blocker fails to contain opponent	• Failure to maintain a stable base of support	• Bend the knees and widen the stance.
	• Failure to utilize a shift of body weight into the opponent	• Lean into the opponent as contact is made.
Blocker fouls	• Failure to maintain the position of the arms and hands instead of moving them against the opponent	• Hold the arms firmly; do not try to shift them around or to grasp the opponent.

Error	Causes	Corrections
Block missed	• Failure to make firm contact with opponent	• Keep the head up and watch the opponent; move the shoulder into contact and keep the head to the side, not down; use small, quick steps to adjust position.

DODGING

Error	Causes	Corrections
Poor Timing		
	• Failure to focus on the opponent's movements	• Continuously watch the direction of the opponent's movements.
	• Failure to change directions at the appropriate time.	• Change directions when the opponent is off balance or is taking long strides and has body weight on one foot.
Ineffective avoidance of opponent		
Movements slow and predictable	• Failure to use quick movements of the head and the shoulders	• Use sharp movements of the head and shoulders to fake a shift in direction, then move in another direction.
Dodger off balance	• Failure to control the body weight	• Use small steps and shift the hips quickly while pivoting away from the opponent.

TAGGING

Error	Causes	Corrections
Inability to tag or grab the flag		
	• Failure to focus on the opponent	• Watch the waist or belt of the opponent to avoid being faked out of position.
Loss of balance		
	• Failure to maintain center of gravity over feet	• Keep the arms out to the sides; avoid crossing one foot in front of the other; use short, quick steps.
	• Taking long steps or lunging at the opponent	• Take short steps; try to stay on your feet (if you lunge and miss, there is no second chance).

(Cont.)

KICKING

Error	Causes	Corrections
Misses ball		
	• Failure to focus or concentrate on the ball throughout the movement	• Watch the ball throughout the approach and the leg swing.
Inaccurate		
Ball goes to right or left of target	• Failure to contact the ball with the top or the inside top of the instep	• Point the toe and swing the foot through the center of the ball, making contact with the instep or the top of the foot.
	• Failure to follow through toward target	• Swing the kicking leg straight toward the target.
Ball goes too high or too low	• Improper position of the ball	• Hold or drop the ball so that one end is angled down and forward and the other end points in the general direction of the kicker's head.
	• Improper contact point on ball	• Contact the lower back of the ball with the prescribed part of the foot angled downward.
Weak		
Ball goes only a few yards or falls short	• Failure to utilize an effective approach	• Step forward into the ball using at least two lead-up steps; use more steps when possible.
	• Failure to utilize a large range of motion in the preparatory movements	• Swing the kicking leg rearward and bend the knee on the backswing; pull the leg forward forcefully.
	• Failure to utilize the whipping action of the leg	• Use sequential action at the trunk, hip, knee, and ankle to whip the kicking foot forward.
	• Ineffective leg position	• Contact the ball when the leg reaches full extension.
	• Failure to get lift and spiral spin to the ball	• Flex the ankle slightly at the end of contact and the beginning of the follow-through; swing the leg through the ball; make contact slightly below the center of the ball.

Chapter 8
Soccer

Soccer developed from a variety of kicking-type games that were played in many parts of the world. Greeks and Romans played a variation, and the Romans are presumed to have taken it to Great Britain. The Irish in ancient times also had kicking-type games. The game was probably brought to the New World by immigrants from England.

In the early 1900s, there were two main types of football, as it was called. One version allowed the player to catch and run with the ball; this developed into rugby and football. The other type prohibited hand contact; this evolved into soccer. Soccer, as we know it now, was first called *association football* to distinguish it from rugby and football. From the abbreviation of the word *association* (assoc.), the name of soccer was derived. The term *football* is still the preferred term in Europe.

Soccer is the most popular sport for participants and spectators in many parts of the world, such as Europe and South America. It was little known in the United States until after World War I, although a few intercollegiate games were played by men in the latter part of the 19th century. The United States Football (Soccer) Association was formed in 1913, and the game began to spread as standard rules were developed.

It is believed that the first college in the United States to introduce soccer for women was Bryn Mawr in 1911. They played a modified game that eliminated personal contact and roughness of play. In 1927, the first women's rules were published by a section of the American Alliance for Health, Physical Education, Recreation and Dance. Rules are still published regularly by this organization. Through the years, women's and men's rules have merged and are now identical.

Many communities have noted a developing interest in youth and adult soccer in the 1970s and 1980s as part of the trend toward fitness activities. High schools are adding the sport to their instructional and interscholastic programs for girls and boys. The game provides a suitable coeducational activity in secondary schools because most students start at the same skill level and progress together. In addition, the sport does not require extensive or expensive equipment; soccer balls, pinnies, and goals are sufficient.

Purposes and Values

Soccer is a valuable coeducational activity that can be easily included in the physical education curriculum. It contributes to the program in unique ways by providing an opportunity for the development of eye-foot coordination and dynamic balance that no other sport equals. It improves endurance and general fitness and encourages the vigorous exercise needed to promote cardiorespiratory fitness. Learning to dribble, kick, and field the ball effectively requires the coordinated use of many body parts. However, most of the skills involve gross body movements that can be practiced and enjoyed by youngsters who have difficulty with refined motor skills. Soccer can be played by girls and boys in fifth grade as well as in high school. Modified soccer activities and lead-up games are also appropriate with younger children.

Soccer is a sport in which cooperation is essential. Educational objectives in the affective domain can be emphasized and players encouraged to develop helping relationships.

Soccer also enables large groups to participate simultaneously in vigorous activity. Twenty to 30 players can be comfortably accommodated on one field, and field measurements may be adjusted to fit the available space.

The cost of incorporating soccer into the curriculum is minimal. Balls and some sort of goalposts are the only essential items. In summary, soccer meets the objectives of the physical education program with regard to fitness, neuromuscular development, social interaction, and cost-effectiveness.

The Game

Soccer, like field hockey, is played with 11 players on a team. These are usually divided into five *forwards*, three *halfbacks*, two *fullbacks*, and one *goalkeeper*. The objective of the game is to protect the *goal* at your own end of the field while trying to kick or *volley* the ball into the goal that your opponents are defending. The ball may be kicked or hit with any part of the body except the hands and arms and advanced with a *dribble* or with a *pass* to a teammate.

Play is begun by one team having a *kickoff* (an unguarded *placekick* in the center of the field). After each goal is scored, the opposite team starts play again with a kickoff. All goals score one point. In case of a tie at the end of the official playing time, extra periods may be played. The procedure for overtime play varies with the level of play and specific league rules.

The ball is put back in play after going out of bounds at the sideline (also called *touch line*) with a *throw-in* by an opponent of the person who last touched the ball. When a ball is sent over the end-line (also called *goal line*) but not between the goalposts by a member of the attacking team, the defenders are awarded a free, unguarded kick, or *(goal kick)*, from the goal area (Figure 8.1). When the ball is sent over the goal line not between the goalposts by a defender, the attacking team is awarded a *free kick*, or *(corner kick)*, from a spot near the closest *corner* of the field. A player taking a kickoff, a throw-in, or a free kick may not touch the ball again until after another player has contacted it.

Goalkeepers have special privileges that allow them to catch, throw, punt, *dropkick*, and bounce the ball while inside the penalty area. A foul is called on any other players who touch the ball in any way with their hands, except for a sideline throw-in. These fouls are usually penalized by awarding a free, unguarded kick to the opponents on the spot where the foul occurred. Fouls committed by defending players in the penalty areas may be penalized by awarding a *penalty kick* at goal.

Soccer is played in quarters, which may be 10 to 20 min in length for younger players, or in halves of 40 to 45 min for adults. Overtime periods vary from 8 to 10 min.

Playing Area

The soccer field is from 100 to 120 yd long and 60 to 75 yd wide with a center circle and *penalty areas* in front of each goal. For play in coeducational classes, it is desirable to have fields that are regulation size. Smaller fields accommodate younger players sufficiently, and fields at least 70 by 60 yd provide adequate space for effective use of strategy. A diagram of the regulation field is shown in Figure 8.1.

The field markings for soccer may be varied for instructional programs. If field hockey will be played on the same field, the same semicircular goal area could be used (or the penalty area of soccer might be used for field hockey). The field should have a marked center line. The center circle is useful but may be omitted.

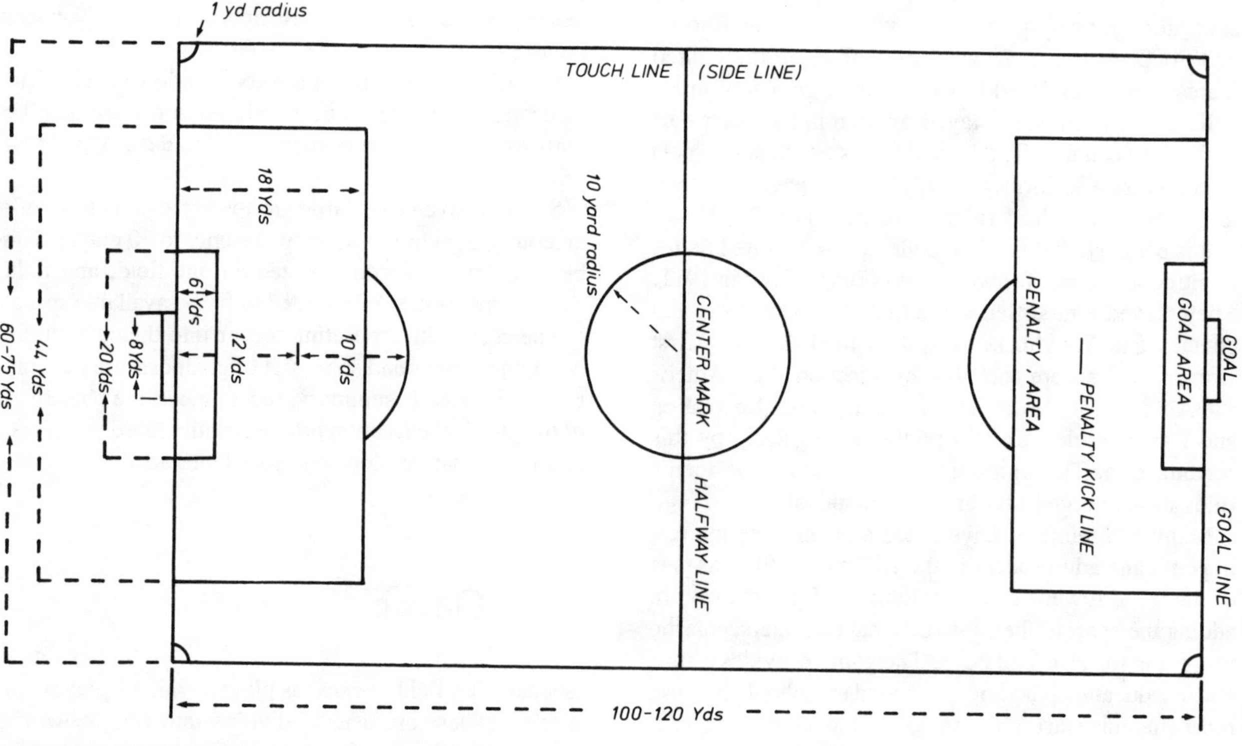

Figure 8.1. Soccer field

Equipment

A minimal amount of equipment is needed in soccer. The following equipment is recommended.

Goals

The goal cages for soccer should be centered on each goal line and are 8 yd wide and 8 ft high. They may be made of 4-by-4-in. wooden posts or of iron pipe. If pipe is used, sleeves of larger pipe can be recessed into the ground to serve as holders for the goals to permit a change of goal cages to be implemented with little difficulty. Loose nets attached to the backs of the goals permit more accurate evidence of goal scoring and help to reduce time lost chasing balls during practice, but these are not essential.

Balls

Soccer balls may be made of leather, plastic, or rubber and should be between 27 and 28 in. in diameter. Although official game balls must be leather, rubber balls are cheaper and usually more practical for general use. Leather absorbs moisture and eventually becomes heavy and hard. Rubber balls can be used both indoors and outdoors and are more durable, although they tend to sting more on contact with the body. When working with young children, the use of lightweight plastic, Nerf, or Styrofoam balls is recommended until the players master the basic skills and are able to adjust to the weight and force of the regulation ball. One ball for every two players is advantageous, although one for every five or six is acceptable.

Footgear

The use of soccer, field hockey, or turf shoes is recommended because of the rapid and erratic movements needed to play soccer. These all have pegs or rubber cleats, which help to prevent slipping. Leather uppers are also advisable to give extra protection from the ball and the feet of others.

Shin Guards

Shin guards should be worn by beginning players to protect against damage to the lower leg. These can be of leather or fabric with plastic inserts and straps to secure them to the leg, or they can fit inside the socks. Shin guards for field hockey and soccer are interchangeable.

Pinnies

As with other sports in which teams interact directly with each other, pinnies are helpful in differentiating one team from another. Instructors may find it useful to use one color of pinnies for forwards and another color for defensive players on the same team. This enables the instructor or coach to see where the players are going and to evaluate position play more easily.

Suggestions for Coeducational Play

Boys and girls usually begin at about the same skill level in soccer. Therefore, the same experiences can be provided for all novices. Middle school girls may need to be encouraged to be more aggressive in attacking the goal or tackling an opponent but should be able to master the skills as readily as can boys.

A difference in strength and speed may be evident between genders at the high school level. When this occurs, instructors should handle it the same way they would handle differences within groups of one gender. Stronger or faster players are assigned to *mark* (guard) similar opponents, and weaker or slower players oppose those of similar skills. As long as teams are balanced in overall ability, competition can be successful and motivational.

Often it is helpful to distribute players so that each team has approximately the same number of good players. Having captains choose their own teams may not accomplish this in certain classes. Younger students tend to pick teams based on friendship and not on athletic ability. Teachers may wish to exercise more control over team selection to equalize competition.

Students could be divided into motor skill ability groups. Teams could then be formed by assigning a specified number of players from each ability group to each of the teams. Motor skill groups might be subjectively designated by the instructor or determined on the basis of scores achieved on pertinent skill tests. For example, all students could be timed on an obstacle dribble and tested for passing accuracy. Each student's score on both tests would be combined and the best one-third assigned to the top group; those with scores in the bottom one-third would be assigned to the low-skill group, and the remaining students would be in the middle group. It might be better to select the best one-fourth for the high-skill group and the lowest one-fourth for the low-skill group. Most of the students would fall into the middle, or average, group. Teams would then be comprised of an equal number from each group.

Requiring students to rotate positions frequently also improves opportunities for all to participate in play. This limits the opportunity for stronger, more aggressive players to dominate the action and moves the more reluctant players into key positions. Players who start games as forwards move to defensive positions after 7 to 10 min of play, and the backs then move into the forward lines. It might also be necessary to move those in the center of the field to side positions and vice versa. Goalkeepers who choose this position because they wish to stand around and do little must be rotated into more active positions.

Team play must be encouraged. Do not let a few players run all over the field and follow the ball wherever it goes. Insist that players stay in their own positions and learn to pass to teammates. One way to keep players in their own areas is to divide the field from end line to end line with four lines, each parallel with the sidelines. The lines should be 12 to 15 yd apart to divide the field into five equal areas, or zones (use only three lines if using the four-player attack pattern). Each attack player is then assigned a zone in which to play. This forces a spread across the field and eliminates crowding around the ball. Each defensive player is also assigned a zone or a person to guard. Thus, the defense is also spread out and must learn to develop better teamwork. This idea works better when using the traditional 5-3-2-1 pattern of play (see Figure 8.19 and the section on offensive formations).

Dividing the field into a smaller number of segments will also work when using other offensive or defensive patterns. There will be fewer segments but larger zones. Each attacker and the backup players are assigned zones. The defenders function with fewer restrictions. Perhaps they would be limited to their own half of the field or to one quadrant.

Sometimes rules can be added to equalize play more effectively. Some of these include the following: (a) At least one player of each gender on a team must play the ball before a goal can be attempted; (b) Two successive shots at goal may not be made by players of the same gender (alternate boy, girl, boy, etc.); (c) Girls must take all free kicks, throw-ins, and so on; (d) A throw-in or a free kick must be received by a player of the opposite gender.

Effective officiating will also help to improve coeducational play. Students should be taught to avoid dangerous and wild kicking and to avoid body contact while tackling. Rules related to these should be enforced during play even if it becomes necessary to penalize offending players by removing them from the game.

Teaching Progressions

Skills presented in this chapter are grouped according to fundamental movement relationships to one another and commonality of purpose for ease of understanding and analyzing. This does not imply that the skills should always be presented to players in that order.

The following are suggested teaching progressions for the various skill levels. The suggested progression is only one of many that might be utilized to suit the particular needs of a specific class or instructional group. Instructors should move on to intermediate or advanced skills when players have adequately mastered the simpler skills.

Progression for Beginning Players

I. Dribbling
   A. Inside of the foot
   B. Outside of the foot

II. Passing
  A. Inside of the foot
  B. Outside of the Foot
  C. Instep

III. Trapping
  A. Sole
  B. Lower leg

IV. Volleying
  A. Knee
  B. Shoulder

V. Tackling
  A. Front
  B. Side

VI. Kicking
  A. Punt

VII. Goalkeeping
  A. Stance
  B. Throw

VIII. Game play

Additional Skills for Intermediate Players

I. Passing
  A. Toe

II. Trapping
  A. Thigh
  B. Chest/abdomen

III. Volleying
  A. Head

Additional Skills for Advanced Players

I. Passing
  A. Heel

II. Trapping
  A. Chest

III. Tackling
  A. Hook

IV. Kicking
  A. Dropkick

Techniques and Practice

Dribbling, Passing, and Shooting

The *dribble* in soccer consists of a series of light taps given to the ball by a foot to keep control of the ball while running downfield. The dribbler should learn to keep the ball close to the feet without stepping on it and to dribble equally well with either foot. The player should be prepared to stop, change direction, or pass the ball to prevent interception by an opponent. The dribble does not advance the ball as quickly as does a pass, so it should not be used extensively except to draw the defense to the dribbler and free other teammates to receive passes.

The three main styles of dribbling use the inside of the foot, the outside of the foot, and the toe. The first two are preferred because the beginner using the toe dribble tends to lose control and kick the ball too far ahead.

The *pass* is executed with the feet. The types of passes are similar to the dribbling styles and use the inside of the foot, the outside of the foot, and the instep (top of foot). The pass or kick off the tip of the toe is difficult to control and should be used only by intermediate and advanced players. The ball may be kicked with the heel of the foot, but this is used primarily to stop the ball's forward momentum or as a short backward kick to a trailing teammate. This also is a more advanced skill. Beginners tend to misjudge and step on the ball, so this pass could be hazardous to them.

Shooting is also a kicking skill executed with the feet. Shots can be taken when the ball is either stationary, rolling, or airborne. The two basic kicking techniques for shooting use the inside of the foot and the instep. Players should develop the ability to shoot effectively with either foot. Ball manipulation while playing soccer is useless unless shots on goal are taken.

Generalizations

The skills of dribbling, passing, and shooting are unique forms of striking in which the lower limbs are used to impart force to the ball. In general, the three skills are different in specific purpose, which also affects general execution. Skill executions are differentiated relative to the amount of force to be imparted to the soccer ball. The general characteristics of kicking in dribbling, passing, and shooting are similar.

The preparatory motion begins with a step forward with the foot opposite the kicking foot. The length of the step prior to kicking is dependent on the desired force application to the ball. The length of the last step increases as the need for force application increases. The longer step provides for a larger range of motion at the hip. The plant foot is placed slightly to the rear and lateral to the ball or where the ball should drop if airborne. The position of the plant foot relative to the ball is also dependent on the desired magnitude of force application. The smaller the force application needed, such as in the dribble, the closer the plant foot is to the ball. The hip is hyperextended (backward) with accompanying knee flexion in preparation for the force-production phase. The degree of hyperextension at the hip and of flexion at the knee also depend on the magnitude of force required. Larger amounts of hyperextension at the hip in combination with large amounts of flexion at the knee occur for forceful applications to the soccer ball.

The force-production phase begins with a downward and forward swing of the leg accompanied by rotation of the pelvis toward the ball. In more forceful kicking, which generally excludes the dribble, the leg demonstrates a whipping action. The first movement is flexion at the hip until the thigh comes forward and is approximately perpendicular to the ground. Extension at the knee then opens the leg as it swings toward the ball. The leg follows through the arc of motion until the momentum of the leg is dissipated.

The amount of force imparted on the ball is dependent on the placement of the plant foot, which affects the possible range of motion at the hip and knee. In addition, force application is dependent on the speed of both flexion at the hip and extension at the knee. The faster the leg moves toward the ball, the more force will be transferred to the ball. The force imparted to the ball is directly related to the distance traveled by the ball. The dribble requires and demands the smallest application of force of all three skills. Therefore, the dribble technique has a small range of motion at the hip and knee with a slower speed of leg extension toward the ball. These qualities are increased for passing medium distances. The range of motion and speed of movement is optimized for power in shooting and long passing. Accuracy of ball placement should never be sacrificed for power or force application.

The two types of ball trajectory are the ground ball and the lofted ball. These are determined by the placement of the foot on the ball while striking. The ground ball is used for dribbling, shooting, and short passes. The lofted ball is used primarily for long passes. The foot contacts the ball at the center or slightly above the center for the ground ball and under the center of the ball for the lofted ball.

A further differentiation within the techniques of dribbling, passing, and shooting is the part of the foot used in striking the ball. Any part of the foot can be used to strike the ball, but the larger the surface area used in striking, the more ball control is possible. Therefore, the larger surface areas of the inside, outside, and instep of the foot should be mastered before attempting to use other parts of the foot. Players should also be encouraged to learn dribbling, passing, and shooting skills with both feet.

Placekick

The *placekick* is taken when the ball is stationary and usually by a defensive player on the field after the opponents have fouled or kicked the ball over the goal line not between the goalposts. The kicker takes three or four approach steps and contacts the ball with the top of the instep or the inside of the foot.

Inside Kick

The inside of the foot is used in both techniques of advancing the ball and shooting (Figure 8.2). The technique is performed as mentioned in the generalizations of dribbling, passing, and shooting. The unique aspect is that the striking foot is brought forward with the side of the foot at right angles to the supporting foot. The ball is struck with the inside of the foot. The foot swings through the ball to complete the follow-through.

The inside of the foot provides the largest flat surface area for making contact with the ball and gives good ball control. The inside kick is used to tap the ball ahead as the dribbler runs. This is the easiest of the two preferred styles of dribbling for beginners to learn. When alternating the feet to tap the ball, the inside-of-the-foot dribble keeps the ball in front of the body. This dribble can be converted easily into a short pass and can also be used for an accurate and powerful shot on goal.

Outside Kick

The outside kick is used for both dribbling and passing (Figure 8.3). The ball is struck with the outside surface area of the foot. The kicking technique is the same as previously discussed, but the ankle is flexed and inverted (rotated toward the inside) to position the foot for striking. After striking the ball, the foot continues in the swinging action to the side to complete the follow-through.

The outside kick for dribbling is more difficult for beginners, but mastering this enables the player to be more deceptive in the game. A tap with the outside of the foot can be used to change direction, to dodge a tackler, or to pass to a teammate.

Instep Kick

The instep kick is used for passing and shooting. The ball is struck with the instep (top of the foot). Generally,

Figure 8.2. Inside-of-the-foot dribble

Figure 8.3. Outside-of-the-foot dribble

there is less accuracy or control with the instep kick due to the rounded surface area making contact with the ball. The general kicking technique is the same, but the ankle is flexed. The foot comes underneath the ball. Lofted balls are easily accomplished with the instep kick.

Toe Kick

The toe kick can be used for dribbling. The toe dribble is sometimes referred to as the *fast dribble*. In this dribble, the ball is tapped lightly with the toe of the foot as the foot swings forward to take the next step. It seems to be a natural movement, but it usually results in the ball being kicked far ahead or the dribbler stepping on the ball and falling. It is suggested that this be taught only to intermediate or advanced players.

Common Movement Problems and Suggestions

The following are common movement problems encountered in the general technique of kicking as well as in dribbling, passing, and shooting. Instructional suggestions are also presented.

The following are common technique errors in the general skill of kicking.

- Players many times plant the nonkicking foot in a position that restricts or limits the kicking performance. Placement of the plant foot should not be too close to the ball but should vary relative to the range of motion at the hip needed for the appropriate application of force.
- The largest single error in kicking is improper force application. Players tend to kick the ball too forcefully or too softly. Accuracy should be emphasized over forceful or power kicking. Practice different lengths of kicks to learn how much force is needed to achieve the objective.
- Beginning players tend not to focus on the ball at contact. Generally, this can cause the player to miss the ball or not strike the ball when the foot is moving the fastest. Watch the ball.
- A common error is to strike the ball in the wrong place. Striking the ball too high or too low can cause the ball to travel in an unintended direction.
- Many players will swing the leg across instead of through the ball. This can cause unnecessary spin on the ball, resulting in less accuracy, and can deplete the force applied in the kick.
- Inadequate force application may be due to poor balance techniques during the kick. Body symmetry and a firm base of support around which the kicking leg can swing are essential.
- Loss of balance is a common problem for the beginning kicker. This is generally caused either by the ball being too far away from the kicker or by a failure to shift body weight over the plant foot.

The following are common technique errors that are unique to dribbling.

- Dribblers need to look up and not continuously focus on the ball. Failure to look up can cause players to lose their sense of direction.
- The most common error is to apply too much force on the ball, which puts the ball too far in front of the body. This creates the greatest opportunity for interception.
- Additional errors are caused by disruptive timing or nonrhythmical motion while dribbling. This makes the player appear jerky in the dribble.
- The player should practice changes of speed and acceleration of the dribble as an offensive strategy.
- The player should incline the upper body slightly forward to protect the ball and use shorter strides when near an opponent.

The following are common technique errors that are unique to passing.

- The passer should learn to pass the ball quickly and to conceal the intended direction.
- All players should be encouraged to use the simplest pass because of the better chance of success.
- The most common passing error is the inability to control the speed of the ball. The speed must be correct to ensure accuracy of placement and to enhance control by the receiver.

The following are common technique errors that are unique to shooting on goal.

- Players should be encouraged to use the simplest and most basic kicking technique with accuracy and power whenever possible. Always emphasize that accuracy is more important than power in shooting.
- The speed of a player's approach and body balance greatly influence the player's ability to kick the ball forcefully with accuracy.
- Players should be encouraged to shoot low and quickly. Players should always follow the shot toward the goal in case a follow-up shot is possible.

Dribbling Practice Drills

The following are practice drills for dribbling only. Practice drills for passing follow the analysis of trapping in the next section. The two skills should be practiced together. Shooting and long-kick drills are described after the section on tackling.

Individual Drills. Individual drills maximize a player's participation. The following are individual practice drills.

1.0. The procedure that maximizes dribbling practice when there is enough equipment is to give players balls and have them run (slowly at first) around the outside of the field while dribbling.

1.1. Set up obstacles along the route so that the dribblers must stop, change direction, or maneuver around an object. Be sure that all are running in the same direction to avoid collisions. Encourage players to keep their heads up and to be aware of what or who is around them.

2.0. If there is sufficient equipment for only half the class, put the players in pairs. Place one from each pair at one end of the field and the other at the other end. One partner dribbles down and the other dribbles back, either changing the style of dribble or using the same one.

2.1. One of the partners dribbles around the outside of the field while the other waits; then the second person dribbles while the first one recovers. They continue to alternate, one dribbling and one resting.

Group Drills. The following are group drills for dribbling. The drills presented here are in progressive order for introduction. However, all drills need not be taught.

1.0. Single-Column Formation (Figure 4.2). The leader dribbles the ball to a designated line or cone marker and back to the next person in the column. The dribbler then goes to the end of the column, and the next player dribbles. This continues until all players have had an opportunity to dribble. Variations include the following:

1.1. The dribbler must dribble around a cone, an Indian club, or a chair at the opposite end. This facilitates the learning of control.

1.2. Devise conditions to require control for beginners, such as that the dribbler must stop the ball between two designated lines (e.g., a line and the end wall in a gymnasium) before dribbling back to the start. This promotes control rather than a kick-and-chase pattern. Dribblers who fail to stop the ball must go back to the start and repeat the drill.

1.3. Place cones or other obstacles about 8 ft apart in front of the dribbler, who must move in and out around them (i.e., in an extended figure 8).

1.4. Replace the cones with human obstacles. As skill levels improve, allow the human obstacles to move one foot in an attempt to get the ball. Be sure that the human obstacles are replaced frequently. The first dribbler could take a turn and then replace the first human obstacle, who goes to the end of the column. The second dribbler replaces the second human obstacle, and so forth, until all have been replaced. This drill is good practice for dodging also.

1.5. Make the drills into a relay race. Be sure the skills do not disintegrate into kicks without control under the stress of competition.

2.0. Circle Formation (Figure 4.13). One player dribbles around the outside of the circle and back to place. The next person takes the ball and does the same thing. This continues until all players have had an opportunity to dribble around the circle. Try to stay close to the circle. This gives practice in control and direction changing. Variations include the following:

2.1. Persons in the circle should be about 6 ft apart. Dribble in and out around the players in the circle. This would be good for control and dodging practice.

2.2. Change direction and dribble the other way around the circle.

3.0. Shuttle Formation (Figure 4.8). Columns of individuals are 25 to 30 ft apart. The leader of one column dribbles the ball across to the leader of the other column and goes to the end of that column. The leader of the second column dribbles back to the first column and goes to the end of that column. This continues until all players have had an opportunity to participate.

Trapping

A *trap* is executed to stop and control the ball with the feet, legs, or body. Trapping should be taught along with passing so that players can practice both together. During class the players should be encouraged to use the feet at all times to control the ball and to avoid handling the ball even when retrieving an errant pass or dribble. The instructor should set an example by avoiding the use of the hands as much as possible.

Generalizations

The purpose of trapping is to control the movement of the ball in motion or flight. Players should use the largest body surface area possible for controlling or stopping the ball. In all trapping or controlling skills, the surface area making contact with the ball should be withdrawn, or retracted, from the moment of impact until the ball is under control or stopped. Retraction is accomplished by moving the total body or body parts toward the ball in motion until the moment of impact. Just prior to or immediately following impact, the body parts are retracted or the total body is retracted by taking steps backward. The retraction of body parts or the total body dissipates the force of the ball until it is stopped or drops to the feet.

Trapping With the Foot and the Leg

The common foot and leg traps are executed with the sole of the foot and the inside or front of one leg (also called the *instep trap*). The sole-of-the-foot trap is quick and effective against a ball that is rolling smoothly toward the trapper. This is more useful in the gym on a level floor than it is outside. The inside-of-the-leg (calf) trap is used to field a low-bouncing ball to one side of the body. This should be practiced with each leg, not just the preferred one. The front of both legs (shin or thigh areas) gives a wider surface for trapping a bouncing ball coming head on.

Sole-of-the-Foot Trap. The player moves directly in front of the ball's path of motion. Just prior to the ball reaching the player, the player lifts one leg while balancing on the opposite leg. The foot is raised by flexing the knee. The toe should be held higher than the heel of the foot. The foot should be just high enough to trap the ball between the sole of the foot and the ground (Figure 8.4). Once contact is made with the ball, the player can withdraw or retract the foot to dissipate the force of the ball further.

Figure 8.4. Sole-of-the-foot trap

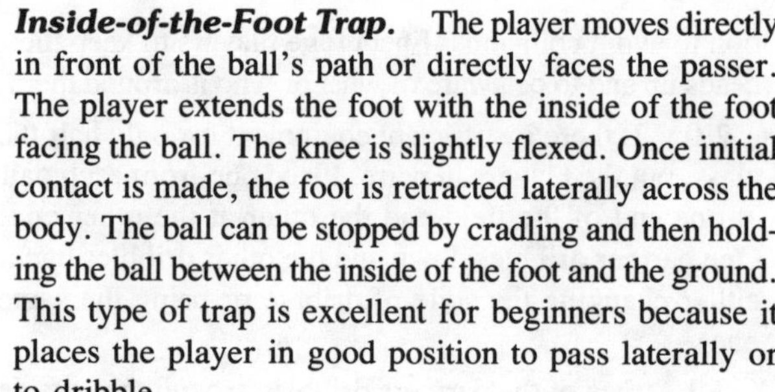

Inside-of-the-Foot Trap. The player moves directly in front of the ball's path or directly faces the passer. The player extends the foot with the inside of the foot facing the ball. The knee is slightly flexed. Once initial contact is made, the foot is retracted laterally across the body. The ball can be stopped by cradling and then holding the ball between the inside of the foot and the ground. This type of trap is excellent for beginners because it places the player in good position to pass laterally or to dribble.

Outside-of-the-Foot Trap. As in other traps, the player moves directly in front of the ball's path. The outside of the foot is advanced toward the ball with the knee slightly flexed. The ankle is inverted (toes turned in) to have the outside of the foot facing the ball. Once contact is made, the foot is retracted to dissipate the force of the ball. The controlling or trapping of the ball with the outside of the foot is one technique used to alter play or as an element of surprise.

Instep/Lower-Leg Trap. The player moves directly in line with the path of the ball. The hip is flexed with the thigh positioned a little higher than the horizontal. The knee and ankle are flexed. The ball is contacted with the top of the instep and the front of the lower leg. Once contact is made, the foot is lowered by flexing the knee to carry the ball to the ground (Figure 8.5). The ball is then trapped between both the instep and the lower leg and the ground.

Thigh Trap. The player can rush the ball and use the thigh to control the ball. The thigh is raised toward the dropping aerial ball by flexing at the hip. The knee is also flexed. At the moment of ball contact, the thigh is retracted by extending at the hip. This action permits the ball to drop to the ground. This type of trap permits

Figure 8.5. Instep/lower-leg trap

the player the ability to rush the ball and place it in a good position to dribble, pass, or shoot.

Advanced Traps. The advanced traps or means of controlling the ball are usually those of aerial balls. All the previous traps can be used for aerial balls. The following techniques are considered advanced techniques for intermediate and advanced players.

Other parts of the body are also used for controlling the ball when it is higher in the air. This is sometimes called *collecting* (or blocking) the ball instead of trapping, but the effect is the same, which is to stop and control the ball before dribbling or passing. The player should withdraw with the ball and try to drop it softly to the ground in front of the feet. Collecting may be done with the inside of the foot raised in the air or with the inside of the thigh. The abdomen or chest may also be used to stop the ball. Players may cross the arms in front of the chest if desired when using the chest block. However, the arms must be kept in contact with the body; the elbows may not be lifted to propel the ball. Women may feel more comfortable with the arms protecting the chest. Some special drills for practicing the stomach (abdomen) and chest drills are included at the end of the passing and trapping practice drills.

Common Movement Problems and Suggestions

The following are common movement problems encountered in the general techniques of trapping. Instructional suggestions are also presented.

- Players sometime fail to move directly into the path of the ball, causing them to make unnecessary lateral moves or not to use the best surface area for controlling the ball.
- Players may lack ball control because of using an uneven or rounded body-surface area. Players should use the largest body-surface area possible to control the ball.
- Mistakes are sometimes made because players do not make an early enough decision on what part of the body to use in ball control. Players must maintain concentration on the tasks of the game.
- Improper maintenance of balance causes unnecessary motions that limit ball-controlling performance.
- Players may offer too much resistance with the body part and cause the ball to bounce away. This can also occur when the player does not retract the ball-controlling body part.
- Players should be encouraged to move toward the ball to receive it when opponents are close.
- Players should be encouraged to make conscious decisions early on what to do after receiving the ball.

Passing and Trapping Drills

The following drills combine both passing and trapping. Both partner and group drills are presented.

Partner Drills. When plenty of equipment and space is available, players should work in pairs. Some of these drills may be used as lead-up games for younger children and as indoor activities if inclement weather prohibits outdoor play.

1.0. Partners are spaced 10 to 14 ft apart. They trap and pass the ball back and forth to each other. Different styles of passes and traps should be used.

1.1. As skill improves, increase the distance between partners.

2.0. Draw a target or a line on the gymnasium wall about 2 ft above the floor. Partners stand side by side about 15 ft from the wall. One passes the ball to the target; the partner moves up to trap the rebounding ball and passes it back to the target. The original passer then traps and passes the rebound. Play continues with this repetition.

Group Drills. The following are group drills utilizing both passing and trapping. Drills are presented in the suggested order of introduction.

1.0. Circle Formation (Figure 4.13). Players stand about 10 ft apart in a circle. The ball is passed with the inside-of-the-foot pass around the circle. The inside of the left foot is used to pass counterclockwise; the inside of the right foot is used to pass clockwise. Sole-of-the-foot or inside-of-the-leg traps are used.

2.0. Double-Line Formation (Figure 4.10). Lines are about 10 ft apart. Players pass one ball back and forth between the lines using only legal traps to control the ball. The ball should be kept low.

3.0. Shuttle Formation (Figure 4.7). The leader of one column passes to the first person in the other column, who traps the ball and passes it back. Players go to the end of their own column. Different passes and traps may be used in this drill.

4.0. Double-Column Formation. A target 4 ft wide and 3 ft high is drawn on the wall of the gymnasium with tape or water-color paint (Figure 8.6). One column is stationed about 15 ft in front and about 8 ft to the side of the target. The other column is the same distance to the other side. Player X1 passes the ball with the inside of the right foot to the target (Pass a) and goes to the end of the other column. Player X2 fields the ball (b),

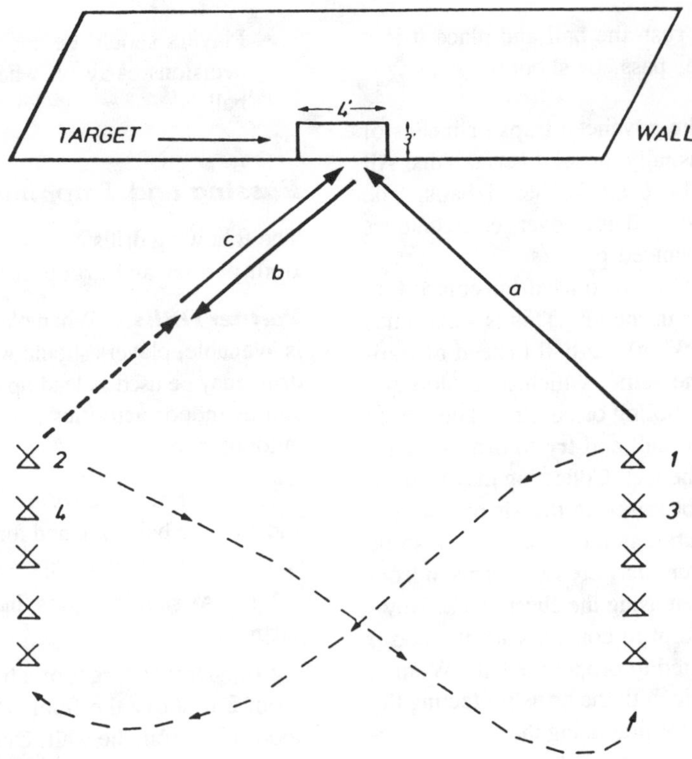

Figure 8.6. Pass-and-trap drill with target

passes it to the target with an inside-of-left-foot pass (Pass c), and goes to the end of the other column. Player X3 traps and passes to the target, and play continues sequentially. Variation: Use the outside-of-the-foot pass.

5.0. Column Formation with Leader (Figure 4.3). The leader is about 20 ft in front of the column. The leader kicks the ball slightly to one side or the other of the first person in the column, who must move in front of the ball, trap it, pass it back to the leader, and go to the end of the column. This will help players learn to move quickly to get in line with the ball to intercept it. As skill improves, the leader may kick the ball farther away from the receiver. The leader should be changed periodically.

Chest/Abdomen. Beginners tend to be afraid of blocking with the torso. Therefore, special drills that lead up to using the torso to block may alleviate some of the fear, help players learn to do it correctly, and gain confidence in using it. Intermediate players should be able to use this skill.

1.0. Column Formation with Leader (Figure 4.3). The leader should be about 6 ft in front. The leader tosses the ball softly at waist height to the first person in the column, who blocks or collects it with the stomach, drops it to the ground in front of the body, kicks it back to the leader, and goes to the end of the column. Change leaders periodically. Be sure the tosses are soft and accurate. The balls may be partially deflated, or volleyballs may be used at first to soften the impact. As the trappers gain confidence, the leader moves farther away and throws the ball a little harder.

2.0. Use the same formation as in Drill 1.0. The ball is tossed higher, and the trapper blocks the ball with the chest. The arms may be crossed over the chest for safety and comfort, but this provides an uneven surface and limits control. Variation: The leader passes the ball into the air to the trapper with an instep kick.

Volleying

A *volley* is executed when an aerial ball is hit with a part of the body or leg in an effort to direct it to a teammate, a space, or a goal. The most common volleys are done with the foot, knee/thigh, hip, shoulder, and head.

A volley should be utilized by the player only when performed with control. The player who lacks experience can develop a reliance on its use to clear the ball or get rid of the ball quickly. This dependency should be discouraged. Control must be emphasized and its use a matter of choice, not panic. The development of control centers around developing a touch on the ball that enables the player to exert the necessary force to project the ball the appropriate distance and direction needed in a variety of situations. In addition, concentration and maintenance of good balance are essential.

Foot Volley

Foot volleys are similar to all the previously mentioned foot skills. The inside, outside, and toe areas of the foot can be used for volleying. Foot volleys are used when the ball is slightly airborne and are accomplished by lifting the striking surface parallel to the ground when striking the ball.

Knee/Thigh Volley

This is used for bouncing balls or those that are knee to hip high. The volleying knee is lifted to meet the ball while the player balances on the opposite foot with the arms out to the sides. The ball contacts the top or the side of the knee or the widest top part of the thigh, depending on the desired ball direction. Contact with the flatest body-surface area gives the most accuracy.

Hip Volley

A ball that approaches about waist high may be volleyed with the hip. The player turns the torso and pushes the hip out laterally to meet the ball and direct it. The arms should be kept up and clearly out of contact with the ball.

Shoulder Volley

This volley would be used to direct a ball that is above the waist but too low for a head volley. Some novice players prefer it to the head volley. A forward stride is taken with the feet. The opposite foot from the shoulder used to strike is forward in the preparatory phase. The striking shoulder is then turned toward the ball with the arm on that side folded against the body and the weight shifted to the foot on that side. The player flexes at the hips, knees, and ankles. The player thrusts the shoulder upward by rapid extension of the hips, knees, and ankles. This generally lifts the player into a jump. The ball is contacted with the platform created by the upper part of the arm and shoulder.

Head Volley

Heading is used to direct a ball that comes above the shoulders. This is considered an advanced skill by some and should not be taught to elementary school children unless very lightweight balls are used. Most high school classes could learn the technique, but it is not recommended that individuals be required to use it. Instructions should be given so that those who choose to head the ball do so with less risk. Others could use the shoulder volley.

Heading can be accomplished while on the ground (diving header) or by jumping into the air to meet the ball. The latter should be taught initially and is covered here. The diving header should be used only by experienced and well-conditioned players.

Heading begins with a forward stride directly under the ball with the knees flexed to create a stable base of support from which to push. The body weight is shifted rearward. The body is extended upward into the air to meet the ball by a rapid extension of the ankles, knees, and hips. The body weight is shifted forward during this extension. The head (forehead) makes contact with the ball just prior to reaching the apex of the jump. The chin is down, and the muscles of the neck are tightened. The player projects the head through the ball while using the arms for balance.

Common Movement Problems and Suggestions

The following are the most common movement problems in volleying skills. Instructional suggestions are also presented.

- Players do not always align themselves directly under the ball during their preparations. This can cause adjustment types of movement that limit the effectiveness of the performance.
- Players should be encouraged to concentrate on the task and to maintain good total body balance throughout.
- Players sometimes do not impart enough force onto the ball. This error could be caused by the player not striking through the ball with the body part. Insufficient follow-through can cause the player not to make contact at the maximum speed.
- Poor timing can also create an impact with less than desirable speed.
- In heading, players tend to close the eyes naturally just prior to contact. Emphasis should be placed on keeping the eyes open.
- Heading is a skill that creates apprehension in novice players. Novice players are many times afraid to strike the ball with the head. It is suggested that beginners hold the ball and throw it lightly against the forehead as a beginning movement. They should throw the ball progressively harder. After players are at ease with this, they can toss the ball into the air before heading it.

Volleying Practice Drills

Care must be taken when starting to work on volleying to avoid having players get hurt by the ball. Youngsters who suffer pain when the ball hits them will naturally avoid a repetition of such contact. One way to lessen this problem is to use softer balls. Volleyballs, foam balls, playground balls, and plastic beach balls would be suitable. If these are not available, partially deflate the soccer balls. The tosses used to put the ball in the air for the volley should be soft, short tosses at first. Tosses should be used instead of kicks because they are more accurate and controlled.

Partner Practice. Paired practice maximizes the activity for each learner but requires a ball for every two players. The following are partner drills.

1.0. One partner (about 6 to 8 ft away) tosses the ball to the other. Make five underhand tosses to each side for each of the foot, knee, hip, and shoulder volleys. Tossers take a turn at volleying after five tosses for each player.

2.0. Using the preceding formation, make five high tosses for the head volley. The person doing the volleying tries to direct the ball back to the tosser. After practicing from soft tosses, partners could move farther apart, and the tosses could be higher and harder.

3.0 As skill levels improve in Drills 1.0 and 2.0, the tosses could be kicked passes.

Group Practice. The following are group drills for volleying. Begin with the simpler drills and progress to the more complex ones.

1.0 Single Column with Leader (Figure 4.3). The leader tosses the ball to each player in turn, who volleys it back to the leader. Variation: The leader may pass the ball with the foot if skilled enough.

2.0 Circle Formation (Figure 4.13). The leader in the center tosses the ball to each person, who volleys it back. Vary the toss so that all types of volleys are practiced. The leader rotates into the circle, and a new leader takes over after each round or as designated by the instructor.

3.0. Shuttle Formation (Figure 4.7). Leaders are about 8 ft apart. The leader of one column tosses the ball to the leader of the other, who volleys it back. This continues until each player has a turn. Each player goes to the end of the same column after volleying. Players should attempt to keep the ball in the air. The ball may be volleyed with anything except the hands or arms. Variation: This can be made a competitive drill by having groups count the number of successive volleys they make. Every time the ball gets away or someone touches it illegally, the group must start counting over. The ball may be allowed to hit the floor but should be raised to volley level again. The group with the highest number of volleys at the end of the playing time (2 to 5 min) wins.

4.0. Triangular Formation (Figure 8.7). Player X1 tosses the ball to Player X2, who volleys it to Player X3. Player X3 traps it, then tosses it to Player X1, who volleys to Player X2, and so forth. Players X1, X2, and X3 could each head columns as shown in Figure 8.7, in which case each player goes to the end of the same column after handling the ball. Vary the height and placement of the tosses to allow practice of all the volleys.

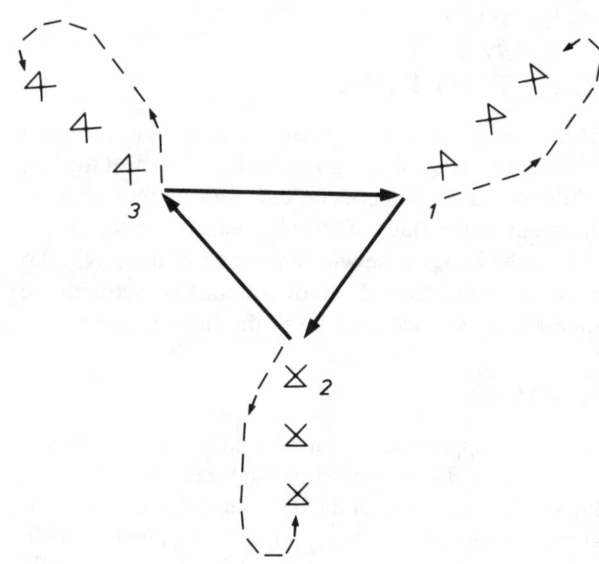

Figure 8.7. Volleying practice

5.0. Circle Formation (Figure 4.13). Players begin with a short pass (with the foot) across the circle. The ball is volleyed or passed back and forth to everyone in the circle. Variation: Competition can be added by counting the number of successive volleys or passes without losing the ball out of the circle or touching it with the hands or arms.

Tackling

A *tackle* consists of taking the ball away from an opponent who is dribbling or controlling the ball. Pushing the opponent away from the ball is illegal. Players should also avoid any other body contact. The key to the successful tackle is timing. The tackler tries to contact the ball when it is away from the dribbler's foot (perhaps 8 to 15 in. ahead) or when the dribbler is off balance and unable to change the direction of the ball. The tackler need not always gain possession of the ball but may deflect it to a teammate or merely interrupt a drive on goal.

The most commonly used tackles are those that are done when facing the opponent (i.e., the straight, or front, tackle and the hook tackle) and the side tackle, which is done from the side of the opponent while running the same direction. The split and the slide tackles are more advanced skills and are not discussed here. The slide tackle is not recommended for use in classes due to the potential for injuries that may result from poor timing or lack of skill.

Generalization

The player should approach the opponent in preparation for the tackle. When making the tackling movement, the nontackling leg should be bent at the knee for force absorption and balance. The tackling foot is elevated slightly with the knee abducted (turned outward) and the ankle firm. The inside of the foot should be directed through the center of the ball. The ball is either pushed or kicked away from the opponent.

Straight/Front Tackle

The straight, or front, tackle is done when the dribbler is moving directly toward and in front of the tackler. The tackler approaches the dribbler and tries to reverse the direction of the ball by blocking or kicking it to the side and out of reach of the dribbler. The tackler tries to contact the ball when it is away from the dribbler's foot. In these tackles the ball may be captured by the tackler or deflected away from the dribbler.

Hook Tackle

The hook tackle is used when the dribbler is moving toward the tackler who is to the side of the dribbler's path. The tackler shifts the weight to the foot away from the dribbler, bends that knee to increase stability, and extends the leg near the dribbler to hook the ball with the toe and draw it away. Attempts by unskilled players to use this tackle may result in tripping. Players should be encouraged to keep their balance and to avoid touching the opponent.

Common Movement Problems and Suggestions

The following are common movement problems experienced by tacklers. Instructional suggestions are also presented.

- Unsuccessful tackles are many times due to the lack of determination and aggressiveness of the tackler.
- Leaning the body away from the tackling leg causes the player to have an ineffective force for capturing the ball.
- Being caught off balance often causes missed tackles. Tacklers should take small, quick steps and be ready to shift weight for changing directions quickly.
- A flexible foot at the ankle can cause not only an ineffective tackle but possibly a situation in which injury can occur. Keep the ankle firm.
- Timing is essential to a good tackle. The most successful tackle occurs when the ball is positioned away from the opponent.
- The ball and the dribbler must be watched carefully for indications of change of direction.

Tackling Practice Drills

The following tackling practice drills are broken down into categories of those tackles that occur from the front and those that occur from the side. Both partner and group drills are presented under each type.

Front Tackle Drills. Paired practice provides the most efficient use of time if balls are plentiful. Players should be paired with another of comparable size or skill. One partner dribbles toward the other, who tackles. Players reverse roles after a predetermined number of tackles.

1.0. Shuttle Formation (Figure 4.8). Columns of individuals are about 20 ft apart. The leader of one column dribbles toward the leader of the second column, who comes forward and tackles the ball. The tackler passes to the second person in the first column and goes to the end of that column. The dribbler goes to the end of the tackler's column. When the drill starts, the dribblers should be cooperative and dribble loosely at moderate speed. After accomplishing the basic tackle, dribblers should dribble more closely and make the tackler work on timing. Variation: Move the columns farther apart. The successful tackler dribbles back toward Column 1, and the next person in that column moves out to tackle. They continue the pattern back and forth: dribble, tackle, dribble, tackle, and so on. Practice the straight tackle first and then the hook tackle.

2.0. Stationary Tackle Drill. If players have difficulty tackling a moving dribbler, the instructor may wish to revert to this simpler drill. Do not waste class time on this drill if most players can handle the moving tackle. The dribbler stands with the ball about 6 in. in front of the feet. The tackler approaches slowly from in front of the dribbler, lifts or hooks the ball away, and dribbles once or twice. The next step is for the dribbler to wait until the tackler is about 2 ft away and then tap the ball lightly while the tackler tries to block it and reverse the direction of the ball.

3.0. 2-on-2 Game. Four columns are arranged as in Figure 8.8. Players in Columns 1 and 2 are dribblers, and those in Columns 3 and 4 are tacklers about 25 yd away. Players X1 and X2 advance downfield, dribbling and passing one ball back and forth. Players X3 and X4 try to tackle or intercept the ball. This is similar to a 2-on-2 in basketball. Once the ball goes behind the dribblers, the turn is over, and the next person in each column starts a turn. Players go to the ends of the opposite columns when finished. Each tackler should guard one dribbler.

Variations include the following:

3.1. Add two columns of players (one at each end) and play 3-on-3.

3.2. Continue to add until there are five dribblers and five tacklers as in a game situation. At least half a soccer field would be needed for 5-on-5. Have different columns start the ball so that play is not always in one area of the field.

Side Block Tackle

The side block or tackle is done when the dribbler and tackler are side by side. The tackler must accelerate slightly ahead of the dribbler and reach with the tackling foot to capture the ball as it is positioned away from the dribbler.

Side Block Tackle Drills. As in other skills, paired practice is best if enough balls are available. Partners start out side by side facing the same direction; one dribbles, and one tries to tackle. The instructor should have partners reverse roles regularly.

1.0. Double-Column Formation (Figure 4.9). Players in columns are about 4 ft apart. Designate a finish line about 20 yd downfield. The leader of Column 1 dribbles downfield. The leader of Column 2 runs alongside and tries to gain control of the ball and move it back to the starting line. After reaching a certain line or making a successful tackle, players go to the end of the opposite column, and the next two players begin. Change the dribbling to Column 2 after several practice trials so that players get a chance to practice the side block tackle from each side. Variation: If tackled, the dribbler may tackle back using the side tackle. Watch for players dominating play when using this variation. Evenly matched opponents may exchange possession of the ball several times. End the drill after 1 or 2 min of play by the same two persons.

2.0. 2-on-2 Game. See Drill 3.0 for the front tackle. Play as described previously, allowing side tackles to be used. Variation: Add more players up to five on each side as described previously and expand the space allocated.

3.0. Triangular or Zigzag Drill with Tackling. A double-column formation of players is placed near the end line. Add two columns of individuals at the side (Figure 8.9). As Players X1 and X2 start to pass back and forth downfield, Players X3 and X4 move out to act as tacklers. The passers try to dribble, using the triangular passing pattern to evade the tacklers. If the dribblers reach the center line or the tacklers get the ball back to the start, play ends, and the next person in each column starts the drill. Dribblers go to the end of the tacklers' columns and tacklers to the end of the dribblers' columns. At least two groups of passers and tacklers could start at each end line and work toward the center line, or two groups could start at one end line and two groups at the center line going toward the opposite end line.

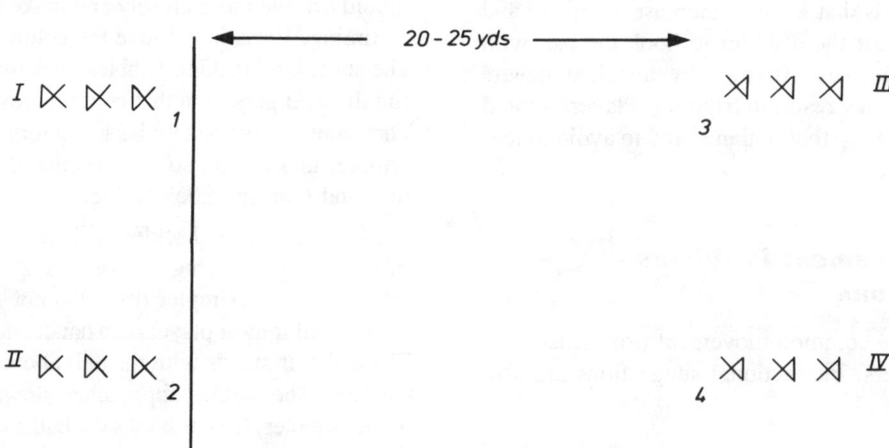

Figure 8.8. 2-on-2 tackling drill

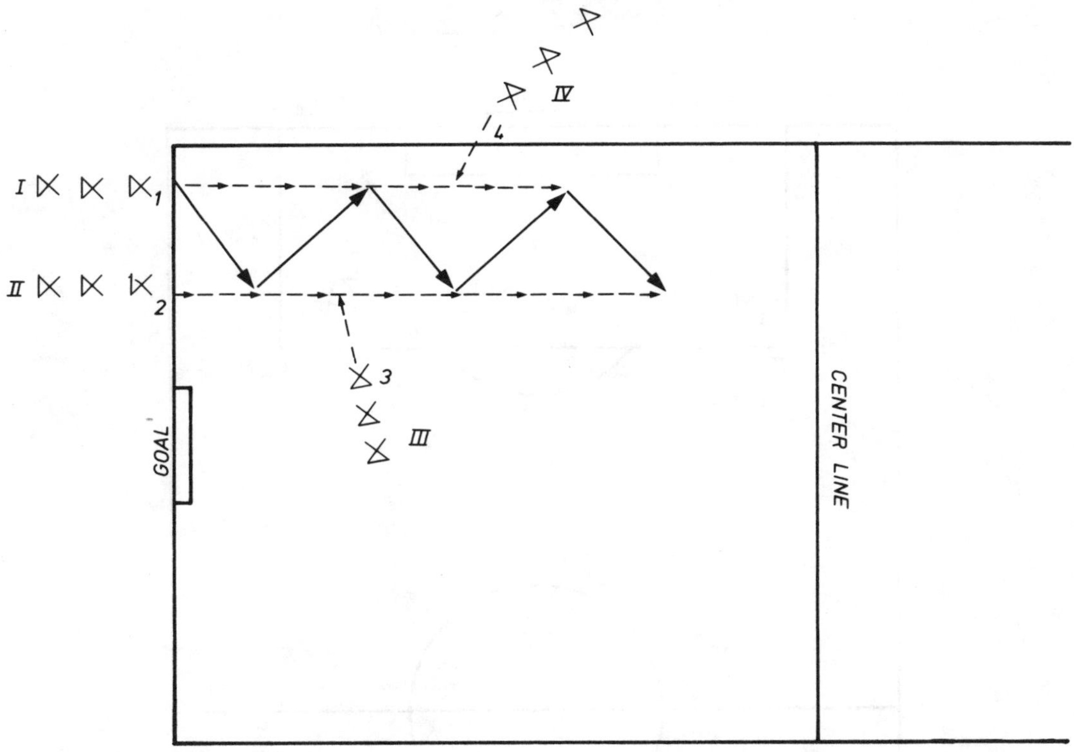

Figure 8.9. Triangular passing to avoid tacklers

Dodging/Feinting

The *dodge* is the movement made by a dribbler to avoid a tackler. The key to effective dodging is to keep the ball close to the feet and to make rapid directional changes, pulling the ball to one side or flicking it out of the reach or over the foot of the opponent. Dribblers should learn to take small steps so they can change feet quickly without losing balance.

The *feint* (fake) is an essential element of dodging. Players should learn to dribble and pass with the inside and the outside of both feet so that the tackler cannot easily predict where the ball will go. An example of a dodge that may be used against an opponent moving in for a straight or hook tackle is to feint a kick to the right with the left foot, then pull the ball left with the outside of the left foot.

Other types of dodges involve stopping the ball with the sole of the foot to interfere with the tackler's timing and using a *heel pass* to reverse the direction of the ball. The latter is a more advanced skill; beginners may step on instead of in front of the ball and lose their balance.

Practice Drills

All the drills listed as tackling drills may be used for dodging practice. The dribbler, instead of being cooperative, tries to dodge the tackler and retain possession of the ball.

Shooting and Kicking Practice Drills

The analyses of shooting and long-kick techniques were presented earlier in this chapter. It is suggested that these variations of the kick be practiced after the other ball-manipulative skills have been taught.

1.0. Double-Line Formation (Figure 4.10). Lines of players are 15 to 20 yds apart. Players kick the ball back and forth using all the kicks and trying to get the ball to a specific person. Receivers may practice traps. Instructors should make sure all players get an opportunity to practice.

2.0. Placekicking Practice. Column Formation and Line Formation (Figure 8.10). The players in Columns 1 and 2 take turns placekicking the ball toward the upper corners of the goal. Players in Columns 3 and 4 combine at the start of the drill, field the balls and return them along the ground to the kickers. Players in Columns 1 and 2 go to the ends of their own columns after taking a turn. After everyone in Columns 1 and 2 has had a turn, rotate so that Columns 3 and 4 become kickers and

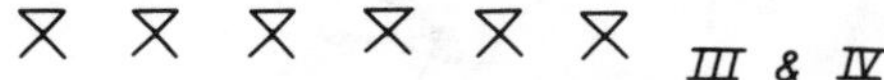

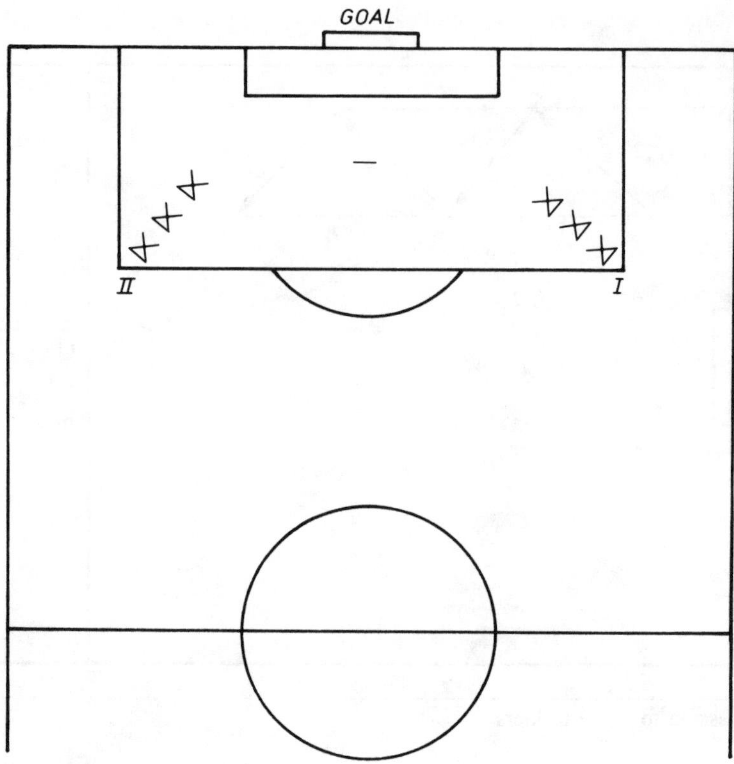

Figure 8.10. Placekicking practice

Columns 1 and 2 combine to retrieve balls. This can be done with three groups instead of four. Variation: Move kickers back to the edge of the penalty area and have retrievers move up to the end line and act as goalkeepers. The goalkeepers return the balls to the kickers with short punts. This drill requires more skill at kick placement, and it is doubtful whether beginners will benefit much from it. They would probably spend most of their time chasing balls all over the field.

Throws

The use of throwing fundamental skills is legal in only two game situations. The goalkeeper has the option of throwing the ball as a means to start an attack after capturing the ball. Generally, the goalkeeper uses a one-handed overarm throw to project the ball the longest distance. The second use of throwing skills is the *throw-in* to restart play after a ball has gone out of bounds. The player uses a two-arm overarm throw. There are many tactical aspects of the throw-in. The rules require that the ball be thrown into play by a player positioned with both feet outside the sideline (touchline).

Two-Arm Overarm Throw

The player takes a straddle or forward-stride foot position. The ball is held equally in both hands overhead. Simultaneously, the arms flex at the elbows, the knees flex, the trunk and head arch backward, and the ball is positioned behind the head. The force-production phase of the throw is initiated with an extension of the elbows and knees while the trunk is brought forward to add momentum to the movement. The ball is released either directly overhead or in front of the body. Contact with the ground must be maintained with both feet. The follow-through is a continuation of the forward motion of the upper body.

One-Arm Overarm Throw

The goalkeeper is the only player with the privilege of using the one-arm overarm throw. The preparation for this skill involves a rearward body-weight shift as well as a clockwise rotation of the hips, spine, and shoulders (for the right-handed thrower). The throwing arm is also retracted rearward to a maximum backswing position. The force-production phase is an uncoiling action that begins with a reversal of the preparatory motions. The body weight is shifted forward; the hips, spine, and shoulders rotate counterclockwise; and the arm moves forward to the point of release. The ball is released tangent to the target. The arm continues forward and downward after the release in the follow-through.

Common Movement Problems and Suggestions

The following are common movement problems encountered during instruction of the goalkeeper's throw and the throw-in. Instructional suggestions are also presented.

- Insufficient force in the throw can be caused by not utilizing a full range of motion.
- Insufficient force can also be caused by not using the whipping sequential action of the upper extremities.
- Lifting one or both feet before releasing the ball can result in a depletion of force application and/or a loss of balance.
- The player may not be fully extended at the point of release.
- Inaccuracy is generally due to a poor release. The early or late release can cause directional problems.
- Players throwing the ball into play should do so quickly to avoid allowing the opponents to get into good position.
- Always encourage players to direct the ball to an unmarked player or to an open space accessible to a teammate.
- The throw should always be directed toward the direction of attack.

Goalkeeper Skills

Goalkeepers must have quick reflexes, jumping ability, accurate kicks, aggressiveness, and good judgment. They have special privileges, such as punting, dropkicking, catching, and throwing the ball, but only within the penalty area. Goalkeepers must be aware of where their teammates are as well as the positions of attackers. Good goalkeepers can initiate an attack on the opponents' goal by making accurate passes or punts to teammates downfield. Long kicks just to clear the ball are usually ineffective because they simply go to the opponent's defensive players, who send the ball right back toward the punter. In an emergency, send the ball on an angle to the sidelines but know the positioning of your own forwards. The dropkick is not used often; most goalkeepers prefer the punt or the more accurate throw.

General Stance and Positioning

The goalkeeper's stance is a shoulder-width straddle position with the knees flexed. The trunk is flexed slightly forward with the body weight forward. The elbows are flexed next to the body with the palm of the hands forward (wrist hyperextended). The fingers are spread and pointing up.

Goalkeepers (often called goalies) must practice playing the angles to reduce scoring possibilities. Figure 8.11 shows two possible positions (A and B) for a goalkeeper to stand to defend the goal. In Position A, the shooter (X1) has space on either side to score a goal. A player at Position A cannot possibly protect the whole area. In Position B, the goalkeeper has moved closer to the shooter and has reduced the space available for the shot. A player at Position B has a good chance to deflect a shot on goal but is closer to the attacker and will need to react faster to the shot.

In Figure 8.12, the attacker is farther to the side of the goal and closer to the end line but almost the same distance from the center of the goal. This reduces the potential area for a shot on goal. In this situation, the goalkeeper (XG) does not need to go out as far from the goal to protect both corners effectively. The same situation would occur on the extreme angle on the other side of the goal.

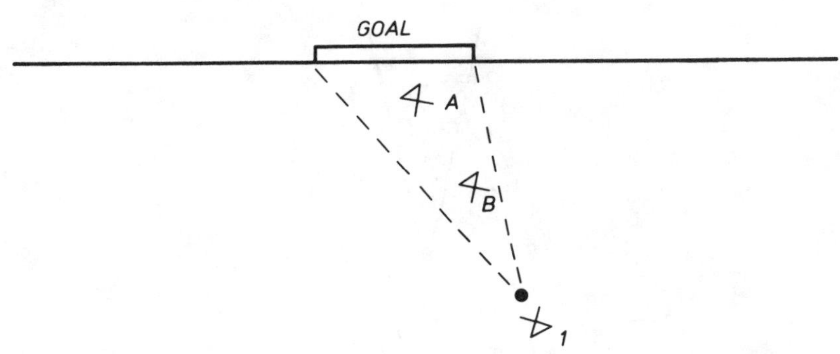

Figure 8.11. Goaltending angle: Side front

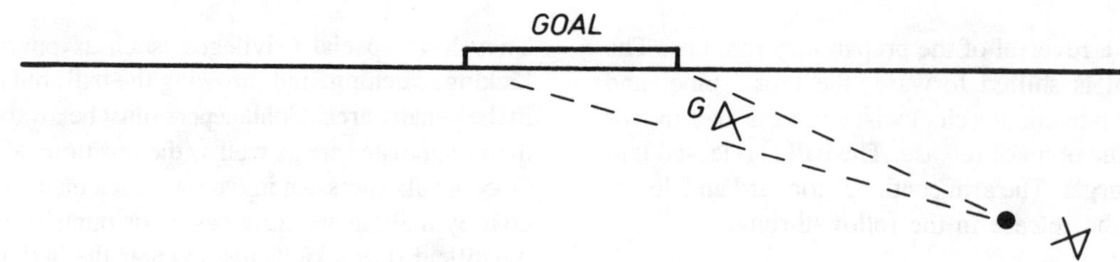

Figure 8.12. Goaltending angle: Side

Figure 8.13 shows the area that must be covered if an attacker approaches from the front. The goalkeeper is Position E would have little chance of stopping a shot at either side of the goal. In Position D the open spaces have been reduced, and it would take a very accurate kick to pass the goaltender and enter the goal cage.

Specialized Kicking

The dropkick and the punt are used by the goalkeeper to launch an attack after gaining possession of the ball from the opponent. The general technique in both kicks is similar. The preparatory phase begins with a step forward with the foot opposite the kicking foot while holding the ball in front of the body with both hands. During the step, the pelvis is rotated clockwise (for a right-footed kicker). The leg is hyperextended (bent backward) at the hip and the knee flexed. This positions the leg appropriately for force production.

The force-production phase begins with a rapid counterclockwise rotation of the hip and forward motion of the thigh (flexion at the hip) toward the ball. The flexion at the hip slows when the thigh is perpendicular to the ground. The knee is very rapidly extended, which moves the foot toward the ball. After contact is made, the leg continues in the arc of motion to complete the movement.

Punt. The kicking technique is considered a punt when the ball is dropped in front of the body and kicked before the ball has an opportunity to touch the ground. The eyes must be focused on the ball to make a good contact. The instep of the foot should contact the ball by applying force through the ball's center of gravity in the line of the intended trajectory. The punt has the capability of more distance than does the dropkick.

Dropkick. The dropkick is different from the punt in that the ball is contacted after bouncing from the ground after the drop. The ball is held in front of the body and then dropped. The instep of the kicking foot contacts the ball immediately after the ball rebounds from the ground. This kick generally does not achieve the same long distances as does the punt, but the slight delay may cause the opponents to be off balance or out of position.

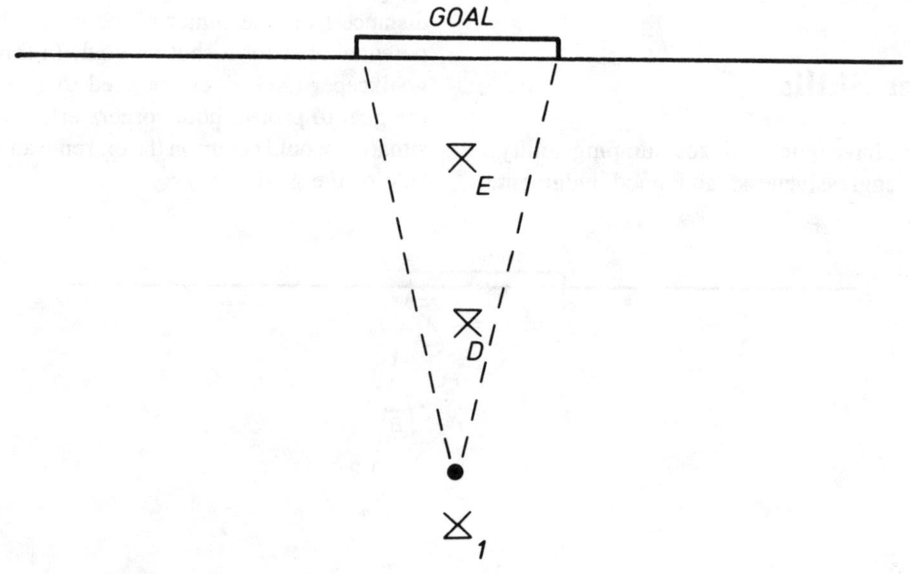

Figure 8.13. Goaltending angle: Center front

Common Movement Problems and Suggestions

The following are movement problems encountered during instruction of goalkeeper kicking. Additional instructional suggestions are presented.

- Players may use an inappropriate final approach step length. A step that is too long causes the kicker to be reaching too much forward to contact the ball. This causes weak contact made very low or close to the ground. A final step approach that is too short causes the player to contact the ball too early in the leg extension with the ball too high off the ground.
- Placement of the support foot should be positioned behind and lateral to the area where the ball will drop. This foot position provides the most stable position for the kicker. Balance can be further enhanced by using the arms in opposition to the legs after the ball has left the hands.
- Players may not hold the ball far enough in front of the body for a good kick. If the ball is dropped from a position too close to the body, the kicker is cramped and cannot contact the ball with the leg fully extended.
- Force application may be depleted if the kicker does not utilize the whipping action of the leg.
- The most common error is in utilizing the proper timing during the kick. The rhythm of the punt is even, and the foot should contact the ball when the foot is moving the fastest. The rhythm is uneven for the dropkick. Novice kickers tend to wait too long to make contact with the ball and project the ball with more height than is needed.

Goalkeeping Practice Drills

Beginning goalkeepers need to have balls kicked or volleyed gently to them. Close shots should be controlled and soft. Long shots may be somewhat harder but not at maximum force. After goalkeepers gain confidence, the shots on goal may be harder. However, never allow more than one player at a time to kick at the goalkeepers, as they need time between shots to prepare for fielding. Only advanced players should try to field kicks in rapid succession.

1.0. Double-Column Formation as in Figure 8.10. One of the retrievers in Columns 3 and 4 steps into the goal and acts as goalkeeper. Columns 1 and 2 kick the ball toward the goal as described in Shooting and Kicking Drill 2.0. After every five shots, that goalkeeper goes to the end of the column, and the next player in the column goes to the goal. Rotate after everyone in Columns 3 and 4 has had a turn tending goal. Columns 1 and 2 rotate to goaltending and retrieving; Columns 3 and 4 rotate to kicking.

2.0. Four-Column Formation (Figure 8.14). Players in Columns 1 and 2 work together, and players in

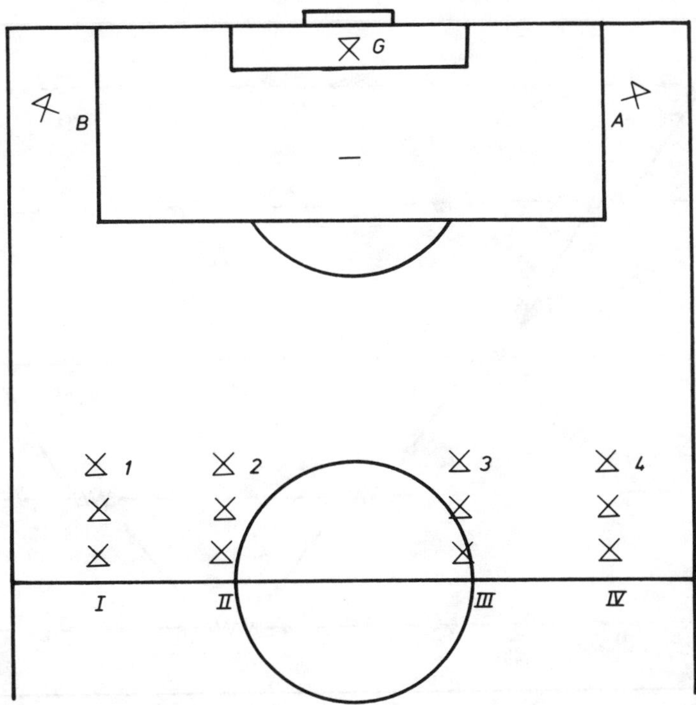

Figure 8.14. Goalkeeping and shooting practice

Columns 3 and 4 work together. Players X1 and X2 dribble and pass toward the goal and then shoot when they get within range. The goalkeeper (XG) moves out and tries to prevent a goal. Player X1 goes to the end of Column 2 and Player X2 to the end of Column 3. Then Players X3 and X4 dribble and pass toward the goal and shoot while the goalkeeper defends. Goalkeepers are encouraged to use their hands and shooters to shoot from at least 15 ft out. Player X3 goes to the end of Column 4 and Player X4 to the end of Column 1. The next players in Columns 1 and 2 then go, and play continues alternating approach sides. Unless there is a ball for every two players, the balls must be rolled back to the next players after a goal or a successful defense is made. The instructor should rotate goalkeepers frequently. Variation: Players XA and XB are stationed on either side to receive a clearing pass from the goalkeeper.

3.0. Goalkeeper Defense Against Five-Player Attack. Players line up in five columns. The leaders of each column start downfield together. They dribble and pass across the field, and shoot at the goal (Figure 8.15). The goalkeeper defends against the shot on goal. To allow more players to participate, two sets of columns could line up at the center line with one group moving toward each goal. A goalkeeper at each end of the field defends. After finishing, players go back down the sidelines and return to their own columns; or the columns could be numbered, and players return to the next-numbered column (Column 5 goes to Column 1). This gives all players a chance to play each of the typical forward positions. Those returning should do so along the sidelines. Then the second lines could start without interference as the first lines finished. When the full field is used, the second line starts as soon as the first line gets to midfield. Balls must be passed back to other dribblers unless there are enough for each attacking line to have one. It may be necessary to require that shots on goal be made from outside the goal area or just inside the penalty area. This is safer for beginning goalkeepers and gives them more time to get in position and react to the kick.

General Practice Drills

1.0. Circle Formation (Figure 4.13). Players in one half of the circle are on one side of a line (on the gymnasium floor or soccer field), and the other half is on the other side. Players are about 3 to 4 ft apart. Players on each side of the circle try to kick the ball out of the circle between the opponents. The ball must not be kicked above the waist. Each time a team manages to kick the ball out legally between the opponents, it gets a point. The team scoring the most points in a given time wins.

2.0. Line Soccer (Figure 8.16). The class is divided into two teams. The teams line up 30 to 40 ft apart. This game may be played indoors or outdoors and can be adapted to the space and lines available. Younger players

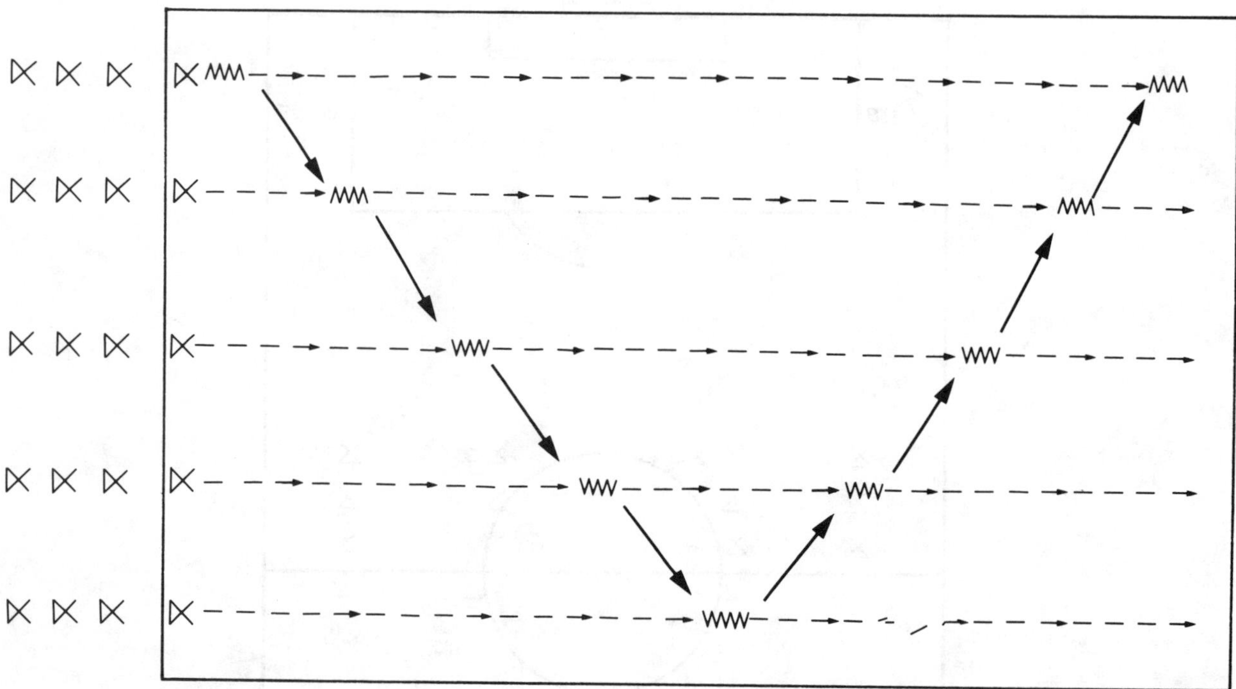

Figure 8.15. Forward line passing drill

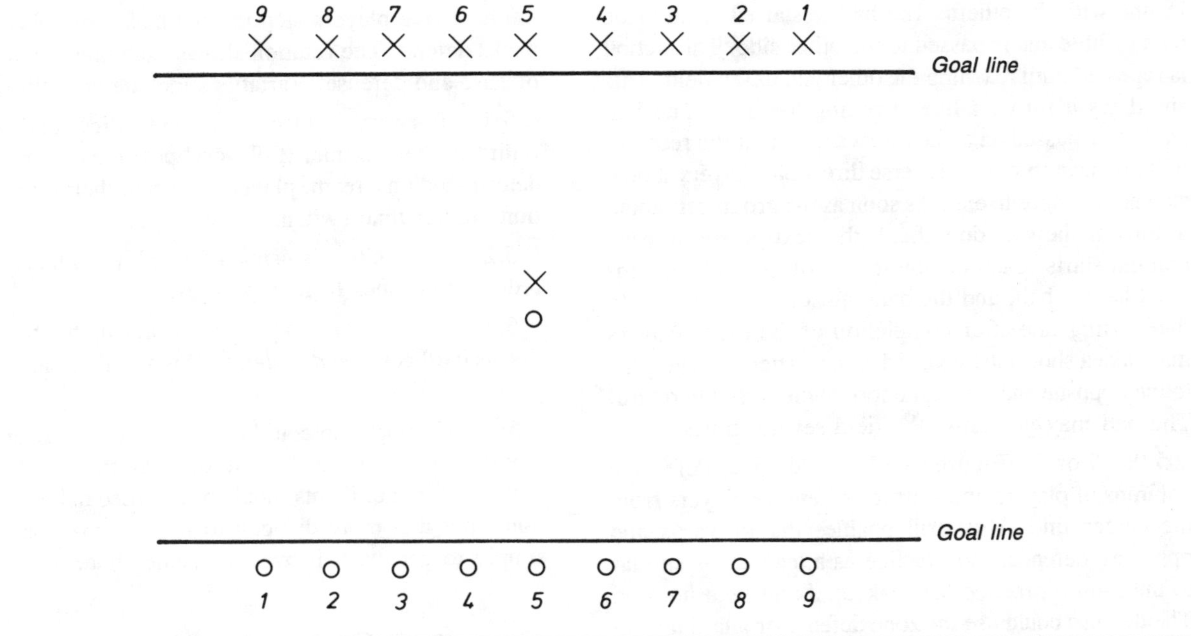

Figure 8.16. Passing and trapping practice: Line soccer

should be placed closer together; older players can be farther apart. One person from each line goes to the center. The ball is rolled out between them, and each tries to kick the ball through the opponents' line while helping to defend against the other team scoring. The sideline players try to keep the ball from crossing their line. For safer play, the ball should be kept below the waist, and any kicks that cross the lines above waist height do not score. High school students may be skilled enough to allow the ball to go to shoulder level. Because of the closeness of the competitors, head-high kicks should never be permitted. An additional safety factor is to draw or designate a restraining line 10 to 12 ft from each goal line. Center players may not go beyond these lines to kick the ball toward the opponents. Variations include the following:

2.1 With older players, two (or even three) players from each team can go to the center at once. This allows the use of teamwork and strategy.

2.2. Consecutively number the players in each line. Start numbering from diagonally opposite ends of the lines (e.g., start numbering one line from the east end and the other from the west end). The ball is placed in the center of the area. The instructor calls out a number. The two players with that number first run to touch the line defended by the opponents and then to the ball and finally try to kick it through the opponents' line. If they run directly to the ball, they tend to collide or kick each other, and injuries could occur. By having to touch the opponents' line first, the players are coming toward the ball from the opposite side and must maneuver around the ball or dribble the ball to the correct side first.

2.3. Goalposts or cones may be set up at each end of the playing area. Each sideline team is assigned one goal to defend. Designated players move out from their sideline positions and attempt to score at the opponents' goal. This arrangement also alleviates the problem of players crashing head on into one another as they rush to kick the ball toward the opponent and simulates a game situation better.

3.0. Triangular Passing Drill. Double-Column Formation (Figure 4.9). This is sometimes called a *give-and-go*. Parallel columns of players are 8 to 10 ft apart and near an end line of the field. The leaders of each column begin running downfield passing a ball back and forth. Caution should be taken that the passes are angled ahead of the receivers so that players do not have to stop or back up. The players run straight downfield staying away from their teammates. The passes form two sides of the triangle and the path of the runner the third side. On reaching the center line, passers stop, return the ball to the next persons in the columns, and wait for all to finish. If there are more than five in each column, the players could return around the sidelines of the passing area to the ends of the starting columns. Otherwise, after all are at the center line, the drill is repeated going back toward the start.

4.0. Five Parallel Columns (Figure 8.15). Columns of players are lined up at one end of the field. The first person in each column starts running downfield staying in line with the others. The ball is started at one side by a dribble and is passed to the other side. This action is repeated until reaching the other end of the field. This simulates a forward line attacking the goal. The ball should be passed on a slant forward so that the receiver will not have to stop or reverse direction. Players should stay at the opposite end. As soon as the group gets about a third of the way downfield, the next person in each column starts. Each person in one of the end columns must have a ball, and the balls must be kicked back to the starting line after completion of the drill. Players may take a shot at the goal if desired. After all have gone to the opposite end, the same formation is used to return. The ball may go across the field several times.

5.0. 5-on-5 (Figure 8.17). Add five defensive columns of players and start the offensive players from the center line. This drill enables the forwards and opposing defenders to practice as a team. It is similar to the 5-on-5 practice for basketball and field hockey. The defense could use the zone defense or guard the opponents 1-on-1. Players X1, X2, X3, X4, and X5 (forwards) start downfield dribbling and passing. Players X6, X7, X8, X9, and X10 (backs) move out quickly to tackle or intercept before the forwards make a goal. After the ball goes over the goal line or back to the center line, players go to the ends of the opposite columns, and the next five players step up to attack while five new backs defend. The rotation allows each player a turn at offense and defense. Variations include the following:

5.1. Forwards return to the center line, and backs return to the end line. If players' positions are already determined on a team, players return to their own positions rather than switch.

5.2. A team that is using a four-player attack could reduce both lines to four persons.

5.3. Add one or two players to back up the forward line as halfbacks (*midfielders*). This simulates an actual game situation.

5.4. Competition could be introduced by awarding 2 points for a goal and 1 point for a ball that is returned to the center line. Points should be awarded in both situations, but it is more difficult to score a goal than it is simply to get the ball over the center line.

Special Situations

Kickoff

The *kickoff* is a placekick taken from the center of the field to start each half and to resume play after each goal

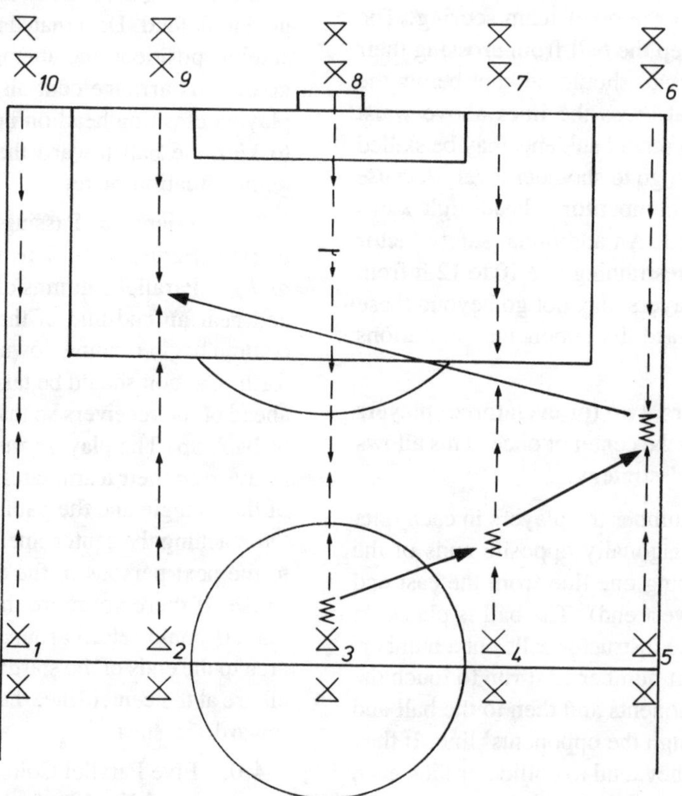

Figure 8.17. 5-on-5 practice

has been scored. At the time of the kickoff, all players must be in their own halves of the field and opponents not within 10 yd of the kicker. The ball must be kicked toward the opposing goal by at least the ball's circumference; usually, it is kicked on the diagonal toward one side or the other so that a teammate of the kicker can gain possession of the ball before the opponents. The kicker may not touch the ball a second time until someone else has played it.

Forwards on both teams should move toward the other goal quickly when the kickoff is taken. Teammates of the kicker try to receive the pass and the opponents try to intercept. Halfbacks (midfielders) must move quickly up to tackle or to act as a backup to their teammates. The kicker may try to pass to an inside forward, who kicks to the opposite winger, thus swinging the play to the other side of the field after drawing the defense to one side.

Throw-In

A *throw-in* is taken by an opponent of the player who last touched the ball before it passed over the sideline (also called the touch line). It is taken from the point where the ball left the field of play. This must be a two-handed overhead throw taken with both feet touching the ground out-of-bounds and facing the direction of the throw.

The player taking the throw-in may not play the ball again until another player has touched it. No defensive player may guard the thrower actively. No goal may be scored directly from the throw-in.

A side halfback generally would take the throw-in so that the forwards may advance ahead to receive the pass. A wing should take the throw-in when deep in the opponents' territory. The teammates of the thrower should try to move ahead quickly or circle around to receive the pass. The center forward might move to the sideline while the inside forward near that side moves to the center of the field and the wing moves downfield to draw the defense away from the play. Competitive teams should have several plays to use when taking a throw-in. These plays vary depending on whether the throw-in came near the center of the field or near the goal line. See sideline play as depicted for field hockey in chapter 6 (Figures 6.13. and 6.14).

Drop Ball

A *drop ball* is taken when two opponents simultaneously send the ball over the sideline, simultaneous fouls are called on opponents, or a time out is called while the ball is in play (as for an injury). The referee drops the ball from waist height between any two opponents, each of whom is facing the opponents' goal. Other players may be anywhere on the field. The ball is dropped at the point the offense occurred or 5 yd from the boundary where it occurred, with the exception that no drop ball may be taken in the penalty area. The ball must hit the ground before it can be touched by a player.

Some teammates of the persons taking the drop ball should try to distribute themselves behind and to the side of the spot of the drop, whereas others should move downfield and guard their opponents. The person taking the drop ball should kick to the side (not directly into the opponent), hook the ball, or volley to a teammate.

Free Kick

Most fouls committed on the field outside the penalty areas result in a *free kick* being awarded to the opponents. This is a placekick taken at the spot where the foul occurred. The ball may be kicked in any direction and may not be played again by the kicker until someone else has touched it. All opponents must be at least 10 yd away when the kick is taken. For some fouls, an indirect free kick is awarded; this means a goal may not be scored directly from the kick (see soccer rule books for further rules analyses).

The free kick is generally taken by a halfback or back so that the forwards can move ahead to receive the pass. Players should move very quickly to take the kick to prevent the opponents from getting into good defensive formation. If no backfield player is available to take the kick quickly and teammates are moving into position to receive the kick, a forward may take the kick.

When an opponent is taking a free kick, all players should fall back into defensive positions. Defending forwards should move into a semicircular formation around the kicker when play is anywhere other than near their own goal. Even in this situation, *wings* (wingers) or *insides* (inners) may drop back to help defend near the sidelines.

Goal Kick

When the attacking team sends the ball over the goal line not between the goalposts, the defending team is awarded a *goal kick*. The ball is placed in the goal area near where it went out of bounds and must be kicked out of the penalty area before it may be played by anyone else. All opponents of the kicker must be outside the penalty area at the time of the goal kick. The kick usually is taken by the goalkeeper or a back. When it is taken near the side of the goal area, a defensive back may kick so that the goalie can stay near the goal.

Defending teammates of the kicker should face the other end of the field and try to move into a space near the side of the penalty area to receive a pass. Offensive teammates of the kicker should move downfield and try to evade the opposing defenders to collect a long kick and initiate an offensive play.

Opposing forwards should spread themselves around the edge of the penalty area to intercept the ball as it comes out (Figure 8.18). Opposing midfielders fill in the spaces between the forwards. The team backs should be alert to intercept long passes to forwards breaking downfield.

Corner Kick

The *corner kick* is an unguarded placekick taken by an attacker from the corner of the field. It is awarded when the defense kicks the ball over its own goal line but not between the goalposts or when players take a free kick outside the penalty area and kick the ball directly into their own goal. All opponents of the kicker must be at least 10 yd away, and the kicker may not play the ball again until someone else has touched it.

Defenders may line up solidly in front of their own goal to prevent a shot, but this often causes them to interfere with each other and the goalkeeper. It is good for several players to assist the goalkeeper, but others should be assigned to try to intercept passes and prevent shots. One or two defensive forwards (usually insides or one wing) may drop back to assist the defenders. The goalkeeper must have a clear view of the play and should not allow teammates to get directly between the goalkeeper and the ball. The goalkeeper should stand near the goal line and toward the side of the cage from which the kick is being taken.

Attacking players should develop plays to facilitate shots on goal from corner kicks. The kicker may try a long, high kick across the goal for teammates to try to volley or may initiate a series of short passes designed to lure the defenders away from the goal to permit a backdoor shot. Sometimes attackers line up in column formation and break different ways with the kick to confuse defenders. Whatever they do, they should stay apart, move quickly along erratic paths, and be ready to volley the ball with the head, shoulder, or foot.

Penalty Kick

A *penalty kick* is awarded when players commit certain fouls inside their own penalty areas. These fouls are usually ones that have prevented a goal. The ball is placed 12 yd in front of the goal and a placekick taken by an attacker. The goalkeeper must stand still on the goal line until the ball is kicked but may then try to prevent the goal. All players except the goalkeeper and the kicker must be outside the penalty area in the field.

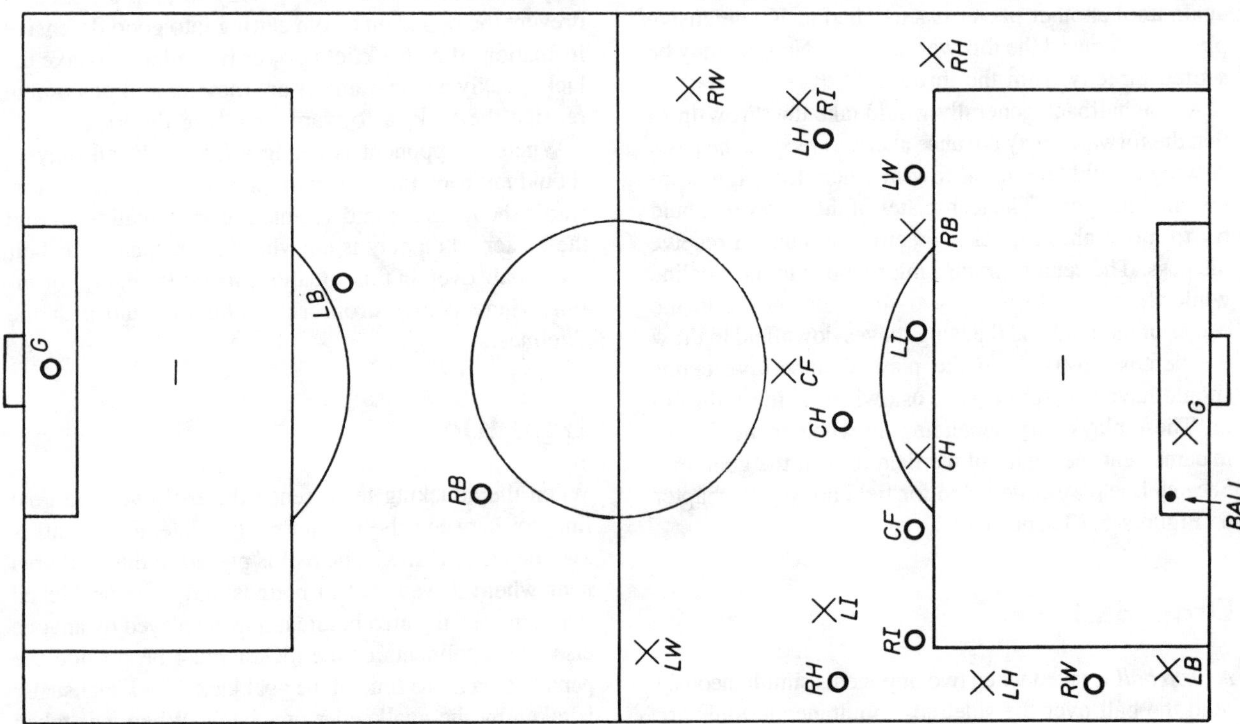

Figure 8.18. Goal kick formation with Team X goalkeeper taking the kick

The kicker must kick for the goal and may not touch the ball again until another player touches it. No other player may participate in the play unless the goalkeeper gains possession, in which case the goalkeeper puts the ball back in play.

During a penalty kick, all defensive backs and attacking forwards should be ready to move to attack or defend if the goalkeeper gains possession of the ball. Forwards on the defending team should be ready to break downfield should the goalkeeper be successful. If a goal is scored, play is restarted with a kickoff. Otherwise, a goal kick or a free kick is used to resume play.

Offense

Offensive Formations

The traditional offensive lineup for soccer is the pyramid arrangement (Figure 8.19). In this pattern, the forwards are the attackers. The halfbacks or midfielders back up the forwards and also mark (guard) the opposing wingers (also called wings) and center forward on defense. The backs are mainly defenders and mark the opposing inside (also called inner) forwards. The goalkeeper plays only defense. This provides a balanced attack and defense.

There are several variations of offensive patterns currently preferred. The 4-2-4-1 lineup uses four forwards, two midfielders (or links), and four backs. This gives a strong defense but a weaker attack. However, it can be very effective if the midfielders are mobile and have good endurance.

The 3-3-4-1 employs four backs, three midfielders, and three forwards. This does not provide a very effective offense. It does allow good coverage of the middle of the field but requires attackers to cover a lot of ground.

Another pattern that is popular among nonprofessional teams is the W-M formation (Figure 8.20). The center halfback drops back even with the fullbacks, and the left and the right inside forwards drop back slightly behind the center forward and the wings. This formation gives strength to the defense and allows a five-player offense with two halfbacks to back up the forwards.

The pattern of play selected depends on the qualities of the players, the amount of practice time available, and the maturity of the players. The more complex patterns should be left to the competitive players and simple ones used in classes.

Individual Strategies

Each individual player, by using certain techniques and strategies, can contribute greatly to the effectiveness of the offense of the team. Some of these strategies include the following:

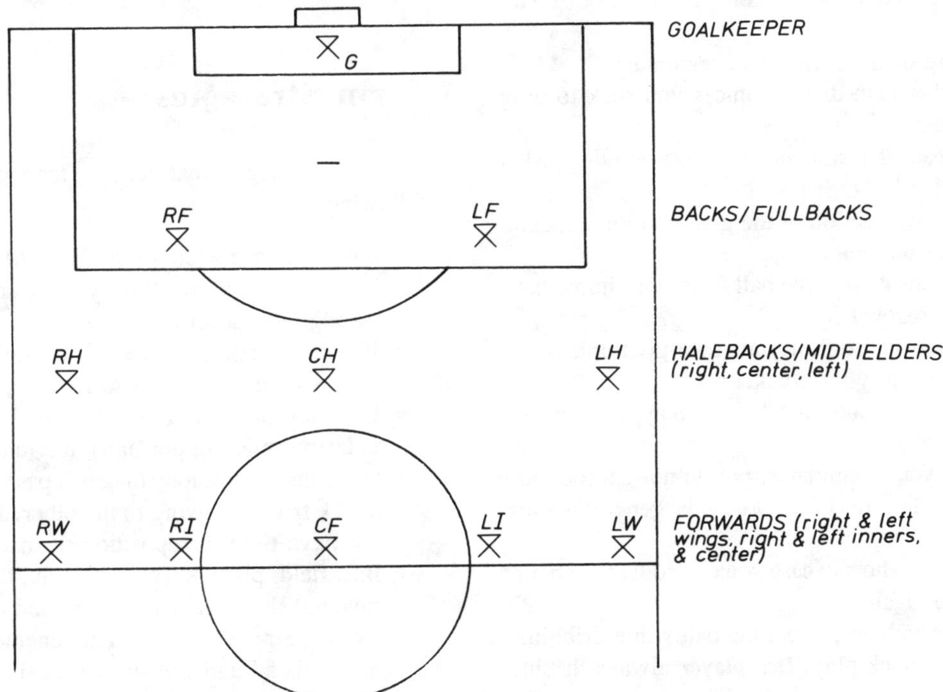

Figure 8.19. Pyramid lineup (5-3-2-1)

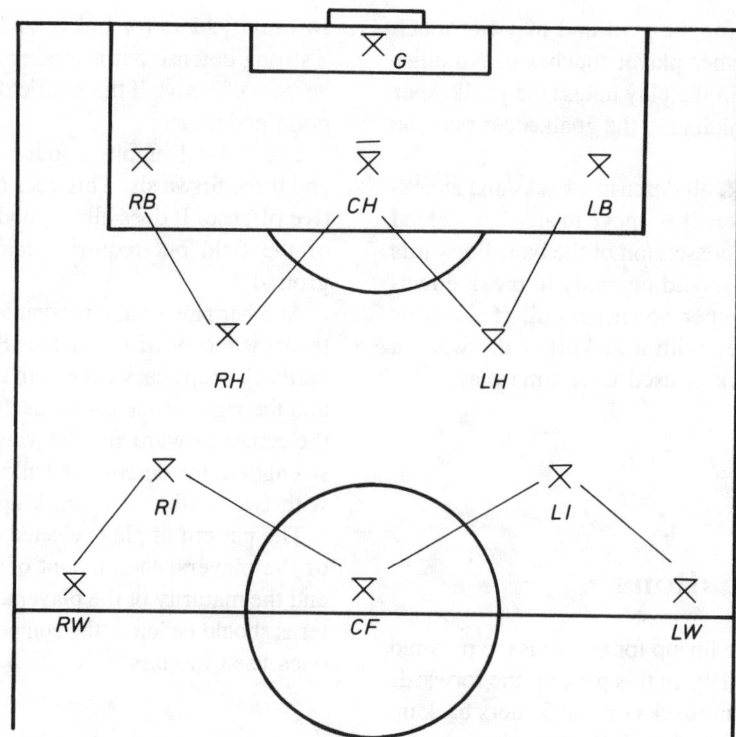

Figure 8.20. W-M formation

- Be alert and ready to shift from defense to offense quickly.
- Stay away from teammates who have the ball. Do not make it easy for one defender to mark two opponents.
- Be aware of the location of teammates.
- Pass rather than dribble unless you seek to draw a defender to you.
- Pass ahead of teammates who are moving. Most passes should be diagonal.
- Face in the direction of the goal you are attacking whenever possible.
- If an opponent takes the ball from you, immediately try to recover it.
- Never pass in front of your own goal unless it is a sure pass to your goalkeeper.
- Always try to center the ball when approaching the opponents' goal.
- Back up your teammates, but do not get too close to them. Ten to 15 yd away is generally close enough.
- Follow your shots in case you can collect a rebound and shoot again.
- Use your body to protect the ball while dribbling.
- Vary the attack play. If a player always dribbles or passes the same way, the defense can predict the action.
- Move to the ball when it is passed to you. Do not wait for the ball to come to you because someone else may get there first.

Team Strategies

Offensive strategies that improve team play include the following:

- Use the entire width of the field. Make the defenders spread out to allow your teammates to slip through the spaces.
- If two defenders are near you, look for your free teammate and try to pass to that player.
- Use short passes most of the time. Long passes provide too much opportunity for interception.
- Occasionally use long diagonal passes to change the attack from one wing to the other. Defenders may not have time to reposition themselves.
- Backfield players (generally halfbacks or midfielders) should take throw-ins and free kicks away from the penalty area. This enables forwards to move ahead and prepare to receive the ball.
- Do not act predictably. Have different team plays and vary the strategies.

Defense

Two traditional types of defensive patterns are used in soccer (as seen in basketball previously): the 1-on-1 *marking defense* and the *zone defense*. Usually, defenses employ a combination, that is, 1-on-1 when the opponents are close to the goal you defend and a zone pattern when your own forwards are attacking and some of your defense is backing them.

In more advanced play, other systems of defense may be developed. These defenses require a lot of team interaction and practice that are difficult to master in a class or recreational setting but that should be employed in interscholastic competition. Most of these more complex defenses rely on zone defense in certain areas while specific defenders are left free to move to help teammates wherever the ball goes. Forwards are also called on to assist with these defenses.

1-on-1 Marking

Each defensive player is assigned to guard (*mark* in field sports) a particular opposing attacker. The usual pattern is to have the side halfbacks mark the opposing outside or wing forwards. The center halfback marks the opposing center forward, and the fullbacks mark the opposing inners, or inside forwards. Assignments for using this strategy must be somewhat flexible so that if a forward gets around the marker, another defender moves in to cover until the bypassed defender recovers. Forwards may be marked loosely when they are in their own territories or near the middle of the field but should be marked closely when nearing the scoring area. The defender should try to stay between the opponent and the goal and to watch the ball to prepare to intercept a pass intended for an opponent.

Zone Defense

The zone defense requires each defender to be responsible for a certain area of the field. The defender marks any player who enters that zone. This system is very effective against forwards, who often interchange positions, but it can be troublesome if attackers cluster in one zone.

Generally, the field is divided into five zones by imaginary lines running parallel with the sidelines. Each backfield player (halfbacks and backs) is responsible for one zone (Figure 8.21). The positions are left halfback (LH), left back (or fullback) (LB), center halfback (CH), right back (RB), and right halfback (RH). Sometime the halfbacks take the three middle zones and the backs the two outside zones.

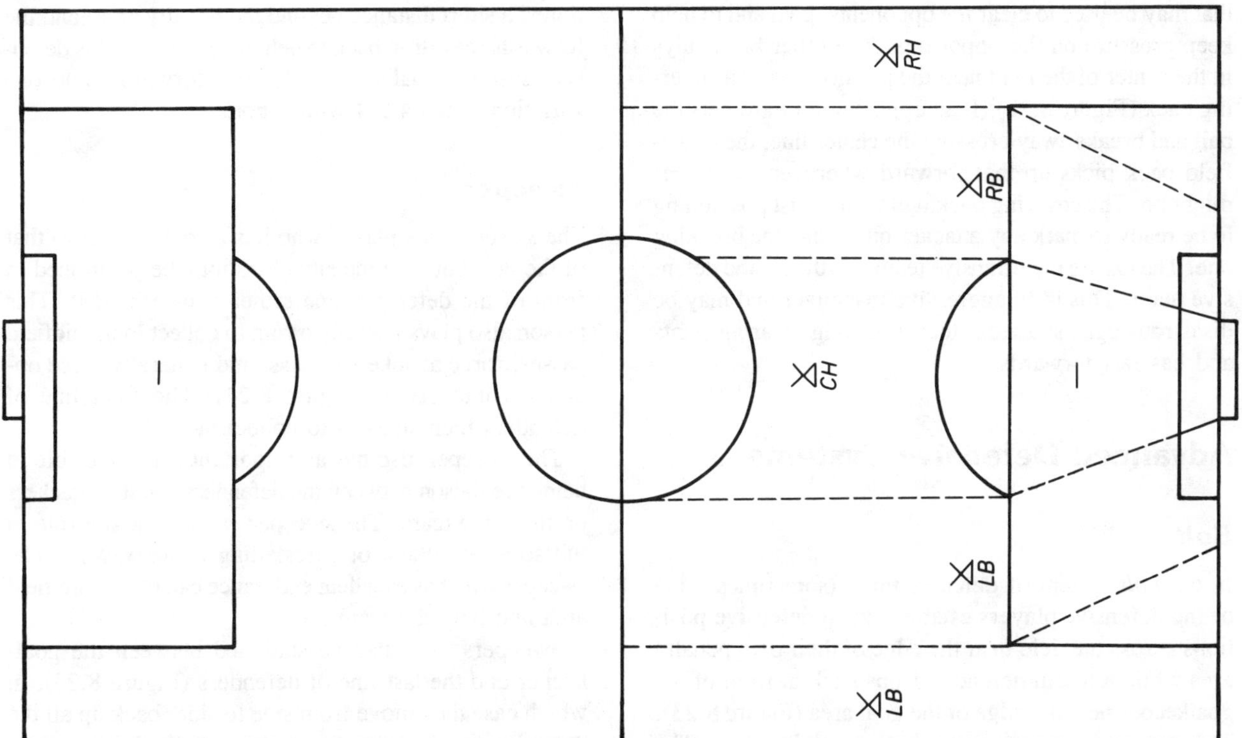

Figure 8.21. Zone defense positions

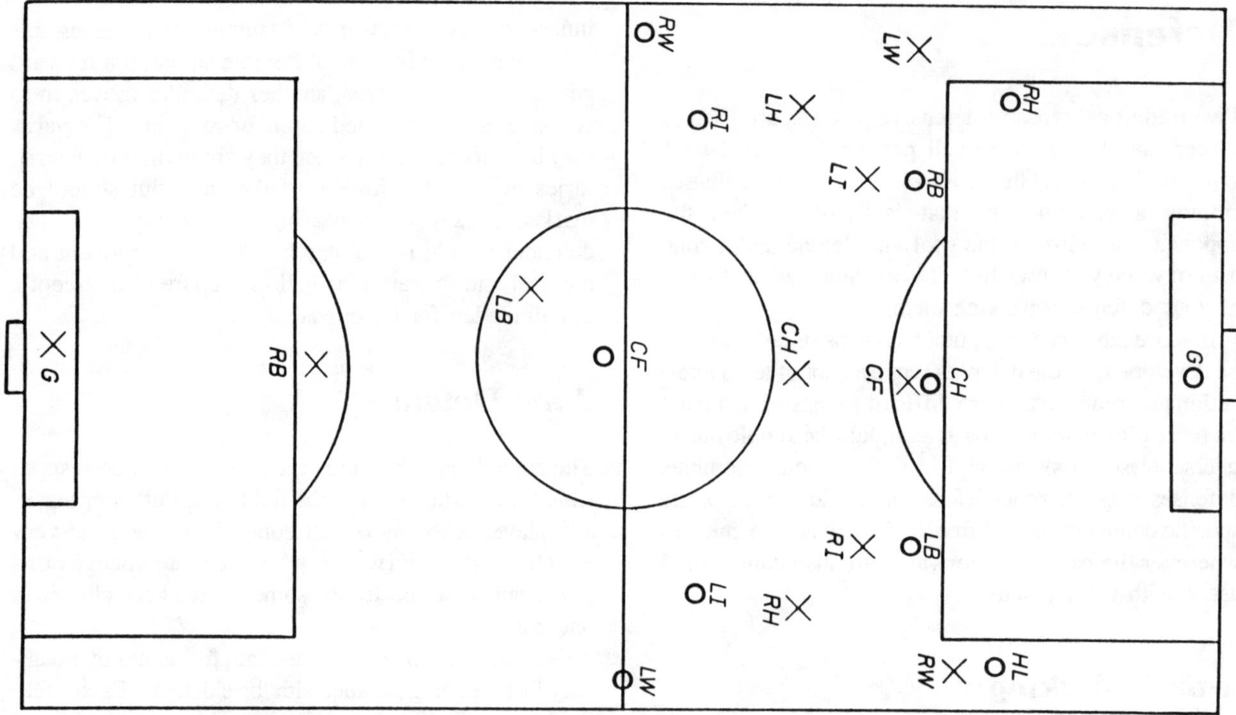

Figure 8.22. Zone defense with covering back

A variation of this zone pattern has one of the backs moving well downfield to pick up long defensive kicks that may be used to clear the opponents' goal and to help keep pressure on the opponents. The other back stays in the center of the field near the penalty area as a covering back (Figure 8.22). If an opposing forward gets the ball and breaks away crossing the center line, the downfield back picks up that forward wherever the player might be. The covering back will then adjust positioning to be ready to mark any attacker other than the breaking one. The Os are the offensive team and the Xs the defensive team. This is an aggressive maneuver and may be disastrous against a team that uses long clearing punts and has fast forwards.

Advanced Defensive Systems

Bolt

In the *bolt* system of defense, three (sometimes four) of the defensive players establish zone defensive positions across the field near the edge of their own penalty area while a fourth defender drops back in front of the goalkeeper near the edge of the goal area (Figure 8.23). This person is known as the *bolt*, or *sliding bolt*. The bolt must move laterally near the goal area on the field as the ball is passed and back up whatever defender is tackling or trying to intercept. The midfielders are stationed a short distance beyond the penalty area, and the forwards may drop back to help defend also. This defensive system usually has only four forwards, and one variation is the 4-2-4 with a bolt.

Sweeper

The *sweeper* is a player who has a role similar to that of the bolt but in some situations may be positioned in front of the defensive line rather than behind it. This person also plays laterally trying to collect long midfield passes, force attackers to pass, and generally force opponents into errors (Figure 8.24). The final line of defenders then steps in to collect the ball.

The sweeper also has an important offensive role in being the liaison between the defenders and the attackers on the same team. The sweeper can play a key role in initiating an attack or forestalling a breakaway. The sweeper who has excellent endurance can play more field area and help the team more.

Sweepers may also be stationed between the goalkeeper and the last line of defenders (Figure 8.23), in which case they move from side to side, back up all the defenders, and sweep up whatever balls they can get. The sweeper in field hockey usually plays this pattern.

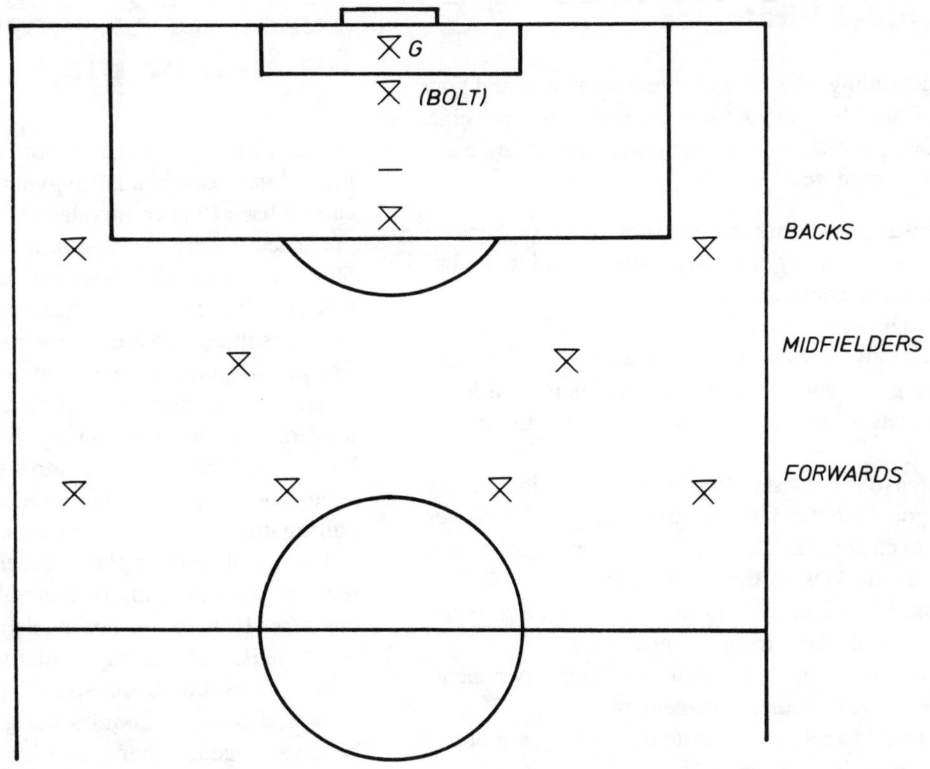

Figure 8.23. Bolt defense system

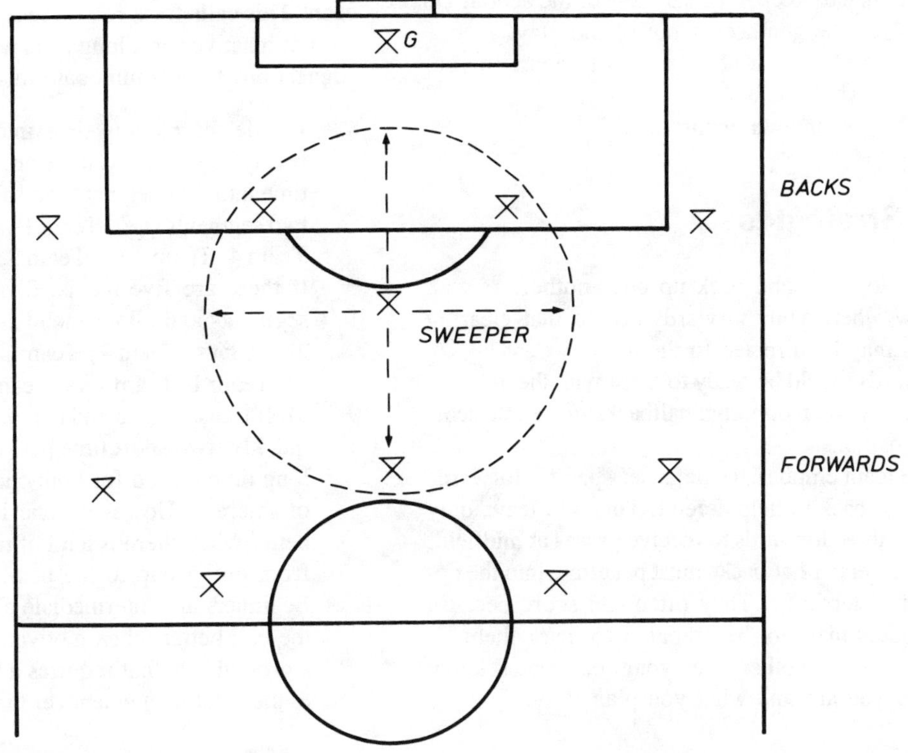

Figure 8.24. Sweeper defense

Individual Strategies

When defending, stay between your opponent and your goal with your back to your own goal whenever possible. From this position it is easier to kick or volley away from your own goal.

- Forwards who lose the ball should not quit; tackle back immediately or try to pursue the ball until your defensive backs arrive.
- Forwards should not drop back near their own goal. They only interfere with the defense. Fast forwards may go to within 20 to 25 yd of their own goal, whereas slower ones should stay near the center line.
- Defensive kicks should go toward the sidelines or diagonally toward the side of the center line. Never try to clear the ball in front of your own goal except for a safe kick to the goalkeeper.
- Raised kicks or volleys are most effective when clearing the ball from the goal area.
- Never double up with a teammate on one opponent. This leaves another opponent free.
- Be ready to help a teammate by marking the opponent who is now unmarked.
- If you are passed by your opponent, recover quickly and either pursue that player or mark the player left free by a teammate who has moved to tackle your opponent.
- Leave the goalkeeper a clear view of the action. Do not block the goalkeeper out of the play.
- Do not stand and wait for a pass to come to you. Move toward the ball.
- Build up your own endurance.

Team Strategies

- Work together and back up one another.
- Know where your forwards are so that clearing kicks may be directed to them.
- Forwards should be ready to assist with the defense, especially when opposing halfbacks move into scoring positions.
- If the team emphasizes defense, specific forwards must go back to help defend. This will leave only two or three forwards to receive passes at midfield.
- Midfielders or halfbacks must penetrate into the opponents' territory. They often can score because defenders may not be prepared to mark them.
- Talk to one another. Let your teammates know where you are and what you plan to do.

Teaching Suggestions for Indoor Play

Soccer can be practiced indoors as well as outdoors. If the indoor space is a large gymnasium, the entire area can be used to accommodate 11 players on a team. If the space is only the size of a basketball court (94 by 50 ft) or smaller, the players per team should be reduced to seven. Players in this situation probably would be assigned as three forwards, three backs, and a goalkeeper. For indoor play, it is recommended that the side walls be considered inbounds so that a ball rebounding from the side wall remains in play. This will expedite play because beginners lose control easily. The drop ball should be used when two or more opponents trap the ball against the wall to reduce kicking injuries.

The use of foam or plastic beach balls for indoor play reduces chances of injury caused by hard kicks in close quarters. If these are not available, old volleyballs or soccer balls that are only partially inflated are suitable.

The goals could consist of pylons, free-standing volleyball posts, or floor hockey goals. Goalposts should be closer together than the official distance when playing on a reduced court. The goal lines should be at least 6 ft from the end wall to allow a safety area for attacking forwards.

When the space is small and the classes are large, there may need to be four or five teams with seven players each. This calls for a rotation plan so that some players are not inactive for a long time while others play. Two suggestions to accommodate this problem follow:

- Divide the playing time into small segments and rotate frequently. If there are four teams, divide the time into four segments and allow each team to play two segments (i.e., Team 1 vs. Team 2, Team 3 vs. Team 4, Team 1 vs. Team 3, Team 2 vs. Team 4). If there are five teams, divide the time into five segments and allow each team to play twice (i.e., Team 1 vs. Team 2, Team 3 vs. Team 4, Team 5 vs. Team 1, Team 2 vs. Team 3, Team 4 vs. Team 5). If transitions in and out of the game can be made quickly, two short time periods are better than one long time period for both endurance and retention of interest. However, one longer time period is better when there is a lot of time lost in the change from one group to the next.
- Beginners and intermediate players learn to control the ball better when motivated to do so. Establish a ground rule that requires a team to rotate out (go to the sidelines) whenever they are responsible for

kicking a ball that goes out of bounds at the sidelines (or end line if desired). This will encourage everyone to try to control the ball rather than kicking or blocking wildly. Because the ball will go out of bounds frequently, this rule will result in rapid rotation. Teams A and B could play while Teams C and D wait. As soon as the ball is kicked out at the sideline, Team A or B rotates out and Team C goes in. Team D goes in after the next error, followed by the team that rotated out first, and so on. The team that controls the ball has the opportunity to play longer. Rotation to the sidelines could also follow a goal, but this makes some players see goal scoring as a negative motivator.

There are official rules for the indoor soccer game that may vary from those of outdoor soccer. These rules call for only seven players on a team. They could be used for indoor play in classes. Rules are available in the United States from the Major Indoor Soccer League.

Terminology

Back (fullback)—Defensive players who generally stay in their own half of the field and try to prevent goals

Bolt—A defensive player who plays near the edge of the penalty area and attacks any offensive player who comes near

Collecting—Fielding or stopping the ball legally with the body, legs, or feet

Corner—The intersection of the end line (goal line) and the sideline (touch line); the position where a corner kick is initiated

Corner kick—A free kick taken near the corner of the field by an offensive player and awarded when a defensive player sends the ball over the goal line not between the goalposts

Cover—To protect an area; to take over for a teammate who is out of position

Defensive team—The team not in possession of the ball trying to prevent a goal

Dodge—Abrupt change of direction done to avoid an opponent

Double marking—Two defensive players guarding one opponent

Dribble—Controlling the ball while running by using a series of short taps made with the feet

Drop ball—A method of restarting play after a double foul or certain out-of-bounds plays in which the referee drops the ball between two opponents

Dropkick—A ball that is kicked as it rebounds from the ground after being dropped from the hand(s)

Feint—Movement made with the head, shoulders, or one foot in an attempt to mislead an opponent about the direction the person will move; a fake

Forwards—The players who lead the attack and generally play from their own midfield area to the goal at which they are shooting

Free kick—An unguarded placekick awarded to the opponent of one who fouls (usually taken at the point where the foul was made)

Fullback—See Back

Goal—A 1-point score awarded for kicking the ball into the goal; the target formed by two upright posts and a horizontal crossbar designating the scoring area

Goalkeeper (goalie)—The person designated to protect the goal who is given special privileges such as catching and throwing the ball

Goal kick—A free kick awarded to the defensive team when the offensive team sends the ball over the goal line not between the goalposts

Goal line—The end line of the field

Halfbacks—Players who back up the forwards on offense and also help the backs on defense, generally playing in the area between the two penalty areas

Heading—Volleying the ball with the head

Heel pass—A backward pass contacted with the heel of the foot

Insides (inners)—Forwards who play an attack position between the center of the field and the wing positions

Kickoff—An unguarded placekick in the center of the field used to start each half and after each goal is scored (the team not scoring takes the kickoff)

Mark—To guard an opponent

Midfielders—Players who play both offense and defense and move from penalty area to penalty area on the field (similar to halfbacks)

Offensive team—The team in possession of the ball trying to score a goal

1-on-1 defense—A defensive system characterized by having each defensive player mark (guard) one specific opponent

Pass—Propelling the ball with the feet or other legal body part

Penalty area—An area in front of each goal within which the goalkeeper has special privileges

Penalty Kick—A free kick toward the goal awarded at the penalty kick line to the offensive team for certain fouls committed by the defenders within their own penalty area

Placekick—A ball that is kicked from a stationary position on the ground

Punt—A ball that is kicked before it hits the ground after being dropped from the hand(s)

Save—A deflection or catch of the ball by the goalkeeper that prevents a goal

Striker—A player who is primarily a scorer; a forward who concentrates on attacking the goal

Sweeper—A defensive player who roams from side to side on the field and plays either in front of or behind the other defenders (except the goalkeeper) and who attempts to intercept all long downfield passes by the opponents

Tackle—Taking the ball away from an opponent by use of the feet and without body contact

Throw-in—A two-handed overhand throw used as a means of putting the ball in play after it goes out of bounds at the sidelines

Touch line—The sideline of the field

Trap—Fielding or stopping the ball with a part of the body other than the arms or hands

Volley—Striking an aerial ball with a body part other than the arms or hands

Wings (wingers)—The forwards or attacking players who play near the sidelines of the field

Zone—A defensive system characterized by having each defensive player assigned to protect a certain area and to guard any players who enter that zone

Selected Readings

Beim, G. (1977). *Principles of modern soccer*. Boston: Houghton Mifflin.

Ford, G. (1982). *Basic soccer: Strategies for successful player and program development*. Boston: Allyn & Bacon.

Miller, D. & Ley, K. (1963). *Individual and team sports*. Englewood Cliffs, NJ: Prentice-Hall.

National Association of Girls and Women in Sport. (1986). *Soccer rules*. Reston, VA: American Alliance for Health, Physical Education, Recreation and Dance.

Thompson, W. (1980). *Teaching soccer*. Minneapolis: Burgess.

Soccer Skills Errors and Corrections

KICKING (GENERAL)

Error	*Causes*	*Corrections*
Weak		
Ball fails to reach target	• Failure to maintain stability in order to have a firm base on which the kicking leg can swing	• Balance the body weight over the non-kicking foot while swinging the kicking leg.
	• Planting the nonkicking foot in such a way as to restrict the range of motion at the hip	• For a short kick, plant the support foot close to and left of the ball. For a longer kick, plant the support foot 2 to 3 ft behind and to the left of the ball or the desired contact point (for a right-footed kick); point the toe of the support foot toward the target; swing the kicking leg freely from the hip.
	• Failure to extend the leg rapidly toward the ball	• Straighten the leg strongly as contact is made; increase the speed of the leg movement to increase force. The faster the leg swings through, the more force will be applied to the ball.

Error	Causes	Corrections
	• Failure to hold the ankle rigid when contacting the ball	• Point the toe; hold the ankle and foot firm as the ball is kicked.
Inaccurate		
Ball goes to left or right of target	• Failure to focus on the ball	• Watch the ball until the foot makes contact; use the peripheral vision to monitor the surrounding action.
	• Failure to strike the ball through its center	• Contact the ball at a point in line with the intended path; striking the ball too low will cause the ball to rise into the air as the foot slides under it; striking too high results in a stubbed kick that stays low to the ground and usually travels only a short distance.
	• Failure to swing the leg straight through rather than across the ball	• Point the foot toward the target; shift the weight forward toward the target as the ball is contacted.

DRIBBLE

Error	Causes	Corrections
Lack of ball control		
Ball goes too far ahead	• Too much force applied to the ball	• Keep the ball close to the foot (within 1 to 2 ft); tap the ball with the inside or outside of the foot rather than with the toes.
	• Failure to see potential disruptions	• Keep the head up; alternate glancing down at the ball then up to assess the position and opponents.
	• Failure to protect the ball with the body, arms, and stance	• Incline the upper body forward and use short steps when nearing an opponent; keep the ball close to the feet.
Ball follows predictable path	• Failure to vary speed and direction	• Move slowly and then quickly in an erratic path to make it difficult for the opponents to intercept.
	• Failure to utilize both sides of the feet to kick	• Practice contacting the ball with the inside *and* the outside of both feet; vary the practice to encourage control.
Lack of body control		
Body is unbalanced	• Failure to maintain balance over the nondribbling foot	• Use short steps, bend the knees, and keep the body weight low to facilitate balance and to be able to change direction quickly; keep the arms extended to the sides; swing the arms to assist with direction change.
Run is interrupted	• Failure to make the dribble a part of the running stride	• After tapping the ball with the foot, step forward on that foot; alternate tap-step on one foot, tap-step on the other foot, etc.; avoid dribbling with the same foot all the time.

(Cont.)

DRIBBLE (Continued)

Error	*Causes*	*Corrections*
Lack of ball control		
	• Disruptive timing (arrhythmic action)	• Incorporate the dribble into the running stride; avoid hopping on one foot while kicking with the other (also see the previous correction).

PASSING

Error	*Causes*	*Corrections*
Lack of ball control		
Ball bounces too far away from feet	• Failure to stop the ball before kicking	• Stop the ball with the feet or body before attempting to pass it.
	• Failure to use the side of the foot	• Use the side of the foot rather than the toe to present a broader and smoother surface for contact.
Ball goes too far left or right	• Failure to position the body over the ball as it is kicked	• Lean the body weight forward as the ball is fielded; step onto the kicking foot after the kick.
Ball kicked too hard	• Failure to control the speed or force applied to the ball	• Learn to judge distances; swing the leg backward a short distance (1 to 3 ft) for a short kick; use a longer backswing for a longer kick.
Weak		
Ball fails to reach target	• Failure to kick the ball through its center	• Extend the leg and foot directly through the center of the ball toward the target.
	• Failure to maintain body balance	• Balance on the nonkicking foot during the kicking leg's backswing and start of the forward swing; shift the body weight forward as the ball is kicked; extend the arms out at the sides to assist balance.
Inappropriate strategies		
	• Failure to use the simplest pass for better accuracy percentages	• Keep the passes low to the ground whenever possible; avoid forcing teammates to use more difficult trapping skills; use soft passes for teammates who are nearby.
	• Failure to kick ahead of the receiver	• Aim the ball well in front of a moving teammate so that the receiver will not have to slow down, stop, or change direction.
	• Failure to pass the ball quickly	• Pass the ball when the opponents get near, usually about 6 ft away; do not wait until the opponents are too close, or they will be able to intercept; plan in advance and know where teammates are.
	• Failure to conceal the intended direction	• Avoid looking directly at the intended receiver; use the inside or the outside of the foot to direct the ball; use small steps when near the ball; practice passing with both feet and use the nonpreferred foot often.

SHOOTING*

Error	Causes	Corrections
Inaccurate		
Ball goes to right or left of target	• Failure to focus on the center of the ball during the kick	• Watch the spot on the ball where the foot will make contact as you approach the ball.
	• Failure to contact the ball properly	• Kick near the back center of the ball to keep it low.
	• Failure to emphasize accuracy rather than power	• Aim the ball at the corners of the goal or away from the goalkeeper; avoid the goalkeeper; do *not* try to power the ball past the player.
Weak		
Goalkeeper intercepts ball	• Failure to use the speed of the approach to add momentum to the kick	• Take several running strides toward the ball before kicking it whenever there is time.
	• Restricting the full leg and body extension	• Lean the trunk away from the ball and straighten the leg at the hip, knee, and ankle to add power.
	• Limiting the backswing of the leg	• Swing the leg backward from the hip; flex the knee and point the toes; reduce the back-swing for a quick shot.
	• Kicked ball moves too slowly	• Swing the leg forward strongly; straighten the leg and flex the ankle.

*Shooting is a specialized form of passing. See error correction chart for passing. A few errors especially relevant to shooting are included here.

TRAPPING

Error	Causes	Corrections
Lack of ball control		
Ball is missed	• Failure to be in line with the ball	• Move the body into the path of the ball quickly, then move forward toward the ball if there is time; keep the weight balanced on both feet ready for movement while waiting for the play to develop.
	• Failure to make a quick decision about which body part to use for the trap	• Monitor the path of the ball; get in line with the path; be prepared to trap with any part of the body; decide which trap to use and avoid changing after starting the trap.
Contacted ball is *not* controlled	• Failure to use the best area of the body for ball control	• Use the largest and flattest body surface available to receive forcefully kicked or aerial balls; use the feet for low or softly kicked balls.
	• Failure to absorb force	• Retract or withdraw the body parts when contact occurs to prevent a rebound; give with the ball.

(Cont.)

VOLLEYING

Error	Causes	Corrections
Inaccurate		
Ball missed	• Failure to focus on the ball throughout the volley	• Watch the ball carefully; avoid distractions by other players.
Ball misdirected	• Failure to be aligned with the path of the ball	• Move directly under or in line with the ball as it approaches.
	• In heading, closing the eyes too soon	• Keep the eyes open and on the ball until just before contact.
Weak		
Ball falls short	• Player off balance	• Keep the weight over both feet, lean toward the approaching ball; widen the stance.
	• Failure to strike the ball through its center	• Project the body or body parts toward the ball, trying to hit through it along the intended ball path.
	• Poor timing	• Use a sequential forward motion of body parts toward the ball.
	• Failure to utilize a full follow-through	• Strike through the ball; do not stop as contact is made.
Uncontrolled force		
	• Failure to compromise between force application and force absorption	• Volley with control; retract body parts slightly on contact with forceful kicks and then propel the ball in the desired direction.

TACKLING

Error	Causes	Corrections
Ball missed completely		
	• Improper timing	• Contact the ball when it is away from the dribbler's foot; do *not* attempt to tackle a ball that is in contact with the dribbler.
	• Body off balance	• Take small, quick steps and keep the knees bent when approaching the opponent; be prepared to make quick directional changes; avoid lunging at the ball.
Weak		
Ball not retained	• Failure to remain upright	• Keep the body erect; do *not* lean away from the tackling leg.
	• Failure to control the ball after contact	• Hold the ankle firm as the ball is blocked; rotate the foot to direct the ball only when the opponent is not within reach of the ball.

Error	*Causes*	*Corrections*
	• Failure to tackle with determination and aggressiveness	• Once the tackling action is begun, follow it through strongly; be aggressive; if the tackle is missed, go after the ball and attempt another tackle.

SPECIALIZED KICKING (PUNT AND DROPKICK)

Error	*Causes*	*Corrections*
Weak		
Kick lacks distance	• Failure to add body momentum to the kick	• Use a running approach to the ball; take several steps before the kick.
	• Failure to extend the kicking leg fully	• Shorten the last step; drop the ball farther in front of the body; "whip" the leg through from the hip and knee so that full extension occurs at contact with the ball.
	• Contacting the ball with the top of the toes rather than with the instep	• Lengthen the last step; kick through the ball; follow through toward the target; drop the ball slightly closer to the body.
	• Improper position of the non-kicking foot	• For a forceful kick, plant the nonkicking foot firmly about 3 ft behind and to the left of the ball (right-footed kicker).
	• Failure to utilize a full back-swing of the leg	• Extend the kicking leg back at the hip and flex (bend) the knee; reach backward with the leg.
Lack of control		
Ball goes to right or left of target	• Failure to focus on the ball	• Watch the ball throughout the approach until the foot contacts it.
	• Improper timing	• Maintain an even rhythm with the steps for the punt; the rhythm for the dropkick is uneven, requiring a hesitation before the forward swing of the kicking foot.
	• Failure to follow through	• Extend the leg directly toward the target
	• Body off balance	• Extend the arms out to the sides after releasing the ball; drop the ball in front of the kicking leg (slightly to the side of the center of the body).
	• Improper ball position	• Extend the ball in front of the kicking leg far enough so that the leg can be extended before contact; drop a ball to be dropkicked farther in front to accommodate the delayed kick as momentum takes the body farther forward.
Too high		
	• Improper contact point	• Contact the ball with the instep more behind the center of the ball (less underneath).

(Cont.)

SPECIALIZED KICKING (PUNT AND DROPKICK) (Continued)

Error	*Causes*	*Corrections*
Too high	• Off balance	• Keep the weight forward; do *not* lean backward with the kick.
Lacks height	• Improper contact point	• Contact the ball more underneath and behind the center.
	• Ball too close to the kicker	• Be sure the ball is in front of the body and the leg is extended at the knee when the kick is made.

GOALKEEPING

Error	*Causes*	*Corrections*
Unsuccessful ball interception	• Failure to maintain focus on the ball	• Watch the ball, not the opponent; avoid distractions by the teammates and other players.
	• Having vision obscured by teammates	• Keep teammates to the sides; never allow them to line up directly between the ball and the goalkeeper.
	• Failure to keep balance	• Keep weight forward on the balls of both feet; take small, quick shuffling steps; avoid crossing one foot over the other.
	• Failure to block the ball	• Move the body quickly in line with the ball; field (block) the ball before attempting to clear it; move toward the shooter with small quick steps.
Poor clears	• Failure to direct the ball to the side instead of in front of goal	• Shift weight to outside foot (one nearest a sideline) and sweep the inside of the opposite foot across and in front to kick ball toward the nearest sideline; learn to clear with each foot.
	• Failure to know where teammates are	• Keep the head up; use peripheral vision to keep track of teammates.
	• Failure to direct the ball to a space	• Look for open spaces between opponents; clear (throw, bat, or kick) the ball into spaces toward the nearer sideline.

THROWS

Error	*Causes*	*Corrections*
Weak		
Ball fails to reach target	• Failure to have a firm base of support	• Keep the feet on the ground when throwing; stride in the direction of the target with the foot opposite the throwing arm.
	• Failure to have a sequential action of the upper extremities	• Pull the ball through with sequential action beginning at the hips and trunk and culminating with hand and ball being "whipped" rapidly forward.
	• Failure to utilize a full range of motion	• Rotate the body and the arm clockwise (for right-hander) in the preparatory phase and strongly counterclockwise in the forward throwing phase.
	• Failure to extend at the point of release	• Reach as far as possible toward the target with the hand(s).
Inaccurate		
Ball is misdirected	• Failure to release at the appropriate point	• Release the lofted ball when the hand is under the ball; release when the hand is behind the ball for a horizontal throw.
	• Failure to follow through	• Extend the fingers and arm(s) toward the target.
Inappropriate strategies		
	• Failure to throw quickly	• Take throw-ins and goalkeeper throws quickly to prevent opponents from getting into defensive positions.
	• Poor placement of the ball	• Know where teammates are; throw to spaces ahead of teammates or toward which they are moving; direct the ball toward the direction of the attack; throw controlled passes.

Chapter 9
Softball

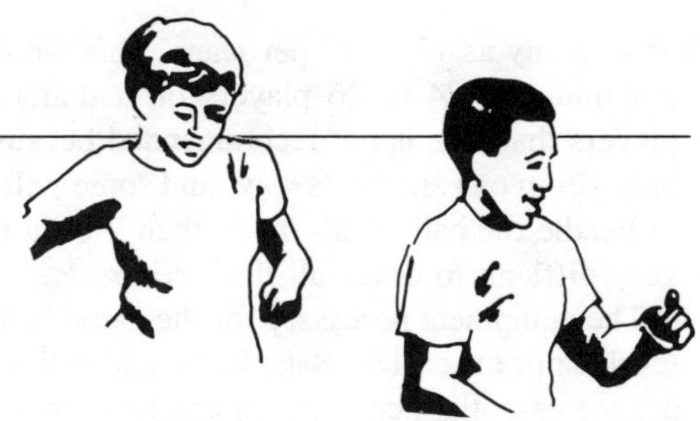

Softball is a variation of baseball that was originally adapted for indoor play and later taken outside to the playgrounds around the country. Although Abner Doubleday is credited with designing the diamond-shaped base path and positioning of players for baseball in 1839, George M. Hancock is generally considered to be the one who suggested the larger ball and a smaller bat used in softball. The first game of indoor baseball, as it was called, is thought to have been held in 1887 in Chicago, where an old boxing glove and a broom handle served as a ball and a bat.

The game quickly moved outdoors and was adopted by playgrounds, recreation centers, and schools all over the United States because it could be played more safely with fewer injuries by less skilled people of all ages. The game was known as indoor-outdoor baseball, mush ball, playground ball, scrub, kitten ball, and other names until the early 1930s, when the name *softball* was accepted.

During the early part of the 20th century, rules differed from community to community (e.g., the number of players on a side, pitching distances, and the length of base paths). In 1903, the American Sports Publishing Company printed a handbook of softball rules, but many other organizations still used their own rules. In 1926, Gladys Palmer compiled softball rules for women, which the American Physical Education Association adopted in 1927. It is estimated that there were at least 12 sets of rules prior to 1933, when organizations sponsoring tournaments in the United States met and established the Amateur Softball Association, which organized a joint rules committee to standardize the rules of fast-pitch softball.

The fast-pitch game took over playgrounds into the 1960s, by which time pitchers had become so skilled that they dominated the game, and batters were unable to score many runs. Play became less exciting, and spectators and average players began to lose interest. Slow-pitch softball grew as a result of an effort to put excitement back into the game by giving the hitters more of a chance. The slow-pitch game also enables players of lower skill and older people with slower reaction times to participate and enjoy play. In the early 1980s, slow-pitch softball became the most popular of the variations of the sport.

Purposes and Values

Softball is a sport that is played informally as well as in leagues all over the United States. Youngsters should learn the basic skills so they are able to participate in pickup games in social or recreational settings as well as participate in softball as a lifetime sport. Most communities throughout the country have softball leagues for adults and young people.

Playing softball does not require extensive conditioning and cardiovascular fitness; there are many opportunities for rest between plays in the game. Certainly, the player who is in top cardiovascular condition will be able to run farther and play longer. However, the average once- or twice-a-week player will be able to enjoy the game and will benefit from the activity without investing the time and effort necessary for maximum fitness. Such players should warm up carefully before games by stretching the muscles of their legs, back, and arms. Additional warm-up exercises could include throwing and catching. Proper warm-up should help prevent injury caused by fast or sudden starts, stops, and hard throws.

The mastery of softball requires development of the fundamental skills of throwing, catching, hitting, running, and perhaps sliding. Players should also develop eye-hand coordination, flexibility, and agility. Players must have good depth perception and eye-tracking ability (coincidence anticipation) to judge fly balls and to hit the pitched ball. They must strive for quickness of movement and be able to stay alert while waiting for the action to start. Softball is one of the few team sports in which strength and height are not significant factors because players do not participate directly against one another. In addition, skill can be more important than power.

Another advantage of softball for class use is that it can accommodate various sizes of groups. Although there are 9 players on a team officially (10 in slow pitch), the game can be comfortably played with as few as 7 or as many as 12 or 13 per team. This would mean a maximum of 24 to 26 players on a diamond. More players than this is not recommended because players only get in one another's way, and some will never get to handle the ball. With fewer than 7 on a team, it is very difficult to cover all the territory.

The equipment necessary for the game is neither extensive nor expensive. Bats, balls, and catcher's masks are the essential items. Bases can be homemade, and, with the right kind of soft softballs, gloves would not be necessary. An official diamond field is desirable, but any flat grassy surface would be suitable. The game can be played on asphalt or other hard-topped surface, but then sliding should not be permitted. Sliding is discouraged with younger players or novices due to the injury potential.

Some of the lead-up games and skill practices of softball can be played by only two or three persons. Hitting fly balls or grounders to each other and playing a between-base rundown game (hot box) are interesting and motivating activities.

Because many boys have a variety of experiences playing softball or baseball outside of school while many girls do not, it is important to teach all students the basic skills early in their school years and to encourage them to practice whenever possible. Instructors or coaches may have to give special attention to improving girls' skills through positive instructional suggestions and longer practice sessions.

The Game

Softball is a variation of baseball that uses a larger and softer ball, lighter weight bats, and a smaller field. To play the game, members of one team take turns batting while the opposite team in the field tries to put the batters *out* by (a) catching the batted ball on the fly, (b) tagging the runner with the ball while the player attempts to reach first base or the next base, (c) causing the batter to accumulate three *strikes*, or (d) holding the ball and touching the base ahead of a runner who must advance. The batting team becomes the fielding team after 3 outs are made. Each team is allowed 3 outs per *inning*. The team scoring the most runs (completed circuits of the bases) at the end of 7 innings is the winner.

There are 9 players on each team for the fast-pitch game and 10 players on each team for the slow-pitch variation. The *diamond* and general positions of players are shown in Figures 9.1 and 9.2. Except for the pitcher and the catcher, players may play anywhere in fair territory legally.

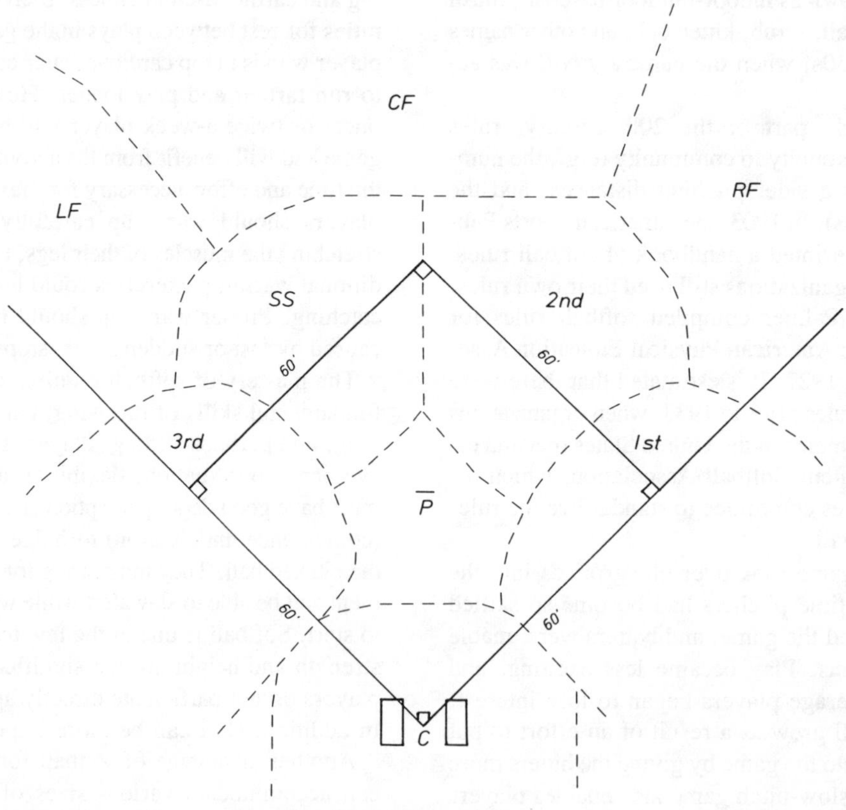

Figure 9.1. Typical field coverage for the fast pitch game (9 players)

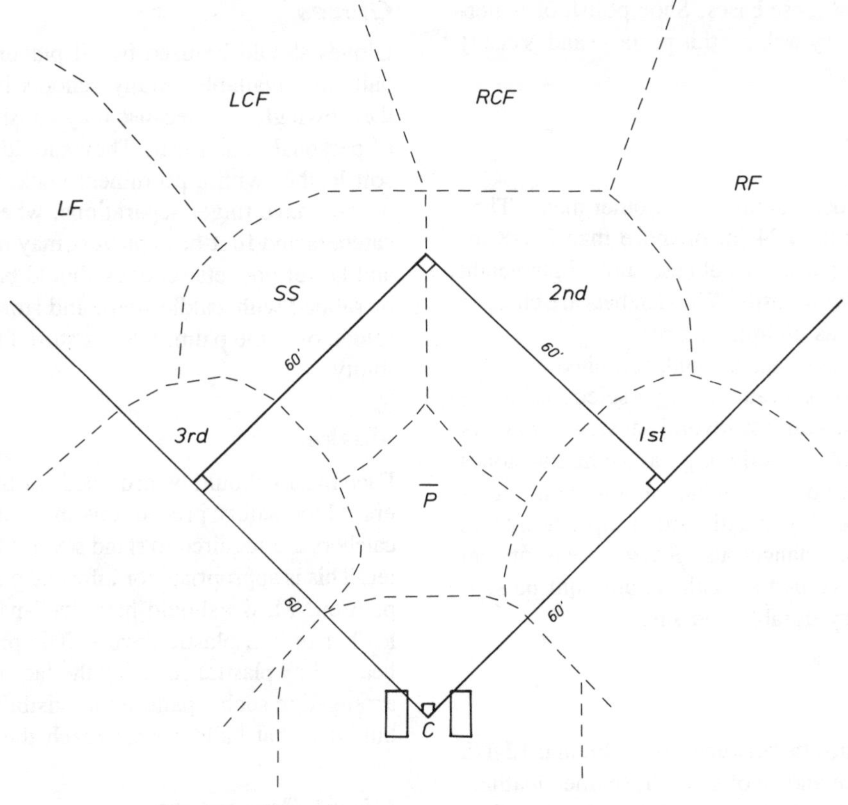

Figure 9.2. Typical field coverage for the slow-pitch game (10 players)

There are several variations of softball played in different areas of the country or to suit specific groups. The fast-pitch and the slow-pitch games will be considered here. The main difference between the two is in the pitching style. In fast pitch, the pitcher tries to throw the ball hard and parallel with the ground in an effort to make the batter miss the ball. In slow pitch, the pitcher must throw the ball with a perceptible arc no higher than 10 ft. The strike zones differ somewhat, and in slow pitch the batter may not attempt to run to first base if the catcher fails to catch the third strike. Other rule variations will be discussed later in this chapter.

Playing Area

The regulation softball field has a grassy outfield area and a smooth dirt infield without grass (Figure 9.1). The *infield* is the area inside the base paths and a short distance behind the lines between first and second bases and second and third bases. Instruction and class play can easily be conducted on any level area, although it is safer to use a grass-covered area than a hard surface like asphalt in case players fall or slide. A backstop should be placed at least 25 ft from home plate behind the catcher's position. The minimum recommended distance from home plate to the limits of the *outfield* is 200 ft (longer if adults are using the field). The distance between bases is 60 ft, although this may be increased to 65 ft for adults playing the slow-pitch game.

Home plate and the *pitcher's rubber* are made of hard rubber, plastic, or wood and should be embedded in the ground flush with the playing surface. The pitching distance for men is 46 ft and for women 40 ft. A pitching distance of 40 ft is suggested for secondary school classes.

Equipment

The following is a description of the equipment necessary for softball play. Standards for equipment and recommendations on equipment use are also included.

Bases

Bases should be 15 in. square and made of kapok-filled (or other fiberfilled) canvas. They should have straps anchored to spikes that can be driven firmly into the ground. Bases that slide around are hazardous to runners and any base player. If baserunning skills or games are practiced indoors or on hard surfaces, plastic bases that adhere to the floor are recommended. It is better to paint bases on the floor or blacktop surfaces than to risk injury by using loose bases. Shoe polish or water-color paint works very well for this purpose and is easily removed with water.

Bats

Bats are made of wood, aluminum, or other metal. They may not be longer than 34 in. or more than 2-1/8 in. in diameter. Young players should use short, lightweight bats that they can swing easily. Wooden bats are cheaper but not as durable as aluminum ones.

When classes are large and the budget limited, wooden bats are recommended because a larger selection can be provided. Such bats can last several seasons if players are taught to use them properly (e.g., avoid hitting stones with them). Cracked or broken bats should be immediately removed from play and discarded. Splinters from these could be very dangerous. Rough areas on bat handles should be sanded smooth. Aluminum bats, if affordable, are very durable and safe.

Balls

Official softballs must be between 11-7/8 in. and 12-1/8 in. in circumference and be of smooth, seamed leather. Beginners find leather balls easier to handle after they have been used a while. Leather balls become softer with use, but those that have been wet tend to become heavy and hard after drying. Rubber balls or those with synthetic covers are more durable and are cheaper and may be more practical for instructional purposes. However, they are often quite hard, and beginners tend to try to avoid catching them.

There are several good soft softballs available today. These are recommended for use with younger players or in situations in which all players do not have good gloves. Whiffle balls or mush balls make indoor play in restricted areas safer. Mush balls provide a more realistic situation and can be used with regular bats. The whiffle balls are usually cheaper but should be used with plastic bats.

Gloves

Gloves should be used by all players unless modified balls are available. Many schools have players bring their own gloves, because they consider gloves an item of personal equipment. They should be constructed of soft leather with a prominent pocket. Fielders' gloves usually have finger separations, whereas mitts used by catchers and first-base players may have more padding and larger pockets. Gloves should be kept clean, oiled or rubbed with saddle soap, and stored with the thumb folded over the palm. Gloves stored flat soon lose flexibility.

Masks

Face masks should be provided for the use of all catchers. Good safety precautions mandate their use unless catchers are required to stand several feet behind the batter. This is appropriate for informal play but not for competition. Masks should have well-padded frames with leather or soft plastic covers. The protective wires (or heavy-duty plastic) covering the face must be sturdy and arranged in such a pattern that visibility is not impaired but such that balls cannot reach the face.

Chest Protectors and Shin Guards

Chest protectors are advisable for all fast-pitch play in competitive situations. They are not usually needed for slow-pitch or casual play, when catchers can stand back from the batter. Shin and knee guards are recommended for fast-pitch advanced play but are unnecessary for most classes.

Shoes

Tennis shoes are recommended for class use. Turf or field hockey shoes with short rubber cleats are appropriate. Metal cleated shoes with leather uppers should be worn only by experienced players in competitive leagues.

Suggestions for Coeducational Play

Boys often have developed more softball skills than have girls by the time they reach the secondary grades. Care must be taken that boys do not dominate opportunities to handle the ball to the exclusion of the girls. On the other hand, if girls make errors whenever they handle the ball, motivation and enjoyment are lost for all players. Girls must be encouraged to develop the basic skills of the sport.

Physical education classes are conducted for the purpose of learning, not just recreation. Students who have not mastered the subject matter should have homework assignments just as they would in other classes. Those who are weak throwers or uncertain catchers should work on these skills outside of class. Playing catch with someone for 15 to 30 min per day after school or during free time such as recess or lunch will help improve these ball-handling skills.

Teachers can emphasize the affective domain of learning by encouraging cooperative skill development. The highly skilled players in a class can be made responsible for helping the less skilled to learn. Those who have mastered the skills can be assigned to work with one or two of the poorer skilled players. This could be considered a teamwork homework assignment to be accomplished before or after class.

Teams should be comprised of a balance of stronger and weaker players. However, the stronger players must not be allowed to play the key positions all the time. Frequent rotation of positions during game play will give all players more opportunity to practice the skills. A common pattern to distribute play is to alternate a boy and a girl at each defensive position each inning. For example, if a boy plays first base the first inning, a girl must do so the second inning. Be sure that girls are not always assigned to right field, where the ball is rarely hit.

Rules might be established to require alternating boys and girls in the batting order also. This gives all a chance to bat, and the players can learn some of the strategies of arranging a batting lineup for competitive play (trying to get runners on base before your strongest hitters come to bat).

Selecting appropriate equipment is a key factor in promoting the development of skills. Hard softballs and poor gloves can impede learning. Younger or novice students should use softer balls or mush balls when learning. These balls do not sting the hands or induce fear and withdrawal and are less apt to cause injury if the player is hit with the ball. Although some players in a class may be capable of handling harder balls, the softer ball should be used until a large percentage of the players are competent. Gloves should fit the wearer, and instruction in their use is important.

Batting tees can help to develop batting skills when timing is a problem. Players in a game might be given the option of hitting off a tee or hitting a pitched ball. This gives the lesser skilled player a chance to concentrate on the hitting technique while the more skilled player practices judging pitches, timing, and hitting. Most players in this type of situation will be motivated by their peers to advance to hitting the pitched ball and not stay with the tee too long.

A skilled pitcher can do much to improve hitting skills and help a batter develop confidence. The teacher or a skilled student would be able to place pitches where the batter could more easily hit them. Umpires should not call balls and strikes in most class situations. Make the batters hit the ball in order for all players to get more practice. In regular play, accumulating three strikes is an out, but with younger players this rule can be ignored.

Using a pitcher who is a member of the batting team assures sympathetic pitches. When pitchers are members of the batting team, they try to put the ball where the batters can hit it. Pitchers in this situation should be prohibited from playing batted balls. Only the defensive players do that. They should also be rotated out of the pitching position frequently to get a turn at bat.

Teaching Progressions

Skills in this chapter are grouped according to fundamental movement relationships to one another and commonality of purpose for ease of understanding and analyzing. This does not imply that the skills should be presented to players in that order.

The skill level of players in softball classes may vary greatly. Although the progressions suggested have been developed to accommodate many groups, the instructor should evaluate each class carefully and adjust the program to meet the needs of each specific situation. Some players will have had many softball experiences. These players will be able to move quickly into the intermediate or even the advanced skills. Other groups may need to spend more time on throwing, catching, and batting skills to the exclusion of other fundamentals.

Progressions for Beginning Players

I. Throwing and catching
  A. Underarm
  B. Overarm

II. Fielding
  A. Fly balls
  B. Ground balls

III. Pitching: Underarm throw
  A. Fast pitch (horizontal throw)
  B. Slow pitch (lobbed throw)

IV. Batting: Full swing

V. Baserunning

VI. Base play
  A. Force play
  B. Tag play

VII. Game play

Additional Skills for Intermediate Players

I. Pitching
  A. Whip or slingshot
  B. Windmill

II. Straight slide (optional for use with coached teams, not classes)

III. Rundown of runner between bases

Additional Skills for Advanced Players

I. Sidearm throw

II. Bunting

III. Pitching
  A. Curves
  B. Floater

IV. Slides
  A. Hook
  B. Dive

Techniques and Practice

Throwing and Catching

Throwing and catching should be taught together. By the time the children are ready to begin softball play, they should have had basic instruction in throwing and catching skills. They should then be ready to work on refining the skill of handling a rather hard, small ball.

Students of secondary school age should concentrate on the overhand throws and try to improve force and accuracy. The underarm throw is usually only used for short distances. The sidearm throw may be practiced by the more advanced performers but should not be introduced to novices.

Underarm Throw

The underarm throw is used effectively when a quick release is needed. Generally, the player is very low to the ground and does not have the time to stand and execute an overarm throw. The underarm throw should be used only for short distances of 15 ft or less. This throw is used to place the ball very quickly into the hands of a fielder.

The underarm throw begins after the player has fielded the ball. The player grasps the ball with the fingers of the nongloved hand while the gloved hand moves away, exposing the ball to the receiver. The thrower pivots toward the receiver. The leg on the nonthrowing side should be forward. At the same time, the throwing arm and hand drop perpendicular to the ground. The fingers are behind the ball and the palm of the hand facing the receiver. The arm is then hyperextended at the shoulder to swing the arm rearward in the backswing. The height of the backswing depends on the throwing distance needed. The larger the distance, the more backswing is needed for force production.

The force-production phase begins with flexion at the shoulder, which creates a pendular swinging of the arm forward. Accompanying the arm swing is a forward shift of body weight. The ball is released when it is tangent to the receiver's target catching area. This is usually near the bottom of the pendular swing. Enough force should be generated for the ball to travel as fast as possible and in a straight line to the receiver. The follow-through is a continuation of the arm motion in the direction of the throw.

Common Movement Problems and Suggestions. The following are common movement problems that occur during underarm throws. Instructional suggestions are also included.

- The most common problem occurs due to the improper timing on release. The thrower could have an early or a late release, which affects the direction of the ball. The most common type of errant release is a late release, which puts too much arc on the ball.
- Another common error is failure to generate enough force to get the ball to the receiver quickly. This

is generally caused by an insufficient backswing, improper or lack of body-weight transfer, inadequate speed of the arm swinging forward, or insufficient follow-through.

- Instructors should check the throwing hand of the performer. The ball should be held in the fingers with the palm of the hand not touching the ball.
- The thrower should be taught to emphasize the lifting motion of the throw and to permit the ball to roll off the fingers.

Overarm Throw

The overarm throw is one of the most fundamental skills of softball. The overarm throw is essential for all players regardless of playing position or gender. The player should throw the ball only when the playing situation dictates it and the purpose of the throw is clear. Unnecessary throws generally result in playing errors. Therefore, the player must prepare for the throw mentally. Each time the ball is thrown, the player must make decisions about the receiver, the distance to be thrown, and the speed of the delivery.

The initation of the throw in softball begins with a transfer of the ball from the glove to the throwing hand (Figure 9.3). This should be done as smoothly as possible. The ball is held with the tripod, or three-finger, grip. The tripod grip has the index and long fingers behind the ball with the thumb and other two fingers coming forward on both sides of the ball to complete the grasp. The three-finger grip is identical with the tripod except that the index, long, and ring fingers are behind the ball. The three-finger grip is more suitable for beginners and players with small hands.

The preparation phase begins with a step or pivot to face the throwing target. The leg opposite the throwing arm is forward, and the hip and shoulder opposite the throwing arm are pointing toward the target. A clockwise rotation of the trunk and hips occurs for a right-handed thrower. The nonthrowing arm raises up in front to maintain balance as the throwing arm drops down and rearward in the early stages of the preparation. The elbow of the throwing arm flexes with the forearm laid back. The arm is moving above the horizontal in a lateral and backward motion during this *backswing* phase. The body weight is shifted rearward and might cause the forward foot to lift off the ground slightly.

The force-production phase begins with a shift of body weight forward, which is caused by a counterclockwise, or forward, rotation of the trunk and hips toward the target (right-handed throw). The arm is brought forward by this action and begins to rotate medially at the shoulder. The elbow is above (or slightly above) the shoulder level. The upper arm is almost facing the target. The whipping action of the forearm now positions the hand for release. This action is a rapid extension at the elbow. The hand releases the ball when it is tangent to the target. The arm continues to move forward after the release. The arm moves diagonally across the body with continued medial rotation. Further explanation of the overarm throwing motion can be found in chapter 3.

Common Movement Problems and Suggestions. The following are common movement problems encountered during the execution of the overarm throw. Instructional suggestions are also presented.

- The thrower that fails to rotate the hips and trunk rearward restricts the range of motion of the total movement. Generally, a complete transfer of weight does not occur. These problems deplete the potential force production that can be transferred to the ball.
- The most common problem is the error of permitting the forearm, wrist, or hand to lead the motion. The most proximal upper-limb segment (upper arm)

Figure 9.3. Overarm throw

moves forward first with the most distal segment (hand) moving forward last. The elbow should lead the action and be above (or slightly above) the shoulder.

- Holding the arm too close to the body causes the skill to appear cramped. Generally, this also causes the performer to release the ball without a fully extended arm.
- The performer can also have a limited follow-through. Correction of previous errors can sometimes eliminate the limited follow-through.
- Additional analysis questions that focus on errors can be found in the section on the overarm throw in chapter 3.

Sidearm Throw

This throw is used as a quick throw by infielders to get the ball to a base without taking the time to straighten up or take a full backswing. Because the arm swing is a circular movement, it tends to result in poorly directed throws and should not be taught to novices. A drill to practice this skill is presented after the skill analyses.

The distinguishing feature of the sidearm throw is the horizontal plane in which the throwing arm moves. Force production is generated by the forceful rotation of the pelvis and trunk in combination with the rapid extension of the arm at the elbow.

The preparatory actions are similar to the overarm throwing skill. The hips or pelvis lead the force-production action by rotating forward toward the target. The hips stop rotation when they are facing the target. The arm is then extended at the elbow and swings horizontally (*adduction*) at the shoulder. This brings the arm forward along the horizontal plane of motion. The elbow still leads the motion, and the ball is released when tangent to the target. The follow-through is a continuation of the arm motion in the direction of the throw. The arm medially rotates and crosses in front of the body.

Common Movement Problems and Suggestions. The following are common movement problems experienced when performing the sidearm throw. Instructional suggestions are also presented.

- Failure to rotate the pelvis rapidly can greatly decrease the force production for transfer to the ball.
- The most common problem with the sidearm throw is accuracy. The timing of the release is difficult due to the horizontal, or arc, motion of the arm. Forward motion of the shoulders through trunk and hip rotation and a forward stride can flatten the throwing-hand arc and create more time to execute an accurate release.
- Supination of the arm can also lead to additional problems with ball-trajectory direction. Throwers should be encouraged to begin the medial rotation of the arm just prior to release.
- A shortened backswing or follow-through are also movement problems that restrict force production and accuracy.
- Additional analysis questions and comments found in chapter 3 in the section on the sidearm throw may be helpful in identifying errors.

Catching Generalizations

Catching thrown and batted balls that are in the air is done in the same way. Fielding balls that bounce along the ground requires a somewhat different technique. In both cases, key points are to get in front of the ball, watch it until it gets to the hands, and use both hands in the catch whenever possible.

Fielding the Thrown Ball

Fielding the thrown ball is a primary skill for the infield players. There are basically four types of thrown balls that must be caught: high (chest height or above), medium (around waist level), low (below the waist), and wide (forehand or backhand side). The techniques for all four are similar with the exception of arm positioning.

The receiver should focus on the ball through the entire flight. The receiver begins by positioning the body directly in line with the path of the ball. The stance is slightly wider than the shoulders for stability. The player extends the arms toward the ball in flight. The position of the arms depends on the flight path of the ball. The gloved hand always has the palm facing the ball-flight path. The nongloved hand follows the gloved hand also with the palm of the hand facing the ball flight path whenever possible. When the ball is high or at chest

Figure 9.4. Catching a thrown ball

height, the arms, hands, and fingers are positioned up with the thumbs close together. When the ball is low or below waist level, the arms are extended downward with the little fingers close together and the fingers of both hands pointing downward. When catching a ball wide to either the forehand or the backhand side, the player reaches laterally with the catching arm and hand. Whenever possible, both hands should reach for the ball. If the ball is on the forehand side, the movement is a simple lateral lunging motion with knee flexion and weight transfer on the ball-flight side. If the ball is on the backhand side, the receiver must reach across the body with the glove hand to receive the ball. Again, the knee must flex, and body-weight transfer occurs on the ball-flight side. Both situations of catching wide balls involve a semilunge to the ball-flight side.

The hands should be open and relaxed for the catch. The ball is always caught in the pocket of the glove. The force of the ball is dissipated by flexing the elbow or drawing the ball rearward toward the center of the body. If additional force absorption is necessary, a step backward can provide a larger retraction distance for force dissipation. The extent of all force-absorption movements is dependent on the force of the ball being caught. The nongloved hand closes over the ball after it is in the glove. This places the throwing hand on the ball in a ready position for the next movement sequence (Figure 9.4).

Common Movement Problems and Suggestions. The following are common movement problems experienced when fielding a thrown ball. Instructional suggestions are also included.

- Many players are not aggressive about reaching toward the ball. Any shortening of the reach toward the ball limits the possible retraction distance for force absorption. Encourage players to be more aggressive in receiving.
- Beginners might forget to reach with both hands, or, when they do use both hands, the nongloved hand gets in the way.
- Relaxation of the fingers and opening the glove prior to impact should also be emphasized. In addition, closing the glove over the ball after impact is essential. Failure to do either of these can cause the ball to rebound off the glove.
- Another common error of the beginner is to close the glove too soon. This can also cause the ball to rebound off the glove.
- Beginners who are fearful of receiving tend to close the eyes on impact. The best way to eliminate fear is to provide the performer with positive experiences in catching. This can be done by using a very soft ball or catching from short distances until the skill is learned effectively. Harder softballs and longer distances or more forceful throws can then be introduced to the performer. Once the fear of receiving is controlled, the instructor should emphasize focusing on the ball throughout the receiving sequence of movements.
- Failing to flex the elbows immediately after impact (giving with the ball) and stepping backward causes the ball to sting the hands or to rebound off the glove. The primary purpose of receiving, which is dissipation of force, should be emphasized.
- Whenever possible, players should be encouraged to back up the catch by placing the body behind the ball.

Fly Balls

The *fly ball* is caught at or above chest height whenever possible. One of the most important aspects of receiving fly balls is making a correct judgment on the ball's flight. There are many things that affect the ball flight. The receiver must make judgments on the speed of ball flight, the angle of ball trajectory, the effects of gravity on the ball, air resistance, and any other environmental circumstance such as wind, sun, or lights at night.

Once the receiver makes a judgment about ball direction, the player should move toward the site where it is anticipated the ball will drop. The sooner the player reaches the site, the more time is available for small position adjustments. It is better to move farther back than is necessary than to move directly to or ahead of the ball site. When the player is positioned slightly back from the ball site, it is easier to move forward to the ball than to try to move backward to receive the ball. The player should keep focused on the ball at all times. The player should call for the ball to communicate with teammates the player's intentions. This will also permit the player to remain focused on the ball and avoid collisions with teammates.

Once reaching the receiving site, the player should assume a comfortable and stable stance. The stance is a forward stride with the foot on the throwing side slightly forward. The knees are slightly flexed. The arms should extend upward toward the ball with the gloved hand in front of the throwing shoulder. The fingers in the gloved hand are pointing upward with the palm of the glove open and facing the approaching ball. The actual catch and dissipation of force is identical to receiving a thrown ball (see previous discussion).

The advantageous position for receiving is with the shoulder on the nongloved side pointing toward the throwing target. This enables the receiver to initiate a rapid throwing action following the catch.

Common Movement Problems and Suggestions. The following are common movement problems unique to receiving fly balls. All errors discussed previously in the section on fielding a thrown ball also apply to the fielding of the fly ball. Instructional suggestions are also included.

- The most common problem in fielding a fly ball is a judgment error on the direction of ball flight. The instructor should provide as many experiences as possible in all types of situations in many environmental conditions. Only experiences and observations will eliminate these judgment errors.
- Beginners should practice catching fly balls from short distances. This should build confidence in catching and permit enlarging the distance. Increase distance as skill levels increase.

Ground Balls

The *ground ball* refers to receiving a ball that is rolling or bouncing along the ground. The fielder must judge the path or flight of the ball by attending to many clues. The player needs to focus on the path of the ball as it comes off the bat or is thrown from a teammate. Low or ground balls sometimes result when a teammate misjudges the distance between players. The receiver should attend to the speed, spin, angle, and direction of the ball.

The receiver should move aggressively toward the ground ball to save time and reduce the amount of ball bouncing. The body should be positioned directly in front of the ball's path. The body acts as a barrier behind the gloved hand in case the ball is not caught directly.

When a player is fielding the ground ball, the body should be in a crouched position with one foot slightly behind the other and both hands held low in front of the body. From this position a rapid throw can be made by taking a step toward the target on the foot opposite the throwing arm (Figure 9.5). Many right-handed fielders prefer to have the left foot slightly behind the right. Then, as the ball is caught, the right foot is used as a pivot, and the left foot steps toward the target with the throw. If the fielder must move to the right, the player should pivot on the right foot, cross the left foot over in front, and take the first step with the left foot. When moving to the left, the right foot crosses over using the left foot as the pivot foot. Other aspects of catching the ground ball are similar to those covered under receiving the thrown ball.

Common Movement Problems and Suggestions. The following are common movement problems that are unique to fielding a ground ball. Other movement problems discussed under fielding a thrown ball also apply to the fielding of a ground ball. Instructional suggestions are also presented.

- Players make poor judgment errors when they wait for the ball to come to them. Any additional rolling or bouncing on the ground can create more possibilities for ball-direction changes. Encourage players to be aggressive in moving toward the ball.
- Players that do not put the total body behind the catch can lose total control of the ball. The ball bouncing off the body keeps the ball within playing distance for that player.
- If the player lifts the head in anticipation of the catch, the body can raise up enough to lift the glove and miss the ball. Emphasize focusing on the ball at all times.

Throwing and Catching Practice Drills

The following are throwing and catching drills. Partner, group, and sidearm drills are included.

Partner Drills. Practice in pairs is best for the overhand throwing and catching skills. Each player will have a partner and practice throwing and catching with that person.

1.0. Start with partners about 15 ft apart (20 for older players) and gradually increase the distance until most

Figure 9.5. Catching a ground ball

are throwing about as far as they can without lofting the ball high in the air. All players participating in this practice should be lined up so that they throw back and forth in the same direction (e.g., north and south). This will provide a safer situation and help prevent accidents caused by poorly thrown balls. This is also a good warm-up activity to use prior to games to help prevent sore arm muscles. The distance between partners should be kept short if the group is using regular softballs and have no gloves. When gloves or mush balls are used, the distances can be increased. Unskilled players may move to about 40 ft apart; those more adept may finish the practice about 60 ft apart, which simulates the distance between bases.

1.1. More skilled players can be encouraged to practice throwing by giving them a challenging objective. Have one partner hold up a glove, which the other must try to hit. This provides a situation in which the ball must be thrown so accurately that the receiver does not have to move the hand to catch the ball.

1.2. After practicing throwing the ball straight to the receiver, players can also practice catching fly and ground balls in the same pattern. For fly-ball practice, the thrower arches the ball into the air, and the catcher must move under the ball to catch it before it bounces. Players may need more room between pairs when doing this because they tend to be less accurate than with direct throws.

2.0. To practice fielding ground balls, one partner throws a bouncing ball to the other, who fields it and throws it directly back in the air with an overhand throw. This is done so that the person fielding the ground ball becomes accustomed to throwing it immediately as in a game situation. Encourage overhand throws to the fielder because underhand throws tend to roll unrealistically along the ground. Throwers and fielders rotate after every 10 ground balls.

2.1. Beginners should try to throw directly to the fielder at first and then throw 3 or 4 ft to the side so that the fielder will have to move to get in line with the ball. More advanced players should throw hard ground balls to each side, making the fielders stretch and move quickly to get the ball.

Group Drills. When there are not enough balls for paired practice, the following group drills are suggested. Direct throws, fly balls, or ground balls may be practiced using these drills.

1.0. Leader-Class Formation (Figure 4.6). The leader, about 15 to 20 ft in front of the class, throws the ball to each in turn. The catcher returns it to the leader.

2.0. Double-Line Formation (Figure 4.10). Lines of players are placed about 15 ft apart. The ball is started at one end and thrown back and forth down the line and back. As skills improve, the distance between the lines should be increased.

3.0. Column With Leader (Figure 4.3). The leader could be one of the more skilled players in a novice group or could be changed frequently in a more skilled group. The leader throws the ball to the first person in the column, who catches (or fields) it, throws it back, and goes to the end of the column. The leader then throws to the next player. This continues until all players have participated. Players should move quickly into position to catch and throw.

4.0. Shuttle Formation (Figure 4.7). The first person in one column throws the ball to the first person in the other column and goes to the end of the player's own column. The first person in the other column throws the ball back to the second person in the first column and goes to the end of the player's own column. This continues until all players have participated.

5.0. Shuttle Formation With Base (Figure 9.6). Place bases 40 ft apart (60 ft for advanced players). Players line up in columns behind the bases. Player X2 steps in front of the base, receives the throw from Player X1 (Throw a), and tags the base with one foot. Player X3 steps in front of the other base, receives the throw from Player X2 (Throw b), and tags that base with either foot. This continues back and forth. Players go to the ends of their own columns after throwing the ball. Emphasize accurate throws and continuous action. Variation: Players stay behind the base. As the ball is caught, they bend to touch the edge of the base with the glove (or the ball) as if tagging a runner.

Motivation can be enhanced in all these drills by adding competition. This is more important for the advanced beginners or the intermediate players who think that their skills are better than they really are. These are

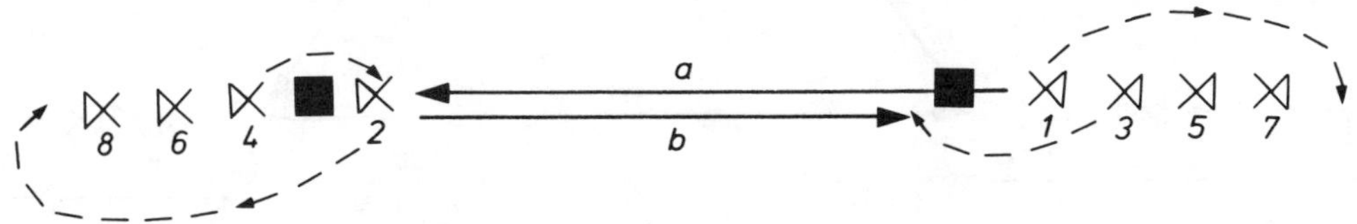

Figure 9.6. Throw and catch with base tag

the ones who want to avoid skill practice and go directly to the real game without having the ability to do so. Beginners are usually motivated by improvement in the skills they practice; advanced players recognize the need for refinement of skills. Therefore, these latter groups need less extrinsic motivation.

To make the drills competitive, add a counting procedure. Count the number of successful catches in a row without dropping the ball. The teacher starts all groups at the same time, stops them after 2 to 5 min, and compares scores. This could be repeated several times for each drill used. Avoid using procedures that eliminate those who make errors because this causes those who need the most practice to be the ones who get the least.

6.0. Softball Field (Figure 9.1). Three to six players are lined up behind each base outside the base paths. The ball is thrown around the diamond with players rotating in to take a turn and then go to the end of their own line. More experienced players may practice throws also from home to second base and from third base to first base.

Sidearm Throw. The following is an example of a drill for practicing the sidearm throw. This drill also includes practice receiving ground balls.

1.0. Triangular Formation (Figure 9.7). Player X1 throws a ground ball to Player X2 (Throw a). Player X2 fields the ball and throws sidearm to Player X3 (Throw b), who catches the ball and throws a ground ball to Player X4 (Throw c). This pattern continues until all players have participated. Note that players who field a ground ball use a sidearm throw, and those who catch a sidearm throw, throw a ground ball. Players go to the ends of their own columns after throwing the ball. After several turns, reverse the direction of the throws.

Pitching

The two main variations of softball are *slow pitch* and *fast pitch*. The types are distinguished by the pitching styles, although each requires an underhand throw. Both the slow-pitch and the fast-pitch deliveries are discussed here.

Slow Pitch

More schools are playing the slow-pitch game because (a) young and inexperienced players can bat the ball more easily, (b) there is no opportunity for dominance by one player (the pitcher), (c) there is less stress on children's arms when throwing the slow pitch, (d) the game employs 10 fielders rather than 9, (e) catchers can play well back from the batter and need not wear cumbersome (and expensive) equipment, and (f) base stealing is not allowed, and thus sliding is discouraged.

The pitched ball in slow-pitch softball must arch into the air at least 6 ft and drop down over the plate within the strike zone. This is between the batter's highest shoulder and the knees while in a natural batting stance. The pitching distance is 46 ft, but this may be reduced to 40 ft or even 38 ft for younger players.

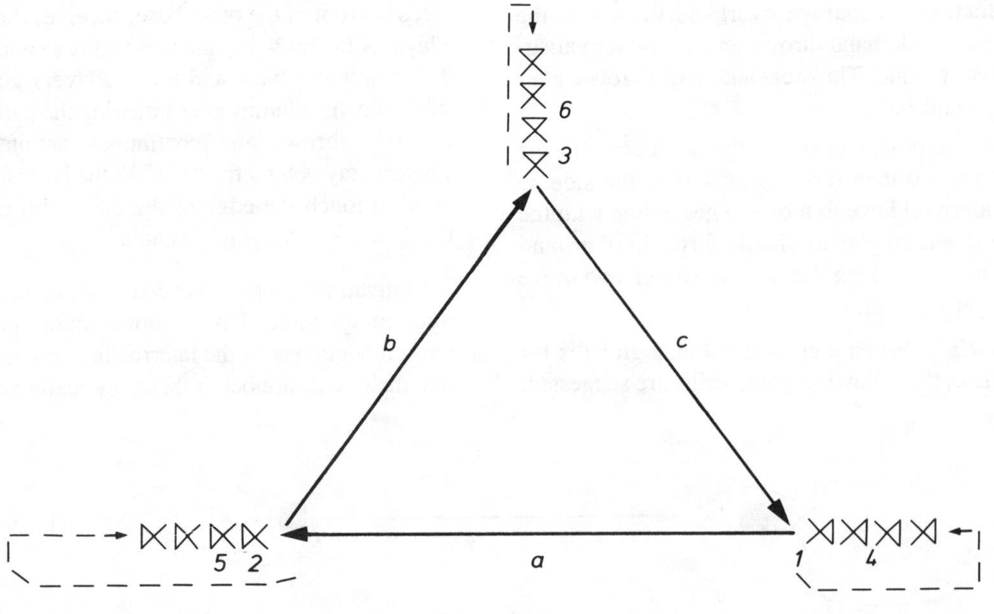

Figure 9.7. Sidearm throw drill

Pitching involves several sequential procedures. The pitcher should stand in a slightly forward stride facing home plate. The foot opposite the throwing arm is slightly forward of the other foot. No particular hand position or arm swing is required for the pitch, although beginners should be encouraged to use a simple underhand backswing and to release the ball with the palm under and slightly behind it. The simple underhand swing begins by bringing the ball down and back in a semicircular swing. Pitchers should step toward home plate on the foot opposite the throwing arm to maintain better balance and to be ready to field the batted ball. As the pitcher steps forward, the pitching arm swings forward and down toward the point of release. The wrist is flexed rapidly (snapped) just prior to the point of release and with a feeling of lift being placed on the ball. The follow-through is a continuation of the throwing motion and leads to an additional step on the leg of the throwing side. This enables the pitcher to be in the fielding position and ready for any action to follow.

Common Movement Problems and Suggestions. The following are common movement problems observed by instructors when players perform the slow-pitch technique. Instructional suggestions are also included.

- The most common problem in pitching is accuracy, which depends primarily on the timing of the release. Accuracy should be emphasized by using a target when practicing. Speed, spin, and arc should be attempted only after control is evident in the pitcher.
- If the player has difficulty achieving the force necessary to get the ball to the plate, emphasis should be placed on a sufficient backswing, the speed of the forward swinging motion of the arm, a forward transfer of body weight, and a sufficient follow-through.
- Emphasis should also be placed on the lifting motion of the ball at release and on assuming field position after the follow-through.

Fast Pitch

The fast pitch for the unskilled or average player consists of a ball that is thrown horizontally with little arc. Accuracy of placement is the only factor of importance to beginners using this type of pitch. Pitchers should try to throw to the batter's weak areas (i.e., inside, outside, high, or low). Only skilled pitchers can take full advantage of the various types of pitches that can be thrown because the ball must have speed before it will be affected by air currents that cause it to curve. Beginners and intermediate players should strive to develop control and some speed before trying curves and sliders.

The fast pitch can be varied in two ways. First, the skilled pitcher can learn various windups, such as the sling shot, figure 8, or windmill. Second, the pitcher can vary the type of delivery, which could be various types of curve balls, such as the incurve, outcurve, sinker/drop, or riser.

Whip/Slingshot/Half Windmill. The stance is a side-straddle position with the nonthrowing shoulder facing home plate. After the windup is learned, the pitcher can add a step that adds momentum to the throw. When using the step, the foot on the nonthrowing side is behind the other foot and steps forward during the backswing of the arm and plants just prior to release. This step also provides for greater rotation of the trunk, which builds more momentum.

The hands are vertically down in front of the body at the start of the pitch. The hands separate with the throwing arm flexed at the elbow. The throwing arm moves backward in a pendular motion with the nonthrowing arm swinging forward for balance. The body weight is shifted rearward and the hip and shoulder on the throwing side rotated back. The throwing arm swings rearward and above head level with the back of the hand facing home plate.

The force-production phase begins with the forward swinging motion of the arm downward. The knee on the throwing side flexes to initiate a forward shift of body weight. The hips and trunk rotate forward toward home plate at the same time. The hips and trunk stop when they are facing the batter. The upper arm leads the action and stops as it reaches the hip or becomes perpendicular to the ground. This creates a situation in which the lower arm can extend rapidly at the elbow and whip forward to the point of release. This is the slingshot action referred to in the name of the windup. Just prior to release, the forward leg flexes slightly at the knee for stability as well as for flattening the throwing arc to increase the chance of an accurate throw. The ball is released at a level between the hips and knees. The shift of body weight forward continues through the follow-through. The pitching arm continues the action by moving forward and upward. The direction of the follow-through will depend on the type of delivery.

Figure 8. The *figure 8* windup starts in the same stance as described in the slingshot pitch. The motion begins with a swinging action of the pitching arm from chest height to an outward, downward, and backward motion that makes a loop behind the back. At the same time, the trunk is rotated clockwise (for a right-handed player). The figure 8 looping motion is made as the arm moves from the preparatory backswing to the force-producing forward swing. Force production is begun by the forward trunk rotation (counterclockwise) as the pitching arm and hand are brought forward very rapidly.

The release and follow-through are similar to those described in the slingshot windup.

Windmill. The distinguishing feature of the *windmill* is the full circular motion of the pitching arm. The stance is a forward stride with the foot on the throwing side forward and facing the batter. The ball is held with both hands in front of the body. The weight is shifted forward as both arms with the ball are stretched forward and out from the body. The body weight shifts rearward as the throwing arm swings up and overhead starting the full circular motion. The gloved arm remains forward and out in front of the body for balance. The pitching arm continues its circular motion by swinging over the head or around the top of the circle. As the arm starts down and back in the circular motion, the leg on the nonpitching side begins a step forward. As the pitching arm is fully extended and starts forward toward the release, the stepping foot is firmly planted. The release and follow-through are identical to those described in previous pitches.

Common Movement Problems and Suggestions. The following are common problems experienced when performing fast-pitch windups. Instructional suggestions are also included.

- Pitchers should hold the ball in the fingers, not against the palm of the throwing hand, because this can cause a slow or hindered release of the ball.
- Pitchers having difficulty generating enough speed on the ball may have problems with the forward weight transfer to generate momentum and a rapid forward swinging speed of the arm to complete the follow-through.
- A common problem in pitching is accuracy. The release can be early or late; both cause inaccuracy. If the release is early, the throw tends to be too low. If the release is late, the throw tends to be too high.
- A pitched ball that is too wide (right or left) tends to be due to a failure to swing the throwing arm parallel with the body. The wide pitch can also be caused by too little or too much rotation of the hips. When the pitcher does not rotate the hips enough, the pitcher never completely turns to face the target or batter. Rotating the hips too much can cause the pitcher to rotate beyond facing the target or batter.
- When the body is not in equilibrium or balance during the final stages of force production, the throw will generally be weak or less than forceful (fast).
- Timing is essential to the fast pitch. When the pitch is timed correctly and the total body synchronized, the throw will appear smooth and continuous without pause or hesitation.
- At the conclusion of any pitch, pitchers should position themselves in the fielding position. This prepares them for the subsequent action.

Curve Ball

The fast-ball pitcher may also work on throwing the spins that cause the ball to *curve* as an incurve, an outcurve, a drop, or a riser. The ball will curve in the direction of the spin; thus, if the nose or leading part of the ball is spinning to the right, the ball will curve to the right (Figure 9.8); if it is spinning to the left, the ball will curve to the left (Figure 9.9). Figure 9.10 illustrates the effect of topspin and backspin on the ball. If the nose is spinning down, the ball will drop (A); if it is spinning upward, the ball will rise or at least not drop (B).

After mastering the fastball, pitchers should learn to throw a change-up or a slow ball to confuse batters. The key to an effective change-up is to make sure that the delivery pattern looks the same as that for the fastball so that the batter won't recognize it until too late. The hand position on the ball is the significant factor. The ball is usually held in the palm of the hand or with the knuckles on the ball. Either position inhibits the wrist action, so the usual wrist flick is absent even though the arm swing is the same as when throwing the fastball. The ball tends to lack spin and speed, giving the ball the appearance of floating to the plate.

Practice of these advanced skills should be done on an individual basis. Special drills are not presented for group use.

Incurve Delivery. The grip for this curve ball has the thumb on one side with the index and long fingers vertical on the back of the ball and slightly lateral and parallel to the center of the ball. The little and ring fingers are directly opposite the thumb on the side of the ball. The curve is created by placing spin on the ball, which is also more affected by air current. To impart the spin for a curve ball, the hand rotates under the ball just prior to the point of release. The palm is rotated outward away from the body. The rapid wrist flexion (snap) occurs late in the release as the hand comes under the ball. The arm follows through with a diagonal motion across the front of the body.

The incurve is effective for the batter who is too close or crowds the plate. The ball is directed toward the center of the plate but then breaks toward the inside corner and the batter.

Outcurve Delivery. This pitch is performed the same as the incurve with the exception of hand movement on the ball. The wrist flexes (snaps) late in the release, but the hand moves under and over the top of the ball in a counterclockwise motion. The palm rotates inward toward the body.

The outcurve is effective for the batter who is too far back in the *batter's box* or who backs away from the plate during the swing. The ball is directed toward the center of the plate, but breaks toward the outside corner and away from the batter.

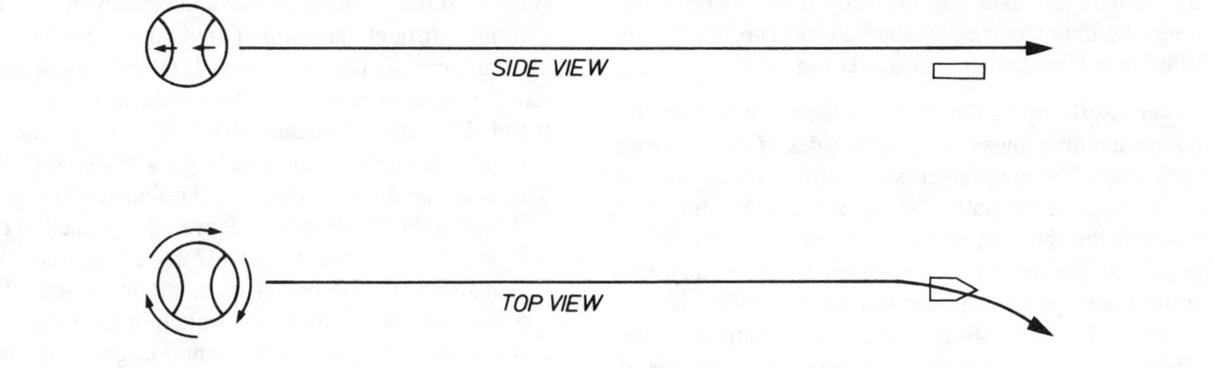

Figure 9.8. Curve to right (incurve)

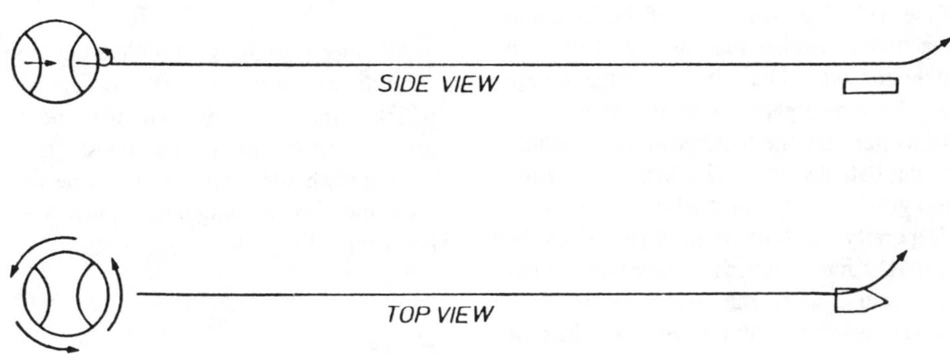

Figure 9.9. Curve to left (outcurve)

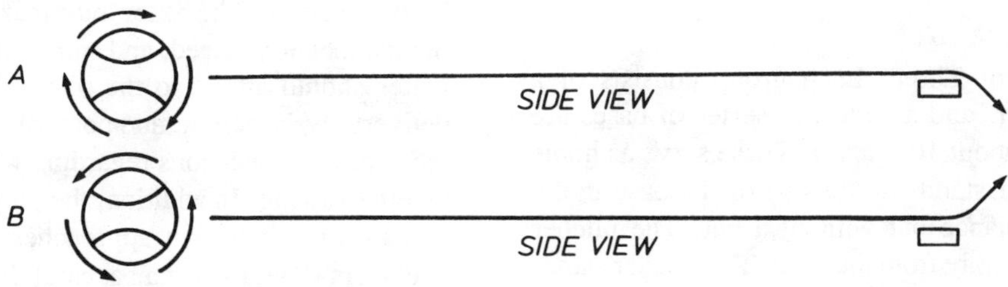

Figure 9.10. Effects of spin on the ball: (A) drop, (B) riser

Incurve and outcurve balls that are too slow or do not curve are generally caused by lack of speed in wrist flexion (snap), holding on too loosely to the ball, or not using a forceful transfer of body weight. The ball will not curve or break if thrown into an opposing wind to the spin, if the wrist is incorrectly snapped relative to timing and direction, or if an improper stride or follow-through is executed.

Drop/Sinker Delivery. The grip for a *drop pitch*, or *sinker*, is with the index, long, and ring fingers positioned vertically on the back of the ball. The thumb is on top of the ball and the little finger on the lateral side of the ball. Just prior to release, the thumb comes off the ball. Wrist flexion occurs at release and as the fingers come up the back of the ball, thus creating topspin. The slower the ball, the more drop the ball experiences. A slower ball can be created by shortening the forward stride prior to release. A compromise must be made between speed of ball delivery and magnitude of ball drop.

The drop pitch is excellent for the batter who is very tall in the batter's box or holds the bat high. The drop pitch is too low or too slow when the pitcher shortens the stride too much or releases early or has a loose grip on the ball. The ball will not drop if the stride is too long, the thumb comes off the ball too late, the ball is lifted at release, or the release is too late.

Riser Delivery. The grip for the *riser* is with the thumb and little finger on opposite sides of the ball from each other. The long finger is extended vertically on the center back of the ball. The tip of the index finger is touching the ball between the thumb and the long-finger positions. The index finger is flexed at each of its joints so that the tip of the finger touches the ball.

On the forward swing during force production, the elbow of the pitching arm is brought toward the side of the body. To create the necessary backspin, the release includes a lifting and inward rotation of the hand so that the back of the fingers are toward the plate just before the release of the ball. The ball rolls off the long and index fingers in such a manner that the top of the ball rotates toward the thrower. The follow-through is high and the stride is long to create lift on the ball.

The riser is excellent for the batter who is unusually low or high in the batter's box and when anticipating a bunt. It is also good for the batter who is deep in the batter's box. Generally, the ball does not rise when the elbow is not brought into the body, when weak wrist hyperextension occurs, when the stride is too short, when using an incomplete follow-through, or when the hand is not maintained under the ball.

Practice Drills

The following are pitching drills for groups of three or more.

1.0. Groups of Three. Each group consists of a pitcher, a catcher, and a batter. A series of bases are placed in a row about 10 ft apart. These serve as home plates. The batter stands to the side of the base in the regular batting stance but without a bat. The pitcher stands 25 to 30 ft away from the plate. The catcher stands behind the plate. This gives a strike zone as the target. The pitcher practices pitching to the catcher, who holds up a glove or hand as a target. After every 10 pitches, they rotate; the batter becomes pitcher, the pitcher moves to catch, and the catcher goes to the batter's position. Variation: Intermediate to advanced players could add a fourth person to the group to act as an umpire. This player would stand behind the catcher and practice calling balls and strikes.

2.0. Column Formation (Figure 4.2). Targets 17 in. wide and 30 in. high are drawn 15 in. above the floor on a solid wall. Each column of four to six players is lined up at a line in front of a target and 30 ft from the wall. The first player steps on the line using it as a pitching rubber and throws five underhand pitches at the target, then goes to the end of the column. The next player steps onto the pitching rubber and repeats the pattern. Continue through the column until all players have had several turns. As players gain skill, the pitching line may move to 40 ft from the wall. This is the distance recommended for coeducational class play. Variation: Competition may be included by adding a scoring procedure. This could be done by assigning 3 points (or 1) to every ball pitched inside the target. Players keep track of their own scores. A larger target (42 by 29 in.) could be drawn around the 30- by- 17-in. target on the wall. Then 1 point could be awarded for a pitch in the larger area and 3 points for a pitch in the center target. The player (or team) accumulating the most points wins. If these targets could be left on the walls, they would provide good practice stations for individuals to use before or after class or during recreational time.

Advanced pitchers who have developed a fast pitch should learn to throw at the corners of the *strike zone*, which is the area over home plate between the batter's armpits and the top of the knees. They may also use a slant (a pitch that is released near one side of the pitcher's area and thrown diagonally toward the other side of home plate).

Batting

Batting is essential to the offense of any team. Unless players can hit the ball and get on base, they can never score runs. Every player on the team has the responsibility of batting. The batter must make judgments regarding the location, speed, and spin of the pitched ball. The batter should attend to the pitcher's grip on the ball, delivery, wrist action, and point of release to help make the necessary decisions regarding whether to swing and where to swing. In addition, the player should maintain focus on the ball as it approaches the plate.

Players should select a bat carefully. The batter should be able to hold the bat parallel with the ground when the bat is extended at arms' length over the plate. If the tip of the bat sags toward the ground, the swing will be low and under the pitch. This will result in hitting pop-ups or missing the ball altogether. If there are several bats available, use the one that feels a little heavy but can be held as noted. If there is little choice, move the hands away from the end of the handle until a good balance point is reached.

A light bat can be held with the hands at the end of the handle. This allows the bat to extend over home plate farther to reach pitches on the outside of the strike zone. For a medium-weight bat, slide both hands up the handle about 2 in. from the end. This shortens the reach a little but allows better control. When the bat is heavy, move the hands farther from the end of the handle (3 to 5 in.).

This is called *choking up*. It shortens the reach considerably but does allow better balance and control. It also keeps the bat from being tip-heavy and promotes a swing that is parallel to the ground. Whatever grip is used, the hands should always be kept close together.

The handle or grip of the bat should be small enough to let the thumb overlap the fingers when grasping the bat and large enough to prevent the fingernails from digging into the palm of the hand. Cork or taped handles usually provide a better gripping surface. Metal bats should have handles with a rough surface.

Full Swing

The batter swings through a large semicircular arc when executing the full swing. The batter must prepare mentally for the pitch by making the necessary judgments in a very short time period. Once the batter is committed to the full swing toward the ball, the intent is to hit the ball with maximum force to a specific field location. The amount of force that can be transferred to the ball is dependent on the momentum of the bat, which is the product of the mass and velocity (speed) of the bat at the moment of impact. Bat momentum is tempered with control for the purpose of accuracy.

Batting is a sidearm striking fundamental skill. The stance is parallel with the distribution of body weight forward and equal over both feet. The knees are slightly flexed and the trunk inclined slightly forward. The hips and shoulders are held level or parallel with the ground (See Figure 9.11).

The bat is held at shoulder height and slightly behind the head by flexing the shoulders and elbows. The head is turned toward the pitcher. The nondominant arm is diagonally positioned in front of the body and parallel with the ground. The dominant arm is bent with the elbow directed downward and slightly rearward. The wrists are hyperextended (cocked) to extend the bat vertically at an angle over the shoulder of the dominant side.

Figure 9.11. Batting stance

The swing forward begins with a forward stride or shift of body weight toward the pitcher. The striding foot is that foot closest to the pitcher. If the striding foot moves toward the plate and in front of the back foot, the hips are blocked from a complete rotation, and the ball contact will be early, thus directing the ball more to the right. This is referred to as a *closed stance*. If the striding foot steps back slightly with the toe of the foot pointing more out than straight ahead, the hips are open for more rotation, and the ball contact is late, thus directing the ball more to the left. This is referred to as an *open stance*.

The hips of the right-handed batter start the force production by rotating counterclockwise toward the pitcher. The arms with the bat continue to rotate toward the pitcher by rotating at the shoulders. The bat should be brought around level or parallel with the ground. The arms are extended at impact, and the wrists snap. The ball is contacted in front of the forward hip.

The follow-through is a continuation of the forward swinging. The bat remains level or parallel with the ground during the follow-through and is dropped to the ground at the conclusion of the follow-through.

Common Movement Problems and Suggestions. The following are common movement problems during the full swing. Instructional suggestions are also presented.

- Many players restrict the full swing by assuming the wrong stance in the batter's box. The incorrect stance can influence the entire swing. Therefore, this error should be corrected first.
- A common error is holding the elbows too close to the body. This cramps the swing and makes swinging awkward. This can be caused by standing too close to home plate.
- The force production of the swing can be depleted by not transferring the body weight during the swing, not swinging the bat rapidly, or not following through completely.
- Another common problem is lifting the head or closing the eyes just prior to impact. Generally, this causes the batter to miss the ball totally or to misdirect the hit.
- Instructors should emphasize the proper head position and focusing on the ball thoughout the swing.
- Instructors should check bat weight and grip. Many times this error in a player's choice of a bat creates

all types of errors in the swing itself, especially if the bat is too heavy.

- Many beginners continuously hit ground balls or pop-fly balls. This is generally caused by not swinging level. Diagonal swings upward create pop-fly balls and diagonal swings downward create ground balls. Observe the shoulders to be sure they stay level. A high leading shoulder results in a pop-up and a low leading shoulder in a chopping motion.
- Throwing the bat at the conclusion of batting can be very dangerous. Dropping the bat should be taught as a part of the skill even before running to first base is introduced.

Practice Drills. The following are batting drills. Beginners need practice swinging the bat and hitting a ball. They should not have to work on timing simultaneously. The use of a batting tee is appropriate for elementary school children. The ball just sits there on the tee ready to be hit. There are also commercial batting devices that allow the ball to be held steady for beginning practice. It is possible to make a batting device out of a rotating clothes-drying stand with straps attached. Velcro is sewn onto the straps, and pieces of Velcro are glued onto several old softballs, which are hung from the straps for the batter to hit. If a rotating clothes stand is used, the batter can take several hits in succession before stopping to reattach the balls. Drills 1.0 through 3.0 require the use of a batting tee or similar device.

1.0. Groups of Five to Seven. One person is the batter, another the catcher, and the others are fielders. The batter hits the ball off the tee, and the fielders retrieve it and throw it to the catcher, who puts it back on the tee. Be sure the catcher steps out of the way before the batter swings. Rotate after every five hits so that the batter can go to the outfield, catcher to the batter, and one outfielder to the catcher. The outfielders can be numbered for rotation order if necessary.

2.0. Groups of Six (Figure 9.12). The fielders form a semicircle 8 to 10 yd from the batting tee. The batter (B) tries to hit the ball firmly without using a full swing to each of the fielders in turn. The fielders return the ball to the catcher (C), who replaces it on the tee. This helps beginning batters learn to direct the ball to a certain area. They should learn to move the stance forward or back to change the direction of the ball.

3.0. Modified Softball Game. Players take positions and play as in a regular game except that the ball is hit off the tee, which is placed on home plate, rather than having a pitched ball. The pitcher acts only as another fielder.

4.0. Pepper. Six to eight players are positioned as in Figure 9.12, with four to six fielders. The batting tee

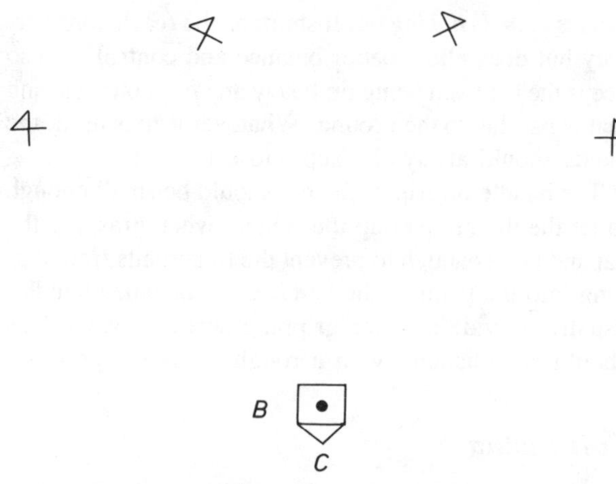

Figure 9.12. Batting and fielding with a tee

is removed. A fielder tosses the ball to the batter, who hits it. The player who fields the ball tosses it quickly back to the batter for the next hit. The tosses should be soft and easy at first but could become fast as skill improves. The batter should choke up on the bat, concentrate on meeting the ball with the bat, and try to hit ground balls. A full swing is unnecessary for this drill. Rotate players so that all get a chance to bat. Variation: Advanced players may use Pepper as a warm-up activity with these modifications. Number all players. The batter is Number 1, the catcher is Number 2, and fielders are Numbers 3 through 8 from one end of the line to the other. The fielders try to pitch the ball quickly enough or hard enough to make the batter miss or hit a foul ball. When this occurs, all players move up one position, and the batter goes to the end of fielders. This is a good drill to help players learn to watch the ball as it comes to the bat.

5.0. Groups of Eight or Nine. Set up home plate and a pitching rubber for each group. Each group has a pitcher, a catcher, two batters, and four or five fielders distributed about the field. One batter warms up and gets ready while the other batter hits the pitched balls. After five hits (not five pitches) the batter goes to the outfield, and a fielder comes in to warm up while the second batter hits. This continues until all fielders have batted. The pitcher and catcher then go to bat while two of the fielders take their places. Whenever possible, select a pitcher who is fairly accurate; time will be wasted chasing wild pitches. When there are several groups doing this drill, be sure that they are spaced far apart or are all hitting in the same direction to avoid collisions or players being hit by misdirected balls. If the practice time is short and the pitching poor, the number of hits may be reduced to three. In some instances with small classes, the instructor or coach may pitch to the batters if the instructor or coach can throw accurately.

Bunting

The *bunt* is a batting skill used by the more advanced players in the fast-pitch game only. It is not legal to bunt in slow-pitch softball. Teaching the bunt to beginners or even intermediate players is not recommended. They should learn to hit the ball first before moving on to the more refined skills. In addition, it is not fair to allow players to bunt the ball unless the catcher is close enough to home plate to field short bunts. This requires the catcher to wear full protective equipment, which most schools do not provide. The bunt is a soft hit of the ball in an attempt to have the ball roll to a stop about 8 or 10 ft from home plate near one of the base lines. This makes it difficult for the fielding team to reach the ball and throw it to a base in time to beat the *batter/baserunner*.

There are two types of bunts: those used as a base hit to get to first base and those planned as a *sacrifice* bunt, where the batter expects to be thrown out at first base but wants to move a baserunner ahead to another base. Both are executed the same way, except that the former should always come as a surprise to the fielders and be done when infielders are in their normal positions slightly behind the base paths.

Bunting is a combination of striking and force-receiving fundamental skills. The batter assumes a normal full-swing batting stance (as discussed previously under the full swing). The top hand on the bat is a loose grip. As the pitcher releases the ball, the batter turns to face the pitcher. The back foot of the right-handed batter moves counterclockwise to position the batter. As this step is in progress, the top hand on the bat slides upward on the bat. The hand slides midway up the bat with the palm of the hand on the back of the bat and the fingers clenched tightly against the palm. Avoid wrapping the fingers around the bat where they will be hit by the ball. The shoulders and bat should be parallel with the ground and the knees slightly flexed (Figure 9.13).

At the moment of impact, the bat is retracted by flexing the elbows. This procedure dissipates the force of the pitch. To direct the bunt, the batter can angle the top end of the bat. If the top end of the bat is retracted (back), the ball can be directed to the right. If the top end of the bat is forward, the ball can be directed to the left. When the bat is level or facing the pitcher, the ball can be directed toward the center. The reverse directions occur for the left-handed batter. Another method of directing the ball is to push the bat in the desired direction. This is used if the pitched ball approaches slowly.

Figure 9.13. Bunting position

After the ball rebounds off the bat, the batter drops the bat to the ground to begin running toward first base.

Common Movement Problems and Suggestions. The following are movement problems frequently encountered during bunting. Instructional suggestions are also presented.

- The most common problem is permitting the ball to rebound too much. This makes the playing of the ball easy for the opponent. This is generally caused by not retracting the bat (giving with the ball).
- Directing the ball incorrectly, such as popping the ball up in fair territory, is generally caused by not meeting the ball squarely or with a level bat.
- Improper placement of the sliding hand on the top end of the bat can lead to hand injuries. The hand becomes exposed to possible ball contact in this situation. Practicing with softer balls when first learning the skill of bunting should be helpful. Emphasize keeping the fingers retracted against the palm.
- Players need to recognize the different pitches to use them to the best advantage in bunting. The best type of pitch for bunting is the low pitch.

Practice Drills. The following are drills for practicing the bunt. Only advanced players would use these drills.

1.0. See Figure 9.11. This drill pattern can be used for bunting practice if the tee is removed. The batter turns to face the fielders, who are about 5 yd away, and bunts the balls that are tossed as in Pepper (Drill 4.0 for batting). Variation: Batter turns side to fielders and assumes regular batting stance. As toss is made, the batter turns to face the fielders and bunts the ball. This gives practice in the pivot turn to achieve the bunting stance. Players rotate after five bunts or as described in Drill 4.0 for batting.

2.0. Modified Game. Players are positioned as in a regular game. The batting team must bunt rather than swing at the ball. The first- and third-base players can move closer to home plate to be ready for the bunt. Batters bunt five balls and run to first base after the fifth bunt, trying to reach the base before the ball is thrown there. Fielders and batters exchange places after everyone on the team has had a turn.

3.0. As in Drill 2.0 for Bunting (Modified Game). A member of the batting team is placed at first base as a runner. The batter bunts the ball down the third-base line and runs out the hit. Fielders try to throw out the baserunners at second or at first. Variations are as follows:

3.1. Add a baserunner at second base. The bunt could roll along the first- or the third-base lines.

3.2. Move the baserunner to third base. The bunt should be along the first-base line in this case to avoid hitting the baserunner, who is attempting to score from third base.

Place Hitting

Batters who can place a hit anywhere on the field are a definite asset to a team. Generally, right-handed batters tend to hit to left field and left-handers to right field. Defensive players learn to expect this. *Place hitting* the ball to the *opposite field* (right for right-handers and left for left-handers) or to spaces between the fielders will open more scoring opportunities and confuse the defense. The placed hit may not go as far as a regular hit because the bat is choked up on for better control. This causes some loss of power, but, because the ball is placed to spaces between fielders, this is of less importance.

Footwork. Besides choking up on the bat about 2 or 3 in. (or using a lighter-weight bat), the hitter should stand well away from the plate and stride toward the direction the hit is to go (Figure 9.14). Players should be sure not to step out of the batter's box. A hit made while out of the batter's box is an out. The ball should be hit firmly, but the backswing may be somewhat shorter and the follow-through extended in the direction of the hit ball. A level swing is essential. For a right-handed batter, an outside pitch is easier to hit to right field, and an inside pitch generally goes to left field. The reverse is true for a left-handed batter.

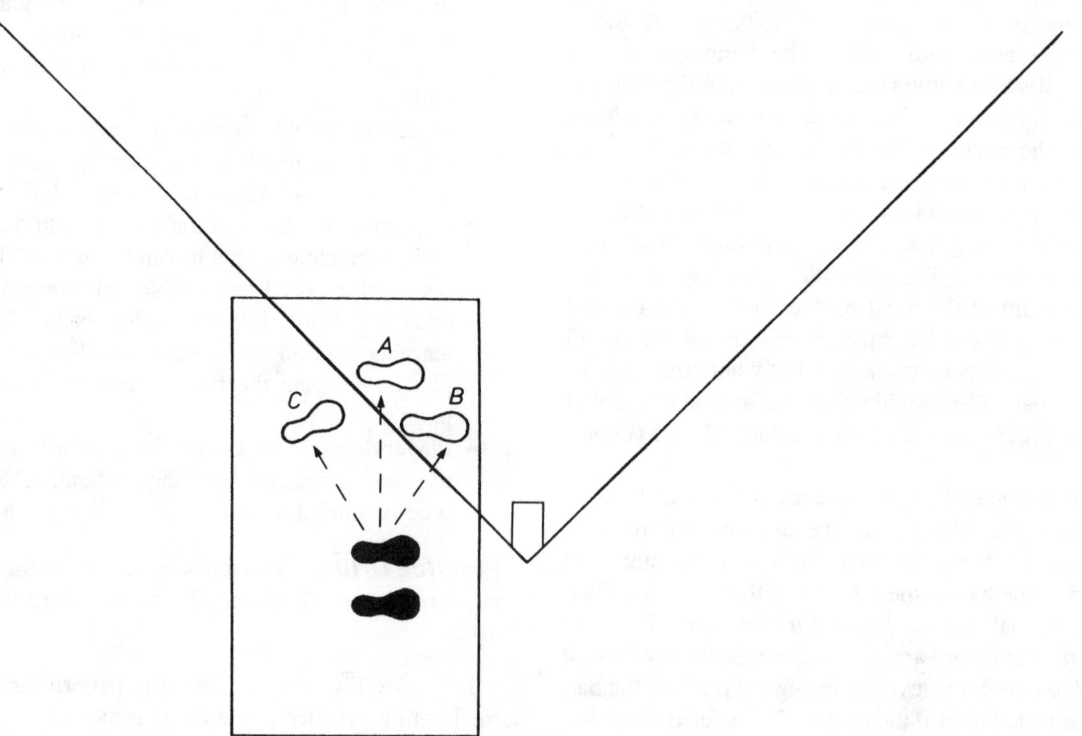

Figure 9.14. Right-handed batter's stride for place hitting: (A) straightaway, (B) right field, and (C) left field

Practice Drills. The following are drills for place hitting. Fielding skills of other players can be practiced simultaneously with place-hitting practice.

1.0. Divide into groups of seven or eight players. Each group consists of a catcher, a pitcher, a batter, and four or five fielders (Figure 9.15). Play on a regular diamond or establish a pitcher's plate and a home plate for each group. Groups should be at least 50 to 60 ft apart and all hitting in the same direction if this close. The fielders are in a semicircle about 50 or 60 ft from the batter. The batter chokes up on the bat slightly and tries to hit to each fielder in turn. This is like the game of Pepper (Drill 4.0 for batting) except that the fielders are farther from the hitter, who uses a full or almost a full swing. Rotate after five or six hits so that all players get a chance to place hit.

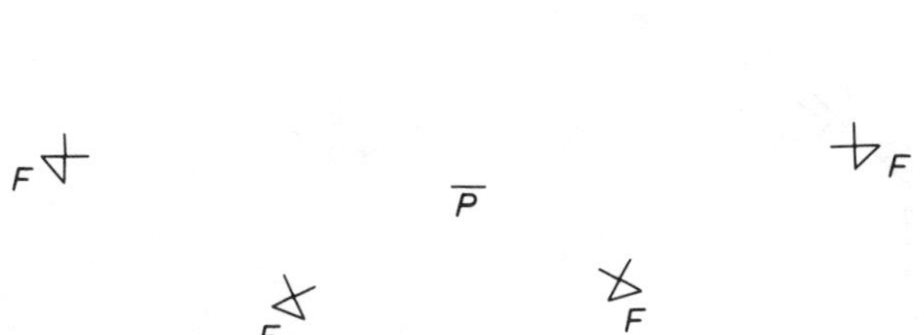

Figure 9.15. Place hitting: C = catcher, B = batter, P = pitcher, and F = fielders

2.0. Place hitting also can be practiced using the batting drills and most of the general practice drills.

Baserunning

Good baserunning can be the key to winning games. Players must learn how to get a quick start and how to get to the next base as fast as possible. The general mechanics of running can be found in chapter 3.

Batter Becoming Baserunner

When a batter hits the ball, the weight will be on the forward foot. Therefore, the first step toward first base should be on the other foot or the back foot. This would be the right foot for right-handed batters and the left foot for left-handed batters. The body should be kept low with the arms pumping strongly for the first few steps. The running action should begin as soon as the ball is hit. To avoid wasting time, the batter should not wait to see where the ball is going.

Because there is no need to stop at first base, batter/baserunners should continue to run until they pass first base. They do not stop at the base because this causes them to slow down before getting there. The runners should not leap or lunge at the base but should use a normal running stride, touching the outside of the base (near the foul line) to avoid colliding with the first-base player. Batter/baserunners may overrun first base without jeopardy as long as they return directly to first base and make no obvious movement toward second base. Runners should not overrun second or third base or they can be put out with a *tag* while off base.

The baserunner that hopes to get more than one base after hitting the ball would move 2 or 3 ft outside the base path on nearing first base, curve around the inside of the base touching the inside corner with the left foot, and run on toward second base. The same pattern would be used any time a runner expects to round one base and go on to the next (Figure 9.16).

Practice Drills. The following are baserunning drills. When the bat is used in the drill, emphasize not throwing the bat.

1.0. Column Formation (Figure 4.2). Players are about 4 ft apart in the column. Columns of individuals are parallel and about 10 ft apart. All players take a regular batting stance, holding an imaginary bat, with their sides toward one wall or line, where a pitcher will be. On the verbal signal "Hit" or a whistle sounded by the leader, all swing as if hitting a ball, pivot on the lead foot, and take three or four steps at a 45° angle to the right (225° for the left-handed batter). This simulates where first base would be. All players return to their columns. This could be repeated several times until the players get the feel for the footwork. With younger players, the instructor or coach should specify a point of reference toward which to run that approximates a 45° angle.

2.0. Column Formation Near the Side of the Batter's Box (Figure 9.17). The first person in the column steps into the batter's box, swings the bat, drops it, and starts toward first base. After running about halfway to first (Point A), the player returns to the end of the column while the next person steps into the box. Emphasize stepping toward first base on the back foot, dropping (not throwing) the bat, and swinging the arms to help with the running start. Variations include the following:

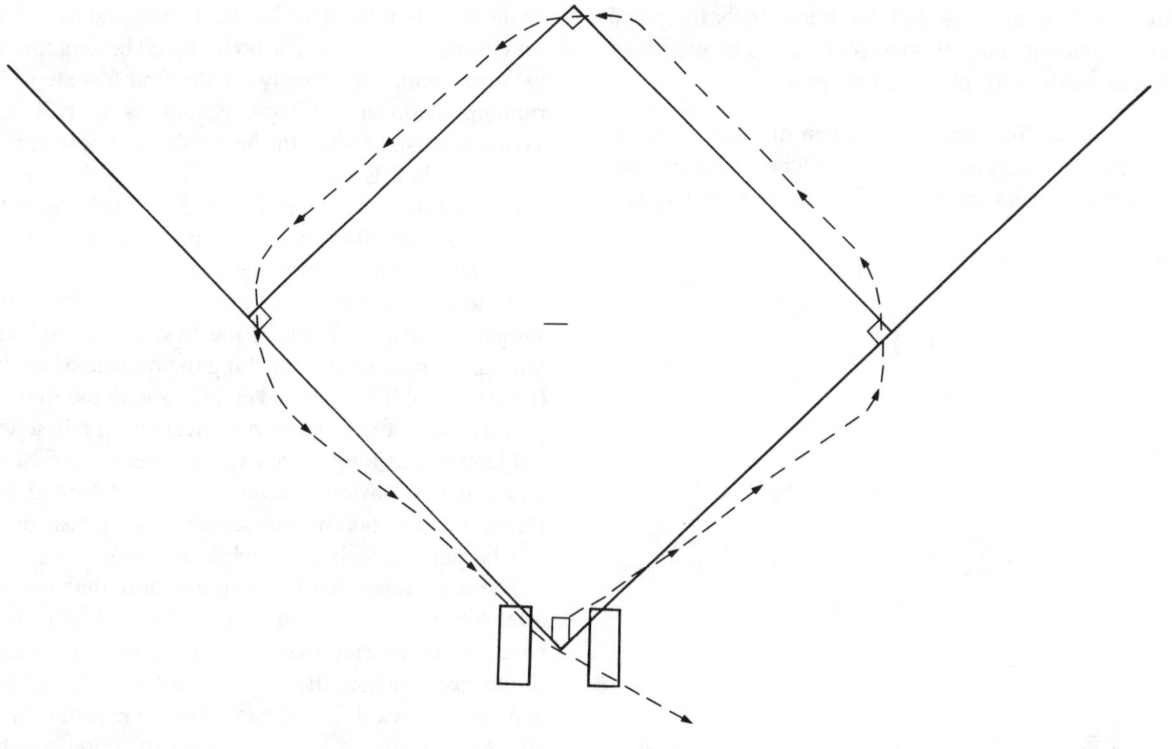

Figure 9.16. Path of baserunner rounding bases

2.1. The batter/baserunner continues past first base and runs toward second base (Point B) to practice the rounding pattern.

2.2. If space is limited, a second column could be positioned using second base as home plate. These players would run toward third base after swinging the bat.

2.3. The formation shown in Figure 9.17 may be used for timing baserunners. This could be done for motivational purposes or as a means of selecting players for a team. The first player steps into the box and, on a signal from the timer, swings the bat and runs to first base (or farther). The time starts at the signal and stops when the specified base is touched. The timer may wish to start timing after the swing or as home plate is crossed.

Baserunner Advancing

Once a player reaches a base and play has stopped, this player must be ready to move on to the next base as soon as play resumes and the opportunity arises. In slow-pitch this means waiting for the next hit before moving to the next base. *Base stealing* is not allowed in the slow pitch game. Runners must remain in contact with the base until the pitched ball reaches home plate or is hit by the batter. However, they should be alert and ready to run with each pitch. Many coaches prefer that runners start as the pitched ball reaches home plate so that they will already be in motion when the ball is hit. If it is not hit, they must return to their base.

The baserunner in the fast-pitch game may leave the base when the pitcher releases the ball (actually when the heel of the nonpivot foot crosses the pitcher's plate). This allows the baserunner to leave the base before the ball gets to home plate and to be in motion if the ball is hit. If the ball is not hit, the baserunner may have to stop and quickly return to the base to avoid being caught off base by a quick throw from the catcher.

Very fast runners can take advantage of this *leadoff* opportunity to steal a base, especially second base, which requires a long, accurate throw from the catcher. Slower runners have to watch the catcher and wait for a misplay or a poor pitch before attempting to steal.

Several stances are used by fast-pitch baserunners when leading off. In one stance, the baserunner faces the catcher with the left foot touching the base. The runner uses side-sliding steps 6 to 8 ft along the base path as the ball leaves the pitcher's hand. This position allows a good view of the play and a fast return to base but requires a pivot before getting into full running stride. This is a typical style of baseball players who are allowed to leave the base before the pitch.

In another style of leadoff, the baserunner takes a sprint-start position facing second base in a slight crouch with the toe of the back foot braced against the base and

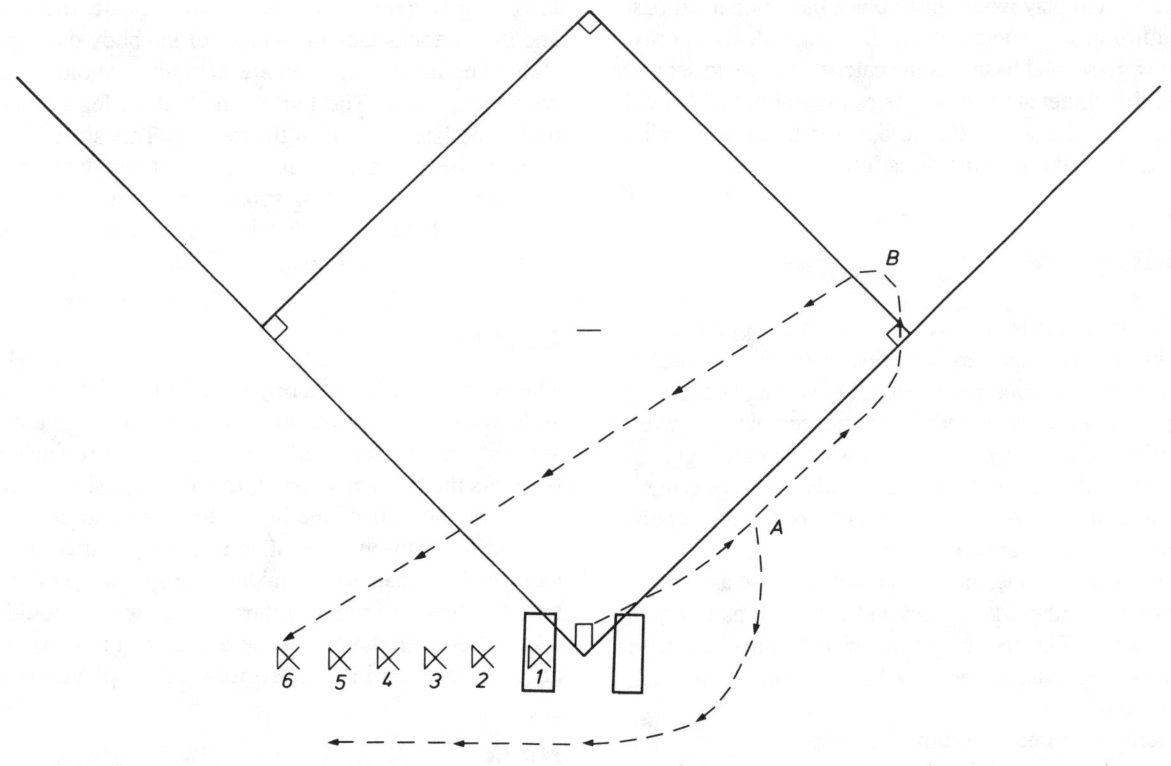

Figure 9.17. Baserunning drill

the front foot 12 to 18 in. down the base path. This positions the runner for a good push-off as the pitched ball is released. This style allows for faster movement from the base without the need to pivot if a full running stride is necessary. It does not allow as good a view of the batter and catcher or as fast a return if no advance is possible.

A third style of leadoff utilizes the sprint-start position but has the front foot on the edge of the base nearest the next base and the back foot behind the base. The runner can then start in motion as the pitcher begins the forward arm swing because by the time the runner's front foot leaves the base the pitched ball should be on its way to the plate. This style allows the fastest start from the base but requires an agile and alert runner if a quick return to base is needed.

A baserunner who is directed to steal a base or who is committed to run should use the sprint start and avoid turning to watch the catcher (this would slow the runner). If runners do this, they should use the sprint start for every leadoff; otherwise, the opponents will know when they plan to steal a base.

Baserunners who wish to advance to the next base after a fly ball has been caught should also use a sprint start. The runner must remain in contact with the base until the ball touches the fielder and then may advance with the liability of being put out. If the play is in front of the runner, the runner should watch the ball carefully and be prepared to start the instant the fielder touches it. If the play is behind the runner (e.g., runner at second base and fly ball to right field), the runner could watch the third-base coach, who would watch the ball and signal the runner when to leave base.

Practice Drills. The following are drills for baserunner advancing. Batting drills 3.0 and 5.0 and bunting drills 2.0 and 3.0 could also be used for baserunning practice. Also see General Practice Drills.

1.0. Mass Formation. Players spread out 5 or 6 ft apart facing the instructor or coach. All players practice the slide-step leadoff and the sprint start. The instructor gives a signal to denote the hit or the released pitch, and the players move as if leaving a base.

2.0. Groups of Seven. Place defensive players on the diamond as first-, second-, and third-base players as well as pitcher and catcher. The other two players will be baserunners at first and second bases. As the pitcher pitches the ball, the baserunners practice moving off base several times as allowed by whichever rules apply. Then the baserunners (one or both) attempt to steal. This also gives the catcher a chance to practice throws to bases. Although slow-pitch players are not allowed to steal a base, this drill gives them practice moving off the base quickly as they would when the ball is hit. Rotate players after each stealing attempt until all players have had a chance to practice baserunning. A variation for fast-pitch play would be to place baserunners at first and third bases. The runner at first base steals to draw a throw to second base. As the catcher throws to second base, the runner at third base tries to steal home. Infield players could also use this to develop a defensive plan to deal with the stealing situation.

Sliding

Sliding into base is an advanced skill that should not be taught or encouraged in the average secondary school class. Many instructors do not allow sliding because of the potential for injury with inexperienced players. Even experienced players often get abrasions on the legs, especially if they do not wear protective leg coverings. Information on sliding is presented here for the benefit of coaches of advanced players.

The purpose of the slide is to reach the base as quickly as possible without going beyond it as well as to try to evade a tag. Players should never slide into first base because they usually need not be concerned with a tag at that base.

There are three recommended types of slides: the straight (feet first) slide, the hook slide, and the bent-leg slide. The head-first slide or dive should be discouraged. The potential for injury in the dive is too great.

Technique Generalizations

Sliding is a receiving-of-force fundamental skill. Sliding simulates controlled falling. The slide is initiated by leaning back at the appropriate distance from the base. This leaning lowers the body to the ground. The sliding begins when a body surface meets the ground with a substantially small amount of friction. Sliding is initiated when less friction than is necessary to adhere two surfaces together occurs. This is accomplished in sliding by thrusting the side of the foot against the surface. As the player continues to lean, or lower, the body to the ground, more body-surface area comes in contact with the ground. The more body surface area in contact with the ground, the more friction is created. The increasing friction accompanies increased deceleration or slowing down of the total body. The gradual increasing of friction between the body and the ground is essential to successful sliding.

Straight

The straight slide is done with the body stretched out, usually partially on the side, although some prefer the back. It should be done from the full stride. As the runner starts the slide about 10 to 12 ft from the base, the top leg is extended straight toward the base while the lower leg is flexed. The outside of the calf, the thigh, and the buttocks take the weight of the body during the slide. The hands and head are held up to avoid contact with the ground. The foot of the bottom leg is tucked under the knee or calf of the top leg. This slide is used to reach the base as soon as possible without overrunning it. If the slider is wearing spiked shoes, be sure that the spikes are held up so that they do not stick into the ground and do not impale the fielder.

Bent Leg

The bent-leg slide is merely a variation of the straight slide with the body on the side. Instead of remaining straight, the top leg is allowed to flex as it touches the base. As the top leg is flexed, the player pushes up with the knee and calf of the leg underneath and comes to a standing position. This slide is usually started a little closer to base than is the straight slide so that the momentum will help the runner return to the feet. It should be used whenever there may be a chance to advance to another base, as in an overthrow or misplayed ball.

Hook

The hook slide is done primarily to evade a tag. The body is launched past the side of the base, and the toe of the top leg is stretched out to hook the near corner of the base as the legs slide by the base. The knee of the top leg is flexed so that the toe remains hooked on the base until the body stops moving (Figure 9.18).

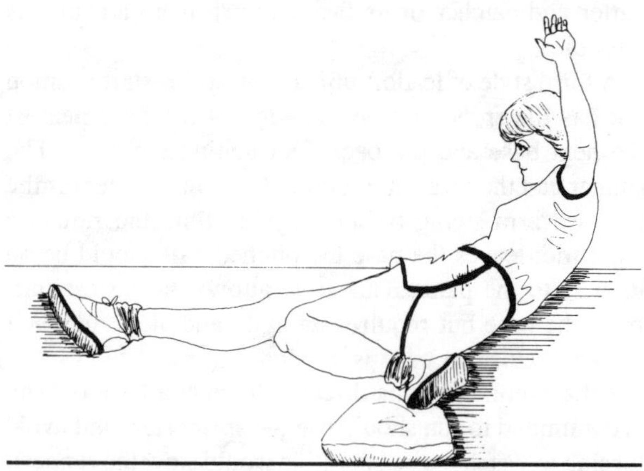

Figure 9.18. Hook slide

Common Movement Problems and Suggestions

The following are common problems during the execution of sliding. Instructional suggestions are also presented.

- One common problem is catching the cleats in the ground or having too much body surface make initial contact with the ground. The slide may cause an injury in this situation or decelerate the slider too fast, making the player too slow.
- If the player tries to catch the body with the hands or forearm when leaning back, an injury is very possible. Progressive instruction to alleviate the fear of sliding should remedy this problem.
- Players may make poor judgments as to when the initiation of the slide should occur. Early initiation of the slide might slow the slider or even prevent the player from reaching the base. A late initiation of the slide can cause the player to slide past the base. A fast runner should start the slide action about 10 ft from the base.

Practice Drills

Practicing the slide is difficult because if the runner does not start with good speed, no slide will occur. It cannot be done in slow motion. A modified practice can be done with little chance of injury if there is a large sand pile (such as a jumping pit) or a beach nearby. Players can practice running and sliding in loose sand without harm; however, they should wear long pants or sliding pads.

A rather steep, grassy (or sandy) slope can also be used for practicing the slide. Players stand sideward on the slope near the top, lean toward the uphill slope, put one hand on the ground, lift both feet, push off down the slope, and land on the side of the bottom leg (the one nearest the hill). The top leg stretches out as if toward a base. Practice sliding on each side. Good players can hook slide to either side of the base.

The next step is to go to a moderate-speed run and try the slide on the ball diamond. Make the sliding area as safe as possible by removing all stones and any hard objects or surface protusions.

General Practice Drills

There are several good games and drills that can be used to practice combinations of softball skills simultaneously. These can be used after most of the basic skills have been learned to add motivation and stimulate interest.

1.0. Infield Practice. A defensive infield lineup is placed on the field (three base players, a shortstop, and a catcher). A leader or instructor stands near the batter's box and hits balls to each of the fielders in turn. The player fields the ball and throws it to the first-base player, who returns it to the catcher. The batter receives the ball and hits to another fielder. Two or three persons could line up at each of the positions and rotate in after each player has a turn. Variations include the following:

1.1. Throw the ball to second base and then to first as in a double play.

1.2. Throw to third base.

1.3. Throw directly to the catcher.

1.4. Add outfielders.

2.0. Outfield Practice (Fungo Hitting). Several fielders scatter about in an outfieldlike area. A batter tosses the ball up to him- or herself and hits fly and ground balls to the fielders. Players field all the balls that come to them. A catcher can be used to receive the balls from the outfield and then toss them to the batter, or the batter can receive the balls directly. If a catcher is available, two balls can be used. While one is being returned to the catcher, the other one is hit. Variations include the following:

2.1 Fielders form a column in the outfield area. The first person in line fields the first hit wherever it goes, throws the ball to the catcher, and goes to the end of the line. This procedure continues for all subsequent players in the line. This variation is effective only if the hitter can direct the ball reasonably well.

2.2. After a fielder catches two fly balls or four ground balls, this player becomes the batter, and the batter goes to the outfield. This might be varied to three fly balls or six ground balls if there are only a few players. The count could be cumulative from one batter to the next or start over with each new batter.

3.0. Hit and Lay Down (Hit the Bat). A batter and several scattered fielders (3 to 10) are arranged as in general practice drill 2.0. The batter hits the ball to a fielder and lays the bat down perpendicular to the path of the throw coming back to the batter. The fielder throws or rolls the ball trying to hit the bat. If successful, that fielder becomes the batter, and the batter goes to the field. If the ball does not touch the bat, the batter hits again and continues until someone hits the bat with the thrown ball. This is not a good practice drill for beginners because many cannot toss balls up to themselves and hit them.

4.0. Batting, Fielding, and Pitching Practice. A full defensive lineup is placed on the diamond, and there are three or four assigned batters. Each batter hits three to five balls, then goes to the field to replace a fielder who comes in to take a turn batting. Players who field a ground ball throw it to first base. Caught fly balls are returned to the pitcher. The batters may practice base-running by running to the base on the last hit. This drill is good for use by regular teams as a practice session. Variation: For fast pitch players, have the batters bunt the last hit and run to first base trying to beat the throw. This gives bunting practice, too.

5.0. Work-Up. Players are distributed in the field and given numbers as follows: catcher (1), pitcher (2), first base (3), second base (4), third base (5), shortstop (6), left fielder (7), left center (8), right center (9), and right fielder (10). Four or five players are assigned as batters. The batters try to hit safely, and the fielders try to get them out. Batters continue as hitters and baserunners until they are put out, when they take the place of Player 10 (the right fielder). Then all defensive players move up one position. The catcher becomes a batter, the pitcher moves to catcher, and the first-base player moves to pitcher. This continues until a full rotation occurs with all players changing positions. Variations include the following:

5.1. There may be as few as 7 defensive players or more than 10.

5.2. Batters may be required to go to the field after scoring 3, 4, or 5 runs. This will give more players a chance to bat and would be particularly useful if the skills of a few players were clearly superior to the others.

5.3. With beginners who are unable to pitch well, one selected player or the instructor may wish to pitch continuously to expedite the game. The other players would then rotate around this position.

6.0. One-Pitch Softball. A regular softball field is used. The group is divided into two teams. One team is in the field while the other team is up to bat. Assigned pitchers from each team pitch to their own teammates. Only one pitch is allowed to each batter. The ball must be hit, or an out is declared; there are no alternatives. Once the ball is hit, regular rules apply. Teams change places after 3 outs. Pitchers may begin pitching as soon as the first batter is ready. They do not need to wait for the fielding team to get into defensive position. This encourages fast changes from field to batting and vice versa, which helps keep players alert. The team scoring the most runs wins the game. The pitcher must be a player who has reasonably good control. Change pitchers periodically (e.g., after 3 innings) to allow pitchers a chance to bat. Variations include the following:

6.1. Instead of changing from batting to fielding after every 3 outs, every member of the batting team goes up to bat before the teams switch. The team scoring more runs in the same number of innings wins the game. The teams should be composed of an equal number of players.

6.2. If the batter hits a foul ball, a second pitch is allowed.

6.3. This game can be played indoors readily using a mush ball or whiffle ball and a bat.

Base Play

The offensive players (baserunners) and the defensive players (baseplayers) must all learn to play the bases. Skilled offensive play at the bases helps to score runs. Skilled defensive play results in more outs. Both types of skillful play are essential for safe play.

Offensive

For the baserunner this means learning where to touch the base. Baserunners who are rounding a base to go to the next one should touch the inside corner of the base with the left foot if possible. This allows a pivot on the left foot and less deviation from the base path. However, the runner should not break stride (interrupt the running movement) just to touch base with the left foot. In this case, the right foot can be used (also see the section on baserunning).

Defensive

The defensive baseplayer needs to know how to tag the base in a *force-out* as well as how to tag a runner when there is no force play. The force play occurs when a runner is forced to run to a base because the player hit the ball and must go to first base or because someone else hit the ball and the other baserunners must advance. Note that if there is an empty base behind a baserunner, then that baserunner does not have to run when the batter hits the ball. Thus, there is no force play for that runner.

When preparing to tag a base to force a runner out, the baseplayer should stand on the side of the base closest to where the ball is and wait for the throw from a teammate. As the ball comes, the baseplayer touches the near side of the base with one toe (usually the foot opposite the catching hand for maximum reach) and reaches out toward the ball with the glove hand. Care should be taken to maintain contact with the base but to leave the baserunner room to touch the base. This is done so that the baserunner does not hit or step on the player's foot. Baseplayers should step away from the base as soon as the ball has been caught to reduce the chance of a collision with the runner.

Tagging the runner calls for different positioning. If the runner is not sliding into the base, the fielder should try to stand beside the base path and tag the runner with the ball held in both hands as the runner goes past. The ball itself does not need to touch the runner as long as the hand (or glove) holding the ball makes contact. The hands and arms of the fielder should give way with the contact (i.e., follow the path of the runner) to avoid having the ball knocked from the grasp. The fielder may even spin away from the runner to help absorb the force of the contact.

The baseplayer facing a sliding runner should straddle the base with one foot on each side of the base path being used by the runner. The ball should be held in the glove hand just above the ground between the base and the runner so that the slide carries the runner into the glove. The baseplayer must watch the runner so that if a hook slide is executed, the glove and ball can be moved to the appropriate corner of the base. Baseplayers should never stand between the base and the slider because injury is quite possible in this position. As with any tag play, the hands should give with the contact to absorb the force and retract quickly after the touch. This helps prevent a fumble and also allows the baseplayer to prepare for the next play.

Practice Drills

When there are enough balls, players may be paired to practice playing the base. Each partner stands near a base or a base-sized area defined on the ground. Partners throw the ball back and forth practicing touching the base with one foot while reaching for the thrown ball.

Practice tagging a runner can be done the same way, except that the player straddles the base, receives the ball, and bends to hold the ball near the ground at the side of the base as if tagging the runner. The thrower should practice aiming low toward the base so that the baseplayer does not have to move much after the catch. Additional base-play practice will be described in the General Practice Drills.

Offense

A good offensive team relies on batting and baserunning to score runs. Baserunners must be alert and use the skills and techniques described earlier. Batters need to be able to hit the ball hard and get away from home plate quickly.

Batting Order

The arrangement of the *batting order* can help the team in its offense. The best hitters should come to bat when there are runners on base to maximize scoring. Therefore, the best arrangement is to have high-average short-ball hitters bat first to get on base. Then the home-run or long-ball hitters come to bat to bring them home.

The first batter should be a consistent hitter (not necessarily a long-ball hitter) or one who gets walked frequently and can run fast. The second batter should be a good place hitter and a fast runner who can beat out short hits and advance the first batter around the bases. In fast pitch, the second batter must be good at bunting. The third batter should be able to hit hard to the outfield to either score the previous batters or get one player to third base. The fourth batter is the strongest and best hitter on the team (the cleanup batter). The fifth batter is the next-best hitter, and so on down to the 9th or 10th hitter, who would be the weakest hitter on the team. Some teams prefer to have the pitcher bat in the last position to allow more rest time. The 9th or 10th batter on a team does not bat as often as those higher in the batting order. However, pitchers who hit well should be placed higher in the order.

When a team is using a designated hitter (fast pitch) or an extra hitter (slow pitch), these batters should be worked into the lineup using the same strategy noted. Usually, they would be superior hitters and would bat in the third, fourth, or fifth place in the order.

Base Coaching

For formal or informal game play the use of base coaches is recommended. League teams no doubt have coaches or specific players who could serve in this capacity. Games played in class or as casual recreational activities should also have coaches to assist base runners. These coaches would probably be members of the batting team who are not scheduled to bat for a while (e.g., the eighth or ninth batter during the first inning). They need not be the same persons throughout the game. In classes, nonparticipating players could be the base coaches. This gets them involved and provides them with relevant learning opportunities.

The first-base coach should watch the hit ball, encourage the batter/baserunners to get to first, and tell them to round the base if there is a chance for an extra base. If the team is using signals to give instructions to the batter or baserunners (e.g., bunt, *hit-and-run*, or take a pitch), the first-base coach should make those signals for right-handed batters. This coach is responsible for baserunners from the time they leave home plate until they reach second base.

The third-base coach assumes responsibility for baserunners when they are on second base. These coaches must make important decisions related to scoring runs. They either stop runners at third base or send them on to home plate. Most runners coming in to third base have their backs to the play being made by the defense. They must watch and rely on the third-base coach to let them know what to do. Runners rounding second base should immediately look to the third-base coach for advice about advancing to third base.

Base coaches must use hand signals to give information to approaching runners. The noise level may be too high for voice commands to be heard, and opponents may also be yelling commands to confuse the runner. Common signals are the hands held palm out toward the runner (stop), the hands held palm down toward the ground (slide), and one arm (or both) waved toward the next base (go on to that base).

Signals to tell batters what to do are used only in more advanced play. These vary widely and are not discussed here.

General Strategies

All batters should do the following:

- Watch the pitched ball carefully.
- Start the swing as the ball is released and stop if the pitch is poor.
- Hold the bat off the shoulder when the pitcher gets ready to pitch.
- Avoid swinging at pitches outside the strike zone.
- Hold the bat firmly but avoid tensing the entire body.
- Be ready to hit every pitch.
- Move to the back of the batter's box for a fast-ball pitcher and choke up or use a lighter bat.
- Move toward the front of the batter's box for slower pitchers or in the slow-pitch game.
- Run out each hit even if it looks like a foul ball or a sure out. Fielders can make errors.
- Be ready to hit when stepping into the batter's box. Do not make a lot of preliminary movements while in the box such as swinging the bat and shuffling the feet. An alert pitcher will watch for these and pitch the ball before the batter is ready to hit.
- Learn to place hit. With a runner on second or third base, a hit to right field gives the runner more time to advance.

Baserunners should do the following:

- Be ready to run with each pitch.
- Watch the base coaches for directions, especially when the ball is behind the runner.
- Try to advance until there is an empty base behind you. This eliminates the possibility of a force play.
- Move a short distance down the base path when a short fly ball is hit to the outfield. If it is missed, continue on; if it is caught, return to base quickly.
- Stay on base when a long fly ball is hit and there may be a chance to advance after the catch. This might occur on a hit to right field with the baserunner on second base. The throw to third base would be a very long one.
- Know how many outs there are.
- After 2 outs, run on every hit even if it is a fly ball. If the fly is caught, it will be the third out; if the fly is missed, the runner has a good start.
- Know where the other runners are positioned at all times. Do not catch up to or overrun them.
- Never have a change of mind in the middle of a slide. This is how sliders get injured.

Defense

Defense in softball requires alertness in all fielders. Each person should be ready to move with each pitch. If the ball is hit, the defensive players can move quickly into position, whether to field the ball, cover a base, relay a throw, or back up a teammate. Every player has a job to do whenever the ball is hit. In general, infielders field ground balls and infield hits and cover the bases. Outfielders field long hits and fly balls, and back up the infielders and one another. Besides catching pitches, catchers field bunts and cover home plate. Pitchers may have to back up play at the bases.

Before each pitch is made, every defensive player should mentally review the situation and determine what to do if the batter hits the ball. Plans must be made for several options: (a) a ground ball hit to yourself; (b) a ground ball hit to a teammate; (c) a fly ball hit to yourself; or (d) a fly ball hit to a teammate. Other relevant factors to be considered are (a) whether runners are on base, (b) whether a runner is in position to score, (c) the number of outs, and (d) the speed of the batter and the baserunners. When beginners first start to play in gamelike situations, the instructor or coach may wish to question defensive players as each new batter comes to bat to make sure that they know where to throw the ball if it is hit to them. For example, if there is a runner on first base and only 1 out, where should the ground ball be thrown if fielded by an infielder? Who should cover second base in this instance? This type of questioning takes only a few seconds, and it can help young players learn to plan their moves so that they do not waste time trying to figure out what to do with the ball after they field it.

Defensive players must be prepared to move in any direction when the ball is batted (Figure 9.19). They should assume a ready position with each pitch. The feet may be parallel with each other or one slightly ahead in a comfortable stride position. The knees should be slightly flexed with the body leaning forward. The hands could rest on the knees until the ball is pitched. The body is tensed, the hands come up in front, and the weight is shifted to the balls of both feet as the ball is pitched. When moving backward to get to a ball hit over the head, turn the body around with the back to the pitcher and watch the ball over the shoulder. Do not try to run backward; it is much too slow.

Backing Up Teammates

Players must learn that they have a job to do every time the ball is hit. If the ball is hit to them, they must field it; if not, they must either cover a base or back up a

Figure 9.19. Ready position for fielder

teammate. When backing up a play, fielders should first try to get in line with the hit or the throw and then move closer to the play. Try to stay 12 to 20 ft away from the play to have time to react to an overthrow or misplay. Some of the general backup responsibilities for specific players are listed in Table 9.1. Players with no particular responsibility should try to line themselves up with anticipated plays to help if necessary.

Sometimes coaches may wish to modify the backup assignments due to the skills of particular players. An outfielder with speed and outstanding throwing ability may be expected to try to back up all long hits, or a shortstop with a long hard throw may serve as the relay person for throws from any outfielder whenever possible. Pitchers may need to conserve their strength and be relieved of backup and covering responsibilities.

Table 9.1 General Backup Responsibilities for Specific Players

Player	Backs up
Right fielder	First-base player Second-base player Center fielder Overthrows at first base
Center fielder	Second-base player Shortstop Right fielder Left fielder
Left fielder	Third-base player Shortstop Center fielder Overthrows at third base
Third-base player	Shortstop Second base for throws from right field
Shortstop (covers second base on hits to right side of diamond)	Third-base player Second base when second-base player is covering base Relay throws from left and center fielders
Second-base player (covers second base on hits to left side of diamond)	First-base player Shortstop when taking plays at second base Relay throws from right field
First-base player	Second-base player (occasionally) Home plate on throws from outfield after long hits Second base (on throws from left fielder if second-base player is covering the base)
Catcher	First base on throws from right side of diamond and no runner on second or third base
Pitcher	Third base after a long hit Home plate after long hits or if first-base player is occupied Second base on throws from center field
Extra center fielder (slow pitch only)	Either second base player or shortstop Other center fielder Either right or left fielder

Relaying the Ball

When long balls are hit to the outfield and fielders will be unable to throw the ball all the way back to the infield or home plate, teammates must move to help them *relay* the ball to the desired location. These relay players are usually the second-base player or the shortstop. The second-base player moves toward right field as the relay person on the right side of the field, whereas the shortstop makes relays on the left side of the field. When one runs out to relay a throw to the infield, the other watches the baserunners and calls out advice about where to throw the ball. This way the relay person who is facing away from the play can receive the ball, pivot, and throw to the correct base.

Specific Situations

Responsibilities of players in specific situations are described in the following diagrams. These indicate typical situations and again may be modified to suit special player skills or deficiencies.

No One on Base, Hit Toward First Base (Figure 9.20).

1. The first-base player fields the ball. If there is plenty of time, the base player calls the others off by voice and runs to the base for the force-out.
2. The second-base player moves to back up the first-base player and then on to cover first base.
3. The pitcher moves toward first base but covers it only if the second-base player must stop to field the ball. Some prefer the pitcher to cover the base, especially in slow pitch.
4. The catcher moves down the foul line to back up the throw.
5. The right fielder backs up the first-base player.
6. The shortstop covers second base.
7. Others back up or cover the next potential play if an error occurs.

No One on Base, Long Hit to Right Field (Figure 9.21).

1. The right fielder fields the ball. If the right fielder is far away, throw to a relay player.
2. The center fielder backs up the right fielder.
3. The second-base player moves to short right field to relay the throw if necessary.
4. The shortstop covers second base.
5. The third-base player covers third base.
6. The left fielder backs up a throw from right field to second base.
7. The pitcher backs up third base.
8. The first-base player moves to back up the catcher if a home run is anticipated.

The right fielder must decide where to throw the ball. The shortstop or first-base player should call out instructions because the second-base player will be facing the outfield.

No One on Base, Long Hit to Left Field (Figure 9.22).

1. The left fielder fields the ball and uses a relay if necessary.
2. The center fielder backs up the right fielder.
3. The shortstop moves to short left field for a relay throw.
4. The second- and third-base players cover their bases.
5. The right fielder backs up second base in case of a throw from the left fielder.
6. The pitcher backs up third base.
7. The first-base player backs up the catcher.

The left fielder must decide whether to throw to second base or third base or to use the relay person. The second- or third-base player should call advice about where to make the play.

Double Plays

When there is a runner on first base and fewer than two outs, infielders should try to get 2 outs when fielding a ground ball. This is called a *double play*. The easiest way to complete a double play is to throw the ball first to second base and then to first base. The runner advancing to second base will be forced out (no need to tag the person) and then the batter/baserunner will be forced out at first base. If the batter/baserunner is put out at first base before the other runner is out, there is no longer a force play on that runner, and the runner must be tagged before reaching second base.

If there are runners on first and second bases, double plays may be made by tagging third or second base before throwing to first base. A double play may also be made by touching third base and then throwing the ball to second base.

Three double plays with backup patterns are shown as follows. Note that all defensive players have a role to play.

Ground Ball to Second-Base Player (Figure 9.23).

1. The second-base player fields the ball and tosses it to the shortstop (b).
2. The shortstop steps on second base, receives the toss, and throws to first base (c).
3. The first- and third-base players cover their bases.
4. The right fielder backs up the second-base player and then may move to back up first base.
5. The left fielder backs up shortstop at second base.
6. The center fielder backs up the second-base player.
7. The pitcher backs up first base. (Some coaches prefer to have the catcher do this.)

Ground Ball to Shortstop (Figure 9.24).

1. The shortstop fields the ball and tosses it to the second-base player (b).
2. The second-base player receives the toss while touching second base and throws to first base (c).
3. The first- and third-base players cover their bases.
4. The left fielder backs up third base.
5. The center fielder backs up the shortstop.
6. The right fielder backs up second base.
7. The pitcher backs up first base. (Some coaches prefer to have the catcher do this.)

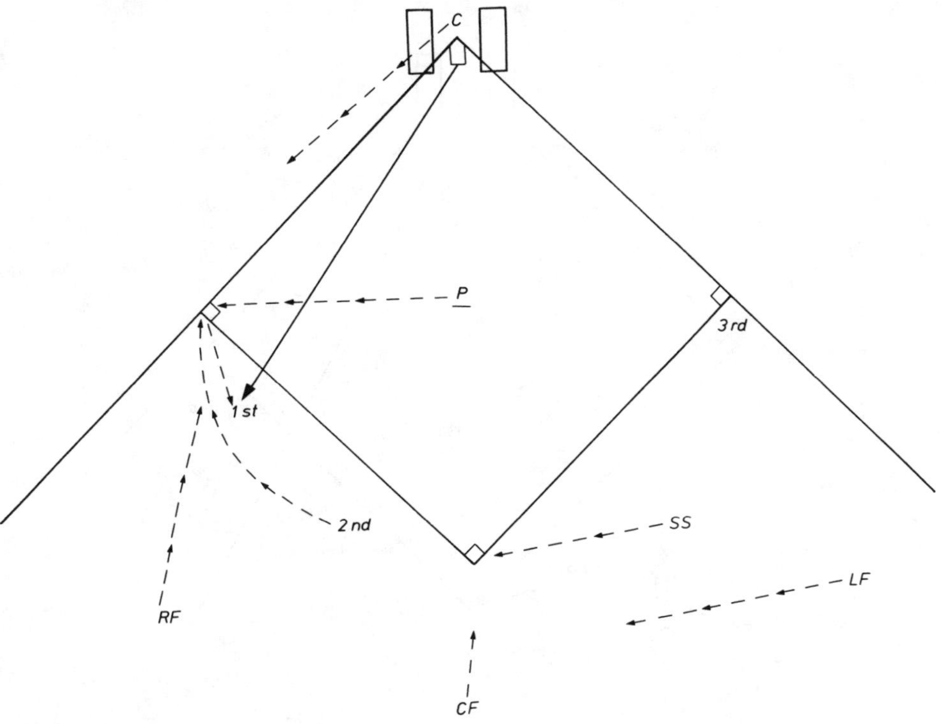

Figure 9.20. Defensive play: No one on base, hit toward first base

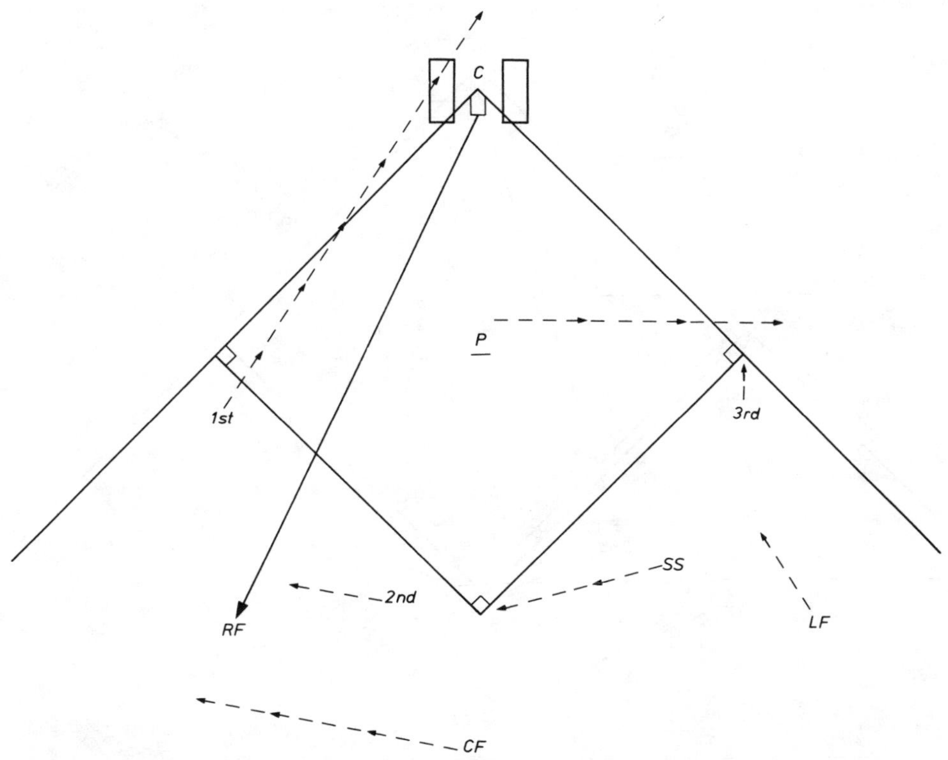

Figure 9.21. Defensive play: No one on base, long hit to right field

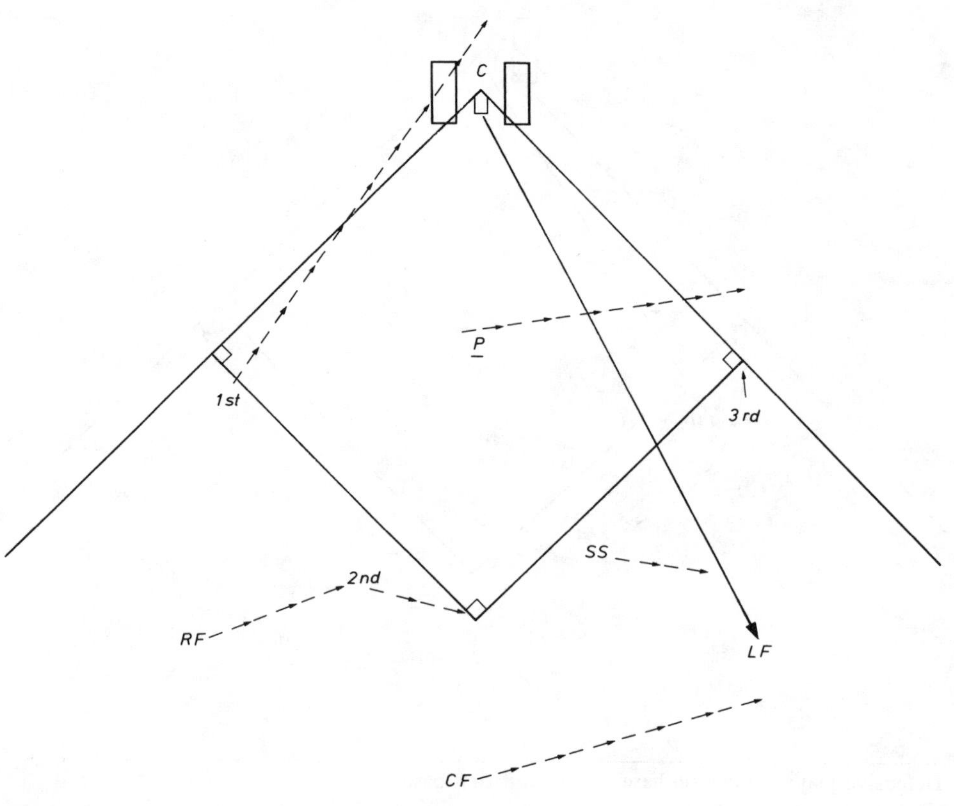

Figure 9.22. Defensive play: No one on base, long hit to left field

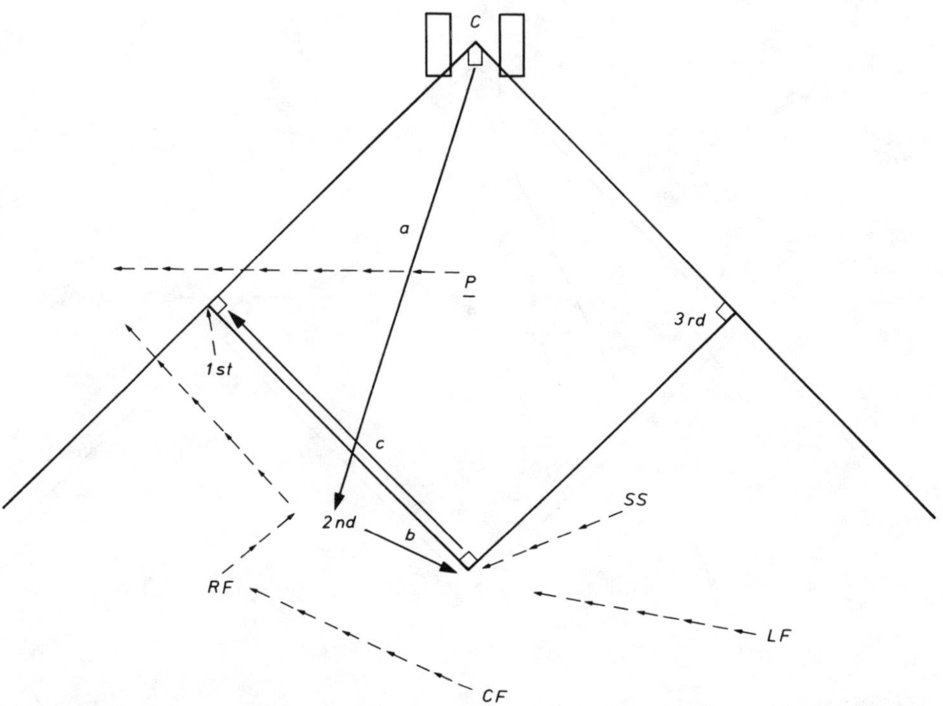

Figure 9.23. Defensive double play: Runner on first base, less than 2 outs, ground ball to second-base player (a = hit ball, b and c = thrown balls)

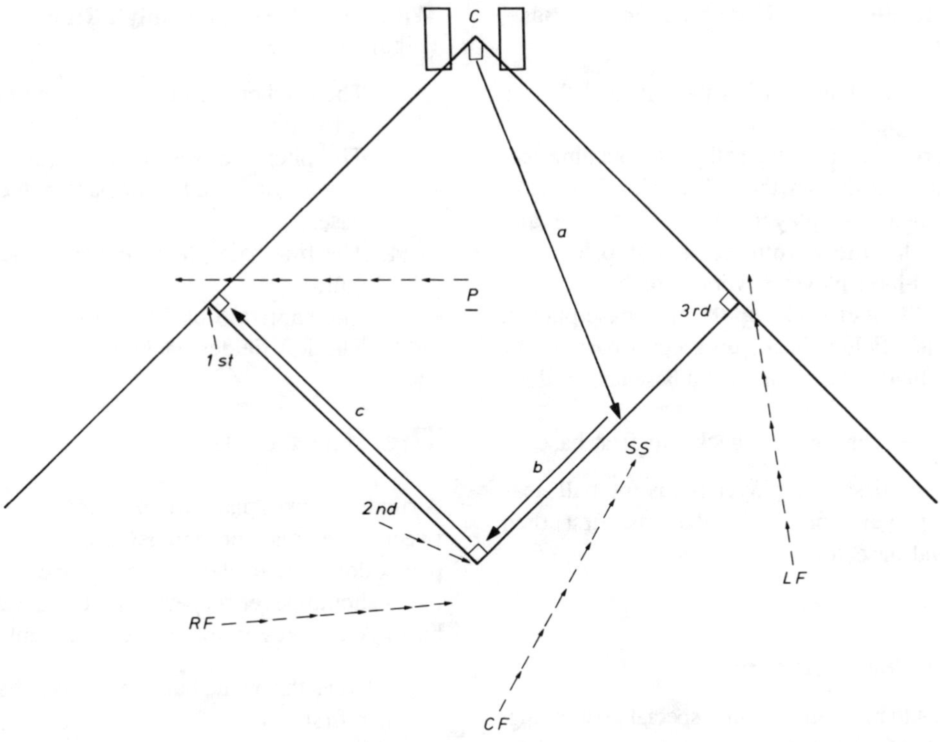

Figure 9.24. Defensive double play: Runner on first base, less than 2 outs, ball hit to shortstop (a = hit ball, b and c = thrown balls)

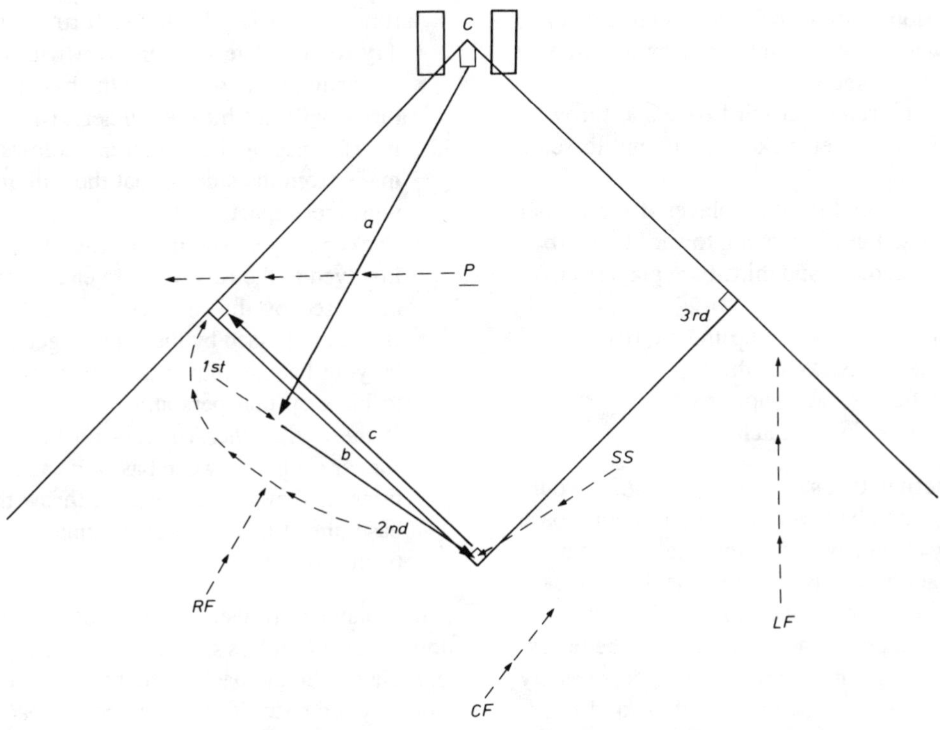

Figure 9.25. Defensive double play: Runner on first base, less than 2 outs, hit pulls first-base player off base (a = hit ball, b and c = thrown balls)

Ground Ball to First-Base Player Pulled Off Base (Figure 9.25).

1. The first-base player fields the ball and throws to second base (b).
2. The shortstop catches the ball while touching second base and throws the ball to first base (c).
3. The second-base player covers first base and receives the throw from the shortstop.
4. The third-base player covers third base.
5. The right fielder backs up the first-base player.
6. The center fielder backs up second base.
7. The left fielder backs up second base and/or third base.
8. The pitcher (or catcher) backs up first base.

Note that if the first-base player fields the ball near first base, that player should touch that base first, then throw to second base for the tag play.

Other Defensive Situations

A few common situations that require special positioning are illustrated here. Advanced players would need to know many others.

Runner on Third Base, Less Than 2 Outs, Ground Ball to Shortstop (Figure 9.26).

1. The shortstop fields the ball and has three options:
   a. Throw to home plate if the runner at third base starts for home (b_1).
   b. Check the runner at third base and throw to first if the runner makes no attempt to score (b_2).
   c. Throw to the third-base player if the runner is off base but not running toward home (b_3).
2. The first-, second-, and third-base players cover their bases.
3. The center fielder backs up the shortstop.
4. The left fielder backs up third.
5. The right fielder backs up first.
6. The pitcher backs up catcher.

A similar pattern to that shown in Figure 9.26 would be used if the ground ball were hit to the second-base player. The only change would be that the center fielder back up the second-base player, who is fielding the ball, and the shortstop cover second base.

Note that where a play at home plate might be necessary to prevent a run from scoring, the infielders usually play inside or on the base paths. The first- and third-base players also move closer to home plate when expecting a possible bunt. Infielders may assume a position on the base path when the ball is pitched but may not stay there and interfere with a runner unless they are fielding a batted ball.

Wild Pitch (Fast Pitch Only), Runner on Third Base (Figure 9.27).

1. The catcher runs to retrieve the ball and throws it to home plate.
2. The pitcher covers home plate.
3. The second- and third-base players cover their bases.
4. The first-base player moves to help retrieve the ball.
5. The shortstop backs up the pitcher.
6. The left fielder backs up third.

The Rundown

A rundown takes place when a baserunner is caught between bases and the defensive players try to run the player down and tag her or him. Runners caught between bases should never be permitted to advance to the next base. A few key points to help prevent this follow:

- Always throw the ball to the base ahead of the runner first.
- Force runners to run back toward the bases they left. At least they may not gain another base if there is a misplay.
- The player with the ball should run hard toward the runner to make that player commit to a change of direction and then throw the ball. Do not allow the runner to jockey back and forth with little steps.
- Try to complete the rundown with one throw.
- Play slightly to the side of the base path so that the throw will not hit the runner. This also prevents interference by the fielder and allows the tag to be made from the side so that the ball and glove give with the impact.
- Backup players should be ready to step in if those involved in the rundown are caught out of position or passed by the runner.
- If you are passed by the runner, get out of the way; let your backup player take over and circle around to back up that person.
- If there are other runners on base ahead of the runner caught between bases, be alert to their positions. If they try to advance, throw the ball to the base ahead of the leading runner (especially one trying to score).

Baseplayers are usually the ones involved in a rundown, but outfielders should take backup positions. The right fielder should back up first base and on some occasions second base. The center fielder backs up second base sometimes, and the left fielder would back up third base. Pitchers also should assume backup positions for rundowns.

A typical example of a rundown between first and second bases starts with the second-base player chasing the

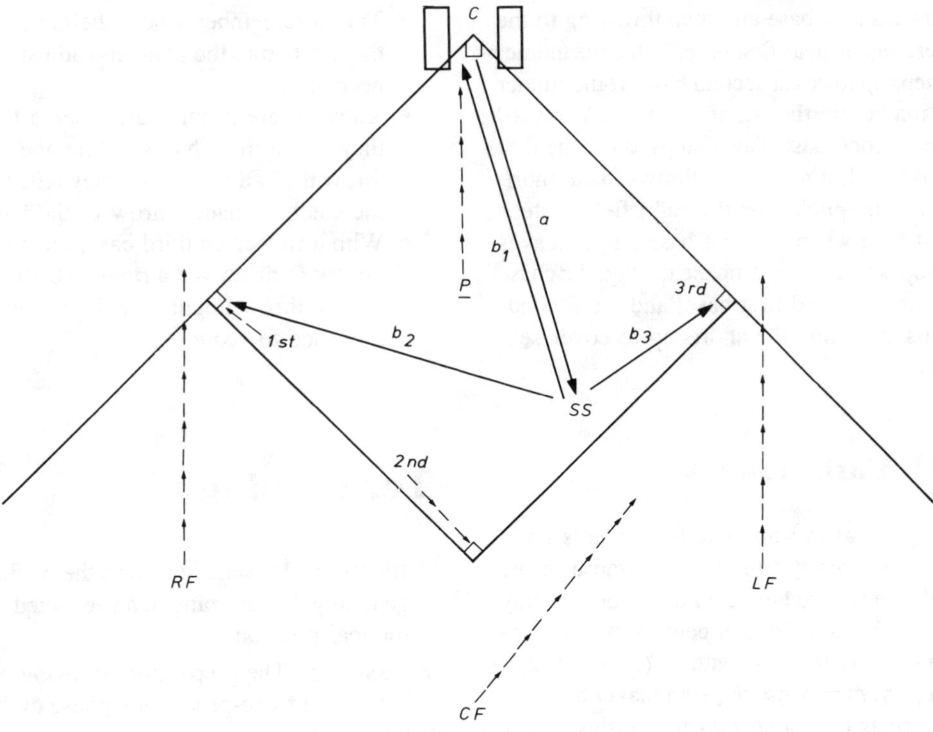

Figure 9.26. Defensive play: Runner on third base, less than 2 outs, ground ball to shortstop (a = hit ball, b_1, b_2, and b_3 = throw options)

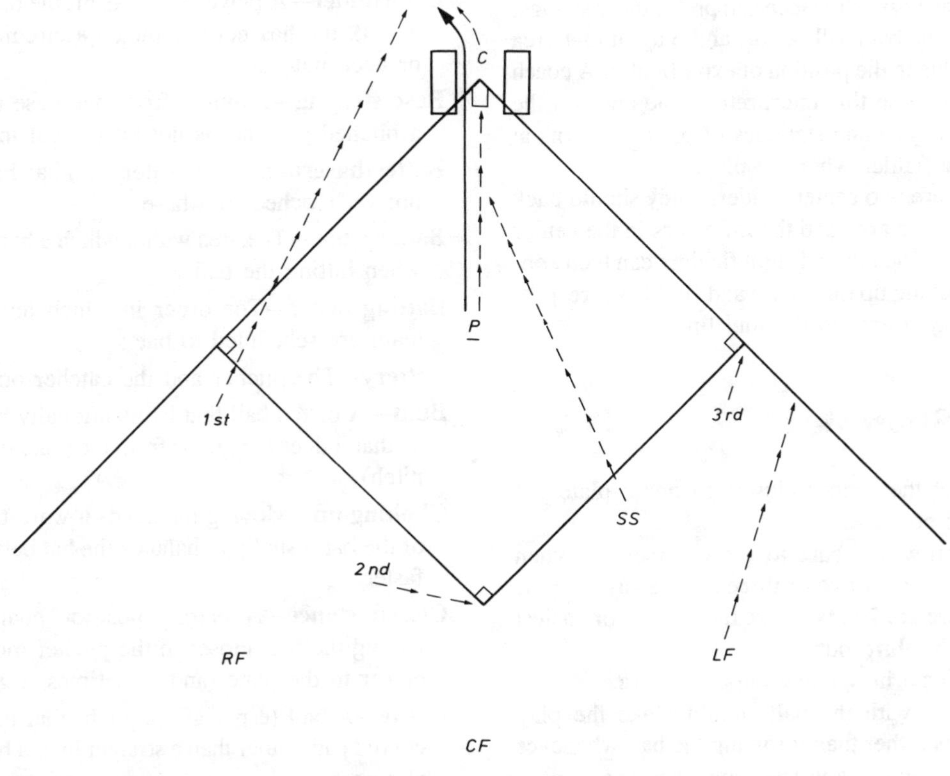

Figure 9.27. Defensive play: Wild pitch, runner on third base

runner back toward first base and then throwing to the first-base player, who is near first base. In the meantime, the shortstop steps up to cover second base. If the runner changes direction before the tag and runs back toward second base, the second-base player steps aside; the first base-player chases and, if necessary, throws to the shortstop for the tag. The pitcher or the right fielder steps in to cover first base when the first-base player leaves it. If the shortstop is unable to complete the tag, the chase reverses once more toward first base, and the second-base player falls in behind the shortstop to cover second base again.

Slow-Pitch Variations

The slow-pitch game allows an extra fielder; this gives the defense the opportunity to spread out more in the field. The usual pattern is to have four outfielders evenly spaced throughout the outfield. For beginners and intermediate players this is the best pattern (Figure 9.2).

More skilled players may use the 10th player to better advantage. The rules do not specify where this player must stand, so the player may move about depending on the needs of the defense. Against a strong left-field hitter, the team may want two left fielders. If the batter frequently hits *line drives* over second base, a short fielding position behind second base might be best. A player who can look at a batter's stance and preliminary swings, predict where the ball will be hit, and play in that area can be invaluable in the position of extra fielder. A coach may wish to assume this interpretive role and, on the basis of the analysis and statistics of previous turns at bat, signal the fielder where to play.

When there are two center fielders, they should back up the second-base area and the infielders in the center of the diamond. The left and right fielders can then concentrate on backing up third base and first base, respectively, and play nearer to the foul lines.

General Strategies

- Try to get the runner closest to home plate out whenever possible.
- Do not throw to a base to get a runner out when the runner is only two or three steps away from it.
- When there are 2 outs, make the nearest or easiest play for the third out.
- Always know how many outs there are.
- Baseplayers with the ball should make the play themselves rather than throwing the ball whenever possible. Every throw risks an error.
- Try to remember where the batter hit the ball on the last trip to the plate and adjust your position if necessary.
- Know where runners are when a fly ball is hit. If they leave their bases before the catch is made, throw the ball to the base they left. If they run after the catch is made, throw to the base ahead.
- With a runner on third base, most catchers should not try to throw out a runner stealing second base. Such a throw might give the runner on third base a chance to score.

Terminology

Adduction—Movement toward the midline of the body, generally the returning of an abducted limb to the anatomical position

Backswing—The preparatory drawing back of the arm before the force-production phase of throwing or hitting the ball

Ball—A pitch that does not go over the plate within the strike zone and at which the batter does not swing

Base on balls—Being awarded the right to go to first base after being pitched four balls (same as a *walk*)

Baserunner—A player who has hit the ball or received a walk but has not completed a circuit of the bases or been put out

Base stealing—Running from one base to another on a pitched ball that is not hit (illegal in slow pitch)

Batter/baserunner—A batter who has hit the ball but not yet reached first base

Batter's box—The area within which a batter must stand when hitting the ball

Batting order—The order in which individuals on a team are scheduled to bat

Battery—The pitcher and the catcher on a team

Bunt—A batted ball that is intentionally hit very softly so that it does not go far from the plate (illegal in slow pitch)

Choking up—Moving the hands toward the heavy end of the bat, usually to balance the bat better and swing faster

Closed stance—A batting position characterized by having the foot closer to the pitcher moved forward closer to the plate (and sometimes slightly toed in)

Curve—A ball (especially a pitch) that moves along a curved path rather than a straight line; a ball with lateral spin

Diamond—The area within the softball (or baseball) base paths; in general, a softball field

Double play—Making two outs in one continuous play

Drop pitch—A pitch that moves lower (drops) as it approaches the plate (also called a *sinker*); a ball with topspin

Error—A mistake in fielding, throwing, or catching made by the fielding team

Fair ball—A hit ball that is within or over a baseline as it bounces into the outfield or that lands within the foul lines in the outfield

Fast pitch—A softball game comprised of nine players per team in which the pitcher throws the ball approximately parallel with the ground

Figure 8—A style of pitching characterized by the pitching arm moving in a figure 8 pattern

Floater—A pitch thrown with as little spin as possible so that it seems to float through the air

Fly ball—A batted ball that is lofted into the air

Force-out—An out made at a base when the baserunner need not be tagged

Fungo—A ball that is hit into the air to give the fielders catching practice; a self-tossed hit

Grounder—A batted ball that bounces along the ground

Hit-and-run—An offensive play in which the runner starts to run to the next base as the ball is pitched and the batter must attempt to hit the ball to help the runner advance (usually used only in fast pitch)

Home plate—The base at which the batter stands to hit the ball and behind which the catcher is positioned

Infield—That area of the field within and including the base paths and a short distance behind them; the area of the field from which the grass has been removed

Inning—A turn at bat for each team; 3 outs for each team

Leadoff—A baserunner moving away from contact with a base as soon as the ball is pitched (illegal in slow pitch)

Line drive—A hard-hit ball that travels almost parallel with the ground

Open stance—A batting position characterized by having the foot closer to the pitcher drawn back away from the plate and the toe of that foot pointing slightly to the side

Opposite field—Right field for a right-handed batter and left field for a left-handed batter; the field to which most batters do not usually hit the ball

Out—Failure of a batter to reach first base safely when completing a turn at bat or failure of a baserunner to reach the next base safely

Outfield—The area of the field outside the base paths; the grassy area beyond the area where the grass has been removed

Pitch—An underhand delivery of the ball to the batter

Pitchout—A pitch deliberately thrown out of the reach of the batter to prevent that batter from hitting the ball

Pitcher's rubber—The wooden or hard rubber strip near the center of the diamond that marks where the pitcher stands

Place hit—Hitting the ball to a desired part of the field or "placing" the hit where you want it to go

Plate—See Home plate

Pulling the ball—Hitting the pitched ball too far in front of the plate (results in a foul ball to the left for a right-handed batter and to the right for a left-handed batter)

Relay—Assisting a teammate to get the ball to a certain base by moving into position in the path of the throw, catching the ball, and throwing it on

Riser—A pitch that rises (or appears to rise) as it approaches the plate; a ball with backspin

Rundown—Catching a runner between two bases and throwing the ball back and forth until one fielder is able to tag (or run down) the runner

Sacrifice—Deliberately hitting the ball in such a manner that the baserunner may advance even though the batter is put out (often a bunt)

Sinker—See Drop pitch

Slingshot—A style of pitch characterized by a long backward and forward whipping action of the pitching arm (also called a *whip* pitch)

Slow pitch—A softball game comprised of 10 players per team in which the pitcher must pitch the ball with a perceptible arc

Steal—Running from one base to another on a pitched ball that is not hit (illegal in slow pitch)

Strike—A pitched ball that is swung at and missed; a pitched ball that goes over the plate in the strike zone at which the batter fails to swing

Strike zone—Fast pitch: The area over the plate that is between the batter's knees and armpits. Slow pitch: The area over the plate that is between the batter's highest shoulder and the knees

Tag—To touch a runner who is off base to put that runner out

Tag up—To return to a base after taking a leadoff or starting to advance to the next base

Walk—See Base on balls

Whip—See Sling shot

Windmill—A style of pitch characterized by an almost 360° circle of the pitching arm

Selected Readings

Drysdale, S., & Harris, K. (1982). *Complete handbook of winning softball*. Boston: Allyn & Bacon.

Joyce, J., Anquillare, J., & Klein, D. (1975). *Winning softball*. Chicago: Henry Regnery.

Kneer, M., & McCord, C. (1966). *Softball: Slow and fast pitch* (2nd ed.). Dubuque, IA: Wm. C. Brown.

Mushier, C. (1983). *Team sports for girls and women* (2nd ed.). Princeton, NJ: Princeton Book.

National Association of Girls and Women in Sport. (1987). *Softball official rules*. Reston, VA: American Alliance for Health, Physical Education, Recreation and Dance.

Walsh, L. (1979). *Coaching winning softball*. Chicago: Contemporary Books.

Whiddon, N., & Hall, L. (1980). *Teaching softball*. Minneapolis: Burgess.

Williams, H. (1983). *Perceptual and motor development*. Englewood Cliffs, NJ: Prentice-Hall.

Softball Skills Errors and Corrections

UNDERHAND THROW (USED MAINLY FOR PITCHING)

Error	*Causes*	*Corrections*
Weak		
Ball does *not* reach target or does *not* travel in a horizontal path	• Insufficient backswing	• Rotate the hip of the throwing arm backward; increase the arm backswing until it is at least parallel with the ground.
	• Failure to transfer the body weight	• Step forward on the foot opposite the throwing arm; lengthen the stride to help increase force.
	• Failure to swing the arm forward	• Straighten the throwing arm and swing it vigorously forward from the shoulder.
	• Failure to get the wrist action needed	• Bend the hand backward (hyperextend) while swinging the arm forward; snap (flex) the wrist strongly as the ball is released.
	• Failure to complete the follow-through	• Swing the arm past the point where the ball is released.
	• Ball held incorrectly	• Hold the ball in a modified tripod grip between the thumb and first three (or two) fingers; avoid resting the ball against the palm.
	• Failure to utilize a lifting motion	• Flex the wrist to provide lift and added speed to the ball at the moment of release.
Inaccurate		
	• Improper release point	• Release the ball at the point in the swing when the ball is traveling toward the target (usually just past the bottom of the arc).
	• Failure to flex the forward knee in the stepping action.	• Bend the forward knee as the weight transfers forward and the arm swings (this flattens the throwing arc and helps improve accuracy in directing the ball).

Error	*Causes*	*Corrections*
Too much height		
	• Releasing the ball too late	• Release the ball when the palm of the hand is toward the target and the arm is just passing the line of the body (the hip); avoid holding the ball until the hand is palm up (see also previous correction).

OVERHAND THROW

Error	*Causes*	*Corrections*
Weak		
Ball does *not* reach	• Failure to hold the ball properly	• Hold the ball in the fingers; avoid letting it touch the palm; use all four fingers and the thumb if the hands are small; otherwise use three fingers and the thumb.
	• Failure to rotate the hips and trunk	• Rotate the entire body clockwise (right-hander) to maximize the range of motion in the preparatory action.
	• Failure to transfer body weight	• Step forward on the foot opposite the throwing arm.
	• Failure to utilize a "whipping" action	• Start the power phase of the arm action with the shoulder and the upper arm, which causes the elbow to move forward; following sequentially with the forearm and the hand movements.
	• Failure to extend the arm fully	• Extend the arm fully forward at release.
	• Failure to reach rearward fully (cock the arm)	• Extend the upper arm backward at the shoulder on the backswing; flex the elbow to approximately 90°.
	• Insufficient follow-through	• Extend the entire throwing arm and shoulder toward the target.
	• Holding the elbow of the throwing arm low	• Keep the elbow at or above shoulder level; avoid letting the elbow point downward.
Inaccurate		
Ball goes to right or left of target	• Failure to face the target	• On the power phase of the movement, rotate the trunk counterclockwise (right-hander) so that the hips face the target.
	• Failure to reach toward target	• Extend the arm and hand directly toward the target.
	• Failure to apply force behind the ball	• Release the ball with the fingers and the palm facing the target and the hand directly in line with the flight path.

(Cont.)

UNDERHAND THROW (Continued)

Error	Causes	Corrections
Too high		
	• Ball released too soon	• Extend the arm and hand directly toward the target.
Too low		
	• Ball released too late	• Extend the arm and hand directly toward the target.
	• Ball held in palm of hand	• See the first correction (holding the ball properly).

SIDEARM THROW (SEE COMMON ERRORS FOR THE OVERHAND THROW)

Error	Causes	Corrections
Weak		
Ball fails to reach the target	• Failure to use a full back-swing	• Rotate the trunk and shoulders and reach backward with the arm.
	• Failure to "whip" the arm through	• Rotate the shoulder of the throwing arm forward and swing the arm vigorously out to the side; snap the wrist.
	• Failure to transfer the body weight	• Step toward the target on the foot opposite the throwing arm.
	• Failure to rotate the hips rapidly	• Rotate the hips counterclockwise (right-handers) as the arm is pulled around in a horizontal pattern.
Inaccurate		
Ball goes to right or left of the target	• Releasing the ball at the wrong time	• Release the ball as the palm faces the target; an early release results in the ball going too far right; a late release results in a throw to the left (right-hander).
	• Failure to lower the shoulder of the throwing arm	• Lean toward the throwing arm side and lower that shoulder slightly.
	• Failure to rotate the arm medially (inward) just prior to release	• Rotate the shoulders counterclockwise (right-hander) as the arm is pulled around in a horizontal pattern.

CATCHING

Error	Causes	Corrections
Inability to intercept the ball		
Player does *not* reach the ball	• Closing the eyes as the ball approaches	• Keep the eyes open and focused on the ball until it is in the hands (glove).
	• Improper body position	• Move quickly to get in line with the path of the ball; then move toward the ball.
Lack of ball control		
Ball is *not* caught and held	• Improper hand position	• When catching above the waist, point fingers up and keep thumbs together and palms toward the ball; for catches below the waist, point fingers down and keep little fingers together and palms toward the ball.
	• Failure to catch with both hands	• Reach toward the ball with both hands; when using a glove, center the glove webbing in the path of the ball and hold the throwing hand ready to close over the ball.
	• Failure to relax the fingers	• Cup the hands and relax the fingers; avoid rigidity.
	• Failure to reach toward the ball	• Extend the arms toward the ball; bend the elbows slightly.
	• Failure to absorb the force	• Flex the arms and step backward to cushion the impact and avoid hurting the hands.
	• Improper use of the glove	• Hold the glove open in the path of the ball; let the ball come into the pocket area; close the glove around the ball; close the free hand over the ball.

FIELDING FLY BALLS

Error	Causes	Corrections
Inability to intercept		
Player does *not* get to the ball	• Failure to judge ball flight pattern correctly	• Watch the ball continuously from the time it leaves the bat; practice judging different flight paths; watch the ball while moving into fielding position.
	• Improper body position	• Move into the path of the ball as quickly as possible; then move forward in line with the ball if there is time; move under the ball so that it can be caught in front of the shoulder of the throwing arm.

(Cont.)

FIELDING FLY BALLS (Continued)

Error	*Causes*	*Corrections*
Lack of ball control		
Ball is *not* held	• Ball bounces off the glove	• Let the ball come into the open pocket of the glove; close the glove quickly after the ball contacts it.
	• Improper glove position	• Hold the glove so that the webbing (pocket) is in the path of the ball; hold the free hand to the side with the palm facing the ball, ready to close over the ball in the glove; glove fingers point upward for balls above the waist and downward for balls below the waist.

FIELDING GROUND BALLS

Error	*Causes*	*Corrections*
Inability to intercept		
Player does *not* get to ball	• Improper preliminary waiting position	• Stand with the feet slightly more than shoulder width apart, the knees bent, and weight balanced over the balls of both feet; lean forward; watch the ball and move into its path as soon as possible.
	• Improper body position at the ball	• Position the total body in line with the ball.
Lack of ball control		
Ball is *not* held	• Failure to move forward toward the ball	• Do not wait for the ball to come to you (the more bounces a ball takes, the more chance it has to change direction).
	• Failure to maintain focus on the ball	• Visually monitor the progress of the ball until it reaches the glove (hands); avoid looking up.
	• Lifting the head or the glove just prior to the catch	• Keep the head down; extend the glove and free hand low, almost touching the ground in the ball's path.

SLOW PITCHING (SEE COMMON ERRORS FOR THE UNDERHAND THROW)

Error	*Causes*	*Corrections*
Weak		
Ball does *not* reach the plate	• See first four causes and corrections of underhand throwing errors	
	• Inappropriate follow-through	• Swing the arm well past the vertical downward line of the body; release the ball as the arm is about 45° past the vertical; reach upward and outward to arc the ball.
Inaccurate		
Ball has insufficient arc	• Failure to utilize a lifting action	• Keep the palm of the hand under and behind the ball at the release; flex the wrist on release to put arc on the ball.
	• Poorly timed release	• Release the ball as the arm nears 45° past the vertical downward line of the erect body; if ball goes too high, the release is too late; if ball does not arc, the release is too soon.
Ball goes to right or left of target	• Improper arm swing	• Swing the arm backward and forward in the same plane as the intended ball path; avoid the horizontal rotation or wrapping the ball around the body.

FAST PITCHING (SEE COMMON ERRORS FOR THE UNDERHAND THROW)

Error	*Causes*	*Corrections*
Weak		
Ball *not* reaching the plate	• Improper grip on the ball	• Hold the ball in the fingers and the thumb; avoid letting the ball rest against the palm of the hand.
	• Failure to transfer the body weight	• Step forward firmly on the foot opposite the pitching arm; extend the stride to increase ball speed.
	• Shortened forward stride	• Lengthen stride toward the batter.
	• Failure to maintain balance	• Keep the upper body nearly vertical; avoid leaning sideward.
	• Use of an incomplete backswing	• Swing the pitching arm backward to shoulder level or above; rotate the hips and trunk to add backward reach (when using the windmill windup, the forward power phase of the movement begins above shoulder level in back).

(Cont.)

FAST PITCHING (Continued)

Error	*Causes*	*Corrections*
Weak		
Ball *not* reaching the plate	• Failure to provide forward force with the arm	• Swing the arm as rapidly as possible; develop a sequential action utilizing the hips, trunk, shoulder, elbow, and wrist.
	• Improper follow-through	• Extend the arm and reach toward the target; let the momentum of the arm swing pull the entire body forward to face the batter.
	• Insufficient wrist action	• Just before releasing the ball, flex (snap) the wrist strongly and let the ball roll off the fingertips.
Ball too high		
	• Ball released too late	• Release the ball just as the arm passes the vertical line of the body.
	• Improper synchronization	• Lengthen the forward stride to increase the arm-swing range of motion and provide more forward momentum and slightly delay the release.
Ball too low		
	• Ball released too soon	• Hold the ball firmly in the fingers; snap the wrist when releasing the ball at the bottom; wait until the bottom of the swing.
Horizontal inaccuracy		
Ball goes too far to the left or right	• Improper hip rotation	• Let the hip be drawn back naturally as the shoulder rotates with the backswing; avoid more than 90° rotation.
	• Failure to swing the arm parallel to the body	• Swing the arm vertically forward past the body; avoid a horizontal action in the forward phase of the pitch.

BATTING

Error	*Causes*	*Corrections*
Weak		
Ball hit only a short distance	• Inappropriate bat or grip on bat	• Select a bat that can be easily held parallel with the ground while the arms are extended; choke up on a bat that is too heavy (slide both hands toward the center of the bat).
	• Limiting the range of motion	• Stand with the left side toward the pitcher (right-hander) and the feet apart; rotate the upper body backward in preparation for the swing.

Error	*Causes*	*Corrections*
Weak		
Ball hit only a short distance	• Failure to transfer the body weight	• Step toward the pitcher on the leading foot as the swing starts.
	• Insufficient follow-through	• Swing through the ball; avoid trying to stop the swing as contact is made; allow the bat to slow down as it circles the body.
	• Inhibiting the arm swing	• Keep the elbows up and out from the body; direct the left elbow toward the pitcher and the right elbow downward and slightly behind the body (right-hander); stand far enough from the plate so that the bat can swing over it when the arms are extended.
Inaccurate		
	• Poor timing	• Swing the bat so that it contacts the ball over the front part of the plate; adjust the start of the swing to allow this contact point.
	• Failure to have a level swing	• Extend the bat so that it is in line with the extended arms; slide both hands up on the handle if the tip of the bat droops; swing the bat parallel with the ground.
	• Failure to focus on the ball	• Watch the ball continuously as it approaches; bend or extend the knees to lower or raise the swing depending on the height of the pitch.
	• Stepping away from the ball	• Generally, step toward the pitcher with the foot that is nearer; avoid stepping away from the pitch with the foot closer to the catcher.
Ball hit too high		
	• Contact made under the center of the ball	• Swing the bat parallel with the ground; avoid swinging diagonally upward; keep the right shoulder up (right-hander).
Ball hit too low		
	• Contact made above the center of the ball	• Swing the bat parallel with the ground; avoid chopping at the ball; hold the tip of the bat low at the start of and throughout the swing.

(Cont.)

BUNTING

Error	*Causes*	*Corrections*
Missing the ball		
	• Improper stance	• Square the body around to face the pitcher; move the feet parallel with each other with the toes pointing toward the pitcher.
	• Improper hand position on the bat	• Slide the top hand about 6 to 8 in. toward the center of the bat; retract the fingers on that hand so that they do not encircle the bat (hold it between the thumb and the fore-finger).
Inaccurate		
Ball misdirected or fouled	• Failure to control the ball	• Hold the bat parallel with the ground; hold the left hand slightly ahead of the plate to bunt to first base; hold the left hand slightly behind the plate to bunt toward third base (right-hander).
Ball hit too hard or soft	• Failure to apply correct force	• Give with the ball to absorb part of the force; push the ball only if the pitch is slow.

Chapter 10
Speedball

Speedball was developed by Elmer D. Mitchell as an outdoor alternative activity to football and soccer. It combines the skills of soccer, basketball, and football. Speedball is played on a soccer-type field. It was first played in 1921 at the University of Michigan, where Dr. Mitchell served as director of intramurals. Because speedball can be adapted for large groups and provides for vigorous activity, many school programs include the sport.

In 1930, the National Section on Women's Athletics of the American Alliance for Health, Physical Education and Recreation (AAHPER) published women's rules, which were a modification of the men's rules. Speedball rules for girls and women continued to be published by AAHPER for some years. Rules for men have changed little since the original publication in the 1920s.

Speedball, like soccer, is an excellent game for coeducational play. The skills are varied and include kicking, throwing, dribbling, and catching, which need not be highly refined. The required equipment, such as soccer balls, pinnies, and goals, is inexpensive.

Purposes and Values

Speedball, like soccer and field hockey, is an excellent outdoor activity for coeducational play in Grades 8 through 12. It is recommended that soccer and basketball be taught first and that speedball be introduced after the basics have been mastered in those sports because it combines the skills of both.

Speedball requires vigorous running, passing, catching, kicking, volleying, and dodging. It contributes to the players' fitness and balance, body control, ball-handling, kicking, and speed-of-movement skills. Players must learn to think quickly and be able to vary their responses to different levels of play (e.g., an aerial ball may be caught, but a ground ball must be kicked or volleyed with the body).

Speedball is an inexpensive addition to the program. In fact, if soccer fields and equipment are already available, nothing else is required. It meets the same program objectives as soccer and can involve many students at one time in strenuous exercise. Students rarely have experience with speedball games outside of school; therefore, they are all novices, and the skill variations are minimal at the start of the unit. Care must be taken in later competitive play to equalize teams by assuring that some more skilled and some less skilled players are on each team.

The Game

Speedball is a combination of basketball and soccer with a little football added. It is played with 11 players on a team. Positions usually include (like soccer) five forwards, three *halfbacks*, two *fullbacks* (sometimes called *guards*), and a *goalkeeper*. The forwards play mainly on offense, the halfbacks back up the forwards and also play defense, and the fullbacks play mainly defense. The goalkeeper is exclusively a defensive player but may play an important role in initiating offensive strategy. The goalkeeper in speedball has no special privileges. The object of the game is to score points at the end of the field your opponents defend while keeping them from scoring at your own end.

The main difference between soccer and speedball is that the latter permits the use of the hands to *pass* or to score once a ball has been converted to an *aerial ball* (sometimes called a *fly ball*). An aerial ball may be passed back and forth as in basketball and may be air dribbled once; however, if it hits the ground, it becomes a *ground ball* and may be only kicked or volleyed with the body as in soccer until it is again lifted into the air from a foot or both feet (to oneself or another player). Players may not run with the ball but may take one step if catching the ball while stationary or two steps if catching on the run. A *dribble* with the feet is permitted, and one air dribble to oneself is legal.

There are several ways to score in speedball (Table 10.1). The following are the different methods of scoring.

- Field goal. This is the same as in soccer; a *field goal* is a ball that is kicked or volleyed with the body over the goal line within the *goal cage*.

- Touchdown. A *touchdown* is a forward pass that is caught by an offensive player anywhere over the goal line.
- Dropkick. A *dropkick* is a ball that is dropkicked over the crossbar of the goal from more than 5 yd from the goal line.
- Penalty kick. A *penalty kick* is a free kick on goal awarded for a foul by the defenders that passes between the goalposts under the crossbar.
- End goal. The *end goal* is a ball that is kicked over the goal line not within the goal cage from within 5 yd of the goal line. This is used in men's rules only.

For coeducational play it is recommended that the scoring be a combination of both touchdowns and points by kicking. Most goals scored by beginners are touchdowns. Allocating touchdowns only 1 point will encourage players to try other variations. The successful use of dropkicks and field goal attempts should be rewarded with 2 points. Penalty kicks should stay at 1 point unless it is necessary to penalize players more forcefully for fouling; then they should count 2 points. The use of the end-goal scoring procedure is not recommended unless the skill level is very low and other means of scoring are unsuccessful.

Play is begun with a placekick in the center of the field by one team (as in soccer). Each team must be in its own half of the field at the start of the game, after which they may move freely about the entire field. After each score, play is resumed as at the start of the game by the opponents of the team scoring points. Fouls and balls going out of bounds are played as in soccer.

Table 10.1 Points Awarded for Scoring in Speedball

Method	Women's Rules	Men's Rules	Suggested
Field goal	2	3	2
Touchdown	2	1	1
Dropkick	3	2	2
Penalty kick	1	1	1
End goal	. . .	1	. . .

Playing Area

The playing area for speedball should be at least 60 by 100 yd, but any soccer, field hockey, or football field may be used. Smaller areas are recommended for younger players. A center line and 5-yd lines at each end of the field are special markings (Figure 10.1).

Equipment

The equipment used in speedball is similar to the equipment used in soccer. The following equipment is recommended.

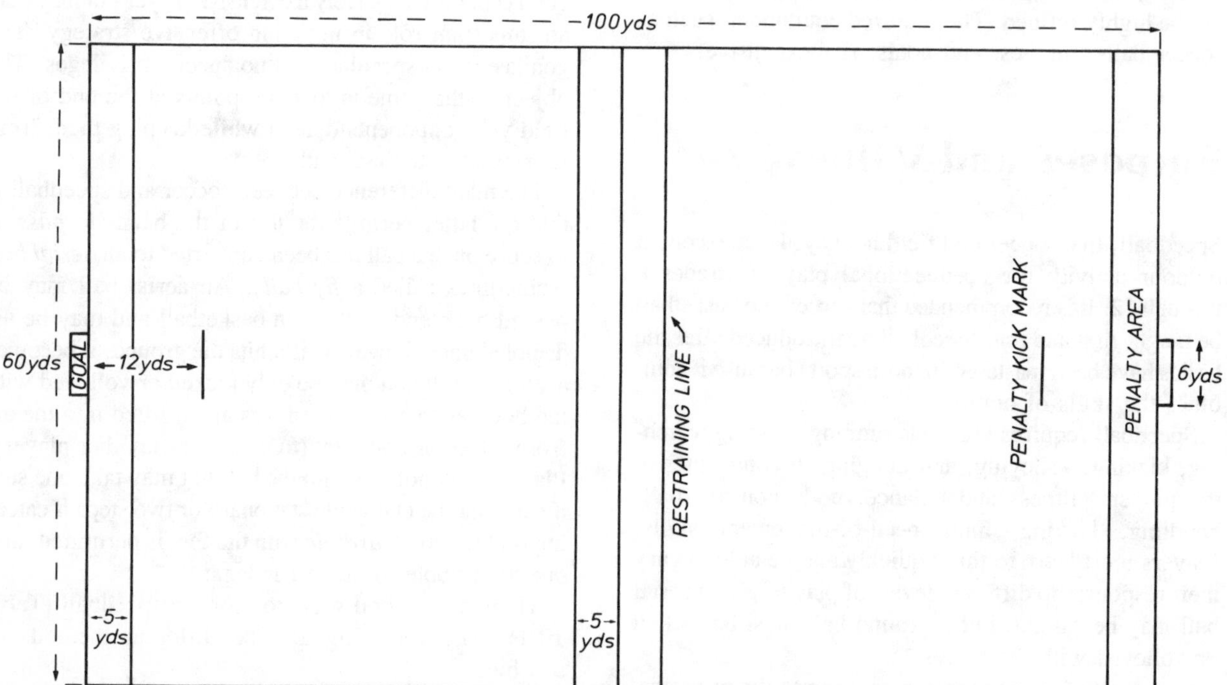

Figure 10.1. Speedball field

Goals

Soccer goals are regulation, but field hockey or football goals may be used.

Balls

Soccer balls are appropriate, although a regulation speedball, which is slightly larger than the soccer ball, could be used. In the interest of economy, soccer balls are suitable. At least one for every five or six players should be available.

Footgear

Shoes and shin guards appropriate for soccer or field hockey are suitable for speedball.

Pinnies

Pinnies or vests are essential when games are being played.

Suggestions for Coeducational Play

Many of the suggestions to make coeducational speedball play more effective are similar to those of soccer and basketball. Having teams composed of a variety of skill levels provides more equitable competition. The use of 1-on-1 guarding with the better players opposing each other and the less skilled opposing those of similar skill is best. Although zone defensive play is appropriate for advanced competitive play, it may not be the best system to use in classes where team composition changes, practice time is limited, and skill levels vary greatly.

Students should be encouraged to employ teamwork and to try to involve all players in the game. The use of sympathetic passes is imperative. Players should learn to recognize which teammates can handle hard passes and which ones need softer, more direct passes.

Rules might be enforced that require alternating passes between boys and girls or having at least one girl handle the ball before a goal is attempted. Another possible but less desirable rule is to limit the scoring opportunities to kicks and volleys for boys and to allow only girls to score by passing and catching the ball.

Teaching Progressions

The teaching progression for speedball depends on previous instruction. Speedball combines basketball and soccer skills, so it is strongly suggested that those sports be taught prior to speedball. A typical progression for speedball under these conditions would consist of a review of the pertinent skills from the other sports followed by a review of the unique skills of speedball. If the skills of one or both of these sports have not been taught, most of the beginning skills of the two sports would have to be presented prior to the speedball skills.

I. Review of throwing and catching skills (see chapter 5)

II. Review of foot-dribbling and kicking skills (see chapter 8)

III. Conversion of ground balls to aerial balls
   - A. Kick-up to teammate
   - B. Lift to oneself
     1. Two-foot lift
     2. One-foot toe lift
     3. One-foot roll up

IV. Review of tackling skills

V. Review of guarding skills

Techniques and Practice

Throwing and Catching

The throwing and catching skills in speedball are identical to those used in basketball (see chapter 5). The chest pass, the one-handed shoulder pass, and the two-handed overhead pass are the ones most frequently used in speedball. The drills described in chapter 5 may be used to practice the passes. Emphasis should be placed on passing to a moving teammate and running out for a pass as in touch football.

Dribbling and Kicking

Dribbling and kicking skills are described in the soccer unit (see chapter 8). The drills in that chapter may be used to practice these skills in speedball. More work should be done on the punt and the dropkick through practice. The punt can be used by any player to advance the ball downfield and the dropkick to score goals.

Tackling and Guarding

A player playing an aerial ball may be guarded just as in basketball. When the ball becomes a ground ball, the ball handler may be tackled as in soccer, using little or no physical contact.

Goalkeeping

The goalkeeper in speedball is responsible for the goal-cage area only. Touchdown passes are the responsibility of the backs. The goalkeeper has no special privileges but should be skilled at punting, which may be used to clear the ball toward the sidelines or to initiate an attack by sending the ball over the heads of the opponents to waiting teammates near the center of the field. Punting drills are described later in this chapter.

Women's rules allow the goalkeepers to take one bounce with the ball. If play around the goal area is congested, this may be desirable to reduce the chance of injury from close-quarter kicks or throws.

Conversion of Ground Balls to Aerial Balls

Kick-Up to Teammate

A ground ball can be converted to an aerial ball by kicking it or lifting it with the toe so that a teammate is able to catch it before it bounces. This technique is essential to the strategy of speedball.

The *kick-up*, or *lift*, skill is performed identically to other kicking skills with the exception of foot placement on the ball. The foot must strike under the center of the ball. This lifts the ball to make it airborne. Striking the ball in this location is accomplished by contacting the ball close to the ground. The kick-up technique with the instep requires a slightly more plantar flexed ankle (extended). The kick-up with the inside of the foot requires a slightly more inverted foot (rotated inward).

Common Movement Problems and Suggestions

The following are common movement errors made while performing the kick-up to a teammate. Instructional suggestions are also included.

- Failure to loft the ball is generally caused by not positioning the foot properly at impact with the ball or not following through sufficiently. An extended follow-through with the correct foot position can enhance the probability of making the ball airborne.
- Another cause of not creating an airborne ball is failure to strike the ball under its center.
- The stationary kick-up should be practiced prior to attempting this skill with a moving ball.

Partner Drills

The kick-up skill can be most effectively practiced in pairs if there are sufficient balls and space. Any type of lightweight ball could be used, such as volleyballs, playground balls, beach balls, or soccer balls. Basketballs may be too heavy.

1.0. Partners stand 10 to 15 ft apart and use a toe-lift to pass the ball back and forth to each other, attempting to pass accurately. Pairs should be well spread out on the field for safety and should all be lifting back and forth in the same direction (e.g., north and south). Emphasize that the movement is a lift and not a kick. The receiver may catch the ball and place it on the ground or may trap it as in soccer.

2.0. Partners stand side by side about 10 ft apart facing the same direction with one ball. Both players begin running straight ahead while one of them foot dribbles the ball. After a few steps, the dribbler toe lifts the ball to the partner, who catches it, drops it to the ground, dribbles, and lifts it back. Play continues until reaching the end of the field.

Group Practice Drills

The following are practice drills for the kick-up. The drills are in order of suggested introduction.

1.0. Double-Line Formation (Figure 4.10). Players are in lines about 15 ft apart. Players kick or toe lift the ball back and forth between lines and try for accuracy and control. Players catch the aerial ball, put it on the floor, and kick it back to the other line. To improve motivation, add competition by having the pairs count the number of consecutive successful kick-ups they can do in a specific period of time (e.g., 2 to 4 min).

2.0. Shuttle Formation (Figure 4.7). The first person in Column 1 kicks the ball up to the first person in Column 2 and goes to the end of Column 1. The receiver catches the kick-up, places the ball on the floor, kicks it up to the second person in Column 1, and goes to the end of Column 2. This continues until all players have participated.

3.0. Shuttle Formation (Figure 4.8). The drill starts as the previous drill does except that the receiver throws a ground ball back to the second person in Column 1, who must block the ball with the body, gain control, and then kick it up to the next person in Column 2. This continues with Column 1 fielding the ball without using the hands and doing a kick-up to the person in Column 2, who catches the ball and returns a thrown ground ball. Players go to the end of the opposite column after completing a turn.

4.0. Double-Column Formation (Figure 4.9). Players are about 20 ft apart. The first person in Column 1 starts dribbling a ball downfield. The first person in Column 2 runs parallel with the dribbler, who attempts to execute a kick-up to the other player. Both continue downfield passing back and forth, using the feet or body for ground balls and throwing and catching aerial balls. Variation: The players in the columns line up near the center of the field. As the players near the goal, they attempt to score by a dropkick, a kicked goal, or a thrown pass. The instructor or coach may specify which one or allow any legal maneuver.

Two-Foot Lift

The *two-foot lift* is a lift to oneself and is used to convert a ground ball to an aerial ball while keeping control of it. It should not be used when a player is closely guarded or when quick action is needed because it usually is slower than a pass or a kick-up to a teammate. Practice drills for the lifts are described at the end of all the lift analyses.

The two-foot lift begins by applying light pressure against the ball with the feet (Figure 10.2). The ball is held against the inside of the foot between both feet. The player jumps vertically by flexing and then extending at the hips and knees. The pressure on the ball by the feet is increased during the initial phase of the jump. Once the player is airborne, the ball is lifted to the downward-stretched arms by both feet. The player grasps the ball firmly with both hands. The ball is now held with a hand on each side of the ball.

Common Movement Problems and Suggestions

The following are common movement problems experienced by the player attempting the two-foot lift. Instructional suggestions are also included.

- Failure to lift the ball can be caused by positioning the feet inproperly on the ball just prior to jumping. The ball should be held firmly between the ankles and the toes of both feet turned inward toward the ball for further security.

Figure 10.2. Two-foot lift to oneself

- Failure to catch the ball may be due to an inadequate lift of the ball. This jump must be of sufficient height to ensure an adequate lift.
- In addition to the jump, the failure to bend at the hips when catching the ball can cause the player to miss the ball during the catch.
- Failure to flex at the waist and reach down with the arms can also cause the lift to be ineffective.

Roll-Up

The techniques used in the *roll-up* are the one-foot toe-lift and the one-foot roll-up. Each is used to convert a ground ball to a caught ball held in the hands. This conversion can occur by either lifting the ball with the foot or rolling it up the inside of the leg.

One-Foot Toe-Lift

The technique of the one-foot toe-lift begins with the leg semiflexed and the sole of the foot directly on top of the ball (Figure 10.3). The leg extends at the knee and flexes at the hip to draw the foot backward over the ball. As soon as the foot loses contact with the ball, the toe is extended under it with maximum plantar flexion at the ankle. Once the foot is under the ball, the ball is lifted upward to the hands by flexing the knee, which elevates the foot with the ball resting on it. Both hands grasp the ball firmly, one hand on each side of the ball.

One-Foot Roll-Up

The one-foot roll-up begins with the ball held firmly between the insides of the feet. The player uses one foot to pull the ball against the inside of the opposite leg and vertically roll the ball up the inside of that leg. Once the ball reaches within arms' length, the ball is caught firmly with both hands.

Common Movement Problems and Suggestions

The following are unique movement problems for the one-foot toe-lift and the one-foot roll-up. Each of the skills will be referred to individually.

- The most common error in the one-foot toe-lift is a misdirection of the lift. This is generally caused by not placing the sole of the foot directly on top of the center of the ball. In addition, if the player pulls the foot backward in a diagonal direction, the desired ball direction will be altered.
- The most common error in the one-foot roll-up is not applying enough pressure or force to hold the ball firmly against the inside of the opposite leg. Players should use firmness in holding the ball against the leg. In addition, players should keep the foot under the ball to roll the ball up the leg.

Practice Drills

Individual practice is best using any kind of large ball like a volleyball or playground ball in addition to speedballs or soccer balls. Basketballs may be used by older players, but these are rather heavy and difficult to lift with the toe. Both the two-foot and the one-foot lift should be practiced.

1.0. Double-Line Formation (Figure 4.10). Players in lines stand about 15 ft apart. The player with the ball lifts it up to him- or herself and then rolls it to a player in the opposite line. That player lifts it with one foot, catches it, and rolls it back to the first line. This con-

Figure 10.3. One-foot toe lift

tinues until all players have had an opportunity to participate. Variation: Instead of lifting the rolling ball with one foot, the player must trap the ball, hold it stationary with the foot for a moment, and then kick it up to oneself.

2.0. Circle Formation (Figure 4.13). Players must stop the ball and control it without using the hands and then lift it to oneself and pass or roll a ground ball to another player in the circle.

3.0. Column Formation (Figure 4.2). Each player in the column dribbles the ball about 20 yd, stops it, kicks it up to oneself, throws a ground ball back to the next player in the column, and returns to the end of the column. The next player in line must stop the ball with a trap or block as in soccer before beginning to dribble. Specify a line or use markers to designate the stopping area.

General Practice Drills

1.0. Five-Parallel-Column Formation (Figure 8.16). The first players in each column begin to run downfield while passing and kicking the ball from one to another. This resembles Drill 4.0 for general soccer practice (see chapter 8) except that a player may catch an aerial ball and pass it by hand to a teammate. If the ball falls to the ground, it must be kicked or blocked as in soccer until it is again raised by the foot to become an aerial ball.

If an entire field is available for this practice, start at one goal line and go the full length of the field. Players stay at that end after completing the drill. The second person in each column may start when the first line completes one-third of the distance or reaches midfield. After all players have completed the drill, the columns should re-form and repeat the drill back to the other end of the field. Players should rotate positions so that they will not always be in the center of the field or near the sidelines. For example, Column 1 moves to Column 2's position, Column 2 to Column 3's, and so on. This continues until all players have been in columns or a specific time period has elapsed.

If only half a field is available, start the drill at the center line. Players should then return to the original starting column around the outside of the field (outside of the sidelines) after completing a turn. Be sure they do not return within the field area, where they would interfere with the next group. The second group could start when the first group gets about halfway to the goal line. Players return to different columns to vary their positions on the field. Variations include the following:

1.1. Include scoring a goal in this drill. Require a field goal attempt (kicked goal as in soccer) one time, a touchdown (ball thrown and caught in the end zone as in football) another time, and a dropkicked goal the next time.

1.2. Add five defensive players to defend the goal. These should be stationed at midfield near the sidelines and should move onto the field as the players start downfield. The five players completing a turn and attacking the goal move to become the next defensive group. Defenders go to the attacking-drill columns after their defense is successful or a goal has been scored.

2.0. Punt Practice: Column Formation (Figure 10.4). Players in Column A line up at the center line near the sidelines of the field. Column B lines up near the goal line facing Column A. Two more columns may be positioned on the other side of the field as are Columns C and D. The first person in Column A (and C) punts the ball toward the goal line. The first player in Column B (and D) tries to catch the ball, or retrieves it and returns it to the next person in the punting column. Players go to the ends of the opposite columns. Variation: If there is plenty of space, Column A punts to Column B, and Column B punts the ball back. Players then go to the end of their own column after each turn.

3.0. Dropkick Practice: Column Formation (Figure 10.5). Players in one column line up about 15 ft in front of the goal. Another column lines up parallel with the goal line about 20 ft out of bounds. The first person in Column A dropkicks the ball toward the goal and goes to the end of Column B. Player B1 retrieves the ball,

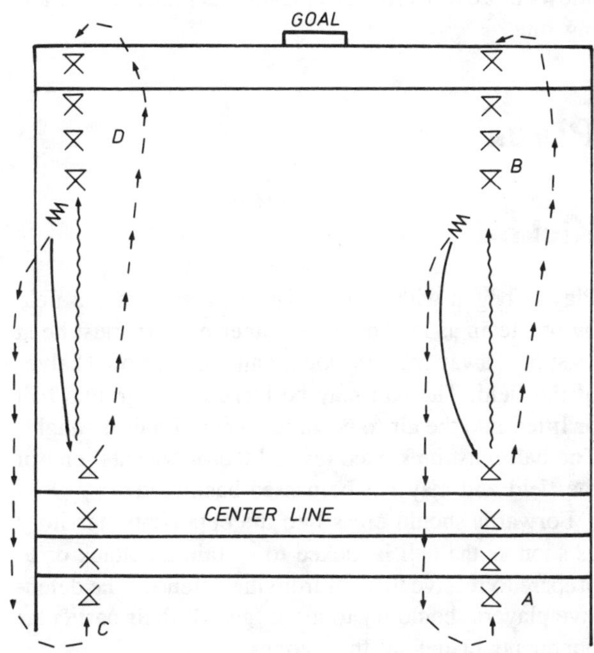

Figure 10.4. Punt drill (wavy line indicates path of kicked ball)

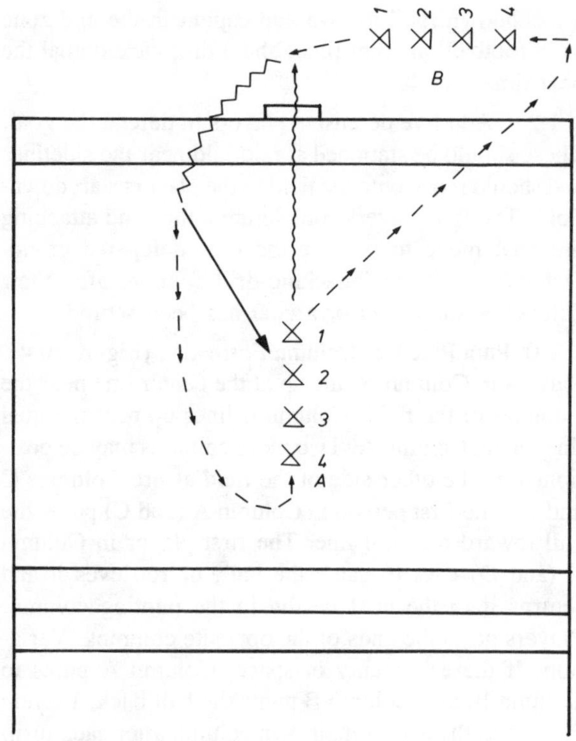

Figure 10.5. Dropkick drill

dribbles it back onto the field, lifts it to the next player in Column A, and goes to the end of Column A. If there are two or three balls available, Player A2 can dropkick while Player B1 is returning the previous kick. Player A3 then kicks while Player B2 is returning the ball. This allows more turns for each player and reduces the waiting time.

Plays

Kickoff

Play is begun with a *kickoff* in the center of the field by one team as in soccer. All other players must be at least 5 yd away from the kicker and in their own halves of the field. The ball may be kicked as a ground ball or lifted into the air to become an aerial ball if caught. The ball must be kicked toward the opponents' end of the field and may not be passed backward.

Forwards should cross into the opponents' territory as soon as the ball is kicked to sustain an attack or to prepare to receive the ball from the defense. The defensive players should try to mark (guard) their particular opponents or defend their zones.

The kicker may try a medium kick to a space in the opponents' defense or a short kick toward the side to a teammate, who breaks downfield with the kick. Long kicks deep in the opponents' territory usually are easily intercepted by the defense, which can then pass the ball back to its own forwards.

Throw-In

When the ball goes out of bounds over the sidelines, it is put back in play by a *throw-in* by an opponent of the player who last touched the ball before it went out. This thrown ball may be played as either an aerial ball or a ground ball. Any player may legally take the throw-in; however, the halfbacks should usually take them to allow the forwards to move downfield and prepare to receive the pass. The push-in plays of field hockey and the throw-in plays of soccer are suitable for use here (see chapters 6 and 8).

The wing forward should take the throw-in when the ball goes out near the goal line the team is attacking. The halfback on that side of the field and the center halfback may move close to be in position to receive the pass and center the ball or may try for a goal. The use of a halfback as an aggressive attacker will sometimes confuse opponents, especially if they are using a 1-on-1 marking defense.

A ball that goes out of bounds over an end line (other than when a goal is scored) must be put in play by an opponent of the person who last touched the ball. The ball can be put back into play with a throw-in, punt, dropkick, or placekick.

Toss-Up

A *toss-up* is used whenever two or more opponents simultaneously (a) hold the ball, (b) trap the ball against their feet, (c) send the ball out of bounds, or (d) commit double fouls. The ball is tossed up between two opponents at the spot where the incident occurred except not within 5 yd of a boundary line. It is played like a jump ball in basketball. All other players must be at least 5 yd away until the ball is tapped. Jumpers face the opponents' goal as in the basketball jump ball.

Players near the toss-up should try to guard opponents as in the basketball jump-ball situation. Some of the forwards should move toward the opponents' goal to be in position to receive a pass should their team secure the ball. Defenders must be alert to mark opponents who try to maneuver behind them, especially if the toss-up occurs near the goal they defend.

Free Kick

A *free kick* (placekick) is awarded to the opposing team when a player commits a foul, such as picking up a ground ball, running with the ball, holding the ball too long, or using unnecessary or rough bodily contact. The free kick is taken at the spot where the foul occurred unless the foul was made by a defender within the player's own penalty area, in which case a penalty kick is awarded.

The fullbacks or the goalkeeper should take all free kicks within 25 yd of the goal they defend. This gives forwards a chance to move ahead to receive the kick and halfbacks a chance to spread out to receive the ball if all forwards are covered. The halfbacks generally take the free kicks in the midfield area. The forwards should take free kicks near the opponents' goal line. In this case, a kick back to a trailing halfback may open a new line of attack and should be considered.

End Line Out of Bounds

When the ball goes out over the end line and no score is made, the opponents return the ball to play with a throw-in or a kick at the spot where the ball went out. This generally occurs when there is an unsuccessful touchdown or field goal attempt or when a defender sends the ball over the end line.

Penalty Kick

A *penalty kick* is awarded to opponents when a defensive player fouls within the player's own penalty area or behind the player's own goal line. The latter may occur when defending against a forward-pass scoring attempt. The ball is dropkicked toward the goal from the penalty mark (12 yd from the goal) by any player on the attacking team. Only the goalkeeper may defend the goal. Teammates of the penalty kicker must be in the field of play and outside the penalty area until the ball is kicked. Teammates of the goalkeeper may be behind the goal line (outside the goal) or on the field of play outside the penalty area. A field goal may not be scored on a penalty kick. If the dropkick is unsuccessful, the ball continues in play.

The penalty corner lineup for field hockey (see chapter 6, Figures 6.17 and 6.18) can be modified to accommodate the penalty kick. The backs behind the goal line move outside the goal posts, and one of the offensive players moves to the penalty kick line.

Offense

The biggest problem of beginning players is clustering around the ball. It is not unusual to have 18 or 20 young players all trying to kick the ball while only the goalkeepers stand isolated near their goals. Players must remember to stay spread out across the field. Only two players, one from each team, should be trying to control the ball at once. Two to four teammates may be 4 to 8 yd away to back up these contenders, but all others should remain a distance away to be in position to receive or intercept a pass.

The most common offensive lineup is the traditional soccer pattern (Figure 10.6). This is the recommended positioning for class use in situations where players get little chance to plan plays and there is only informal group coaching. The position variations related to soccer (see chapter 8) may be introduced if more advanced levels of play are to be developed.

The V formation is frequently employed to start an offense from the team's own backfield. When a team is on the defense, the V formation for the forward line has the center forward moving to about 20 yd from the player's own goal. The inners move to about 30 to 35 yd from their own goal, and the wings linger near the center line. This enables the center forward to collect balls that the defense deflects near the center of the field and to pass or kick the ball out to the wings to start the attack.

The inverted V formation is a common variation often used. This has the wings moving back toward their own goal line while the center forward stays near the center line. Because defensive players should try to clear the ball away from the center of the field and move it toward the sidelines, this pattern allows the wings to be in position to get the ball and start an attack. However, clearing the ball to the sidelines is less important in speedball than in soccer or field hockey because the forward-pass scoring possibility in speedball spreads out play along the entire end line.

Throwing is usually a more controlled way than is kicking to advance the ball downfield. Passes must be quick and accurate. Players should not follow their passes but should move parallel with the receiver to get in position for a return pass. Try to pass near the sidelines until approaching the goal area. This spreads out the defense so that it is easier to find spaces to move into or pass to, and no defensive player can guard two attackers at once. The forward-pass method of scoring should be utilized if the defense clusters in front of the goalposts and ignores play near the sidelines.

Different methods of scoring should be tried. The team

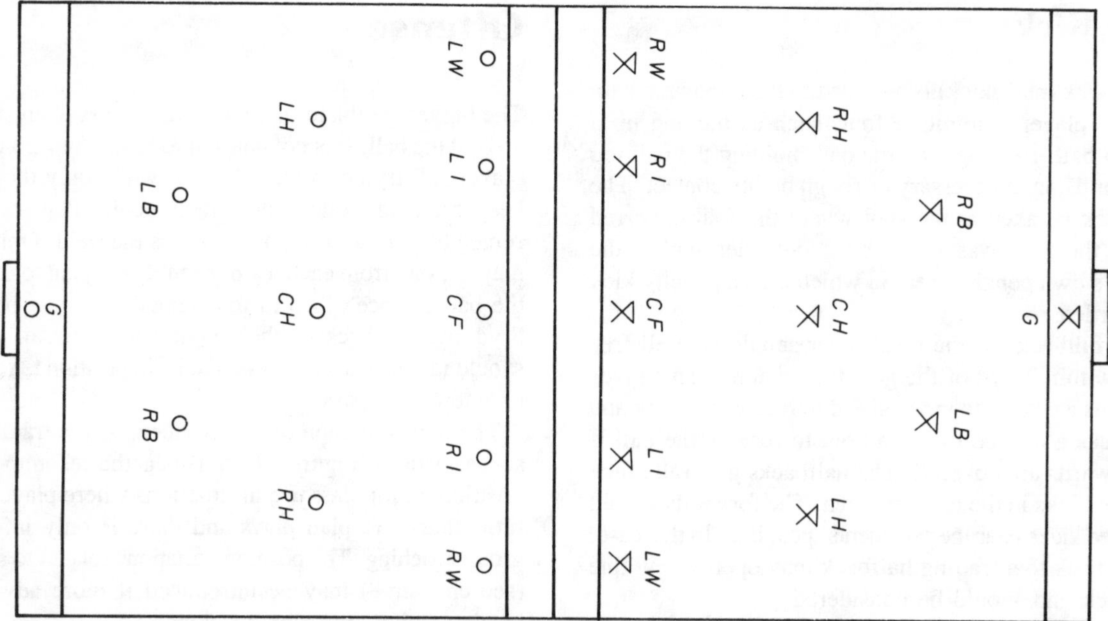

Figure 10.6. Starting positions

that uses primarily one method is too predictable; the defense will soon adapt to it. If the defense goes into a concentrated coverage against the pass, a dropkick or a field goal may be effective. If the offense attempts field goal kicks primarily, the defenders will marshal their forces in front of the goalposts and reduce those scoring opportunities.

There is no offsides rule in speedball; therefore, players may position themselves well ahead of the ball. A diagonal pattern of the forwards may be useful. As soon as a wing or an inner gains possession of the ball, forwards move ahead to form a diagonal line that slants ahead of the ball to the other side of the field. This allows for quick passes across the field. As soon as a player passes the ball, the player must run quickly downfield and try to invert the diagonal so that the passes or kicks may then be made back across the field. This is similar to Drill 4.0 for general soccer practice (see chapter 8).

Halfbacks have a dual role. They must play offense and back up the forwards, and yet be ready to convert to defense when the opponents gain possession of the ball. They can be very valuable on offense, especially if the opposing backs are using a 1-on-1 defense, in which case no one may be guarding the halfbacks (unless the opposing forwards drop back). A quick pass back behind the forward to a trailing halfback may divert the opponents long enough for a player to break clear over the goal line to receive a pass.

When the offense wishes to get the ball downfield in a hurry, the punt or placekick is most effective. Long, random kicks are not appropriate, because they usually go directly to the opposing backs and are returned. However, if forwards have a chance to get in the clear downfield, kicking will get the ball to them faster than will aerial passes. Players should not hesitate to place an aerial ball on the ground and kick it in this type of situation.

Defense

The best defense to use against a team that plays the traditional lineup is the 1-on-1 pattern. Each defensive back is responsible for one opposing forward; usually, the side halfbacks guard the wings, the backs guard the inners, and the center half guards the center forward. This defense is especially effective against a team that tries a lot of touchdown passes. It enables the defenders to stay close to their opponents and to prevent them from getting the ball. The same individual guarding stance used in basketball is appropriate, with the defender always trying to stay between the attacker and the goal (see chapter 5).

When the forwards bunch in one area or interchange positions often, the 1-on-1 defense is less effective because the backs may get in each other's way or wear themselves out chasing the offense around. In this case a zone defense would be more efficient. As in basketball, the zone defense may be a straight zone, a shifting zone, or a combination of these.

Defensive players should mark the spaces when in the ground game to intercept passes. As the attackers approach the goal area, the defenders must move in close to them to prevent open shots on the goal or dropkicks. The player catching an aerial ball has fewer options than the one playing a ground ball. The player with the aerial ball may not move with the ball and therefore need not be closely guarded unless in position to kick for a goal. The defenders can position themselves more effectively if they cover the potential pass receivers or open spaces in this situation. However, some defenders must be prepared to move in quickly if the attacker converts to a ground ball and starts to dribble.

Defenders who gain possession of the ball should immediately try to get the ball to one of their forwards to start an attack. The use of the outlet pass (or kick) to the sidelines clears the ball from the goal area but, on the other hand, may open up a touchdown opportunity for the opponents. The forwards and the defense on the same team must work together closely. The forwards should position themselves where the defense expects them to be so that the defense knows where to pass the ball without looking around. If the wings are able to move well back toward their own goal line (as with the inverted-V offensive formation), they will be in position to secure a sideline pass and also to help defend against a touchdown pass near the sideline.

Some teams concentrate on keeping the ball near the center of the field on offense as they would in soccer and field hockey. In this case, the center forward may be very useful in moving toward the goal her or his team defends to assist the defense. A review of the field hockey defensive patterns suggests other strategies (see chapter 6).

Terminology

Aerial ball—A ball that has been legally lifted into the air by the foot and caught in the hand(s); a ball that may be thrown from player to player as long as it does not touch the ground

Dribble—Moving the ball along the ground using taps with the foot as in soccer

Dropkick—A ball that is kicked as it rebounds from the ground after being dropped from the hands; a 2- or 3-point score made by dropkicking the ball over the crossbar of the goal

End goal—A 1-point goal scored by kicking the ball over the end line not within the goal cage

Field goal—A 2-point goal scored by kicking or volleying the ball into the goal cage

Free kick—An unguarded placekick awarded to the opponents of players who commit certain fouls, such as illegally handling the ball

Fullbacks—Defensive players who generally stay in their own half of the field and primarily protect the goal (also called *guards*)

Goal cage—A soccer goal or the area of a football goal under the crossbar and between the goalposts

Goalkeeper—The one player of a team whose primary responsibility is to stay near the goal and prevent the opponents from scoring

Ground ball—A ball that has hit the ground and may legally be played only with the feet or body as in soccer

Guard—See Fullbacks

Halfbacks—Players who generally play between the forwards and the backs, back up the forwards, and play defense

Kickoff—A free kick taken in the center of the field at the start of each half and after each goal

Kick-up—Lifting the ball up to oneself or a teammate with the toe of the foot (also called a *lift* or *lift-up*)

Lift—See Kick-up

Pass—Moving the ball from one person to another using the hands if an aerial ball or the feet if a ground ball

Penalty kick—A free kick at the goal awarded to the offense for certain fouls by the defenders; a 1-point score made by a successful penalty kick

Roll-up—Using one foot to roll the ball up the other leg and into the hands, which are reaching down; placing a toe under a ball that is rolling and letting the ball roll up the leg to the hands

Throw-in—The means of restarting play after the ball goes out of bounds at the sidelines (taken by the opponent of the one who caused the ball to go out)

Toss-up—A ball that is tossed up between two opponents who jump to tap the ball to a teammate (as in basketball). Used to put the ball in play whenever two opponents simultaneously hold the ball, send it out of bounds, or commit fouls

Touchdown—A 2-point (1 in some rules) score made by catching a forward pass behind the end line

Two-foot lift—Lifting a ground ball into the air using both feet

Selected Readings

Casady, D. (1974). *Sports activities for men*. New York: Macmillan.

Miller, D., & Ley, K. (1963). *Individual and team sports for women*. Englewood Cliffs, NJ: Prentice-Hall.

Mushier, C. (1983). *Team sports for girls and women* (2nd ed.). Princeton, NJ: Princeton Book.

Speedball Skills Errors and Corrections

KICK-UP

Error	*Causes*	*Corrections*
Unsuccessful loft		
	• Failure to contact the ball with the proper position of the foot	• Contact the ball with the top of the instep.
	• Failure to follow through sufficiently	• Extend the foot and toes toward the target.
Too low		
	• Failure to strike under the ball	• Make contact under the center of the ball; lift the foot into the air.
Too high		
	• Failure to maintain a firm ankle	• Keep the ankle rigid through the ball; flex the knee for short kick-ups.
	• Too much force applied	• Reduce the backswing of the kicking leg; slow down the approach to the ball.
	• Failure to control ball	• Field or block the ball before attempting the kick up; do *not* try to kick up a bouncing ball but control it first.
Too far		
	• Improper contact point	• Contact the ball with the top of the foot near the toes; contact the ball under the center; reach forward with the leg to make contact.
	• Too much force applied	• Reduce the backswing of the kicking leg; slow down the approach to the ball; avoid contacting the ball directly behind the center.

TWO-FOOT LIFT

Error	*Causes*	*Corrections*
Unsuccessful lift		
	• Failure to position the foot on the ball properly just prior to jumping	• Place one foot on each side of the ball with the toes turned slightly inward.

Error	Causes	Corrections
Unsuccessful lift		
	• Failure to hold the ball firmly	• Hold the ball firmly between the ankles; apply equal pressure from both feet.
	• Failure to flex (bend) the knees for the jump	• Bend the knees and ankles just prior to the jump; keep the ankles against the ball.
	• Failure to jump off both feet simultaneously	• Distribute weight evenly over both feet; execute the jump without shifting the feet apart or away from the ball; keep the toes pointed inward slightly; lift the ball upward.
	• Failure to lift the ball adequately	• Bend vigorously at the knees and hips to raise the ball upward; keep feet in contact with the ball briefly after the feet leave the ground as the knees and hips flex.
Unsuccessful catch		
	• Failure to focus on the ball	• Keep the head down; look at the ball.
	• Failure to jump sufficiently	• Push off firmly against the ground; jump vigorously
	• Failure to flex (bend) at the hips when catching the ball	• Contract the abdominal muscles strongly to curl the body down toward the ball; flex at the hips.
	• Failure to reach down with the arms	• Reach downward with the arms; avoid using the arms to help achieve jumping height as in the usual jumping pattern.

ROLL-UP TO ONESELF

Error	Causes	Corrections
Unsuccessful		
Body off balance	• Failure to hold the ball against the opposite leg	• Keep the weight balanced over the stationary leg; apply sufficient pressure with the free leg to hold the ball firmly against the inside of the stationary leg; extend the arms out to the sides at first to assist balance.
Ball not raised high enough	• Failure to roll the ball up the leg	• Slide the lifting foot slightly under the ball; rotate the lifting foot inward so the sole faces the stationary leg; let the ball slide against the lifting foot as it rolls up the other leg.
Ball not converted to held ball	• Failure to control the ball with the hands	• Bend at the waist and hips and reach the arms down toward the ball; place one hand in front of and one behind the ball as the ball nears the knees; grasp the ball with both hands.

(Cont.)

ROLL-UP TO LIFT

Error	*Causes*	*Corrections*
Lack of lift	• Improper foot position initially	• Place the sole of the foot directly on top of the center of the ball.
	• Failure to get the foot under the ball	• Pull the foot on top of the ball firmly toward the body causing the ball to roll; quickly place the same foot flat in the path of the rolling ball; allow the ball to roll onto the tops of the toes before lifting.
	• Improper timing	• Flex the ankle and lift upward with the toes as soon as the ball rolls onto them; extend the foot toward the target when lifting to a teammate.
Inaccurate pass	• Lack of ball control	• Extend the foot and leg toward the target as the ball rolls on top of the toes. Balance the ball momentarily on top of the foot.
	• Improper timing	• Flex the ankle and lift upward with the toes as soon as the ball rolls onto them; extend the foot toward the target when lifting to a teammate.

Chapter 11
Volleyball

Volleyball is one of the few sports that originated in the United States and then spread throughout the world. It was developed to provide an indoor game to be played during the cold winters in the northeastern states. William C. Morgan is credited with originating the game in 1895 in Holyoke, Massachusetts, where he was a YMCA physical education director. He needed a game that could be played by men of various ages and skills, that was not quite as strenuous as the new game of basketball, and that could accommodate more players.

The original game was played by hitting the inflated bladder of a ball over a rope. This game was quickly modified to use an elevated tennis net and a ball designed by Morgan specifically for the game. The ball used today is very much like that ball devised in 1895.

The YMCA promoted volleyball throughout the United States and in some foreign countries in the early part of the 20th century. During World War I, the game spread even more because it was used extensively as a recreational activity by men in the United States armed forces.

The first volleyball rules were published by the YMCA in 1897. The game spread quickly to playgrounds, recreation centers, and schools in other parts of the United States. Modified rules for women were published in 1924. The United States Volleyball Association was founded in 1928 to promote and encourage volleyball on the national and international levels. Each of these groups had their own rule variations until the late 1950s, when concentrated efforts were made to develop common rules. Women's rules continued to differ from men's until the early 1960s, when most differences were eliminated. A strong motivation for the development of common rules for all groups of competitors was the acceptance of volleyball as an Olympic sport for men and women in the 1964 Games held in Tokyo, Japan.

Volleyball has developed and changed significantly from the early days, when it was used to provide moderate activity to large groups of relatively unskilled people, to the present-day game of power volleyball. It still remains one of the few games that can appeal to and be played by novices and experts, by large and small groups, by boys and girls, and by coeducational groups. It can be modified easily to suit younger players by lowering the net or using a plastic beach ball. It can be enjoyed by the highly skilled by reducing the number of players on a side to four or even two. Doubles play is popular in some recreational and competitive groups. The number of players on a team can be increased to maximize participation in large classes; however, this usually results in lower skill development because each person has less opportunity or need to hit the ball.

Purposes and Values

Volleyball is a sport that can accommodate a large number of players at one time. The best play and skill development occurs when there are only 5 or 6 players on a team, but more can be used if it is necessary to involve more students in activity. When classes are large and space is small, teams could have as many as 9 or 10 players. However, this does not provide a good practicing or learning situation.

Volleyball requires agile, quick movements; good eye-hand coordination; hand and arm strength; and mental alertness. Cardiorespiratory endurance is not important for beginners, but skilled players must be in good condition. The hands, arms, and shoulders should be strengthened through an exercise program before the volleyball unit begins. This training provides players with more opportunities for successful performance of these skills and helps eliminate some of the finger injuries.

Reaction time is very important to skilled play. The ball may travel at high speeds, and rapid responses are necessary. Although there is doubt that reaction time can be improved, response time can be improved through training and experience. Players need to learn to adopt a ready position and watch the opponents carefully. As the opponent hits the ball, the player must analyze the backswing, the position of the hand at contact, and the position of the hitter on the court, and then try to interpret the effects these will have on the path and speed of the ball. The player must learn which cues to attend to and how to respond in the most effective manner. This can make it easier to defend against the attack hits made by the opponents.

Volleyball is of special value in a coeducational program because it is one of the few team sports in which girls and boys begin at approximately the same skill level. Boys do not usually practice these skills outside of class and therefore do not have a skill advantage. Additionally, there is no direct contact between players, so height and weight differences are less significant than they are in activities such as soccer and basketball.

Care should be taken to avoid situations in which the taller, stronger boys dominate play. This is not usually a problem until the eighth or ninth grades. Instructors and coaches should emphasize the need for cooperative teamwork among players. Emphasis on the affective domain of learning fits appropriately into this unit.

The net may be lowered to allow more success for middle school or junior high students at skills such as spiking and blocking. It is advisable to adapt the net height to the height and skill of the participants. Appropriate challenges to performers can enhance participation without causing undue frustration.

The Game

Volleyball is played by two teams of six players each by hitting a ball back and forth over a net. The objective is to prevent the ball from touching the court on your side of the net while attempting to make the opponent miss the ball or hit it out of bounds. The ball may not be caught or thrown (a *held ball* foul) but must be clearly hit by the players.

A team consists of six players (Figure 11.1): right *forward* (RF), center forward (CF), left forward (LF), right *back* (RB), center back (CB), and left back (LB).

The game is begun by the RB player on one team serving the ball over the net into the opponents' court. Each team is permitted three hits to return the ball to the other side. Players may not hit the ball more than once in succession. Only the serving team may score points. If the serving team wins the *volley*, it scores a point; if the receiving team wins the volley, *side out* is declared, and the receiving team becomes the serving team.

The usual *match* is won by winning two out of three games (three out of five for more advanced players and for some tournament play). A game consists of 15 points; however, a team must defeat the opponent by 2 points to win; otherwise, play continues. Timed games may be played when a tournament schedule must be followed or for informal class play.

The right back on one team begins the game by serving from out of bounds behind that team's end line. The server continues to serve as long as that team scores points. A clockwise *rotation* of players one position occurs each time the receiving team becomes the serving team. Players must be in the same positions relative to their teammates at the time of the serve but may move

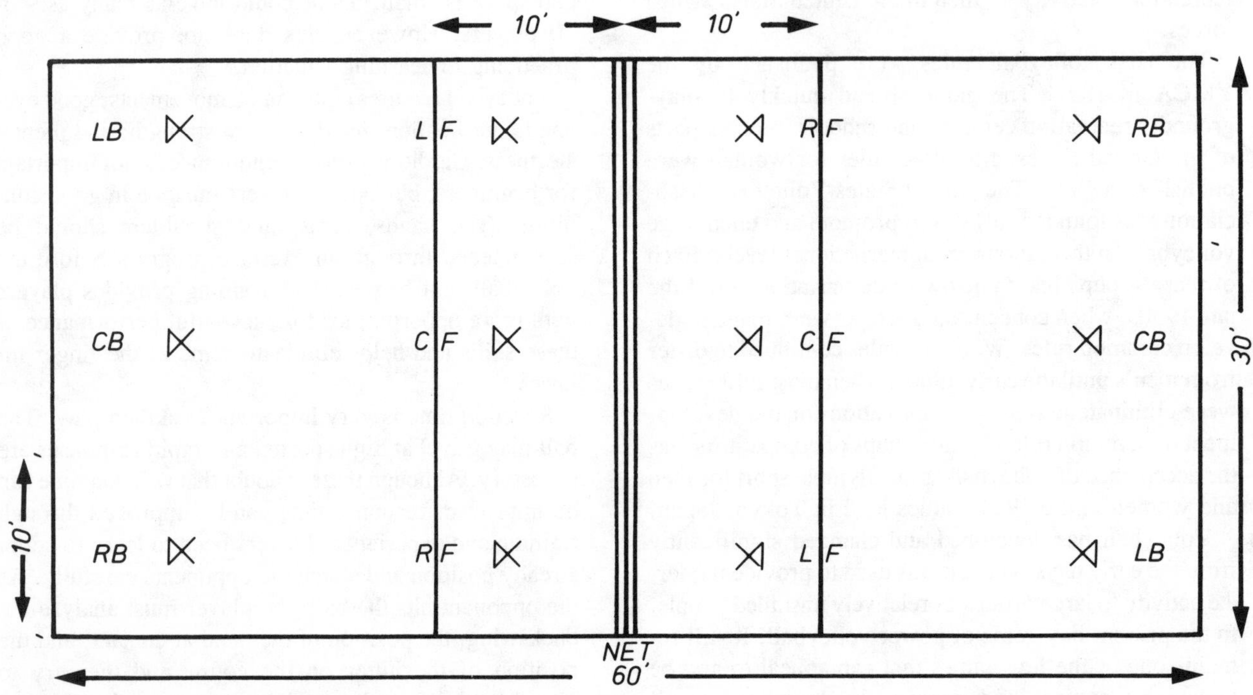

Figure 11.1. Volleyball court and team positions

about on the court after the ball has been served. Players may leave the court to play the ball.

Playing Area

The volleyball court is 60 by 30 ft. A net bisects the court into two 30-ft-square playing areas. A *center line* directly under the net separates one side of the court from the other. Two more lines, called *attack lines*, run parallel with the center line on each side of the net and 10 ft from the center line. The outside lines should be 2 in. wide and are within the boundary limits (Figure 11.1).

Smooth flooring provides the best surface for volleyball, but any firm surface is adequate. Recreational play on sand beaches is very popular in some areas of the country. Each court should have at least 6 to 8 ft of space around it to reduce interference with play on other courts. The ceilings should be at least 23 ft high, although the game can be played under modified rules in gymnasiums with lower ceilings, in which case the ball may be allowed to continue in play off the ceiling if it returns toward the floor on the same side of the net. However, a ball that deflects off the ceiling to the opposite side of the net should be ruled out of bounds.

Equipment

The following is a description of the equipment necessary for volleyball. The only equipment required for volleyball are the net, net supports, and balls. Standards for equipment and recommendations on equipment use are also included.

Balls

Regulation balls have leather covers and need to be kept properly inflated. Some balls have panels glued onto the inner rubber bladder. Such balls should be inspected often and any loose corners of leather reglued immediately before the entire panel peels off. Rubber balls are recommended for outdoor play because they are more durable, but they are usually harder and sting the hands. Beginning and younger players have difficulty learning volleyball skills under these circumstances. Even leather balls may cause discomfort for the beginner who is practicing a skill repeatedly. To alleviate this problem, balls can be made softer by removing some of the air, using older worn volleyballs, or even using lightweight plastic beach balls to begin the unit.

In the teaching situation, it would be ideal to have a ball for every two students in class. However, effective instruction and practice can be organized with one ball for every five or six students, in which case classes could be divided into permanent squads to expedite class management.

Nets

The volleyball net should be adjustable in height to accommodate adult men's and women's play as well as school children. The official net height for men's play is 7 ft 11-5/8 in. and for women's play 7 ft 4-1/8 in. A lower net may allow individual success practicing skills like the spike and the block and thus motivate younger players to master these skills. The supports should not interfere with play on the court and should be sufficiently firm to enable the net to be drawn taut.

Suggestions for Coeducational Play

Volleyball lends itself readily to coeducational play because it does not involve body contact, it depends more on skill than on strength, and it permits adjustments for height differences. Experiences in this sport outside of school are limited for both boys and girls. Therefore, students generally approach the activity with similar skill backgrounds in the relevant basic skills.

The use of partially deflated balls, Nerf balls, or beach balls will help beginners overcome the initial fear of being hurt by contacting the balls with the hands or arms. After a moderate level of skill is achieved, regular volleyballs can be introduced.

Teachers should assess the height of players in classes and adjust the net height accordingly. When the net is so high that only a few can spike successfully, others are discouraged from trying it. The girls in a high school class are generally shorter than the boys and therefore are often deprived of the chance to spike. As skill levels increase, nets can be raised to present further challenge. The recommended height for coeducational play for senior high students and adults is 7 ft 8 in. This is about halfway between the official heights for men's and women's play.

Some teaching suggestions for encouraging teamwork and preventing some players from dominating play include establishing special class rules. The team that violates one of the following rules could lose the service or a point.

1. There must be three hits on a side before the ball is hit over the net.
2. The bump must be used to receive the ball, or at least one pass made before the ball crosses the net.
3. If two or more players on a team hit the ball, at least one must be a girl.
4. Teams must line up alternating boys and girls.
5. Players must play their own positions.

Whenever there are a lot of students on each court (more than seven or eight), the players are so close together that a few players dominate the game. When this happens, the less aggressive players stand around and do nothing. Keep the numbers low so that each player has an area to cover and more opportunity to participate. Substitute with other players frequently.

If players do not stay in their own positions, divide the court with water-color paint or shoe polish. The players are then required to stay in their own sections unless making a save on the third hit.

Teaching Progressions

The following outline suggests skill progressions for instruction in volleyball. Those groups at the intermediate level should review the beginning skills and move on quickly to practice the intermediate skills. The experienced players should spend most of the instructional time learning the advanced skills, refining those skills previously learned, and working on advanced strategies. Both intermediate and advanced groups should spend more time than should beginning groups in game play.

Progression for Beginning Players

I. Passes
   A. Overhead
      1. Front set
      2. Back set
   B. Underhand pass/bump

II. Serves
   A. Underhand
   B. Sidearm (high school novices)

III. Game play

Additional Skills for Intermediate Players

I. Passes
   A. Dig

II. Serves
   A. Sidearm
   B. Overarm (overhand)

III. Offensive and defensive skills
   A. Spike
   B. Block
   C. Dink

IV. Game play and simple strategy

Additional Skills for Advanced Players

I. Serves
   A. Spins
   B. Floaters

II. Offensive and defensive skills
   A. Smash
   B. Rolls and dives

III. Game play with offensive and defensive patterns of play

Techniques and Practice

Fundamental Techniques

A player must be alert and in a ready position to react to any ball in flight that has been directed to him or her by a teammate or opponent. The player must also approach the ball in order to play it. The ready position and the approach with various footwork skills are utilized in passing, setting, and some defensive receiving.

Ready Position

The ready position is a stance of shoulder width with the body weight equally distributed over both feet (Figure 11.2). This permits the performer to be stable but at the same time to move quickly with a forward shift of body weight onto the balls of the feet, causing the heels to move slightly upward off the floor. The knees are flexed ahead of the toes and the trunk flexed (inclined or leaning) forward. The arms are extended downward and are adjacent to the inside of each knee.

Figure 11.2. Ready position

Approach and Footwork

The performer must determine the ball destination and move quickly to that court area. In the straight approach, the performer can move quickly by taking small steps and keeping the center of gravity low. Players should attempt to position themselves behind and under the ball with their bodies facing the intended direction of ball flight. After positioning themselves properly, players should stop and assume a balanced or stable position for the passing and setting.

When a straight approach is not possible, the side step or the crossover and run are useful approaches. Sidestepping is utilized for short distances and is initiated by sliding the foot on the side of the intended movement laterally. The trailing foot quickly follows the lead foot. Several of the side steps can be taken in a sequence to reach the desired court position, after which the lead foot stops slightly forward and faces the direction of the intended hit. The trailing foot closes the gap by creating a stance of about shoulder width. When there is a greater lateral or diagonal distance to cover, the crossover and run is more appropriate. This approach is initiated by the inside foot (opposite the side of intended motion) crossing over in front of the outside foot (side of intended motion). The inside foot is planted in the direction of the run. This places the body in a position to execute a run to the desired court location. At the conclusion of all approaches in the passes and sets, the performer takes a stance of approximately shoulder width with one foot slightly ahead of the other.

Overhead Passing and Setting

The *overhead pass*, or *front set*, is the basic hit used to pass a high ball to a teammate or to set the ball into position for a teammate's offensive hit. Short players who may have difficulty mastering attack plays at the net should learn to perform this skill well to be an asset to their teams.

The overhead pass or front set is a pushing skill (Figure 11.3). The performer has already performed the ready position or the approach and resumes an appropriate stance of stability before executing the overhead pass. The appropriate stance in this situation is with the knees flexed and the head tilted back sufficiently to focus on the ball. The arms move forward and upward until the upper arms are parallel with the floor and the elbows flexed and pointing out to the sides. The hands are hyperextended (bent backward) at the wrist and the fingers spread and hands slightly cupped. The thumbs and index fingers form a triangle.

The action of the overhead pass or front set begins with extension of the legs and arms simultaneously into the ball. The fingers contact the ball (the palms do not touch the ball) above and in front of the forehead. The fingers close in a grabbing action once contact is made. The wrist and fingers act like an uncoiling spring during contact. Extending the fingers at contact without making an illegal hit permits more ball control. The follow-through is executed with continuous upward extension of the entire body through the ball in the direction of the hit.

Practice Drills

The ideal way to practice the set is for each person to have a ball and clear wall space. The ball is tossed into

Figure 11.3. Overhead pass or front set

the air and then volleyed against the wall in a continuous manner. As players improve, a motivational element may be added by having them count the number of successive hits they can make. Whenever the ball falls to the floor or is caught, the count starts again. The person with the highest score wins.

Players can also learn to set the ball directly over their heads rather than using a wall. They toss the ball overhead to start and then continue to volley straight up. As skill improves, the player can be required to keep one foot stationary or to stay within a small area on the floor. Encourage players to hit the ball 6 to 10 ft overhead.

Partner Drills. Pairing players to share a ball works well if there is enough equipment and space to accommodate the entire group. This maximizes practice time for each learner.

1.0. Beginners should start by having one person toss a high lobbed pass to the hitter, who volleys it back to the tosser. Players usually are more accurate with a toss than with a set. After a given number of tosses (perhaps 5 to 10), the tosser becomes the hitter and the hitter the tosser. Emphasize accuracy and high passes.

2.0. When each player has had sufficient practice from the tossed ball, the partners could set the ball back and forth to each other. This type of practice is safer if all passes are going back and forth in the same direction (i.e., all north and south or all east and west).

Group Drills. The following are group drills for the overhead pass or front set. Emphasize placement accuracy.

1.0. Circle Formation (Figure 4.13). Players volley the ball back and forth across the circle using the overhead pass. Emphasize keeping the ball above shoulder level. If the ball drops below chest level, catch it and start over with a high toss. Scoring may be added for motivation. Count the number of successive hits. Start over if the ball hits the floor or is caught.

2.0. Circle Formation with Leader in Center (Figure 4.15). The person in the center sets the ball to each person in the circle. After each circuit, another leader enters the circle. Motivational variation: See which group can complete all circuits first.

3.0. Leader and Class Formation (Figure 4.6). The leader passes the ball down the line from one end to the other. Change leaders frequently.

4.0. Column Formation With Leader (Figure 4.3). The leader tosses the ball to the first player in the column, who hits it back and goes to the end of the column. The leader volleys the ball to the next person. This continues until all players have had an opportunity to pass. Change leaders periodically.

5.0. Shuttle Formation (Figure 4.7). The leader of one column sets the ball to the leader of the other column, who sets it to the second person in Column 1.

This pattern continues until all players have passed. After players hit the ball, they go to the end of their own or the opposite column. This drill can also be done with one column of individuals on each side of the net.

6.0. Two Columns at Right Angles (Figure 11.4). Player X2 sets the ball to Point A (Pass a). Player X1 runs to Point A and volleys the ball back to Player X4 (Pass b). Player X4 volleys back to Point A (Pass c), where Player X3 receives it and volleys to Player X6. This procedure continues until all players have participated. Each person goes to the end of the opposite column after volleying the ball. Emphasize high passes to allow time to get into position. This drill works best with at least three persons in each column.

7.0. Circle Formation Facing Clockwise (Figure 4.14). All players begin to run around the circle in a clockwise direction. The ball is volleyed back and forth as they run. Change to a counterclockwise movement and repeat.

Back Set

The *back set* is used to hit the ball to a teammate who is behind the *setter*. This is an excellent deceptive move and should be mastered especially by the shorter players.

The back set is also a pushing skill, and it is similar to the overhead pass, or front set. The preliminary movements of the back set—ready position, approach, body positioning, stance, and striking preparation—are performed the same way as in the front set. However, the back set has a different execution in the force-production phase of extension. In addition to the forceful extension of the ankles, knees, and trunk at the hips, the hips move forward at ball contact, causing the back to arch slightly and the body weight to shift forward onto the front foot. The arms extend over the head with the palms up and fingers pointing behind the player as the ball is projected in a high arc behind the hitter. The thumbs point upward after the ball is contacted. As in the front set, the head and body follow through in the direction of the intended ball flight.

Practice Drills. The following are practice drills for the overhead pass, or front set, and the back set. Emphasize accuracy in the sets.

1.0. Column Formation (Figure 4.9). Players are positioned in columns about 6 ft apart. The first person in a column tosses the ball overhead and back sets to the person behind, who then sets to the next player behind. After the ball is passed, players turn around to face the other direction. This continues until the ball reaches the end of the column. The last person in the column may volley the ball back up the column or may catch the ball, turn around, and start it back up the line.

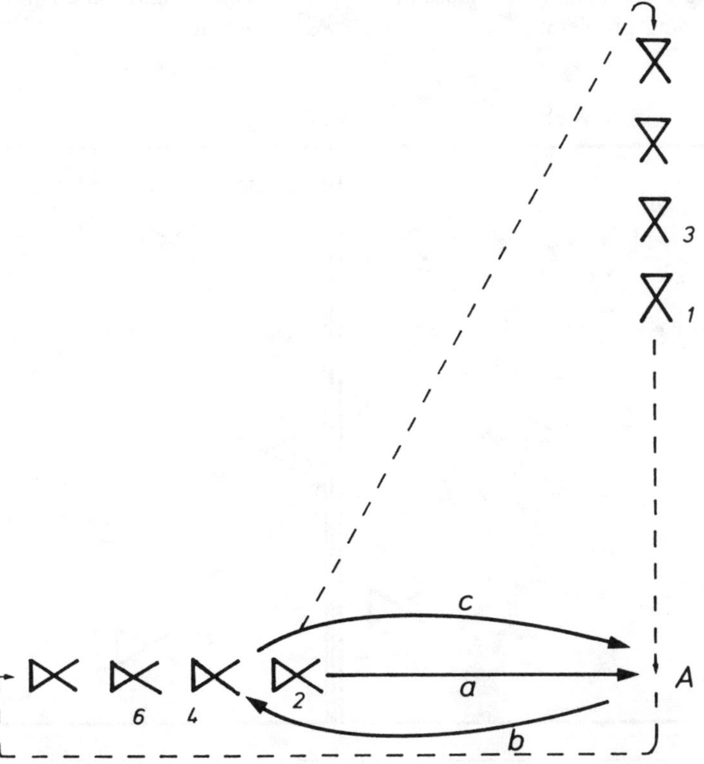

Figure 11.4. Passing drill: Two columns at right angles

2.0. Column with Net (Figure 11.5). Three groups may be assigned the same court. Players assigned to the X1 positions set the ball high to players in the X2 positions, who have their backs to the net. Players in the X2 positions back set over the net. Players in the X3 and X4 positions receive the volley and return the ball to those in the X1 positions. This drill may be started with a toss rather than a set for beginners. When three groups are all using one court, the middle group should be working in the opposite direction from the outside groups. If there are more than four persons per group, the extra players should be on the retrieving side or behind the setter awaiting a turn to be setter. Players should rotate after four or five trials so that each gets an opportunity to front and back set. The ball should be returned under the net to Player X1 to avoid more confusion and the danger of hitting someone in the head. As skills improve, the ball could be volleyed back to Players X1 or X2.

Common Movement Problems and Suggestions

The following are common difficulties encountered in passing and setting. Suggestions are also included for instruction.

- A common movement problem is to start the approach too late. This does not permit players to set or stabilize their positions or stances before hitting. During drills, cueing players might help those individuals with this timing problem.
- A limited range of motion in the lower body and especially in the upper body determines the distance and height of the pass or set. Players should practice passing and setting different distances and heights by varying the range of motion.
- In the back set, players frequently fail to get the ball behind them. Remind them to move under the ball so that it is dropping toward the top of the head. Players should also point the fingers behind the head. If the fingers are allowed to point forward, a throw or carry may result.
- The pass or set requires a soft touch with precise control and accuracy. A soft touch is achieved when the entire body accelerates consistently prior to contact through the follow-through. Fingers should be relaxed and the primary contact on the ball from the thumb and the index, long, and ring fingers simultaneously. The little fingers act as the directors or steering mechanisms of the ball. Striking the ball with the palms or heels of the hands can cause a loss of ball control.
- Some players appear to execute the skill properly, but the ball does not go in the intended direction. This may be caused by an improper hand position or angle. If the fingers are not flexed, the ball could go backward over the head. If the hands are vertical or perpendicular to the floor on ball contact, the ball will be netted or go under the net. The thumbs should be at right angles to the index fingers to give support under the ball and to help project the ball upward.

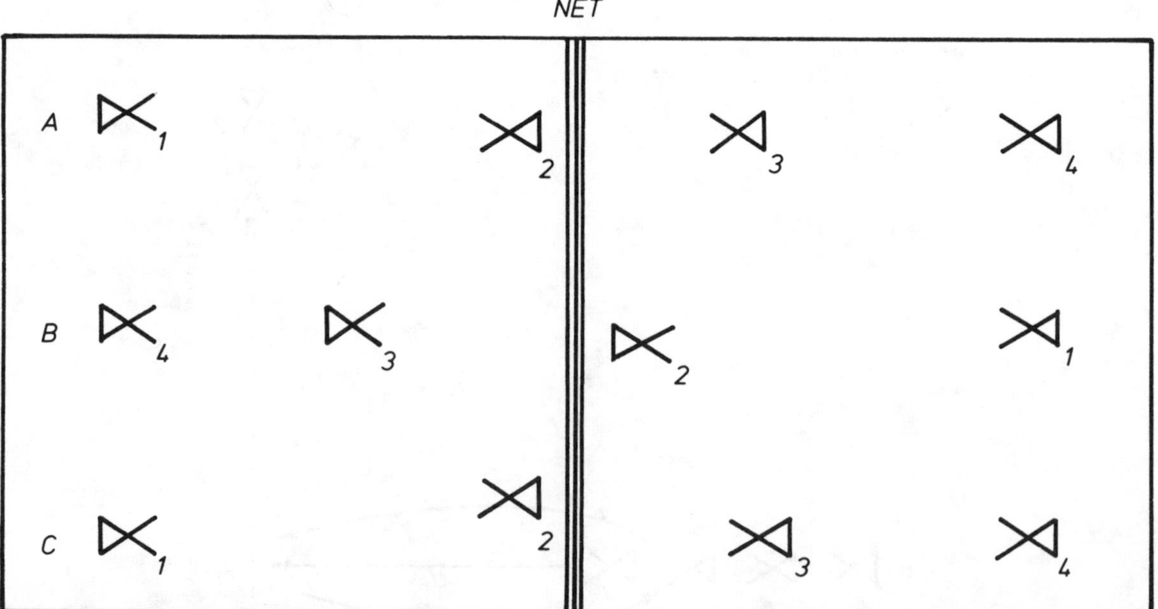

Figure 11.5. Back set drill

- The overhead pass (front set) and the back set should be taught without an approach before being combined with the approach. The overhead pass or front set should be taught before the back set.

Underarm Pass, or Bump

The *underarm pass* is used to volley a ball that has dropped below waist level. The ball must not be lifted or held but must be hit sharply and crisply. The two-handed underhand pass is also called the *bump*, or forearm, pass. It is usually executed in front of the body but may be used to either side.

The underarm pass or bump is an underhand striking skill (Figure 11.6). The performer executes the appropriate approach and establishes a stable stance with the appropriate set position prior to the execution of the underhand pass. The performer can step forward into the ball with either foot. Arms are brought forward and together in front of the body to form a surface for striking. The hands are held in the interlaced or interlocked position (Figure 11.7). The player positions the body to accommodate playing the ball as close to the body's midline as possible.

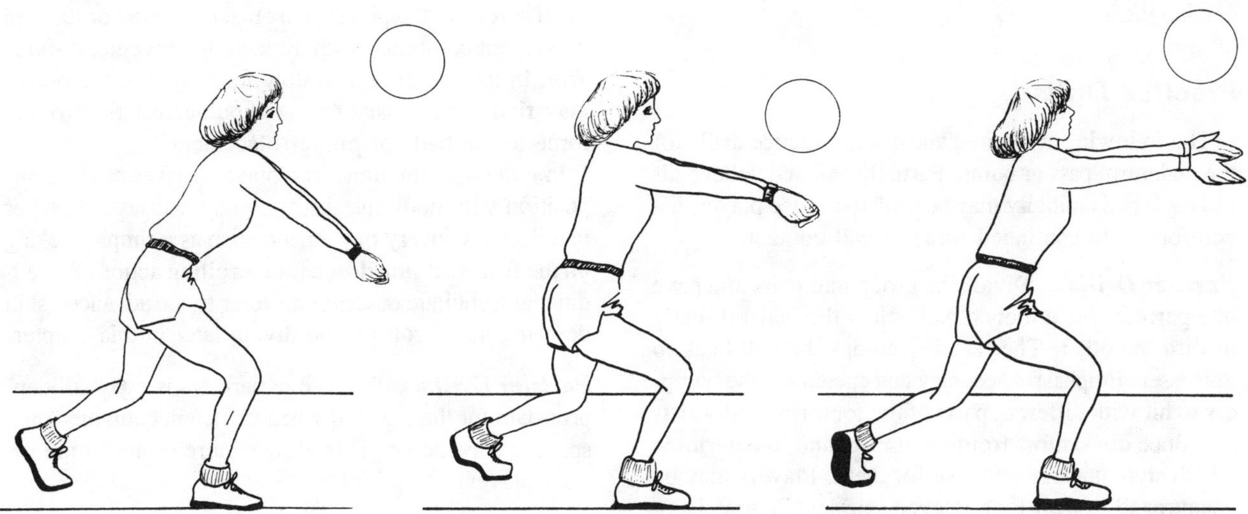

Figure 11.6. Underhand pass or bump

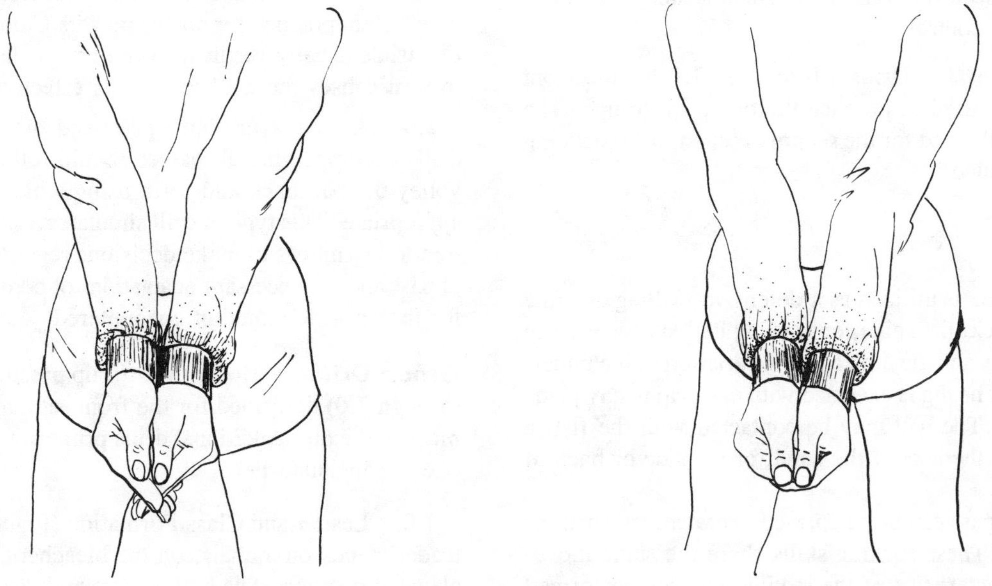

Figure 11.7. Interlaced and interlocked hand positions

The strike occurs on the forearm about 2 to 3 in. above the wrist. This is the preferred contact point. Extension only at the shoulders creates the arm swing, which immediately follows ball contact. This action causes the shoulders and arms to move forward and slightly upward without flexing the elbows.

When the ball cannot be contacted close to the midline of the body, a lateral underhand pass is needed. The approach involves a sideward lunging movement. The shoulder on the opposite side of the lunge drops while the shoulder on the same side of the lunge rises.

The follow-through is in the desired ball direction. The positioning of the arms during contact determines the ball direction. The body remains flexed at the knees and the body weight forward and the arms straight at shoulder height.

Practice Drills

The following are paired and group practice drills for the underarm pass or bump. Partially deflated volleyballs or beach balls initially may be used to reduce player discomfort from continued forearm-ball contact.

Partner Drills. Divide the group into pairs and have one partner toss a lobbed ball below the waist directly toward the other. The receiver bumps the ball back to the tosser. Emphasize accuracy and encourage the bumpers to hit with different parts of the forearms and wrists to reduce discomfort from the impact and to determine which style is more effective for them. Players may be encouraged to wear long-sleeved shirts while practicing this skill.

One partner should toss at least 10 times to the other before they switch roles. Beginners usually need quite a few consecutive trials before being able to achieve reasonable control.

Group Drills. Drills 1.0 through 7.0 for the front set may be used to practice the bump in groups. The partner drills used for the set are excellent for practicing the bump also.

Dig

The *dig pass* is utilized as a defensive skill against the power attack, the spike, or varying ball speeds used in some spikes and the dink and is a variation of the underarm pass. The dig is executed with one arm in any plane of motion. The ball may be contacted with the fist, a firm palm, the heel of the hand, or the side or back of the hand.

The dig pass can be performed overarm, sidearm, or underarm. These striking skills share the same movement characteristics of the stiking patterns performed in the same plane of motion. The primary difference between the dig and other forms of passing is the singular limb involvement. The arm action and body positioning vary regarding the type of dig utilized and the game circumstances.

When receiving a *smash*, or hard spike, the dig takes on unique movement characteristics. The positioning of the arm requires a very firm position and very little flexion at the shoulder and very little or no backswing. Due to the momentum of the ball in this situation, arm motion increases the momentum of the hit ball and results in losing control.

The dig is also used to receive balls of varying speeds. These off-speed spikes and dinks create an uncertain situation for the receivers, who do not have sufficient time to approach the ball and set their positions for the hit. Therefore, the player must make a diving or lunging movement combined with a reaching movement of one arm. In the situation of a slow-moving ball, the player may find it necessary to use shoulder rotation to add force to the ball for proper placement.

In most dig situations, the player arrives at the court position with body instability, which causes the player to utilize a recovery movement, such as a simple rocking on the feet, additional steps, or a rolling action. For additional technique description, refer to the advanced skill descriptions of rolling and diving later in this chapter.

Partner Drills. Practice in partners is especially appropriate for the dig skill when sufficient equipment and space are available. This allows more on-task time for each player.

1.0. One partner tosses the ball low (knee to waist height) to each side of the partner receiving. The lateral toss encourages the hitter to lunge and reach out to strike the ball with one arm or hand. Ten tosses to each side is sufficient practice for novice players. Additional practice trials usually result in sore arms or hands, which in turn causes the drill to lose its effectiveness.

2.0. After players have practiced the dig, partner drills encompassing all passes should follow. Partners volley the ball back and forth using whichever pass is appropriate. This type of drill simulates a game situation by forcing hitters to make decisions regarding the type of pass and the necessary adaptations of body positioning for the specific situation encountered.

Group Drills. Most of the group passing drills (1.0 through 7.0) described for the front set may be used to practice the dig. Additional drills primarily for dig practice are included here.

1.0. Leader and Class Formation (Figure 4.6). The leader stands on a chair, on the bleachers, or in some elevated position. The ball is thrown downward and to the side of each player in turn. This simulates the action of the spike. Throws should be easy for beginners and get more difficult as the skill level increases. Change leaders periodically. A variation of this drill is to have each person go to the end of the column after taking a turn at digging the ball.

2.0. Net Recovery Dig (Figure 11.8). Player X1 throws the ball into the net (preferably just above the bottom tape). Player X2 digs the ball into the air as it rebounds from the net. Player X3 volleys it over the net. Player X4 catches or retrieves the ball and returns it under the net to Player X1. The net should be tight and the ball thrown hard at first so that it rebounds well. Players in the X2 positions should be close to the net in a crouched position and should try to hit the ball high in the air and slightly backward or to the side to allow a teammate easy access to it. Of course, if the net ball resulted from the second hit in a game, the digger would have to attempt a hit over the net. After several trials, the players rotate positions. Extra players may be assigned either to the X3 positions to volley the ball over the net or to the X4 positions to retrieve balls.

Common Movement Problems and Suggestions. The following are common difficulties encountered in the underarm passing skills. Additionally, suggestions are included for instruction.

- Inability to reach the appropriate court position can cause a player to make poor ball contact and is generally due to initiating the approach too late. Success is primarily dependent on agility (fast footwork) and proper body positioning. Practicing approaches at varying speeds should help to eliminate this error and develop the proper timing of approaches based on the speed of the ball.
- Some players hit the ball incorrectly due to poor body positioning. Players should position themselves behind and under the ball for the bump and make ball contact close to the midline of the body. When players are practicing their approaches, check their set positions (body position relative to stance) for the location of the line of gravity in relationship to their base of support. This can be tested by applying pressure to them in the set position to check their stability.
- Novice players may miss the ball totally. This could be due to the situations just reviewed or to not remaining focused on the ball.
- Many times players make contact with the ball just to have it go out of bounds or off at an unexpected angle. Ball contact with the bump should be on the fleshy part of the arms, which should be parallel and level (flat). The angle of ball trajectory is determined by the flatness of the striking surface and the height of the arms at contact. Elevation of the arms prior to contact can detract from the velocity imparted to the ball and cause the ball to move too vertically or possibly backward over the head.
- The quickness (speed or velocity) of the arms at the shoulder just prior to contact and the velocity of the ball into the arms determine the amount of force applied to the ball. Provide practice receiving the

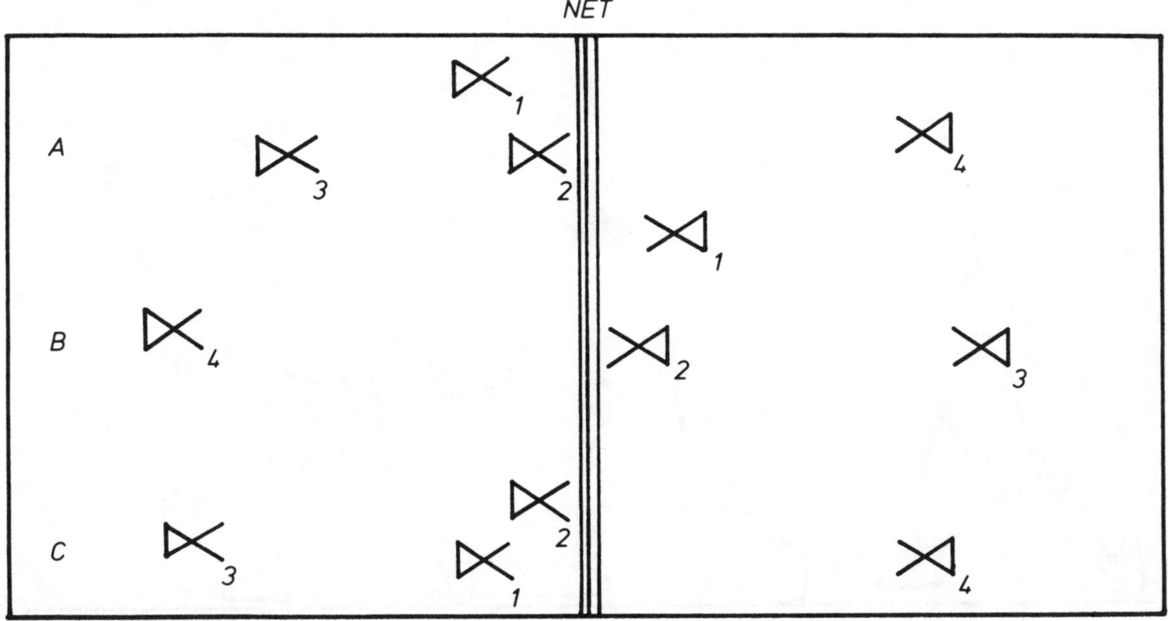

Figure 11.8. Net recovery dig drill

ball at varying speeds and utilizing varying degrees of motion at the shoulder to help the player develop the proper judgment of movement for projecting the ball with accuracy.

- The approach and underarm pass (bump) without the approach should be taught separately. Competence in each skill separately will facilitate the execution and timing of the two skills combined.

General Passing Drills. The following drills may be used to practice all of the passing skills. Emphasize maintaining the volley using any appropriate pass.

1.0. Double-Line Formation (Figure 4.10). Lines of players face each other about 10 ft apart. Players overhead pass or bump back and forth down the lines. Start lines close together; as skills improve move them farther away. A variation would be to place one line on each side of the net and volley over the net.

2.0. Team Formation on Court. Distribute groups of 5 to 10 players on each side of the net. Start the ball with a toss and volley back and forth over the net.

3.0. Circle Formation (Figure 4.13). Players kneel on the floor and volley the ball back and forth. Use small circles. Variation: Players sit instead of kneeling. These drills are for intermediate to advanced players and require good ball control and the use of vigorous arm and shoulder movements.

4.0. Single Column Facing Wall (Figure 4.2). The first person in the column sets the ball against the wall and immediately goes to the end of the column. The next person moves toward the rebound and volleys it back up against the wall. This pattern continues until all players have had an opportunity to set the ball against the wall. Competition can be added by counting the number of successive volleys for a squad or the number of times the team can go through the column without missing. This competition is more suitable for the advanced player.

Serves

The *serve* is used to put the ball into play. Because players must rotate to each position on the court, everyone must learn how to serve. There are three main types of serves (as well as variations): underhand, sidearm, and overhead. Players should be encouraged to work toward mastering the overhead serve, which is the most difficult to return. Beginners and younger players may need to start with the underhand serve but should advance to the sidearm or overhead serve as soon as possible.

Underhand Serve

This is the easiest serve to perform because the ball is contacted underneath and goes in an arc over the net. With a good backswing to generate power and a strong forward stride to add momentum, anyone can learn to serve consistently this way. The underhand is also the easiest serve to return. Its flight pattern allows time for the receiving team to get into position and plan an effective attack.

The underhand serve is an underarm striking movement pattern. The server stands facing the net in a forward stride with the body weight forward and knees slightly flexed (Figure 11.9). The forward foot is the

Figure 11.9. Underhand serve

foot opposite the striking arm. The nonstriking hand cradles the ball in front of the body at approximately waist height. The ball is positioned in line with the path of the swinging arm and hand. The striking arm is held either in close proximity to the ball or down at the side.

In preparation for the swing, the striking arm is moved rearward to approximately shoulder height in a swinging action that is facilitated by a clockwise rotation, or opening, of the hips. The body weight is shifted rearward onto the back foot at the same time. At the top of the backswing, the player can either toss the ball slightly upward or remain in contact with the ball until just prior to contact.

The force-production phase begins with a counterclockwise rotation of the hip for the right-handed hitter. Immediately following the start of the hip rotation, a rapid downward- and forward-swinging motion of the striking arm occurs. At the same time, the body weight is beginning to shift forward. The hand is held in either an open and cupped position, a half fist for striking with the heel of the hand, or a fist.

Just prior to ball contact, the trunk and knees begin to extend. In addition, the nonstriking hand holding the ball swings laterally away from the ball. The ball is contacted to the side and in front of the body at approximately waist height. It is essential to make contact behind and under the ball.

The follow-through consists of continued forward and upward swinging of the arm in the direction of the intended ball flight. The front foot is also pointing in this direction. The trunk continues to extend at the hips until the body is upright.

Sidearm

The sidearm serve can be projected over the net in a more level path than the high arc of the underhand and thus is more difficult to return. It also tends to be more difficult to control and is less accurate than the underhand serve. If mastered, the sidearm serve can be given various spins and be very effective.

The sidearm serve is an underhand throw coordinated with the sidearm striking pattern. The server stands with the side of the body that is opposite the side of the striking arm toward the net. The feet are shoulder-width apart and the knees slightly flexed in the stance. The weight is equally distributed over both feet. The nonstriking hand holds the ball in front of the body at or slightly below waist height.

The preparation phase begins with a rearward weight shift as the ball is tossed vertically into the air. The ball is tossed upward so that it can be contacted directly in front of the shoulder of the striking arm. At the same time, the striking arm moves rearward in preparation for the force-producing forward swing.

The force-production phase for the right-hander begins with a counterclockwise rotation of the hips, which rotates the trunk toward the target. At that time, weight begins to shift toward the left foot. The tossing arm moves down, and the striking arm begins its forward swinging motion. The arm is held in a reasonably extended position with the upper arm lagging behind the shoulder, the forearm behind the upper arm, and the hand behind the forearm. This provides the serve with the whipping action needed to impart velocity to the ball. Just prior to ball contact, the weight is equally distributed over both feet. This provides a stable base on which the striking arm can also increase the acceleration (whip action) toward the ball.

The hips and shoulders are open (facing the net or target) at the point of contact. Contact with the ball is made either through the center of gravity of the ball or slightly below that point in the direction of the intended ball flight. Contact is made with the heel of the hand or with the fist, and the palm faces the target at the moment of contact.

The follow-through is a continuation of the swinging action of the arm. The body weight is transferred forward onto the front foot. The arm swings in the direction of the ball flight.

Overarm (Overhand) Serve

This serve is the most difficult to return because the flight path is almost parallel with the ground and gives the opponents little time to respond. The ball should be tossed above the shoulder of the striking arm and contact made behind the ball.

The server faces the net in a stride stance with the foot opposite the striking arm forward (Figure 11.10). The ball is held in both hands in front of the body and the arms extended and parallel to the floor. The tossing hand cradles the ball underneath, and the striking hand rests on top of the ball.

The server can either start in a stride stance or step forward into the stride stance just prior to the ball toss. In either case, the weight is forward on the front foot prior to the ball toss. The ball is tossed vertically upward about 2 ft in front of the striking shoulder. The striking arm moves rearward through the horizontal plane at approximately shoulder height. At the same time, the elbow flexes, permitting the forearm and hand to drop behind the head. This is similar to the preparatory arm swing of the overarm throw. The shoulders and pelvis rotate clockwise for the right-hander (open), thus allowing for a forward rotation in the force-production phase. The body weight is shifted on the back foot at this time also.

The ball toss occurs just prior to the beginning of the force-production phase. The ball is tossed vertically over

Figure 11.10. Overhand serve

the striking shoulder at the desired forward position for ball contact. The force-production phase begins with a counterclockwise rotation of the pelvis or the hips (closing). This is followed immediately by a forward rotation of the arm at the shoulder. The forearm lags behind the upper arm and hand behind the forearm. As the body moves forward, the weight shifts forward. Contact is made above the head and slightly in front of the striking shoulder with the hand moving through the center of gravity of the ball and the wrist held firmly extended. The point of contact on the ball and the positioning of the wrist may be altered if a variation (e.g., a floater or a spin) is attempted. The palm of the hand is facing the desired ball flight direction.

The arm follows through after contact in the direction of ball flight. A step forward may occur, but only after contact has been made.

Common Movement Problems and Suggestions

The following are movement problems that occur the most frequently when teaching the serve. Suggestions for correcting such problems and teaching progressions to facilitate instruction are also included.

- Beginners should not be encouraged to toss the ball when first learning the underhand serve. If the performer tosses the ball, poor performance sometimes results from a poor toss, which alters the spatial positioning of the ball for contact. Practice of the skill by making light contact can emphasize the timing and the proper ball area to contact.
- When the skill is performed adequately but inaccurate ball placement occurs, emphasize and pay special attention to the following:
  a. Shoulders should be facing the net on ball contact.
  b. Follow-through motions that move to the right or left rather than in the direction of the intended ball flight will cause the ball to move in that direction. This is sometimes caused by a diagonal arm swing, such as the outside-to-inside swing in the underarm serve.
  c. An improper stance can permit or restrict the pelvic (hip) rotation. This is generally indicated

when the right-handed player projects the ball too far to the right and the left-handed player too far to the left.

d. The ball will travel in the direction of the follow-through. Emphasize this point by having players finish their swings by pointing with their arms in the direction they wish the ball to go. However, make sure focus remains on the ball until after the contact.

- Players may have difficulty getting the ball over the net due to striking the ball too softly or without sufficient velocity. To increase ball velocity, emphasize the following:

a. The intentional and forceful body-weight shift or forward stepping action can add momentum to the swinging arm.

b. Increasing the backswing will permit more time and distance to build momentum in the swinging arm. This is especially important if the player has shortened the backswing.

c. The striking arm should remain firm and swing through the ball. Any flexion (giving) or momentary slowing down of the arm prior to or at contact will deplete the momentum available for transfer to the ball.

Variation: Spins

Most served balls spin somewhat. However, the server who can cause a rapid spin on the ball has a good offensive weapon. A fast-spinning ball tends to curve in the direction of the spin (Figures 11.11 and 11.12). If the

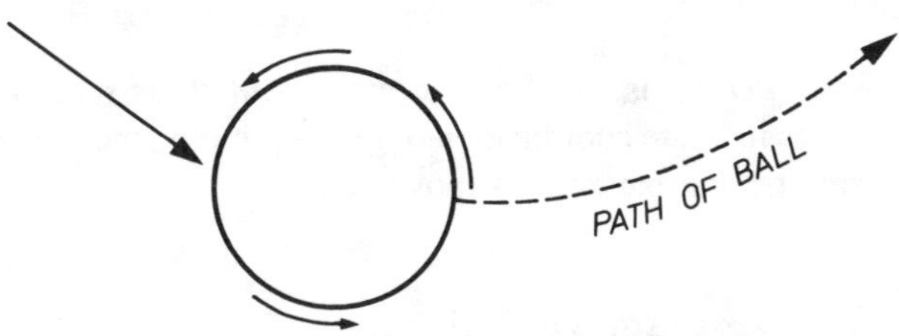

Figure 11.11. Top view of ball with counterclockwise spin

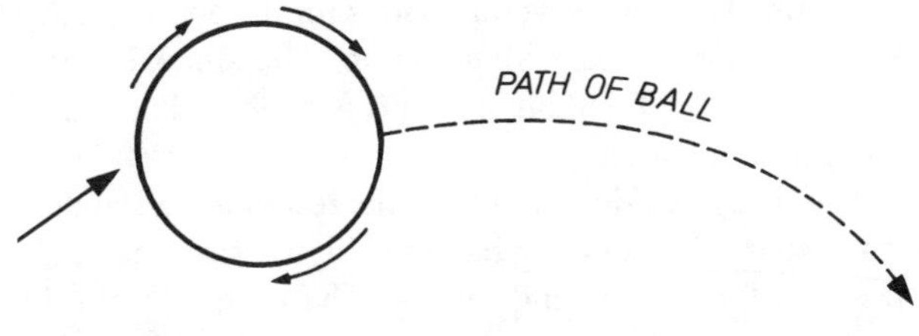

Figure 11.12. Top view of ball with clockwise spin

nose of the ball (side toward the net) is moving to the right, the ball will curve to the right. A spin to the left causes a curve to the left. A ball that is hit with topspin will drop, and a ball given backspin will rise.

Spin is created by the hand position on the ball and the action of the hand during ball contact. Any spin is created by contacting the ball away from the center of gravity of the ball opposite the direction of the intended spin. Force application applied at any point on an object other than in line with the center of gravity initiates rotation. Additional spin is imparted by a snapping (flexion) of the wrist while in contact with the ball. The wrist snap permits the server to maintain contact with the ball longer and thus apply more spin to the ball. An extended or exaggerated follow-through also permits more time in contact with the ball for imparting spin.

The spin most difficult to initiate with an overhand serve is topspin (the top rotates forward). Topspin is created by contacting behind the ball and below its center of gravity. This action is accompanied by a forward snapping (flexion) of the wrist at ball contact. Again, an extensive or exaggerated follow-through permits more time in contact with the ball for imparting spin. The follow-through is diagonally across the body and down.

Variation: Floater

The floater, or *punch serve*, is a ball that is hit directly from behind with little follow-through. It is a punch or push type of movement. The air valve should be positioned so that it is in front of the ball on contact. This slight variance in the ball's balance and the lack of spin cause it to float or waver through the air, and receivers will find it difficult to predict its flight path. The person who does not have a hard overhand serve may find this serve to be very effective. It is usually done from an overhead position but may be initiated underhand.

Contact occurs on the center back of the ball in the floater, directly through the center of gravity of the ball in the desired ball direction. Contact through the center of the ball limits the spin of the ball. The follow-through is short and quick, thus limiting the duration of ball contact and thus the opportunity to impart spin. Firmness (held extension) of the wrist is essential to making direct contact for a short time period.

Practice Drills

Paired and group practice drills are listed here. Use the paired drill whenever there are sufficient balls and space.

1.0. Dividing the group into partners and having one on each side of the gymnasium provides for the most practice in a limited amount of time. Each pair has a ball that they serve back and forth to each other. Players need not use the same ball every time but may serve any ball that comes to them. The distance between partners should be 40 to 60 ft, and players should be warned to stay alert for any off-target serves that may come their way. Be sure that all balls are flying in the same general direction (e.g., north and south). With young players or very large classes, one ball for every two pairs might be safer. This drill can be done with or without nets.

The placement of the serve is a very important consideration, especially for those who do not have a *power serve*. Players should practice directing the serve to specific areas of the court. With this skill, they can take advantage of weaknesses in the receiving team's defense or place the ball between two opponents in an effort to cause confusion. Generally, the best areas to place the ball are near the back of the court and between the front and back rows near the sidelines (Figure 11.13).

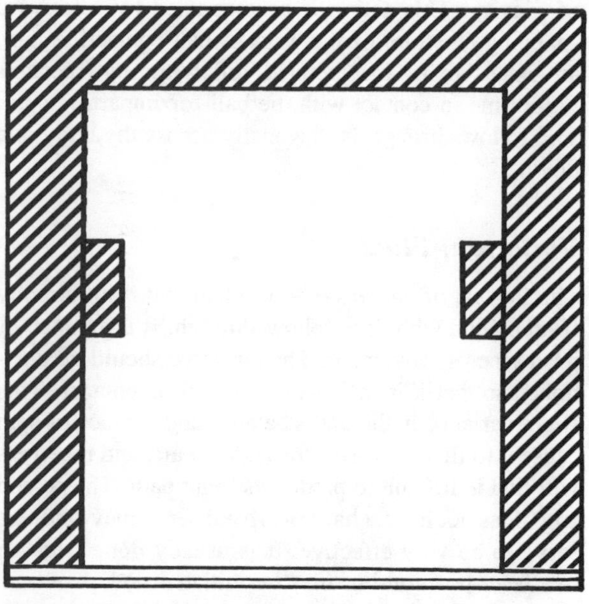

Figure 11.13. Target areas for serves

A team that receives the serve with the center back near the back line may have an open spot near the center of the court. If the center back plays near the middle of the court, the middle of the back end line is vulnerable.

2.0. Line Formation Facing Wall (Figure 4.5). One ball per group. The line should start about 15 ft from the wall. The ball is served against the wall above a 12-ft mark. The player getting the rebound serves next. Have the player make sure that everyone has a turn before second turns are taken. After success at this distance, move back farther until eventually reaching 30 ft. Keep the same level on the wall.

3.0. Single-Column Formation (Figure 4.2). This is the same as Drill 2.0 except done in column formation. The server retrieves the ball, gives it to the next person, and goes to the end of the column.

4.0. Players are distributed on the court as if for a game, one ball per court. Any back-row player steps behind the end line and serves the ball. The ball is volleyed back and forth until it is missed. The ball is then given to the closest back-row player, who steps out of bounds and serves. Be sure that every back-row player gets to serve. Then have front and back lines switch positions on the court.

5.0. Divide the court into zones by drawing lines parallel to the net with tape, shoe polish, or water-color paint (Figure 11.14). The 10-ft line delineates the first zone. The area between the 10-ft line and the end line is divided into three more zones. One team stands behind each end line and serves to the opposite court trying to place the ball into the high point areas (e.g., back of court). There may be one ball per court or one ball for each team. Designate one person to be the scorer for each team. The scorer may score either for teammates or for the team on the opposite side of the net. The latter arrangement is preferred if the scorers are also participants, because they are in a better position to observe the balls that land on their side of the net than those that hit on the other side of the net. After a certain amount of time, play can be stopped and scores compared.

Attack Hit Skills

An *attack hit* is an offensive movement skills that involves intricate coordination of the run, jump, and overarm striking patterns of movement.

Fundamental Techniques

Attack hits require not only a ready position with the approach but also a jump that is coordinated with proper arm positioning for striking. The fundamentals necessary for attack hits are the ready position, the approach, and the jump. There are several options for the approach that must be coordinated with the jump. The attack hits can also be executed without an approach when dictated by the game situation.

The ready position for attack hits resembles a standing track start. The standing height is higher than the ready position for passing and setting. The more upright the standing position, the more it facilitates the approaches utilized in the attack hits.

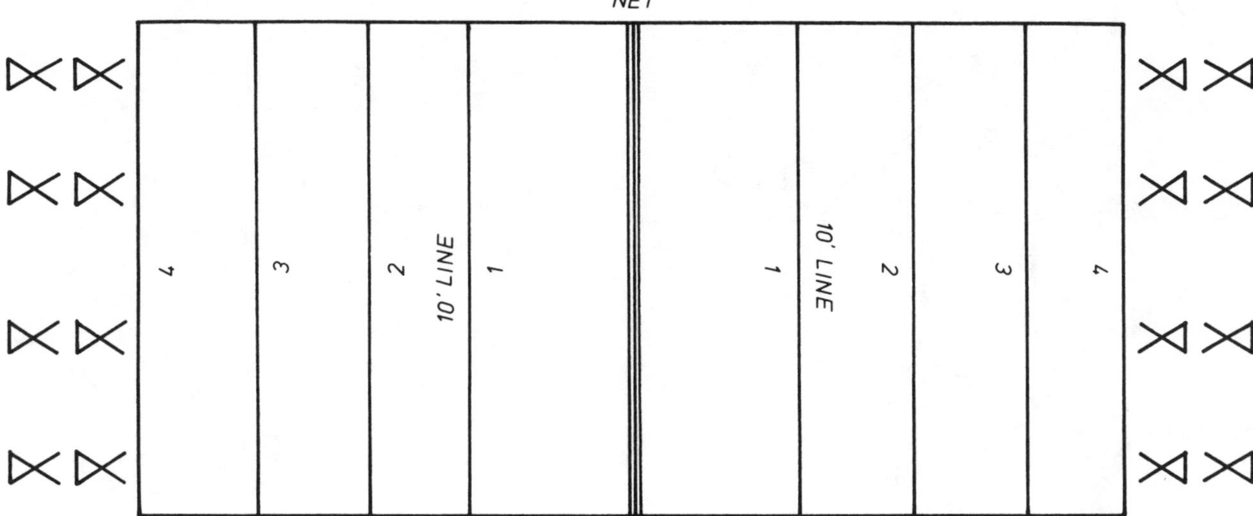

Figure 11.14. Serving practice

The approach is essential to the proper positioning and timing of the jump for the attack hit. There are three common types of approaches: the step-hop, the three-step, and the four-step. A player should attempt all approaches, but generally a player will adopt one style of approach. Selection of approach is usually a personal preference.

The step-hop approach consists of a hop and a jump movement. The player takes the necessary running steps toward the ball before taking a step-hop and jump onto both feet. The player lands on both feet to begin the preparation for the jump, which lifts the player vertically to strike the ball.

The three-step close approach is initiated with a short step forward with one of the feet. The opposite foot steps forward and plants in position for the jump while the arms are swinging backward. The initial foot now closes by coming forward and planting next to the other foot to establish the stance for the jump to strike. This third (closing) step is done onto the toes and involves flexion at the knees and hips in preparation for the jump. The performer is now in position to execute the jump.

The four-step close approach is identical to the three-step approach except that an extra step is taken. The first two steps are short running steps. The third and fourth steps are identical to the last two steps of the three-step close approach.

The coordination of the approach with the jump is essential for vertical lift in the jump and proper timing for the attack hit. On the last step or hop, the body drives downward by flexing at the ankles, knees, and hips with the shoulders facing the net. An immediate simultaneous extension at the knees and hips propels the body upward into the jump. Assisting this vertical propulsion is the forward and upward swing of the arms. Smooth, quick transition from one movement to the next is important for attaining the necessary height, preparing the arms for motion in the hit, and achieving the necessary force production. Practice is essential to developing the timing necessary for arriving at the peak of the jump at the appropriate aerial ball placement.

The preparatory striking arm motion is identical regardless of the type of attack hit. The arms are held close to the body in the forward and upward swinging action. The back becomes moderately arched as the shoulders and hips open (rotate clockwise). During this same sequence of movement, the striking arm moves in a straight horizontal path rearward as in the overarm throwing pattern. The nonstriking arm is extended forward and upward for dynamic balance of the total body. The different attack hits are similar but vary in the forward striking arm swing, the point of contact on the ball, and the type of contact made. The similarities in approach, jump, and preparatory striking arm motion permit the player to deceive the opponent regarding the type of attack hit.

Spike

The *spike* is the most effective offensive skill, and all players should attempt to master it. Almost every player can jump high enough to reach above the net. Short players need to have good sets that drop the ball near the top of the net (see Player A in Figure 11.15). Players can then spike a ball that is only 6 to 8 in. above the net. Tall people or good jumpers can spike balls that are farther from the net and still get a good downward angle (see Player B in Figure 11.15).

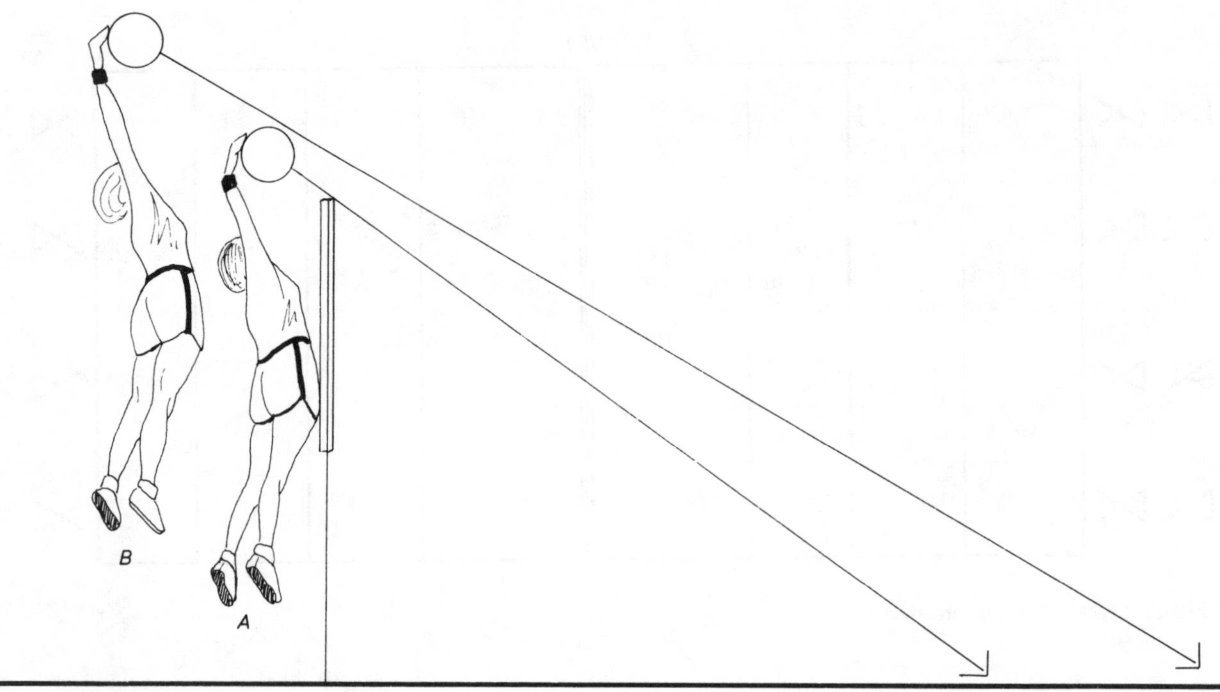

Figure 11.15. Spike sets

Players should try to spike the ball so that it hits the floor between the 10-ft line and the net, unless an opening in the defense has been sighted, in which case the spike should be directed to the uncovered space.

The spike is also referred to as the *power attack* (Figure 11.16). The force-production phase begins—after the approach, jump, and preparatory striking arm motion—with the counterclockwise rotation of the hips

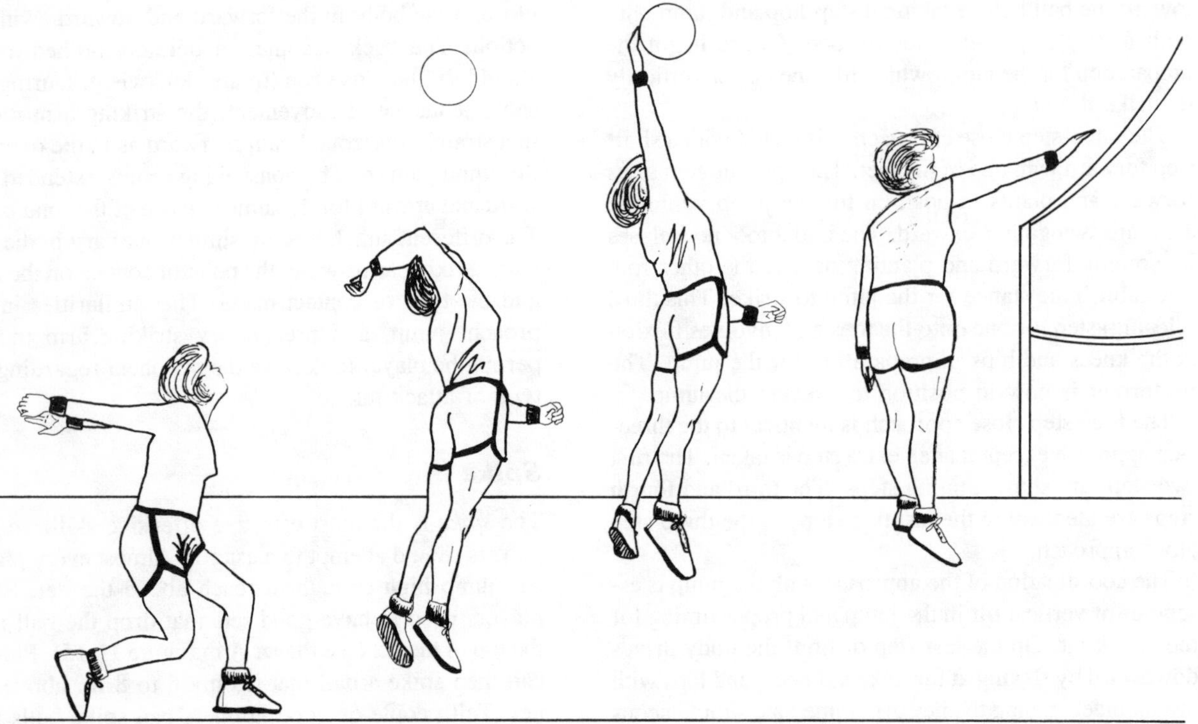

Figure 11.16. Spike

(right-handed player), initiating the forward rotation of the trunk toward the ball. After the hips begin to rotate, the striking arm starts forward at the shoulder. The elbow begins its extension while the wrist is hyperextended (bent backward). The upper arm lags behind the shoulder, the forearm behind the upper arm, and the hand behind the forearm. This action permits the whipping or uncoiling of the arm as it approaches the ball. The arm is fully extended at contact and the wrist still hyperextended. Contact is made in front of the body above the shoulder at a height equal to the length of the fully extended arm. The ball is contacted slightly above its center and with the entire hand. A snapping (fast flexion) at the wrist helps transfer velocity to the ball. The arm continues in the direction of the previously established motion. The trunk flexes forward with the snapping of the wrist through the follow-through.

Practice Drills. The spike should first be practiced without a net. After players become accustomed to the basic pattern, practicing at a net that is just above head level will provide an opportunity for a successful spike without having to jump. The next step is to have the ball supported just above a net that is at regulation height. The learner then jumps vertically and executes the spike without being concerned with timing. Finally, the entire sequence is used with the player spiking a tossed or set ball over the net.

Individual and paired drills provide more practice opportunities and should be used whenever possible. The following are individual and paired practice drills.

1.0. A player with a ball stands about 10 ft from and facing a wall. The ball is tossed overhead and slightly ahead of the right shoulder (left shoulder if left-handed). The ball is hit downward to the floor so that it rebounds into the wall and returns to the hitter. The spiker should try to hit the ball so hard that the rebound from the wall goes high in the air on the return. The ball then may be spiked again directly from the return. This permits a continuous series of spikes.

2.0. The same formation can be used with partners who alternate spiking the ball. Be sure the ball hits the floor before hitting the wall.

The following group practice drills are also effective.

1.0. Column Formation Facing Wall (Figure 4.2). The leader of the column stands about 10 ft from the wall. The leader tosses the ball up to him- or herself, spikes it to the floor 2 to 4 ft from the wall, and goes to the end of the column. The next person steps forward and attempts to spike the rebound. Otherwise, the player catches the ball, tosses it into the air, and spikes it. Emphasize trying to achieve continuous action so that each player spikes the previous spiker's rebound.

2.0. Spike at Net. The squads are distributed on the court as in Figure 11.8 except that the players in the X2 positions are at least two long steps from the net and turned so that the nondominant arm is toward the net. Players at the X1 positions must position themselves to face the X2 players. Player X1 tosses the ball high in the air near the net and close to Player X2, who steps forward, jumps, turns, spikes the ball, and lands facing the net. Be sure that tosses drop near the net but not over it. Players X3 and X4 (and any others in the squad) retrieve the ball and return it to the tosser. After several trials, players rotate. The nets may be lowered at the start of this practice drill to allow for more success. As skills improve, raise the net to the regular height used for class or competition. Variations include the following:

2.1. The tosser sets the ball instead of tossing it.

2.2. Player X3 initiates play by hitting the ball to Player X1, who sets to Player X2, the spiker.

2.3. Spikers move several feet from the net and take a two- or three-step approach before spiking.

Smash (Advanced Skill)

The *smash* or *backcourt spike*, is executed from the mid- to the backcourt, so it cannot be directed downward (Figure 11.17). As the overhead ball is hit with the palm of the hand, the wrist is flexed strongly to impart topspin. This stroke is similar to an overhead serve. The ball should travel almost horizontally until the spin causes it to curve downward.

The smash is a power attack performed identically to the spike with the exception of the point of contact on the ball and the follow-through. Players also may prefer to eliminate the jump. The ball is contacted behind rather than near the top and is hit almost parallel with the ground. The snapping of the wrist, which moves the hand over the ball, imparts topspin on the ball rather than the hard direct vertical downward motion caused in the spike.

Practice Drills. Distribute players on the court as in Figure 11.5. Player X2 sets to Player X1, who smashes the ball over the net. Players X3 and X4 retrieve. Extra players may line up behind Players X1 or X4. Rotate after several trials so that all players get a chance to attempt the smash.

Dink

The *dink*, or *soft spike*, is the countermove by the offense to avoid the block. It should be presented and practiced following instruction in the block. It consists of hitting the ball lightly with the fingers so that it arches over

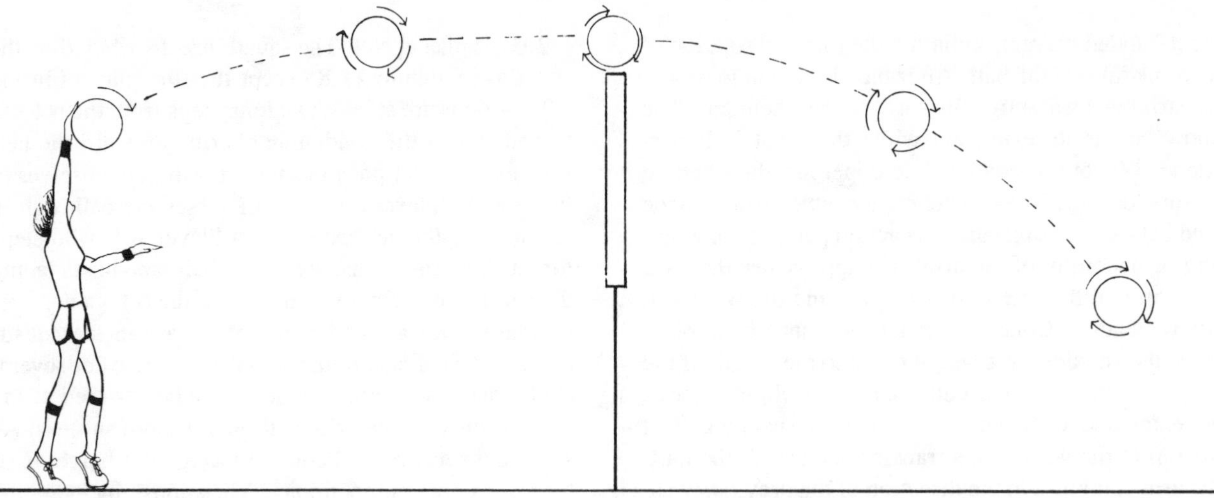

Figure 11.17. Smash with topspin

or around the outstretched hands of the blocker and falls to the floor directly behind the blocker so that other players cannot reach it.

Surprise is important to the effectiveness of the dink. The hitter should jump as if to spike and then, after the blocker jumps, give the ball a little tap over the blocker. The blocker is already in the air and is unable to adjust quickly enough to handle the dink. An attempted dink that lands beyond the 10-ft line on the court will be easily fielded by the blocker's teammates. The dinker must hit the ball lightly.

The dink may also have preliminary movements identical to those of the spike and smash except for the slowed action of the arm prior to ball contact and the hand action on the ball. The ball is hit with the fingertips or knuckles and tipped in an inverted-U pattern. The strike is a soft contact with the wrist held firm. The dink does not employ the snapping of the wrists or the trunk flexion during the follow-through that the other two attack hits have.

Dink Practice Drills. The following are practice drills for the dink skill. Emphasize a soft touch on the ball.

1.0. Column Formation (Figure 4.2). The leader of the column stands near the net, tosses the ball upward, dinks it over, and retrieves it. The leader goes to the end of the column, and the next person goes through the same procedure. Each person may take three or four trials before going to the end of the column. There could be three columns at each net. If one column of individuals is on one side of the net and the other two columns on the opposite side, those awaiting a turn could retrieve for the hitters on the opposite side of the net.

2.0. Distribute players on the court as in Figure 11.8 with Player X4 close to the net. Player X1 tosses or sets, Player X4 blocks, and Player X2 dinks. All others on the squad are retrievers. After several trials, players rotate until all have had a chance to practice the dink. Variations include the following:

2.1. Player X3 bumps or sets the ball to Player X1, who sets to Player X2, who then dinks while Player X4 blocks.

2.2. This is the same as the first variation except that Player X2 may either spike or dink. If Player X4 does not block, Player X2 spikes. If Player X4 jumps to block, Player X2 dinks.

Common Movement Problems and Suggestions

The following are common movement problems encountered in the attacks. Suggestions are made to facilitate the instruction for such problems.

- When first learning the spike, players may have difficulty with the timing. Suspending a ball from an overhead structure by a rope or holding a stationary ball for initial trials allows the player to concentrate on performing the skill. After achieving the spiking motion pattern, players can work on timing with a tossed or a set ball.
- A common error of the novice player is to start the approach too soon. This generally causes a stop or pause in the movement between the approach and the jump. Sequential practice of the approach and timing practice with tossed balls should help this situation. The appropriately timed approach can be

combined with the jump for perfecting the jump and overall timing. The last step is to combine all this with the striking action.

- If the purpose of the attack hit is power and the player is not achieving the desired ball velocity, consider the following possible causes:
  a. Limiting the range of motion in the hips limits the force production by restricting the range of motion of the total body.
  b. Many players do not achieve the power on the attack hit due to lack of arm-and-shoulder range of motion. Instruct players to exaggerate their arm movements.
  c. Novice players tend not to use the whipping action for maximum force production. This is observable when the elbow moves ahead of the shoulder, the forearm moves ahead of the upper arm, or the hand moves ahead of the forearm. Instructors can demonstrate this to the player by restricting or delaying the action of the forearm and hand with their own hands.
  d. When the movement pattern appears correct but the desired speed is not attained, have the player speed up the movement of the arm.

Block

The *block* is the defensive play used against the spike. It requires the defender at the net to jump high in the air and hold up the hands and arms in an effort to cause the spike to rebound back to the spiker's side of the net. The hands and arms must be held firmly so that the hard-driven spike will not pass through. A *blocker* must remember to keep the head back and to slant the arms and hands forward to deflect the ball downward. The block may be performed by one, two, or three players at once. The multiple block is more effective because it covers more area.

Timing is very important in the block. The jump should be timed so that it begins immediately after the spiker jumps. Tall players may jump at the same time as the spiker because their extension above the net is higher and they can still block a spike on the way back down to the floor. Short players must be at maximum jumping height as the ball reaches the net and so must allow time for the spike to occur. Some instructors prefer to have the blocker jump at the same time as the spiker to counteract the tendency to be late with the block. Blockers cannot wait for the arm action of the spiker to start before initiating a block move. They will be too late.

When a blocker must approach the net in order to block, the sidestep approach for short distances and the crossover approach for longer distances are suggested. Both approach techniques were covered in detail in the previous section on fundamental techniques. The ready position for the blocker is established once reaching the position of 1 to 2 ft from the net (Figure 11.18). The blocker's stance is parallel with the feet shoulder-width apart and the knees flexed. Hands are held at shoulder

Figure 11.18. Block

height, the elbows are flexed, and the forearms are parallel with the net.

The preparation for the jump consists of flexion at the ankles, knees, and hips with the trunk slightly flexed (inclined or leaning) forward to assume a half-squat position. Force production begins with a forceful and rapid simultaneous extension of the ankles, knees, and hips. The arms are extended vertically over the top of the net on the vertical jump. The fingers are spread, and the total arm (including the hand) is held firm for ball contact. Just prior to contact, the player turns the shoulders, arms, and hands as a unit toward the center of the opponent's court. The reach should be sustained as long as possible. The blocker can hyperextend (bend backward) at the wrist to deflect the ball upward if desirable. This is referred to as the *soft block*.

The landing is executed by reaching for the floor with the legs. On contact with the floor, the blocker gradually permits flexion of the ankles, knees, and hips, in that order, bringing the blocker safely back to the ready position assumed prior to the jump.

Common Movement Problems and Suggestions

The following are common movement problems encountered during instruction. Suggestions are made to help resolve these problems.

- More than a half-squat position in preparation for the jump detracts from the force production or vertical lift possible in the vertical jump.
- A common foul for the blocker is touching the net. This is generally caused by starting the block too close to the net, flexing the trunk too far forward, reaching too far over the net, jumping into the net, or extending the arms toward the ball rather than allowing the ball to rebound off the hands or arms.
- When the ball rolls down the front of the blocker, it is generally caused by the blocker's being positioned too far from the net, extending the arms and hands too slowly, or spreading the arms apart too far.
- Novice players tend to withdraw the arms from the extended position over the net too soon after reaching the peak of the jump. It should be emphasized that blocking can be done on the way down from the vertical jump also.
- Instruction and practice for landings are essential for avoiding physiological problems in the legs.
- Instruction and practice for single blocks should precede the instruction and practice of double or multiple blocks.

Practice Drills

The following are practice drills for blocking. Blockers can practice individually or in pairs.

1.0. Double-Column Formation. Columns of individuals are lined up near the net post about 2 ft apart (Figure 11.19). The first person in each column takes two or three steps forward, faces the net, jumps up, and claps hands with the other leader over the top of the net.

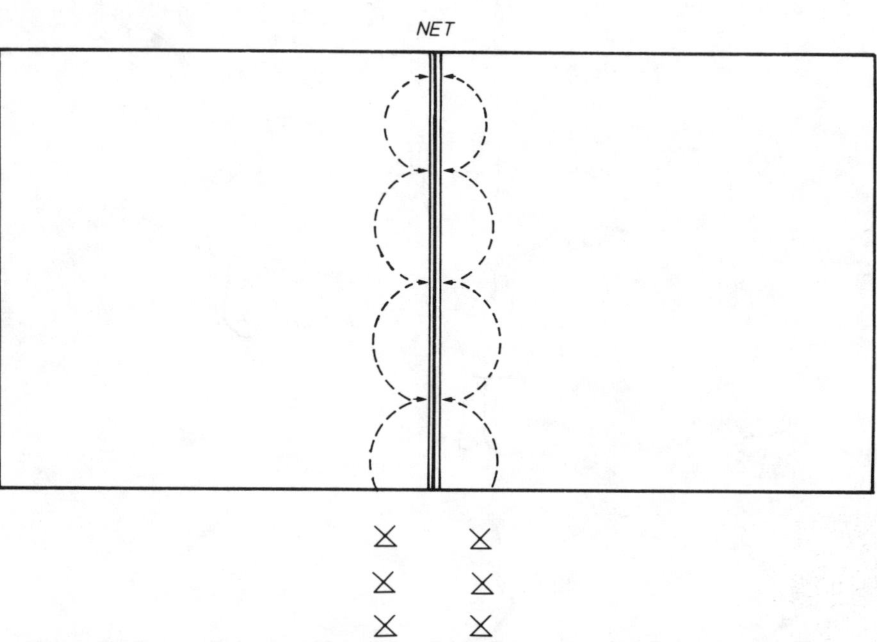

Figure 11.19. Block practice

After landing, each takes two or three more steps to the side and jumps again. This continues the length of the net. As soon as the leaders start the second jump, the next two people begin the drill. The players may use slide steps or running steps between jumps. Some may be able to touch only the fingertips above the net. Players remain at the opposite side of the court until all have finished, then return in a similar manner. The net may be lowered for short or younger players.

2.0. Squads are distributed on the court as in Figure 11.8, except that Player X4 moves close to the net. Player X1 tosses or sets the ball to Player X2, who spikes. Player X4 attempts to block the spike. Player X3 and others in the squad retrieve the balls. After four or five trials, players rotate so that all get a chance to practice both the spike and the block.

Advanced Skills: Rolls and Dives

The *dive roll* and the *dive* are used to save a ball that is low or far enough away that normal movements would be ineffective. Some instructors and coaches believe that skills involving rolls should be taught before the dives because it is less threatening to learners to do a roll on the floor than to land flat on the stomach. Others believe that the dive should be taught first because dives are dangerous if not done properly. All are advanced skills and should not be presented to novices or junior high classes. Some high school classes might be ready for these skills, but most are not. High school varsity players should have few problems mastering them.

Dive and Shoulder Roll

The dive roll is used after a dive or a lunge to the side to retrieve the ball. It should only be used when the ball is too far away for players to remain on their feet.

After the ball is hit with the back, side, or heel of the hand, the arm swings under the body. The shoulder of the arm is tucked under the body. The shoulder hits the floor, and the momentum carries the body onto the other shoulder and back up into a crouched ready position. Care must be taken to tuck the shoulder under so that the back of the shoulder contacts the floor. The free hand is positioned in front of the body on the floor to help push the body over. The legs tuck to permit the player to come up to a squat position on the feet. Just prior to becoming erect the arms push the body up by extending against the floor in front of the body.

Common Movement Problems and Suggestions. The following are common movement problems and teaching suggestions for the dive roll.

- Beginners often land on their hands and knees when trying this movement for the first time. Emphasize tucking the leading shoulder under and rolling onto it. Encourage them to keep the weight on the toes until going into the roll.
- Lifting the ball illegally with the open palm is a frequent error. Players should attempt to hit with the thumb-side (or back) of the hand or with the fist to prevent this.
- Remind players to complete the roll and return to the feet quickly to be ready for continued play.
- Emphasize tucking the head to the side away from the floor as soon as the ball is contacted to expedite the roll and to reduce the chance of hitting the head on the floor.

Practice Drills. The following are practice drills for dive rolls. The dive and dive rolls should be practiced first on mats to cushion the impact and avoid injury.

1.0. Players are scattered about (preferably on mats) in a deep crouch position. Players reach across in front of the body with the right arm, tuck the right shoulder under, roll onto it across the upper back, and continue to the hands and feet. Practice the same pattern rolling to the left. A variation is for players to tuck both the shoulder and head and to push forward with the feet. The player rolls over the shoulder as in a tumbling shoulder roll and across the back from shoulder to hips, then returns to the feet.

2.0. Partners. One partner tosses the ball low and to the side of another player, who starts in a crouched position. The receiver reaches out, digs the ball, tucks the shoulder under, and rolls back onto the feet. Five tosses should be made to each side before the players switch places. The tosses should be arched and fall about 4 ft to the side of the receiver. As skills improve, the toss can be changed to a direct throw.

3.0. Column with Leader Formation (Figure 4.3). The leader tosses the ball low and to the side of the first player in the column who lunges out, digs the ball, tucks the shoulder under, and shoulder rolls back onto the feet. After regaining her or his balance, the player goes to the end of the column and the leader throws the ball to the next person. Leaders should throw some balls to the right and some to the left to enable practice to both sides. Change leaders occasionally so they may practice the dive roll too.

Dive

The dive is executed when the ball is straight ahead and too far away to reach while maintaining balance on the feet. A step is taken toward the ball, the knees are flexed (bent), and the body is projected through the air in a low dive (horizontal position). The ball is best hit with the back of the hand because the palm is then ready to touch down on the floor first. As the palms hit the floor, the arms flex (bend) to help cushion the body from the force of impact with the floor. The body is lowered to the chest and stomach. The body then slides between the hands, ending in a prone, or face-down position. The dive should not be used if a dive roll is possible because the player can regain the ready position more quickly with the roll added.

Common Movement Problems and Suggestions. The following are some of the most common movement problems when performing the dive. Suggestions are made regarding the progressive teaching of this skill.

- The major risk involved in the diving action is the possible contact of the head and face on the floor. To avoid this problem, emphasize the arch of the back.
- Players should experience the arching position of the back while lying prone on the floor before attempting this in the dive.
- Players should also experience the sliding action on the stomach before attempting this movement in the dive. This can be done by having one player hold another player's legs in the wheelbarrow position, which resembles the diving position when contact is first made with the floor. The player then executes pulling and flexing movements of the arms while arching the back.

Practice Drills. The following are practice drills for dives. Mats should be used whenever possible.

1.0. Players Scattered About on Mats. From a crouch position, players push themselves into a low dive, catch themselves on the hands, lower the body to the mat, and slide on the chest and stomach between the hands. Be sure the hands are slightly more than shoulder-width apart when they contact the mat. Transfer the movement to a wooden floor. Do not practice this skill on cement or a rough-textured surface.

2.0. Partners. One partner softly tosses the ball about 6 to 8 ft in front of the other, who dives, hits the ball, and catches the body as above. Reverse roles.

3.0. Column and Leader Formation (Figure 4.3). This is the same as Drill 3.0 for the dive roll.

Offense

Much of the offensive play of a team depends on a player's ability to evaluate an opponent's position, to make accurate passes, and to take advantage of team strengths. Players must learn to try for a spike or an attack hit (smash) each time they are on offense. Merely getting the ball over the net is not sufficient except for the earliest beginners.

The best plan of offensive play is the bump-set-spike attack. The person who receives the ball from the opposite side (usually a back-row player) bumps the ball to a designated setter in the front row. The setter sets the ball to a spiker, who executes the attack hit. This would normally be a spike; however, if blockers are in place, it could be a dink.

Spikers should learn to control and direct the spike. Figure 11.20 shows several vulnerable areas for a corner spike. If a blocker covers one of these areas, try to utilize another path.

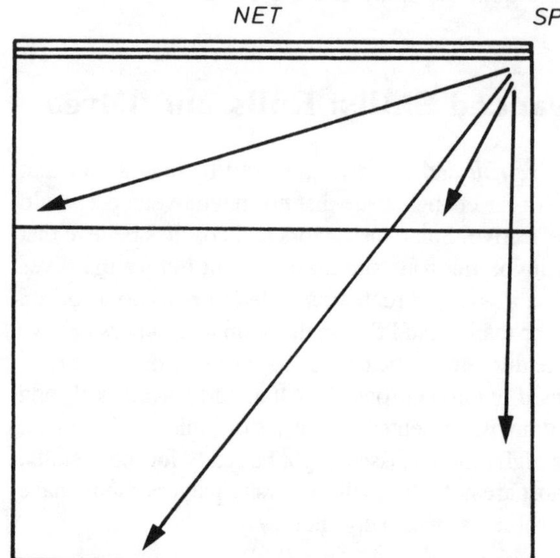

Figure 11.20. Pathways open for the corner spiker

The center spiker has more potentially vulnerable areas at which to aim. Figure 11.21 shows several options. If blockers cover the middle, the spiker should hit toward the sidelines or try to go between the blockers. Hits in the seams (areas between opponents) are also advantageous.

The ideal offensive lineup is to have every player skilled at passing and spiking. Then it does not matter who makes the sets or the spikes. Because this rarely occurs, however, the setters and the spikers should be separated on the court so that there is always at least one spiker and one passer in the front row. Consider the rotation pattern when distributing players. If there are three spikers and three setters (passers), they should be distributed as in Figure 11.22. If there are only two passers (or two spikers), they should be positioned as in Figure 11.23. This is the 4-2 offense: four spikers,

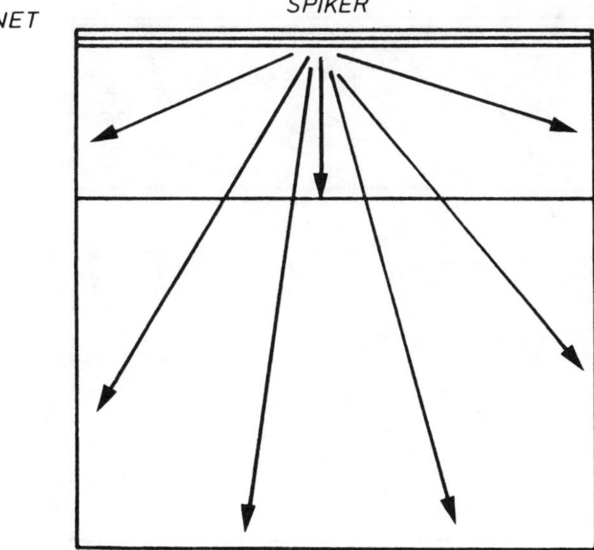

Figure 11.21. Pathways open for the center spiker

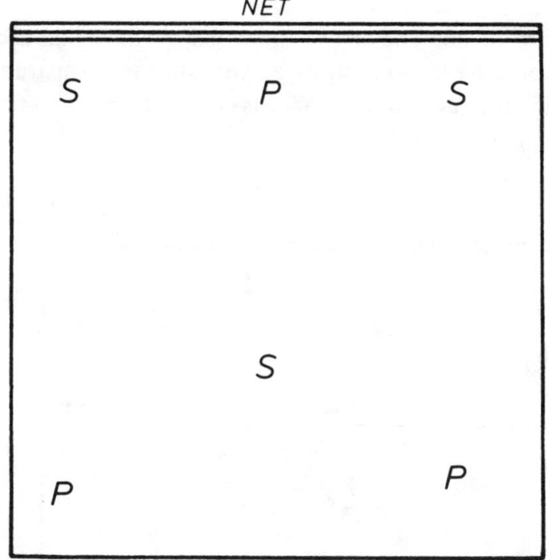

Figure 11.22. 3-3 offense: Three passers (setters) and three spikers

two setters. Note that in both of these patterns there will always be at least one passer and one spiker in the front row as rotation occurs.

One of the common lineups considered appropriate for a good offense is the *M formation* (Figure 11.24). This is also good defensive placement against a hard serve. The M formation allows five players to be ready to receive the serve and initiate the first pass. The center forward must be a setter and take the second hit. The left and right forwards move back toward the net as soon as the serve has been received in order to be in the proper position for spiking. If the center forward is not a setter, the player moves back to a wing of the M, and the left or right forward moves up. The side forward must remember to be closer to the sideline than is the center forward when the ball is served; otherwise, an out-of-position foul could be called.

The best position for the setter is the center of the front row (except for some advanced play). From here the setter can set to either the right or the left forwards and provide some deception. The player receiving the ball should try to pass it to the center-front position. If the

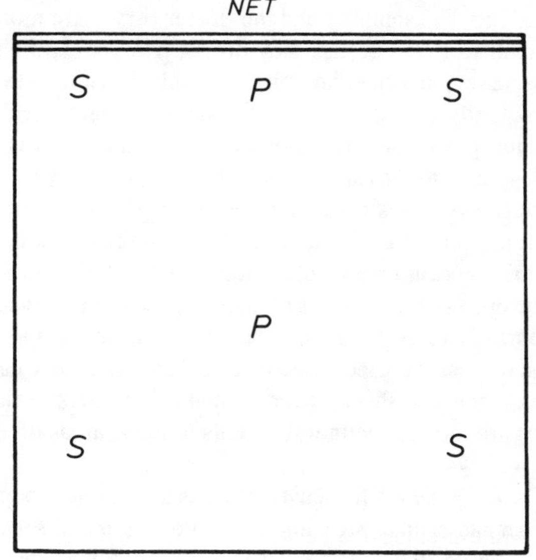

Figure 11.23. 4-2 offense: Two passers (setters) and four spikers

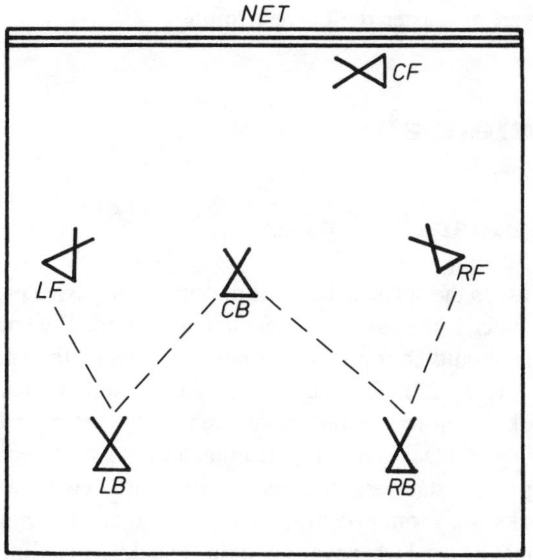

Figure 11.24. M formation for offense or defense

designated setter is not in the center of the front row, the player should move to that spot as soon as the ball is put in play. This is called an *interchange* or a *switch*.

Immediately after the server contacts the ball, players may move anywhere on the court. However, they must return to the original serving-order rotation pattern before each serve; otherwise, an *overlapping* foul is committed.

The serve can be an important offensive weapon. Servers should learn to place the ball in unprotected areas, between players, or near the backcourt. The serve that travels almost parallel with the ground and just barely clears the net is more difficult to return than is a highly lofted hit. The spinning and the floater serves are more difficult to field because they do not travel in straight lines. Every intermediate player should learn to serve consistently and accurately. Advanced players should develop power or a deceptive action in their serves.

Beginners tend to all move toward the ball. They must learn to avoid this because it leaves large areas of the court unprotected. The alert offensive player will watch for this to occur on the opponents' court and hit the ball to the open space, which is often in the back of the court. Accurately directed hits are valuable offensive maneuvers and can be used effectively by the team that has weak spikers or short players. The back corners of the court are the most vulnerable. Hits to those areas often win volleys.

The *quick set* is a maneuver that sets the ball just above the net rather than high in the air. For the quick set to be effective, the spiker must leap as the ball is set in order to meet it before it falls below the level of the net. The change in timing of this set-spike usually causes the defense to be caught without blockers. This is an advanced skill and should not be attempted by beginners. It takes much practice by the setter and the spikers involved to master the correct timing.

Defense

Against the Spike

Just as the spike is the most important offensive play, the block is the most important defensive one. The entire team should shift positions to defend against the spike (Figure 11.25). The player opposite the spiker tries to block. Front-row teammates move to *cover* the probable angles of attack. Back-row teammates must try to cover angles of attack and the rest of the court. Two-player blocks are more effective than one-player blocks and should be used whenever possible. The defensive lineup for a two-player block at the right corner is shown in

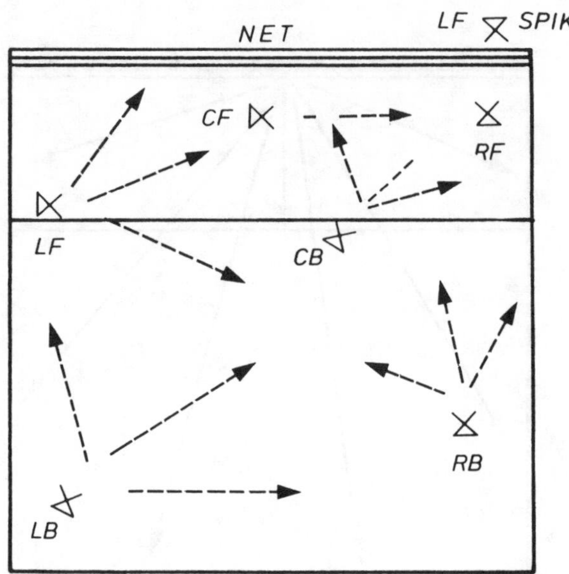

Figure 11.25. Defensive position with one blocker against a spike from opposing left forward (LF)

Figure 11.26. The arrows show the territory that each player must try to protect. Players shift in comparable positions to the left if the spike is coming from the opposing right forward.

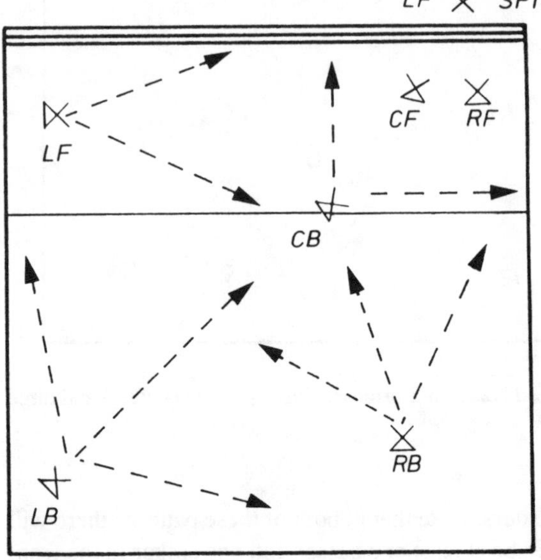

Figure 11.26. Defensive positions with two blockers against a spike from opposing left forward (LF)

Defense against a center spiker is more difficult because there is a wider range of options for the spiker (Figure 11.21). The defensive lineup against this spike is shown in Figure 11.27. The center forward attempts

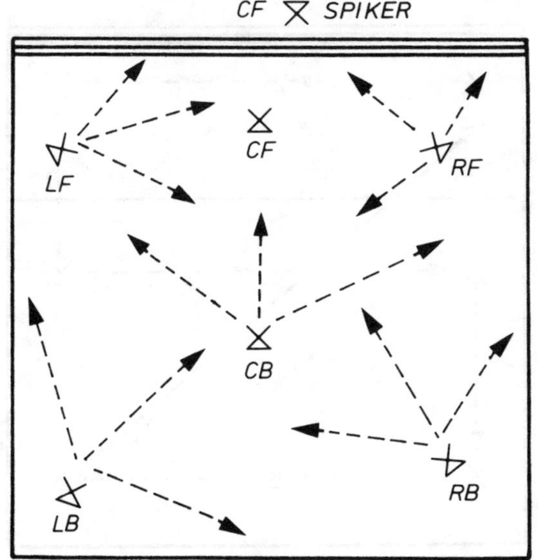

Figure 11.27. Defensive positions against a center spiker

the block while the rest of the defense tries to cover other possible outlets. Two or three defenders should try to block. The block is really the only good defense against a good center spiker.

Against Hard Services

The *W formation* is a common defensive lineup used when the serve is hard and toward the back of the court (Figure 11.28). This can lead into the 5-1 offense for a team that has five spikers and a setter. This is a variation of the M formation.

This defensive pattern allows the three back players to stay well back on the court. The side forwards drop back to help receive the serve. The setter stays close to the net to receive the first pass from that player's team. If the best setter is at right or left forward, then that player stays at the net near the corner, and the center forward drops back to a point of the W. Remember that the center forward may not be closer to a sideline than is the forward on that side when the ball is being served.

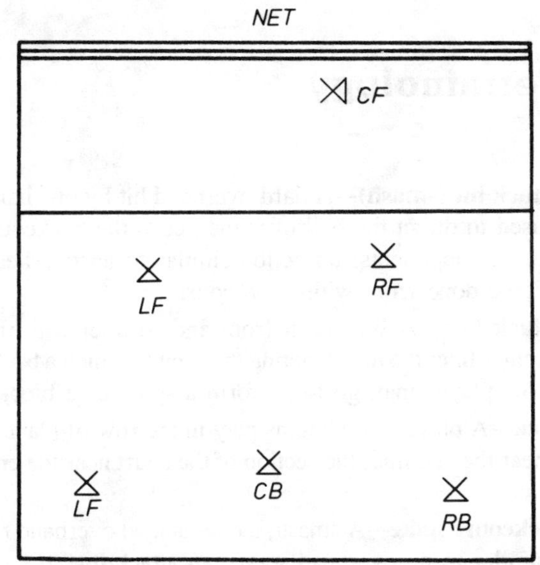

Figure 11.28. W formation for defense

General Strategies

Players must be ready to back up their teammates at all times. If a player runs out of position to make a play, the player's teammates must cover the empty area, and the player must try to recover and return as soon as possible. Players may run out of bounds to play the ball; however, the ball must pass over the net between the sidelines when being returned to the opponents. It may not go around the net or over the portion of the net that is out of bounds.

When players have been pulled out of position and the team is in disarray, a high hit to the back of the opponents' court may give the team time to regroup. This usually makes it easy for the other team to form a new attack, but the defenders would have time to get ready for it.

Teams and players must be able to shift quickly from offense to defense and vice versa. Players must also be flexible and innovative. A versatile team has an advantage over one that always uses the same style of play. Occasional variation from the bump-set-spike pattern may surprise the defense and win volleys.

General Teaching Concepts

When the instructor wants to move into a game situation after drill practice, the last drill should involve play over the net, such as Drill 2.0 for passing and setting (Figure 11.5). This provides a natural grouping for game play. Those on each side of the net constitute teams for the game.

A legal serve requires that the ball be tossed or dropped into the air before being hit by the server. It may not be hit directly off the other hand. This rule may be waived for beginners in class situations.

Do not keep the net so high that players cannot spike or block. Lowering the level of the net to 6 or 6-1/2 ft makes game play and skill performance easier for elementary and middle school students. Seven feet may be appropriate for high school play.

Plastic inflated beach balls are very good for beginners. They neither hurt the hand nor travel as fast as volleyballs, but they do simulate the flight of a volleyball and allow the development of hitting skills. To encourage the use of specific skills, award an extra point (or points) to a team that executes that skill (e.g., a spike or a block).

Modified games can be played early in the volleyball unit to motivate performers. This could come as soon as the overhead pass, the bump, and the serve have been taught.

Teams of 8 to 10 players can be assigned to a court. Two ways to handle this overload follow:

- Six players go on the court, and the others on the team line up at the sideline. Every time the team wins the serve, one player rotates out and a sideline person goes in. This allows rapid substitution, and no one stays out very long. This should be used by intermediate and advanced players.
- Place all the team members on the court. The recommended lineup and rotation order (box, or square, rotation) for eight players is shown in Figure 11.29. The lineup for nine or more players and a modified rotation plan are shown in Figure 11.30. This is called the *S rotation*. Extra players are added to each row, starting with the front row. This might be used with beginners, but the court often becomes too crowded for the development of good play.

An effective way to teach scoring and basic rules to groups is to place all players on one court, where the

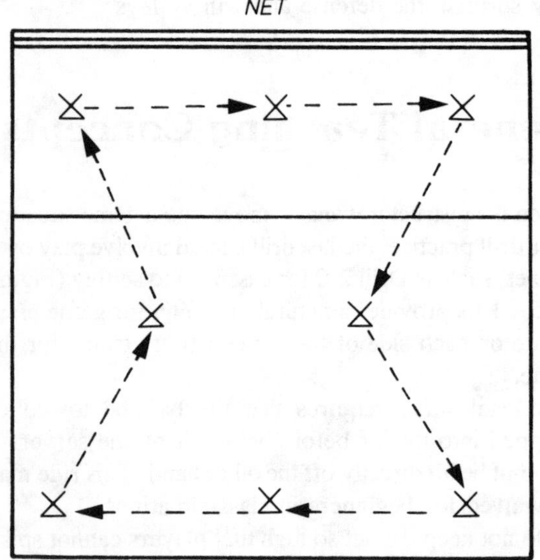

Figure 11.29. Eight-player lineup and rotation pattern

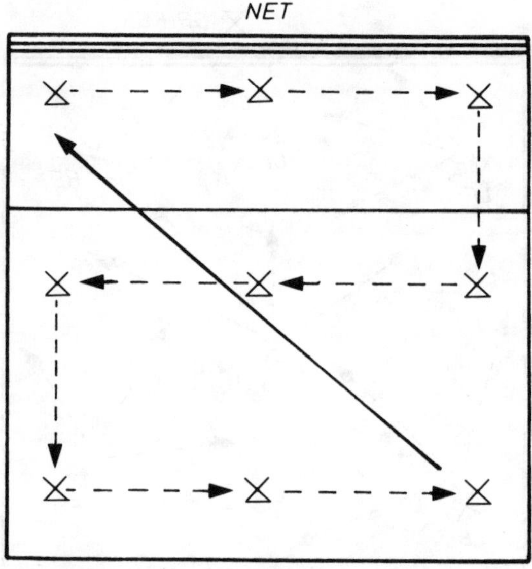

Figure 11.30. Lineup for nine or more players and S rotation

instructor can officiate and closely supervise everyone at once. Critique of techniques, reinforcement of rules, and comments on strategy can be made easily for all to hear as play is conducted. Rotation may need to be modified because of the number on each team. If it is not feasible to place all players on one court, try to consolidate them on two adjacent courts. The instructor can then move back and forth between the courts to instruct and assist as much as possible. This class organization plan should be continued perhaps for only one class period. Then players should be dispersed more to encourage the development of individual skills and team concepts.

Terminology

Attack hit (smash)—A hard overhand hit by one hand used to direct the ball over the net to the backcourt of the opponents; an action similar to an overhead serve done from within the court

Attack line—A line 10 ft from and parallel with the center line; the line denoting the limit to which a back-row player may go to perform a spike or a block

Back—A player who begins play in the row of players near the end line; the section of the court near the end line

Backcourt spike—A smash; a one-handed overhand hit similar to an overhead serve; an attack hit

Back set—An overhead pass that sends the ball behind the passer

Block—To stop the ball with the hands or arms as it crosses the net (or in some instances as it nears the net) so that the ball rebounds back to the opponents' side of the net

Blocker—A front-row player who attempts to stop the ball before or as it crosses the net

Bump—A two-handed underarm pass of a ball that is below waist level; a pass done with the hands or forearms (preferred)

Center line—The line directly under the net that divides one side of the court from the other or one team from the other

Cover—To protect an area or space between teammates; to protect an area left vacant by a teammate

Dig pass—A one-handed pass generally used only when the player is unable to get in position to use two hands; a pass performed by allowing the ball to rebound from the fist, forearm, or hand (side or back)

Dink—A softly arched hit designed to send the ball over the upraised hands of blockers; a countermove to avoid a block

Dive—A horizontal lunge of the entire body in an attempt to reach the ball

Dive roll—A lunge to the side to reach a distant ball which is performed by leaving the feet, hitting the ball, and then doing a shoulder roll to regain balance on the feet

Double hit—One player hitting the ball twice in succession; allowing the ball to rebound from one hand (or other legal body part) and then another body part (usually illegal)

Floater—See Punch serve

Foot fault—A foul committed either by stepping completely over the center line or by stepping on or over the end line before contacting the ball on a serve

Forward—A player who begins the play in the front row or near the net

Front set—See Overhead pass

Held ball—A foul caused by not hitting the ball clearly; a ball that is lifted, thrown, or caught briefly

Interchange—To exchange places on the court after the ball has been served

Jump serve—A served ball that is hit while at the height of a jump

M formation—An offensive formation that assumes an M shape and that strengthens the center of the court

Match—The means of determining the better of two teams; the winner of two out of three games (or three out of five)

Overhead pass—A two-handed pass of a ball that is above waist level generally used to direct the ball to a teammate; (sometimes called a *front set*)

Overlapping—An illegal team arrangement in which players are not clearly within their assigned positions relative to one another when the ball is served

Power serve—A strong overhead serve

Punch serve—A serve executed by punching the ball and that has little spin and appears to float through the air (also called a *floater*)

Quick set—A low set just above net height designed to confuse the opponent and prevent a block (sometimes called an *off-speed set*)

Rotation—A specified pattern of movement designed to shift players sequentially around the court

Serve—To put the ball in play by a one-handed hit from out of bounds behind the right back of the court; to start the ball in play

Setter—A player whose primary responsibility is to lob high passes to teammates who will spike the ball over the net

Side out—The term used to designate the loss of the serve or a change of service from one team to the other

Smash—Same as Attack hit

Soft spike—See Dink

Spike—A sharp downward hit of the ball from above net level toward the floor on the opposite side of the net; an attack hit originating near the net

Switch—See Interchange

Underarm pass—See Bump

Volley—To hit the ball before it bounces; to hit the ball back and forth over the net

W formation—A defensive pattern that assumes a W shape, characterized by moving two forwards away from the net to strengthen a team's ability to defend against a strong serve or attack hit

Selected Readings

Cherebetiu, G. (1969). *Volleyball techniques*. Hollywood, CA: Creative Editorial Service.

Gozansky, S. (1983). *Championship volleyball techniques and drills*. West Nyack, NY: Parker.

Mushier, C. (1983). *Team sports for girls and women* (2nd ed.). Princeton, NJ: Princeton Book.

National Association of Girls and Women in Sport. (1987). *Volleyball rules*. Reston, VA: American Alliance for Health, Physical Education, Recreation and Dance.

Scates, A. (1984). *Winning volleyball drills*. Boston: Allyn & Bacon.

Thompson, D., & Carver, J. (1974). *Physical activities handbook*. Englewood Cliffs, NJ: Prentice-Hall.

United States Volleyball Assocation. (1987). *Official volleyball reference guide*. Colorado Springs: USVBA.

Volleyball Skills Errors and Corrections

OVERHEAD PASSING/GENERAL

Error	*Causes*	*Corrections*
Inappropriate timing		
Ball missed or hit low	• Failure to start the approach at the proper time	• Get in line with the ball quickly and wait for it to descend toward the forehead; use small, quick steps to move the body under the ball.
	• Lunging forward at the ball	• Contact the ball above the forehead and push upward.
Move telegraphed to opponent	• Arching back too soon in the back set	• Keep the trunk erect until the last moment; arch the back for the back set as the arms and hands begin force production.
Weak		
Ball hit too softly	• Failure to face toward the target	• Square the shoulders toward the intended flight path of the ball.
	• Failure to set the feet	• Plant both feet firmly about shoulder-width apart; keep one foot slightly ahead of the other.
	• Inadequate use of the legs	• Flex the knees; extend them vigorously as the ball is passed; keep the feet in contact with the floor; avoid jumping at the ball.
	• Insufficient range of motion in the upper body	• Thrust the shoulders up and slightly forward as the arms extend toward the ball.
	• Insufficient range of motion in the arms	• Flex the elbows and draw the hands back to the shoulders in preparation for the pass; thrust the arms and hands upward with the pass.
Passing ball too low		
Lack of height	• Positioning the hands vertically (perpendicular to the floor)	• Bend the wrists so that the backs of the hands are toward the floor and the palms are slightly upward.
	• Holding the elbows too low	• Keep the elbows up about shoulder level and out to the sides.
	• Failure to have the thumbs under the ball	• Point the thumbs toward each other and slightly downward under the back of the ball; form a ''window'' with the thumbs and index fingers in front of the forehead and watch the ball through the window as it approaches.

Error	*Causes*	*Corrections*
Inappropriate timing		
Ball missed or hit low	• Failure to position the body correctly	• Move underneath the ball so that it is descending toward the forehead.
Lack of ball control		
Ball misdirected	• Slapping at the ball	• Relax the fingers; cup the hands; contact the ball with the end pads of the fingers.
	• Failure to accelerate the entire body consistently prior to contact	• Simultaneously thrust upward and slightly forward with the legs, body, and arms.
	• Failure to use both hands effectively	• Draw both hands back and push upward simultaneously with both arms; position the body directly in the path of the ball.
	• Failure to flex the fingers on contact with the ball	• Push at the ball; do *not* relax the fingers so much that the ball goes through the hands.

UNDERARM PASS/BUMP

Error	*Causes*	*Corrections*
Lack of ball control		
Ball missed	• Failure to initiate approach soon enough	• Stand in the ready position while awaiting the serve or a volley from the opponents; move as soon as the ball is hit.
Ball hit too low or to side of target	• Failure to get in position and to make ball contact close to the midline of the body	• Move in line with the path of the ball; stand with knees bent to absorb force.
	• Failure to maintain balance	• Get set in a forward-stride position with the knees bent.
	• Failure to position the arms in line with the ball	• Hold the arms together in the path of the ball; if the ball is to the left of the midline of the body, drop the right shoulder forward; if the ball is to the right of the midline, drop the left shoulder forward.
Ball rebounds erratically	• Failure to have the arms together and straight	• Clasp the hands together securely and extend the arms; keep the wrists, forearms, and elbows close together.
	• Failure to make ball contact with the best surface	• Contact the ball with as flat a surface as possible (the forearms).
	• Failure to focus on the ball	• Watch the ball until it contacts the arms.
Ball hit too high (or backward)	• Flexing the elbows	• Keep the arms straight at contact.
	• Lifting the arms to meet the ball	• Allow the ball to come to the arms as they are angled toward the floor in front; avoid raising the arms to a horizontal position.

(Cont.)

UNDERARM PASS/BUMP (Continued)

Error	*Causes*	*Corrections*
Ball hit too high (or backward)	• Improper body position	• Lean forward from the hips; do *not* stand erect; hold the arms away from and in front of the body.
Weak		
Ball does *not* go high enough	• Allowing the arms to absorb too much force	• Hold the arms firmly in position except for very hard hits, then give with the ball.
	• Failure to utilize a quick lift of the arms at the shoulder just prior to contact	• Swing the arms slightly forward and up from the shoulders as the ball is contacted (not appropriate when fielding hard serves or spikes).
	• Poor body position or balance	• See the first three corrections.
Lifting or carrying the ball		
(illegal hit)	• Improper hand position	• Clasp one hand inside the other; avoid using the hands in an open palm-up position; hold the wrists firm without flexion.
	• Improper body position	• Move quickly into position; avoid being indecisive—decide which pass to use and carry it out.

SERVE

Error	*Causes*	*Corrections*
Weak		
Ball fails to go over net	• Failure to use a full backswing to permit more time and distance to build force	• Rotate the trunk and swing the serving arm backward in the preparatory action.
	• Failure to use a forceful body-weight shift	• Increase the stride length of the forward step; step forward on the foot opposite the serving arm.
	• Failure to keep the striking arm and hand firm during contact	• Tighten the muscles of the hand and arm making contact with the ball; contact with a harder surface such as the heel of the hand or the fist.
	• When executing an overhand serve, failure to whip the hand through	• Keep the elbow of the serving arm up; elbows move forward as the arms move around the shoulder; whip the hand through.
Excessive height		
Ball goes too high	• Improper contact point on ball	• Make contact more behind the ball and less underneath; swing a little later; toss the ball farther in front; strike the ball when it is lower to the ground (between the knees and hips for the underhand serve).

Error	*Causes*	*Corrections*
Excessive height		
Ball goes too high	• Improper ball toss	• For the underhand, toss the ball about 1 ft in front and to the inside of the striding foot; for the sidearm, toss the ball about 1 or 2 ft in front and to the outside of the side-striding foot; for the overhead, toss the ball about 2 ft above and slightly forward of the striking-arm shoulder.
Inaccurate		
Ball goes out of bounds at sidelines	• Improper body position	• Have the shoulders facing the net to begin the serve (except for the sidearm serve, when the nonstriking-arm shoulder points to the net).
	• Failure to direct the follow-through motion	• Reach straight toward the target with the serving arm.
	• Failure to maintain focus on the ball	• Continue to watch the ball until contact is completed.
	• Restriction of hip rotation	• Step forward on the foot opposite the striking arm.
	• Contacting the ball in the wrong place	• Make contact with the ball directly behind the intended line of flight; strike through the ball.

DIG

Error	*Causes*	*Corrections*
Lack of ball control		
Ball rebounds erratically	• Poor body position	• Move quickly to get to the ball; lunge toward it if necessary.
	• Failure to contact the ball with a flat surface	• Contact the ball with a flat part of the fist (fingers or side near thumb), the back of the hand or the wrist.
	• Failure to follow through	• Reach out toward the direction of the target with the striking arm.
	• Failure to contact the ball at the proper point	• Contact the ball below and slightly behind the center; attempt to hit the ball upward.
Weak		
Ball hit with insufficient force	• Failure to keep the hand and arm firm on contact	• Hold the hand and arm rigid; let the ball rebound from the hand or arm.
	• Failure to contact the ball with an appropriate part of the hand or arm	• Make contact with the forearm, the heel or back of the hand, or the fist; avoid letting the ball contact the open palm and fingers.

(Cont.)

ATTACK HITS (SPIKE AND SMASH)

Error	*Causes*	*Corrections*
Weak		
Ineffective hit	• Failure to utilize the full range of motion	• Rotate the hips clockwise about 90° (if hitting with the right hand); rotate the trunk so that the shoulder of the nonstriking arm points forward.
	• Failure to utilize a whipping action of the striking arm	• Lead the forward arm motion with the elbow; whip the forearm through.
	• Failure to utilize wrist action	• Flex (snap) the wrist as contact is made.
Poor timing		
Ball missed	• Failure to start the approach at the proper time	• Start the two-step approach to the ball as it is set by a teammate; move toward the spot quickly.
Body position poor	• Running too far under the ball	• Position the body so that the ball is above and slightly in front of the shoulder of the striking arm.
	• Failure to contact the ball as high as possible	• Jump and reach up as high as possible; contact the well-set ball at its peak or just as it starts to drop.
Ball hit into net	• Contacting the ball too late	• Hit the ball before it drops below net level; make contact behind and slightly above the center; when spiking, contact closer to the top of the ball.
Net contact made		
(Foul)	• Failure to jump straight up	• Plant the forward foot (or both feet) ahead of the center of gravity and lean back just before jumping; lift the arms strongly to help convert horizontal momentum to a vertical jump.

BLOCKING

Error	*Causes*	*Corrections*
Inadequate jump		
Jumper fails to reach above net	• Failure to utilize appropriate flexion of the knees	• Flex the knees to maximum efficiency (depth of squat should *not* exceed the sitting position).
	• Failure to drive legs downward	• Push hard against the floor with both feet.
	• Failure to use the arms to gain momentum	• Lower the arms down and back before jump; swing them vigorously forward and upward with the jump.

Error	*Causes*	*Corrections*
Inadequate jump		
Jumper fails to reach above net	• Failure to jump directly upward	• Jump straight up or slightly backward to avoid net contact.
Poor timing		
Ball missed	• Failure to get into position quickly	• Move toward the net where the ball is expected to cross; crouch and prepare to jump.
	• Jumping at the wrong time	• Begin the jump before the spiker's toes leave the floor.
	• Failure to intercept the ball	• Extend the arms quickly upward and hold as long as possible; flex the wrists slightly to direct the ball downward.
Failure to block		
Arms and hands improperly positioned	• Failure to keep the arms extended and firm	• Hold the hands and arms close together and rigid.
	• Blocked ball not crossing the net	• Move closer to the net; extend the hands (and forearms if possible) over the net or directly above it.
	• Ball going between the arms	• Keep the arms close together, the hands spread, and the head back.
Making net contact		
(illegal)	• Playing too close to the net	• Stand about 3 ft from the net while waiting for the play to develop; take one step toward the net and jump; move farther away if a running approach is used.
	• Jumping into the net	• Move and jump on an angle toward the net; avoid moving straight toward it.
	• Flexing the trunk excessively	• Jump slightly backward; bend at the waist so that the buttocks move away from the net as the arms extend forward over the net.
	• Reaching too far over the net	• Draw the arms back quickly when descending from a block attempt; know the limitations of your reaching ability.
	• Downward follow-through	• Hold the hands and wrists rigid; avoid flexing the wrists and hitting downward.